BEFORE TEMPLES

sidestonepress

BEFORE TEMPLES

Rectangular structures of the Low Countries
and their place in the Iron Age belief system

R. DE LEEUWE

© 2023 R. de Leeuwe

Published by Sidestone Press, Leiden
www.sidestone.com

Imprint: Sidestone Press Dissertations
This book was originally written as a dissertation and successfully
defended at Leiden University in 2023.

Lay-out & cover design: Sidestone Press
Photograph cover: Stock.adobe.com | Oscar

ISBN 978-94-6428-060-9 (softcover)
ISBN 978-94-6428-061-6 (hardcover)
ISBN 978-94-6428-062-3 (PDF e-book)

DOI 10.59641/4u9131xg

Contents

Acknowledgements	**9**
1. Introduction	**11**
1.1 Prologue: a semantic problem	11
1.2 The problem of interpreting a rectangular structure	12
1.3 The problem of the 'ritual' in a rectangular structure	13
1.4 The problem of the environmental context and date of a rectangular structure	15
1.5 Research questions	16
1.6 Dataset and limitations	16
1.7 Variables	17
1.8 Approach and outline of the study	18
2. The belief system in the Iron Age	**21**
2.1 Introduction	21
2.2 The soul and the ancestors	21
2.2.1 Different concepts of the soul	22
2.2.2 Communication with the dead	23
2.2.3 Creating monuments in the Bronze Age	24
2.2.4 Immortality of the soul in the Iron Age	25
2.3 Phenomenology and the natural world	26
2.3.1 Bronze Age conceptualisation of phenomena	26
2.3.2 Sacred trees	28
2.3.3 Gods and spirits in natural places	29
2.4 The 'ritual of exchange'	30
2.5 Objects of exchange	32
2.5.1 Offerings and depositions	32
2.5.2 Pottery as the sacrificial object	33
2.5.3 The ultimate sacrifice	33
2.5.4 Sacrifice in times of war	34
2.6 Before temples: a place for depositions	35
2.6.1 Roman cult places in the Low Countries	36
2.7 Conclusion	37

3. Geographical framework: the 'archaeotypical' sanctuary   **39**

3.1 Introduction   39

3.2 The sanctuaries of Northern France   41

    3.2.1 The archetype   41

    3.2.2 A war memorial   44

    3.2.3 A place for the ancestors   47

    3.2.4 A weapon depository   48

    3.2.5 A place for communal gatherings   49

    3.2.6 Variety in sanctuaries   52

3.3 The rectangular structures of Germany   54

    3.3.1 Viereckschanzen   54

    3.3.2 The sanctuaries of Manching   57

    3.3.3 Community gathering and offering places   59

3.4 Shrines, enclosures, and causeways in England   59

    3.4.1 Shrines   60

    3.4.2 Causeways and depositions   62

    3.4.3 Enclosures   63

3.5 Conclusion   64

4. Rectangular structures in the Late Bronze Age – Early Iron Age   **67**

4.1 Introduction   67

4.2 Rectangular structures in urnfields   67

    4.2.1 Surrounding features   67

    4.2.2 Relation to Bronze Age barrows   72

    4.2.3 The (medio) Atlantic tradition   73

4.3 Rectangular structures in Early Iron Age settlements   74

4.4 Conclusion: the urnfield as a point of origin   75

5. Rectangular structures in the Middle Iron Age   **77**

5.1 Introduction   77

5.2 Burial traditions and the treatment of human remains   77

    5.2.1 Burial traditions   77

    5.2.2 Human remains in wet contexts   79

    5.2.3 Human remains in a settlement context   81

5.3 The 5th century BCE   82

    5.3.1 The pottery deposition of Kooigem   82

    5.3.2 Deposition of whole pots   84

5.4 Rectangular structures and their relation to graves   85

    5.4.1 Rectangular structures surrounding graves   85

    5.4.2 Rectangular structures surrounding and near graves   89

    5.4.3 Rectangular structures near contemporary graves   93

5.5 Discussion on rectangular structures in the Middle Iron Age   95

5.6 Conclusion   97

6. Rectangular structures in the Late Iron Age — **99**

6.1 Introduction — 99
6.2 Transition into the Late Iron Age — 99
6.3 Continuation of burial traditions — 100
    6.3.1 Including the ancestors — 101
    6.3.2 Respecting the ancestors — 104
    6.3.3 Burial enclosures — 105
6.4 Rectangular structures and field systems — 110
    6.4.1 Rectangular structures in fields — 110
6.5 Diverse use and variable contexts of rectangular structures — 113
    6.5.1 Rectangular structures in settlements — 114
    6.5.2 Structural elements — 116
    6.5.3 A place for deposition — 119
6.6 Synthesis: the varied use of rectangular structures in the Late Iron Age — 122
6.7 Conclusion — 123

7. The environment and context of rectangular structures — **125**

7.1 Introduction — 125
7.2 Aalter-Woestijne — 125
    7.2.1 Function of the linear ditches — 127
    7.2.2 Incorporation of rectangular structures — 128
7.3 Harelbeke and Kortrijk — 129
    7.3.1 Ditch systems — 129
    7.3.2 Roads — 130
    7.3.3 Iron Age landscape use in the Harelbeke-Kortrijk region — 130
7.4 Oss-Ussen — 131
    7.4.1 Early to Middle Iron Age cemetery — 132
    7.4.2 Settlement C and rectangular structures R49 and R50 — 133
    7.4.3 The central position of rectangular structure R25/R26 — 133
    7.4.4 Iron Age landscape use in Oss-Ussen — 134
7.5 Diachronic landscape use and the rectangular structure — 134

8. The function of a rectangular structure — **137**

8.1 Introduction — 137
8.2 The rectangular structure as a functional earthwork — 137
    8.2.1 Field boundaries and landscape structuring — 139
    8.2.2 Defences — 139
    8.2.3 House and settlement ditches — 140
    8.2.4 The temporality of a ditch — 140
    8.2.5 The concept of a rectangle — 141
8.3 The rectangular structure as a cemetery demarcation — 142
    8.3.1 Associated finds — 144
8.4 The rectangular structure as a symbolic boundary — 145
    8.4.1 Formulation of the afterlife — 145
    8.4.2 Monuments without remains — 146
    8.4.3 The impact of conflict — 147

8.5 The rectangular structure as a deposition space 149

    8.5.1 Pits 149

    8.5.2 Postholes and enclosed structures 151

8.6 The rectangular structure as a liminal place 152

    8.6.1 In-between the high-low dichotomy 153

8.7 Epilogue: evaluating Oss-Brabantstraat 154

9. Conclusion **157**

9.1 Iron Age beliefs 157

9.2 Warriors and missing persons 158

9.3 A place for communication 159

9.4 Some answers and more questions 160

References **163**

CATALOGUE OF RECTANGULAR STRUCTURES IN THE LOW COUNTRIES **187**

Acknowledgements

Writing a dissertation is mostly a lonely pursuit, but ultimately cannot be achieved without the aid of others. First of all I would like to thank prof. dr. Harry Fokkens for giving me this opportunity and prof. dr. David Fontijn for believing I can pull it off. They guided me through the process into the right direction. I thank the reading committee prof. dr. Mette Løvschal, prof. dr. Guy de Mulder, and dr. Karen de Vries for the useful suggestions that improved the quality of the manuscript. Furthermore I like to thank several people who helped me gather data on the sites. On several occasions this required some digging: Hendrik de Meeuw (RAMS) for helping find my way in the depot in Meerwaarde collecting data on Kooigem, colleague Mieke van de Vijver for providing data on Belgium sites, specifically Aalter-Woestijne, Ron Bakx for sending me all available information on Bouchout, and keeping me updated with other publications, Anna de Rijck for information on Brecht, Bart Cherretté and Arne Verbrugge (SOLVA) for information on Ronse and Erembodegem, and Gérard Bataille for information on the site of Villeneuve-au-Châtelot.

I will not forget that nearly all sites cited in this dissertation concern commercial digs, resulting in 'grey literature'. The ground work for the contents of all these excavation reports was done by field archaeologists, who are often underappreciated and subjected to a lot of hassle, complaints, time pressure, tight funding, complicating circumstances, bureaucratic paperwork, quality checks, qualification requirements, weather conditions, uninterested clients, overactive volunteers, unwanted metal detectorist, hostile land owners, untrusting and/or inexperienced authorities, rushing excavator operators, collapsing profiles, failing equipment, high groundwater levels, local wildlife, misquoting journalists, and underpaid wages. My warm sympathies to all of you, and especially the ones I call my friends. Keep up the good work!

Additionally, I convey my gratitude to Marjolein Kok for sending me her dissertation. It was helpful in writing the theoretical framework. I also thank Go Fuji for the translation of the Japanese signs around the sacred Nagi in Shingu City. Many thanks to Paul Judge for reading the whole thing and correcting my 'England', specifically in regard to the use of commas. Further gratitude to Richard Jansen, Minja Hemminga and Annette Schmidt for reading chapters and finding discussion points, to the Netherlands Forensic Institute and RAAP for allowing me time to work on this dissertation, and of course special thanks to my Andy for his support, patience and understanding all these years.

1

Introduction

1.1 Prologue: a semantic problem

Most archaeological dialogues start with a discovery. The subject of this dissertation is no exception. In 2007 a couple of colleagues and I were digging trial trenches in Oss (southern Netherlands), along the Brabantstraat, when we came upon several parallel ditches. These narrow ditches looked different from previous encountered features on the site and their appearance suggested an Iron Age or Roman date. In another trial trench the parallel ditches continued at a 90-degree angle, evidently part of a larger rectangular structure. In the subsequent excavation in 2008, the southern half of the structure was uncovered. To find out if our theories were correct, the northern half was excavated as well in 2010. The entire structure measured 32 × 23m and consisted of four parallel, concentric rectangular ditches. The scarce finds gave little indication for its use. The rectangular shape however, appeared to be an extensively debated phenomenon under many different names, such as 'rural open air cult place', 'ritual enclosure', 'Iron Age religious site', 'shrine', and 'sanctuary' (e.g. De Laet 1966; Brunaux 1986; Slofstra & Van der Sanden 1987; Woodward 1992; Annaert 1993; Van der Sanden 1994; Haffner 1995; Fitzpatrick & Powell 1997; Fontijn 2002a; Van Enckevort 2007; Van Zoolingen 2010, 153-162). All authors suggested these types of structures were related to religion or a type of cult activity. Some authors (e.g. Brunaux 1986; Slofstra & Van der Sanden 1987) even derived requirements that a rectangular enclosure should meet in order to identify it as a sanctuary or a cult place. By lack of a better theory at the time, I indiscriminately used their models as analogies and interpreted the Brabantstraat site as a cult place (De Leeuwe 2011).

The main problem with this interpretation is the underlying processual semantic assumption that is based on the shape of the structure. The rectangular design instigates a biased tendency to label the structure as a 'cult place', imposing an inexplicit set of characteristics that require critical examination. However, is there actually any evidence for this interpretation? Provided a 'cult' is a demonstrable possibility, what would this entail and how does it relate to the religious belief system of the period? The structure in Oss dates from the Late Iron Age or Early Roman era. Of the latter period we are certainly aware of the use of structures for religious actions: Roman temples. The purpose of a temple was, and remains, worship and communication with a god, or several gods, or all of them. Even in the outer reaches of the Roman Empire such as the Low Countries, temples were used as places for religious acts such as offerings. Examples are the temple for Nehalennia in Zeeland (Hondius-Crone 1955; Bogaers 1955, 11-20; Bogaers & Stuart 1971), two different locations with temples in Elst (Bogaers 1955; Van Enckevort 2007), one in Empel (Roymans & Derks 1994), a temple complex in Tongeren (Mertens 1968; Nouwen 1997, 106-108, 135-141; Cosyns 2013) and the recently discovered temple complex in Zevenaar (Verhelst & Norde forthcoming). However, what was used in the Iron Age, if any, as a place of worship or offerings before the introduction of temples?

Despite what the title suggests, this thesis is on the use of rectangular structures as so-called sanctuaries or cult places in the Iron Age seen as a diachronic development from

INTRODUCTION   11

the (Late) Bronze Age, in contrast to the more common approach as a retrospective from Roman times. During the Iron Age, communities in the Low Countries changed over into the organised tribal territories that Caesar described in his *Gallic Wars*. In the 700-year course of the Iron Age, communities based on traditional symbolism and control over luxury commodities trade routes since the Late Neolithic, changed over into market economies, with well-equipped armies and political centres (Cunliffe 1999, 268-274; Wells 2011). The Early Iron Age was the stage of ornate Hallstatt chiefdoms, who controlled trade routes and maintained contacts with central Europe (e.g. Fokkens & Jansen 2004, 84-87; Wells 2011; Van der Vaart-Verschoof & Schumann 2017). From the 5th century BCE, the expansion of the La Tène culture over large parts of central and west-Europe introduced a new sense of identity, expressed in a warrior elite and a distinct material culture (Cunliffe 1999, 268-274). In the Low Countries, the population increased, specifically in the later Iron Age (Fokkens 2019, 190-192; Jansen 2021, 480).[1] People rearranged and structured the landscape on a large scale for the first time, new trade routes and new commodities (such as salt) emerged, bringing with it new contact zones and alliances, and ancient belief systems were largely overturned (Gerritsen 2003, 235-254; Løvschal 2014). In the midst of all these fundamental socio-cultural changes, the rectangular structure is introduced. Evidently, these structures fulfilled a particular need rooted in Iron Age societies, and expressed in a manner unique to the Low Countries.

1.2 The problem of interpreting a rectangular structure

With the incorporation of the Valetta Treaty in the first decade of the 21st century, the amount of archaeological research in the Low Countries increased (Lammers 2017). The Valletta Convention, in effect, mandates that archaeological investigations are done before any soil disturbance is carried out, paid for by the disturber. This produced a large increase in archaeological fieldwork and as a result a massive amount of 'grey literature' (excavation reports that are the result of commercially initiated digs and that are difficult to access), including an increasing number of rectangular structures. Specifically in the Low Countries these ditched structures often portray a lack of finds, complicating the interpretation. Despite that deficiency, the structures are generally interpreted as cult places or open-air sanctuaries.

At this point the terminological distinction between a cult place, a shrine, a sanctuary, and an enclosure need an explanation (table 1.1).

The designations 'cult place', 'shrine', and 'sanctuary' commonly refer to constructed sites, often containing a small building, where a particular action was repeated, visible in the archaeological record by multiple features and an abundance of finds of one or more specific categories. The difference between them is regional, as in France the structures are referred to as sanctuaries or *lieux de culte*, *Heiligtümer* in Germany, in Britain they are usually called shrines, and in the Low Countries cult places or open-air sanctuaries. The term 'enclosure', in contrast, refers to an anthropogenic structure that encloses a certain area, not specifying what this enclosed space was used for. In this dissertation, the term 'rectangular structure' will be used to denote a manmade structure without pre-determining its purpose or duration of its use. The function can therefore be limited to host a singular event, unlike the utilisation of a cult place as defined above. *De facto*, to identify sites as cult places there should be an abundance of finds. For the Lower Rhine Region Empel, Kessel-Lith, and Elst are named as Late Iron Age examples of cult places (Roymans & Derks 1994; Roymans 2004, 103-193; Roymans 2007; Heeren 2014; Fernández-Götz & Roymans 2015). While these sites produced a large number of deposited Iron Age finds, such as bones, fibulae, coins, and weapons, there is insufficient evidence of an associated Iron Age structure. The excavated structures in Elst and Empel contain Roman temples, with some Iron Age finds suggesting the existence of a predecessor. The finds in Kessel-Lith were all dredged up along with the remains of a Roman temple (Roymans 2004, 141-143; Meffert 2014, 74-75; Heeren 2014). These sites are comparable to deposition sites, apart from the aspect that it is *assumed* a preceding structure stood at these places in the Late Iron Age, even though the actual structure was never documented. Such rich cult places served as a public space for social and political gatherings, to forge identities in the construction of ethnic communities, where feasts and meetings of 'inter-group cult communities' were held (Roymans 2007; Fernández-Götz 2014, 171-182). This theory is mainly based on sites in France that revealed a similar assemblage of finds (Roymans 1990, 62-75).

The work of Brunaux in the Picardy-region in the north of France was influential on the discussion on the interpretation and origins of these rectangular structures. After the excavation and publications on the sites of Gournay-sur-Aronde (Brunaux & Méniel 1983; Brunaux, Méniel & Poplin 1985, Brunaux 1986) and Ribemont-sur-Ancre (Brunaux 1997; Brunaux 1998; Brunaux *et al.* 1999) the interpretation of other sites was generally modelled on these publications and used as an analogy for new discoveries (Slofstra & Van der Sanden 1987; Brunaux

---

1   Extrapolated from a calculation by Jansen (2021, 340, footnote 50), by the Late iron Age the Low Countries had an estimated population of about 300.000-400.000 inhabitants mostly living on sandy and clayey soils.

Term	Definition
Cult place	Constructed site, often containing a small building within a demarked space, where one or more repeated actions took place, like offerings, visible in the archaeological record by multiple features and an abundance of specific types of artefacts; the alleged Iron Age predecessor to a Roman temple
Enclosure	Space enclosed by a physical feature (bank and/or ditch, palisade etc.)
Heiligtum	Term for a cult place in Germany
Sanctuary	Common term for a cult place in France, also referred to as 'lieu de cult' occasionally also used in Britain and the Low Countries
Shrine	Term for a (small) cult place in Britain
Open-air sanctuary	Term sometimes used in the Low Countries for a type of cult place without a roofed building
Viereckschanze	Phenomenon almost exclusively found in southern Germany, initially interpreted as cult places, and now commonly identified as a large square area with a surrounding ditch and bank, likely with a defensive function, generally interpreted as Celtic manors or the centre of a rural settlement, dating to 2nd and 1st century BCE.
Offering site	Place used for offerings, in the archaeological record commonly visible by a deposition of one or more objects, which can be a natural place such as a river, bog, tree, cave, etc.
Rectangular structure	In this this thesis defined as an archaeological feature with a specific shape made out of a ditch and possibly a bank, and/or on rare occasions a palisade, a description referring only to the appearance of the structure, not to function.

Table 1.1. Definitions of terminology.

et al. 1999; Lejars 2001). These sites in France have both an abundance of finds and an associated structure that served a cult-related purpose, resulting in the title 'cult place', 'sanctuary', or 'shrine' commonly being applied to structures associated with many finds, demonstrating repetitive actions or offerings.

The interpretation of such sites is influenced by references made by classical authors (Wait 1985, 203-204; Brunaux 1995). Caesar (Gallic Wars, VI, 17, trans. Macdavitt 2012) described how, after a conflict, Celtic warriors sacrifice captured animals, and deposited other things into 'consecrated spots', where they were heaped into piles that nobody dared to touch. Diodorus Siculus (Diodorus Historical Library, V, 27, 4, trans. Oldfather 1939) mentions religious sanctuaries or enclosures throughout the Celtic regions, many with temples or shrines, sometimes near water. Strabo (Geography, IV, 4, 5, trans. Jones 1927) mentioned that he heard of human skulls being attached on the porch to a sacred area. For extensive summaries of classical sources on sanctuaries in Belgium Gaul[2] and related subjects I refer to Wait (1985, 203-204) and Brunaux (1995).

More recently, the status of Gournay as an archetype 'Celtic cult place' with the large amounts of metal objects and human bones has come under debate (Fontijn 2002a; Lejars 2007). This particular site might actually represent an exception rather than an example. The same could be stated for Ribemont-sur-Ancre, where two-hundred decapitated warriors along with their weapons and armour were found. Other sites in France are mostly Gallo-Roman sanctuaries with a presumed Iron Age predecessor based on the finds (Roymans 1990, 62-75; Fauduet 2010, 147-148). Large numbers of weapons, mainly swords, spearheads, and umbos, were found on sites with Gallo-Roman temples as well as having been dredged up from rivers (Roymans 1990, 75-90). Other finds at temple sites include depositions of coins, fibulae, purposely made miniatures such as wheels, diverse animal bones, and human bones.

So, while the evidence of depositions is accumulating, the associated Iron Age structures are still elusive. According to the description of a typical Iron Age sanctuary as ascertained by Brunaux, the primary requirement is a demarcation surrounding a sacred place in the form of a wall and/or ditch system (Brunaux 1986, 29-30; Brunaux 1995). In the Low Countries the discovered rectangular structures generally contain few finds. However, finds have been discovered outside structures or research areas, often metal detector finds or accidental by-catch that was dredged up from an aqueous context. As a result, the evidence necessary to interpret an Iron Age site as a cult place is lacking: either the structure lacks the associated finds, or finds are not associated with a structure.

1.3 The problem of the 'ritual' in a rectangular structure

A dissertation on the Iron Age belief system could easily get entangled in the web of definitions surrounding ´ritual´. The word 'ritual' is often used to express acts of a religious or superstitious nature. Bell (1992, 7) argued for 'ritual activities' to be removed from their isolated position as special paradigmatic acts and restored to the context of social activity in general. She proposed an alternative

---

2   Belgium Gaul is defined by Caesar (Gallic Wars, I, 1) as the space between the Seine and the Rhine, or, according to Strabo (Geography, IV, 4, 3), from the mouth of the Loire to the Rhine (Brunaux 1995). The research area would for the larger part be situated in this region.

framework for understanding ritual behaviour. Many rituals can be integrated into everyday activities without further reflection on the issue; in a world without the cognitive distinction between sacred and profane (Fernández-Götz 2014, 171). It has even been argued that our modern distinction between profane and sacred is entirely meaningless for the understanding of Iron Age human behaviour, as they 'formed two layers that seem to have been precisely superimposed' (Bradley 2005, 120). Or, in the words of the pragmatic approach by Grimes (2014, 41), that 'a fundamental premise of ritual studies is that a ritual is embedded'.

As Brück (1999) has argued, the word 'ritual' has to be used with care as the notion of ritual as a distinct category of practice is not a common concept to all societies. When the word 'ritual' is used to designate actions that resulted in certain finds or features observed in the archaeological record, it implies there are also actions in the opposite realm of the domestic sphere that are 'profane', 'technological' or 'practical'. This dichotomy is arguably a modern rationalist thought and it suggests that archaeologists implicitly define ritual and non-ritual as two mutual exclusive practices (*Ibid.*). Brück (1999) further states that ritual is frequently described or defined as a non-functional, irrational action, even though based on anthropological analogies it becomes apparent that the actors do not make such a distinction. Actions that by our functionalistic point of view would be described as 'ritual', could have been perceived by Iron Age people as perfectly logical. It is entirely conceivable no such distinction was made between ´domestic´ and ´ritual´. The motive behind a certain act cannot be described as either ritual or practical, irrational or rational, religious or secular. Defining a deposition as the result of a 'ritual' act, would not do justice to the complex worldview underlying the motivation of the act. Nonetheless, it will become apparent in this dissertation that depositions and 'uncommon' or 'symbolic' features have been used by many archaeologists as the basis for the identification of cult places. The underlying motivation of the act that resulted in these assemblages of finds and features of the archaeological record will be a reoccurring topic in this thesis, without the emphasis on either 'ritual' or 'domestic/profane'.

Not until critically reviewing the site in Oss again in 2018, I discovered I had overlooked a piece of essential information (De Leeuwe & Jansen 2018; Ch.6.5 in this volume). Three pits with evidence of fire were quite conveniently enclosed by the structure. At the time of the first publication, I left them out of the consideration as their primary use predates the cult place. How could 5th century BCE wells possibly be connected to a structure four centuries younger? However, their final use might have coincided with the utilisation of the rectangular structure. The top fill of all three pits contained layers of burned material. The secondarily burnt pottery fragments, charcoal, and loam from the pits revealed glimpses of information about the utilisation of the place. If so, was this act of burning or deposition related to the function of the rectangular structure?

Finding burned pottery and loam is not uncommon in an Iron Age settlement context. Depots containing burned pottery and loam in postholes of structures are interpreted as abandonment depositions for the related house or settlement (Van den Broeke 2002; 2015). The burned pieces in those cases were carefully selected and stacked. However, charcoal was missing from these depositions, unlike the material in the pits of the rectangular structure.

Few finds could be directly related to the structure in Oss. Fourteen Roman coins were found that seemed to be dating to a subsequent use of the site (De Leeuwe 2011, 112). As a collection of coins is often regarded as an indicator of votive offerings, the focus again turned towards the French sanctuaries. The assemblage of votive objects in Roman Gaul is interpreted as requests for aid in military victory, healing, fertility, or agricultural success among other purposes from different deities (Roymans 1990, 84). Roman sanctuaries have been described as 'spaces intended for the worship of one or more cosmological powers, separate from the profane world, in which the members of the cult community regularly gathered in order to perform their personal or collective rituals before a ritual focus' (Derks 1996, 108-109). The physical focus point here could be a pit, hearth, post setting, statue or altar. As find assemblages in French Iron Age sanctuaries often contain weaponry depositions, Brunaux (1995) interprets the Iron Age sanctuaries as war trophies. He suggests two distinct types of activities take place in sanctuaries:

1. Activities performed by warriors, an important social category within Celtic society. According to Brunaux (1995), the behaviour of a warrior is 'ritualized' to the extreme, from their initiation until their return home after conflict. Assemblies would be held in a central place, where wars were decided and ended, with the agreement of the priests, in particular the druids. Sanctuaries were also the places where the bodies of the conquered enemies along with their armour and weapons would have been on display as an offering to the gods.
2. Activities performed by priests (druids) and related to features in the enclosed space.

The French sanctuaries in question have some comparable characteristics and Brunaux (1995) gives a specific description of their lay-out. It shows a quadrangular ground plan, enclosing an area of around 2500 m^2, commonly delimited by a ditch, sometimes a wall, and sometimes bordered by a bank on each side of the ditch. In the centre of the enclosed space, the sacred area, a large pit is found. This supposedly represents the presence of a substantial altar. The shape is usually round or oval, 2-4m in diameter, and of a depth that can reach more than 2m. This pit is surrounded by several smaller pits arranged in a circle and covering a space of 20-25 m². The whole structure is interpreted as a subterranean altar devoted to chthonic deities.

According to Derks (1996, 148-149), the emergence of new cult places in the Late Iron Age was the result of increasing hierarchisation of northern Gallic society caused by internal changes such as the use of oppida, coin circulation, differentiation in artisanal production and growing numbers of imports from the Mediterranean. In his definition of this north-Gallic region, Derks (*Ibid.*, 24) included the Low Countries below the Rhine. In this thesis I will argue that the north of France knew a set of different traditions than the Low Countries and even though some aspects can be compared they are basically regional phenomena. The description of the rectangular ground plan of these sanctuaries may resemble the structures found in the Low Countries. However, the arrangement of the enclosed space and the finds do not match. The often modest number and the types of finds do not support the theory of a long use of the structure, or the use as a place for regular assemblies or feasts. The expected evidence for a 'cultic' interpretation often seems to be lacking in these structures. How then should we interpret the rectangular structures in the Low Countries and their meagre find assemblage? Are these even used for 'cult'-orientated assemblies? Is it a different type of gathering where objects have no part, or perhaps a local adjustment of the same act? One theory suggested by several authors is that most of these Low Country structures are cult places that functioned on a local level related to an ancestral cult (Fontijn 2002a; Gerritsen 2003, 167; Fernández-Götz 2014, 171-182; Roymans & Derks 2014). The proximity of most structures to graves and cemeteries was the basis for this theory. In cases where no burials were found it was suggested the burials were destroyed by ploughing or other recent activities (Fontijn 2002a, 155; Hiddink 2014, 255). From the connection to burials, it could be concluded that the action performed at the structure was a burial tradition. The problem with that theory is that not all burials are related to one of these structures. In fact, most cemeteries in the Middle Iron Age do not have a rectangular structure in the vicinity (Gerritsen 2003, 132-133; Hiddink 2003, 7-10). Some of the Middle and Late Iron Age burials themselves are surrounded by small ditches resembling urnfield features rather than sanctuaries (Gerritsen 2003, 135-137; Hiddink 2003, 27). In short, what type of purpose or act did these rectangular structures serve and how can it be described?

1.4 The problem of the environmental context and date of a rectangular structure

A single piece of burned human remains was all the evidence of a possible cremation grave found in relation to the structure in Oss (De Leeuwe 2011, 54). Clearly, the environmental context of this structure cannot be described as a cemetery. Unfortunately, areas to the east and west were not excavated and the contextual setting of the structure therefore remains elusive. As will appear from the description of many of these structures in this dissertation, the lack of context is a recurring problem in the interpretation of the structures. Only a few were excavated on a large-scale excavation. Some were barely excavated beyond the outline of the structures and some of the older excavations cover only a part of the structure.

The lack of contemporary features in the vicinity of the structure in Oss supports the theory that suggests cult places become detached from cemeteries in the Late Iron Age. Roymans distinguishes two types of cult places: local and supra-local, also referred to as regional and supra-regional (Roymans 2004, 12-14; Derks & Roymans 2009, 7-8; Roymans & Derks 2014, 230; Fernández-Götz & Roymans 2015). While the local ones still had links to cremation cemeteries, the supra-local sanctuaries are dissociated from funerary contexts. According to Fernández-Götz & Roymans (2015) supra-local sanctuaries were positioned away from settlement sites or cemeteries and played an important role in the creation of a shared identity. The emergence of the supra-local cult places in the Lower Rhine region is placed in the La Tène D2 period, or possibly D1, immediately preceding the Roman temples (Roymans 2004, 13). The number of supra-local sanctuaries in the Lower Rhine region is limited to the examples of Kessel-Lith, Elst, Empel (Derks & Roymans 1994; Roymans 2004), and perhaps the in 2022 discovered temple complex at Zevenaar.

The theory of the emergence of supra-local structures is heavily based on sanctuaries found in oppida in the Middle Rhine-Moselle region dating to the second and first centuries BCE, and the theory that a group of local cult places was already in use in northern France and the Lower Rhine. These supra-local cult places would have functioned from the 3rd century BCE, were the result of hierarchisation of society and were allegedly related to ancestor worship and burial customs (Derks 1996, 148-149; Roymans 2004, 11; Roymans & Derks 2014, 230; Fernández-Götz & Roymans 2015, 26). The problem with this latter theory is that it is based on only a few sites which are situated in different environmental contexts: near a settlement or in a cemetery. The actual use of these sites is assumed to be for gatherings of the local 'cult community' (Gerritsen 2003, 163-167). Again this suggests a longer use of the structures and reoccurring actions that would have taken place there. Excavations in Belgium show however, that some of these structures were not meant to be visible demarcations for a longer period. Research of a rectangular ditched structure in Ursel provided evidence that the ditch had been filled in shortly after it was dug and possibly even in a single act (Bourgois, Semey & Vanmoerkerke 1989). This observation does not correspond to a repeated use of the structure as a regular gathering place. Also, the find assemblages on these sites do not provide a solid basis to support the theory of a long utilisation. In fact, it is difficult to accurately assess the construction date and changes in utilisation.

1.5 Research questions

The central research question of this dissertation is focused on the identification and utilisation of a particular type of rectangular structure that is generally interpreted as a cult place. I seek to understand what these structures were really used for. To avoid using the sometimes confusing above mentioned multitude of names for these structures such as cult place, enclosure or sanctuary, the more neutral term 'rectangular structure' is used.

Deriving from the problems mentioned above, the basic research questions can be formulated as follows:

1. Which finds and features define an Iron Age rectangular structure in the Low Countries?
2. How were rectangular structures used in the Iron Age?
3. What socio-cultural purpose did these structures serve within Iron Age societies?
4. What is the environmental and social context of the rectangular structures and does it change over time?
5. Can these structures be identified as the cult places described by classic writers such as Caesar and Diodorus in the final stages of the Iron Age?

1.6 Dataset and limitations

Ideally, the collected data needed to study an archaeological phenomenon related to religion should reflect all aspects described by Bell (1992, 94-101) as the interactions of individuals and society (the 'ritualised body') with the structure (the 'ritual place') and the structured environment (space/environmental context). This trinity of body, space and place are integral parts of a religion. This thesis is centred around the place component: the archaeological remains of a constructed feature from which clues to the associated actions and the structural environment might be derived. This includes the manner in which a structure can be used, why it was there and how it was related to the landscape around it. The pragmatic reality is that the archaeological record offers limited possibilities.

For inclusion in this research, the data was compiled using only a few basic criteria that a site must meet. First of all, the site needs to contain a constructed feature that was interpreted as a cult place, sanctuary or 'ritual' structure, or at least thought to have a religious significance. Depositions of objects in a natural place, such as a river, lake or bog, are excluded in this study by lack of a constructed place. Inherently, the structure has to be dated to the Iron Age. Preferably more precisely to a sub-period (Early-Middle-Late) of the Iron Age, so that chronological developments might be determined with respect to a possible typology, function, and to changes in the structures and associated actions.

As the dataset will demonstrate, dating both the foundation and the abandonment of these structures can be challenging. The foundation date is defined as the construction of the structure, materialised in the archaeological record by the digging of the ditch (or another manifestation of the construction). In theory this action was preceded by a need and a decision, followed by choosing the location and determining the dimensions. All these actions may have had an accompanying tradition that never left a trace in the archaeological record. Digging was merely the first action in a line of acts that left visible evidence.

Furthermore, the fieldwork data of the site needs to contain sufficient information on a selection of variables to work with. To analyse an archaeological site the excavation data must contain information on the construction of the excavated structure and the associated features and find assemblage. The latter could express the interactions of the individuals or a society that represent actions of the 'ritualised body' within the designated space, or in other words, the acts. The main variable to study is the dimensions of the structure itself and the methods by which it was constructed. The dimensions may reflect the size or importance of the group for which the structure was made, the effort put into building it, the visibility and the degree of impact on its surroundings. Construction methods can for example, entail both a ditch and bank, representing an open structure with a limited visibility of a temporary nature in the landscape, or a bedding trench that used to contain a wall, representing an enclosed space in which actions took place that were not visible for the outside world.

Following the above-described criteria, seven Late Bronze Age to Early Iron Age structures were selected, seventeen Middle Iron Age, and twenty-three Late Iron Age ones. Totalling 47, the number of structures in the dataset is the primary limiting factor for analysis of the data. The size of this dataset would not be considered enough in a statistical analysis to test for patterns. The dataset is merely a sample of an unknown number of Iron Age sites in the Low Countries. The research area that the dataset covers is the southern part of the Netherlands including the riverine area with the Rhine/Old Rhine as the northern fringe, excluding the peat area, and Belgium excluding

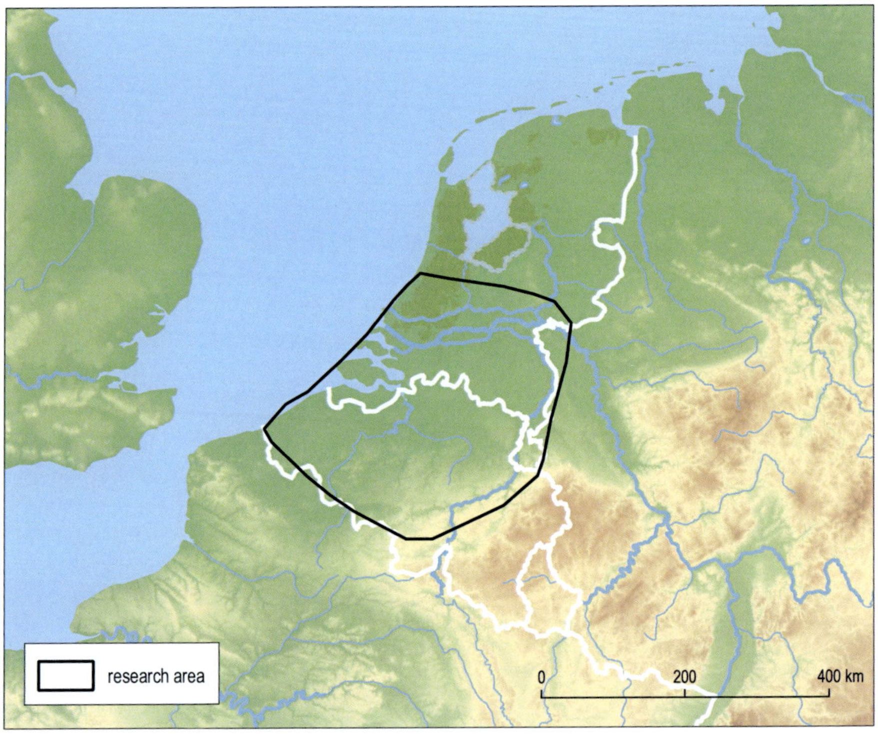

Figure 1.1. Research area (approximation), in the Low Countries.

the Ardennes (combined referred to in this thesis as 'the Low Countries', fig. 1.1). In the northern Netherlands rectangular structures of the Iron Age are either not interpreted as cult places, have different dimensions, or are absent altogether (see also Ch.4.2.1).

The interpretation of the sites is another factor influencing the analysis, as it is obviously subjective. Authors searched for analogies of their excavated structures and found the same references again and again, commonly referring to an article by Slofstra and Van der Sanden (1987). This article contained the description of six sites with rectangular structures, five of which were Roman, interpreted as cult places based on the analogy with Iron Age French sites. The early publication, accessibility, and repetitive use of the article created circular reasoning, prescribed by the shape of the structure. This resulted in the subsequent interpretation of many rectangular structures as cult places, without scrutinising the context or the evidence. Inadvertently, the six sites generated a slow-growing dataset consisting not only of Roman but also Iron Age structures, while at the same time no other types of constructed Iron Age features related to the belief system were identified. As a consequence, the main starting point for investigating Iron Age cult places remains this dataset of predominantly rectangular shaped features. To summarise, this dataset is compiled out of structures with a similar shape and a possible cult place interpretation. It is conceivable that the shape was not as relevant to the makers of the structure, but fundamentally it is the only data available.

Two other aspects of Iron Age behaviour are relevant for a holistic approach as they are inextricably linked with the use of rectangular structures: burial traditions and depositions. Exploring these subjects in full is outside of the scope of this thesis. Burial customs of the Early Iron Age have been covered by other researchers such as De Mulder (2011) and Louwen (2021). The number of Middle and Late Iron Age cemeteries in the Low Countries is estimated at a few hundred (see chapters 5 and 6). A comprehensive study of these cemeteries, and also additional research into deposition practices, is needed in future research. In this thesis a limited sample of either will serve as an analogy.

1.7 Variables

A catalogue describing the Iron Age sites in the Low Countries cited in this thesis is available in the appendix. Each site description starts with the general appearance of the structure in question and its excavated dimensions. The dimensions of a structure will be given in metres at the excavation level, in a 'heart-to-heart' distance (the centre of the ditch on one side measured to the centre of the ditch on the opposite side). However, at the time of construction the surface of the ground was likely at another level than at the time of excavation. During its use, the structure may have been changed, reused, had parts added, altered or destroyed, thereby resulting in excavated features that are a palimpsest of different phases. Thereafter, inevitable post-depositional processes changed the site. In many places ploughing destroyed the upper layer of the features in the soil while equalising the relief. As a result a ditch dug in the Iron Age ends up at the archaeological surface level as a shallower and narrower feature than when it was originally dug. Over thousands of years, trees growing on the site and burrowing by animals may have had a destructive impact, making features less visible. An understanding of these processes, the interpretation by the excavator, and a reconstruction where possible, gives essential insights into the appearance of the structure.

Associated features like accompanying pits and postholes, along with the find assemblage, assist in understanding the utilisation of the structure. Pits may have been used for the deposition of offerings, or possibly even communicating with chthonic deities associated with the earth or subterranean underworld (Brunaux 1986, 137-148; Aldhouse Green 2006, 129-135; Bradley 2005, 170-171). Postholes used to have posts in them that made structures or fences. In many cases the structure remains unclear and in reconstructions the posts are often depicted as representing merely upright wooded posts. More likely, they were part of a structure, were connected to each other (by planking for example) and served a purpose as (roof-) supports, or even represented a totem or a pillar. A similar statement can be made with respect to the evidence for trees. Trees or forests may have been involved in certain Iron Age religious beliefs and symbolism (Green 1997, 212-214; Aldhouse-Green 2015, 156-161). With their roots and their branches, trees reflected a link between the upper and the underworld. In the archaeological record a 'tree throw' or 'tree fell' can easily be identified, although unfortunately it is often impossible to date when the tree grew there. Nonetheless, where possible, all of these associated features will be described. In the accompanying figures of each site, only features that were contemporary and those directly preceding the use of the rectangular structure have been depicted. In all the figures north is up. The description of the finds is limited to those recovered from the structure itself and from associated features, along with other contemporary finds. Dates are given in years Before the Common Era (BCE) or in the Common Era (CE), where possible using Oxcal 4.3.2 for (re)calibration.

When considering the use of a structure, the surrounding environment has to be taken into account. The specific location could have been chosen for a reason. Hence, the context and geographical location within the landscape are integral parts of the archaeological reconstruction. The context could have been near or in a settlement related to daily life, or in or near a cemetery related to ancestors or particular burial customs. The position in the landscape can be described as on a hill, near a river or stream or some other prominent natural feature, perhaps a clearing in a long-gone forest, or a manmade feature such as a crossing of roads that are now no longer visible. Reconstruction of the context and the geographical

positioning within the landscape could explain for example the orientation and choice of location of the structure. Some excavations, specifically the somewhat older ones involving strenuous manual labour, extended marginally beyond the dimensions of the structure itself and covered little of the surrounding area, therefore making a contextual reconstruction problematic.

1.8 Approach and outline of the study

To provide a basis for the analysis of the Low Countries data, a theoretical and geographical framework is needed. In Chapter 2 the theoretical framework is centred around the question *how rectangular structures could fit in the Iron Age belief system*. What components did the world view and the belief in the afterlife of these people consist of? What is the relation to the ancestral cult as suggested by so many authors? How did people perceive their relation with the natural world and what do votive offerings represent? In Chapter 3 the geographical framework will provide insight into the theories on cult places in bordering regions: France, Germany, and England. The goal for this chapter is providing a reference of *what is generally defined as a cult place in northwest Europe*. The archetype sanctuaries of France will serve as a starting point, followed by a discussion on German structures and available evidence in Britain. This unavoidably includes discussing certain French sites that have been discussed countless times before and the foregone discussion on the interpretation of *Viereckschanzen* as cult related structures.

After the framework is set, chapters 4 to 6 discuss all sites in the Low Countries that form the core of this thesis. Chapter 4 focusses on the intangible topic of the origin of rectangular structures. Both De Laet (1966) and Fontijn (2002a) suggested that *cult places have derived from burial customs in urnfields*. This hypothesis needs to be tested. To this end, the oldest rectangular structures found in the Low Countries and their relationship to cemeteries will be reviewed. In Chapter 5 the theory that *'local open-air cult places' emerged in the Middle Iron Age* is researched. Several authors conceptualise that these rectangular structures would have functioned as community gathering places from the 3rd century BCE onwards (Derks 1996, 148-149; Roymans 2004, 11; Roymans & Derks 2014, 230; Fernández-Götz & Roymans 2015, 26). As many Middle Iron Age ^{14}C-analysis results in a calibrated date between roughly 400 and 200 BCE, this chapter comprises the structures dating between 500 and 200 BCE. Chapter 6 encompasses an even larger number of sites dating to the 2nd and 1st century BCE to provide insight into the theory that suggests *cult places become detached from cemeteries in the Late Iron Age* (Gerritsen & Roymans 2006; Fernández-Götz 2014, 52, Roymans & Derks 2014). Does the association with burials change over time from the Middle to the Late Iron Age? In addition, the question is addressed

18   BEFORE TEMPLES

as to what the find assemblage and the features reveal on the use of the structures or the place.

Chapter 7 shows the additional value of a large-scale excavation around the structures. The diachronic development of the landscape in which these structures first appear can demonstrate an incentive for the location choice, the relation to existing landscape elements, as well as the embedment of the structures in successive field systems. Chapter 8 contains the synthesis of the dataset in which the sites, their finds and features, their context and geographical setting, and ultimately their function, will be discussed. Finally, in Chapter 9 the main conclusions will be summarised, the research questions addressed, and suggestions for further research given.

2

The belief system in the Iron Age

2.1 Introduction

Archaeologists study the Iron Age belief system through the physical remains of actions. This limits us to a circumstantial notion of what the Iron Age belief system in Northwest Europe entailed, what myths were being told, which symbols were used, or even who the participants were. The evidence is indirect as these people did not leave a written record; only texts by contemporary and later Roman authors remain, and the interpretation of the archaeological record (Green 1997, 14). Religions are complex systems where people, deities, sacred places, dates, and objects are all connected by an intricate network of narratives providing explanations and traditions giving meaning to life, the universe and everything. Every religious system is basically a regional phenomenon (Morris 2006, 1). It has been described as an experience, consisting of sensations, perceptions, concepts, and names (Müller 1889, 115).

In this chapter a theoretical temporal framework is established to support the idea that rectangular structures were constructed for a purpose that was intrinsic to the world view of Iron Age people. These people deemed the construction of the rectangular structures a logical necessity or requirement under certain circumstances. The aim of this thesis is not to understand the whole of Iron Age religion, but to focus on the generative principles that resulted in the construction of these features and the deposition of related find complexes.

2.2 The soul and the ancestors

At the base of the temporal framework is a belief that is referred to by Durkheim (1995 [1912], 57) as the 'original type of all religions': the ancestral cult. Ancestral worship or 'the ancestral cult' is an often used but ill-defined term to describe the belief system of the Bronze and Iron Age communities in the Low Countries. Mostly the term is applied by archaeologists to describe burial customs, without considering what ancestral worship actually entailed for the practitioners.

Ancestor worship can be defined as a form of animism based around the notion that people, or possibly all living creatures, have a soul. The soul is believed to be attached to a bodily form from which it rarely exits (Tylor 1873, 113ff, as cited by Durkheim 1995 [1912], 48-49). As described by Durkheim (1995 [1912], 48-49), the soul can become a spirit when transformed by metamorphosis, usually upon death. Once the body is destroyed, the separation of body and soul is considered final. Detached spirits can move around, enter inside bodies to either cause disorders or aid vitality, and they also have needs and passions. A population of souls (or spirits) is formed around the living, and their number grows over time. Since souls have control over health and sickness, and over good and bad, it is therefore considered wise to satisfy them with offerings, sacrifices, and prayers. In this way the dead become ancestors and ancestors become spirits or even gods. Durkheim (*ibid.*, 49) states that the first rites were funerary rites, the first sacrifices involving food offerings were meant to meet the needs of the deceased, and the first altars were their tombs.

2.2.1 Different concepts of the soul

The belief in the soul is complex and is conceptualised and practiced in many forms around the world. From the description given by Durkheim, it would appear that the general idea is that human beings possess one soul. However, in Europe before the 5th century BCE, a dualistic concept of the soul was more likely the norm (Bremmer 1983, 14, 66-69). Humans were thought to have a 'free' soul that was not necessarily bound to the body as it could wander in states of sleep, trance, or transmigrate after death (*Ibid.*, 14-52, 63-66). The second soul is referred to as the 'body' or 'ego' soul. In Archaic Greek literature (attributed to Homer, 8th century BCE), the free soul is identified as *psychē* and the bodily soul consists of three major parts called *thymos, noos,* and *menos* (*Ibid.*, 54). *Thymos* was only active when the body is awake and controls emotions, *noos* is related to the intellect, and *manos* to impulses (*Ibid.*, 53-61). Animals and plants were also thought to have souls, although not the *psychē-* or the *noos*-type (*Ibid.*, 125-131).

Upon death, *psychē* was believed to leave for Hades while the bodily parts of the soul expired with the physical remains (Bremmer 1983, 15). To enter Hades, a river had to be crossed which could only be achieved if the body was cremated, preferably on home grounds (*Ibid.*, 89-92). People who committed suicide, children, adolescents or slaves had a different status in Greek society and were inhumated instead of cremated. Also, the souls of people who died an untimely or violent death in ancient Greece had a different fate (*Ibid.*, 101). In the Classical period (5th-4th century BCE), the common practice was for fallen warriors to be buried on or near the battlefield (Kurtz & Boardman 1971, 247-248). The friendlies were cremated, while the enemies and the slaves were buried. Sometimes the cremated remains were covered by a mount, equipped with a rectangular enclosure and the statue of a lion, such as an enclosure measuring 32 × 23m in Thespiae and one of 24 × 15m at Chaeronea. In situations where not all bodies were recovered from the battlefield, a cenotaph was built (Kurtz & Boardman 1971, 257). Offerings were placed at the empty tomb similar to offerings at actual tombs. In case warriors were buried on the battlefield a cenotaph could be erected at home to record names and the event. Sometimes cremated remains were returned home or burials were performed without remains (Kurtz & Boardman 1971, 258). A similar procedure was for instance performed for losses at sea.

Soul dualism is not unique to Europe and used to be central in Chinese traditions before the introduction of Buddhism (Yü 1987). From about the 6th century BCE the soul was considered as *hun* and *p'o,* and by the 2nd century BCE the former was thought of as belonging to the *yang* category (an active and heavenly substance) and the latter to *yin* (the element of receptivity, passive and earthly). It is therefore unsurprising that upon death *hun* left the body for heaven while *p'o* remained on earth (*Ibid.* 1987). So far the European dualist notion of the soul seems comparable. However, the Chinese belief system is illustrative for the variety of ways in which the concept of the soul can be intertwined with all aspects of life. In Chinese folk traditions a soul can be lost due to diseases in children or in adults attacked by supernatural beings, a soul can travel in shamanistic journeys or be replaced by a spirit or god, and a soul can cease to exist when a person is no longer remembered (Harrell 1979). Souls of dead people can become supernatural beings, or even a god if they were powerful in life. In case of a violent death or when there were no descendant to worship them as ancestors a soul can become a ghost. Ancestors are thought to behave in the same manner as living people and have distinct personalities (*Ibid.* 1979).

After the 5th century BCE, many religions held the viewpoint that only one soul controlled the *psychē* as well as the ego, a 'unitary soul' (Bremmer 1983, 14). All religions of the Abrahamic tradition believe humans have one life and one immortal soul that upon death is judged (e.g. Meysami-Azad 2017). In these belief systems the body is only a temporary vessel while the soul represents the real person or permanent identity that is taken onwards to the afterlife. In one of the earliest text of the Vedic tradition, the Rig-Veda (northwest India, c. 15th-10th century BCE), there used to be a similar notion of the continued existence of the soul after death, including continued personal identity (e.g. MacDonell 1900). However, in contrast to the Abrahamic tradition, the remains were cremated instead of inhumated. The dead were provided with all necessities they needed in the next life and in the cremation the spirit of the deceased would rise to the sky with the smoke, and then go on a path foregone by the fathers to the 'other world'. In later Sanskrit doctrine (c. 7th century BCE) the belief system in India has incorporated reincarnation (*Ibid.* 1900). The soul is considered universal and transmigrates after death "into a series of new existences in heavens and hells, or in the bodies of men, animals, and plants on earth, where it is rewarded or punished in strict accordance with its karma or action committed in a former life" (*Ibid.* 1900, 500).

Within the frame of the ancestral cult, the belief in the soul is accompanied by superstitions, and unavoidably, taboos (Frazer 2012 [1911]; Caesar on sacrifices, *Gallic Wars* 6.14). This complex part of the belief system is difficult to comprehend as an outsider, specifically as an atheist archaeologist regarding an ancient extinct religion.

Many superstitions and taboos would not have resulted in remains that became part of the archaeological record. As an illustration the example of the 'abandonment depots' as described by Van der Broeke are used (2002; 2015). He remarked on a pattern of broken and secondarily burned pottery that was left in postholes of settlements structures in the 7th -6th and also in the 3rd century BCE. The pottery was typically found in only one or two postholes of a house or outhouse. His interpretation was that these depositions were intended as abandonment or closing acts, upon leaving a farmyard or settlement. Van der Broeke did not specify at whom this sacrifice was aimed. What if the

pottery offering was meant to keep the soul of a person that died in that house bound to the place? This could even be a motivation for a move, specifically if the deceased in question died what was considered 'a bad death', or if the living relatives believed the place was somehow haunted. The possibilities of accompanying superstitious beliefs are endless. It is conceivable the former house place was considered a place of taboo after its abandonment.

2.2.2 Communication with the dead
In many religions it is believed that upon death, the soul of a person does not automatically become a spirit or

Figure 2.1. Examples of memorial stones in Madagascar. Photos by the author.

deity (Durkheim 1995, 57-59). A qualification is needed for the deceased to become an ancestral spirit, like a certain status in life, a certain manner of death, or an appropriate rite of passage. The outcome can be a spirit, a ghost, genie, demon, deity, or any type of animate and conscious being. Sometimes it is possible to communicate with these (ancestral) spirits or beings, an act that is considered necessary under certain circumstances.

Animistic cultures sometimes use physical means to communicate with spirits. On the island of Borneo a diversity of material representations of ancestors signify and discern the presence of ancestral spirits (Couderc & Sillander 2012, 37-40). For example, the ancestor skulls of the Dayak and the *tojahan* shrines of the Uut Danum represent particular ancestors and facilitate acquisition of potency from agencies associated with them. These objects or sites are worshipped, mediating contact with ancestors or associated spirits. Other objects are used to commemorate, such as funerary posts, or to connect to or communicate with spirits, such as collective bone ossuaries, hearths, and house altars. Wooden figures and erect stones are placed in sacred places in the forest that connect communities. Some objects become relics with attributed special powers. The pelvic bone of an aristocrat is thought to have sexual potency and enables the rebirth of the soul of the deceased by reburial in *kelireng* burial posts. Stones symbolise endurance and can function as portable charms for personal protection. Some large boulders or even mountain ranges are believed to represent petrified mythological ancestors. Stones are also erected to commemorate secondary burials of important people.

Among the Mahafaly and the Antandroy people, who live in the south and central highlands of Madagascar, death is likewise regarded as a rite of passage from life to the realm of the ancestors (Parker Pearson & Ramilisonina 1998; Crossland 2014, 181-195). The spirits of the dead are believed to share the world with the living (Crossland 2018). However, when a person dies far away from home and the body cannot be buried, there is a fear that the soul has no resting place or the wandering spirit can harass the family of the deceased. In the past, this occurred on military expeditions, kidnappings or when people were enslaved and alienated from the ancestral land and tomb (Crossland 2014, 181-195; Crossland 2018). On those occasions a standing stone, known as a *vatolahy* ('man-stone'), was erected by the relatives (Parker Pearson & Ramilisonina 1998). These stones are found in a variety of clearly visible places: on the edge of a farmyard, in a village, along roads, on hill tops or higher grounds and in fields (fig. 2.1).

The stone offers a place for the soul to reside, as well as a place where the living can communicate with the ancestor, not unlike the cenotaphs in Classical Greece.

They were sometimes constructed on other occasions to commemorate events, treaties, and agreements, such as the adoption of a child, the end of a tribal feud, or the foundation of a settlement, while at the same time offering protection (Crossland 2014, 181-195). Also, the stones were used to mark boundaries of territories of different groups, or to 'deflect the malign influence of a tomb whose position with respect to a house or village might affect the living' (Parker Pearson & Ramilisonina 1998).

2.2.3 Creating monuments in the Bronze Age

In the northwest European Bronze Age ancestral worship typifies the burial tradition. The custom of constructing a barrow over a grave has been in use in the Low Countries since the early third millennium BCE (Lanting & Van der Plicht 2001; Furholt 2003, 91-100). This custom steadily continues throughout the second millennium BCE, although between 2100 and 1800 BCE and the centuries preceding the Urnfield period (1400-1100 BCE) there appear to have been hiatuses in barrow construction (Bourgeois & Arnoldussen 2006; Fontijn & Bourgeois 2008; Bourgeois 2013, 31-38). Many barrows had circular structures surrounding them, such as palisade ditches, a bank and a ditch, ring ditches or post circles (Glasbergen 1954; Bourgeois 2013, 30). These structures emphasised the shape and the presence of the barrow, confirming that the barrow is not merely a functional burial practice, but foremost a symbolic one. The barrows themselves and many of their surrounding features would have been intentionally placed on open heathlands, where they were visible in the landscape (Bourgeois 2013, 206). Three observations lead to the conclusion that the barrows were used for ancestral worship:

firstly, there is the shape of the barrows themselves; not spherical but rather flat-topped (*Ibid.*, 105-107). This platform-shaped top might have been used for deposition practices, as remains of pottery and charcoal have been found in these locations (Lawson 2007, 168, cited by Bourgeois 2013, 107-108). A Middle to Late Iron Age barrow near Apeldoorn proved this practice was not exclusively a Bronze Age affair (Van der Linde & Fontijn 2011). With a diameter of nearly 19m this example was exceptionally large for that period. On the flat top two cremation graves were found, one of which was alongside a post. It has been suggested such singular posts functioned as a grave marker (Kooi 1979, 132).

Secondly, the surrounding features such as the post circles seem to have been positioned in such a way as to create a delimited or claimed space, marking the boundary between the internal 'sacral' space for the dead and the outside 'profane' world for the living (Theunissen 1999, 92). The barrow in combination with the surrounding features would have made a significant visual impact (Bourgeois 2013, 116-117). The construction of these barrows can be described as a deliberate and strategic act. The visibility was intended to convey land ownership resulting from the association of communities with real or mythical ancestors (Hanks 2008, 262).

Thirdly, on some sites post alignments and post *alleés* have been discovered (Fokkens 2013). The alignments are positioned in between the barrows seemingly dividing the cemetery, while the *alleés* lead straight up to the central burial. These rows of posts stop a few metres short of the barrow implying they are later additions, possibly Iron Age, to the barrow landscape. Assumingly they represent interactions with ancestors rather than with a primary burial.

The position of the barrows relative to the settlements suggests the ancestors buried within were part of the ancestral worship, in a sense that they still held a central position in Iron Age society (Gerritsen 2003, 249-250; Fokkens 2002). Barrows were reused for secondary graves in increasing numbers during the Bronze Age (Theunissen 1999, 85-86). In a way the barrows and their surrounding features represent religious structures, as Durkheim (1995 [1912], 49) suggested when he proposed the use of tombs as early altars.

2.2.4 Immortality of the soul in the Iron Age

The people that inhabited the Low Countries in the Iron Age still practiced ancestor worship and believed in souls and spirits, and possibly, some form of reincarnation. Wait (1985, 205-206) gives an overview of classic authors who wrote about the Late Iron Age belief in the soul. One of them was the Greek historian Diodorus Siculus. He refers to the immortality of the soul in his work *Bibliotheca historica*, written between 60 and 30 BCE, in which he collectively refers to the people north of the Alps and in Western and Northern Europe as Gauls and sometimes as Upper Celts (*Bibliotheca historica* 5.25.1, trans. Oldfather 1939). Texts like his have limitations for the interpretation of the Iron Age belief system, as the references mainly concern Gaul and only cover the 1st century BCE to the 2nd century CE, as well as contain a certain bias by the writers (Wait 1985, 192-193). Also, Diodorus may not have witnessed the following himself, but copied from others like Posidonius (*Bibliotheca historica*, 5.28.5-6, trans. Edelstein & Kidd 1972):

They invite strangers to their feasts, and do not inquire until after the meal who they are and of what things they stand in need. And it is their custom, even during the course of the meal, to seize upon any trivial matter as an occasion for keen disputation and then to challenge one another to single combat, without any regard for their lives; for the belief of Pythagoras prevails among them, that the souls of men are immortal and that after a prescribed number of years

they commence upon a new life, the soul entering into another body. Consequently, we are told, at the funerals of their dead some cast letters upon the pyre which they have written to their deceased kinsmen, as if the dead would be able to read these letters.

From this text can be extracted that the Late Iron Age belief system included an immortal soul that could transmigrate after death. Caesar, as a Late Iron Age contemporary of Diodorus, gave specific descriptions of the different tribes in Gaul and Belgica, and where they lived (Gallic Wars, I, 1, trans. Macdevitt 2012, 6). Based on his descriptions, the Low Countries were apparently divided into Belgica in the south and part of Germania in the North, the dividing line being the river area with the Meuse, the Rhine and the Waal. Caesar further elaborated on how people believed souls are transferred from one body to another upon death (Gallic Wars, VI, 14). This made for fearless warriors, as '... they think that men by this tenet are in a great degree excited to valour, the fear of death being disregarded'. The belief in the faith of the soul after death may have resulted in certain treatments of the dead, specifically in situations of a violent death and in warfare. This is vividly illustrated by Diodorus writing in the following section (*Bibliotheca historica*, 5.29.5):

In their journeyings and when they go into battle the Gauls use chariots drawn by two horses, which carry the charioteer and the warrior; and when they encounter cavalry in the fighting they first hurl their javelins at the enemy and then step down from their chariots and join battle with their swords. Certain of them despise death to such a degree that they enter the perils of battle without protective armour and with no more than a girdle about their loins. They bring along to war also their free men to serve them, choosing them out from among the poor, and these attendants they use in battle as charioteers and as shield-bearers. It is also their custom, when they are formed for battle, to step out in front of the line and to challenge the most valiant men from among their opponents to single combat, brandishing their weapons in front of them to terrify their adversaries. And when any man accepts the challenge to battle, they then break forth into a song in praise of the valiant deeds of their ancestors and in boast of their own high achievements, reviling all the while and belittling their opponent, and trying, in a word, by such talk to strip him of his bold spirit before the combat. When their enemies fall they cut off their heads and fasten them about the necks of their horses; and turning over to their attendants the arms of their opponents, all covered with blood, they carry them off as booty, singing a paean over them and striking up a song of victory, and these first-fruits of battle they fasten by nails upon their houses, just as men do, in certain kinds of hunting, with the heads of wild beasts they have mastered. The heads of their most distinguished enemies they embalm in cedar-oil and carefully preserve in a chest, and these they exhibit to strangers, gravely maintaining that in exchange for this head some one of their ancestors, or their father, or the man himself, refused the offer of a great sum of money. And some men among them, we are told, boast that they have not accepted an equal weight of gold for the head they show, displaying a barbarous sort of greatness of soul; for not to sell that which constitutes a witness and proof of one's valour is a noble thing, but to continue to fight against one of our own race, after he is dead, is to descend to the level of beasts.

The instantaneous removal of the head is described by Armit (2012, 47) as perhaps the most appallingly brutal act bestowed on the human body, as the head 'is considered the seat of the soul, the basis of our individuality and the part of the body that most defines who we are'. After all, the head gives a person the ability to think, housing consciousness and self-awareness.

Besides archaeological finds, evidence of Iron Age headhunting is provided in the form of iconography (Wait 1985, 198-199). In France, graffiti portraying a mounted warrior with a human head hanging from the neck of his horse was found on a piece of pottery and in Spain several zoomorphic bronze fibulae shaped the same image (Périchon 1987, 678; Almagro-Gorbea & Lorrio 1993 , 231-3; Ill. 2.3; both cited by Armit 2012, 27). The human head either severed or not, had a strong symbolic meaning in the Iron Age. Skulls, or fragments thereof, have been found in Iron Age settlement contexts, or house-related depositions in Britain and in the south of France, forming the link between the occupants and their ancestors (Armit 2012; 2018). According to Armit (2012, 222) the beliefs and practices concerning these depositions change over time from an association with fertility and regeneration before the 3rd century BCE, towards a symbol (or trophy) of an emerging social and political ideology associated with the establishment of new power structures in the Late Iron Age. The emphasis on the human head was a pan-European phenomenon in the Iron Age, part of a belief in which the manipulation of the body and its components evoked the power to mediate between the world of the living and the supernatural world of ancestors, spirits, and gods (Armit 2012, 223-224; 2018). The boundaries between the two worlds were permeable and liminal places such as caves, lakes, bogs, and hilltops were suitable for communication.

2.3 Phenomenology and the natural world

In addition to the soul, natural phenomena also played a part in Iron Age belief systems. Natural religion dwells on the idea that 'nothing is in the mind that was not first in the senses' (Müller 1892, 115). Due to similarities in mythologies among Indo-European peoples, Müller deducted that religious evolution had the same starting point, that is, humans everywhere experienced the same impression of the natural world (Durkheim 1995 [1921], 70-93). Different cultures used different names, but similarly symbolised ideas and functions. According to Müller (1892) a belief system around natural phenomena is formed when natural and cosmic forces, such as winds, stars, the moon, the sun, and the sky, become concrete by superimposing language to describe them, think about them and discuss these concepts with others. Natural elements include not only mountains, seas, and celestial bodies, but also seasons, the weather, natural disasters, and objects or living things, such as animals, rocks, plants and trees.

Two aspects of natural phenomenology are relevant to the Iron Age belief system: the presumed residency of spirits or deities within natural places expressed for example by depositions in those places, and the creation of objects from natural sources such as making pots from clay or metal objects from ore. Making 'something out of nothing' may have been perceived as some kind of magic, although that probably overemphasises the uniqueness of the skillset of the smith (Kuijpers 2008, 51). In the Bronze Age, the 'magical' value was more likely attributed to the created object itself.

2.3.1 Bronze Age conceptualisation of phenomena

The treatment of objects during the Bronze Age gives evidence of how people conceptualized supernatural things in relation to themselves and to other humans (Fontijn 2019, 112). In the Bronze Age and the Early Iron Age large numbers of metal objects, mostly bronzes, that had been previously used as gifts and commodities were bent, broken, wrapped or hit, apparently with the intention to destroy them or make them unusable (Ibid., 3). A selection of objects was deliberately taken out of circulation (Fontijn 2002, 33-35). The mangled remains of these selected objects were buried in certain places in the landscape, sometimes arranged in a specific manner, or they were thrown whole in lakes and rivers (Fontijn 2019, 59).

Not only the mining of metal ores or the possession of precious objects was key in the powerplay of the unbalanced political economies of the Bronze Age (Earle et al. 2015). Equally influential was control over the trade routes, the means of transport used on these routes and having access to specialized personnel, including warriors, craftsmen, and priests. The central stage in this particular political environment was set by the subsequent destruction of the objects and irreparable parting of the valuable items according to specific conventions, in acts of public performance for dramatic effect (Fontijn 2002, 35; Fontijn 2019, 157-158). The objective of these acts was to create a different form of value, removing the created physical object from view and out of reach of the social domain and transforming it into a metaphysical concept permanently kept by supernatural beings (Fontijn 2019, 58-60). A cultural value was created replacing the material one.

Some finds in Scandinavia, Germany, and Switzerland have been described by Kaul (1995) as a Bronze Age interpretation of natural phenomena, providing a glimpse of the Bronze Age belief system. In Denmark, Southern Sweden, and North Germany the ship is a widespread depicted subject in rock art, as well as engraved on bronze objects. Most ship symbols were depicted on razors (eleven in total) and some on knives, tweezers, necklaces, and swords. The earliest examples date to c. 1700 BCE, the latest ones to the 6th century BCE. Depictions of birds, horses, snakes, and human figures are also reasonably common. Other finds provide further glimpses into Bronze Age mythology. In 1999 illegal metal detectorists in Germany found a round bronze plate, measuring 30cm in diameter, which came to be known as the 'Nebra sky disc'. On the plate are gold inlaid depictions of the sun, the moon, two arches (probably used for calculating solstices), stars (including the constellation Pleiades), and the hull of a ship (Meller 2004; Schlosser 2004). The Trundholm Sun Chariot, found in a Danish bog, also made out of bronze, depicts a round disk on a chariot pulled by a horse. The right side of the disk has a gold inlay, depicting the sun, while the backside is a darker bronze, representing the moon (Kaul 2004). The depiction of a horse pulling the sun or moon is also known from rock art and bronzes. Some of these finds seem to symbolise the sun going down in the sea or the ocean in the west and the moon appearing at night. The ship functioned as a medium, being perceived

as a carrier for everything, including the sun (Kaul 1995). Based on these finds, a narrative for Bronze Age mythology was assembled (Kaul 1998; Jensen 2002; Fig. 2.2). This narrative can be summarised as follows: the sun is pulled along through the sky by a horse, and by the evening ends up in the west in the sea on a boat. Underwater at night, it was pulled or guided by a snake or a fish to the east, to be transferred over to the horse in the sky again in the morning. The fact that the Sun Chariot was gold plated on the right side seems to support this hypothesis. When the daily cycle of the sun is viewed from somewhere in the northern hemisphere, the viewer is facing south and the sun appears to be going from left to right (east to west).

In the Bronze Age cultures of Northern Europe, attributes like the Sun Chariot and the Nebra Sky disk are examples of 'transgressive' objects, likely used to visualise the supernatural in re-enactments and repeated performances in which cosmological stories (myths) were conveyed (Fontijn 2019, 132-127). Aggrandized objects were used to transgress the boundaries between the world of the living and the world of the supernatural, the ancestors, and/or the spirits (*Ibid.*, 130, footnote 7). The aforementioned examples are unique, but objects with a similar mythical function are known throughout Northwest Europe. The fact that these transgressive objects were subsequently deposited in a seemingly dramatized performance act, accommodates archaeologists to reconstruct the final part of this theatrical act of exchange. Examples in the Low Countries include the Ommenschans sword, one of six similar ceremonial blades that were found spread out over England, the Low Countries, and France (Fontijn & Amkreutz 2018). Fontijn (2019, 129) emphasises that the deposition practices, that resulted in us now being able to study these objects, have limited interpretative values. Depositions do not inform us of the Bronze or Iron Age conceptualisation of the supernatural, we merely study the place in the landscape where the objects ended up. As for the preceding use, one can only theorise. The reason for the deposition could be explained as the returning of the objects to their rightful owners, who resided in certain places in the landscape (Fontijn 2019, 122).

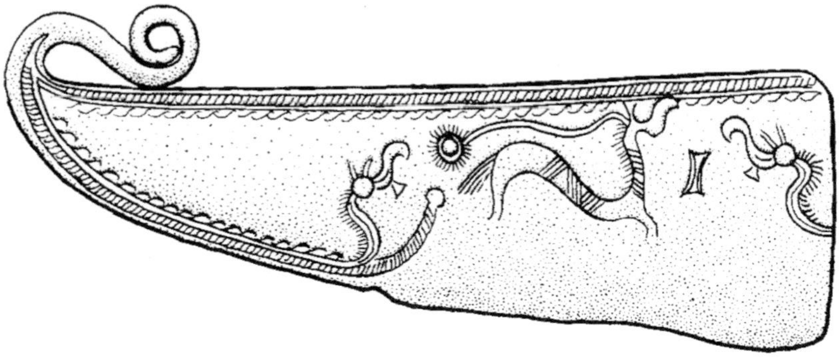

Figure 2.2. Example of a bronze razor with a depiction of a horse and the sun. Razor from Neder Hvolris, Denmark (Bro-Jørgensen 1996; Credits: Bjørn Okholm Skårup).

Figure 2.3. The sacred Nagi in Shingu city (above) and a historical painting portraying the shrine and the tree (photos by the author; painting on information sign at the site).

2.3.2 Sacred trees

Natural religion can focus on more tangible forms of natural phenomena, such as dominant elements in the landscape, sanctifying rivers, lakes, bogs, mountains, trees, and forests. A tree can become sacred through recognition of the power it expresses, providing food, shelter, heat, transportation, and/or medicine (Altman 2017, 10). The location in which the tree grows, for example near a sacred spring, can also make it sacred, as does the association with a religious, historical or mythical event, or an associated spirit.

Sacred trees are widespread. In Japan sacred trees are often planted next to Shinto shrines, or vice versa. The Kumano-Hayatama Grand Shrine in the Kii Mountains was built as a place to worship the three gods who had descended to earth on the sacred rock named Gotobiki.[3] Later a shrine was built in Shingu (new shrine) to 'enshrine' the gods there. The two main residing deities

are husband and wife. The shrine was erected near an old *Nagi* tree that is said to have been planted as a memorial in 1159 (fig. 2.3). The tree serves as a symbol for peace and the symmetrical shape of its leaves supposedly brings benefits for husbands and wives.

The space around a sacred tree can become a sacred place in itself. On the edge of Kirindy forest, on the west side of Madagascar, a large rectangular area is delineated by a wattle work fence around a 500-year-old sacred baobab (fig. 2.4). The enclosure is placed so that the large tree is in one corner of the enclosure, leaving the remaining space open for ceremonies.[4] The lower trunk of the tree is protected by cloths and at the roots of the sacred baobab offerings are left, still visible as a collection of bottles. Young trees inhabit the sacred space and another larger baobab shows horizontal cuts in the trunk, a sign that at one time it was used for climbing. The sacred area can only be entered on bare feet. A notable detail,

---

3   Information sign next to the tree. Transl. G. Fiji.

4   Pers. comm. F. Ravelojaona (guide/interpreter) on location.

Figure 2.4. The sacred baobab (central in the photo) at Kirindy forest, Madagascar, with the fenced enclosure and the entrance to the right (photo by the author).

that could never be reconstructed in the archaeological record, is that footwear has to be left outside the entrance. Removing shoes is also a requirement when entering cattle pens during ceremonies, visiting tombs at burials, at clan gathering places, when entering a house, and at ceremonies in other locations (Parker Pearson 2003, 38).

Another African example is found within Ndembu society where ancestor spirits can feel neglected or forgotten without offerings of beer, food, or prayers mentioning their name at 'living' shrines such as trees planted in the centre of a village (Turner 1967, 9-16). Misfortunes in hunting, female reproduction or various illnesses are associated with the spirits of the dead. A wide range of 'rituals of affliction' are available to cure a victim, performed by a doctor who once had the same affliction. The 'ritual' commonly consists of several stages performed in a certain order, involving treatment, dances, observing certain food taboos, and the construction of a shrine, and/ or a period of seclusion.

In the northwest European Iron Age some species of trees, as well as groves and forests, were considered sacred (Aldhouse-Green 2015, 156-161). Pliny the Elder described in the 1st century CE how oaks in particular were of importance to druids in Gaul. A druid would climb the tree on a predetermined day of the month to cut mistletoe, which would be used in a potion to cure all diseases. Caesar wrote of the Eburones, a tribe that inhabited part of the Low Countries before the Roman armies arrived in the region (Macdevitt 2012, 105). The name of the tribe

allegedly derives from the Germanic or Celtic word for the yew tree (Gysseling 1960, 297). Upon defeat, one of the kings named Cativolcus committed suicide by taking the poisonous juice of a yew tree (Caesar, Gallic Wars, VI, 31). According to Tacitus, Germanic peoples dedicated groves to certain gods and performed religious acts there (Birley 1999, 42). Among the Semnones of eastern Germany no one was allowed to enter the sacred grove without being chained, as an acknowledgment to the local divinity (Tacitus, Germania XXXIX, trans. Birley 1999). If a chained person tripped and fell, they had to crawl out of the grove by themselves. The grove was home to a supreme deity and 'consecrated by the auguries of their forefathers'. It was used for gatherings of the tribes, who allegedly on occasion made human sacrifices.

2.3.3 Gods and spirits in natural places

On the Danish Gundestrup Cauldron, dating to the 2nd century BCE, one of the panels portrays a human sacrifice (Benoit 1955). A man is held by a god, head down over a cauldron. Next to him is a line of warriors with shields. It has been suggested that a large bowl, such as the cauldron, could have been used in an initiation rite for soldiers before battle (Kaul 2011). Another plate on the Gundestrup Cauldron depicts one of the few Celtic gods known by name. He sits with his legs folded and a large pair of antlers on his head, with a torque in one hand and a snake in the other. Surrounding him are different types of animals. In this depiction *Cernunnos*, the 'horned one' has been recognised, known from another source by this name (Green 1997, 59-61). He is presumed to have resided in the forest and was lord of the animals.

Three other deities associated with natural phenomenon were named by Lucan, a mid-1st century CE poet, in his work *Pharsalia*, (Aldhouse-Green 2018). Lucan relates the gods to human sacrifice, druids and the belief in reincarnation (Lucan *Pharsalia* 1, 392-465, trans. Kline 2014):

> The Treviri rejoiced at the army's leaving, and the close-cropped Ligurians who once outdid their long-haired neighbours with flowing locks that adorned their necks, and those who, with pitiful victims, placate their harsh Teutatis, their Esus whose savage shrines make men shudder, their Taranis whose altar is no less cruel than that of Scythian Diana. The bards too who in their verses sing the praise of famous heroes killed in battle, poured out lays at their ease. The Druids laid down their weapons and returned to their barbaric rites and alien modes of worship. They alone are granted the true knowledge, or the false, of the gods and celestial powers; they live in the furthest groves of the deep forests; they teach that the soul does not descend to Erebus' silent land, to Dis' sunless kingdom, but the same spirit breathes in another body. If what they say is true, then our death is merely a moment in the course of continuing life. Thus the tribes on whom the pole star gazes are sweetly deceived, since they are free of the terror of dying, our greatest fear, and the warrior there is eager to meet the steel, is brave in the face of death, convinced it is cowardice to be over-protective of a life that will be renewed.

The god Taranis' name derived from the Gaulish word for thunder, *Taran* (Green 1997, 99-101, 192-193, 205-207; Aldhouse Green 2006, 68-70; Aldhouse-Green 2015, 52-53; Aldhouse-Green 2018). Taranis was probably the sky god who controlled rain and demanded sacrifices by burning. The symbology associated with him is uncertain, but could include the (solar) wheel, the eagle, the oak, fire and lightning. Esus is only known from two images, on which he is depicted as a woodcutter (Green 1997, 93-94, 207-208; Aldhouse Green 2006, 85-86; Aldhouse-Green 2018). The name probably means 'lord', implying a leadership over the natural world. His human sacrifices required hanging from a tree. Symbols associated with Esus are willows, marsh birds and bulls. Teutatis, also known as Toutatis from numerous graffiti, probably was a tribal deity, his name deriving from the word for tribe or polity (Brunaux 1986, 71-72; Green 1997, 208-209; Clémençon & Ganne 2009; Aldhouse-Green 2018). His task would have been to protect the tribe, specifically at a time of war. The

image on the Gundestrup Cauldron holding a sacrificial victim is attributed to Teutatis. Sacrifices dedicated to him allegedly had to be drowned.

Gods and their names were regional specific. In Gaul and the Low Countries several indigenous names of gods were use during the Roman period, often in combination with their Roman name (Roymans 1990, 53-62). It is assumed the name of the indigenous gods were already in use during the Late Iron Age and got assimilated by the Romans or associated with one of their own gods. The Romans assumed their local counterparts more or less had the same function. In Zeeland, the southwest of the Netherlands, the remains of a temple and many altars devoted to a goddess called Nehallenia was dredged up. Etymological research indicates she was a Celtic goddess who was worshipped on the Celtic-speaking coast of the Netherlands and Belgium in Roman times (Kerkhof 2016). She was invoked at a temple on an island by people before they embarked on sea journeys (Stuart 2003). Nehalennia patronized overseas trade, protected the dead on their journey to the afterlife, and also functioned as a fertility goddess and as a goddess of hunting and light (Wagenvoort 1971). She is therefore associated with Diana and is often depicted with a dog by her side.

Magusanus is another example of a god indigenous to the Lower Rhine Region and best known for his Roman association with Hercules (Roymans 2009). He is often depicted with a lion skin and a club. According to Roymans (1990, 59), in reality native gods were likely not as specialized as their Roman counterparts and tended to have similar abilities such as bringing wealth, success in battle, health, protection, and fertility, meeting the basic needs of the regional social group.

2.4 The 'ritual of exchange'

After pleading not to use the word 'ritual', a paragraph is spent here to a specify an act that is often described as a 'ritual'. The use of 'ritual' will be a temporary measure to explore why this way of acting differentiates itself from other practices and why the 'ritual' is actually a strategic and logical way of dealing with the task at hand, which is communication with the dead. Once the idea behind the act is embedded in our perception of the Iron Age world view, the word 'ritual' can again be abandoned.

There is no all-encompassing 'theory of ritual' related to religion available (Grimes 2014, 189-191). There are various theories, opinions, or customary notions reflecting the time and space in which they were formulated (Bell 2009, x). Every religion involves traditions and conventions, and many seemingly 'rational' acts are part of a religion, a superstitious belief, or even a social etiquette (Gluckman 1962, 20-24). Ritual is not exclusively confined to the realm of religion and could be described as any symbolic, formalistic, traditional or invariable practice

Figure 2.5. Vietnamese spirit money, found on the street after a funeral procession passed by (photos by the author).

or performance.[5] Even non-religious people have been known to avoid sitting on row 13, or to knock on wood to avert bad luck. A recent survey by Bullivant *et al.* (2019) revealed that among atheists a surprising proportion (about 10 to 20%) of the population still believe in various supernatural beings or phenomena, such as astrology, reincarnation, life after death, mystical powers, forces of good and evil, and karma.

Many attempts have been made to classify types of ritual, ranging from Durkheim's binary distinction between sacred and profane, to Grimes' classification system of sixteen different categories (Bell 2009, 93). Bell (1997, 93-137) proposed six 'basic genres of ritual action', which by her own definition are not exhaustive: calendrical or seasonal rites, rites of passage, rites of exchange and communication, rites of affliction, fasting, feasts and festivals, and last, political rites. These genres can sometimes be recognised in the archaeological record. For example the early Roman Coligny calendar indicated when certain festivals were supposed to take place and how long they lasted (Brunaux 1986, 49-50). The calendar consisted of a five-year cycle with lunar months of 29 or 30 days. Each month and each year is divided into a 'light' and a 'dark' half (Benigni et al. 2003, 4). The light half of the year started at the winter solstice, when the days are getting longer again.

The best-known genre of religious act, in both anthropology and archaeology, is that in which people make offerings to a god, spirit or deity for reciprocation (Bell 2009, 108). Kok (2008, 46) described offerings as 'religious rituals' in which goods are exchanged between human agents and culturally postulated superhuman agents (i.e. a god, spirit, or deity). Therein the goods refer symbolically to an event that triggers the action and the related agents that invoke the need for the offering. The offering of distinctive artefacts could have different religious motivations, such as removal from circulation

to protect or extinguish their special powers, or they were intended for transmission to another world as gifts to deities, or as provisions in the afterlife for the dead (Bradley 2017, 145-146). In Roman written contracts this principle was called *do ut des*, which translates as 'I give in order to receive from you'. The complex relationships between ancestors, spirits and the living are expressed in 'rituals of exchange, offering and communication' (Bell 2009, 108-114, 136). The ritual commonly involves a physical offering in a distinct culturally understood convention. The offered object varies greatly from smoke coming from burned incense up to the level of slaughtered animals. Intangible offers can involve dancing, songs, and theatre to entertain the gods. Unfortunately the latter leaves limited evidence in the archaeological record. Bell (2009, 110) uses the example of spirit money to illustrate offering. In Chinese, Taiwanese, and Vietnamese societies, large quantities of fake money (fig. 2.5) is used to offer in burial ceremonies or communication with the ancestors. The cash is meant for the ancestors to use in the afterlife, or to placate gods, ghosts or demons or to ask for their favours (Wolf 1974). Objects offered to the dead can only be used by them. Real money would become fake in the spirit world and it is considered inappropriate to treat the dead as if they were the same as the living (Bell 2009, 110). Usually spirit money is burned to transfer it to the other world. This process seems to be a logical consequence of the act of cremation, in which the body is sent to the afterlife by burning. All gifts for the deceased, or necessities, should therefore be sent by the same means.

Burning an offering can be considered as the ultimate rite of exchange: a sacrifice (Bell 2009, 112). In making a sacrifice, the object is consecrated, and during the process it is destroyed or rendered useless. In the Bronze Age of north and central Europe, buried hoards and deposits of objects in water and bogs typify exchange practices on a large scale and over a long time (Fontijn 2002, 276; Fontijn 2019). Many items found in depositions were objects that had previously been used in everyday life, such as axes and sickles or more specific body ornaments

---

5 Summary based on Bell's characteristics of ritual-like activities (Bell 2009, 138-169).

and weaponry, which were subsequently deliberately and systematically removed from society. Deposition practices followed certain conventions, as specific items were selectively deposited in specific contexts. Analysis of the chemical composition of axes suggests that the act of sacrificing precious metal objects was so common that some items might have been specifically produced for this purpose (Kuijpers 2015). Objects were deposited in all sorts of environments: bogs, rivers, lakes, and possibly even at sea (Samson 2006). This exchange was final, as the sacrificed offerings were deformed and/or could not be retrieved from their watery resting place. Based on where archaeological evidence was found, different scenarios for selective deposition were proposed by Fontijn (2019, 29-33). A specific type of object could be deposited in a variety of places, or in one specific type of location such as a river. On some occasions all kinds of objects were deposited in one specific type of location such as a bog. Sometimes objects required specific treatment, and only after this treatment was it allowed to be deposited.

2.5 Objects of exchange

In the Iron Age selective deposition practices changed, but were not discontinued entirely. In Early Iron Age elite graves items were deformed by bending, burning, and breaking before allowing them into the burial context (Van der Vaart-Verschoof 2017, 148). The objects chosen for this purpose reflected a societal role, symbolising the status and identity of the deceased (*Ibid.*, 142). Three of these Early Iron Age elite graves were found in Oss, the Netherlands. They contain a wealthy display of different grave goods. Underneath one large barrow (the *Vorstengraf*) a bronze *situla* was found with the cremation remains of a man, as well as horse tack and a gold inlaid hilted sword which was bent in order to render it unusable (Fokkens & Jansen 2004). The sword is of the Mindelheim-type, which resembles the slightly older Gündlingen-type sword in size and shape (Fokkens & Jansen 2004, 58-59; Van der Vaart-Verschoof 2017, 43-45). This Mindelheim-type is only found in graves whereas the Gündlingen-type was also found in rivers.[6] The Mindelheim-type sword therefore seems to represent a break with the former practice of depositing particular types of objects in wet places. Underneath another nearby barrow the remains of a pyre were found, containing burned wood and bone fragments, accompanied by over 1000 small bronze objects, mostly studs, which were probably part of a decorated yoke and horse tack (Fontijn, Van der Vaart & Jansen 2013). The third large barrow in the same area contained burned pieces of a large oak tree and a single piece of cremated human bone (De Leeuwe 2007; Van Wijk *et al.* 2009; Fontijn, Van der Vaart & Jansen 2013). All three barrows contained different assemblages of objects. However, what they all have in common is that all the objects were made unusable as they were bent, burned, folded, transformed, and/or dismantled before deposition (Fontijn *et al.* 2013, 311; Van der Vaart-Verschoof 2017, 148). Manipulation and fragmentation of grave goods was a regular practice in the Low Countries, and to a lesser extent also in central European Hallstatt cultures (Van der Vaart-Verschoof 2017, 159). This practice, in combination with the intentional destruction of objects, can be interpreted as a 'ritual of exchange'.

2.5.1 Offerings and depositions

The object of exchange in the Iron Age is subject to regional variations, as is the treatment of objects prior to deposition (Bradley 1998, 159-166; Kok 2008). The Early La Tène period is characterised by elite burials in the Marne-Ardennes-Moselle-Middle Rhine-region (Diepeveen-Jansen 2001). In the second quarter of the 5th century BCE to approximately the mid-4th century BCE the burial tradition in the region was predominantly inhumation, whereas previously cremation was customary. New cemeteries were constructed, accompanied by a large increase in the number of graves, both ordinary and elite, displaying a wealth and complexity of funerary practices (*Ibid.*, 209-210). The burials seemed to reflect an increasing differentiation and importance of social relations within the local societies. The elite type inhumations contained a chariot, bronze ware, and/or a dagger, and a sword as grave goods. In the subsequent La Tène B period, during the late 4th to early 3rd century BCE, the burial tradition gradually reverted back to cremation and most of the grave goods lost their significance (*Ibid.*, 212).

In the Low Countries, inhumations as well as 5th century BCE elite burials remain rare. In the Middle and Late Iron Age objects were no longer deposited in graves. The deceased were cremated, sometimes with some of their adornments, followed by the collection of a selection of the burned remains and then were buried in a small pit (Gerritsen 2003, 143). Deposition of objects in wet places continued. Analysis of 100 offering sites (700 BCE-500 CE) in southern Sweden, Denmark, northern Germany, and 22 Iron Age to early medieval sites in the northwest of the Netherlands, showed a large variety in deposited objects (Kok 2008, 46-58). On 118 out of 121 sites the spectrum of offered objects contained tools, defined by Kok as one of the five ontological categories of offerings: persons, animals, plants, natural objects, and tools. The 'tool' category covers all objects made by man and can be subdivided into: household/agricultural, ornament, weapon/equipment, horse tack, wagon/boat, other, and structure. For example nails are a tool sometimes found in

---

6   Mindelheim swords date between the 8th and approximately the 6th century BCE (Fokkens & Jansen 2004, 58; Van der Vaart-Verschoof 2017, 43-45).

watery depositions. Kok (2008, 176) suggests nails are used to bind things together, and can therefore be perceived as a symbol of attachment. Nails could also be associated with healing powers. In contrast to the Bronze Age selections, the Iron Age depositions seem less particular as all five of the categories are found in different combinations together (*Ibid.*, 49). However, some combinations of categories occur more often than others. The combination of pottery, stones, wood, and animal bones is a reoccurring set generally interpreted as linked to fertility rites (*Ibid.*, 54). Similarly, horse tack is often found associated with weapons. In the northwest Netherlands cattle bones were predominant in offering sites (*Ibid.*, 167-171), similar to cattle bones being the most commonly found bones in settlements (e.g. Lauwerier & IJzerreef 1998; Brinkkemper & Van Wijngaarden-Bakker 2005). In addition to bovine bones, parts of horses, dogs, pigs, and goats/sheep were found at offering sites with the percentages of each animal type decreasing in the above mentioned order. This deviates from the assemblage in settlements, as bones of goats/sheep are more common there. On most of the deposition sites in the northwest Netherlands both household and agricultural tools were found.

2.5.2 Pottery as the sacrificial object

Pottery is the most common offering, usually found in a broken form. Kok (2008, 175) points out the symbolic value of a broken object. She states it can bind people, objects, and places. Broken pottery can be recycled (as grog) and thus can symbolise the life-cycle (Brück 2006; Kok 2008, 175). Pottery also has a strong relationship to houses, and not merely in its use as a storage or cookery container. In the southern Netherlands secondarily burned Iron Age pottery is regularly found in postholes of houses and granaries. These depositions of destroyed pots are interpreted by Van den Broeke (2002; 2015) as offerings in an abandonment depot. Pottery was likewise deposited in postholes as foundation depots for houses and granaries, and to a lesser extent during the use of a house in pits in the interior (Bradley 2005, 50-57; De Vries 2021, 114, 128-135; Habermehl 2022, 39-52). Generally, pottery seems to be the most common deposition in a domestic environment. This could be attributed to availability, but there is also an added value to the act as well as the object. Direct links between the symbolic significance of pottery in relation to houses are the so-called 'house urns' (fig. 2.6).

A house urn is a type of ceramic vessel in the shape of a house that was in use in Etruscan Italy and northern Europe during the urnfield period as a container for cremated remains. House urns are quite rare and it is assumed that only a small section of society had the privilege bestowed in their grave (Bradley 2002). Bradley (2002) interprets the northern European examples as symbols of renewal and fertility, comparing them to grain storage facilities, such as

raised granaries and storage pits. The remains of the dead were in this way associated with crops and the yearly cycle of sowing and harvesting. I would like to advance on this idea a little further and suggest that pottery is often used in the Iron Age to emphasise the connection to a house, and possibly also as a metaphor for a home and a prolonged relation with living relatives, and in case of interment, a temporary or permanent place for the soul in the afterlife.

2.5.3 The ultimate sacrifice

Rather extreme cases of transformation in *rituals of exchange* are found in depositions of human corpses in bogs, in an act that was widely known from Scandinavia to Ireland. Dating to the Bronze Age and thereafter, these sacrificed humans all had something in common – their death was a violent one (Glob 2004 [1965]; Van der Sanden 1990; Aldhouse Green 2006, 51-53, 111-135). Many of the peat bodies showed mutilation and trauma that they suffered before, or at the time of death, such as a cut throat or other cut body parts, strangulation or a smashed skull. Some bodies were pinned down in an apparent act to assure that the corpse would stay in place, possibly out of practical considerations to prevent the body floating to the surface as a corpse would normally do during a bloated stage of decomposition. Sacrificial murder victims were not exclusively deposited in bogs. In several British Iron Age hillforts inhumations were found in grain silos and underneath the ramparts (Walker 1984; Cunliffe 1992; Cunliffe 1995; Aldhouse Green 2006, 166-167; Bradley 2005, 170). The incentive for sacrificing a human in a grain silo, a so-called 'pit burial' might have been a fertility rite, while a deposition at the base of a rampart is interpreted as a foundation sacrifice. Both can be interpreted as a *ritual of exchange*. Human sacrifice was only performed

Figure 2.6. Decorated ceramic house urn found in the Banditaccia necropolis, Cerveteri (Lazio, Italy), dated to 650-625 BCE (Vatican Museums, Vatican City).

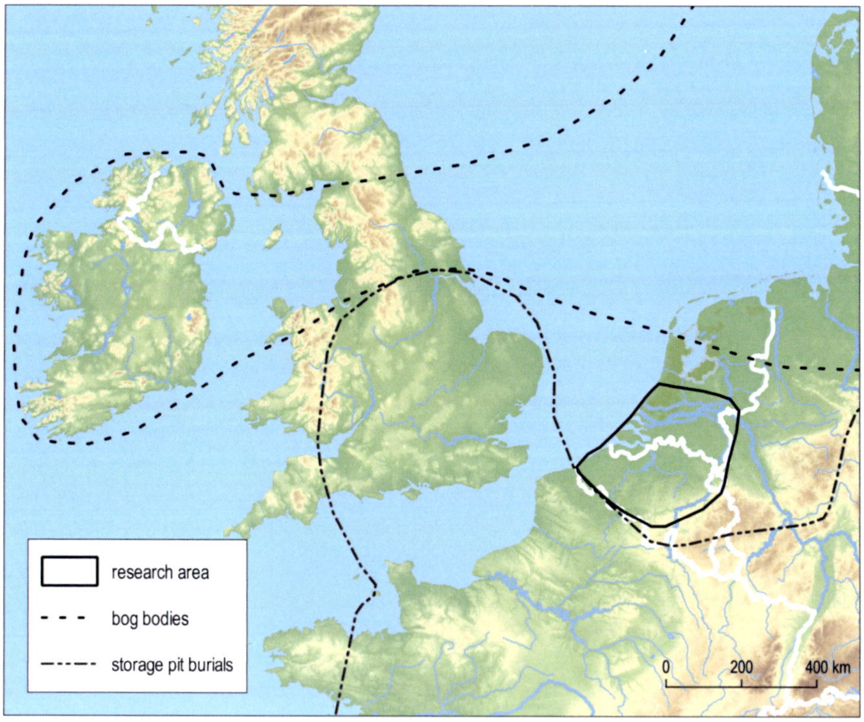

research area

- - - bog bodies

-·-·- storage pit burials

0   200   400 km

Figure 2.7. Map of northwest Europe depicting areas where storage pit burials were performed and peat bog bodies were found (after Bradley 2017, figure 21).

in life-threatening and critical situations to avert evil or catastrophes, placate gods, and to rebuild kinship relations or avoid conflict (Bell 2009, 112-114; Aldhouse Green 2006, 168-169). Commonly the dead were cremated, whereas sacrificed humans clearly were not. Inhumation may have been seen as an inferior method of interment (Wait 1985, 249-250; Lambot 1998; Parker Pearson 2003, 70). Depositing human sacrifices in bogs was a north European custom, in the Low Countries only found in the northeast of the Netherlands, while depositing human sacrifices in storage pits was done further south of the research area, not in the Low Countries (Bradley 2017, figure 21). Notably, neither of these practices were performed in the research area (fig. 2.7).

2.5.4 Sacrifice in times of war

One of the best-known examples of Iron Age war-related depositions was found at the site that defined the later Iron Age: La Tène at the shores of Lake Neuchâtel in Switzerland. In the 19th century the remains of two timber structures were found at the north side of the lake, when the water level was lowered by 3m (fig. 2.8) (Arnold 2009). Part of the site was excavated in the late 19th, the early 20th, and additionally in the 21st century.

In the researched area around 4000 to 4500 votive offerings were found (Vouga 1923, Kanael & Lejars 2009). Most of the offerings were weaponry: hundreds of spearheads and swords, and a few dozen shields. Other finds included human remains, animal bones, wooden yokes, parts of chariots, a few hundred brooches,

knives, razors, bronze cauldrons, and other metal objects. The structures, named 'Pont Vouga' and 'Pont Desor', would have been approximately 70-80m long and 4m wide. Several wooden construction parts were dendrochronologically dated between 269 and 220 BCE, although these parts could not be linked directly to one of the bridges (Gassmann 2009). Under, and slightly downstream of Vouga Bridge, three wooden shields were found, one of which is dated between 225 and 220 BCE (Gassmann 2007). The assemblage of the finds and the ^{14}C-dates extend the use of the site from the second half of the 3rd to the beginning of the 2nd century BCE (Kanael & Lejars 2009). The bones of at least 50 individuals have been found across the multiple excavations the site has seen (Jud & Alt 2009). The distribution of human remains was relatively homogeneous, with a concentration downstream and upstream of the two bridges. Unfortunately, many of the human remains discovered in La Tène have now disappeared. Sixteen skeletons were recently re-evaluated: eight males, four females, three children, and one teenager. One man, aged 30 to 50 years, was beheaded following numerous blows from back to front with one or more cutting instruments. On the skull of a man aged 25 to 40 years there was a series of seven cuts, and the left side of his skull bore a large crack caused by a fall which could have caused death. These are considered not to be the typical traces of a fight. On the skull of a third individual aged 40 to 45 years, two violent blows with a blunt instrument on the back of the skull were the cause of death. Some bones showed evidence of dog gnawing marks suggesting that at least part of the corpses spent a considerable time in the open air before being immersed in the river. Originally the bridges were thought to represent platforms from which votive offerings could be cast into the water as well as transportation to the other side (De Navarro 1972; Bradley 1998, 157-159; Cunliffe 1999, 194; Arnold 2009). More recently the interpretation shifted toward a purpose-built military trophy, a kind of commemorative monument celebrating an important event – probably a battle (Kaeser 2012; 2017). Analogous trophies are also recognised in the 'war'-sanctuaries of Ribemont and Gournay-sur-Aronde, which will be discussed in the next chapter.

War-booty offerings are typified by large amounts of weapons and equipment deposited in a short time-span (Kok 2008, 54-58). The weapons and gear are often found in bundles and many of the objects are intentionally mutilated before deposition. An extreme example is the deposition of a whole 4th century BCE ship filled with weapons, that was sunk in a bog in Hjortspring, Denmark (Randsborg 1995, 20-21). The ship was 19m long with a double prow, a shape resembling contemporary rock paintings. The find assemblage composed of swords, spearheads, mail-coats, and shields that are estimated to have belonged to a crew of 22 warriors. They are likely the remains of a well-equipped army with infantry soldiers and commanders. A ship like that would have been light and fast, with 18 peddlers. The whole army was estimated to consist of around a 100 men on six or seven boats, representing a tribal group of 3000-5000 people (Randsborg 1995, 40-42). Randsborg (1995, 70) points out that the find indicates a quite sophisticated military organization, with elite forces and standardized equipment. Conflicts must have been recurring at the time. The ship and its contents is interpreted as war booty, spoils from a defeated enemy army. Wet depositions are interpreted by Randsborg (1995, 75) as 'sacrifices [that] were beyond a doubt gifts to the supernatural forces of the earth and the underworld, perhaps linked with those of the water'. Furthermore, the act of sacrificing the ship and all of the weaponry, some of which was bend, along with a horse, a dog, a puppy, and a lamb, is interpreted as 'an offer primarily related to a god of war and/or battle' (Randsborg 1995, 88). He further narrates on the comparison of Roman, Celtic, Germanic, and Nordic gods and their attributes and characteristics (Randsborg 1995, 76-86). However, the names of these gods were not known until centuries later. There is no evidence the Hjortspring sacrifice was related to a god. The act of sacrificing the ship and its contents may just as well have been related to animism and the belief in spirits. Perhaps it was considered a taboo to keep war booty that was obtained under certain circumstances, or the sacrifice was related to a superstition. No human remains were found. The warriors themselves were likely killed, enslaved, returned, disarmed, and/or humiliated (Randsborg 1995, 41). It is worth a consideration that in the event that they were killed, their spirits could not come to look for their weapons or haunt their assailants etc., another possible motivation for the sacrifice, unrelated to a god.

In any case, a human sacrifice or weapon deposit seems to represent a larger group (Kok 2008, 70-71). In contrast, depositions of pottery, small animals, and agricultural products are more likely to be offerings by an individual or a family.

2.6 Before temples: a place for depositions

In the Low Countries a similar assemblage of objects was found at the site of Kessel-Lith (Roymans 2004, 103-193). During the 20th century finds were dredged from the Meuse River, dating to the Later Iron Age, Roman, and Medieval Periods. In total twenty-two late La Tène-type (LT-D) swords and scabbards were recovered. Dredge workers testified that many swords were found in a bent condition (Roymans 2004, footnote 262). The site furthermore delivered the same amount of Late Iron Age belt hooks. Belt hooks of similar types were also found in the sanctuary of Empel (Roymans and Derks 1994) and

Figure 2.8. The remains of wooden posts at La Tène in a painting by Auguste Bachelin, dating 1879 (Laténium Museum, Neuchatel).

in seven other sites in the same region (Roymans 2004, fig. 7.6). Some belt hooks seem to be of a particular regional type, a 'Lower Rhine product', while others were possibly imported from North Germany (Roymans 2004, 114-117). Other metal items dating to the Late Iron Age or to the early Roman Era were found at Kessel-Lith: 35 fibulae, five large cauldrons of plated bronze, nine iron socketed axes, several coins, and (parts of) pendants. Besides metal objects, over 100.000 animal bones were found, of which an estimated 64% belonged to cattle, 20% pig, 10% horse, 5% sheep/goat and 1% dog (Ter Schegget 1999). Unfortunately an analysis of this material has not been published to date. Furthermore, 650 fragments of human bones were discovered, belonging to a minimum number of 65 individuals (*Ibid.*). Most of the skeletal material dates to the Late Iron Age, but some to the Roman and Merovingian periods. Approximately 90% of the remains were of adults. The majority (75%), of the bones that could be determined for sex, were male. Several bones had traces of injuries. As the bones showed no signs of weathering or other taphonomic evidence, Ter Schegget (1999, 224) assumes that complete bodies were deliberately deposited in the river bed of the Meuse as part of a sacrifice at a cult place. The site would have been positioned on an important junction of the river Meuse and the river Waal (Roymans 2004, 132-134). As there were no systematic excavations of the site, the interpretation is debatable. Initially the finds were interpreted as the result of depositions at a cult site during the entire Late La Tène period and continuing into the Roman period (Ter Schegget 1999). In the Roman period a stone temple was built at the site, of which tuff stone and limestone building blocks were found in the 1970s. No remains relating to a preceding Iron Age structure were identified. Recently, Roymans (2018) explained the finds as the physical residue of a battle, more specifically the massacre of two tribes by Caesar in 55 BCE, a suggestion originally dismissed by Ter Schegget (1999). As discussed by Van Ginkel (2015) the basis for this reinterpretation is doubtful as the assemblage of the material, dating and isotope analysis did not yield conclusive results. Van Heeren (2014) poses that the site was used as a militarily reinforcement in the 4th century CE. The human bones could be related to that period of utilisation.

The question remains as to what position manmade structures occupied within the animistic cosmological ideology of the Iron Age. Most of the sacrificial acts took place in a natural environment. Deposition events often take place in a liminal space between two opposites (Grimes 2014, 256-262; Habermehl 2022, 275-276). For example the act of depositing weapons in a river takes place at the water's edge such as a river bank or a lake side. The objects could have been thrown from the land into the water or dropped and sunk at a point where

a person could walk into the shallows. The place where the action happens is in the transitional zone where water meets land. A deposition from a bridge or a boat could be perceived in a similar fashion, a liminal space balancing between water and sky, or between dry and wet, or in a more physical way between touchable and untouchable. Space is conceptualised in this dichotomic model of opposites, an 'either/or model' delineated by actions (Grimes 2014, 256). The place can be the leading component of an act, temple rites being among the most prominent examples (Grimes 1999). A temple covers a clearly defined space, bound by conventions of how to act inside and outside, and where practitioners participate in activities that are familiar only to them.

2.6.1 Roman cult places in the Low Countries

In the Low Countries temples are a phenomenon introduced by Romans. It would seem that the expansion of the Roman Empire into northwest Europe brought with it an increase of structures related to religion. These structures are sometimes referred to as Romano-Celtic *fana* (e.g. Wheeler 1928; De Laet 1966; Fauduet 1993) or as Gallo-Roman sanctuaries or temples (e.g. Bogaers 1955; Derks 2002). The main building consists of a square *cella*, surrounded by a *porticus* on four sides. The finds usually entail votive offerings such as animal bones, parts of statuettes and pottery (e.g. Fauduet 2010, 171-206). The *fana* are not of a classic Roman temple type, but some sort of locally implemented adjustment unknown to the Mediterranean region (Haverfield 1912; Derks 1996, 7, endnote 13; 121). These temples were typically places where an indigenous god(s) was/were worshipped. In France, these Roman temples have a long research history. The most recent overview discusses the setting, organisation, and chronology of c. 750 French sites, approximately 47% of which were (partly) excavated, while the majority (53%) are only known by aerial photography (Fauduet 2010). Most structures were constructed in the second half of the 1st century BCE, after the conquest of Gaul by Caesar, and in the 1st century CE (Fauduet 1993, 118-20). On approximately 80 sites it is known that the Roman temple was built on top of an Iron Age site (Fauduet 2010, 144). Examples of Gallo-Roman type temples in the Low Countries were found in Elst, Empel, Domburg, Valkenburg, Nijmegen, Hofstade, Gulpen, Rimburg, Hofstade, Tongeren, and Rijsbergen (fig. 2.9; Bogaers 1955; Mertens 1968, Roymans & Derks 1994). The temple in Empel was dedicated to Hercules Magusanus, an important god to the Batavians (Roymans & Derks 1994, 10-39). At the site coins, fibulae, weapons, and a helmet were found. The temple site was located at the confluence of the rivers Meuse and Dieze. The indigenous name Magusanus,

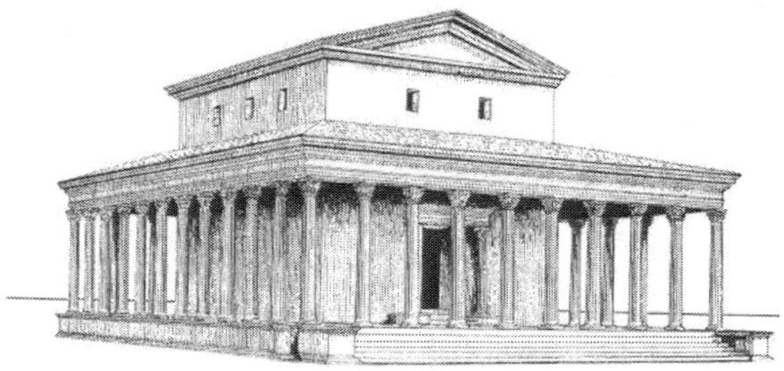

Figure 2.9. A reconstruction of a Gallo-Roman temple in Elst, the Netherlands (drawing by J. Ypey & G.J. de Vries, in Bogaers 1955, pl. 45).

in combination with the oldest objects dating to the late 2nd century BCE, indicate the use of the space as a religious place started in the Iron Age. The Iron Age significance of the place was thereafter incorporated rather than overthrown by the Roman rites and religion.

More common than temples in the Low Countries during the Roman era were so-called rural cult places. These typically consist of an enclosure, lacking the typical *cella* building. Slofstra & Van der Sanden (1987) described six sites, of which four contained apparent linear post rows inside the enclosure. The emphasis in the 1987 article was placed on the similarities between these sites, summarised by the enclosed space and the post rows. When the emphasis is placed on the differences between the sites however, the classification as 'cult place' becomes difficult. The size, the construction, the find assemblage, and even the location context is different for all six sites. However, there is no doubt that rural cult places existed in the Roman Low Countries. A typical Cananefatian rural cult place structure is described by Van Zoolingen (2010; 2011) as a rectangular or square to U-shaped area enclosed or marked by ditches, embankments, and/or palisades. The space can enclosed post configurations and offering pits. The structures are commonly located at the periphery or in isolated parts of settlements and are oriented to the four cardinal directions.

Some of these small, seemingly unpretentious structures are quite rich in finds. A square ditch structure excavated in Den Haag-Rotterdamsebaan contained three deep square pits in the enclosed space (Stokkel 2015, 8-9). Nearby a pottery cup was found, filled with 107 silver *denarii*, six bracelets, a large silver fibula, and part of a necklace. A similar sized square ditch in Lent-Vossepeltlaan NLa1 was situated next to a narrow river channel, in which over 150 fibulae and other metal finds were discovered.[7] The square structure itself yielded two large pits at the north and west corners which contained

burned material and part of a buried horse in a pit on some sort of appendix of the structure. At present at least 50 or 60 of these Roman 'rural cult' sites can be identified, most dating to the Middle Roman Period (e.g. Slofstra & Van der Sanden 1987; Derieuw 2009; Van Zoolingen 2011; Habermehl 2022, 132). Most seem to consist of a simple square ditch and have been used for only a short time span.

2.7 Conclusion

The theoretical framework in this chapter is meant to support the study of Iron Age structures that were assumingly constructed for an activity related to the contemporary belief system. How did these structures and their utilisation fit in the Iron Age belief system? Fundamental to this framework is the belief in the soul. Based on Archaic and Classical Greek literature, the consensus stated that until the c. 5th century BCE the soul had two parts that separated after death. One part stayed with the body while the other transcended onto the afterlife. This coincides with the use of urnfields, most of which were in use until the 5th century BCE (chapter 4). Conceivably, in urnfields one part of the soul remained with the ancestors and one part moved on. The care for the remaining part was expressed in the careful placement of the remains in or under a barrow.

Burial grounds are traditionally recognisable places for activities related to the belief system. Acts related to the burial tradition were of a different kind than the acts performed at the natural places. Archaeological finds indicate this; sets of grave goods tend to differ from the assemblage of items found in rivers. In the Middle and Late Iron Age people were cremated and often interred without any grave goods (chapter 5). If there was anything the dead were thought to need in the afterlife, or in their reincarnated form for that matter, it was most likely burned with their body. The treatment of human sacrifices and war victims or prisoners in the Iron Age contrasts with the contemporary burial tradition. Perhaps only through the cremation of the body could the deceased be accepted into the realm of the ancestors or be assured of reincarnation.

After the 5th century, the basis of the belief system was likely that human (and other animals?) contained only one soul to which a variation of things could happen after death, one of which was remaining with the body (when not cremated) and another was to reincarnate or transmigrate to the afterlife. The change in burial customs with the deposition of cremation remains in inconspicuous graves and small unnoticeable cemeteries indicates that the physical remains lost relevance to the detached soul (and perhaps not to the next of kin either).

The different things that could happen to the soul after death could be influenced by the living. Perhaps

---

7 Excavated in 2009, unpublished to this date; information obtained from Archol BV, Leiden.

not all souls qualified for reincarnation or becoming an ancestral spirit, depending on status, manner of death, or manner of passage. In conflicts, the souls of the conquered were manipulated in different ways, a violent passing preventing the soul reincarnating or becoming an ancestor, or possibly even returning home.

In European Iron Age belief systems, as in Madagascar, there could have been a fear among the surviving relatives that the soul had no resting place when a person died far away from home and the body could not be buried, as would conceivably occur in battle. The abundance of weapon deposits indicates conflicts and, at times, a violent society. Some of the weapons ended up in the water. In the Low Countries there is a long tradition of offerings in watery places and during the Iron Age all sorts of objects were sacrificed. Besides trees and forests, rivers, lakes, and bogs were clearly significant places, or at least considered to be appropriate liminal places where people could communicate with gods or spirits. Offerings in these places could be substantial, specifically when offered by a group of people, such as large amounts of weapons, accumulated multiple tools and even human sacrifices. Offerings by an individual or a family are considered to be simpler, such as pottery or small animals.

As a result, a place with a structure for an activity related to the belief system would presumably have functioned for communication and exchange with the ancestors, the souls of the dead, or particular gods and spirits. The acts in relation to these structures can be differentiated from the acts in wet places, as it is likely that other deities or ancestors were addressed. The structure may aid the communication and/or the exchange. It is to be expected that the object of exchange, or the assemblage of objects, is different from finds in wet places. Another possible function for a structure related to the belief system is the use of space for calendrical rites, seasonal feasts, and gatherings

3

Geographical framework: the 'archaeotypical' sanctuary

3.1 Introduction

Before temples there were sanctuaries. That is at least the assumption based on classical sources (Bogaers 1955, 5) and a few archetypical archaeological examples. The excavation and publication by Jean-Louis Brunaux of Gournay-sur-Aronde and thereafter the site of Ribemont-sur-Ancre in the 1980s and 90s shaped the perception of Iron Age cult places for decades afterwards. Specifically Gournay is often used as an analogy in the Low Countries (e.g. Slofstra & Van der Sanden 1987; Van der Sanden 1998; Van Enckevort 2007; Van Zoolingen 2010; Overbeke, 2012; Hiddink 2014; Kalshoven & Van der Linde 2017; Reyns, Verbeeck & Bruggeman 2018). Likewise, the Germany phenomenon called *Viereckschanzen* used to be considered a valid analogy for rectangular structures found in the Low Countries (e.g. De Laet 1966; Slofstra & Van der Sanden 1987; Derks 1996, 146-147; Van der Sanden 1998; Annaert 1993; Bosquet & Preud'homme 2000; De Logi *et al.* 2007; Van Zoolingen 2010; Groenewoudt 2011; Demey 2012; Demey 2013; Ter Wal 2013; Kalshoven & Van der Linde 2017).

How reliable is this geographical frame of reference for the study region? The Low Countries have a distinct physical geography that differs from other Northwest European regions and that effects all aspects of human subsistence (fig. 3.1). This is reflected most prominently in the regional difference of settlement development. In many central and southern regions of Europe more densely populated urbanised settlements emerged during the Iron Age as a consequence of increasingly hierarchical and specialised societies, long distance trade, and warfare, giving rise to the Late Iron Age fortified oppida (Wendling 2013; Fernández-Götz 2018). Like all towns, oppida were political and religious centres (Fichtl 2013; 2018). Typically covering an area of at least 10 to 15 ha, their fortified walls surrounded different types of buildings that were arranged in large urban courtyards of the elite, representing and displaying economic and military power (Wendling & Winger 2014). Armed conflict played an important role during the Iron Age of northwest Europe, specifically in the later Iron Age (Løvschal 2014; James 2018; Pope 2021). Fortified sites, cattle raids, plundering gangs, and local power struggles characterise Iron Age societies (Løvschal 2014). Evidence of conflict is provided by depositions of large amounts of weapons and human skeletal remains with weapon-related injuries (Wells 2001, 50-83) and by the increasing fixation and formalisation of visual boundaries in the landscape as an expression of ownership and the right to use the land (Løvschal 2014). This includes the site at La Tène as described in the last chapter, many French sites, some of which are described below, and several German and British sites.

In the Low Countries, conflict was either uncommon or expressed in a manner that left few visible traces in the archaeological record. However, societies in the Low

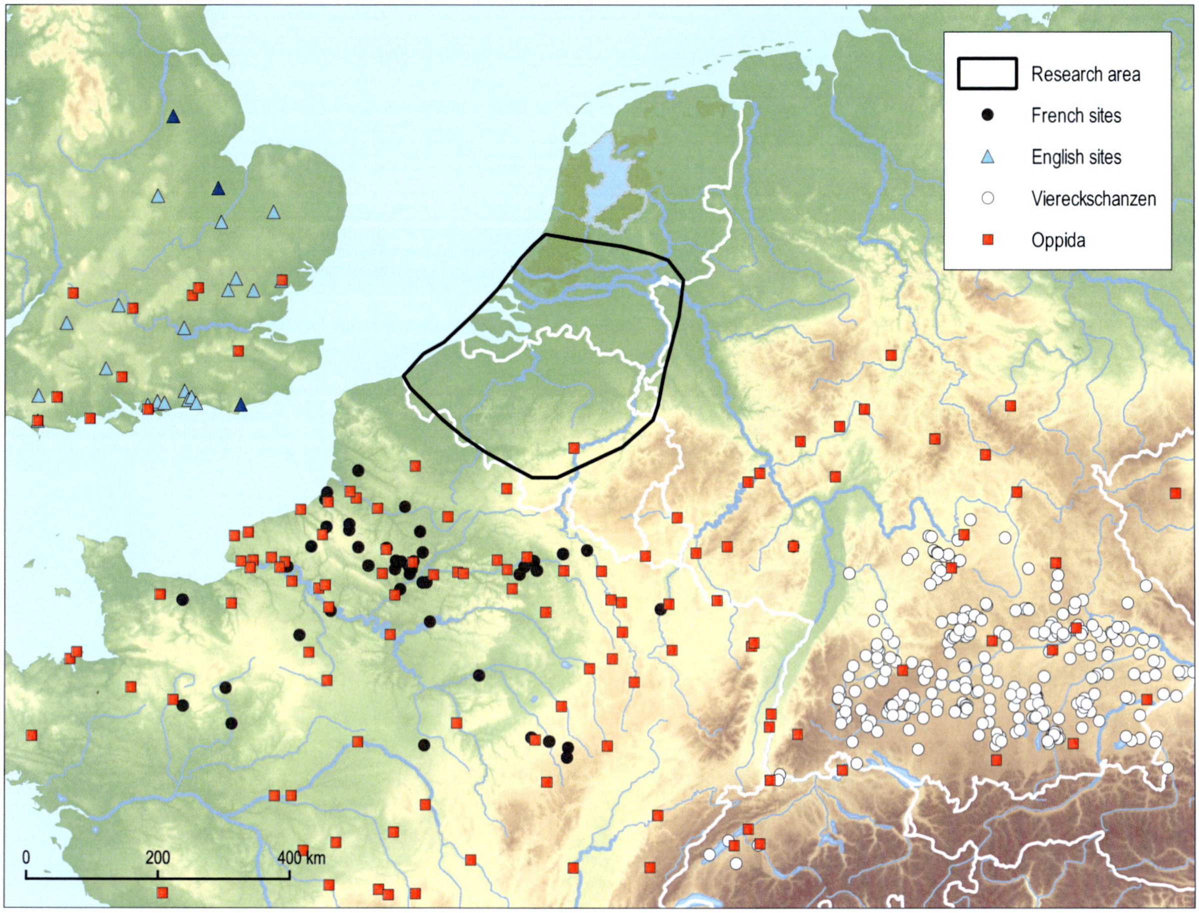

Figure 3.1 Part of Europe showing the distribution of the oppida in the region (based on Schwarz 1959; Wells 1993; http://www.oppida.org), English sites, French sites (based on Fauduet 2010, 319-336) and Viereckschanzen (based on Schwarz 1959; Bittel et al. 1990; Wieland 1999; Pfister 2000).

Countries must have been confronted with a certain degree of conflict (e.g. Gerritsen & Roymans 2006). It can be inferred from the deposits of weapons found in the water that they did. The socio-political organisation of the Low Countries, at least in the Late Iron Age, was fundamentally segmented (Roymans 1990, 43-45; Gerritsen & Roymans 2006). Reasonably autonomous groups, called *pagi* by Roymans (1990) after their Latin name, were part of a large tribal area, or *civitas*. Some of these tribes are known by name at the time of the Roman conquest in the mid-1st century BCE, such as the Menapi in the coastal region, the Frisii in the northwest Netherlands, the Nervii and the Aduatuci in central Belgium, and the Eburones in the southeast of the Netherlands (Roymans 1990, fig. 1.1). Settlements were mostly open and dispersed, with minimal display of either hierarchy or defensive systems (Roymans 1990, 169-190; Schinkel 1998, 162-166; Gerritsen 2003, 109; Fokkens 2019, 193). Drenthe, in the northeast of the Netherlands, is an exception. Nine walled settlement structures were excavated in this region

dating to the mid-4th/3rd century BCE to the 1st century CE (Waterbolk 1977). Waterbolk (*Ibid.*, 163-168) describes them as small fortified enclosures that served for stocking cattle and harvest products that were on occasion used for 'normal' domestic activities. He compares the structures to hillforts, or even *Viereckschanzen*, that served as chieftain seats portraying power and wealth rather than having had the function as refuges.

At least some parts of the Low Countries were reasonably densely populated, specifically in the Late Iron Age (Fokkens 2019, 190-192). Iron Age societies were to a certain point independent operating entities, essentially focused around self-sufficient nuclear families (Schinkel 1998, 162-166). Societies in the Low Countries would have had long-distance trade of goods and ideas with northern France, Germany and across the North Sea with England. To what extent the exchange with those neighbouring regions influenced the building of structures that formed the basis for, or resulted from, the transmutation of religious ideas is one of the central questions in this chapter.

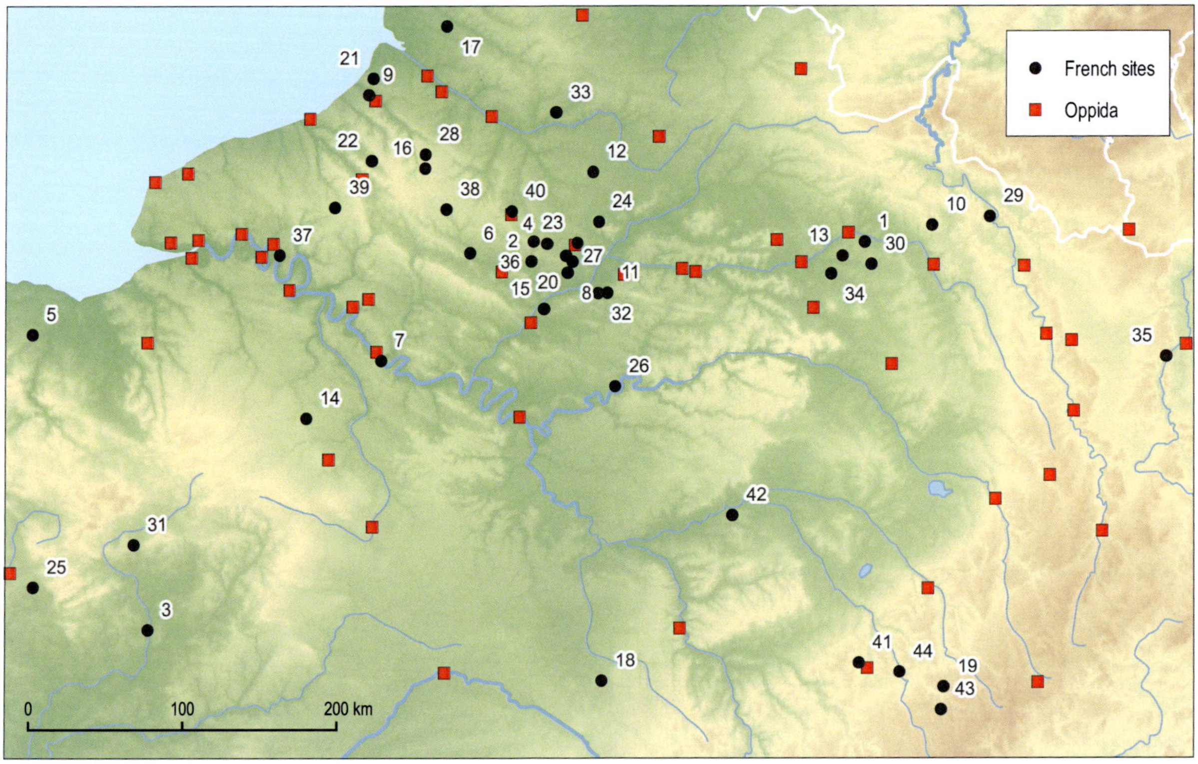

Figure 3.2. Map of northwest France showing Iron Age sanctuaries (After Fauduet 1993; 2010; Brunaux et al. 2003, figure 2).
1-Acy-Romance; 2-Airion; 3-Allonnes; 4-Angivillers; 5-Baron-sur-Odon; 6-Beauvais; 7-Bennecourt; 8-Blincourt; 9-Bois
l'Abbe; 10-Bouvellemont; 11-Champlieu, Orrouy; 12-Chilly; 13-Chateau-Porcien-Nandin; 14-Corneuil; 15-Creil; 16-Digeon;
17-Dompierre-sur-Authie; 18-Déversoir à Montbouy; 19-Essarois; 20-Estrées-Saint-Denis; 21-Eu; 22-Fesques; 23-Gournay-
sur-Aronde; 24-Gury; 25-Jublains; 26-Meaux; 27-Montmartin; 28-Morvillers-saint-Saturnin; 29-Mouzon; 30-Nanteuil-sur-Aisne;
31- Oisseau-le-Petit; 32-Orrouy; 33-Ribemont-sur-Ancre; 34-Roizy; 35-Ste-Ruffine; 36-Saint-Just-en-Chaussée; 37-St-Martin-de-
Boscherville; 38-St-Maur; 39-St-Saëns; 40-Vendeuil-Caply; 41-Vertault; 42-La Villeneuve-au-Châtelot; 43 Villiers-le-Duc; 44 Vix /
Mont Lassois.

3.2 The sanctuaries of Northern France

Whenever an author is in need of an example of an Iron
Age cult place Gournay-sur-Aronde is used. Therefore,
discussing this site is unavoidable in this dissertation. Many
sites that were interpreted as Iron Age cult places have
been excavated in France, particularly in the northwest
(fig. 3.2, black dots). The extent of their publication varies.
In this section five examples are used to illustrate the
diversity of sites rather than emphasise the similarities
between them, an approach advocated by Lejars (2001).

3.2.1 The archetype

When the site in Gournay-sur-Aronde was first discovered
in 1975, the attention was focused on several Gallo-Roman
structures that had been revealed by ploughing activities
(Brunaux 1975). Subsequent excavations uncovered a
rectangular enclosure, which was apparently modified
in several phases (Brunaux 1980). The structure had
rounded corners and a 3m wide opening on the northeast
side (fig. 3.3). It measured 45m in length northwest to

southeast. The oblique dimension was estimated at 38m,
but the southwest side was destroyed in the 1960s by the
construction of a road.

The inner ditch was likely the oldest part of the
structure dating to the late 4th (or early 3rd) century BCE
(Brunaux 1986, 17-18). It had a V-shaped cross section and
was at its widest on the east side: 2.5m, with a depth of
c. 1.8m. The sides and bottom of the ditch were probably
lined with wood (Brunaux et al. 1985). The function of the
lining might have been for easier maintenance and to keep
the ditch free from plant growth. From the start of the
use of this construction, this ditch served as a deposition
repository (Brunaux & Méniel 1983).

In a second phase a wooden palisade or wall was added
on the outside of the inner ditch, probably to obscure
the view of the inner ditch and the interior (Brunaux
et al. 1985b). Other French sanctuaries had a similar
wooden wall (Fresque, Chilly and Mirebeau) and in the
sites of Saint-Maur and Morvillers a wall was placed in
between two parallel ditches (Lejars 2001; Brunaux et al.

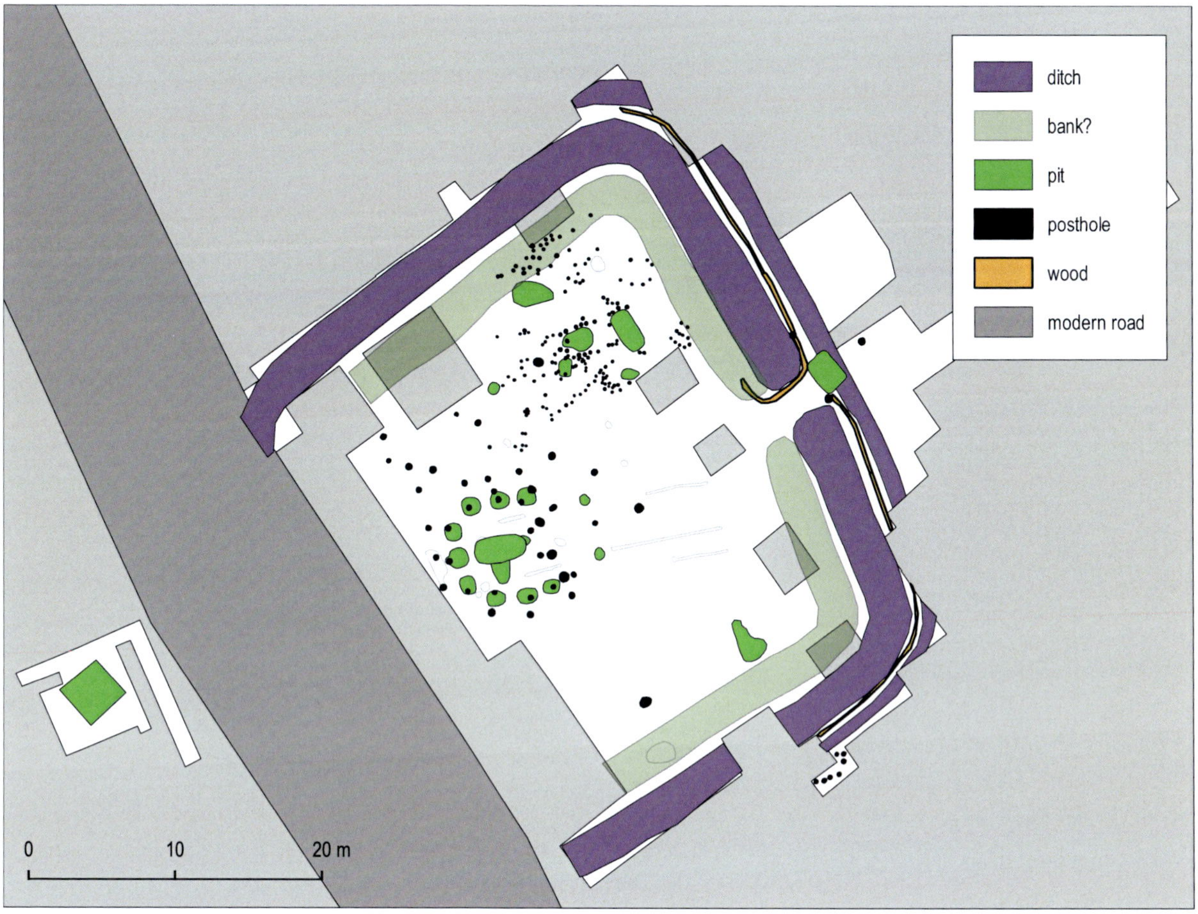

Figure 3.3. Site map of the Gournay sanctuary (after Carpentier 2015, fig. 4; Brunaux et al. 1985b; Brunaux, Méniel & Poplin 1985a, figures 30, 45 and 58).

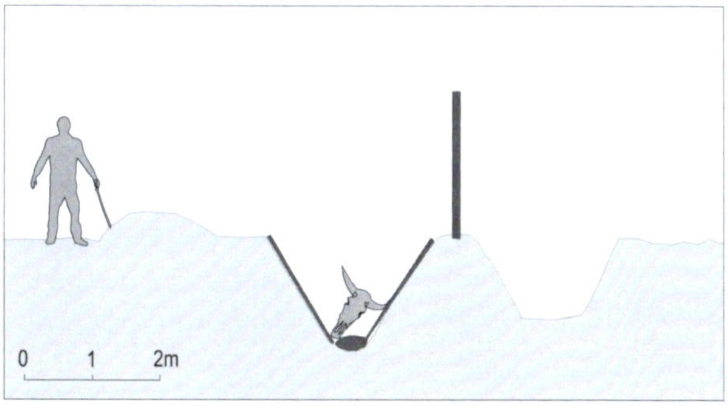

Figure 3.4. Reconstructed section of the palisade and ditches of the sanctuary at Gournay during phase 3 and 4 (after Brunaux et al. 1985b, figure 41, Brunaux 1986, 29). The inside is to the left.

2003). Another outer ditch was added in a later phase (Brunaux *et al.* 1985b; fig. 3.3). The outer ditch seemed to be entirely uninterrupted. For entry, people had to pass over a bridge, under a gate. An uninterrupted ditch or a pit in front of the entrance that had to be crossed when entering, is a feature also seen in the same sites that featured the double ditch and fence (Saint-Maur and Morvillers). Both the palisade and the outer ditch showed signs of maintenance and modifications in

their existence, until the late 2nd century BCE. The layered filling of the inner ditch suggests it was used as a depositional receptacle for a period as long as two centuries (Brunaux *et al.* 1985). In the first half of the 1st century BCE, the site was levelled and reused in the Early Roman Era.

The entrance was modified several times. In the first phase it was just a 3m wide interruption of the inner ditch. Simultaneous to the placement of the wall, a rectangular pit of c. 2-2.5m wide was dug in front of the entrance. This was also the width of the entrance at the time. Some sort of bridge might have been used to cross over the pit and later the outer ditch; perhaps a 'rite of passage' was needed in order to enter the sanctuary (Brunaux *et al.* 1985b). In its final phases the entrance was probably quite impressive. Brunaux reconstructed it as a porch with eight columns, a floor over the ditch and decorated doors (Brunaux *et al.* 2003). The porch may even have been decorated with weapons, and human and cattle skulls that later ended up in the ditch on both sides of the entrance.

Most of the finds were uncovered in the inner ditch (Brunaux and Méniel 1983; Poplin, Brunaux and Méniel 1985; Brunaux, Méniel and Poplin, 1985a). Three categories of remains were found: bones (2800 animal, 80 human), metal objects (2063 fragments, parts and broken weaponry, among which were found 100 swords, 150 scabbards, 220 shield umbos, 70 lance heads and 80 fibulae), and ceramics (270 fragments and four complete vessels). Different sections of the ditch were used for different types of depositions. Human bones are grouped in prime areas: limbs in the corners of the

ditch and vertebrae near the entrance (Brunaux *et al.* 1985). The largest concentrations were deposited on both sides of the entrance. Between the entrance and the corners mostly pig and sheep bones were found, as well as halfway along the sides (Brunaux 1986, 12-13; Méniel 1991). Several complete horses were placed in the ditch in different locations, both in the 'pig/sheep' areas as well as in the 'human' areas. The metal objects show indications of deliberate destruction before deposition (Brunaux and Méniel 1983). The weapons were bent, broken and cut. Scabbards were dismantled, twisted and fragmented. Shields umbos were pressed, hammered, drilled, and cut. Fibulae were opened and folded.

Inside the enclosure a smaller structure was found. This structure also went through several phases of remodelling: different post arrangements and one phase with nine square pits (Brunaux 1986, 17-18). These were large pits of 1.2m in length and more than 1m in depth, arranged in a U-shaped fashion around a central oval pit that was even larger: 3.5m long, 2m wide, and 2m deep (Brunaux *et al.* 2003). The use of the large pit seems related to the discovered animal remains on the site and also to some anatomical parts found at the bottom of

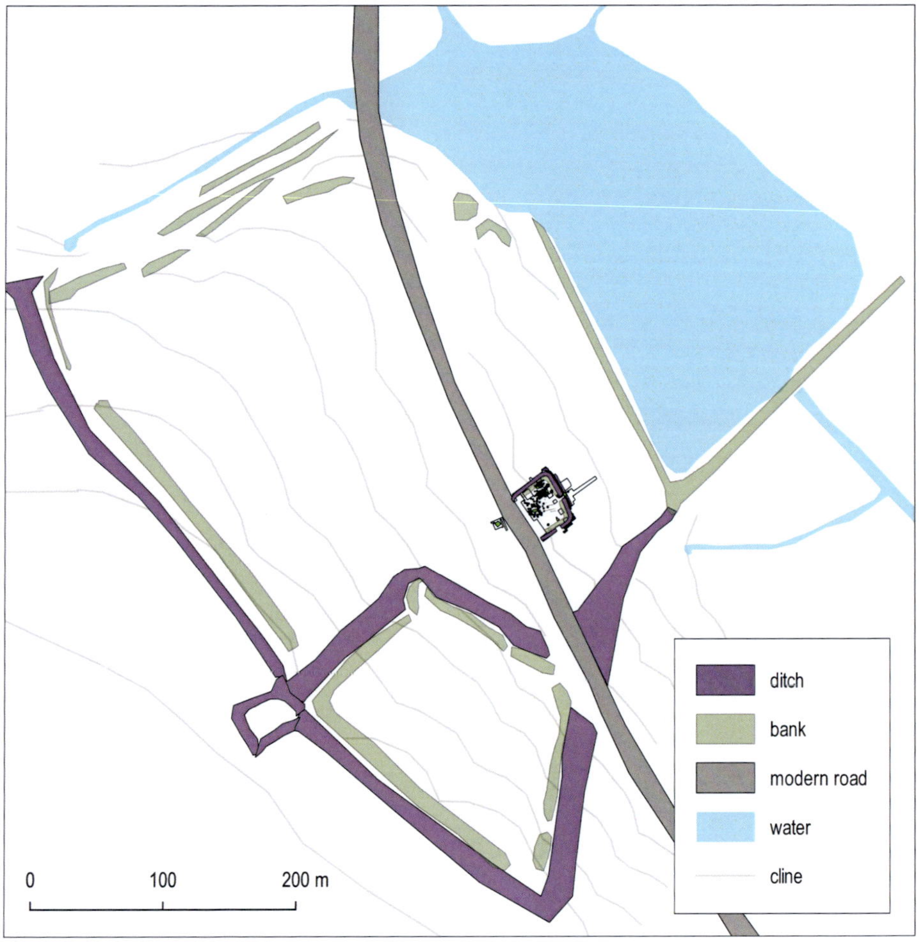

Figure 3.5. Position of the sanctuary at Gournay within the oppidum. Situation plan at the time of excavation. Highest point is the southwest side of the oppidum, the site is sloping down towards the water. 1: sanctuary enclosure; 2: 2.5m square pit with ceramic vases (after Brunaux 1980, figure 1; Brunaux 1983, figure 1; Brunaux 1986, 16).

the pit. The pit is regarded as another typical feature of an Iron Age sanctuary (Lejars 2001). Similar central pits are known from excavated structures in Fresque, Bennecourt, Saint-Maur and Vendeuil-Caply, although not as deep. Recently, it has been suggested that the pits may have functioned to accommodate standing (wooden) statues (Poux 2019). The argument by Poux (2019) is that the pits did not deliver enough evidence that would be expected of an offering receptacle (i.e. animals bones). Also, the cross-sections resemble postholes that were redug several times.

In the north corner of the sanctuary is a seldom discussed cluster of five pits and 173 postholes (Brunaux, Méniel & Poplin 1985a). The small posts were placed in clusters and some are arranged in short rows. The pits held few finds apart from charcoal in the top fill, and they seemed to have been filled in quickly. Notably wooden branches were found scattered over the area. In contrast, the southwest part of the sanctuary was rather devoid of features.

Just 10m west of the enclosure on the other side of a modern road, a 2.6m square pit was found with twenty 4th century BCE La Tène vases (Brunaux 1975; Brunaux, Méniel & Poplin 1985a). The pottery was placed along the vertical walls, seemingly arranged by size and type of vessel. This 'pit of the vases' predates the use of the sanctuary. The 25cm shallow pit did not contain burial remains and was not filled immediately after the deposit of the vases, but was kept open for a while, filling in gradually. The pit itself was dug in a mound or deposit of soil, of which the dimensions were unclear at the time of excavation, except that the pit was probably dug north of the centre of the mound.

The site of Gournay was never fully excavated (fig. 3.5). In fact, the excavation barely extended beyond the outer ditch. The only contextual information is that the features were situated within an oppidum, near the source of the Aronde River, and located at the edge of a plateau, on a slope (Brunaux 1980; 1983; 1986; Lejars 2001). A few small trial trenches were dug in the oppidum that provided a meagre amount of information (Brunaux 1983). Any relation between the excavated features and the oppidum or settlement they were situated in, is unknown, or even what type of activities took place just beyond of the ditches. Likewise, the mound in which the pit of the vases was recovered has not been researched. It is conceivable this concerned an older barrow. As a result, the role of this structure remains unclear, in regard to the local society as well as the oppidum. It is conceivable that the oppidum housed a particular group of people, who at times, maybe at time of conflicts, used the sanctuary for specific acts. Given the number of weapons discovered this could have involved warriors, and given the animal bones and pottery it could have involved their families too or even the whole community.

3.2.2 A war memorial

The next example of an Iron Age cult place seems to be serving an even more specific purpose, related to warriors and conflict. The site of Ribemont-sur-Ancre, about 50 km north of Gournay, was already known as a Gallo-Roman temple complex since it was discovered by aerial photography and excavated from 1966 onwards (Cadoux & Massy 1970). Scattered human remains and fragments of umbos and lance heads had been found there before, but not until the 1982 excavation revealed a large ossuary with strangely arranged human skeletal elements, was the presence of a preceding Iron Age sanctuary suggested (Cadoux 1982; 1982a; Didier & Cadoux 1982). The ossuary was discovered at the foot of the Roman temple and was surrounded by a rectangular ditch of approximately 50m across (fig. 3.6).

From 1990 onwards, the further excavation of the site was left to Brunaux (Brunaux *et al.* 1999). In subsequent excavations of the site, other ossuaries were discovered within the boundaries of the rectangular ditch (Brunaux 1998, Brunaux *et al.* 1999). The site was dated to the late 3rd century BCE and seemed to have been in use for a much shorter period than Gournay, as it was probably dismantled or left to decay around the early 2nd century BCE (Fercoq du Leslay 1996). The two phases of utilization of the site, in the middle La Tène and in the Roman period, had a prolonged hiatus in-between. The Roman temple was built in the late 1st century BCE directly over the La Tène site, disturbing some parts of the older features. Due to the preservation of the Roman temple, only parts of the La Tène structure could be excavated.

The rectangular ditch marked the main activity area of the site, but not the entire utilization (fig. 3.6). Deposits extend beyond the ditch: at least 10m to the east and 20m to the south. The southwest side of the ditch was added later (Brunaux *et al.* 1999). The 3rd century BCE cross section was originally V-shaped and around 2-2.65m deep (Fercoq du Leslay 2000). The bottom of the ditch was flat or slightly bowl-shaped and measured 30-45cm wide, with its sides sloping at steep 65° angles and a width of approximately 2.50m at the top. It gradually widened by erosion and then filled with eroded material (visible by thin layers) to a depth of 1.2-1.3m. It remained in this state for a while, evident by the growth of plants in the ditch filling. In the Roman phase the ditch was used as a deposition receptacle. The site was 'cleaned' and then redeveloped around 40-30 BCE. Before the Roman phase of the site, whatever remained at the time was destroyed and a container with 573 pieces of iron weaponry was deposited in the southwest corner of the ditch. The deposition contained a combination of swords, scabbards

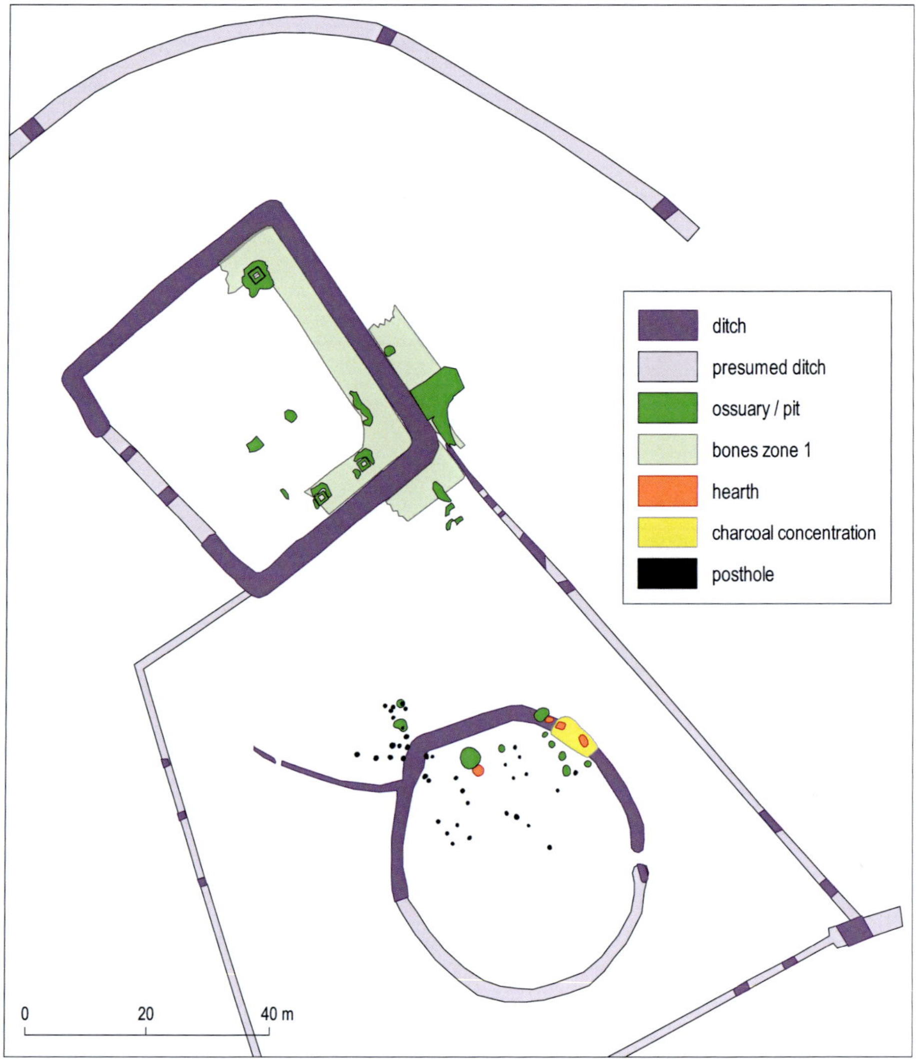

Figure 3.6. Map of the Iron Age sanctuary at Ribemont. The area 'zone 1' contains among loose bones many skeletal parts with anatomical joints (after Brunaux et al. 2003, fig. 19, 37 and 38; Fercoq du Leslay 2000 fig. 3, Delestrée 2001; information at the Centre archéologique Ribemont-sur-Ancre; Fercoq Du Leslay, Bataille & Chaidron 2019, fig. 1 and 2).

and spears from LT C1[8], and swords, scabbards, and belt loops dating to LT D2. In contrast to earlier finds at the site, these weapons did show signs of intentional destruction. The difference in date of the two separate sets of equipment clarified the utilization hiatus (Lejars 1999). A more heterogeneous group of objects dated to the late LT D1 and early LT D2: weapons, tools, around 2000 nails, and other construction parts and assembly elements of Roman military-style decorations, Gallic coins subsequent to the conquest often mixed with Roman coins, ceramics, and amphorae datable to LT D2 (Brunaux et al. 1999). The latter group of objects belonged to the reuse of the site in the Roman period.

The skeletal remains of at least 500 individuals, all adult males, were both documented inside the boundary of the ditch and outside of the ditch (Brunaux et al. 1999; Fercoq du Leslay 2000; Brunaux et al. 2003; Fercoq du Leslay et al. 2019). The remains were manipulated in different ways and the skulls were missing. Four clusters could be identified in similar square arrangements, including the one found in 1982, as well as several large, more random placed bone-mass deposits. The largest bone-mass was found northeast outside the ditch. The bone-mass alone contained around 13.500 human bones and bone fragments in a 30cm thick layer, of at least 114 individuals most of whom were young males (Fercoq du Leslay et al. 2019). Of the bones 77 cervical vertebrae showed evidence of decapitation. In the bone-mass twelve gold coins and a gold torc were found (Delestrée 2001). Isolated skeletal remains were also found spread out over the site. Some of the bones were (partly) in an anatomical position, showing marks of scavengers and weathering, so they must have been left in situ at the surface to decay.

---

8   In France to following definitions are used: La Tène C1: 280-190 BCE, La Tène C2: 190-140 BCE, La Tène D1: 140 – 80 BCE, La Tène D2: 80 – 30 BCE (Arcelin & Brunaux 2003).

Of the four square arrangements (ossuaries) only one was in good condition, located inside the northeast corner of the enclosure (Brunaux *et al.* 1999). Two were in a bad state of conservation and another was crossed by trenches from WWI. Within a pile of bones 3-4m across, the central part of each of these ossuaries consisted of mostly long bones arranged in some sort of square structure that would have been at least 1m high. The most complete example was excavated. It consisted of long bones that were stacked in longitudinal and transverse position in order to make sides. Nearly all of the hand and foot bones were missing, save for the knee caps, heel, and ankle bones (*patella, talus* and *calcaneus*). These articulating parts were found in large numbers at the foot of these 'walls', where they fell while the legs were decomposing. The missing extremities suggest that the legs and arms were already in a state of decomposition when placed in this position. Besides human bones the remains of at least 50 horses were found. Their legs were mostly integrated into the walls, in between the human remains, with many bones showing traces of butchering and dismemberment. The weapons were essentially parts belonging to spears, shield umbos, scabbards and waist chains, and to a lesser degree, swords. None of these objects have traces of intentional destruction, but instead many traces of impacts attributable to battle. Within the 'bone walls' a pit of around 1m deep was discovered, perfectly cylindrical, measuring 30cm in diameter. It contained a complex fill, consisting essentially of splinters of slightly burnt human long bones mixed with charcoal. It may have been a former posthole, that later functioned as a depository. If it was a posthole, the site may have had a previous usage phase (Fercoq du Leslay 1996; Fercoq du Leslay 2000).

Brunaux suggests that these were the remains of (conquered) warriors, of a tribe that suffered a defeat in a unique combat that took place in the immediate vicinity, or even on the location of the enclosure (Brunaux 1996a, 215). The discovered gold coins were probably produced in Armorica (Brittany), providing a suggested origin for the conquered tribe (Delestrée 2001). The whole construction may be a monumental trophy such as described by the classical writers Posidonius and Diodorus (Brunaux 1998, 1999 *et al.*). In Brunaux' reconstruction, the remains of the warriors were on some sort of raised platform, which was part of a building. Many of their weapons were discarded with them. Taphonomic studies prove that it can take years for a body to decompose when raised off the ground.[9] After the building collapsed, many human remains and

most parts of the building would have been left in situ to decay (Brunaux *et al.* 1999). Other parts were rearranged in walls and heap deposits or discarded in the south corner of the ditch.

Just over 30m southeast of the rectangular enclosure another, oval or polygonal example, was found. The oval enclosure was almost entirely excavated, but unfortunately badly preserved (Brunaux *et al.* 2003). This structure was likely older than the rectangular one, predating it by about 50 years (Fercoq du Leslay *et al.* 2019).[10] The length of the structure was probably around the same as the rectangular enclosure. The ditch was also of a similar size, measuring 2m deep. The oval structure was in the centre of a trapezoid enclosed terrain, connected on at least one side to the rectangular structure. Both the trapezoid terrain and the oval structure probably had a wall in the ditch, with a wattle and daub construction. Traces of black and white plaster suggest that the walls of the curved enclosure were painted and could have been be engraved. Inside the oval enclosure 300 human bones and 200 pieces of armaments were found. The human bones, mostly long bones, belonged to a minimum of 40 individuals. The bones showed signs of tool marks and scavenger teeth, and were most likely exposed for a prolonged period. In a large cylindrical pit of 3.50m in diameter and 2m deep, ashy layers were excavated, containing numerous animal bones, some pottery, several weapons and human bones. The archaeological material found in this enclosure was different from the material assemblage found in the rectangular enclosure. Ceramic was abundant in the oval structure and absent in the deposits of the rectangular enclosure. Contrasting with the rectangular one, the oval structure might have been used for funerary rites, or was intended to create a permanent memorial enclosure for the fallen friendlies (Brunaux *et al.* 2003, 37).

The setup of a rectangular and an oval one was also found in Saumeray. Two enclosures about 80m apart, one of 10m square and an oval one of the same length (Hamon *et al.* 2002). Even though these structures resembled graves without the actual burials, the abundance of finds was paramount for an interpretation of them as sanctuaries. In the rectangular structure 6000 pottery fragments, 300 metal fragments, 200 coins and 155 animal bones were found, mostly cranial parts of horses and cattle. The oval structure contained 300 fragments of pottery, 230 metal objects, and 206 bone remains. The metal objects were mostly (parts of) weapons, while the rectangular structure contained besides horse gear and weaponry, fragments of tool parts. The weapons of the two enclosures showed

---

9   Unpublished study of human corpses hanging outdoors from a rope above ground executed by the Anthropological Research Facility (ARF) in Tennessee (ongoing research at the time of visit in 2012). Even in a humid climate ligaments dry out in a temporary stage of mummification and thereby hold the bones together.

---

10   Approx. 300-250 BCE for the oval structure, and 250-200 BCE for the rectangular structure (Fercoq du Leslay *et al.* 2019). The dismantling can be dated around the 2nd-1st century BCE, a phase in which more weapons and pottery were deposited.

typological differences. Both structures at Saumeray seem to have been in use for a limited period of around 50 years in the first half of the 2nd century BCE. The differences in shape and assemblage led the excavators to believe that there was a functional difference between the two structures, which represented two groups of warriors.

Both Ribemont and Saumeray have usages and weaponry deposits belonging to certain events, which the excavators interpret as an indication that the structures were made to commemorate warriors or display victory in battle, possibly representing a single event. These 'war offerings' are also known from Meaux (4th century BCE), Aubigné-Racan, Bennecourt, Saint-Maur, Mirebeau, Montmartin, and Muron, displaying similar assemblages and time frames (Lejars 2001; Marion 2005; Demierre *et al.* 2019). So despite the resemblance in appearance of the continuous rectangular ditch these are different types of sanctuaries than Gournay. Lejars (2001) suggests a commemoration place or memorial would be more appropriate names than sanctuary or community shrine, even though the finds and features may express similar acts.

3.2.3 A place for the ancestors

Gournay is often stated as the oldest example of a sanctuary (e.g. Derks 1996, 142), until an excavation at Vix along the River Seine. In contrast to the above-mentioned sites, Vix has no known weapons depositions. Instead, it was positioned in a cemetery that is mostly known for its rich Hallstatt burials, in particular the famous 'princess of Vix', and its proximity to the hillfort of Mont Lassois (the toponym of Mont-Saint-Marcel). The latter is thought to have been the 'seat' of the Chieftain rulers of the region who were buried on the plain 109m below the flat mount; the interred princess is thought to have been one of the ruling class (Joffroy 1954; 1960; Chaume 2001, 333-360). On the plain, half enclosed by a bend of the River Seine, Late Bronze Age (Ha B3), Early Iron Age (Ha C/D), and Middle to late La Tène (C-D1) burials were found.

From 1991 to 1993, on the site 'Vix-Les Herbues', an enclosure was excavated that subsequently was labelled a sanctuary or cult site. The location of the structure had been known since it was photographed in the early 1960s (Goguey 1968). The enclosure was positioned within the Hallstatt necropolis but did not contain a burial. Results of small-scale surveys of the structure in 1964, 1969, and 1972 were never published (Chaume 2001, 255). The excavation in the 1990s revealed a rectangular ditch 26.4 × 24.8m, of about 2m wide (fig. 3.7). The ditch was interrupted by a gap of 60-70cm on the northwest side, in the direction of Mont Lassois (Chaume, Reinhard & Wustrow 2007).

The site of Les Herbues was significantly eroded at the time of excavation (Chaume 2011, 256-259). About 1m

depth remained of the ditch, that had filled in five phases. The two first (lowest) phases testified of erosion and slow filling. Then a layer containing an assemblage of heterogeneous materials was deposited. This is interpreted as originating from a dismantled building (Chaume 2011). This third layer included the deposition of the remains of two statues near the north side of the entrance. The top of this layer showed a high concentration of organic material showing a stationary situation for a certain length of time. Finally the top two layers consisted of fluvial-transported sediments. Among the finds in the ditch were 2864 fragments of animal bones (Chaume, Reinhard & Wustrow 2007). Of these, 1114 were analysed and revealed 98.8% domestic animals, 0.5% wild animals, and 0.7% birds. The domestic animal bones consisted of 26% cattle, 25% pig, 24% sheep/goat, 10% horse, and 10% dog. Cut marks suggested that these were consumption leftovers. Most of the 548 pottery pieces from the ditch consisted of small rounded fragments from the third layer of the ditch fill (Chaume & Reinhard 2009). The pottery and nine fibulae date the ditch between 530 and 450 BCE. This is contemporary to the famous tomb of the princess, positioned 260m north-northeast.

Near the centre of the enclosure a silo-shaped cylindrical pit was found. The pit was 1.1m deep and had a diameter of 1.2m at its base (Chaume, Reinhard & Wustrow 2007). One third of the pit was filled with stones, the rest consisted of sediments. Unfortunately the pit lacked any dateable material. Another silo-shaped pit was excavated in the east part of the enclosure. This one was 1m deep and had a diameter at the surface of 0.8m

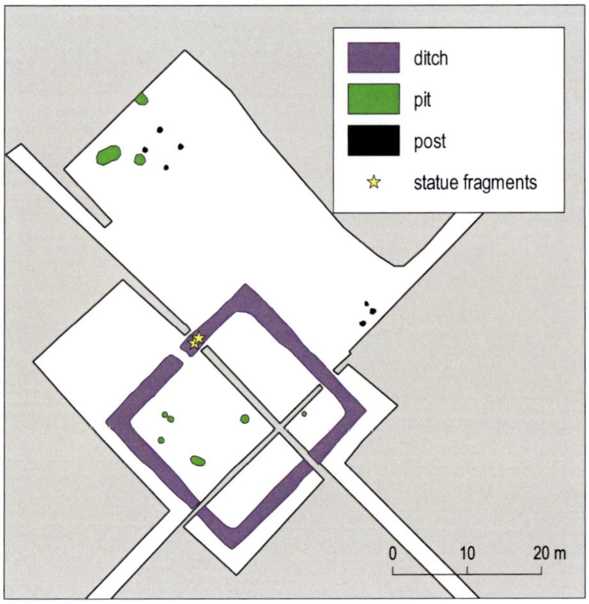

Figure 3.7. The rectangular enclosure at Vix-Les Herbues (after Chaume & Reinhard 2011, fig. 4).

and at the bottom of 1.5m. Like the pit near the centre, it held no datable material.

The remains of the two statues from the ditch are interpreted as the depictions of a male and a female (Chaume 2001, 259-260; Chaume & Reinhard 2011). Originally they would have been around life size. It appears however the statues were deliberately destroyed and part of the remains thrown in the ditch. The largest remaining blocks were 46 × 38 × 51cm ('the male') and 62 × 34 × 51cm ('the female'). The male statue is called 'the warrior' as he had a shield in front of him and weapons at his side. The warrior was in a sitting position with his knees up. The female statue was also in a seated position, dressed in a robe and she had a torc around her neck. The torc was of a model with two balls at the front ends, resembling the real torc made of gold found in the princess tomb. Both statues were missing their head and their feet.

The rectangular enclosure in Vix has been interpreted as a cult structure dedicated to the founding ancestors, who were figures of major political and/or religious power (Chaume & Reinhard 2011). The statues as deified representations of the ancestors were honoured during ceremonies accompanied by 'rituals of exchange'. The animal bones can be perceived as the result of eating or feasting during the ceremonies. The destruction of the site is attributed to the loss of power of Mont Lassois, an event in which the statues were intentionally broken (Chaume & Reinhard 2003, 260; Megaw 2003).

3.2.4 A weapon depository

Both structures at Vix and Ribemont seem to have been made for a specific purpose, one for the ancestors and the latter at a time of conflict. Notably, both were in used on specific occasions. Not all sanctuaries have such a clearly defined role. In 1973 a large coin depot was discovered at a site called Les Grèves in Villeneuve-au-Châtelot (Frézouls 1975, under 'b'). The depot contained two vases with a total of 1128 mainly bronze, and some silver Gallic and early Roman coins. The site was fully excavated in the early 1980s, although how the coin depot fits in the later excavation is unclear. Based on the diversity of finds, the site was in use for a long time. According to Bataille (2007) two Iron Age utilisation phases can be distinguished. The first phase was between c. 330 and 180 BCE (LT B2-C1) with a successive phase that ended around 120-100 BCE (LT C2-D1). In the second half of the 1st century BCE the site was converted into a Roman sanctuary (a third phase).

The main structure consisted of three rectangular ditches (Fig. 3.8). The oldest ditch was incomplete, but probably of a rectangular shape and at least 16m square (Piette 1983). It has a different orientation to its successors and is much narrower. It is unclear how long this ditch had been in use. The main features of the site are two broader parallel ditches, the outer one measuring 26m x 19m and the inner one approximately 20m x 14.5m. From the centre of one ditch to the centre of the other is on average 3.5m distance (Piette 1979). The inner ditch had a U-shaped cross section with vertical sides, up to 110cm deep. The

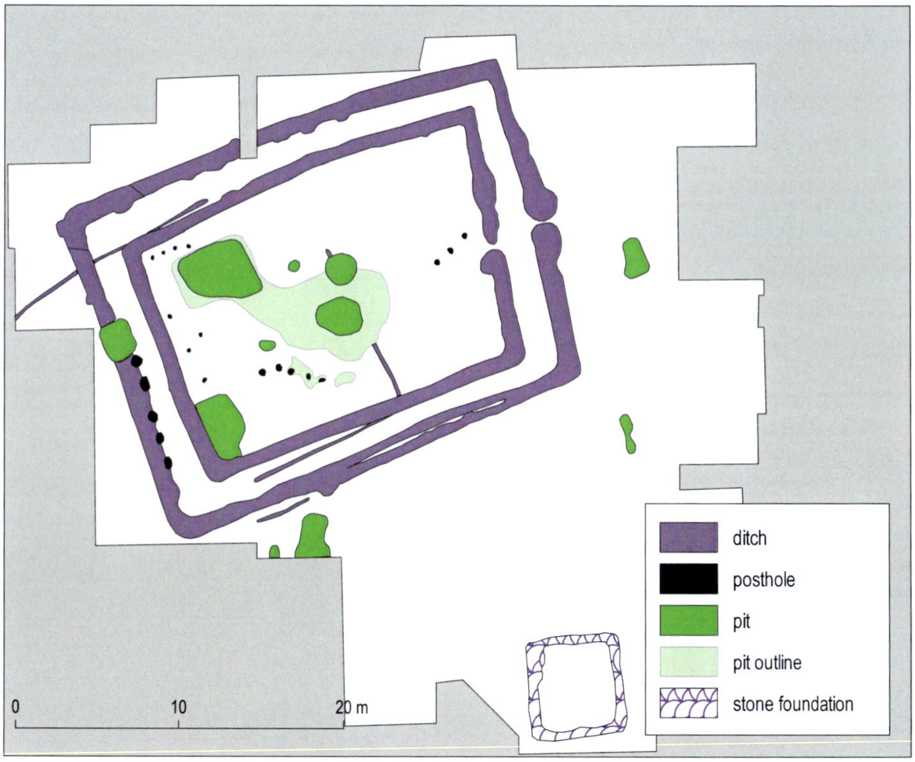

Figure 3.8. Plan of Villeneuve-au-Châtelot (after Piette 1989 as cited by Haffner 1995, fig. 16).

outer ditch was also U-shaped but had more 'flared' sides and split on the south side and c. 80cm deep. Both ditches had a width of about 80 to 100cm. The ditches contained postholes. Both ditches were interrupted on the east side, the inner one by just a few centimetres and the outer one by 30 cm, probably to accommodate a narrow entrance. As no cross sections of the ditches have been published it is unknown whether the ditches were maintained or redug in different phases. Judging by the written description of the cross section and the position of the posts, the ditches can be interpreted as bedding trenches to support walls. These ditches could thus represent a different type of structure from the previous open features described in this chapter.

In the central area a large oval pit was found with an oblong appendix (Piette 1981). In the northwest of the structure a square pit was found. The central pit had been redug and expanded, and was disturbed by a medieval well. Around the central area 110 postholes and smaller pits were identified (Piette 1979; Piette 1981, fig. 13, depicted in a photo, not published on the site plan). These posts were divided into seven parallel lines, in the same orientation as the ditch. They were quite evenly spaced 15-30cm apart and had a diameter of 10-18cm. South of the double ditch structure, the stone foundation of a square building was found that could have been a small Gallo-Roman shrine.

The excavations revealed tens of thousands of metal fragments, which made up a minimum number of 509 Iron Age objects of 40 different types (Bataille 2007). Most objects were found in three concentrations, the largest one at the entrance on the east side. The majority of the Iron Age metal objects were weapons (62%), which made Bataille (2007) define the site as a 'weapon sanctuary'. This would certainly apply to the earliest deposits dating to phase 1, which consisted mainly of weapons (and some fibulae). In phase 2 the assemblage of the depositions changes and a greater diversity of artefacts is represented (from 173 artefacts of nine types in LT C2 to 59 artefacts of 38 types in LT D1). Among the new objects ornaments are emerging (glass bracelets and beads, silver brooches, female belt clips), domestic utensils (pots, knifes, buckets), and elements of chariots and harnesses, but above all tools are heavily represented through iron ploughshares and half-manufactured artefacts. This assemblage certainly differs from the first phase mirroring what must be defined as a shift in the use of the place. The early Roman phase entailed many coins, both Roman and indigenous, and a great number of miniature wheels (*rouelles*) (Duval *et al.* 1994). These were made of gold (N=2), silver (N=34), bronze (N=500), and lead (N=70.000+). Most of the lead wheels were discovered in the inner ditch and 450 made out of bronze in the outer ditch (Piette 1981). The bronze wheels could be associated with Gallic coins. Pottery and bones were found, but their numbers remain unpublished probably due to the focus on the abundance of metal finds.

Overall, the features are poorly publicized, such as the hundreds of postholes that would have been part of one or more structures. The finds are generally interpreted as a cult place that was used over a long time (Lejars 2001). The abundance of a certain dedicated type of object is typical for the end of the Iron Age and the beginning of the Roman era. This includes coins (as in Morvillers-Saint-Saturnin), miniature swords and shields (as in Mouzon), and miniature spearhead (as in Acy-Romance) (Goussard *et al.* 2019). The dedication could have been aimed at a specific deity. The lay-out of Villeneuve, though not the finds, resembles the Oss-Brabantstraat site. This resemblance will be further explored in Chapter 6.5.3.

3.2.5 A place for communal gatherings

Situated 120 km due east of Gournay-sur-Aronde, in the French Ardennes, an entire Iron Age village with 350 structures and parts of the surrounding area was excavated. The excavation extended over fourteen hectares and took fifteen years between 1988 and 2003 (Méniel 2010). The large scale of the excavation allows for a thorough analysis of the relation between acts of sacrifice performed within the context of the village and as well as the burial tradition outside.

The site was in use during the 2nd and 1st century BCE. Northwest of the village five cemeteries were found all surrounded by a rectangular ditch. Three more cemeteries were discovered at a slightly larger distance east of the village (fig. 3.9). A total of 130 cremation graves were excavated within the cemeteries, which may be underrepresented when considering the size of the village and the duration of its existence (Lambot 1998).

The Iron Age village was positioned on a ridge around a Bronze Age barrow that was assimilated into the centre of the village lay-out (Brunaux *et al.* 2003; Lambot & Méniel 2000). The area around the barrow was kept open (the round structure near the middle of fig. 3.9). At the highest point of the hill a D-shaped ditch demarked the community square of 85m in length and 56.5m wide. The square covered an area of almost 3500 m², easily large enough for a gathering of all the inhabitants. The shape of the square probably derived from the shape of the plateau, following its natural curvature. Originally, the ditch was V-shaped in cross section. The remaining width was 0.80-1.10m, to a depth of 0.45-0.75m, and a flat bottom of 10 to 15cm wide. The ditch would have been 1m to 1.5m deep when it was dug. At irregular places postholes were identified within the ditch and the south side of the ditch showed that a fence had been positioned there. According to Lambot & Méniel (2000) this was sufficient evidence that the ditch was originally the basis for a palisade made out of larger posts with smaller ones in between.

In the ditch 780 animal bones were found (Meniel 2010). This is a fraction of the amount found in the

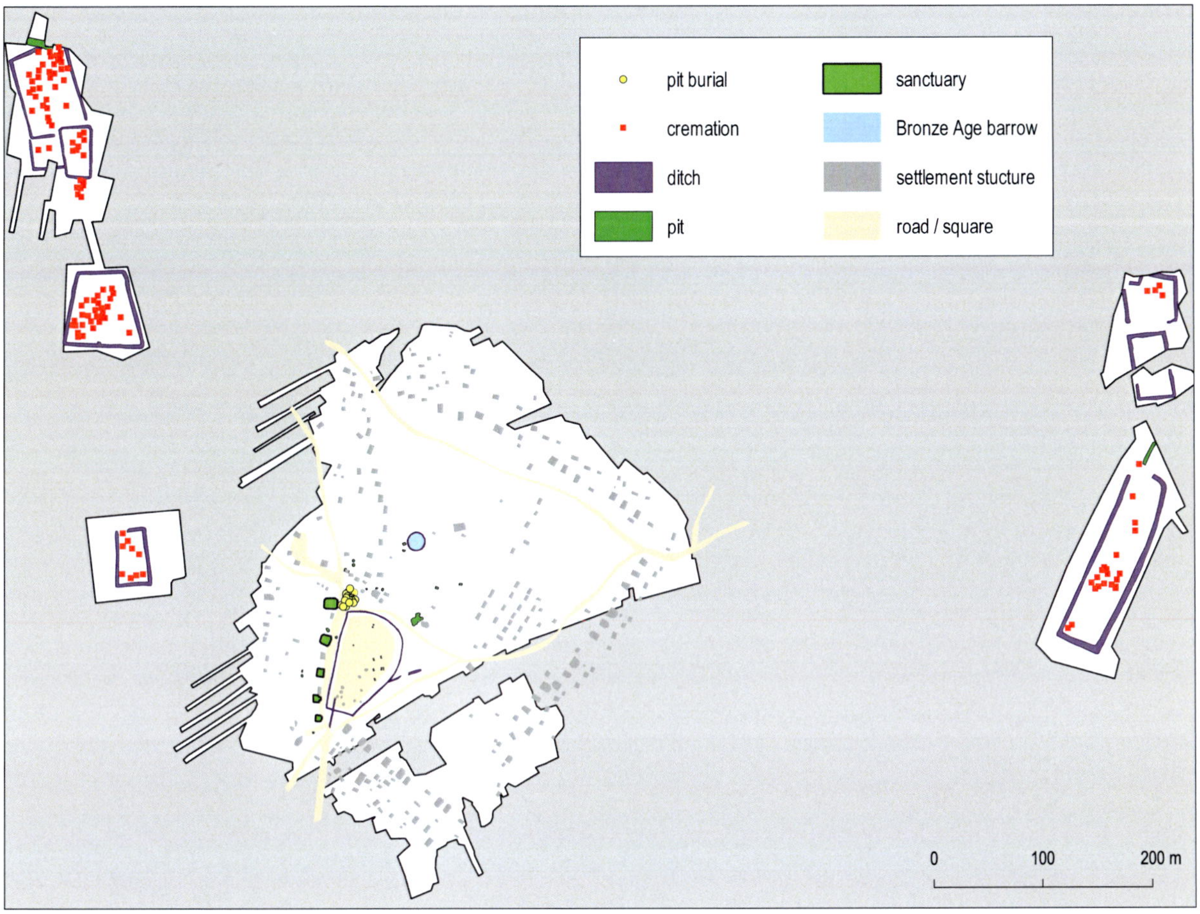

Figure 3.9. Lay-out of the excavations of the Late Iron Age village of Acy Romance and surrounding area with cemeteries and roads (after Lambot 1998; Lambot & Méniel 2000, fig. 11 and 19).

village where a total of 197.000 animal bones have been discovered. The vast majority of the bones in the village belonged to domesticated animals: pig (34%), sheep (25%), cattle (22.4%), horse (8.4%), dog (3.6%), and goat (1%). The remaining part (5.6%) consisted mostly of fish bones. More than half of the animal bones were dumped as waste in eighty filled-in silos (Lambot & Méniel 2000). The remains in the ditch were mainly from cattle (70%) and horse (18%), with a strong representation of vertebrae. In the southern half of the ditch cattle bones were in the majority, whereas in the northern half mainly horse bones were found. On the north side also some fragments of human remains were discovered, mostly teeth and skull fragments.

The square itself was relatively empty of features. On the eastern half of the square six pairs of postholes were arranged in two rows (Lambot & Méniel 2000). The posts could have been part of three constructions, three 'porticos' on four posts, possibly with connecting beams, each construction about 6.8m long. Various functions are suggested for these constructions: decorated totems, space dividers, canopy pillars or supports for skinning and

butchering animals. Given the skeletal finds in the ditch, Lambot & Méniel (2000) propose the latter hypothesis as the most likely. Three postholes, of which two were uncertain, were found in the northern half of the enclosure. A World War I trench disrupted this area and one of the holes could date from this period. Ten treefall pits reveal the presence of large trees scattered throughout the southern half of the site. Their contemporaneity is uncertain.

The only direct access point was from the south on a path bordered by a wooden fence which continued ten metres into the square. The entrance was likely over a plank bridge (Lambot & Méniel 2000). The fence ended in a pit measuring 1 × 1m, with a remaining depth of 20cm. At a distance of 2m outside of the entrance three complete oxen skulls were found. These may have been fixed on the porch or on the fence.

Five buildings stood parallel to the west side of the square aligned with the top of the limestone ridge (Lambot & Méniel 2000). The buildings differ in size, but all seem to have an octagonal ground plan. The smallest building was on the south side of the row (6m across) and the largest one on the north side (11m across). Their dimensions and the distance between them show a regular geometric enlargement with a multiplying factor of 1.25. The entrance was likely towards the square. The postholes of the five buildings contained only a few finds, 60 pottery shards in total, and several iron objects all from the upper fills. The pottery pointed towards a date at the end of LT C2 and the start of LT D1. Two coins found in depressions left by the decay of posts of building II, date the building before 120 BCE. These buildings were interpreted by Lambot & Méniel (2000) as temples because of their lay-out, the finds and features, and their proximity to the square.

Inside the largest building a square 'well' was discovered 2.5m from the entrance (Lambot & Méniel 2000). It was a 7.60m deep square pit that did not function as a water well, as the groundwater level at the site fluctuates around a depth of 60m. Near the top, the remains of a wooden frame were found and at a depth of 5.3m two ledges had been made on the sides with notches in the wall. These were probably designed to support two wooden beams. This construction seems quite specific. Its setting and the proximity to the square and some unusual human burials nearby, indicate according to Lambot & Méniel (2000) that these buildings and the square pit had a sacrificial function. Near the largest temple building, nineteen circular pit-graves were found related to a specific (sacrificial?) act (Lambot 1998; Lambot & Méniel 2000). Each pit contained the remains of one inhumated person in a sitting position, with their knees up and their head between their legs. Most of these had been young adults at the time of death, at least eight were male. The theory presented by Lambot (1998) is that these people had been placed in a small cubical wooden box after death, probably in the square pit mentioned above. After enough time for at least partial mummification they were buried in the same box in a circular pit of about 0.65-1m in diameter, most likely naked and without grave goods. This act seems to have been repeated (annually?) over a limited time period between 100 to 80 BCE. The human remains in these pit burials are interpreted as human sacrifices (Lambot & Méniel 2000).

Another grave on the north side along the largest building was that of a man who had died from an axe blow to his skull. He was buried in a shallow ditch with indications that his hands had been tied. All over the village unburned human remains were found, mostly isolated bones or fragments in pits and silos (Lambot 1998). These represent approximately 50 individuals of all ages. These human remains were treated differently after death from the ones buried in the eight cemeteries surrounding the village (fig. 3.9). In the cemeteries cremation remains were customary, commonly buried in 1.3m long rectangular pits. Some larger graves contained square post settings around them. Grave goods were placed next to the cremation

remains on the east side of the burial pit, along the side. The grave goods consisted of ceramic pots or bowls and sometimes a large iron bucket. Other grave goods were fibulae dating to 180-30 BCE, glass bracelets and beads, and knives that were sometimes found in connection with the remains of animal sacrifices. Rarer grave goods were pincers, axes, and other tools. Only five graves contained weapons. Some of these grave goods had been burned along with the body on the pyre. Most cremation remains weight less than 1kg, which is considered incomplete (it should be at least 1.5 to 2kg). This could be explained by either the cremation method or the method by which the remains are collected after the cremation. At one of the cemeteries, in the centre of the enclosure, a building was found that likely had a collective function (Lambot & Méniel 2000, 114). It surmounted a pit which contained cremated bones and a vase with a broken foot. Another cemetery also had a structure around a small four-posted construction that could have been an altar.

Four rectangular pits near the Bronze Age barrow in the centre of the village served as receptacles for sheep sacrifices (Ibid.; Méniel 2010). The feet or leg bones of 150 sheep were found, along with other parts like ribs and shoulder bones. Most sheep had been three years old at the time of slaughter and some were pregnant, so the time of slaughter of the animals was estimated around the end of December or early January. Another remarkable find was a tapered 5.5m deep pit, at the far south side of the village. It was filled with hundreds of miniature spears, large cattle and horse bones, and some human remains. Several remains showed taphonomic damage, such as gnaw marks made by dogs or weathering patterns caused by above-ground exposure.

The features portray a variety of acts that took place over time in the village. The square and the five adjacent buildings would have been used on multiple occasions as a place of communal gatherings and ceremonies, probably over a longer period. A difficult theory to prove, but likely nonetheless, is that the sacrificial act related to the pit burials took place on a regular or particular occasion. The motivation behind this unusual act can only be pure guesswork. For example, it is conceivable that these sacrifices were made at a time of stress, or they concerned a victim of a rival tribe, or they reflect the reign of only one cruel ruler. Lambot and Méniel (2000, 111) suggested social differentiation is reflected in the manner of burial and could account for the underrepresentation of the cremation burials. The contrast to the 'ordinary' cemeteries is notable, where people were interred according to the more normal custom of cremation. Also, the cremation cemeteries were clearly delimited by a ditch whereas the pit burials were not. Whatever the ditch symbolised, it was not deemed as a necessity for the dead in the pits. Human sacrifices were abandoned when the activities at the five temples ceased around 80 BCE (Lambot and Méniel 2000). Thereafter the act changed and sheep were sacrificed, the remains of which ended in a series of square pits.

Lambot & Méniel (2000, 111) think that the cemeteries were reserved for the dominant population, who mark their power by the importance of the ditches which delimit each family concession. The monumental enclosures and the most powerful mausoleums occupy prominent places within the cemeteries, mirroring the temples and palisaded walls that occupy an equally important position in the village centre.

3.2.6 Variety in sanctuaries

The five sites described above serve to illustrate what is considered to be the 'typical' characteristics of sanctuaries in northern France. The map depicted at the start of this chapter (fig. 3.2) suggests that in a 30 km radius around Gournay at least twelve other cult places are situated: Airion, Angivillers, Blincourt, Champlieu, Chilly, Creil, Estrees-Saint-Denis, Gury, Montmartin, Orrouy, St-Just-en-Chaussée and Vendilieu-Caply. Only four of these have been excavated; the others are known from aerial photos and surveys (Fauduet 1993; 2010; Brunaux et al. 2003). With every new researched site new features and activities are added to the Iron Age compendium. The largest density of sites is around Gournay. It is possible that these cult places are concentrated in a specific regional landscape, or alternatively, the region has been researched more thoroughly since the discovery of Gournay.

The five examples of cult places described above all have different structures, different finds, and so it would seem, were the subject of a variety of activities serving different purposes (table 3.1). The period over which they were used also varies greatly, between several decades and several centuries. Only Acy-Romance contained a large-scale excavation, producing a significantly more insightful understanding of the organisation and diachronic use of the structures. For the other sites the context remains rather speculative. Despite the apparent similarity in shape their lack of uniformity is notable. The

overall size varies, as do the dimensions and the shape of the cross section of the enclosure ditch, the presence or absence of an interruption that served as an entrance, and the interior structures and features.

There are no examples before the Middle Iron Age (the 5th century BCE). In the 5th and 4th century BCE, the Northwest of France was apparently sparsely populated by Early La Tène culture related groups, whose archaeological remains are poorly defined (Brunaux 1995, 141; Brunaux 1996). There was for example hardly any activity in the Vix cemetery between the end of the Hallstatt era (c. 450 BCE) and the reoccupation of the site in the late 3rd century BCE (Chaume 2011). The population density increased significantly in the 3rd century resulting in an abundance of material culture, the first villages, small cremation cemeteries, and apparently the implementation of the first autonomous places of worship (Brunaux et al. 2003). Brunaux continues to state the latter structures were the first to be designed for worship only and not related to settlements or cemeteries. At the same time, monuments first appear surrounding individual burials, both inhumations and cremations (Brunaux et al. 2003, 30). These structures consist of large postholes, sometimes linked to each other by ditches or palisades, set in a quadrangular plan of up to 14m in length. Brunaux et al. (2003, 31) refers to these as mausoleums that accommodate a regular activity, in the form of offerings, or of sacrifice, associated with the burial tradition.

Both sanctuaries and oppida supposedly served certain defined territories (Wells 2001, 84-87). According to Derks (1996, 148-149) the development of the sanctuaries in Northern France were the result of the hierarchisation of society, which caused social differentiation and the need for new conventions and symbolism. Brunaux attributes not only the social changes and the conflicts to the rise of the sanctuaries, but ascribed the movement into the region of ethnic groups collectively called 'the Belgae' in the 3rd century BCE as the cause (Brunaux 1996; Brunaux et al. 2003). It remains uncertain how finds like the pit of the vases, predating the sanctuary at Gournay, fit in this model.

Site	Period BCE	Pottery (N)	Metals (N)	Human bones (N)	Animal bones (N)	Cattle	Horse	Pig	Sheep / goat	Dog	Other animals
Vix	530-450	548	9 fibulae	0	2864	26%	10%	25%	24%	10%	5%
Gournay-sur-Aronde	400-100	270	2063	80	2845	46%	13%	17%	21%	3%	-
Villeneuve-au-Chatillon	330-100	?	509	0	?						
Ribemont-sur-Ancre	250-200	0	Ca. 400	30000+?	0						
Acy-Romance ditch	180-30	A few	A few	A few	780	70%	18%	12%			
Acy-Romance village total	180-30	A lot	A lot?	50 people	197000	22%	8%	34%	26%	4%	6%

Table 3.1. Overview of finds from the Iron Age enclosures of five French sites discussed in this chapter (Roman phases not included).

Function

Most sanctuaries in northern France likely served as a community or (religious) gathering place, as for example Gournay, Saint-Maur, Morvillers-Saint-Saturnin, and probably Vendeuil-Caply, Bailleul-sur-Thérain, and Dompierre-sur-Authie (Brunaux *et al.* 2003). Some served as war trophies, some as a place for specific depositions, and others had likely mixed functions (Demierre *et al.* 2019). Even though they rarely exceed 2500 m² (Ribemont is regarded as the largest in the Picardy region), most structures have a size to accommodate at least a few dozen people. The village square in Acy-Romance is quite exceptional, both in its size and the fact that no less than five religious buildings were bordering it. The smallest enclosure defined as an Iron Age sanctuary in France is Bennecourt which measured 225 m² (Bourgeois 1999). The average seemed to be about 35 × 35m, making the enclosed space notably smaller than in the German *Viereckschanzen*. According to Brunaux *et al.* (2003, 34) the size of the enclosure was proportional to the size of the community, as in burials the size of the burial structure was proportional to the position the deceased held within the community.

The enclosed community gathering place was commonly an open space. The features of the sanctuaries in northern France rarely include buildings, but in the Late Hallstatt and Late La Tène periods they may have had wooden statues as a focal point (Poux 2019). According to Poux (2019), these were not deities but representations of hero ancestors. In Acy-Romance five octagonal buildings could be identified, and in Gournay a building that seemed to change shape with every phase. Possible small buildings were also interpreted on a few other sites (for example Montmartin and Bennecourt; Brunaux *et al.* 2003). Their design consists of a semi-open structure around a large central offering pit (or statue slot?).

Enclosure ditch

The feature that all sites had in common was an enclosure, constructed of a ditch that marked a place in the landscape. This space was materialised in four of the five above mentioned sites as a rectangular feature. The village square in Acy-Romance is the exception, as the shape of the surrounding ditch follows the curvature of the hilltop. Variations on the rectangular ground plan are reasonably common, such as Estrées-Saint-Denis, the round ditch at Ribemont, or the older phase at Fresque.

The ditch commonly had a V-shaped cross section and was an open feature (not filled in, but maintained). In many sites the enclosure was enforced with an adjoining fence, bank or palisade (Brunaux 1986, 2003). These features are believed to have had a different function. The ditch physically marked the 'sacred' grounds, symbolised by the cutting of the soil, while the fence enclosed the activity and

made it invisible to the outside world (Brunaux *et al.* 2003, 19). Other constructions also occur. The vertical sides of the parallel ditches on the site of Villeneuve-au-Châtelot likely represent a function as bedding trenches for a wall of some kind rather than an open feature. The village square of Acy-Romance was likewise reconstructed as a foundation trench for a palisade. The surrounding open ditch often had an additional function as a receptacle for sacrificial objects. These are interpreted as the remains of communal feasting as well as offerings (Lambot & Méniel 2000, 101-102; Lejars 2001; Brunaux *et al.* 2003, 33-34).

Pits

Another common feature is that of one or more pits inside the enclosure. Pits seem to have a similar function as a place for offerings, like the surrounding ditch. In Vix, Gournay and Villeneuve-au-Châtelot central pits were found. In Acy-Romance the pits containing human remains, and other offerings such as animal remains and miniature spears were found outside of the enclosure. Chaume, Reinhard and Wustrow (2007) interpret pits or wells as a mediating structure in a communication system between the living and the dead or the profane and the gods. Pits were generally used for primary deposits, the result of a single event (Demierre *et al.* 2019). In Acy-Romance sheep bones were found in abundance in pits next to the ancestral barrow, indicating that sacrifices may be specific for a place. Additionally, some evidence (treefall pits and pollen) points towards the presence of trees and/or shrubs inside the enclosures (Lambot & Méniel 2000, 28; Brunaux *et al.* 2003), although their contemporaneity is generally difficult to prove.

Finds

A deciding factor contributing to the interpretation of the French sites as religious places, are offerings. In general there are three main categories: metal objects, animal sacrifices and particular treatment of human body parts (Brunaux *et al.* 2003). The ample representation of iron weaponry shows a strong association to warfare. Practices are specific to each sanctuary, based on the find assemblage (Demierre *et al.* 2019). Cattle bones were most abundant in the enclosure ditches, which were also used for weapons. At entrances, rings, coins (in later phases), and weapons are found. Postholes commonly have few finds, which are interpreted as secondary (*Ibid.* 2019).

Brunaux (1986) distinguishes two types of sacrificial rites involving animals: chthonic and commensal. In the first type of rite the animal is slaughtered, thrown into a pit whole and left there to decay as a sacrifice to a (subterranean?) deity. This view is debated by Poux (2019), who argued there is insufficient evidence for systematic animal sacrifices. In the second, more common type of rite, animals were killed for consumption and shared as food between the people (and the gods?) within the sanctuary during a feast. The presence of human bones in sanctuaries is more enigmatic. The number of human bones varies greatly. In Ribemont human remains seem to have been at the foundation of the sanctuary. Notably though, these were not found in the ditch but on the surface, both inside and outside the ditch. The function of the ditch is rather vague here.

Contextual setting

According to Brunaux *et al.* (2003) most sanctuaries were placed in a generally isolated position, at some distance from contemporary residential areas. There are some critical remarks to be made about this hypothesis. A regional study of the area around Gournay to research the relation between the settlements and the sanctuaries has not yet been conducted. Also, it is relevant to consider the limited size of the excavations. From a comprehensive analysis by Fauduet (1993, 102-103), it appears that Roman sanctuaries throughout the whole of France were just as often positioned near a built-up area (49%) as they were in rural areas. Out of the rural examples, 66% appeared to have been placed in an entirely isolated location (one-third of the total number). Geographically around 80% were built on a hilltop or a slope, the remainder in a valley, most likely near a fork in the river or a bridge (Fauduet 1993, 102). The urban examples are commonly Roman and either part of a complex including a theatre and baths, or they are integrated into a housing district.

3.3 The rectangular structures of Germany

Two types of German phenomenon are used as analogies for rectangular structures in the Low Countries. Most referred to are the recurring structures known from Southern Germany, the *Viereckschanze*. The second are a type of smaller cult place that have been identified in several oppida. Both phenomena seem unsuitable for comparison as one is quite unique in both its uniformity and its restriction to a certain region, and the other has an explicit settlement context.

3.3.1 Viereckschanzen

Southern Germany, more specifically the south of the federal states of Bavaria (Bayern) and Baden-Württemberg, along with parts of Switzerland north of the Alps and adjacent areas, is littered with large rectangular ditch-and-bank structures (fig. 3.10). These structures have been called *Viereckschanzen* ever since the name was invented by a Bavarian State Conservator in 1910 (Wieland 1999, 12). The visibility of the structures in the landscape has long since made them the subject of speculation. The earliest interpretation was as Roman military structures, described in the 1830s (Wieland 1999, 16). However, dendrochronological research proved *Viereckschanzen* are actually older, and date exclusively to the 2nd and 1st centuries BCE (Murray 1995, 125). Since the 1950s the function of the *Viereckschanzen* has been a reoccurring subject of debate. Schwarz (1959, 203-214)

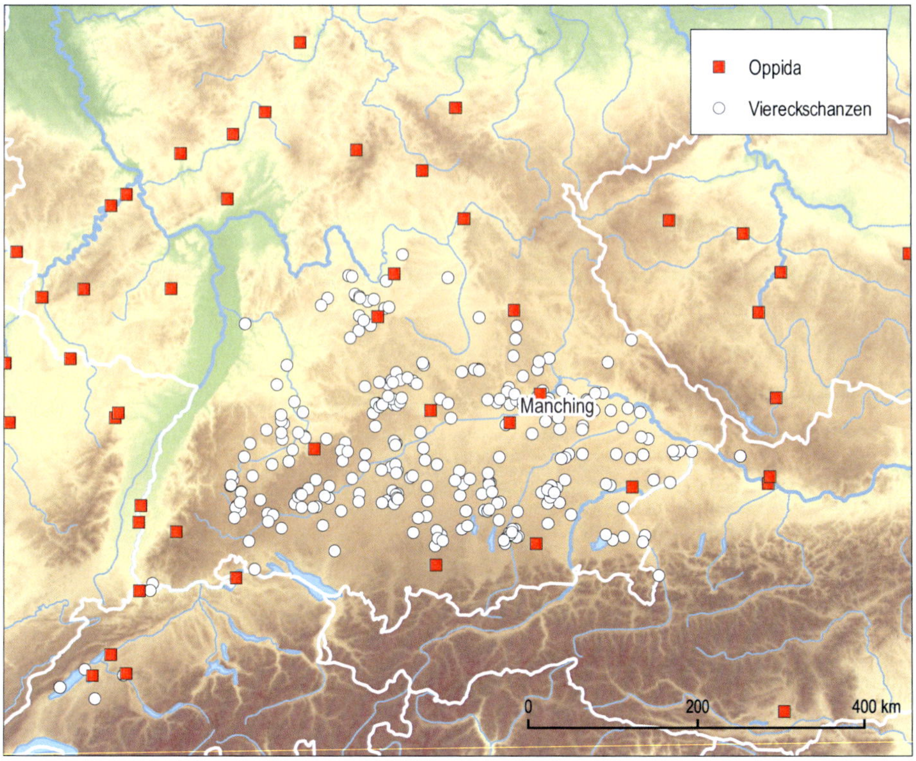

Figure 3.10. Southern Germany and adjoining regions showing the distribution of Viereckschanzen (based on Schwarz 1959; Bittel et al. 1990; Wieland 1999; Pfister 2000) and some of the oppida in the region (based on Schwarz 1959; Wells 1993; http://www.oppida.org).

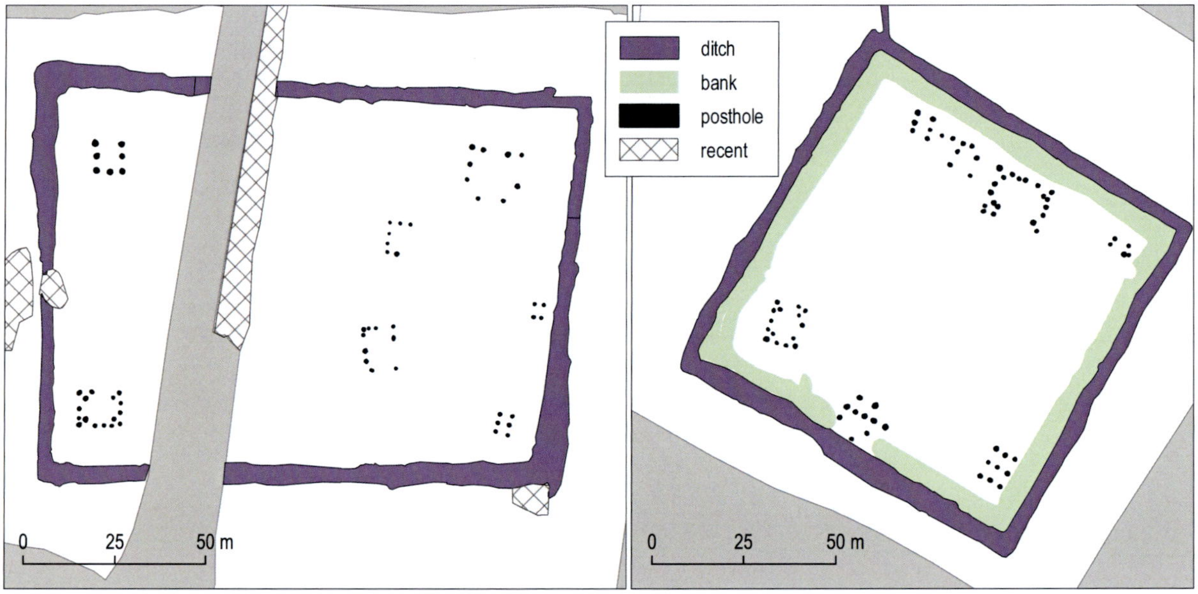

Figure 3.11. Two examples of plans of excavated Viereckschanzen with some of the features (Plattling-Pankofen (left) after Reichenberger & Schaich 1996; Pocking-Hartkirchen (right) after Schaich 1998).

pronounced these structures as cult places on the basis of the excavation of the site in Holzhausen. Not a decade later a multiple function was suggested by Lewis (1966, 5), both sacred and domestic as communal gathering places. Equally debated are the origins of the *Viereckschanze*. According to De Laet (1966) and Reichenberger (1993) *Viereckschanzen* derived from square grave monuments (*Viereckgraben*), while Groenewoudt (2011) saw causality between the shape of Celtic fields and later cult places (including *Viereckschanzen*) triggered by a need to formalise the landscape. It seems to me these authors based their assumption purely on the general shape, disregarding their actual function, geographic distribution, or particular featuring characteristics.

Schwarz (1959) produced an atlas in which plans of most of the known *Viereckschanzen* at the time were depicted. The typical size of a *Viereckschanze* has been described as 80 to 100m long (Drexel 1931, 1). The shape is usually more or less a square, but can be somewhat diamond shaped or rectangular. A *Viereckschanze* covers quite a large area of 1600 to 25000 m² (Van der Sanden 1987, 73), though seldom exceeds 13500 m² (Reichenberger 1993, footnote 11). Deviating dimensions for similar structures are often doubted to be 'true' *Viereckschanzen*, as for example the rectangular ditch and bank in Basel-Gelterkinder, which had a length of over 220m. Initially thought to be a *Viereckschanze*, this structure was later interpreted as an 18th century boundary marker (Reichenberger 1993, 355).

Shortly after the publication of the excavation of the *Viereckschanze* at Holzhausen the functional

theory shifted towards cult sites (Schwarz 1959). The interpretation for Holzhausen as a cult site is based on both the presence of three deep shafts, the deepest of which was 35m, and a small building in one of the corners. The shafts were interpreted as sacrificial pits, as their depth and several curious finds, such as a long meat hook, pointed towards this explanation (Schwarz 1975, 340). Even the deepest one never seemed to reach to the groundwater level, so these shafts were clearly not used as wells. As excavations of *Viereckschanzen* in Tomerdingen, Fellbach-Schmiden, Reidlingen, and Mengen-Ennetach (Wieland 1999, 44-53) also revealed deep shafts, other authors followed suit and the theory of the *Viereckschanze* as a cult site was established. A 20m deep shaft in Fellbach-Schmiden contained among other items several parts of a statue of a sitting person flanked by animals (Planck 1982). In the *Viereckschanzen* in Agen, an 8m deep well contained several layers of metal and wooden objects (Haffner 1995, 40). Most of the objects seemed to be fit for use and therefore could only have been deposited in the well as a deliberate sacrifice. Other 'evidence' of *Viereckschanzen* as cult places came from the apparent position of the entrance of the structure, which was never on the north side, similar to Gallo Roman temples (Schwarz 1975, 344).

Further research into the sacrificial shafts revealed a significant amount of manure inside, either from a stable or from household waste depositions (Fischer 1991; Altjohann 1995; Wieland 1995b; Wieland 1999, 51). This discovery is interpreted as a possibly deliberate destruction of a well by pollution.

The 'cultic' interpretation of *Viereckschanzen* was initially based on a few sites with remarkable finds. When more *Viereckschanzen* were excavated on a larger scale, the viewpoint on the use of the interior space changed as the features appeared to be parts of settlements (Murray 1995, 127). On the basis of the excavation of the *Viereckschanze* of Bobfingen, Wieland (1995; 1996, 30) suggested the place was a homestead of the local elite: a *Siedelwesen* or a *Rechteckhöfe*. Bobfingen was the perfect example of how a rural settlement developed over a period of 300 years and incorporated a *Viereckschanze* in the later phases. The oldest phase dates to La Tène B (3rd century BCE) and holds little more than a dispersed settlement. In La Tène C (2nd century BCE) the settlement has a palisade surrounding it, which is replaced in La Tène D (late 2nd to 1st century BCE) by a *Viereckschanze* (Wieland 1999, 68-9). Other *Viereckschanzen* like Ehningen (Schiek 1985), Wiedmais (Reichenberger 1986), Plattling-Pankofen (Reichenberger & Schaich 1996), and Pocking-Hartkirchen (Schaich 1998) had buildings in the interior similar to the ones found in Bobfingen (fig. 3.11). Generally, these buildings are of a heavier construction than the ones found in settlements or at oppida and often either 8-9m square with four large posts and one or two entrances, or a larger rectangular building of maximum 20m in length (Janson 2000, 10).

The finds in the deep shafts seems to be an exception rather than the norm for the typical *Viereckschanze*. On the whole, the material cultural assemblages from thirty-six excavated *Viereckschanzen* generally proved to be quite uniform (Murray 1995, 130-135). Neither the features inside the excavated *Viereckschanzen* or the artefacts found there gave the suggestion these sites were used as cult places, although the artefact assemblages were not entirely consistent with those found at settlements. Weapons were found at only two of the thirty-six *Viereckschanzen*, while at contemporary oppida these are quite common. The pottery assemblages also diverted from the settlement standard, as for example few identifiable storage vessels were recovered. Based on the finds, Reichenberger (1993, 379-381) argued against the interpretation of *Viereckschanzen* as normal settlements. Additionally, the assemblages showed that activity within the *Viereckschanzen* was not continuous. Murray (1995) suggests that the *Viereckschanzen* were occasionally used for drinking and feasting. He based his theory on the pottery assemblage and descriptions by classical authors such as Phylarchos in the 3rd century BCE as "a wealthy Gaul who hosted his followers with offerings of meat, drink and grain during annual gatherings within fixed enclosures scattered across the landscape" and "attempts by an Arvernian nobleman to maintain a political following by distributing treasure and erecting an enormous rectangular enclosure" by

Posidonius in the 1st century BCE (Murray 1995). Besides the fact that these classical authors refer to Gaul rather than Germania, Murray's theory of *Viereckschanzen* as feasting locations was disputed by Venclova (1997, 134) who argued that some of the pottery assemblages could have belonged to older settlement phases. She saw no substantial difference between the find collections in excavated structures in Bohemia and those in Oppida (Venclova 1997, 140). Based on that, Venclova (1997, 138) suggests that "building fences in the same places as the earlier [...] settlements could indicate an intent to legitimize traditional lineage and power in an area that was previously settled". She also notes that the importance of knowing the broader context of the enclosures has generally been ignored (Venclova 1997, 147). Whether the structures in Bohemia can be compared to the *Viereckschanzen* in southern Germany is another matter. *Viereckschanzen* seem to predominantly occur in a specific region (fig. 3.10). The main area forms a triangle in Bavaria that is bordered by rivers and forested mountain ranges: The Alps to the south, the River Rhine and the Vosges to the northwest, the River Main and the Thuringian woods to the north, while Bohemia lies to the east. The *Viereckschanzen* phenomenon seems to be confined to this region. Other regions are rumoured to have *Viereckschanzen*. In Bohemia, where several structures classified as *Viereckschanzen* were excavated, the term 'quadrangular enclosures' is also used (Venclova 1989). These can have a different, more rectangular shape. The larger structures in France are sometimes designated *Viereckschanzen* (Brunaux 1986, 40; Buchsenschutz 1984, 235). Some sites show similarities such as Lanneray (Robreau and Leroy 1989) and Saint-Arnoult-en-Yveline (Baray 1989) both situated southwest of Paris. In England rectangular enclosures are less common and according to Collins (1989) rarely bear any resemblance to *Viereckschanzen*. Only the central March area in Wales is home to structures that resemble *Viereckschanzen* not only in size and sometimes in shape, but also in numbers. At least 449 sites are known (Wigley 2007, citing Whimster 1989). They are interpreted as settlement enclosures and are likewise a region-specific phenomenon. The sites in Wales consist of a bank and ditch structure with maximum dimensions of about 100 × 100 m.

Viereckschanzen were typically constructed by a ditch and bank. The ditch is positioned on the outside of the structure and the bank on the inside. Some excavations have shown a palisade could have been placed on the top of the bank. Exceptions even indicate a more heavily defensive structure, as for example in Westheim, where instead of a bank a double wooden palisade was used (Bernhard 1986; Fischer 1992). The more typical ditch-and-bank construction is summarised in fig. 3.12.

The ditch was V-shaped, 4-6m wide and on average 2.5m deep (Wieland 1999, 42; Janson 2000, 9). The bank was about 7m wide and 2-3m high, creating a height difference of over 4m. Often the interior was slightly raised compared to the exterior (not depicted in fig. 3.12) (Mansfeld 1989). As this kind of structure suggests a defensive function, even described as a 'massive fortified farmstead' (Wendling & Winger 2014). The dimensions of a typical *Viereckschanze* were clearly of an entirely different category than the aforementioned structures in France. This to me suggests that in contrast, *Viereckschanzen* did have a defensive function instead of a symbolical one.

This raises the question of what was being defended. To protect a community against enemies would be an obvious explanation, although not supported by the lack of weaponry on most sites. One suggestion was to protect cattle against raids, and also against wolves, bears or lynxes (Beeser 1988, 148). Reichenberger (1993, 381) deems an interpretation as cattle pens to be unlikely, arguing it would have been easier and probably more effective to build a fence or a hedge.

Viereckschanzen are often positioned on a slope of a 5% gradient or less (40%) or ridge (30%) sometimes near a steep slope, a further 14% are on top a low hill and always on rock-free soils, not necessarily near water (Müller 1999, 29). These softer soils had agricultural potential and were apparently favourable locations for settlements (Janson 2000).

3.3.2 The sanctuaries of Manching

The dates of the construction of the *Viereckschanzen* in the 2nd and 1st century BCE, are contemporary to another Late Iron Age phenomenon: the *oppida* (red squares in fig. 3.10). *Oppida* were large fortified settlements, commonly on a hill-top, found throughout large parts of Europe from Britain and Spain in the west to Hungary in the east (e.g. Pauli 1980; Wells 1993). One of the first extensively excavated examples is the Oppidum at Manching in the 1950s (e.g. Krämer 1958, 175-202; see hereafter). Finds at Manching and subsequently at other sites confirmed that oppida were the regional centres for trade and crafts, such as iron working, glass making, and coin production (Wells 1995, 173; Wendling 2013; Wendling & Winger 2014). At times of conflicts, the oppida could be used as retreats. In later phases they had a defensive structure with imposing walls (Wells 1993, 3-5; Wendling 2013). Mid-1st century BCE oppida were abandoned, probably due to rapid changes in the region (Wells 1993, 149-155). It has been suggested the oppida were 'groβsiedlungen', seats for regional rulers (Collins 1993, 102-106). They represent a development toward urbanism and societal complexity unlike any other in Iron Age temperate Europe (Wells 2001, 87-88), while *Viereckschanzen* were 'siedlungen', regular settlements, thus representing a difference in size (Krause 1995).

Situated in central Bavaria, on an elevated river bank of the Danube, is one of the largest oppida in Europe (Wendling & Winger 2014; Sievers & Wendling 2014). The entire site measures nearly 2.5km across, a 380ha surface bordered by the residual wall on the south and east sides. Excavations have been on and off since 1955 (Wendling 2013; Brestel 2017, 7-12). The use of the site dates back at least to the Bronze Age, displayed by a few barrows (Wendling 2013). An early Iron Age *Herrenhöfe* (manor) suggests continuous occupation, although not until the 3rd century BCE did the occupation materialise into a rapidly developing urban trade centre. A dense palimpsest of postholes and pits display several centuries of intense occupation, expanding outwards.

Many ditches were found within the boundaries of the oppidum, dug for a multitude of functions (Brestel 2017, 33-58). Ditches for drainage were among the longest. Some ran along the radii of the roundish oppidum to the outer rim, resembling the spokes of a wheel, presumably draining the water downhill. Other ditches served as field or meadow boundaries or surrounded farmyards. Roadsides were also equipped with ditches and several settlements were portrayed as separate entities by surrounding ditches. Besides a functional role, a few ditches had a metaphysical meaning (Brestel 2017, 53). Within the oppidum, four rectangular ditched structures were found that are interpreted as sanctuaries (Müller 1993; Sievers 2010, 89-98; Wendling & Winger 2014; Brestel 2017, 61-66). One structure in the centre of the oppidum is considered the oldest (Sievers 2010, 89-98). The central position was a conscious choice, at an equal distance from the south and east entrances of the oppidum (Eller *et al.* 2012). It would have been near the crossing of several roads (Brestel 2017, 53). The structure consisted of a

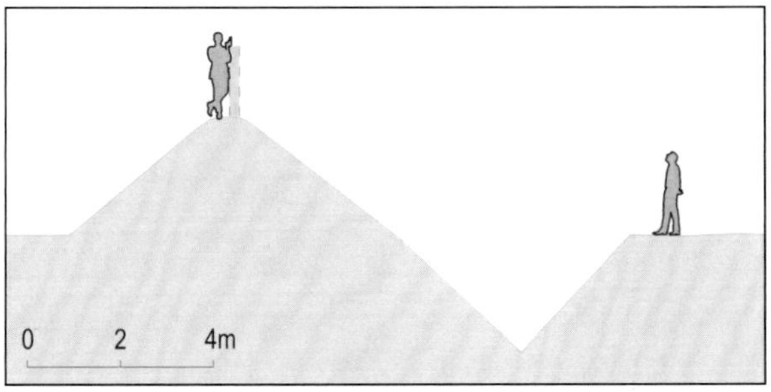

Figure 3.12. Wall and ditch structure of a typical *Viereckschanze* (based on Wieland 1999, 42; Janson 2000, 9). The inside is to the left. Scale: the men are around 1.8m tall. The palisade wall on top of the bank has only been demonstrated on some *Viereckschanzen*.

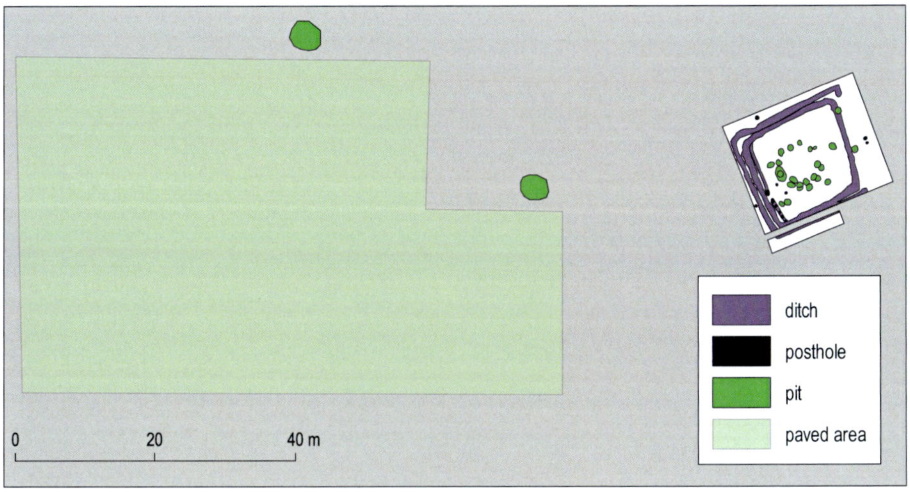

Figure 3.13. Central sanctuary and adjacent paved area in the Oppidum of Manching (after Wendling 2013, fig. 6, and Sievers 2010, fig. 51).

Figure 3.14. Partly excavated cult place in the central area (after Wendling and Winger 2014, fig. 12.2 and 12.3).

rectangular multiple-phased ditch and interior pits organised in a circular fashion (fig. 3.13).

The interpretation of a sanctuary was based on the quality of the associated finds, its long-lasting existence and its form. Even though many weapons were found in the oppidum, the central sanctuary held the only concentration dating to La Tène B2, early 3rd century BCE (Sievers 2010, 50-54). Among the finds were fragments of a Hallstatt sword and early La Tène helmets (Wendling 2013). An area paved with limestone and gravel that was found

approximately 25m west of the sanctuary was interpreted as an assembly place (Sievers 2010, 90-98; Brestel 2017, 62-63). As these features were nominally documented in 1937 when an airfield was constructed at the site, the relation between the sanctuary and the paved area remains unclear. Two depots were discovered adjacent to the paved area ('Depot A12', Sievers 2010, 72-81). These contained whole weapons, parts of weapons, horse gear, parts of fibulae, a glass ring, as well as decorated bronze fragments. In other abandoned storage pits and wells around the site whole pots, animal bones, iron tools, and weapons were deposited (Wendling 2013). Another sanctuary seemed to be positioned in the centre of activities alongside a road (fig. 3.14). A distribution of deposited cattle and horse skulls, fragments of a horse statue and intentionally destroyed weapons surround the structure (Sievers 2010, 108-109; Wendling & Winger 2014). This sanctuary was built over by pits in a later phase, in contrast to the central one.

Wendling (2019) distinguished three levels of activities that took place related to the sanctuaries in Manching. The rectangular structures were primarily meant for the largest scale level, or 'official public worship'. This involved communal gatherings. The second level was represented by for instance funerals, which were categorised as a smaller scale, semi-public rite, performed by a smaller group. Then, at the lowest level were household related rites. These centred around the house and the hearth, and were performed by individuals. Similar type sanctuaries have been excavated in other oppida, as for example in Rosendorf (Austria) where seven sanctuaries were found in three groups (Holzer 2019). These cult places were of limited size (maximum 17 square meters) and each seem to have had their own specialized applications. The smaller sanctuaries were used for pottery deposition and the larger ones for weaponry. Manipulation of human bones played a role in some of the structures, leading Holzer (2019) to conclude that at least some of the activities were related to the liberation of the soul and reincarnation of the dead. Generally, they seem to belong to the oldest phase of the oppidum and were positioned in the centre (Fichtl 2013).

3.3.3 Community gathering and offering places

Viereckschanzen can best be described as uniform, based on their general size and shape (Schwarz 1959; Reichenberger 1993, 381-382). Equally striking is the territory in which these structures occur. Their distribution is primarily limited to the triangular region (fig. 3.10) in southern Germany. Outside of this region, the term 'Viereckschanzen' should be applied with caution. Even though the *Viereckschanzen* have been compared to rectangular ditched structures and sanctuaries in several other countries, such as France, Belgium, the Netherlands, and even Britain (Collins 1984, 146-147; Martin 1993, 22), they differ in their uniformity and their size. *Viereckschanzen* were larger both in the size of the structure as a whole and also the area it covered, as well as the size of the ditch-and-bank structure. Also, there are discrepancies between the period the *Viereckschanzen* were built and the structures in other regions. Therefore the *Viereckschanzen* are a quite unique phenomenon, specific for the Late Iron Age, and cannot be compared to other rectangular structures. Their function is evidently settlement related, although a few features could have been (secondarily) used for deposition. Reichenberger (1993, 383) admits that in theory the common ideas behind their uniformity could be military, with a secondary function as a feasting location, court or religious gathering place for the local community.

Sanctuaries in Oppida seem to have been used for community gatherings and special applications, resulting in specific depositions. Wendling (2013) suggests weapons were on display within a sanctuary and buried or disposed of on special occasions. An (elevated?) building occupied the inner space, surrounded by a palisade with an entrance facing the sunrise and sunset on the equinox. Religious rites at the sanctuaries might have played a fundamental role, with communal activities creating social cohesion and identity within the martial society. It is relevant to consider the context for small cult places, such as the ones found in Manching. The setting within an oppidum is quite particular and the function is likely to be related to the intensive use of the urban environment. Examples were also found in British oppida, and their function is discussed below.

Another type of structured space for depositions was found in Oberdorla, in the northeast of Germany. The site is situated in a distinct non-urban environment, in contrast to the Manching sanctuaries at the edge of a marsh, near a lake and a grove (Behm-Blancke *et al.* 2003, 23-27). From the Early Iron Age the site was continuously used as an offering place until the Early Medieval Period. In the Early Iron Age, twelve separate offering places were constructed, which contained a combination of altars, semi-circular shrines, stone pavements and wooden platforms (Behm-Blancke *et al.* 2002, 7-30; Behm-Blancke *et al.* 2003, 37-43). Each of these seem to have their own particular focus, expressed in the archaeological record by concentrations of bones of cattle, sheep/goat, dog, horses, and pig, pottery, wooden bowls, human bones, and most distinctively, wooden idols resembling humans. Most of these idols dated to the Middle and Late Iron Age and looked like forked branches, with the fork serving as legs and the top shaped as a human head. In the Middle and Late Iron Age phase the use of the site intensified. At least 28 small structures from this period can be distinguished (Behm-Blancke *et al.* 2002, 31-93; Behm-Blancke *et al.* 2003, 43-50). Structures vary from earth 'altars', to semi-circular shrines ('Apsisheiligtum') and a wattle work constructed sort of causeway.

Similar to the interpretation of the different levels for Manching (Wendling 2019), three different sizes of sanctuary can be distinguished in Oberdorla (Behm-Blancke *et al.* 2003, 44): the smallest sacrificial sites are interpreted as private sanctuaries of individual families, the next level contained interconnected small enclosures arranged in rows, and at the largest level were cult places in which a larger 'cult community' presumably offered sacrifices. The large amounts of animal bones are interpreted as leftovers of ceremonial meals on these locations (Behm-Blancke *et al.* 2003, 106-110). The human skeletal remains, many displaying pathological damage, are interpreted as sacrificial victims (Ulrich 2003).

In conclusion, in the urban environment of oppida, some rectangular structures are interpreted as a sanctuaries that can each serve a special function. The structures in Oberdorla fit within a mostly North-European tradition of offering places in wet environments (e.g. Kok 2008). These different types of structures are likewise observed in Britain.

3.4 Shrines, enclosures, and causeways in England

The south and the east of England are the closest part of Britain to the European mainland. As such, it had a number of trade connections to the continent, conceivably contributing to the exchange of ideas (Derks 1996, 144). Two types of phenomena dominate the conception of structures related to Iron Age religion in this part of British Isles (fig. 3.15; Woodward 1992; Hargrave 2018, 3-4). These are small structures commonly referred to as shrines, and causeways related to wet depositions. The identification of 'religious' structures is often problematic. In many sites the structures either lack finds, or finds indicate activity but a structure was not identified (Smith 2001, 74-151; Hargrave 2018, 44-56).

GEOGRAPHICAL FRAMEWORK: THE 'ARCHAEOTYPICAL' SANCTUARY

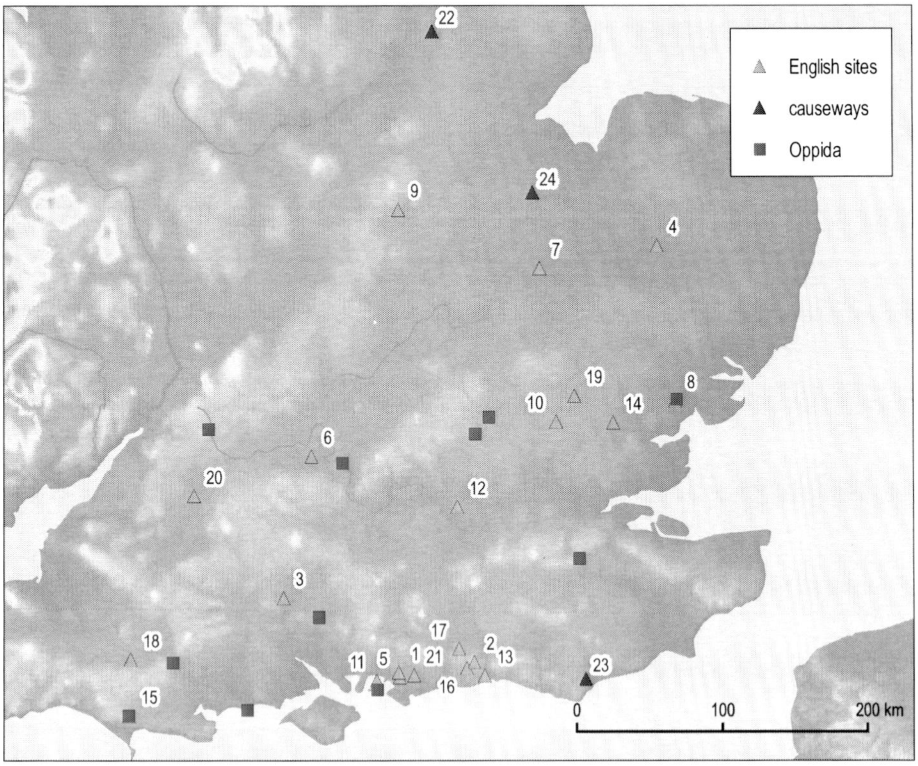

Figure 3.15. Map of part of southwest England. Legend: 1-Bow Hill; 2-Chantonbury; 3-Danebury; 4-Fishbourne; 5-Fison Way; 6-Frilford; 7-Godwin Ridge; 8-Gosbecks; 9-Hallaton; 10-Harlow; 11-Hayling Island; 12-Heathrow; 13-Lancing Down; 14-Little Waltham; 15-Maiden Castle; 16-Muntham Court; 17-Pulborough; 18-South Cadbury; 19-Stansted; 20-Uley; 21-Westhampnett; 22-Flag Fen; 23-Fiskerton; 24-Shinewater (Based on Woodward 1992, figure 1; Fitzpatrick 1997, fig. 115; Crease 2015, fig. 4.3; Hargrave 2018, table 2).

The visibility and accessibility of the English heritage is both an advantage and a disadvantage. The advantage lies in the support and interest of the public, which at the same time is also a disadvantage as metal detecting is an ever-increasing problem. Much of the focus on Iron Age deposition derives from the metal detector finds, which often lack contextual information (Bradley 2017, 66; Hargrave 2018, 205).

3.4.1 Shrines

A sanctuary has been defined by Hargrave (2018, 13) in a non-descript sense as a site of 'specific ritualistic activity', while a shrine more specifically refers to a building believed to have been used directly in relation to religious rites. A sanctuary in this definition therefore does not need to contain a man-made structure. Despite earlier emphasis by Woodward (1992) shrines are now thought to have played only a modest role in Iron Age religion (Hargrave 2018, 204).

Consensus now indicates that shrines are a Late Iron Age phenomenon, contemporary to the increasingly more defined separation of cemeteries from settlements (Wait 1985, 257-261; Bryant 1997; Hamilton 2007). There is in fact no evidence that any of the proposed shrines date before the 1st century BCE (Hargrave 2018, 54, 188). The introduction of this new type of structure at the time, went alongside a notable increase in metal depositions containing coins, fibulae, and horse gear, which Hargrave (2018, 56-57, 198) interpreted as a

possible reaction to Caesar's invasion of Britain in the 1st century BCE and the subsequent Roman conquest in the 1st century CE. Religion and secular power were increasingly intertwined at the end of the Iron Age, also visible in the use of space in oppida and high-status burials (Hargrave 2018, 175-176).

Rectangular buildings are seen as an innovation in this period as the shape deviates from the traditional round house, and also the construction method is completely different (Wait 1985, 154-178; Wait 1985a, 385-393; Hargrave 2018, 50). In sites such as Heathrow, Lancing Down, South Cadbury, and Danebury (fig. 3.16) the structures portray bedding trenches. In for example Danebury the structures consist of a single ditch which would have held upright posts at regular intervals, probably to support a wall (Cunliffe 1984, 81-87).

The largest rectangular ditch in Danebury measures 8.8 × 9m. The interpretation as a religious structure is solely based on the shape, as besides some pottery shards there are no finds to support this theory. The position of the structure within the hillfort, as well as its size, is strikingly similar to the enclosure found in Manching. Nearby three smaller rectangular ditched structures were found, of which the largest (4 × 4 m) is described as a regularly-cut foundation trench for a wall. It has a gap of 65cm on the south-east side, interpreted as an entrance.

Most structures were small, no more than the size of a granary (e.g. Woodward 1992, fig. 18). Larger arrangements

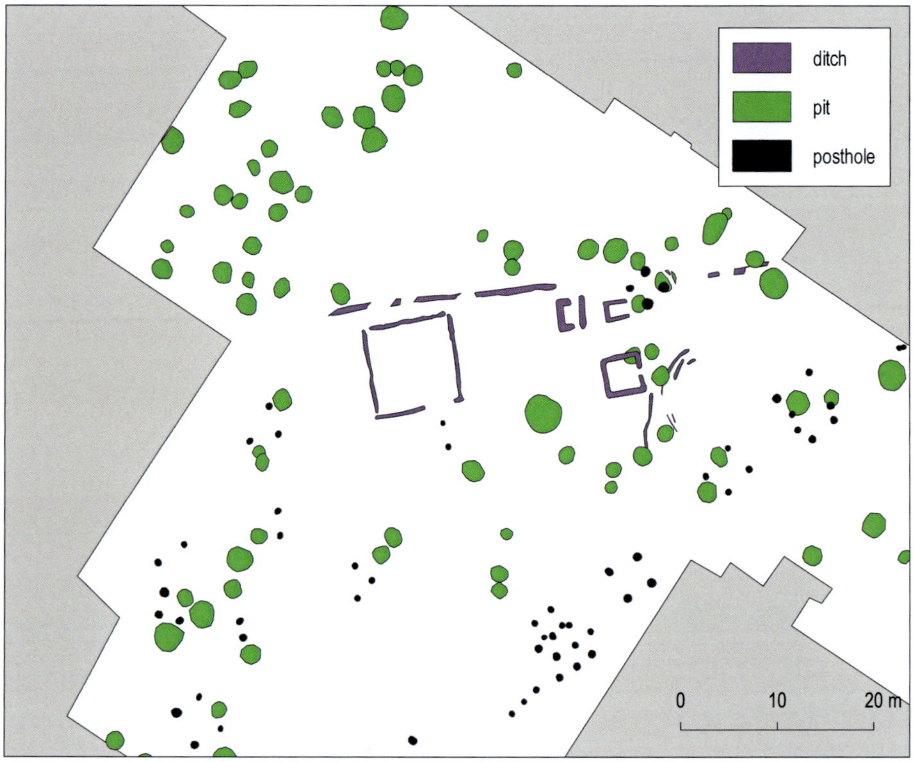

Figure 3.16. Partial plan of the central area of Danebury in the late period, 270-50 BCE (based on Cunliffe 1984, fig. 4.31).

were found in Harlow, Hayling Island, and Fison Way where a round building had been placed in a ditch-and-bank enclosed space. These sites contrast with others in the round shape of the shrine. As the traditional Bronze and Iron Age houses in Britain were round, a rectangular structure stands out (Wait 1985, 156; Woodward 1992, 31; Fitzpatrick 1997, 229-233; Bradley 2005, 56-57; Hargrave 2018, 39). This bias may have influenced the interpretation of rectangular structures as some sort of sanctuary. The alleged rectangular shrines include Heathrow, Uley, Thetford, Stansted, Little Waltham, Cadbury Castle, and the site of Danebury already described above (Drury 1980; Fitzpatrick 1997, 229-231). All of these structures were located in settlements and have a limited find assemblage.

An exception is Hayling Island, a structure rumoured to be a Gaulish-type of import (King & Soffe 2013, 15). The earliest phase of the shrine on Hayling Island dates around the mid-1st century BCE (King & Soffe 1994). It is a rectangular ditch of c. 25 × 25m, and a round inner ditch, both with an entrance aligned to the east. A pit is positioned inside the round ditch (2.5 × 1.7m, and 0.65m deep). The round ditch had a deep slot with preserved plank impressions in places, and substantial square post-holes at the corners and at intervals to support what must have been a plank-built wall. The outer ditch was not so well preserved but might have been of a similar construction. Depositions were primarily within the outer courtyard area and consisted of a variety of objects:

coins, pottery, fibulae, shield parts, iron spearheads, some fragmentary human remains, iron pins, bronze and iron rings, belt-hooks, and animal bones. Unusual objects were a bronze part of a yoke with inlaid red enamel decoration, finger rings, amber beads, iron currency bars, and flints. The flint assemblage consists of scrapers of Neolithic or Bronze Age types. They appear to have been deliberately deposited with the other artefacts. Large mammal bones were mostly of sheep and pigs, with sheep predominating in terms of the number of fragments.

The large number of animal bones in Hayling Island, and also in Hallaton and Harlow, are interpreted as evidence for feasting (Browning 2011; Hargrave 2018, 54, 151-152). These places seem to have been the centres of occasional assemblies, probably in a seasonal, annual event.

Human bones are not commonly found in relation to the shrines. Generally, cemeteries are rare and of the known Iron Age sites in the east of England only around 8% contain human remains, half of which are causeways (Hargrave 2018, 144). In the hillfort of Danebury 300 individual depositions of human remains were recovered in storage pits, indicating distinct patterns of behaviour (Cunliffe 1995, 72-75). Most were single skeletal elements. Some remains were inhumated entirely, before or after decay set in and others only contained parts of the body. Some pits contained multiple bodies. For some reason these deceased were excluded from the normal burial tradition, although Iron Age burial traditions in Britain are described as complicated and regionally specific (Hargrave 2018, 184). These people could have died an unnatural death, or in childbirth, or their disposal could have been sacrificial. The human remains might in some cases have been brought from the burial ground to be reburied in a storage pit. Carbon dating of five individuals showed they all died around the same time (Cunliffe *et al.* 2015). It suggests a mass death event caused by disease or enemy attack, occurring at Danebury early in the 2nd century BCE. Some bodies were flung into pits, while others were left in the open for some time, after which the remains were dumped into disused storage pits. A comparative study of six hillforts including Danebury, taking into account forensic taphonomic studies, suggested three main practices for disposal of human remains, all in use during the southern British Iron Age (Tracey 2012): exposure *in situ* and not on excarnation platforms, whole bodies with evidence of wrapping during decomposition, and the deposition of skull fragments. The exposure of human remains is affirmed by histological analysis of the skeletal material (Booth & Madgwick 2016). The human remains deposited at Danebury had been subject to diverse deposition practices which produced distinctive patterns of articulation and microstructural bio-erosion. Hargrave (2018, 149, 196) suggested that remains of enemies, outcasts or failed royalty were sometimes reused as a commodity for the empowering of defences and pits.

Westhampnett is another exception, where an Iron Age cemetery was found containing 161 cremation graves dating between 90 and 50 BCE (Fitzpatrick & Powell 1997). On the cemetery, pyre burn spots and other pyre-related features were arranged around the eastern perimeter of the graves, bordered by four small ditched structures to the northeast of the cemetery, interpreted as shrines. Three of these contained pottery. A fifth situated further east, contained a four-post structure and a central cremation burial. They were small enclosures, the largest one measuring 6.5m square. The ditches of these structures are wide (c. 80cm) and shallow (c. 20cm) relative to their size, with steep sides as in bedding trenches. Rows of postholes flanked two of the pyre sites on the east side of the cemetery and may have represented a formal physical boundary between the cremation and the burial zone.

In general the shrines were built in close proximity to the sea, on higher grounds and near river estuaries, where rivers run into the sea and fresh and salt waters meet (Willis 2007). It was long thought that deposition places were positioned in remote places, but as more settlements are excavated this hypothesis needs revision. Shrines in Britain appear to be commonly close to settlements, taking the form of depositions in pits, foundation depositions in roundhouses and enclosures, and depots on the edges of fields (Hargrave 2018, 202).

3.4.2 Causeways and depositions

In Britain several structures similar to the bridges of La Tène were found in wetland areas. They are generally referred to as wooden causeways or trackways, constructed directly on peat or as a raised walkway. The causeways are structures thought to have served not just as a bridge or a trackway, but as a deposition platform (Pryor 2001; Aldhouse Green 2006, 24; Parker Pearson & Field 2003; Bradley 2017, 61-65). Like in La Tène, the causeways were in use for a prolonged period, but the British counterparts have an older origin. The oldest example was found at Flag Fen in Cambridgeshire. It was built in stages in the Late Bronze Age and dendrochronologically dated 1365 to 967 BCE (Pryor 2001). Its use probably extends well into the Early Iron Age. The construction comprised of five timber post alignments over a length of about 1 km across the Fenland basin. In the middle of the causeway was a 'platform' of about 2 ha based on an island. A similar construction at least 250m long and made in the late 9th century BCE was found in Shinewater, county Sussex (Greatorex 2003). It was also comprised of a timber causeway that crossed a fenland (the 'Shinewater Track') and a platform in the middle with a solid wooden base (the 'Shinewater Platform'). It was used as a base for buildings during the Late Bronze Age and probably the Early Iron Age. An Iron Age example was found in Fiskerton, Lincolnshire. A peat fen held a 160m long causeway that was dendrochronologically dated 456-321 BCE (Hillam 2003). The construction was continuously repaired and rebuilt and went through at least nine phases.

All these installations produced a rich artefact assemblage in the water next to the post alignments, providing the basis for an interpretation as deposition platform. The Bronze Age assemblage consisted of a great variety of prestige objects, such as gold earrings, brooches, swords, spears, daggers and pins, as well as tools, polished white stones (at Flag Fen), and several human bones. The Iron Age assemblage delivered mostly weaponry (Stead 2003). Apart from four iron swords and eleven spearheads, an ornate bronze sword handle was found in eleven separate pieces, partly inlaid with coral. The sword has only a few known parallels from Germany and Bohemia, and probably dates to the 4th century BCE. In 1826, a complete 4th century BCE bronze shield was found in the river Witham close to the causeway (Jope 1971). It was decorated with a stylised boar. Other finds ranging in date between the 5th century BCE to the 1st century CE were dozens of iron tools, the majority for metal and wood working, 177 shards of pottery, 55 bone spearheads, a jet ring, two amber beads, whetstones, a hammerstone, and a piece of a human skull with damage received from a sharp weapon (Parker Pearson & Field 2003). None of the weapons or tools were deliberately broken before deposition, although all the bone spearheads seem to have been dismantled and many items are incomplete. A lack of deliberate damage is common in Late Iron Age metal deposits in Britain in contrast to similar depositions on the continent (Stead 1996, 65).

Causeways as a form of structured depositional space where deposition practices took place, diminish in importance in the Middle Iron Age in favour of landscape depositions (Hargrave 2018, 131). By the Late Iron Age the number of depots found on land is much larger than those found in water (*Ibid.*, 101-105). This image may be distorted by the easier excess to the land finds by metal detectorists (Bradley 2017, 66-68). Land depots are typically situated within 2 km of a settlement (Hargrave 2018). Notably weapons are never found in land depots, with the exception of miniatures. Typically, land depots consist of metal finds, a picture undoubtedly also distorted by the actions of metal detectorists, although in for example Leicestershire a habit of depositing quern stones existed. Hargrave (2018, 189-194) possibly places too much emphasis on land deposits, stating that they become of increasing importance later in the Iron Age, as many depot consist of coins, a typical Late Iron Age introduction. For many of these depots it remains unknown whether they were part of a deposition platform, which in theory could contain other types of find materials.

One of the few exceptions is the excavation of Hallaton. Surveys and excavations of the site revealed an extensive field system consisting of linear and round ditches situated near a presumed Roman road. Excavation of the main site resulted in a ditch and some sort of entrance (fig. 3.17), interpreted by the excavator as a boundary ditch (Score *et al.* 2011, 18-26). The ditch was 0.9m wide and up to 0.5m deep with relatively deep sides. It is not clear if the ditch continues all around the top of the hill where the site is situated.

The peak of the use of the site was mainly between about 50 BCE and 50 CE, the period between the first invasion and the Roman conquest of Britain, but continued less intensively until the 4th century (Score *et al.* 2011, 16). During that period, at least 16 depots of gold and silver coins were deposited, most of them near the entrance (Score *et al.* 2011, xv). A shallow pit in the entrance held skeletal parts of a dog. The ditch fill contained several Roman depositions such as a depot of helmets, a silver bowl, a silver ingot and a decorated silver mount possibly from a breastplate. East of the entrance a sequence of pits was found, which contained large numbers of animal bones among other finds (Score *et al.* 2011, 26-29). Most of the animal bones had belonged to at least 80 pigs (Browning 2011).

Depots like this once again demonstrate where the archaeological record is lacking when too much emphasis is placed on metal finds. Also, depots usually do not contain mixed materials.

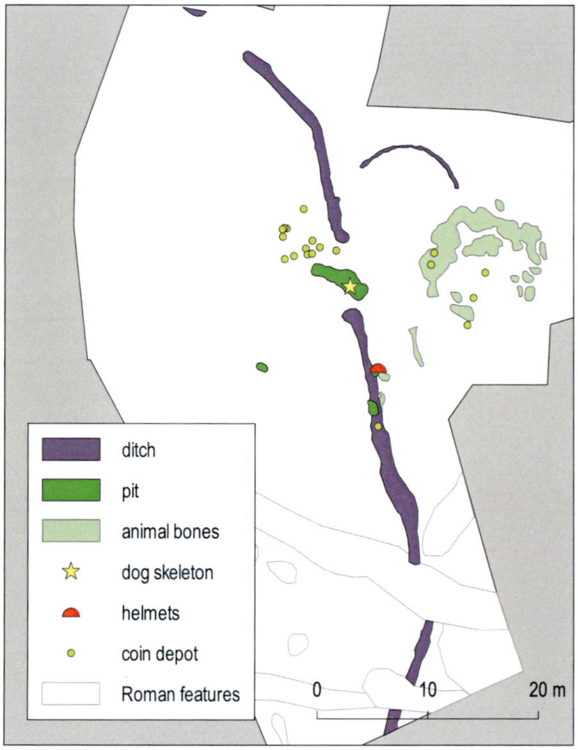

Figure 3.17. Excavation plan of Hallaton (based on Score et al. 2011, figure 7).

Many depots show a preference for a particular type of material, such as silver or gold, and objects were often bent or melted (Hargrave 2018, 134-137). The location of the depots is commonly near a hilltop or on the hillside facing east, although never on the summit. Human remains are sometimes found in a watery context usually not related to metal depositions, with the exception of liminal places, which makes Hargrave (2018, 149) conclude that depositions of human remains and depositions of metals have different purposes within the Iron Age belief system.

3.4.3 Enclosures

In contrast to the continent, rectangular Iron Age enclosures in Britain are generally interpreted as part of settlements (Moore 2006; 2007). Some settlements have a rectangular enclosure around them, commonly around 100m long, and other settlements lack any enclosure. The enclosures occur in clusters in for example Suffolk (Martin 1993), the Severn-Cotswolds region (Moore 2006; 2007), the central Welsh Marches (Wigley 2007), and the Trent Valley (Knight 2007). Enclosures are not isolated in the landscape and some are incorporated into larger field systems. In the Avon valley they appear to be related to linear structures, trackways, and pit alignments (Moore 2007). From around 400 BCE enclosures become smaller, house-hold size, possibly the result of an 'increasing desire for communities to associate themselves visibly with particular locations' (Wigley 2007).

The Welsh Marches are littered with ditch-and-bank enclosures. Some were built as early as the 5th or 4th century BCE, contemporary to the hillforts (Wigley 2007). Their position in the landscape is distinct, as they are all positioned on low ground, with a preferential proximity to rivers. As many as 449 enclosures are currently known, divers in shape and size, 75% of which consist of a singular ditch and 45% are rectilinear. Evidence of maintenance has been found. Some ditches were redug, probably with the help of the wider community.

The Trent valley also has a great variety of enclosures, most of which consist of a single ditch. According to Knight (2007) this represents a variety in function, either ceremonial, or related to burial tradition. Most enclosures would have provided an impressive obstacle, more than would have been required for livestock control or drainage. The role of this barrier could have been symbolic as well as functional, to emphasise group identity and enhance social cohesion (Hingley 1990, Bevan 1997, Chadwick 1999, Giles 2007). This might have been a necessity as land resources were limited and pressure grew during the first millennium BCE. An example is Fleak Close, an enclosure that was frequently recut and gradually expanded (Knight 2007). The enclosure in Barnham was interpreted to have a defensive function due to its impressive ditch-and-bank structure (Martin 1993, 1-22). It consisted of two parallel ditches of about 7.2m wide and 2.8m deep. Based on the resemblance to the German *Viereckschanzen* (measuring c. 1ha) Martin (1993, 22) ventured a cautious alternative interpretation as a cult place. As we now know that *Viereckschanzen* are likewise interpreted as defensive structures related to settlements, Martin's initial interpretation seems like the more plausible one.

3.5 Conclusion

This chapter is meant to provide a frame of reference for the study of the use of rectangular structures in the Low Countries. Are the subjects of this thesis comparable to the sanctuaries in France? As there is no archetypical sanctuary, the decisive factor for the interpretation depends on the finds and the context (table 3.2). The structures in France exhibit a diversity of finds, expressed sometimes in an abundance and sometimes in distinct unusual objects such as the broken statues of Vix. On some sites the array of animal bones testifies of sacrifices interpreted as recurring activities and feasting. Human bones are indications of particular acts that may have taken place at times of societal stress or conflict. In general, sites manifest a rectangular ditch with one or more pits in the enclosed space that served as receptacles for offerings. The duration of use of the structures seem to range between single events to hundreds of years, as was the case in Gournay and Villeneuve.

In the Early Iron Age, sanctuaries in France are rare and Vix appears to be a unique example (table 3.2). In Germany and England the focus centres around (wet) deposition sites. This changes in the course of the 5th-4th century. From that time, sites that have been identified as sanctuaries in France, Germany, or England are all situated in or near a settlement. Starting in the 4th century, in France sanctuaries related to war become dominant. Depositions of weapons, human bones, and bones of other animals are abundant in those places. In the Late Iron Age deposition practices diversify. In sanctuaries situated in an urban environment, but also in other places, all artefact categories are represented.

German *Viereckschanzen* and settlement enclosures in England functioned as defensive structures and seem to have been region-specific phenomena. Only on rare occasions do these large ditch-and-bank structures provide evidence of depositions. Rather, features within the *Viereckschanzen* indicate a habitational use. Having

Type of site / function	Century BCE	Weapons	Pottery	Animal bones	Human bones	Statues	Ditch (and bank)	Context
Wet deposition structure (e.g. causeways)	7th-4th, or later	++	++	+++	+	-	-	Water / liminal place
Late Hallstatt sanctuary (e.g. Vix)	6th-5th	-	+	+++	-	+	+	Cemetery
War related sanctuary (e.g. Gournay, Ribemont, Villeneuve, Saumeray)	4th-1st	+++	++	+++	+++	-	+	Settlement
Urban sanctuary / community gathering place (e.g. Manching, Acy-Romance)	3rd-1st	+	+	+	+	+	+	Settlement / roads
Defensive structure (e.g. *Viereckschanzen*, settlement enclosure)	2nd-1st	+	+	+	-	-	+++	Settlement
Small constructed site for religious rites (e.g. shrines)	1st	+	+	+	-	-	+	Settlement

Table 3.2. types of sites and related finds and features (- = none; + = few, ++ = relatively common, +++ = many).

eliminated *Viereckschanzen* for a cult function, the use of cult places in Iron Age Germany is for now limited to deposition places like Oberdorla and small shrine-like structures in densely populated centres.

From the Bronze Age to the Middle Iron Age causeways and wetland sites represent the main focus for depositions. In Britain, shrines do not occur until the 1st century BCE and even then they are rare, modest in size and mostly unrelated to significant amounts of finds. The main emphasis in Britain is on depositions that are mostly known in the form of Late Iron Age metal depots lacking contextual information due to metal detecting. The limited number of excavations around these depots, like the one in Hallaton, reveal that a structure of some sort may be present at these sites, along with related finds and features. The period between the first Roman invasion of Britain and the conquest in the 1st century CE remains the main focus for land depositions.

Pottery and animal bones are found in all types of sites and in all regions (table 3.2). Notably weapons continue to play an important role in deposition practices during the Iron Age and are found in relation to both causeways and rectangular ditched sanctuaries.

4

Rectangular structures in the Late Bronze Age – Early Iron Age

4.1 Introduction

In the last two chapters I established the remaining evidence of Iron Age religion (chapter 2) and reviewed related structures in regions bordering the Low Countries (chapter 3). Clearly, Iron Age cult places are rare, with the sanctuaries of Villeneuve-au-Châtelot and Gournay standing out in their long utilisation and Vix as the oldest example identified so far in France. In the Low Countries several structures predating Vix are interpreted as cult places. The early date of these structures led both De Laet (1966) and Fontijn (2002a) to the conclusion that subsequent cult places in the region must have had an indigenous origin. In this chapter I will examine this hypothesis and the earliest acclaimed cult places in the Low Countries. One of the structures (Ursel), is part of a more complex site that will be discussed in chapters 5 and 7 as most features date to the Middle or Late Iron Age. The sites were found spread out over a large region, mostly across the sandy areas of the Low Countries (fig. 4.1).

4.2 Rectangular structures in urnfields

Urnfields are a widespread Late Bronze Age to Early Iron Age phenomenon in the Low Countries. They are basically found in all sandy regions and some are known from the riverine areas (De Mulder 2011; Louwen 2021). In the Netherlands at least 689 urnfields are known and in Flanders there are at least 200 (Louwen 2021, 23). The graves in the urnfields are described as having a sober and unpretentious character (De Mulder 2011, 279). Cremation remains are deposited in a small pit with or without an urn and with or without pyre charcoal, under a small barrow. Between 14 and 40% of the graves contain grave goods (De Mulder 2011, 269; Louwen 2021, 153). A broad variety of objects could accompany the deceased in the grave (Louwen 2021, 153-154). Often the objects were burned together with the body. In combination with the types of deposition of the remains and the different monuments, the overall burial tradition is expressed in a diversity of manners. A small number of people were even inhumated instead of cremated.

4.2.1 Surrounding features

Different types of surrounding features occur in urnfields (Louwen 2021, 175-177; fig. 4.2). Over a third of the graves in the Netherlands have their own monument in the shape of a surrounding ditch and/or post setting, commonly of a size less than 10m across.[11] In Belgium, surrounding features occur at approximately one in seven sites.[12] Notable is that

---

11   Louwen (2021, 175); on a total of 3182 graves there were 1360 monuments.
12   Numbers based on De Mulder (2011, 220-223, 264-266); 729 graves of which 98 contained monuments.

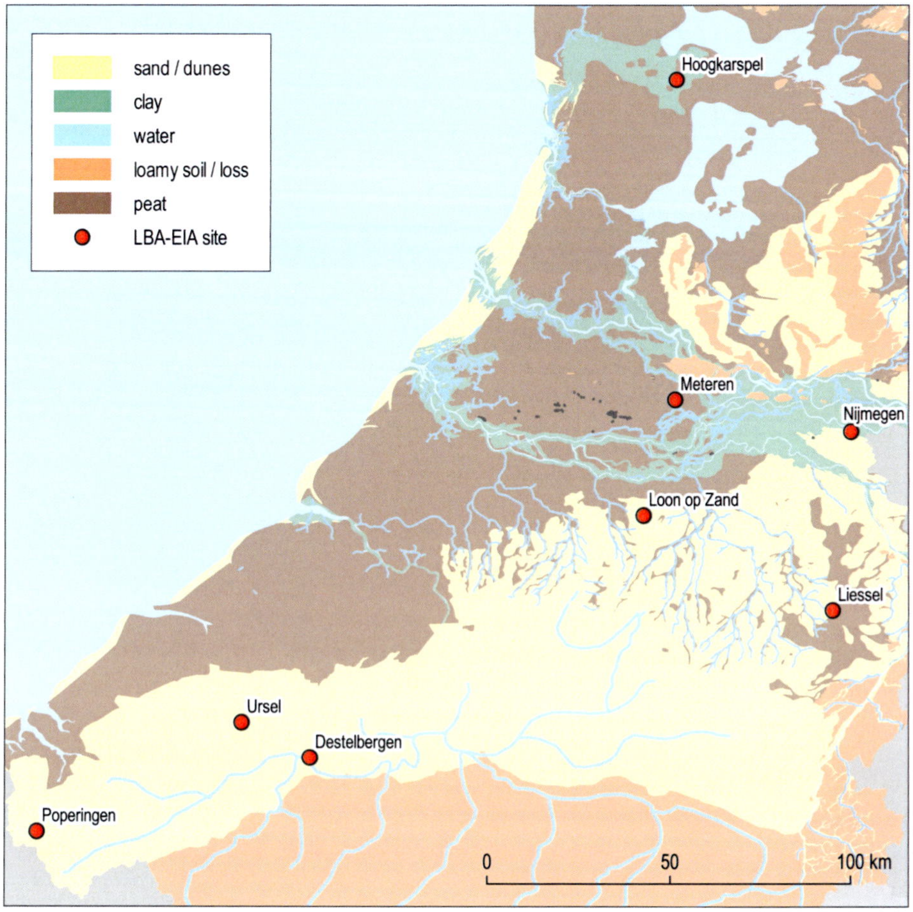

Figure 4.1. Simplified soil map of part of the Low Countries for the Middle Bronze Age-Early Iron Age, with sites featuring rectangular structures mentioned in the text. Paleogeographic map based on Mathys 2009, figure 7.43, Belgium soil map and Vos & De Vries (2013) for the Netherlands around 1500 BCE.

many surrounding ditches were found without a grave (De Mulder 2011, 242). This is likely due to poor conservation, as it can be assumed that originally all surrounding features contained one or more graves (Louwen 2022).

Of the graves with surrounding features found in the Netherlands, round monuments were used 86.5% of the time (Louwen 2021, 176). These features surrounded a barrow and were made in different forms. Commonly, a circular ditch was used (83.5%), but sometimes two or three concentric ditches and/or a post setting. Other types of surrounding features were keyhole-shaped ditches (0.1%), rectangular or elongated ditches (6.3%), and square ditches (2.6%). The keyhole shape was used north of the riverine region and is rarely found further south (*Ibid.*, 175). The shape of the monument is thought to reflect the shape of the mount that it surrounded (*Ibid.*). A square ditch would have surrounded a square(-ish) mount and elongated or oval ditches surrounded (e)long(ated) barrows.

Many types of surrounding features were in used at any moment between c. 1100 and c. 400 BCE. Some general trends are noticeable through time. Circular ditches, as a universal type of monument, occur throughout the (Late) Bronze Age and Iron Age, and thereafter (Louwen 2021,

175). Generally, long barrows are an early phenomenon. In Belgium, long barrows are typically at least twice as long as they are wide and tend to have rounded ends (De Mulder 2011, 249-259). The rectangular surrounding features of this so-called 'Vledder type grave' are generally considered to be the oldest monuments in urnfields, dating to the Late Bronze Age (Van Giffen 1945; Waterbolk 1962; Kooi 1979, 130-131; Verlinde 1985). The graves often have a rectangular post setting inside the ditch, interpreted as the remains of a 'funerary house' (fig. 4.2 left; Kooij 1979, 130). The burial monument as a whole could have developed its rectangular shape because of the wooden funerary house.

Square ditches only came into use in the Iron Age. The earliest square ditch appeared in the urnfield of Destelbergen (Belgium), where it was interpreted as a cult place, after its excavation in the 1960s (De Laet 1966; De Laet *et al.* 1985). The interpretation is illustrative of the fact that it was the first square ditch to be excavated in an urnfield at the time and it also contained multiple graves. In the Destelbergen urnfield only twelve out of 105 graves had a peripheral structure in the form of a ditch. One ditch was round, six were square(-ish) and five were parts of long barrows (fig. 4.3). Twenty-six graves were carbon dated to

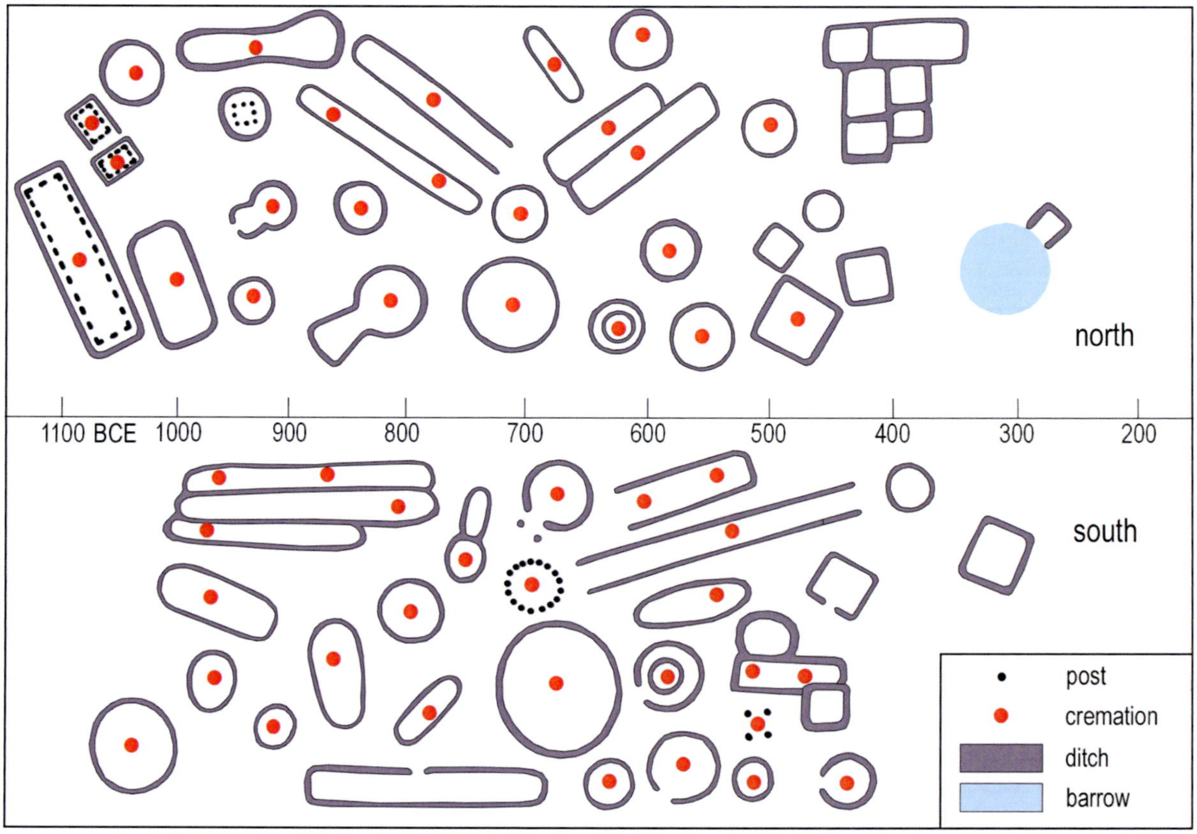

Figure 4.2. Surrounding features used between 1100 and 200 BCE in the north and the south of the Netherlands (after Kooi 1979, figure 145; Hessing & Kooi 2005, figures 28.3a/28.3b).

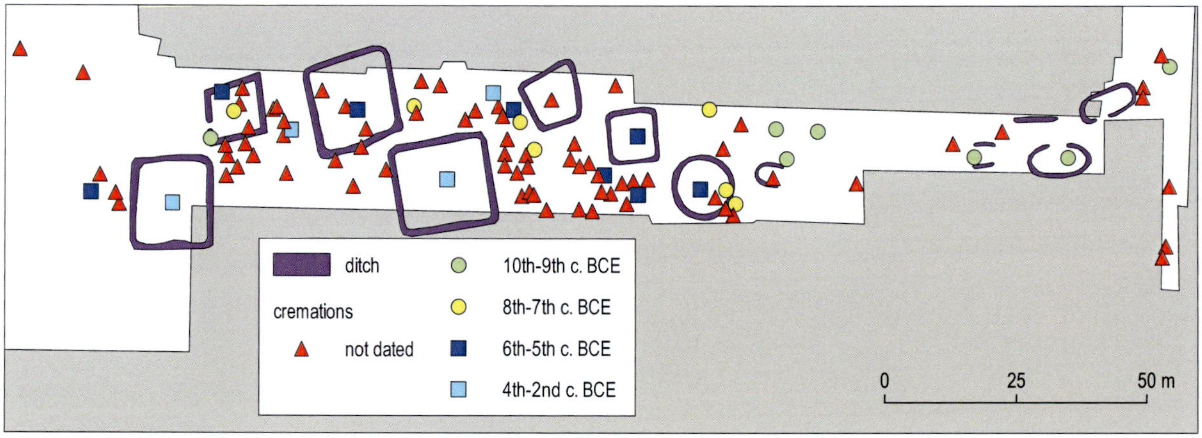

Figure 4.3. Part of the excavation plan of the urnfield of Destelbergen. The structure interpreted by De Laet as a cult place is the second from the left (after De rue et al. 2012, figure 2 and Table 3, dates based on the 'weighted average mean of the probability density function of the calibrated date calBCE').

determine the chronology and utilisation of the cemetery (De Rue *et al.* 2012). The long barrows and associated graves on the east side of the cemetery date to the Late Bronze Age, the others to the Early and Middle Iron Age. Apparently the cemetery spread out towards the west during its use.

The structure in question had a slightly diamond shaped square with sides of 11.6m in length and 1.2m wide (De Laet 1966). On the west side was an opening of 1.2m wide. Openings in a surrounding ditch are an Early Iron Age addition to urnfield features, but

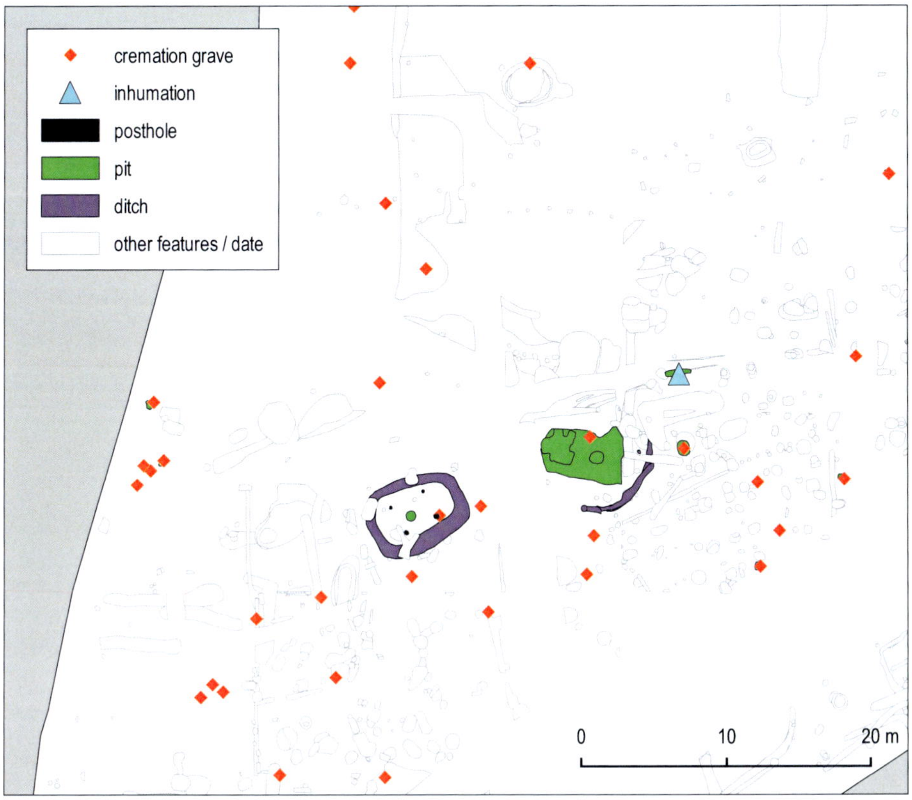

Figure 4.4. Part of the excavation plan of Meteren-Plantage (based on: Jezeer & Verniers, 2012).

the direction is unusual as nearly all openings in surrounding ditches were to the east, southeast or south (Verlinde 1987, table K; Louwen 2021, 175). The diamond shaped ditch enclosed five graves and one was found in the ditch itself just south of the entrance (De Laet 1966). The grave situated in the exact centre of the structure, is assumed to be the reason for its construction. It consisted of a decorated urn with cremation remains placed in a shallow pit. The cremated remains were carbon dated to 783-517 calBCE, making it the oldest grave in the centre of a square ditch (De Mulder 2011, 167-170; De Rue *et al.* 2012).[13] Curiously the structure also contained an even older grave. Since this was the only grave not on the east side of the cemetery dating to the Late Bronze Age, De Rue *et al.* (2012, 644) assumed this grave was exhumed from another part of the cemetery and reburied in the ditch of the square monument, just south of the entrance. This provenance is debatable as there is no evidence, as for example in the form of an empty pit, so the urn and its cremation remains could also have come from another cemetery or from some entirely different place such as a house.

---

13 95.4% probability calibrated date, cremated bone, KIA-34892: 2495 ± 30 BP. Other graves in the centres of square ditches dated: 2320 ± 30 BP (KIA-34887), 2405 ± 40 BP (KIA-37706), 2215 ± 30 BP (KIA-30042), and 2450 ± 30 BP (KIA-37707).

There were no particular finds or features to suggest the diamond-shaped ditch in Destelbergen was anything else than an early example of a rectangular urnfield structure accommodating several cremation graves. Given the distribution of the graves in respect to the surrounding features it is likely that the ditches initially surrounded only one grave. Other urns were added later.

In other urnfields, surrounding features can be less common. In an Early to Middle Iron Age cemetery in Meteren only two surrounding features were found, one of which was merely a fragment. One inhumation grave was found that dated to the 13th to 11th century BCE (Jezeer & Verniers 2012, 43-58). Amidst the Early to Middle Iron Age graves an oval ditch with an overall length of 6.8m and a maximum width of 5m was found (fig. 4.4). The enclosed space held a small structure of four posts with a small pit in the centre.

Initially the feature was suggested to be a cult place because of its central position in the cemetery, although later the interpretation changed to a long barrow (Jezeer & Verniers 2012, 59-62). No finds were directly associated with the oval structure apart from a cremation grave that was found 20cm above one of the postholes.

Two other features stand out in this cemetery. One was the only Iron Age inhumation grave, found 16m northeast of the oval structure (fig. 4.4, triangle). It belonged to a woman in her thirties and could be dated to the 5th century BCE. In between the inhumation grave and the oval structure

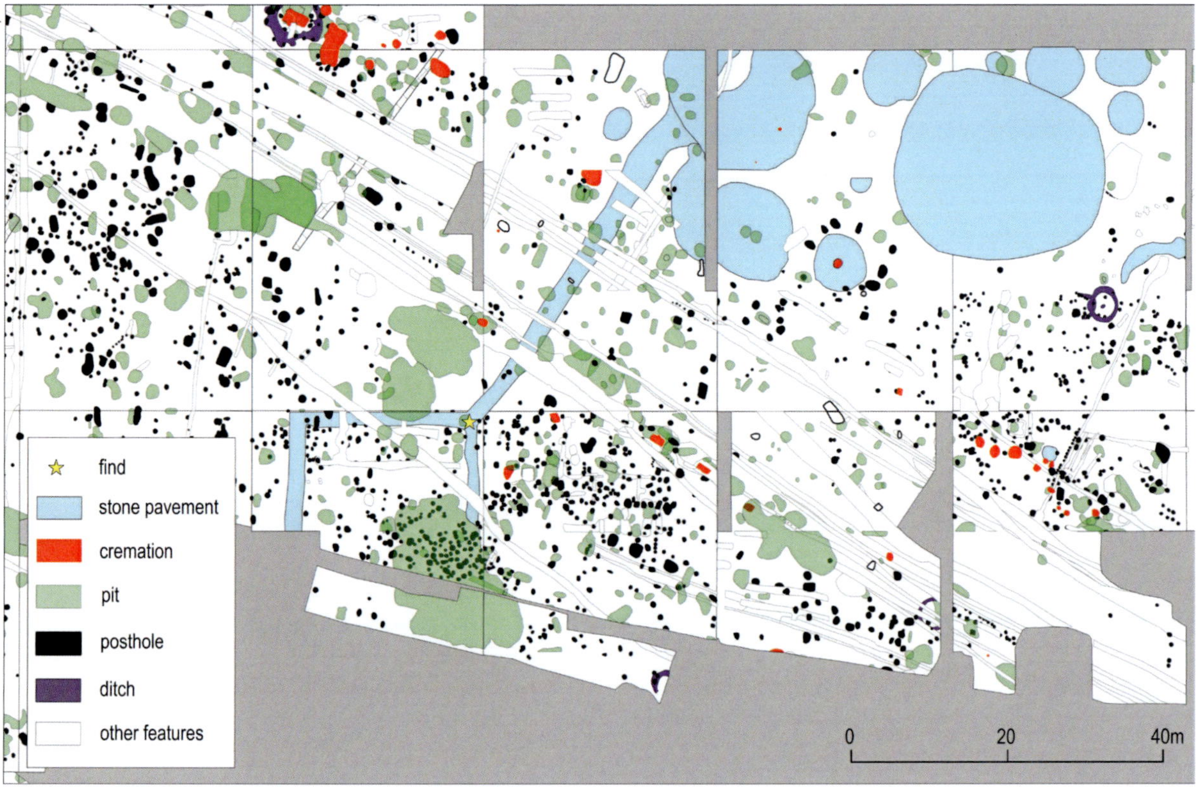

Figure 4.5. Section of the excavation plan of Kops Plateau (Van der Weyden 2013, Odyssee project open access data; Fontijn & Cuijpers 1999, figure 3 and 14).

a charcoal pit was found, 5.5m long and 3m wide (fig. 4.4, indicated as large pit). It looked like fire(s) had been burning in this location. Around the charcoal pit part of a circular ditch was found, also dated to the 6th or 5th century BCE by some associated pottery. This latter feature appeared to be a place where the act of cremating bodies took place. Generally in urnfields, the act of cremation and the act of interment were performed at two separate places (Louwen 2021, 88-89). The spot of the cremation pyre was usually outside the cemetery. In Meteren however, they seem to be situated next to each other.

The four-posted structure within the oval enclosure was interpreted by Jezeer & Verniers (2012, 59-60) as a funerary house. Similar structures are known from other excavations, such as the Bronze Age site of Toterfout-Halvemijl (Glasbergen 1954; Theunissen 1999, 91), and the forementioned Vledder-type grave in the northeast of the Netherlands (Waterbolk 1962, 15-18; Kooij 1979, 130-131; Verlinde 1987, 243-244, 265). Younger examples were found in Mierlo-Hout (Roman era; Roymans & Tol 1993, fig. 11), in Someren-Waterdael III (Late Iron Age structure number 760, Hiddink & De Boer 2011, 140-142), Lomm (Middle Iron Age; De Leeuwe & Prangsma 2011; see Ch.5.4) and Oss-Zevenbergen (two structures dating to the Early Iron Age; Fokkens, Jansen & Van Wijk 2009, 132-133). In

short, four-posted structures are not uncommon in Bronze and Iron Age cemeteries. These structures seem to have had a light construction, sometimes with the posts placed quite far apart, suggesting the structure was not commonly covered by a roof. In general they are interpreted as 'funerary houses' (Kooi 1979, 130; Van Vilsteren 1989; Fokkens, Jansen & Van Wijk 2009, 215-216; De Leeuwe & Prangsma 2010, 105; Hiddink & De Boer 2011, 140; De Mulder 2011, 266-268). A funerary house probably had some kind of plank floor or platform on which the deceased was (temporarily) placed as part of the burial procedure. In Meteren, the charcoal spot 10m to the east was probably the place of the general pyre. It is conceivable that the remains of the deceased were laid out in a funerary house before being transferred to the charcoal pit location and there cremated on a pyre. This burial tradition may have been uncommon in the southern Netherlands, but it was quite typical for northern urnfields.

A noteworthy detail is that both the four-posted structure as well as the pyre location in Meteren were surrounded by a ditch, as if the ditch was made to separate the space during the burial process. Louwen (2021, 178) suggests surrounding features posed a physical boundary between the area where human remains were deposited ('their own space') and the surrounding world. This same

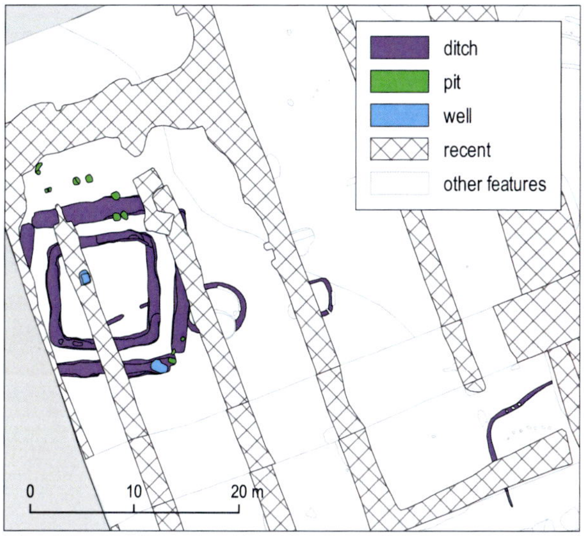

Figure 4.6. Section of the excavation plan of Hoogkarspel (after Jezeer & Roessingh 2019, fig. 11.24).

principle was adhered in Meteren, only not around the graves, but around the places used in the burial rites. This implies that the human remains needed 'fencing off' (or protecting?) during a transitional stage. Conceivably, it kept the spirit(s) or the soul in, or alternatively out, or separated the living from the dead before the deceased entered the realm of the dead. As the cremation graves in the vicinity indicate, a boundary was not deemed necessary after completion of this process. In conclusion, the ditches in Meteren seem to indicate a place where a certain (part of the) burial proceedings took place. The act taken place there could have been comparable to the modern viewing, in a chance to say goodbye to the deceased, perform a wake, memorial or feast, prepare the body before cremation or burial, or prepare the pyre while the body rested.

4.2.2 Relation to Bronze Age barrows

Another rectangular structure associated with the burial tradition was found along Bronze Age barrows and Roman features in Nijmegen (Van Enckevort & Zee 1996; Fontijn 2002a). Situated on the gentler sloped southeast side of the Kops Plateau is a cluster of two stone circles and ten round stone platforms, all made out of a thin layer of cobble sized stones (fig. 4.5).

The features are flanked to the north and east by Neolithic and Bronze Age barrows and an urnfield (Fontijn & Cuijpers 1999). The stone platforms are made of mainly sandstone and some other rock types giving it a desert pavement appearance. Due to their regularity, distinct shape, and the fact that the stones were placed on the uneroded surface, these anthropogenic arrangements differ from all other Bronze and Iron

Age monuments found in the Low Countries. Two stone circles contained a cremation grave in the centre. For most of the stone platforms it is assumed these were covered by a mount (Fontijn & Cuijpers 1999, 43-45). One smaller stone platform was surrounded by pits in which some Middle Bronze Age pottery was found. In the soil above four of the platforms Late Bronze Age-Early Iron Age cremation urns were found, interpreted as secondary graves. A Middle to Late Bronze Age date for the stone platforms is likely on the basis of pottery finds (*Ibid.*, 45-48).

A 42m long and 80cm wide cobble path connects the second largest stone platform to a rectangular feature southwest of it (fig. 4.5). This rectangular, or U-shaped, feature consists of a stone pavement of 1.5-2m wide, marking a rectangular space of 24m by at least 15m (Fontijn & Cuijpers 1999). According to the excavators, the stone pavement was probably placed in a shallow ditch. Part of the south section was destroyed in the Roman period, and another part is situated outside the excavation area, making it impossible to determine whether the structure is either U-shaped or a complete rectangle (*Ibid.*, 55; Fontijn 2002a, 157). The cobble path connection to the platforms (or former barrows) suggests a certain degree of simultaneity, with a time difference between the phenomena of no more than a few generations. The path is interpreted as a possible procession route from the rectangular marked space to the barrows, comparable to post settings and allées (Fontijn & Cuijpers 1999, 59; Fontijn 2002a). Fontijn (2002a, 160-162) pointed out that the rectangular structure marked a symbolic enclosed space where actions could take place and even suggested an ancestral cult, encompassing a ceremony in which the recently deceased were almost literally included among their real or acclaimed ancestors. The (re-) connection of a rectangular structure to an (older) Bronze Age monument is a feature found on other sites (see Ch.6.3.1).

On or in the northwest corner of the structure, a bronze socketed axe was found among the stones, on the exact location where the corner joins the path to the stone platforms (fig. 4.5, star). The type of axe is typical for the second half of the Late Bronze Age to the Early Iron Age (Fontijn 2002, 162). Commonly such axes are known from depositions in wet places and hoards in the Late Bronze Age, making the location of the deposition within the rectangular enclosure on the Kops Plateau an exception (Fontijn 2002, 162; Fontijn 2002a). The interpretation as a cult place was based on the rectangular shape made out of collected cobbles, which could only have represented a symbolic enclosure, in combination with the specific position of the axe. Fontijn (2002a, 164) remarks that the outer edge is a deliberately and carefully chosen position: a transitional place.

In the region of West-Frisia, the northwest of the Netherlands, another type of rectangular Bronze Age structure has been found (Jezeer & Roessingh 2019,

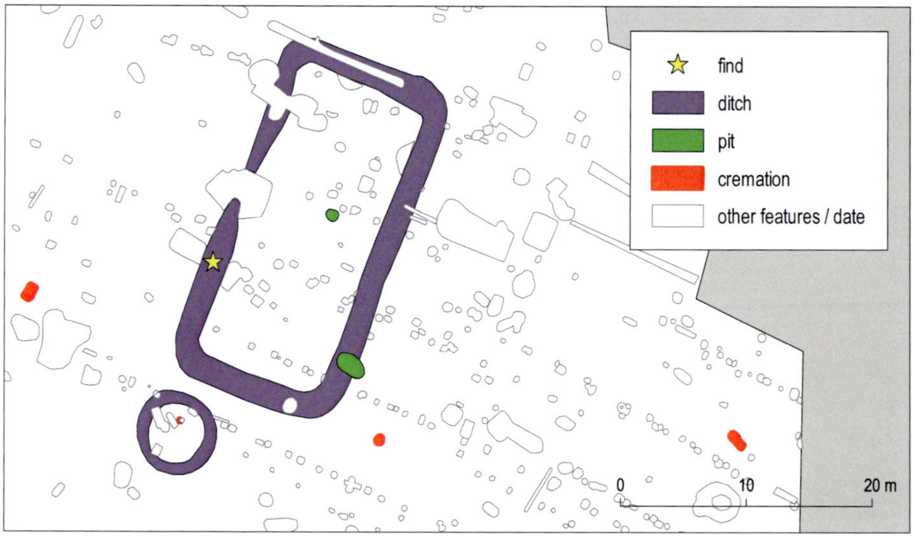

Figure 4.7. Section of the excavation plan of Poperinge (after Van der Linde & Kalshoven 2017).

330-341). A recently excavated rectangular structure consisted of two concentric ditches (fig. 4.6). It was dated 14th-12th century and housed several wells and pits, which held slightly younger material. The function of the structure is unknown. Its position is rather isolated from other contemporary features. Round barrows are known in the area, mostly dating to Middle Bronze Age (Roessingh 2018, 309-311), and some Late Neolithic (Fokkens *et al.* 2017). Some of those have multiple concentric ditches, representing different phases, like the 3-period barrow found near the Watertoren (*Ibid.*, 124-126). Conceivably, the structure can be interpreted as a comparable square grave monument.

4.2.3 The (medio) Atlantic tradition

From the above examples, it can be concluded that – with the possible exception of West Frisia- rectangular structures do indeed first appear in Late Bronze Age and Early Iron Age urnfields. However, these features do not resemble the Middle and Late Iron Age rectangular structures. The urnfield features differ in the limited size of the ditch (width and depth) and the fact that they usually surround one grave.

There is one early exception in the research area, that was found on the southwestern edge near the border with France, in Poperinge. The main excavated structure on this site consisted of a rectangular ditch of 28 × 13.7m, measured on the outside (Van der Linde & Kalshoven 2017, 40). At the excavation level the ditch was 1.7-2.0m wide (fig. 4.7).

The ditch had a V-shaped cross section and a bowl shaped bottom, with a maximum depth of 126cm. According to Van der Linde & Kalshoven (2017, 40-47) the appearance of the fill layers suggests the ditch was an open and dry feature, with the groundwater level below the bottom. They suggest the ditch filled gradually in different phases and no attempts were made for re-digging. On the north side some colluvium was found in the ditch fill indicating the soil from the ditch was used to make a wall on the outside and possibly also on the inside.

The ditch was dated to the 13th-10th century BCE on the basis of finds and carbon dating. Finds that can be directly associated with the Late Bronze Age structure are scarce. During the trial trenches on the site of Poperinge, a nearly complete pot was found standing upright near the bottom of the ditch (Demey 2012, 17). The cup-shaped piece of pottery is identified as a *Henkeltasse*, a type typical for the Late Bronze Age or Early Iron Age (Demey 2012a, 17; Bloo & Weterings 2017, 73). As the pot seems to be deliberately placed at the bottom of the ditch, it was interpreted by the excavators as an offering (Demey 2012a, 14-15). A total of 120 shards of pottery were found in the ditch, belonging to a bowl and two pots most likely dating to the Late Bronze Age. Most pottery was found on the south side of the monument, in the corners, and on the west side of the ditch close to what might have been the entrance. Finds from the ditch also included 35 quite large sandstones, that appeared to be deliberately broken (Van der Linde & Kalshoven 2017, 110).

In, or rather under the ditch on the southeast side, a shaft-like pit was found. Its remaining depth was 1.1m below the bottom of the ditch (Van der Linde & Kalshoven 2017, 44-46). The walls of this feature were probably covered by a wooden lining. The shaft was slightly wider than the ditch and contained no finds. The bottom of the shaft was above the groundwater level. The position of this feature in the ditch, is resembling the wells and pits found in the square structure in West-Frisia. The much later Roman graves indicate that the Late Bronze Age monument remained visible for a long time.

Analysis of macro-botanical samples of the ditch fill demonstrated remains of plants with edible nuts or fruits, namely hazel, hawthorn, blackberry, and oak. According to Van der Meer (2017) this assemblage of plants deviates from samples in contemporary settlements. Especially hawthorn is mentioned for its use in burials, while the act of cutting a hawthorn was thought to bring bad luck (De Cleene & Lejeune 2000, 725-733, cited by Van der Meer 2017). These botanical remains suggest actions at this place that deviated from 'regular' settlement activities.

The large rectangular ditch at Poperinge fits in with a burial tradition described by Milcent (2017) as Late Bronze and Early Iron Age 'medio-Atlantic sub-rectangular funerary enclosures'. Along the coastal regions or northwest France several similar sized features have been found that contained one or more cremation burials. Milcent (2017) argues that this region is not the periphery of the Hallstatt Culture, but part of the Atlantic cultural sphere influenced by exchange networks along the Atlantic coast. Rectangular structures as burial enclosures appear earlier in this region than more central on the continent. The northwest coast of France, including the (southern?) coastal regions of Belgium it would appear, had their own traditions, specifically in the Early Iron Age.

4.3 Rectangular structures in Early Iron Age settlements

Occasionally rectangular structures are found within a settlement context. These are much rarer than rectangular structures in a cemetery context for the simple reason that settlements from the urnfield period are rare. The number of urnfields far surpasses the number of known settlements

from that period (Arnoldussen 2008, 402-417). The singularity of these structures in that context may be the reason that they are sometimes interpreted as a cult place.

An Early Iron Age site in Liessel-Willige Laagt revealed a settlement with mainly settlement associated features (Witte 2012). No cemetery remains are known in the vicinity. A near complete large house plan of a type that is fairly common for the Early Iron Age (Schinkel 1998, 190-191; Hiddink 2014a; Fokkens 2019a) was positioned on a farmyard with similarly orientated features. Apart from the house plan two outhouses, two fences, and a rectangular ditched structure were found (fig. 4.8) The rectangular structure was interpreted as a possible cattle pen, although the possibility of a 'ritual' significance for the inhabitants of the farmstead was suggested by Witte (2012, 38).

The enclosure consisted of a rectangular ditch, measuring 19 × 8m (Witte 2012). Its narrow appearance of 40cm wide (at a remaining depth of 35cm) suggests that it functioned as a bedding trench accommodating a wattle work wall. Two fragments of pottery were recovered from the ditch fill. Three postholes were found flanking the opening on the east side. These might have belonged to posts that were part of a fence gate. A row of double posts was found next to the west side of the ditch. This construction is thought to have been either part of the pen or part of the farmyard, narrowly enclosing the pen. The space inside of the ditch was mostly empty, apart from a few (unpublished) postholes. The fenced

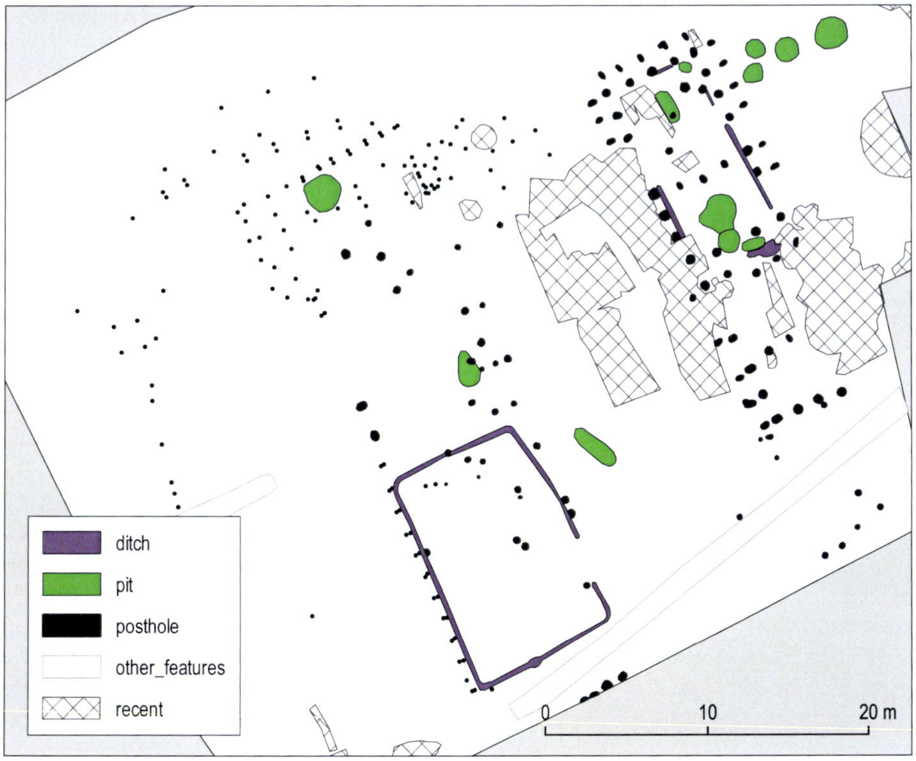

Figure 4.8. Section of the excavation plan of Liessel-Willige Laagt (based on: Witte, 2012, figure 3.30).

farm yard surrounded several interior structures with the same orientation for a multitude of activities, none of them of a religious nature, of which the livestock pen was a key element.

On the western end of the Loonse and Drunense Duinen, a large area of inland dunes and cover sand ridge, a settlement was found consisting of at least five house plans, eleven outhouses, and several storage pits (Roymans & Hiddink 1991). It was occupied from the Middle Bronze Age to Early Iron Age. On the north side of the excavation, 50m from the nearest house plan, the features of an enclosure were found interpreted by Roymans & Hiddink (1991, 124) as either a cattle pen or a cult place. The structure seems to consist of an outer and an inner construction (fig. 4.9).

The outer ditch was made of a 30cm wide trench with a remaining depth of just 10-40cm, while the inner ditch had width of around 35cm and a depth of 15-50cm with steep sides. (Roymans & Hiddink 1991). The narrow ditch with the steep sides led the excavators to the conclusion this had once held a palisade, although no post impressions were observed in the ditch fill. The larger outside ditch had an opening of at least 2.5m on the south side and the inner one an opening of around 1.9m on the southeast side. A round pit was found on the entrance and postholes were found mostly south of the structure (Ibid.). A total of 50 pottery shards from the ditch date the structure to the Late Bronze Age-Early Iron Age. Like the ditch in Liessel, the structure in Loon op Zand appears to consists of bedding trenches that would have contained some sort of wattle work construction. This type of construction in combination with the proximity of the settlement makes an interpretation as a cattle pen most likely.

4.4 Conclusion: the urnfield as a point of origin

This chapter set out to test the proposition that Late Bronze Age to Early Iron Age urnfields are a possible point of origin for cult places in the Low Countries. Beside the fact that few rectangular structures were identified within the study area, there are two problems with this hypothesis.

Firstly, if by a cult place we envision a structure that was used over a longer period of time and served as a central place for ceremonies, feasts, and depositions, than no such structures can be identified. Rectangular structures discussed above were mainly used for a single event or as a cattle pen. The structures in the cemeteries of Meteren and Nijmegen could have been used on multiple occasions in relation to the burial custom. Still, in none of the rectangular structures a repetitive use can be substantiated by the finds.

The second problem with the proposition is the time frame. Some type of rectangular structures were used in the urnfield period, and some even in the

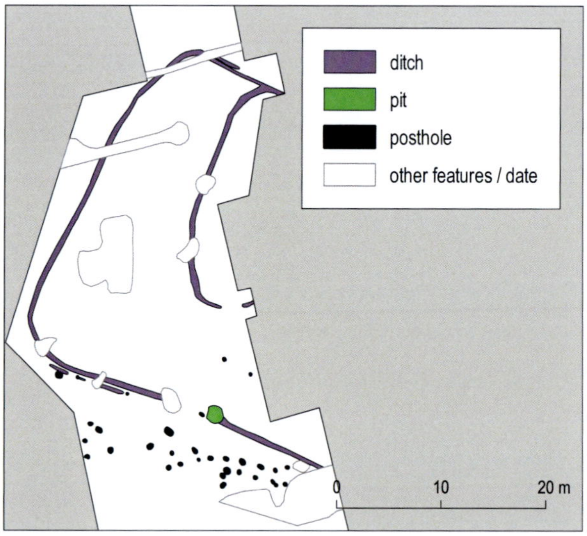

Figure 4.9. Excavation plan of Loon op Zand (after Roymans & Hiddink 1991, figure 15).

Middle Bronze Age. The large rectangular structure in Poperinge and the Middle Bronze Age double ditched structure in West-Frisia appear to be fully developed forms, that were likely related to burial traditions. This indicates that the idea behind the rectangular shape was already established in the (Middle) Bronze Age. Notably, the rectangular structures of the 'Vledder type' (that occur outside the study area), the structures found in the West-Frisia (also situated outside the study area), as well as the large medio-Atlantic type (of which all but one example are outside the study area), all went out of use before the Iron Age even started.

Other type of burial monuments were dominant in urnfields before square monument came into fashion. It is therefore doubtful that the origin of 'cult places', or of rectangular structures in general, is to be sought in urnfields. However, even if urnfields were not the origin, the idea behind the rectangular shape of structures rooted firmly during the Late Bronze Age to Early Iron Age. A pre-existing notion of the meaning behind the shape may have been established by the Early Iron Age when the square burial monument was (re-)introduced. This may have paved the way for the subsequent use of other types of rectangular structures. As Milcent (2017) remarked, the transition from circular to quadrangular funerary enclosures must represent a major mentality change.

5

Rectangular structures in the Middle Iron Age

5.1 Introduction

Continuity and change are two key words used to describe events during a period of transition. In the course of the Middle Iron Age many socio-cultural actions seemed to change, archaeologically visible in cemeteries, depositional practices, house plans, and to a lesser extend in settlement patterns. Most changes are gradual processes, such as the abandonment of the urnfields (De Mulder 2011, 482-484). Another change is notable in the use of rectangular structures. According to several authors, from the early 3rd century BCE onwards rectangular ditches and/or palisade enclosures were in use as 'local open-air cult places' (Gerritsen 2003, 163-167; Roymans 2004, 12; Fernández-Götz & Roymans 2015; Roymans & Derks 2014). They defined these structures as having sides of over 20m, too large for a burial structure although still related to ancestor worship and burial customs since most are located in or near cremation cemeteries. The current discourse is that cemeteries functioned as cult places where gatherings took place. These gatherings played an important role in establishing, maintaining and strengthening community ties. A 'cult community' would have overlapped with a 'burial community' and effectively the burial grounds become the cult place. In this chapter I will examine this theory by researching these structures and the related finds, explore their utilisation and their relation to burials. Because the use of rectangular structures seems related to burials, an outline of funerary procedures and treatment of human remains is given as a starting point. This forms the basis of how people in the Middle Iron Age thought about death and the afterlife.

The Middle Iron Age structures discussed in this chapter, dating to the 5th-3rd centuries BCE, all have been suggested as cult sites (fig. 5.1). Details of these sites are described in the Appendix. Most of the structures were excavated in the loam and/or sandy soil regions of the Low Countries. Only Houten is situated further north in the riverine area with clay soils.

5.2 Burial traditions and the treatment of human remains[14]

5.2.1 Burial traditions

During the 5th and 4th century BCE most large communal burial grounds, generally referred to as urnfields, gradually fell out of use (Gerritsen 2003: 131; De Mulder 2011, 482-484). Some urnfields were reused in or used until the Late Iron Age and Roman Era, like in Someren (Hiddink & De Boer 2011, 135-163). A discourse by Sørensen & Rebay (2008, 57-58), recently adhered by Louwen (2021, 238), suggests to abandon the use of

---

14   This chapter was published in an adjusted version in Metaaltijdenbundel 9 (De Leeuwe 2022).

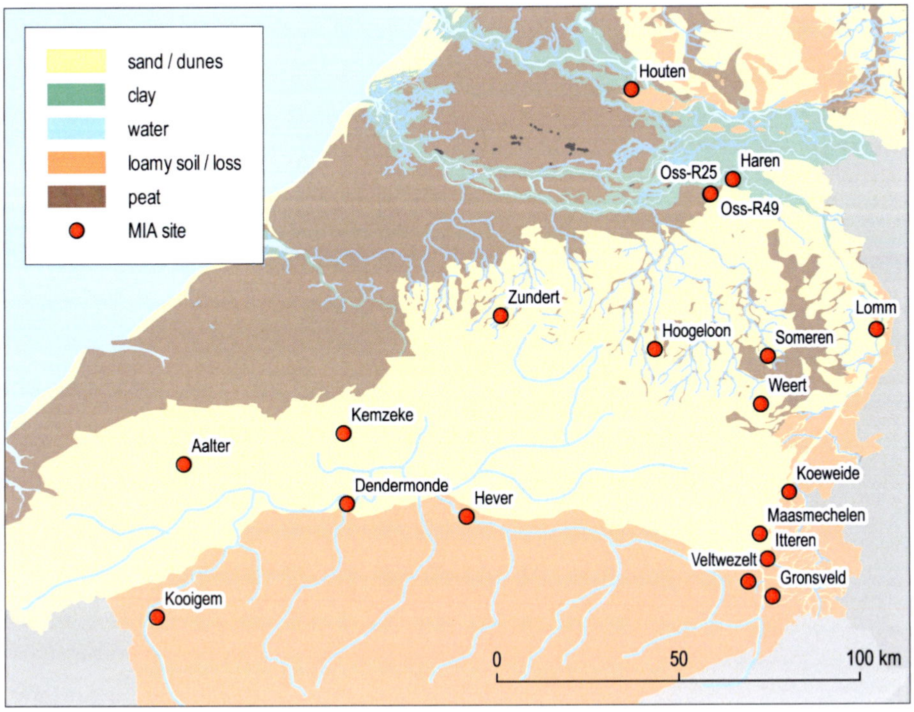

Figure 5.1. Middle Iron Age sites mentioned in the text, on the simplified soil map of part of the Low Countries for the Iron Age. Paleogeographic map based on Mathys 2009, figure 7.43 (Belgium coastline around 2800 calBP), Belgium soil map and Vos & De Vries (2013) for the Netherlands around 500 BCE.

the term 'urnfields' for the reason that not all cremations were buried in an urn during the Late Bronze Age and Early Iron Age. The share of burials that were placed in an urn averaged only around 27% in the Late Bronze Age, increasing to 73% in the Early Iron Age, and decreasing to virtually none by the 5th century BCE (Fontijn 1996; Gerritsen 2003, 128-129; Louwen 2021, 107-109). By then, most large cemeteries were abandoned for smaller ones, although cremation was maintained as the customary mode of final disposition of a corpse. Most burial pits remained unmarked, or marked in a way that did not leave visible remains in the archaeological record, although the use of surrounding graves with ditches was upheld in some places and on a smaller scale. Round as well as square surrounding ditches were used in the Middle Iron Age. In some cemeteries these features were used in conjunction, as in the cemetery of Weert-Laarvelt (Tol 2009; see Appendix). Other cemeteries consisted entirely of square ditches, as in the example of Destelbergen (De Laet 1966; De Laet *et al.* 1985; Ch. 6). Square ditches were used in the Northern Netherlands until about 375 BCE, while in the south this was well into the Roman Era (Lanting & Van der Plicht 2005/2006, 298-306). As in Destelbergen, some square structures in communal burial grounds are suggested to have a 'cult place' function. One example was found in Oosterhout, a larger rectangular square ditch in between several smaller examples. It was part of a large cemetery in use from the Late Bronze Age to the Middle Iron Age (Roessingh *et al.* 2012, 72-73; see Appendix). The structure did not contain any graves, but instead a few

postholes were found inside the enclosure. It was one of many without a burial: of 200 surrounding features in the excavation, 85% were without a related grave and 57 graves were found without surrounding feature (*Ibid.*, 99). The absence of graves was mainly attributed to erosion.

A large ditch with one side of 48m in Zundert was proposed as a cult place, based on the size and despite the fact that a burial was found in the centre (Krist 2005, 66-77; see Appendix). The ditch had an opening to the southeast, a common feature in Iron Age urnfield ditches (De Mulder 2011, 300; Louwen 2021, 175). A total of 35 cremation graves were found in the Zundert cemetery, of which 14 dated to the Middle Iron Age (*Ibid*, 48-56). In the large ditch 145 pottery fragments were found, mostly near the southern end of the interruption on the east side (Krist 2005, 68). About 37% of the pottery was secondarily burned.

A square post setting in the large cemetery of Someren-Waterdael was also proposed as a cult place (Hiddink & De Boer 2011, 127-128; see Appendix). Like the structures in Destelbergen and Oosterhout, it was in some respect divergent from the other burial monuments within the cemetery. It is possible the square structures in Someren and Oosterhout are somehow part of the burial customs, but they differ from the rectangular structures disused in this thesis. They are smaller, the ditch is narrower (or replaced by a post setting), and more relevantly, no finds can be associated with them. Given the large diversity in burial customs, especially in the Middle Iron Age, in all likelihood these were features surrounding a grave.

The large communal burial grounds of the Late Bronze Age-Early Iron Age with their small barrows, were succeeded in the Middle Iron Age predominantly by smaller cemeteries with flat cremation graves without an urn (Roymans 1991, 65; Gerritsen 2003, 138-149; Hiddink 2003, 7-11; Van Beek 2006). These smaller cemeteries occur in a large variety of locations. In the 6th and 5th century BCE some cemeteries contain inhumation graves, specifically in the river area of the Netherlands (Van den Broeke 2014; Kootker et al. 2018). From the 4th century BCE onwards inhumations become uncommon. At least an estimated 100 cemeteries are known in the Low Countries datable to the Middle Iron Age.[15] Most of these consist of small pits with cremation remains in varying numbers per cemetery. A comprehensive study for the research area is not available at the time of writing and outside of the scope of this thesis. For a part of the research area, the Meuse-Demer-Scheldt area, 67 Middle Iron Age cemeteries have been counted containing a total of 505 graves (Van den Dikkenberg 2018, 40). Among these were only 19 inhumation graves (4%).

Unburnt human remains dating to the Middle Iron Age, either in an inhumation or elsewhere, are rare in the Low Countries, as the common burial practice at the time was cremation (Gerritsen 2003, 131-135). In Late Bronze Age-Early Iron Age urnfields approximately 98-99% of people were cremated (Louwen 2021, 85). From about 400 BCE, the cremation practice changed. After the body was cremated on a pyre, a selection of the cremated remains was collected, sometimes with (part of) the pyre remains (Gerritsen 2003, 131-135; Hiddink 2003, 6-13). These were then buried in a small pit without an urn and usually without grave goods. Not only the manner of cremation changed, the location where the remains were buried changed as well. Most urnfields were large collectively used cemeteries, in use for centuries and containing hundreds of graves, while Middle Iron Age cemeteries consisted of several dozen graves at the most, and more dispersed (e.g. Gerritsen 2003, 131-135; Van Beek 2010, 432-440; Norde 2018; Van den Dikkenberg 2018, 46-47). Surrounding features are used considerably less in Middle Iron Age cemeteries, although their use was not completely abandoned. Also the monumentality of mounds declined. Covering a grave with a mount became a rare occurrence. One of the exceptions was discovered in Apeldoorn, where part of a barrow measuring nearly 18m in diameter was excavated (Van der Linde & Fontijn 2011).

In the river area of the Netherlands people were sometimes inhumed during the Iron Age (Van den Broeke 2014). These graves are usually of adults, buried alongside cremation graves. Most of the inhumation graves in the region can be dated from the 7th to the 5th century BCE (Ibid., fig.123, fig.124). Only three inhumation graves can be dated with certainty to the Middle Iron Age (5th-3rd century), all from the site Meteren-De Bogen. According to Van den Broeke (2014), these inhumation graves are of locals who practiced variations in burial practices, possibly altered by influences from other regions, rather than of foreigners or immigrants. A total of 23 inhumated individuals from various sites were sampled for isotope analysis, of which twelve exhibited strontium values of a local signature (Kootker et al. 2018). Therefore, the a priori chance that an inhumed individual was a local is almost 50/50. No such data can currently be generated for cremation remains, so an assumption that inhumation was the preferred burial practice for non-local people cannot be substantiated.

Burial practices and the treatment of the human body after death were divers in the Middle Iron Age. Besides cremation and inhumation, excarnation may have been practiced. In a Middle and Late Iron Age cemetery in Lomm, situated on a bank of the river Meuse, different types of structures were found in between the cremation graves (De Leeuwe & Prangsma 2011). These were linear post rows, and structures with three, four, and six posts. Given the context of the structures, a relation with the use of the cemetery and the performance of burial rites seems evident. The post structures in Lomm were interpreted as platforms or scaffolds, possibly used for excarnation purposes.

5.2.2 Human remains in wet contexts

Unburnt (Middle) Iron Age human remains are also known from contexts other than inhumation burials. Best known are human remains found in the northeast of the Netherlands, quite well preserved in peat bogs (Van der Sanden 1990). Depositions of human corpses in bogs was a wide spread phenomenon from Scandinavia to Ireland. Many of these 'bog bodies' showed mutilation and trauma that they suffered before, or at the time of death, such as a cut throat or other cut body parts, strangulation or a smashed skull. The oldest bodies were deposited in bogs in the Bronze Age, but most date from the Late Iron Age to the 3rd-4th century CE (Ibid., 206-207). Two cases in the Netherlands can be dated to the Middle Iron Age. One was the body of a man found in Exloërmond and the other was a separate arm. The exact location of the latter is unknown, as is the fact whether the rest of his body remained undetected when he was discovered in the 1920s. However, it is conceivable that the deposition concerned only an arm.

In coastal areas of the northwest Netherlands, separate human bones are occasionally found in relation to depositional practices (Hessing 1993; Kok 2008, 111). The practice of offering human bones in wet places,

---

15 Estimation based on searches of ARCHIS3 and DANS-EASY databases for the Netherlands (in 2020) and the CAI database for Belgium (in 2018).

such as creeks, bogs, and the edge of the coastal area, seems to have been performed from the Bronze Age until the 2nd century CE (Hessing 1993; Kok 2008, 206). Some of these bones were apparently stored over a period of time before being deposited, possibly even generations (Kok 2008, 171; Nieuwhof 2015, 283). When human bones were part of a selective deposition, they are commonly found among a spectrum of offered items such as cattle bones and pottery. Human skeletal remains have also been found in large rivers, some of

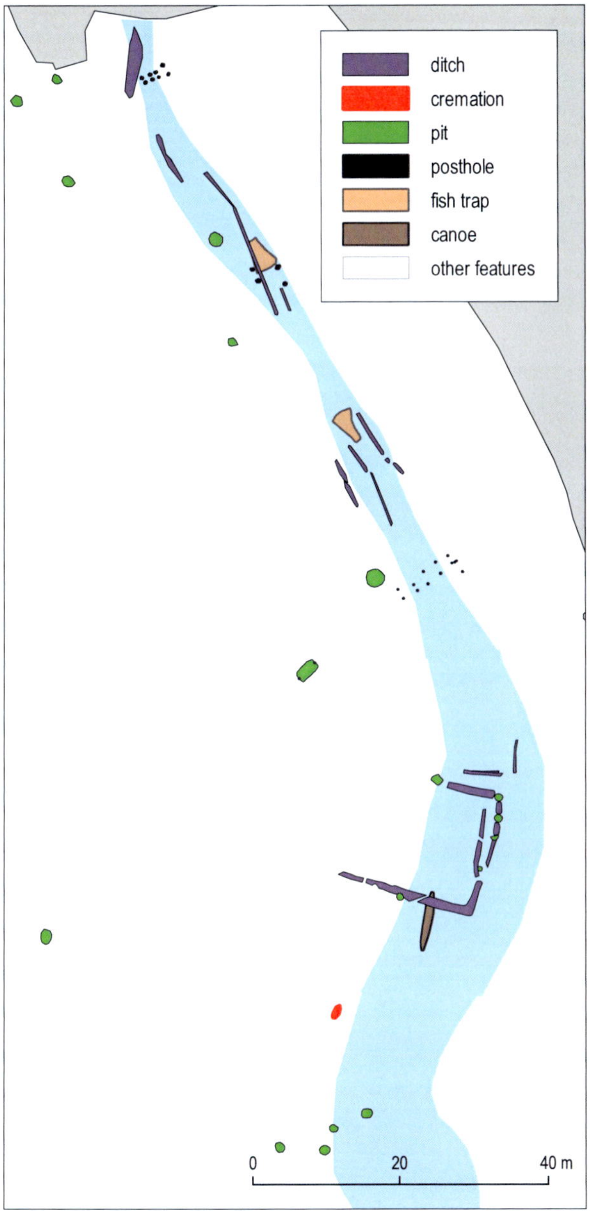

which date to the Early or Middle Iron Age. An example is the human bone material found at Lith-Kessel. Here, the rivers Meuse and Waal converged during the Iron Age (Ter Schegget 1999). Due to currents and erosion, disarticulated bones in rivers are conceivably all without a context, even though they are sometimes dredged up from the same location as other finds such as weapons (Fontijn 2002, 229-230).

Wet deposition practices can be comprehensively illustrated with one of the most prominent deposition sites of the Middle Iron Age: Houten-Castellum. A large scale excavation revealed the residual channel of a small river that had changed its course regularly during the Iron Age (fig. 5.2). The fills of the channel contained over 200.000 finds, more than half of which dated to the Middle Iron Age. The environment on the banks of the river during the Middle Iron Age are described as swampy (Van Renswoude 2017, 115). The landscape was open, with spread out patches of trees and some dispersed willows and alders next to the river, with fields and grasslands nearby (Kooistra 2017). The remains of two small bridges were found with two fish hoop nets in between them. Further south, parts of a rectangular ditch, measuring approximately 18 × 16m, was discovered on the river bank that was interpreted as a 'ritual enclosure used for an ancestral or death cult' (Van Renswoude & Habermehl 2017, 881-883).

Several pits seem to have been dug in the ditch. One pit contained a piece of a human skull and deer antlers with use-wear traces on them. Another pit revealed a whole human cranium, pottery and a spindle whorl. The first skull, and a third skull found in the channel, showed damage that could be ascribed to displaying them on a stake: both craniums were damaged by a force or tool from below (Panhuysen 2017). An incomplete skeleton interpreted as a grave was found only 17m south of the rectangular structure, dated 350-250 BCE, contemporary to the rectangular structure. It consisted of a right leg and a right arm of an 18 to 22 year old individual, seemingly in a crouched position (*Ibid.*). The incompleteness was ascribed to erosion (*Ibid.*), although conceivably the find concerns a deposit of partial remains. Also, four human bones had cutting marks and a further five displayed gnaw marks, both possible indications of excarnation (*Ibid.*). In total 43 human skeletal remains were found that could be dated to the Middle Iron Age, most of them in the channel fills.

Most channel finds (Van Renswoude 2017, 110-111; 815), or even *all* of the Middle Iron Age finds in the channel (Boreel 2017, 64), were attributed to the displaced remains of a Middle Iron Age settlement that may have been situated on the riverbank, of which the features have since been eroded and the finds were washed away to end up in the channel. This is an unlikely scenario for several reasons:

Figure 5.2. Part of the excavation plan of Houten - Castellum displaying the residual channel (light blue) Middle Iron Age features and some of the associated finds (after Van Renswoude & Habermehl 2017, figure 6.8).

- The Middle Iron Age settlement was probably situated elsewhere, away from the active channel. Ter Wal (2012, 54-55) poses that the Houten channel belt was active on the site between the Middle Bronze Age and Middle Iron Age, with the risk of flooding by the main channel. In this period habitation was likely situated on the higher belt levee further from the channel. It seems unlikely that a settlement would have been positioned this near an active river that apparently flooded and meandered frequently. Settlement features dating to the Late Iron Age and Roman period were found on a subsequent river deposit.

- The human bones from the channel are attributed to an eroded inhumation cemetery (Panhuysen 2017). However, the human remains in the pits are interpreted as depositions, as well as for example a rare large pot typical for the period 450-400 BCE (Sinke 2017). Notably, nearly all finds originated from the south side of the excavation, not near the two bridges, but rather around the rectangular structure. The find assemblage in this site resembles deposition places like the English causeways (e.g. Pryor 2001; Parker Pearson & Field 2003; Bradley 2017, 61-65) or Oberdorla in Germany (Behm-Blancke *et al.* 2003). Nieuwhof (2015, 142; 270-275; 280-284) proposes that the bones of the dead were collected and kept for some time, after which they were deposited in pits, ditches or layers at an appropriate occasion. From this perspective the incomplete grave could be perceived as an intentional partial deposition of human remains.

- Several pits dating to the Middle Iron Age were found to be intact. These were dug in the older channel layers. These pits did not indicate they belonged to a settlement context, but rather indicate that the site was used in this period for deposition practices and offerings in pits.

- The amount of pottery and other finds are so numerous and altogether so heavy that it would need a powerful (flash-)flood to move these objects . Also, the conservation of the pottery was good. In none of the contexts pottery was found that was rounded to any extent in such a way that it was recognizable as the result of displacement by washing out (Van den Broeke 2017, 151). Most of the pottery deriving from channel layers were relatively large fragments. The context of the pottery assemblage was described as 'the nature of the layer, the distribution pattern of the finds, in combination with the nature of the find material indicates that the finds were deposited on the spot.' (*Ibid.*, 174, 181).

If from the above it can be concluded that most or all of these finds ended up where they were intended to be, and not displaced by erosion and currents, it is at least worth considering that Houten-castellum is one of the largest Middle-Iron Age deposition sites known in the Low Countries. The tradition of depositing a multitude of objects in a wet spot, specifically until the Middle Iron Age, fits into the north-European tradition as we also know it from Oberdorla or the English Causeways. Unlike these sites though, pottery was the most deposited item in Houten.

5.2.3 Human remains in a settlement context

In the riverine regions of the Netherlands human remains are sometimes found in a Middle Iron Age settlement context. Understandably, there is a certain bias here as the region consists of clay soils. Most Middle Iron Age settlements are found on dryer soils. It is likely that on loamy and sandy soils comparable practices occurred, but preservation circumstances were less favourable and bone did not survive (De Vries 2021, 88). Bones and other organic material are therefore underrepresented in settlement contexts. At the same time, deposition practices in a settlement are not uncommon.

The known examples illustrate that deposition practices may have been varied in settlements, sometimes involving unburnt human remains besides for example pots or shards. In Meteren-De Bogen six human bones dated to the Middle Iron Age were found among Bronze Age settlement features (Meijelink 2002; Robb 2002, 680). They were discovered in two pits and two wells. Another contemporary feature on the site was an oval and a rectangular ditch that were interpreted as features surrounding a grave, although no grave was found in either one. On another site in Meteren, Lage Blok, a human calcaneus (heel bone) and a femur were found in a channel next to a Middle Iron Age settlement (Buitenhuis & Halici 2002, 168). Technically, this is a wet context near a settlement. A similar situation was encountered in Culemborg, where the frontal bones of two or three human skulls were found at the bottom of an old channel fill, along with many animal bones, 40 kg of Early- and Middle Iron Age pottery, and 23 kg of lithic material (Arnoldussen & Van Zijverden 2004). The channel was situated next to a contemporary settlement. Additionally, two fragments of human skull were found lying on the bottom of an Early Iron Age pit in the settlement.

Several human remains were found in the excavation of Kesteren-De Woerd, one of which could be dated to the Middle Iron Age. This particular find consisted of part of the skull of an 8-13 year old child, who had suffered a trauma causing the premature closure of the cranial sutures (Zeiler & Smits 2001). This deformation would inevitably have resulted in neurological disorders and likely a premature death. The skull was deposited in a ditch around the settlement. And in a settlement context in Odijk, part of a human mandible was found in a cultural layer (De Leeuwe 2022a). The layer contained mainly Middle Iron Age pottery and animal bones. The mandible probably belonged to a young male individual (Baetsen & De Leeuwe 2022). Isotope analysis indicated he was likely a local or regional (Kootker 2022). The mandible could have been part of a deposition or of a disturbed inhumation grave in the vicinity.

Besides the central riverine area, the north and northwest regions of the Netherlands have similar depositional practices. For example in Beverwijk/Heemskerk-Broekpolder, a human mandible was also placed in a ditch dated to the Middle Iron Age (Kok 2008, 110-111). In Englum (North-Netherlands) a group of eight human skulls, along with bones of cattle and sheep, were found in a manure layer during the excavation of a *terp* (artificial dwelling mound). In addition, a human skeleton was found, in poor condition and without a skull, and some loose skeletal elements were also scattered around, including a radius and a lower jaw (Tuin 2008). The skulls are dated c. 400-200 calBCE and belonged to at least six adult women and one man without any signs of trauma. As the skulls lacked a mandible they represent decomposed remains, possibly the result of excarnation (Nieuwhof 2008). The manure layer was applied to extend the living space of the terp and interpreted as a means of emphasizing the importance of livestock to the community (*Ibid.*). The event was likely accompanied by a feast that ended with the depositing of the bones in the manure and the partial burning of the remains. Nieuwhof (2008) further more interprets the skulls as a *pars pro toto* offering in an intentional deposition as part of an ancestral rite.

From the above examples it appears that Middle Iron Age human remains found in a settlement context are more uncommon than in wet contexts. What they share, however, is the fact that they are predominantly incomplete in the sense that only parts are found and less often complete burials. This incomplete presence is reminiscent of the treatment that is proposed for the special deposition of other types of finds. De Vries (2021, 186-187), for example, studied pottery depositions in settlements as 'special' deposition practices and demonstrated that these practices invariably consist of deliberate fragmentation, the selection of parts of the fragmented objects, and traces of secondary firing. Human remains found in a settlement context certainly seem selected parts, although intentional burning was only verifiable in Englum.

5.3 The 5th century BCE

In the Marne-mid-Rhine-Moselle region, the 5th century BCE was characterized by graves containing prestigious chariots, tableware and weapons decorated with gold, coral and amber in a new decorative style (Diepeveen 2001, 26).

These objects are known from grave inventories found in wooden burial chambers, covered by large burial mounts, and described as a 'set' having belonged to members of the elite that was part of a new social structure (*Ibid.*, 31, 64). In the Low Countries 36 burials have been found that could be classified as 'elite' burials, containing one or more of the 'set'-items (Van den Dikkenberg 2020). In large parts of Europe, the elite groups lived in fortified hilltop settlements interpreted as their royal residences or *Fürstensitze* (Kimmig 1969; Biel 2007; Nakoinz 2013; Fernández-Götz & Krausse 2016). A well-documented example of a hilltop residence is Mont Lassois near Vix (Ch.3.2.3) with the man-high 'crater of Vix' representing the extreme end of drinking-related vessels. The research area, consisting mostly of a flat or slightly hilly landscape, only hosts a few of such fortified settlements. On the hilltop of the 'Kemmelberg' in the southwest of Belgium for example, excavations in the 60s and 70s revealed several settlement features and large defensive ditch-and-bank constructions that were in use during the 6th, 5th and possibly early 4th century BCE (Van Dorselaer 1974; De Mulder & Putman 2006). The so-called Kemmelware pottery, named after the site, has been suggested to have been made specifically for the elite in the region, as a means for exchange with other elite members (Palmer 2009/2010, 72-73).

5.3.1 The pottery deposition of Kooigem

About 40 km due east of the Kemmelberg lies the site of Kooigem, where another hilltop settlement was found. Limited small-scale excavations revealed several settlement features dating to the 5th and 4th century BCE (De Cock 1987). More relevantly to this thesis, a rectangular structure was uncovered that remains the best documented part of the site (Termote 1987). It consisted of a rectangular ditch of 25.5 × 21.5m, situated on the edge of the plateau, near the top of the western flank (fig. 5.3).

The fills of the ditch can be dated to the late Hallstatt to early La Tène period (5th to mid-4th century BCE). In the soil layer above the recorded feature surface, inside the rectangular ditch, a large quantity of pottery sherds (N=9130) were found, dating to the same period as the finds from the secondary fill of the ditch (fig. 5.3, shaded). Fragments of pots found 5 to 7m apart could be refitted, indicating whole pots may have been broken on the spot. Termote (1987) interpreted the rectangular ditch as a cult place, but the large heap of pottery in the centre as settlement waste. However, three aspect of this find indicate that this was not an ordinary waste heap:

- Firstly, the large quantity was found enclosed by a rectangular ditch. It is unlikely that the primary function of the ditch was to enclose a spoil heap. This particular situation, where such a large quantity of pottery was

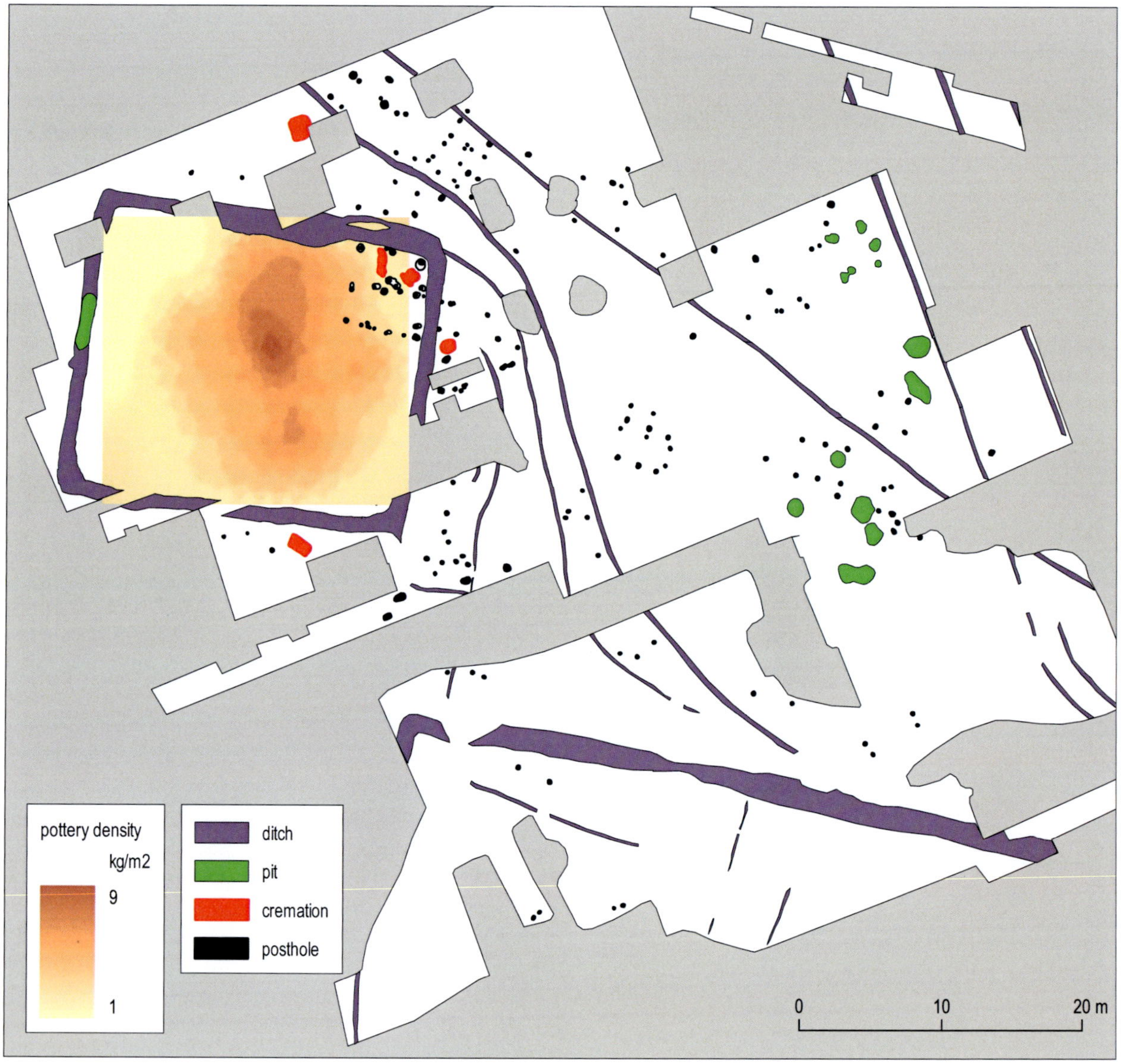

Figure 5.3. Largest part of the available excavation plan of Kooigem Bos (based on excavation data in the RAMS depot, Waarmaarde).

found inside of a rectangular structure is unique for the Low Countries.

- Secondly, the pottery consisted of specific types, two-third of which were *situlae* (*ibid.* 1987). This material deviated from the normal find layer on the site. Seemingly, specific pottery types were selected to be deposited on this location.

- And lastly, the fact that the pottery could have been brought to the location as whole pots and subsequently broken, does not contribute to the theory that this was a spoil heap.

The limited pottery analysis prevents the testing of the hypothesis that the pottery was deposited in a single event, or on reoccurring occasions. Also, it would be relevant to know if the pottery was new or had been previously used as regular table wear. Was this pottery made for a specific occasion, like a feast?

A separate pottery deposition of seven complete pots was found in the fill of the west side of the ditch along with cremation remains. The pottery could be described as a typical 'Groupe de la Haine' depot dating to 350-275 BCE (*Ibid.* 1987; Mestdagh 2008, 39). The pit for this cremation grave was apparently dug into the fill after the initial use of the rectangular structure. Other cremation graves found on either side of the rectangular ditch were undated, although their position suggest they were contemporary or added at a later time.

In the northeast corner a post setting was found, more or less contemporary to the rectangular ditch (*Ibid.* 1987). This was likely a small building of approximately 5.4 × 5.4m, interpreted by Leman Delerive (2000) as a ´domestic´ building. The southern half of this building, made of two parallel rows of posts, might have connected to some sort of bridge over the ditch on the east side. The building appears to be an entrance to the rectangular structure, rather than a regular settlement feature. The northern half of the building stood on the northeast corner and covered two shallow cremation graves. Other cremation graves were positioned outside to the east, south and north of the rectangular ditch, but none of cremation remains have been analysed.

On the east side outside the ditch a row of postholes 2m apart was discovered, possibly leading up to the entrance. Notably several narrow ditches were directed to the same location. Given the dimensions of the cross sections of these ditches, they could be interpreted as bedding trenches. Similar narrow ditches were suggested to be bedding trenches were found on the Kemmelberg (De Mulder & Putman 2006). Unfortunately they were not dated due to lack of finds. If these are bedding trenches contemporary to the rectangular structure and the building in the northeast corner, the whole set-up could represent an impressive entrance.

The large pottery deposit in the interior, the elaborate entrance, and the likelihood the site was visited on more than one occasion, are aspects that could be considered as use of the site as a 'cult place'. Like Gournay, the site is situated near a hilltop settlement, and the type of deposition in the ditch described above reminds us of the 4th century 'pit of the vases' found near the subsequent sanctuary of Gournay-sur-Aronde (Brunaux 1975).

5.3.2 Deposition of whole pots

In the Low Countries, depositions containing whole pots dating to the 5th century BCE are a reoccurring phenomenon. These are regularly found near rectangular structures. In Hever-Stationsstraat (Jezeer 2015; Ch.5.4.2) a half circular structure, enclosed by a large rectangular structure, contained a complete dish that was placed on the bottom of the ditch, dating between 450 and 375 BCE. In Brecht, a deep oval pit was discovered only 2 meters southwest of a square ditch (De Rijck 2019; see Appenix). At the bottom of the pit 173 shards were found belonging to several initially complete pots. Most were of Marne type pottery, dating to the 5th century BCE. The pit also contained cremation remains, although it is unclear if these also derived from the same context as the pottery. Like in Kooigem, this pit seem to have been dug with the intention of placing the complete pots in it, possibly as a grave gift along with cremation remains. Another example in a ditch was the deposit of two early La Tène pots placed in the fill of the ditch around a Bronze Age burial mound at Merksplas (Gheysen & De Mulder 2010).

In Houten-Castellum, a large pot typical for the period 450-400 BCE was found in a layer (Sinke 2017). Details on the location were not described, but the layer also contained the skeleton of a piglet and a thoroughly burned spindle whorl. These finds prove this site was used for depositions since the 5th century BCE. The pit in Houten was positioned next to a creek, which also yielded a canoe dating to the 5th century BCE. Likewise, in a pit on the edge of the historical course of the Bommelaere creek five whole pots were deposited (Beke *et al.* 2017). Two smaller bowls or cups were placed in a larger bowl; a fifth pot leaned against the smallest one.

The act of depositing sometimes seem to have been accompanied by the burning of the objects. In Itteren a pit with a layer of burned material on the bottom was found near a Middle to Late Iron Age cremation cemetery (Meurkens 2011, 93-94; see also Ch.5.3). It contained the shards of at least five secondary burned pots, along with burned stones, burned bones of sheep/goat and pig, charred remains of grains and wild plant, as well as charcoal. The pit was dated to the 8th-5th century BCE. According to Meurkens (2011, 93), this type of pits with a 'rich' content from the Early and Middle Iron Age are known from other sites in the south of the Netherlands. They are notable for large amounts of find material, including secondary burnt pottery, grinding stone fragments and burnt loam, and sometimes the material has been deposited in the pit in a specific manner.

Some of these depositions may have been part of a cremation grave. The cremation cemetery in Kemzeke-Kwakkel contained one grave with a bowl and a situla shaped vase that could be dated to the Early La Tène period, and another that held a different type of bowl typical for the 5th century BCE. Evidently, the 5th century was a time at which whole pots and sometimes various other items, either burned or unburnt, were deposited in pits in or near a location that was subsequently used as a cemetery. In Kooigem the deposition was related to a rectangular structure, in Brecht the pit with the deposition was just outside of a square structure surrounding a grave, in Houten and Bommelaere the pits were next to water (a creek), and in Itteren the deposition pit was found near a subsequent cemetery, while in Kwakkel they were inside of a contemporary cemetery. Perhaps some of these 5th century pits were founder graves, a local variation on the chariot burial.

5.4 Rectangular structures and their relation to graves

From the 4th century BCE onwards, larger rectangular ditched structures become more common (table 5.1). In the Middle Iron Age nearly all of these surrounded,

Site	Ditch date in century BCE	Main structure size (m)	Graves	Post-structure inside	Ditch width x depth (cm)	Ditch cross section	Finds in ditch
Aalter Woestijne	4th-3rd	48 × 27	Inside (5?)	No	200 × 90-200	V	Depot of six pots
Born Koeweide	4th-early 2nd	43.5 × 25-19.5	Inside (2), outside (1)	Yes	170 × 100, 160 × 80	V	Pottery
Boechout Mussen-hoevelaan A, B, C, D	4th-1st	31.9 × 15.6, 24.8 × 14.7, 23.9 × 16.9, 39.3 × 15.5	Inside (2), outside (1)	Yes	150 × 75, 125 × 50, 125 × 50, 120 × 45	V / bowl	Pottery, burned glass bracelet
Brecht Akkerweg	5th-3rd	10 × 10	Inside (2), outside (1)	No	100 × 20-40	Bowl	Pottery
Dendermonde Oud Klooster	?	27 × 23	Outside (4)	No	225 × 90	V?	Pottery
Gronsveld Duijsterstraat	3rd-2nd	12 x ?	Outside? (min. 3)	No	200 × 110	V / bowl	?
Hever Stationsstraat	4th-3rd	38 × 15	Inside (6), outside (17)	Yes	160 × 50-85	V	Pottery
Houten Castellum	4th-3rd	18 × 16	Outside (1)	No	75 × 10-60	?	Grinding stone pieces, human skull piece, human cranium, pottery, spindle whorl
Itteren Emmaus	Late 3rd – early 2nd	47 × 22, 28/22 × 22	Inside (4)	No	160 × 70, 120 × 80, 120 X 70	V	Two pots
Kemzeke Kwakkel, A, B	5th	30 × 20	Inside? (12)	Possible	120 × 50, 150 × 60	Bowl / V	Pottery , iron bracelet
Kooigem Bos	5th-mid 4th	25.5 × 21.5	Inside (2?), outside (10?)	Yes	110-200 × 85	V	Pottery and depot
Lomm Hoogwatergeul	4th-2nd	38 × 33.5	Inside (31), ditch (5), outside (25)	Yes	220 × 80	V	Pottery, sling shot bullet, a Roman fibula, cremation fragments
Oss Ussen R25/26	4th-early 2nd	33.5 × 32.5, 19 × 17	Outside (7)	No	120 × 70, 40-80 × 30	V	Pottery, loom weights, spindle whorls, iron slags, stones
Oss Ussen R49	4th-3rd	19 × 18.5	In vicinity (2)	Yes	100 × 50	Bowl	Pottery, spindle whorls, animal bones, sling shot bullets
Zundert Akkermolenweg	5th-1st	48 x ?	Inside (2), outside (min. 2)?	No	100 × 80	?	Pottery

Table 5.1. Middle Iron Age sites with rectangular structures.

or were found in the vicinity of, contemporary graves. What was the function of these ditches, so often interpreted as cult places? And how can the relation between the burial tradition and the rectangular ditch be defined? The obvious interpretation is that the rectangular structures were used to demarcate a cemetery. A ditch (and likely an adjacent bank) was dug around a rectangular space that was subsequently used to bury cremation remains. This could be perceived as a larger version of the features surrounding one or more graves in urnfields.

5.4.1 Rectangular structures surrounding graves

A cemetery surrounded by a ditch, and maybe also a bank, is a configuration that poses a familiar sight. Most present day cemeteries have a distinct boundary.

In the case of a churchyard this is often a wall around the consecrated burial grounds. Jewish cemeteries are considered holy places and have a status similar to a synagogue. Likewise, Islamic cemeteries ensure the eternal rest of their inhabitants within the burial grounds. In densely populated regions like the Low Countries it is a requisite that these places are demarked to guarantee their undisturbed continuation. Could such a demarcation have had a similar function in the Iron Age?

At first glance, a rectangular ditch that was excavated in Aalter seemed to serve this purpose: the demarcation of a cemetery. An area of 48 × 27m, was surrounded by a 2m wide uninterrupted ditch (fig. 5.4). Originally the ditch would have been sizable, with a 90 to 200cm depth at the time of construction (Langohr & Fechner 1993). It was dug down to the ground water level, where the ditch was

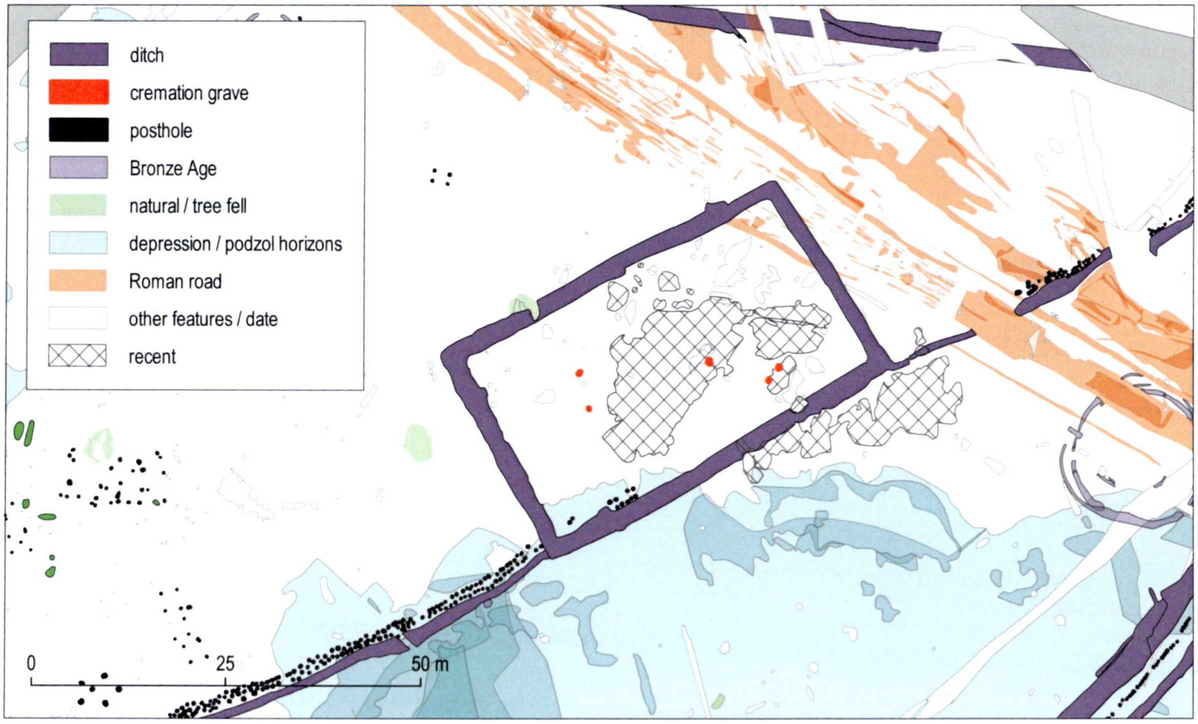

Figure 5.4. Part of the excavation plan of Aalter Woestijne (after Bourgeois & Rommelaere 1991, figure 16 and digital site plan De Groote & Van de Vijver 2019; courtesy of Agentschap Onroerend Erfgoed Vlaanderen and De Vlaamse Waterweg).

at least 50cm wide at the bottom making a slight V-shape in cross section. Such a large feature could easily serve as a boundary to alert people (and perhaps cattle?) of the presence of the cemetery.

The ditch could be dated to the 4th-3rd century BCE on the basis of pottery and charcoal (Bourgeois & Rommelaere 1991; Vijver *et al.* 2016, 114). Several poorly preserved cremation graves were found enclosed by the ditch and many features described as 'burn spots'. Conceivably, the cemetery contained more graves originally, but these were destroyed by later soil disturbances. At first glance, the simple interpretation of a demarked cemetery suffices here.

However, research of the ditch fills suggested that not only was it deliberately closed shortly after construction, the podzol layers of the soil that were taken out during construction were returned in the ditch in the same stratigraphic order (Langohr & Fechner 1993). The fill of the ditch consisted of a layer of large and small lumps of loamy sand at the bottom, suggesting some trampling and a thicker layer of humic soil on top containing charcoal layers and burned bone (Bourgeois & Rommelaere 1991).

In the southwest corner of the ditch a depot was discovered consisting of six secondarily burned and unburned pots, and some calcified bone on a layer of charcoal (Bourgeois & Rommelaere 1991). The pottery is typologically dated to the 3rd century BCE. Apparently,

after the ditch was dug, a pottery deposition has been made, and then the ditch was filled up. The only conclusion here can be that the ditch did not serve as a lasting demarcation.

Only two other cremation cemeteries dating to the Middle Iron Age entirely enclosed all of the discovered cremation graves. One of those, Kemzeke-Kwakkel, has an excavated area that was too limited to determine whether the surrounding area did not contain graves. The only other cemetery where the rectangular ditch could have served as a cemetery demarcation was found in Itteren-Emmaus. Six Middle Iron Age cremation graves were confined within two large rectangular connected ditches (fig. 5.5). The largest rectangular structure was partly destroyed by an old road that crossed it from north to south, which could have demolished additional cremation graves.

Of the Iron Age cremation graves five were found in the large rectangular structure and one in the trapezium shaped ditch. The cemetery was in use in the Middle and first half of the Late Iron Age, and after a hiatus of about 300 years, the space was reused as burial grounds in the 2nd century CE (Meurkens 2011, 74-77; Van de Geer 2011). In contrast to the rectangular ditch in Aalter, the ditches in Itteren showed signs that they were open features for a longer period of time. The ditches seemed to have filled in different phases. According to Meurkens (2011, 74) the bottom fill consisted of thin layers of

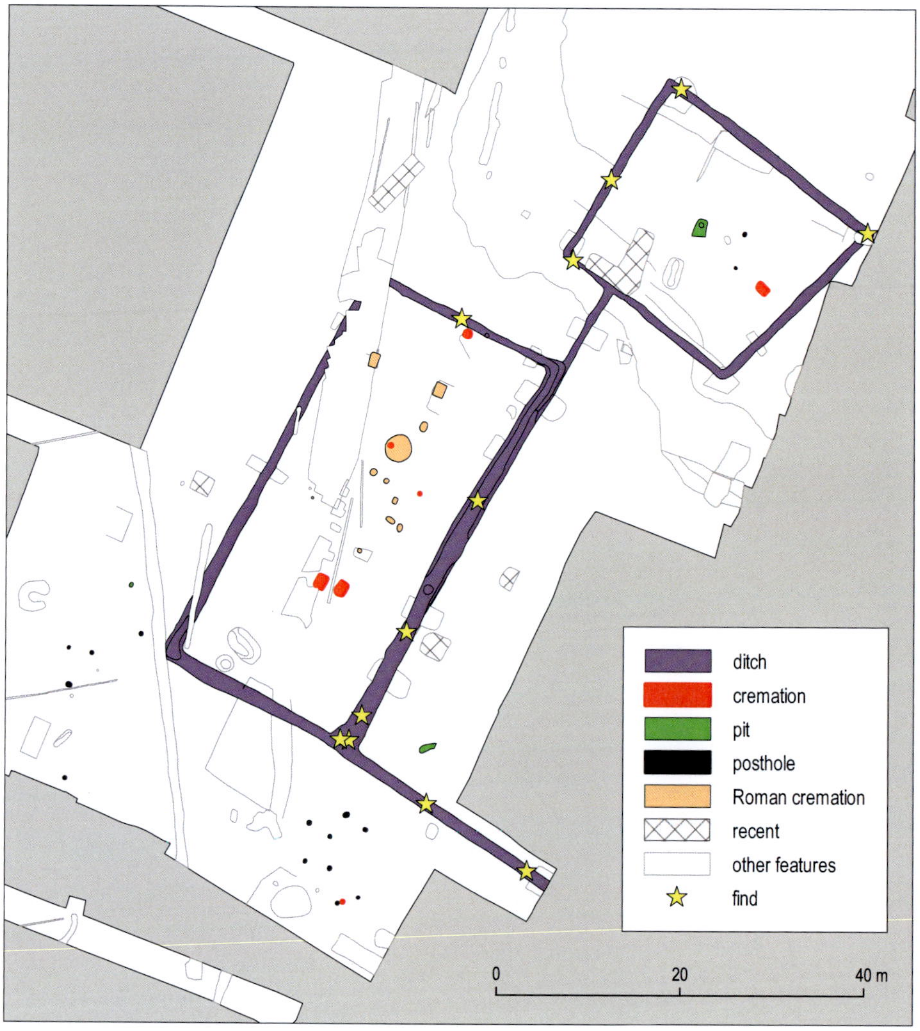

Figure 5.5. Part of the excavation plan of the southern site at Itteren-Emmaus (After Meurkens & Tol 2011, figures 6.1, 6.11 and 8.3).

sediments showing that it filled gradually, although a carbon date from the top and one from the bottom fill had the same result.

The large rectangular structure was reused in the 2nd century CE and therefore must have been visible in some way by the time the cemetery was reused. The upper fill held a mix of Roman and Iron Age finds, an indication the ditch functioned as an artifact trap at the time (Meurkens 2011, 74). But why were two of these needed? And why were they connected? Three aspects to their utilisation might provide insight:

1. The rectangular structures enclosed graves. It is conceivable the northern structure enclosed the grave of one person, similar in function to surrounding features in urnfield. Then, a second, larger rectangular structures was made to enclose one or more graves, after which more were added. This suggests not everyone received their own demarcation, and that on some occasions a new ditch was required. The

connecting ditch could symbolise a relation between the deceased or a relation between the events of their death.

2. Approximately 150m north of the rectangular structures, another cremation cemetery was found with 20 graves (Meurkens 2011, 85-92). It was used during the same time period as the first cemetery. If the two cemeteries were in use at the same time, one with demarcations and one without, perhaps the separate burial grounds had different functions or were these the result of two different groups of people using locations in close proximity of each other. The use of a second cemetery without a demarcation must indicate that the ditch not merely represented a simple cemetery boundary, as apparently not all cemeteries required a demarcation.

3. In several locations, pottery concentrations were found in the fills of the ditches (Fig. 5.5, stars). Some of the pottery was secondarily burned. As there were no settlement features found in the vicinity as a source

Figure 5.6. Part of the excavation plan of Boechout-Mussenhoevelaan (after Bakx, Verrijckt & Smeets 2018, figures 5.1, 5.3, 5.5 and 5.9; digital plan courtesy of R. Bakx, Studiebureau Archeologie bvba).

of pottery waste, the pottery must have been brought to the site to be deposited in the ditches. This activity was apparently only performed on this location, and not in the cemetery to the north.

These aspects imply that the rectangular structures were not merely made to enclose a few graves. A rectangular ditch was only constructed on a specific occasion and used for pottery depositions. On the site of Boechout, even more connected rectangular structures were found (fig. 5.6). There, the rectangular structures outnumbered the number of recovered cremation graves. Structure A and/

or structure B were the oldest (Bakx 2018). Subsequently, structure C, and then structure D were added. The ditches were continuous, apart from one 50cm wide interruption on the north side of ditch D.

Within this large monument, only two cremation graves found in structure A were contemporary, dating to the Middle Iron Age. The cremation grave overcutting ditch D and cremation remains found scattered in the north side of ditch B/south side of C both dated to the Late Iron Age. Cremation remains spread out over the structures are indicative that other graves were destroyed, even though the site was reasonably well preserved and covered by a layer of ploughed soil enriched with sods (Bakx *et al.* 2018, 26, 154).

Middle and Late Iron Age pottery was found in the ditches, but unlike Itteren, the pottery seemed dispersed rather than deposited in concentrations (Bakx *et al.* 2018). As contemporary settlement features were again absent in the vicinity, it must be assumed the pottery was brought to the site and finally scattered in the ditch.

In the interior of structure D six postholes were documented belonging to either one or two separate structures. In the interior of structure C a four-posted structure was found. Small structures with three, four or six posts, in or near a cemetery are not granaries, but possible 'funerary houses'. As a granary is a structure for the storage of crops generally found in fields or settlements, the small structures in Boechout are likely not granaries. Opinions are divided as to how exactly 'funerary houses' were used. Glasbergen (1954) notes that the structures likely served as a temporary residence for the dead before or after cremation and before erecting a funerary monument. According to Van Vilsteren (1989) the structures were part of the cremation itself, as a part of the funeral pyre. In both cases, these structures have a short utilisation related to burial customs.

5.4.2 Rectangular structures surrounding and near graves

Other cemeteries with comparable rectangular structures indicate the ditch was more often ignored as a feature than that it was used to surround a burial ground. At least as many graves were found outside of the structures as enclosed by it. The implication for this observation is that the rectangular ditch was apparently not primarily intended to enclose the entire burial ground or serve as a permanent visible boundary.

An excavation in Born-Koeweide revealed two rectangular structures, resembling the situation in Itteren. The site is also located on a lower terrace of the river Meuse (Van der Leije & Meurkens 2016). The ditch system consists of two connected rectangular ditches, of 43.5m and of 21m in length (Van de Leije 2016, 62-70; fig. 5.7). The smaller rectangular structure was probably slightly younger. As in Itteren, the ditches showed signs they were open features for a while. Only 310 sherds were found in the fill of the ditches, half of which were indeterminable small pieces and some was Late Bronze Age to Early Iron Age settlement waste (Meurkens 2016). Only a small portion was datable to the Middle to Late Iron Age.

Three cremation graves were found, two of which inside the larger rectangular structure. The third grave was found 2m north of the ditches (Van de Leije 2016, 63-65). The cremation remains were deposited in a 10cm deep, round pit, accompanied by a bowl. The burned remains were probably of a male of at least 40 years old, who had suffered from malnutrition (Velseka 2016). More graves could have been destroyed by ploughing. Even though only a few graves remained, their position indicates that the rectangular structures were not intended as cemetery

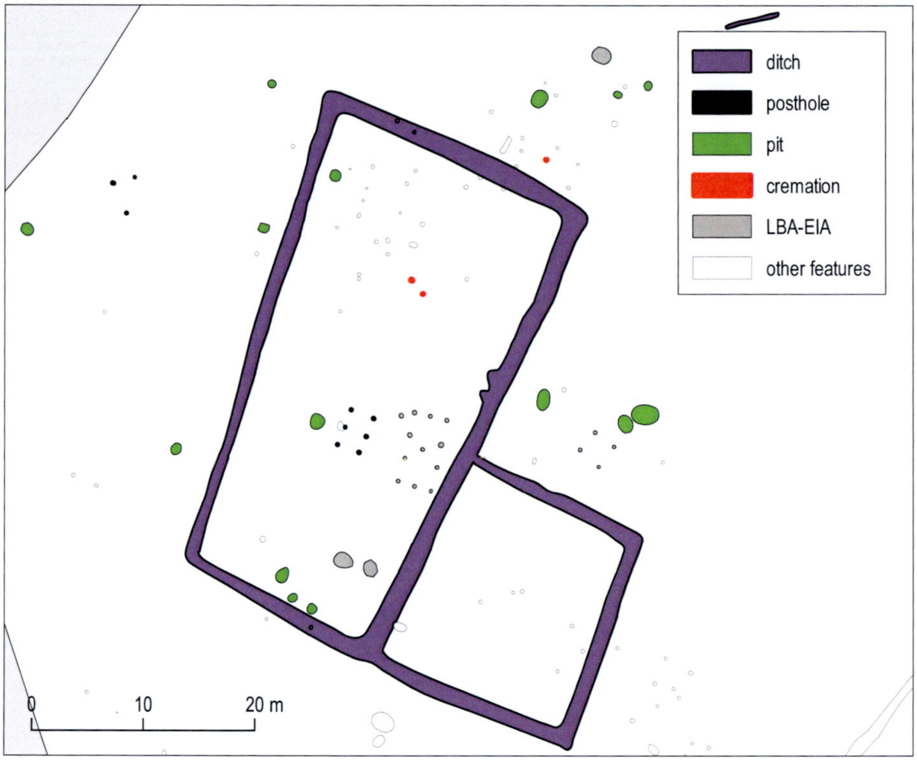

Figure 5.7. Part of the excavation plan of Born-Koeweide (after Van der Leije 2016).

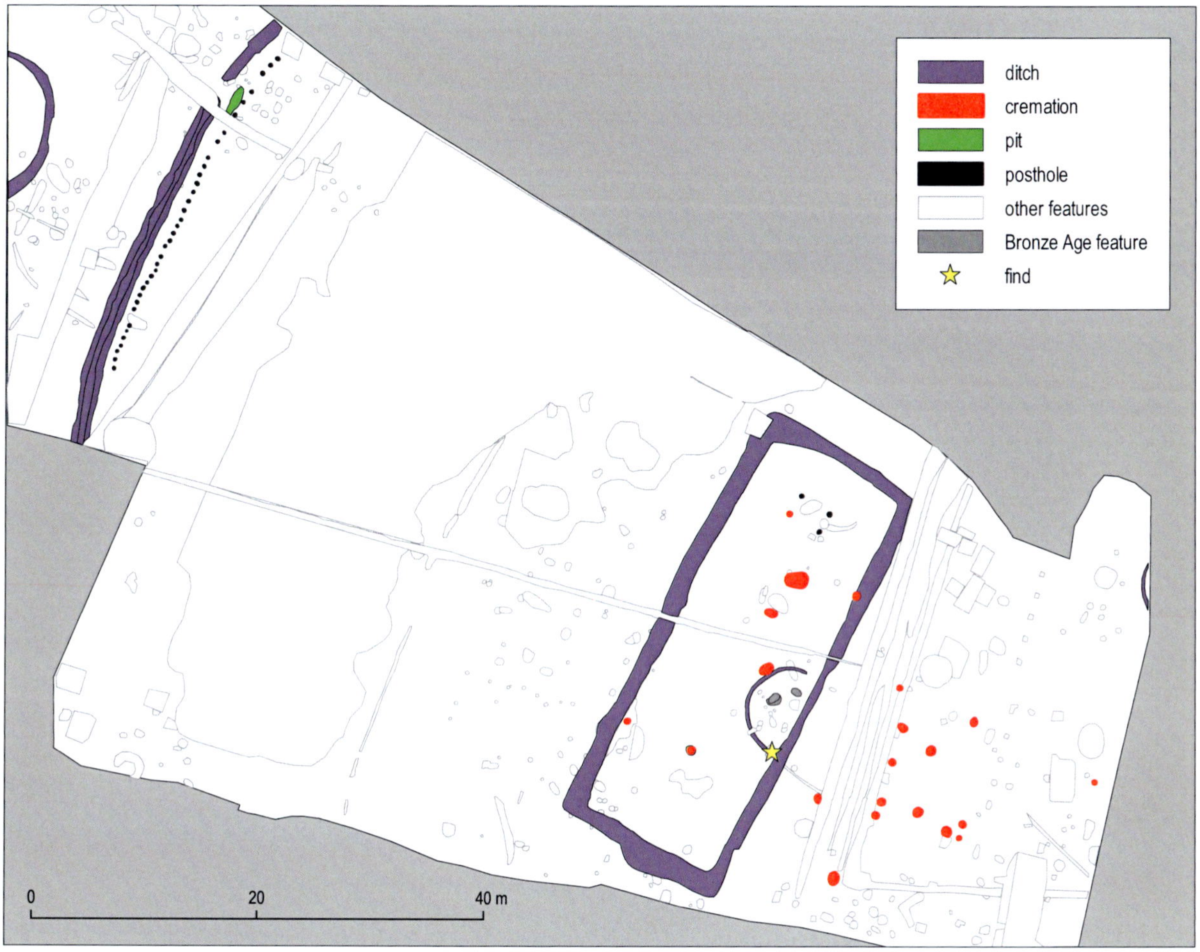

Figure 5.8. Part of the excavation plan of Hever-Stationsstraat. (after Jezeer 2015).

demarcations. The position of a six-posted structure in the centre of the large rectangular structure with the same orientation as the ditch is notable. All the post-constructions on the site are assumed to be part of a Late Bronze to Early Iron Age settlement (Van der Leije 2016, 55-62), but this particular structure was not dated. As a result, it could be related to the rectangular structures as a funerary house used for burial practices.

A comparable situation was excavated in Hever (Jezeer 2015). Within a rectangular structure a small four-posted structure was found. The eastern postholes of this structure contained a lot of charcoal. A single gram of cremation remains was found in the southwest posthole. The four-posted structure was either used as a pyre, or as a funerary house, and thereafter torn down with the open posts holes used as deposition pits. Only 63 pieces of pottery were found in the rectangular ditch, mostly deriving from concentrations in the southwest and the northeast corner, and a 5th-early 4th century pottery deposition, positioned almost on the point where a large rectangular ditch crossed over the circular ditch (*Ibid.*, 21; figure 5.8, star).

A total of 23 cremation graves were excavated on the site, of which only four were carbon dated (*Ibid.*, 26-33). Most were clustered east of the rectangular structure; six were inside the rectangle structure with a seventh in the ditch. One grave lay on the far west side of the excavation, beyond a palisade ditch over 50m west of the rectangular structure. The palisade ditch had a similar appearance to the rectangular feature and assumingly is contemporary. The dark layered fill of the ditches suggest they were left open and gradually filled in.

Jezeer (2015, 18-21) relates the construction of the rectangular structure to the cremation grave and the four-posted structure found along the central axis. It is conceivable the rectangular structure was built for one or more of the central burials. However, most of the graves have been found outside of the ditch, seemingly unrelated to its use. Due to the limited number of dates, it is not possible to determine the development of the cemetery. The ditch was left to deteriorate and ignored with the interment of subsequent graves. The occasion for its construction concerns either one or more of the central graves or is

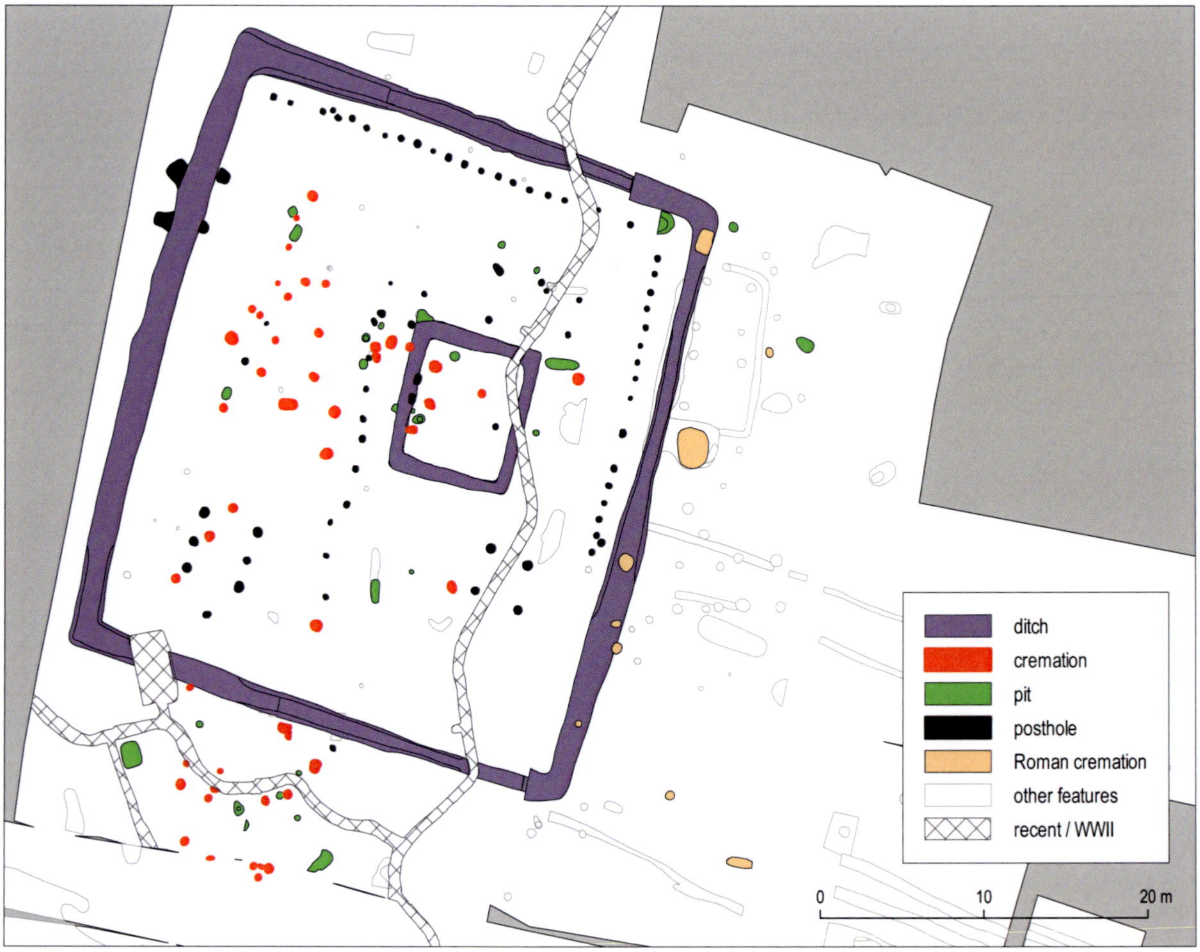

Figure 5.9. Part of the excavation plan of Lomm-Hoogwatergeul with Iron Age features and Roman graves (after Gerrets & De Leeuwe 2011).

related to another specific event. The possible function of the palisade ditch on the west side of the site becomes apparent when the site is compared to Aalter-Woestijne. This will be discussed in chapter 7.

More cremation graves were dated in the cemetery of Lomm-Hoogwatergeul, providing better insight in the development of the cemetery in relation to the rectangular structure (Gerrets & De Leeuwe 2011; Roymans & Derks 2014). The site in Lomm was situated on the east bank of the Meuse, on the sandy clay deposits only about 50m away from the water edge. A total of 61 cremation graves were found, enclosed by and outside of a large rectangular structure (fig. 5.9). More cremation fragments were found in the ditch fills. Two graves were dated to the Middle Iron Age. They were enclosed by the rectangular structure. Four dated to the Middle to Late Iron Age, one of which lay south of the large ditch and the others enclosed. A further eleven dated to the Late Iron Age and nine to the Roman era. The Roman graves are clustered on the east side of the (then filled in) large ditch.

The large rectangular ditch measured approximately 38 × 33m (De Leeuwe & Prangsma 2011). The fill of the ditch consisted of two to four layers, probably representing at least two phases. The initial construction phase was in the 4th-early 2nd century BCE.

Many features seem to be associated with the large rectangular ditch, most noticeable a smaller rectangular ditch inside. As no contemporary settlement was found in the vicinity, it must be assumed all of these features were associated with the cemetery and/or the rectangular structure. In the interior of the large rectangular structure, a six-posted structure was found in the southwest part, two four-posted structures, two three-posted structures, two rows of posts along the inside of the ditch on the north and east sides, and one or two rows just west of the longitudinal axis. Four larger postholes, two on either side of the ditch, on the northwest side, seem to indicate an entrance. Perhaps some sort of small bridge over the ditch was positioned here. The Iron Age graves were positioned inside and south of the

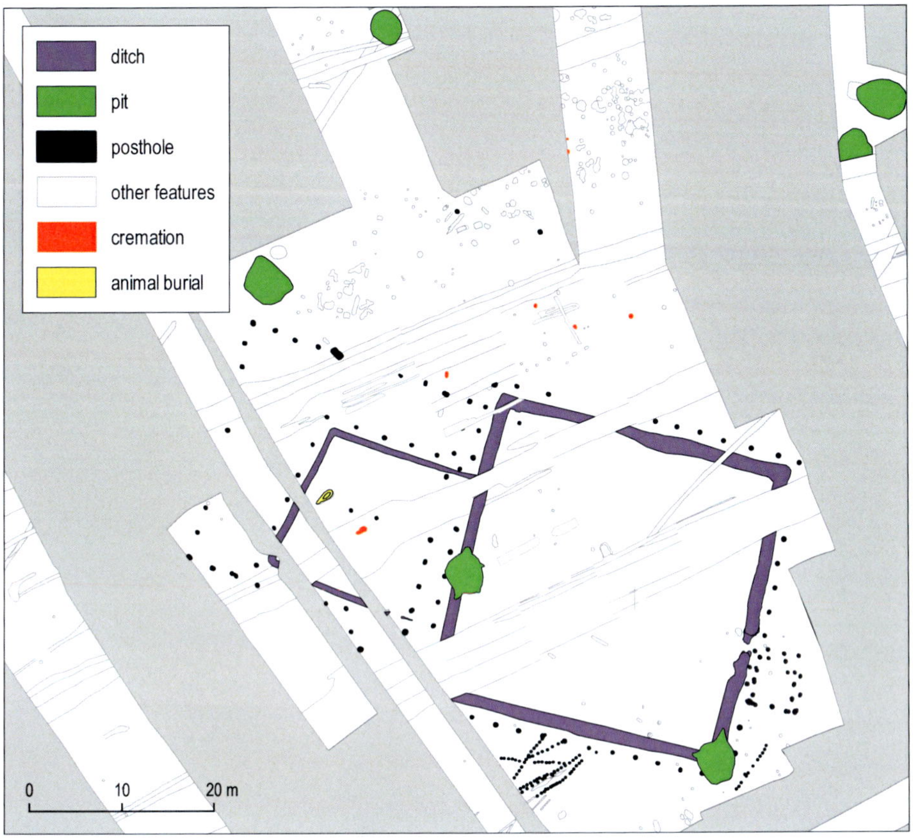

Figure 5.10. Part of the excavation plan of Oss-Ussen with R25/R26 (after data from the library of the University Leiden).

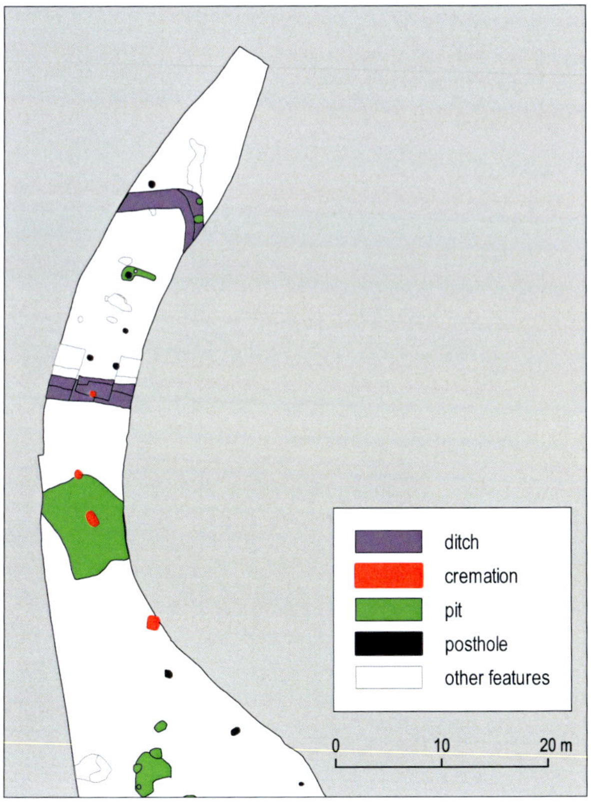

Figure 5.11. Part of the excavation plan of Gronsveld-Duijsterstraat (after Van Dijk 2009).

large ditch. In and around the ditch 31 pits were found, of which unfortunately only 17 were sectioned. Most pits were bowl-shaped in cross section and rich with charcoal, indicating that the burning of material in a pit was a regular occurrence. Their position in-between the cremation graves suggests their fill could be (part of) the cremation pyre remains.

This site seems to combine different burial customs that have been discussed previously in this thesis: a large ditch that functioned as a sort of temporary boundary, a small square ditch that looks like it belonged in an urnfield, and several small posted structures that seem to be associated with the burial customs. Apparently the Iron Age people of Lomm practiced a variety of burial customs. The main conclusion that can be drawn from the site is that apparently the large ditch was probably made around the time of the first burial and subsequently left to fill in slowly. It appears to lose its function or significance over time despite the fact that the location continues to be used as burial grounds. The difference between the burials inside the rectangular structure and those outside can partly be attributed to the period in which the burial took place. Not enough data could be generated out of the cremation remains to determine whether kinship, age, status, gender, or manner of death was a deciding factor for their place of burial.

5.4.3 Rectangular structures near contemporary graves

Due to varying circumstances it can be difficult to relate a rectangular structure to burials or burial rites. Graves in the vicinity still suggest a connection to burial customs, although the function of the structure can no longer be described as the boundary of a cemetery. Another explanation for the construction of a rectangular structure in this context has to be sought.

The centre of the rectangular structure designated as R25/R26 in Oss was crossed over by a recent ditch that may have destroyed a burial or other feature previously there (fig. 5.10). R25/R26 was first described in an article on 'open air cult places' by Slofstra & Van der Sanden (1987) and since then used by many authors as an example of a cult place. It consists of two connected rectangular ditches and post settings. The larger ditch (R26) is a square measuring 32.5 × 33.5m with a distinctly V-shaped cross section (De Leeuwe & Jansen 2018). The ditch seems to have an interruption (entrance?) on the east side. Postholes were found to be evenly placed (2.5-2.8m apart) just outside of the ditch. This is unusual, as R25/R26 along with Kooigem are the only rectangular structures in the Low Countries featuring posts *on the outside*. These posts were likely part of a fence or a wall.

The smaller ditch is connected to the larger one on the west side (Slofstra & Van der Sanden 1987). It is interrupted on the southeast side, but this might have

been the result of poor preservation. Postholes were found on the outside of the ditch as well as in a wider square setting.

Several features can be associated with the structure. Just southeast of the interruption of the large ditch, a small structure made of posts was found (Schinkel 1998, 263). It was reinterpreted as a part of the larger rectangular structure (De Leeuwe & Jansen 2018). The position of the structure next to the opening in the ditch suggests it may have been some sort of entry gate, a small building to pass through, or either a building for actions related to the use of the rectangular structure. Again the site of Kooigem is a good analogy, as a comparable structure can be interpreted as part of the entrance (Ch.5.3.1).

Two large pits were made in the ditch. The one in the southeast corner had a depth of 95cm and the one on the mid-west side was 140cm deep (Van der Sanden 1998, 282-312). Given the overlap, the pits appeared to have been dug after the construction of the ditch, or at least after the adjacent post rows. The ditches contained 1229 fragments of pottery, the southeast pit an additional 1792 fragments, and the western pit 283 (Slofstra & Van der Sanden 1987; Van der Sanden 1998, 325). The pottery from the pits could be dated to 350-250 BCE (Van den Broeke 2012, 34).

Inside the smaller structure a cremation grave was found and at least seven additional cremation graves in the vicinity (Schinkel 1998, sheet 15; see also Ch.7.4). As discribed elsewhere, structure R25/R26 is unusual for a Middle Iron Age feature, especially considering the amount of pottery (De Leeuwe & Jansen 2018). It still could be a theatrically elaborate burial monument although an interpretation as a cult place is feasible considering the different phases, the entrance, and the fence/wall on the outside. A V-shaped ditch like this has been found in Northern France type sanctuaries, also in connection to a wall and sometimes lined with wood, serving as a depositional receptacle (e.g. Brunaux *et al* 1985 figure 41; Brunaux 1986, 29; Lambot & Méniel 2000, fig. 11 and 19). The wall may have prevented looking in by people on the outside. Similarly, the large pits dug into the ditch of R26 served as receptacles for pottery deposits. This topic shall be further explored in chapter 7.4.

Another problem that prevents the testing of the hypothesis that rectangular structures functioned to enclose graves, is a limited excavation surface. An example is the site in Gronsveld where one corner and part of three sides of a rectangular structure were unearthed (fig. 5.11). Despite the incompleteness of the structure the ditches almost certainly belonged to the same structure with a width of about 14m (Van Dijk 2009, 43-45). In the top fill of the ditch stones, burned loam, and six pottery pieces were found. Three postholes were found on the south side of the inner space. Two small pits seem to have been dug in the fill of the ditch on the northeast side.

Figure 5.12. Part of the excavation plan of Dendermonde-Oud Klooster (after Demey 2012).

In the southern ditch of the structure a cremation grave was found with two iron nails (Janssens 2008, 17). Three further cremation graves were uncovered south of the rectangular structure (Van Dijk 2009, 39-43; fig. 5.11). Unfortunately none of the graves were carbon dated. Two of the graves contained some burned loam and several pieces of pottery, one contained an iron fibula typical for the Middle La Tène-period (ca. 250-150 BCE). One grave was in the middle of a large spot of approximately 8 × 9m that contained 275 pieces of burned loam (3 kg) and three stones. The function of this feature is unclear, but the loam could be indicative that a small structure stood on that spot. The site seems to be the result of various activities, likely related to burial practices.

Not as well preserved was a rectangular structure excavated in Dendermonde (Demey 2012, 29-32). The structure is a rectangular ditch measuring 27 × 23m, orientated from the southwest to the northeast (fig. 5.12). The position of the site on the brown loamy sand of Flanders resulted in bad preservation and poor visibility

of archaeological features. As a result, some features were documented as fragments, as for example several parts of the same ditch. The rectangular ditch was barely visible at the excavation level, although at a lower level the bottom was clearer.

In the rectangular ditch 117 pottery fragments were found, in addition to the 100 fragments that were found at the excavation surface while uncovering the structure (Demey 2012, 29-32). Most finds were collected on the northwest side, including a deposit of two situla-shaped pots dating between 400 and 150 BCE.

Several ditches and remains thereof, were found north of the rectangular ditch (Demey 2012, 29-32). Only one could be dated as a contemporary, a fragment found northeast of the rectangular structure. The orientation suggests these two features were once connected, perhaps as some sort of annex. Four features have been interpreted as remains of contemporary cremation graves, even though two contained no bone fragments. One of the graves furthest to the north is an oval shaped pit with a deposition of charcoal and a large

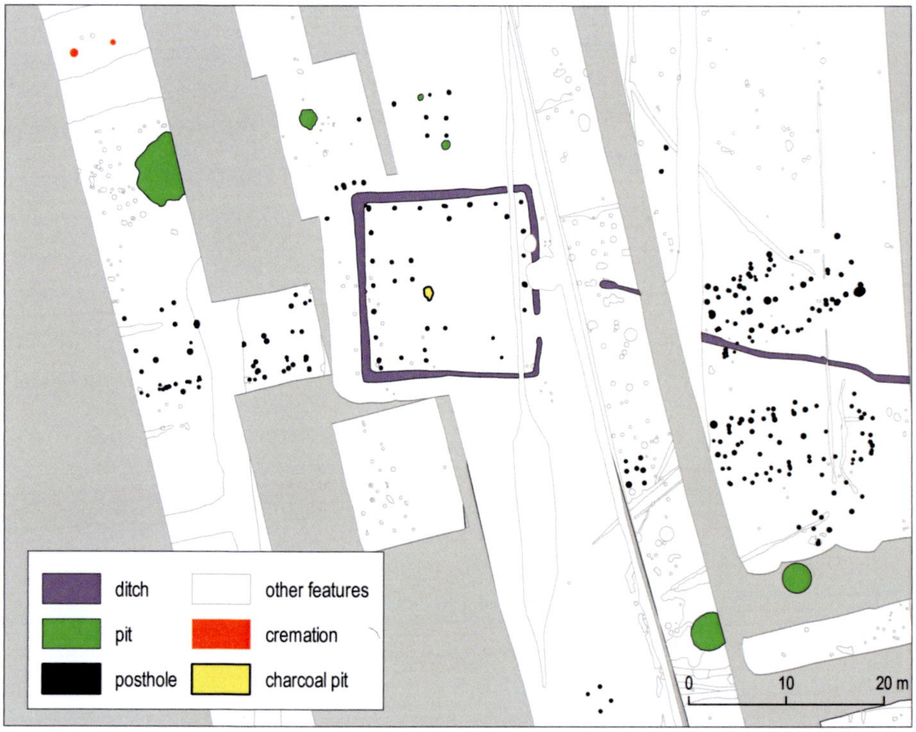

Figure 5.13. Part of the excavation plan of Oss-Ussen with R49 (after Van der Sanden 1998, figure 20; depository of the University Leiden).

burned pottery dish dating 400-150 BCE. Additionally, at least seven Roman period cremation graves could be identified. One of the Roman cremation graves was found in the top of the ditch fill. Due to the preservation state other graves may have been eroded.

The last example in this chapter was also found in Oss-Ussen, structure R49. As in the other examples mentioned above, no graves were associated with the structure. Based on this feature Gerritsen (2003, 167) concluded that cult places were constructed near farmsteads from the end of the Middle Iron Age (early 3rd century BCE), as a 'permanent structure for cults that did not focus on ancestors'.

Like R25/R26, R49 consists of a ditch and a post setting, although the posts were positioned on the inside (fig. 5.13). The ditch measured 18.5 × 19m and showed a 2.1m wide interruption on the southeast side.

Inside the ditch fill over 1100 pottery fragments were found (of which 75% in the western half), along with several sling shot bullets, a spindle whorl, some small stones, and burned and unburned animal bones (Van der Sanden 1998, 315-316, 330-331). The structure is situated 195m north of R25/R26 (De Leeuwe & Jansen 2018). The context of the location will be discussed in more detail in Ch.7.4. As with structure R25/R26, the interpretation of R49 is described elsewhere (De Leeuwe & Jansen 2018). The pottery from different locations in the ditch could be refitted (Van der Sanden 1998, 331). This can be perceived as intentional destruction. Secondarily burned pottery associated with the structure and a 'burn spot' in the centre also testify to destructive practices. The find assemblage is, however, not

different from common Middle Iron Age settlement deposits (Van der Sanden 1998, 315-316). The position of R49 suggests it functioned as a centre of activities within the settlement, including the making of depositions. In regard to the layout of the structure, it could have served as a cattle pen.

5.5 Discussion on rectangular structures in the Middle Iron Age

This chapter set out to test the hypothesis that from the early 3rd century BCE onwards rectangular ditches and/or palisade enclosures were in use as 'local open-air cult places'. From the above it can be established that rectangular structures that are interpreted as 'cult places' were used during the entire Middle Iron Age, from the 5th to the 3rd century BCE. When these sites are compared on criteria that derived from the northern French definition of a cult place, only one site stands out: Houten-Castellum (table 5.2).

The location in Houten-Castellum was used as a place for depositions or pottery, metal objects and animal bones, and probably also for displaying human skulls or heads on a stake. Hence, the type of structure (type 3) in Houten can be interpreted as 'cult place', or a 'wet deposition site' as a reference to sites like Oberdorla, a tradition to which Houten-Castellum seems to be related.

From the structures discussed in this chapter it transpires that three different types of rectangular structures were in use in the Middle Iron Age, distinguishable from each other by their appearance and their context. Notable the majority of the structures were large rectangular ditches enclosing,

Type of site	Century BCE	Weapons	Pottery	Animal bones	Human bones	Statues	Ditch (and bank)	Context
Square ditch as burial surrounding feature in urnfield (type 1)	6th-4th	-	-	-	-	-	+	Cemetery
Rectangular ditched structure (type 2)	5th-3rd	-	+ / +++	+	-	-	+	Cemetery
Wet deposition site (Houten) (type 3)	6th-3rd	+	+++	+++	+	-	+	Water / liminal place

Table 5.2. Types of sites with rectangular structures in the Low Countries and related finds and features (- = none; + = few, ++ = relatively common, +++ = many).

or situated near, contemporary graves containing pottery depositions: the 'rectangular ditched structure'. This is a type (type 2) of structure not recognised in the geographical framework (table 3.2). As the graves were not necessarily enclosed by the ditch, these structures cannot be defined as a burial monument or cemetery enclosure. The relation to graves is not the same as surrounding features in urnfields. Two distinct recurring aspects differentiate the 'rectangular ditched structure'-type from urnfields:

First, in urnfields the rectangular ditches are usually square, have smaller dimensions, are narrower and often with a shallow bowl-shaped cross section (type 1 rectangular structure). Type 2 structures which are the main topic of this thesis discern from urnfield features in their larger dimensions (commonly at least 18-20m long) and their larger cross section (originally approximately 1-2m wide and 60-100cm deep) which is often distinctly V-shaped. Also, their general shape can commonly be described as rectangular rather than square. Similar to ditched structures in urnfields, the ditch is generally of a temporary nature. It is not maintained and seems to have been intended for a specific occasion after which it was commonly left to fill in over time. Some of these ditches were still partly visible or still had some significance in the Roman era, when it was reused as burial grounds, as was the case in Dendermonde, Itteren, and Lomm.

Secondly, pottery depositions in the ditch are habitual. This is also in contrast to ditches found in urnfields. In urnfields, nearly all finds (if any) commonly derive from the graves. The pottery depositions in the rectangular structures are often not related to a grave and concern pottery that was brought to the site for an occasion. As almost none of the structures were found near or in a settlement, the pottery was brought to these structures on purpose and cannot be regarded as settlement waste. It may have been used in a (ceremonial?) meal, subsequently broken and/or burned and then deposited in specific locations of the ditch. This with the exception of some 5th century BCE pottery depositions, which involved whole pots.

On some sites, activities took place that could be referred to as belonging to a cult. The large pottery depositions in Kooigem and Oss-Ussen R25/26 can be considered here, and the manipulation of human remains in Houten. Also, in Lomm, Boechout, Kooigem, Oss-Ussen, Born, and Gronsveld excarnation platforms or 'funerary houses' were used, likely as a part of the burial tradition. However, can these sites be described as the 'local open-air cult places' Gerritsen, Roymans, Fernández-Götz and Derks referred to?

Assuming the total number of known cemeteries dating to this period is at least 100, approximately 1 in 8 or 9 is placed in or near a large rectangular enclosure. The sites either have graves inside the enclosure (N=2-3), both inside and outside of the enclosure (N=6), or one or more graves in the vicinity (N= 3-4). The association with graves was evidently relevant to the function of these structures, although it does not appear to have been the primary reason for their construction. Enclosing graves was not requisite. Ditch systems such as found in Born, Brecht, Itteren, and Boechout, which only contain a limited number of graves, look like they might initially have been made for a particular occasion and only later used as burial grounds. Itteren is illustrative, as most cremation graves on that site were located in a separate burial ground without an enclosure. Sometimes the rectangular structures were extended, with additional structures.

There was no evidence that any of the ditches were redug. The majority was connected to one or more other structures in the form of similar rectangular ditches or a field system. A connection to the land(-scape) was clearly of importance. Notable in this context is the location choice. Nearly all structures were found on a slope, although not on the highest location. This preferential location could be attributed to the perception of the place as a liminal area, or because these areas were in the proximity of settlements and not used or either unusable for fields or grazing pastures. The relationship between the rectangular ditches and linear landscape divisions will be further examined in chapter 7.

5.6 Conclusion

The main aim of this chapter was to test the hypothesis whether in the 3rd century BCE a new type of monument arose that could be referred to as a local cult place. Generally, the term cult place does not apply to these structures as their utilisation period nor the finds substantiate this theory. Neither was any evidence found that suggested that specifically in the 3rd century BCE a new type of structure arose, or that regular community gatherings took place in these structures. These type 2 rectangular structures were likely in use throughout a large part of the research area from the 5th-4th century BCE onwards.

Their primary function was not as a cemetery enclosure, as more often than not the ditch was abandoned or ignored

shortly after construction, nor can they unambiguously be described as a cult place. The only structures that seemed to have been used for repetitive depositions are Oss-R25/26, Kooigem, and Houten. In these sites multiple large pottery depots were found. Other sites also contained pottery, although not in similar amounts. In addition, several sites contained a pit with an Early La Tène pottery depot (Itteren, Brecht, Kooigem, Houten, Hever, and possibly Kemzeke). The relevance of pottery depositions and their significant role in the function of the sites will be further explored in chapter 8.

6

Rectangular structures in the Late Iron Age

6.1 Introduction

In the last chapter it became apparent that different types of rectangular structures were in use during the Middle Iron Age and that they were nearly all related to contemporary graves. As a result the structures were often interpreted as 'cult places' dedicated to the dead, the 'ancestral cult' or used for burial rites. However, through the sparse finds and often ephemeral characteristics it transpires that most of these structures cannot be designated as 'cult places'. The enclosures may resemble the shapes and sizes portrayed in northern French sanctuaries, but the use of the structures in the Low Countries was different. It appears to be a regional specific application. Several authors claim the association with graves changes in the Late Iron Age, as 'cult places become increasingly detached from cemeteries' (Gerritsen & Roymans 2006; Fernández-Götz 2014, 52, Roymans & Derks 2014). This hypothesis was formulated under two assumptions. The first is that 'cult places' were a pre-existing phenomenon at the start of the Late Iron Age. As demonstrated in chapter 5, the Middle Iron Age in the Low Countries did not contain cult places like the examples in France that these authors had in mind. So perhaps structures that can be called 'cult places' developed in the course of the Late Iron Age?

The second assumption is that the Late Iron Age structures functioned as separately operating entities away from cemeteries and the burial tradition, similar to the sociocultural function of temples and shrines in the subsequent Roman Era. If indeed the association with graves is relinquished, is an alternative interpretation such as a cult place a possibility? In this chapter I will examine if the rectangular structures of the Late Iron Age can be interpreted as cult places, and their relation to or detachment from cemeteries. The distribution of the sites mentioned in this chapter is similar to their Middle Iron Age predecessors, primarily on the sandy and loamy soils (fig. 6.1). A few were discovered north of the riverine area. Details of these sites are described in the catalogue in the Appendix.

6.2 Transition into the Late Iron Age

The beginning of the Late Iron Age is not marked by any significant changes in burial traditions like the transition of the Early Iron Age to the Middle Iron Age. The Middle Iron Age and the division between Middle and Late Iron Age was introduced by Verwers (1973) based on the rims of pottery types on several sites in the southern Netherlands. He marked the introduction of La Tène glass bracelets (or arm rings) as the beginning of the Late Iron Age. In the Low Countries La Tène glass first appeared in the second half of the 3rd century BCE (Van den Broeke 1987; Roymans 2004, 16-18; Roymans & Veniers 2009; Van de Geer 2014). In some parts of Belgium the Middle Iron Age was not introduced and the term Late Iron Age covers both periods. While it could be argued that the impact of the introduction of glass on Iron Age societies may have been limited, other

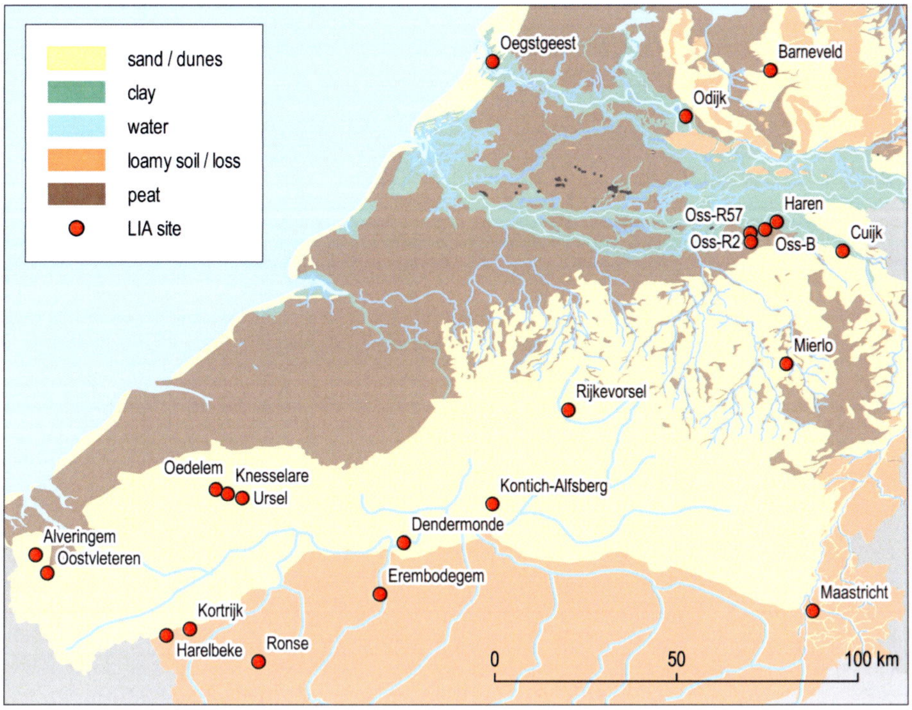

sand / dunes
clay
water
loamy soil / loss
peat
○ LIA site

Oegstgeest
Barneveld
Odijk
Oss-R57   Haren
Oss-R2   Oss-B   Cuijk
Mierlo
Rijkevorsel
Oedelem   Knesselare
Ursel   Kontich-Alfsberg
Dendermonde
Alveringem
Oostvleteren   Erembodegem
Maastricht
Kortrijk
Harelbeke   Ronse
0   50   100 km

Figure 6.1. Simplified soil map of part of the Low Countries for the Roman era, displaying late Iron Age sites. Paleogeographic map based on Mathys 2009, figure 7.45C (Belgium coastline around 1200 calBP), Belgium soil map and Vos & De Vries (2013) for the Netherlands around 100 CE.

observations within the archaeological record indicate gradual changes were taking place. Whereas in the Middle Iron Age farmsteads were dispersed and not rebuilt in the same place (Schinkel 1998, 170-173), in the Late Iron Age settlements became increasingly fixed on a location and were found to be more clustered in certain places of the landscape (Jansen & Fokkens 2002; Roymans & Gerritsen 2002; Jansen 2007; Fokkens 2019b; Jansen 2021, 339-341). A farmstead was rebuilt in the same place and passed down the generations within a kin group becoming a meaningful focal point in the landscape that they farmed (Schinkel 1998, 174-179; Gerritsen 2003, 261; Jansen & Van As 2012; Fokkens 2019b, 202). More permanently inhabited locations invariably occurred in conjunction with the need to secure good soil and exploit natural resources, resulting in the development of boundaries, visible by ditches around farmyards and settlements (Jansen & Fokkens 2002; Jansen 2007; Løvschal 2014; Fokkens 2019b; Jansen & Van As 2012; Jansen 2021a). Several excavations revealed long, linear ditches for which a defensive function was suggested (Jansen & Van As 2012). In a ditch around a Late Iron Age settlement in Oss-Schalkskamp over 200 sling shot bullets were found, interpreted as the dumped inventory of a household after an attack (Fokkens *et al.* 2019, 178).

All of these developments were likely the result from demographic expansion and increased pressure on arable land as is generally the underlying reason for significant changes (Roymans & Kortlang 1999, 37). The clustering of settlements and construction of ditches as

boundaries from the mid-2nd century BCE onwards, fits a general European wide trend. It could be perceived as the Low Countries equivalent of the synchronous development of oppida in other regions: the need for defensive structures, demarcation of territories, and demonstrable ownership of the land. Løvschal (2014) described these boundaries as process-related devices, demarcating social units from their surroundings by explicitly forcing people to cross a physical line. Within this increasingly divided landscape, rectangular structures, likewise made out of a physical and visible boundary, had their own intrinsic place and meaning.

6.3 Continuation of burial traditions
During the second half of the 2nd century BCE larger communal cemeteries of tens or even hundreds of graves were reintroduced (Gerritsen 2003, 147-149). The manner in which this communality is expressed varies locally. Some cemeteries consist of a cluster of 'flat' cremation graves (without surrounding features), while in others the graves were individually surrounded by ditches resembling past urnfields features. The latter type of cemetery could be in use for a longer period of time, well into the Roman era, while small clusters of flat graves are thought to represent a shorter period and a smaller community, such as a household (Jansen 2018). An example of a larger flat grave cemetery was found in Lomm (Ch.5.4.2). The cemetery that started in the Middle Iron Age, was continuously used in the Late Iron Age and into the Roman Era, totalling a minimum of 61 cremation graves.

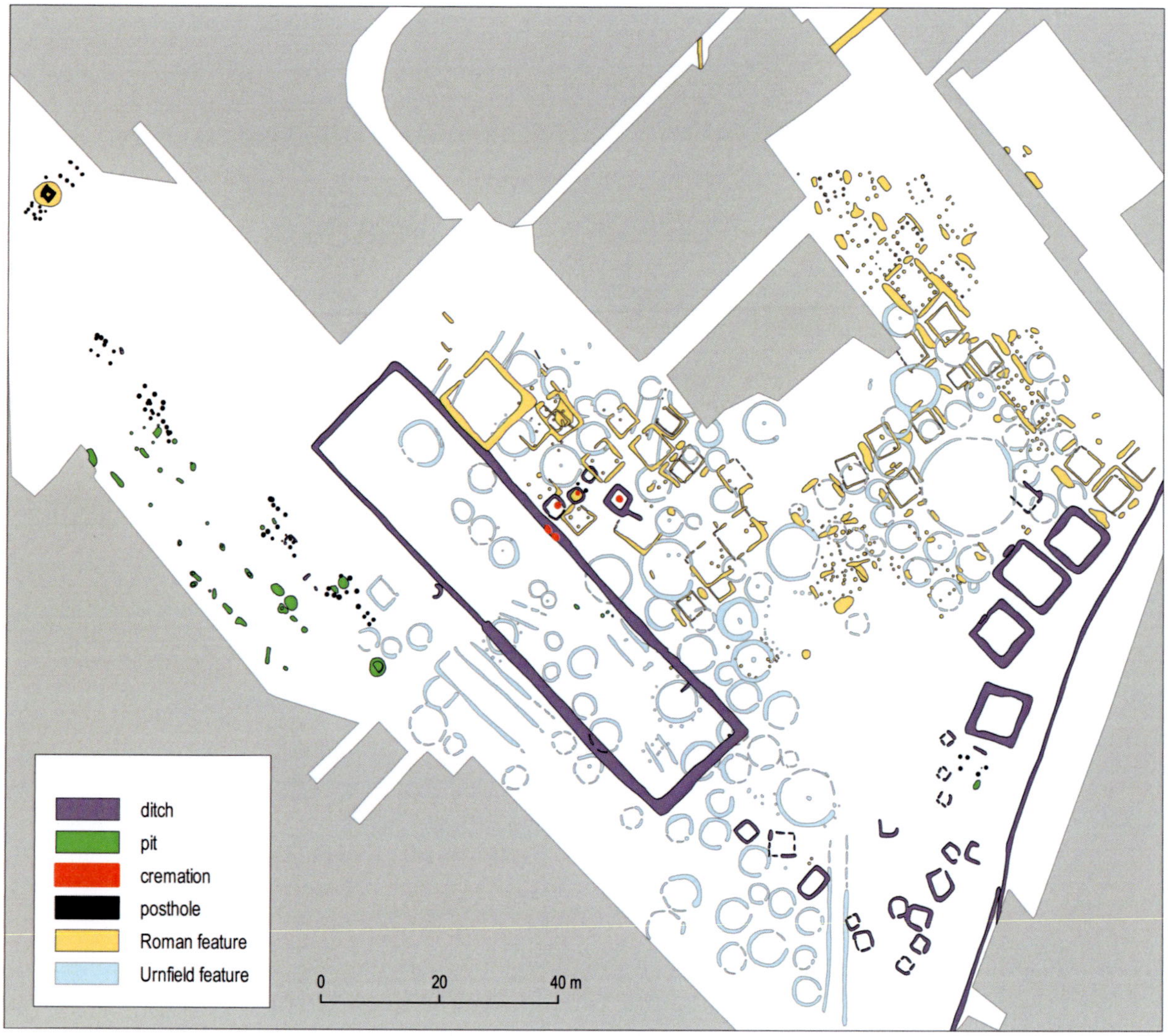

Figure 6.2. Part of the excavation plan of Mierlo-Hout (after Van As, Tol & Jansen in prep.).

Other cemeteries were founded in the Late Iron Age, sometimes on urnfields that were reused from the Late Iron Age onwards. Mierlo-Hout is an example of the latter, a large cemetery with surrounding features that used to be an Early to Middle Iron Age urnfield and was reactivated as burial grounds in the Late Iron Age (Roymans & Tol 1993; Tol 1999; Van As, Tol & Jansen in prep.). A large, 85m long rectangular structure was apparently the first feature to be constructed after the three century hiatus (Tol 1999; Van As, Tol & Jansen in prep.; fig. 6.2). Thereafter square and small rectangular ditches were added that presumably surrounded graves. Due to the poor preservation of the site only a few cremation graves were found in the excavation.

The 85m long rectangular ditch represents one of the largest cemetery structures found in the Netherlands. The fill of the ditch indicated it remained an open feature and it would have been visible for a prolonged period of time. The builders clearly wanted to convey a message by its construction. This statement could refer to the re-commissioning of the burial grounds and/or a 'founders grave' of an important person (Van As, Tol & Jansen in prep.). It is uncertain whether the older monuments, that the large structure crossed over, were still visible at the time of construction. Perhaps this crossing was intentional and the large rectangular enclosure was offered as a replacement for the lost burial monuments. In this scenario, the replacement structure may have served another purpose, to house a multitude of ancestral spirits thought to inhabit the site, rather than merely the singular one of an important person.

6.3.1 Including the ancestors

The manner in which Iron Age people perceived their ancestors is clearly expressed in the incorporation of

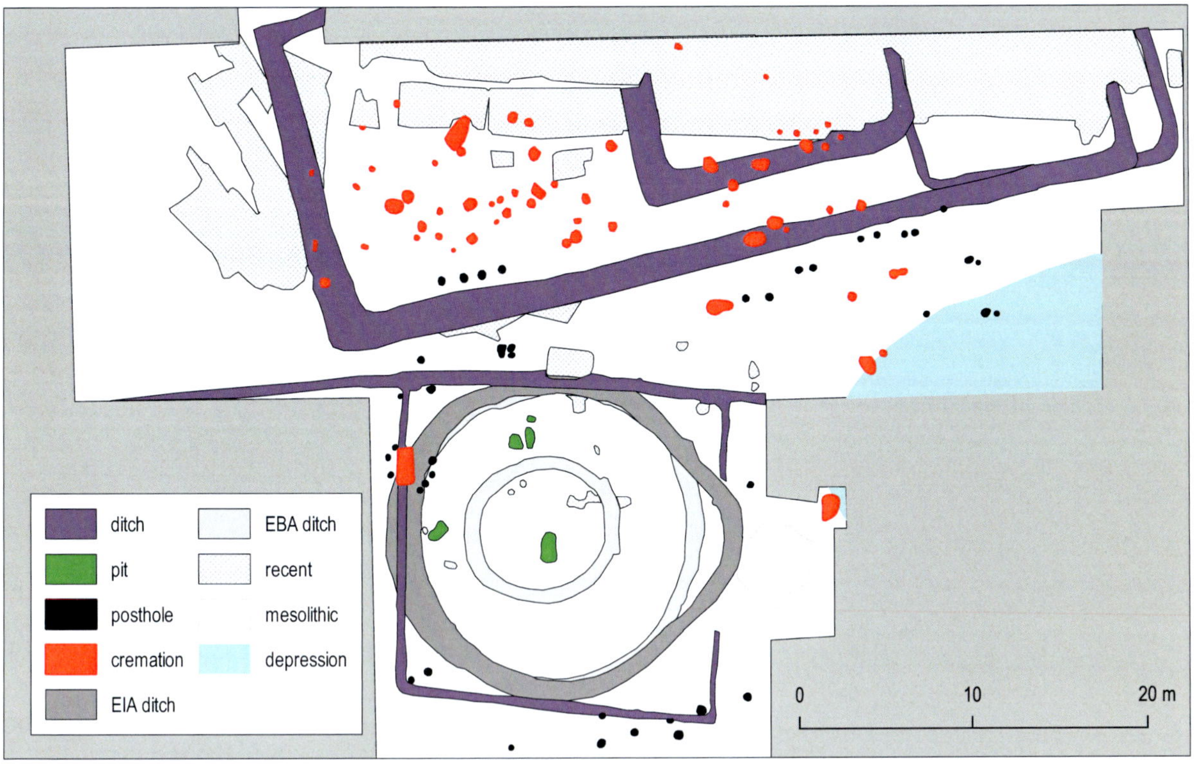

Figure 6.3. The excavation plan of the cemetery in Ursel (based on Bourgeois & Rommelaere 1991).

some of the older graves. Not only the direct relatives, but also the ancient 'mythical' ancestors were acknowledged as Bronze Age barrows were taken into account when the landscape was modified, arranged, and divided in the Late Iron Age. A Middle Iron Age example was found in Zundert. A small Late Bronze Age circular ditch (likely former barrow), was included within a large Iron Age rectangular structure (Krist 2005, 66).

In Ursel-Rozenstraat Late Iron Age structures and a cemetery were found adjacent to an Early to Middle Bronze Age monument (Bourgeois, 1998; Bourgeois *et al.*, 1989). The Bronze Age phase consists of two concentric circular ditches and an egg-shaped ditch overlaying the larger circular ditch. Over a millennium later, a narrow square ditch was dug around the remains of the barrow that used to be there (fig. 6.3). Additionally, three rectangular ditches were made to the north of the barrow, accommodating a cremation cemetery that was continued outside of the ditches. A short row of four posts was placed on the inside of the southwest corner of ditch B, facing the location of the barrow.

The square ditch was shallow and badly eroded. It is assumed to be a demarcation of the Bronze Age monument, constructed at a time when the tumulus was still visible. On the north side the narrow square ditch is connected to another east-west orientated narrow ditch, thereby incorporating the older barrow into a ditch

system. The arrangement shows similarities to Aalter, where two rectangular enclosures were connected to two separate linear ditches (Ch.5.4 & Ch.7.2). The east-west orientated narrow ditch is probably connected to a larger field system found only 200m to the south, that originated in the Middle Iron Age (Mestdagh & Taelman 2008).

Similarly, in Derdermonde-Hoogveld a circular ditch dating to the Middle Bronze Age A of 14m in diameter was found entirely enclosed by a Late Iron Age rectangular ditch (Vandecatsye & Laisnez 2009). Within the ring ditch, on the southwest side, a small row of posts was found (fig. 6.4). Their setting suggests a relation with the ditch or a barrow. These postholes were preserved to a maximum depth of 20cm. It is possible that originally the row enclosed the entire barrow, although one aspect about this row suggests that it did not. The orientation of the whole structure, the rectangular ditch system (ditch A and B), and associated post rows is towards the southwest, the side facing the short post row. What if the short row enclosed by the ring ditch is a significant part of the whole setup of the site? The posts were placed there to support something like a structure or a sculpture, conceivably representing or commemorating the ancestor buried within. In contrast to Ursel, the barrow in Derdermonde was not merely incorporated in the Iron Age arrangement of the landscape. Instead, the whole site seemed to have evolved around it.

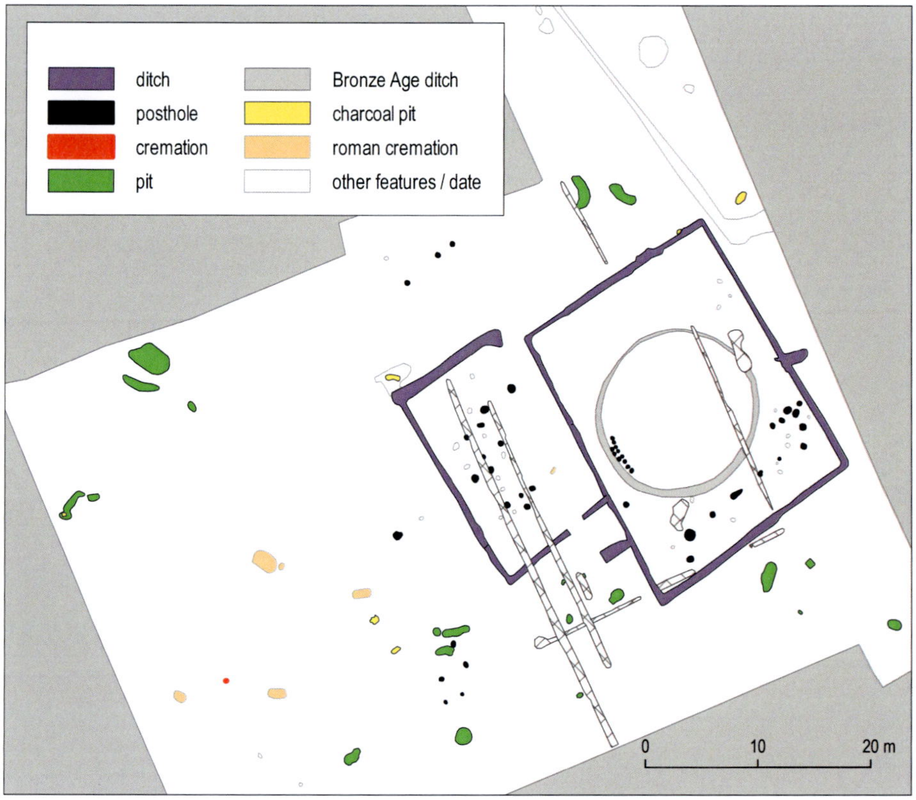

Figure 6.4. Part of the excavation plan of Dendermonde-Hoogveld (after Vandecatsye & Laisnez 2009).

The structures are interpreted as a 'cult place' purposely positioned around the Bronze Age barrow, that played a role in the burials of the deceased and the related customs (*Ibid.*, 27). The relation to the older barrow is undeniable, although the cemetery association is less evident as none of the cremation graves were proven to be contemporary. Is there factual evidence of a 'cult' or are the deposited cremation remains merely a different manner of interment?

To clarify the chronological sequence of events on the site, a description of the diachronic development is helpful:

- Initially, the site was used as a burial place in the Middle Bronze Age A. A ring ditch probably demarked the contours of a barrow, similar to the situation in Ursel.
- A short post row on the southwest represents the location of a possible ancestral 'marker'. The date of this row is unclear, as well as its residual visibility in the Iron Age. However, as Iron Age features align with the row, an Iron Age construction date is conceivable. The row looks similar to the short row of posts found in Ursel-Rozenstraat.
- A single cremation grave indicates the use of the location for burial ground in the Middle to Late Iron Age.
- In the Late Iron Age several features were added, such as two rectangular ditched structures and posts

structures within them. Ditch B is not entirely closed. It appears to have two openings, presumably the entrances. The post structure within ditch B is open towards the barrow, although not aligned with it. It may have supported a half open roofed structure. Cremation remains were by then added in ditch A, along with 19 fragments of pottery (*Ibid.*, 22-23). Several charcoal pits were found in the vicinity that unfortunately were not described in the report by Vandecatsye & Laisnez (2009). The contents of the pits could be ascribed to pyre remains as part of the burial process, or alternatively, to remains of burning material in an attempt to communicate with the spirits of the dead. A large amount of contemporary cremation remains were found in the charcoal rich fill on the east side of structure A.

- The site was used as a cemetery in the Roman Era, when most graves were added (fig. 6.4, red).

The sequence of events that transpired in Ursel-Rozenstraat is comparable to Dendermonde-Hoogveld. The short rows of postholes in both sites makes it more likely that these features originated in the (Late) Iron Age. The difference is the location of one of these within the limits of the barrow ring ditch and of the other within the limits of a rectangular ditch, facing the barrow. The relation to the barrow is in both cases undeniable.

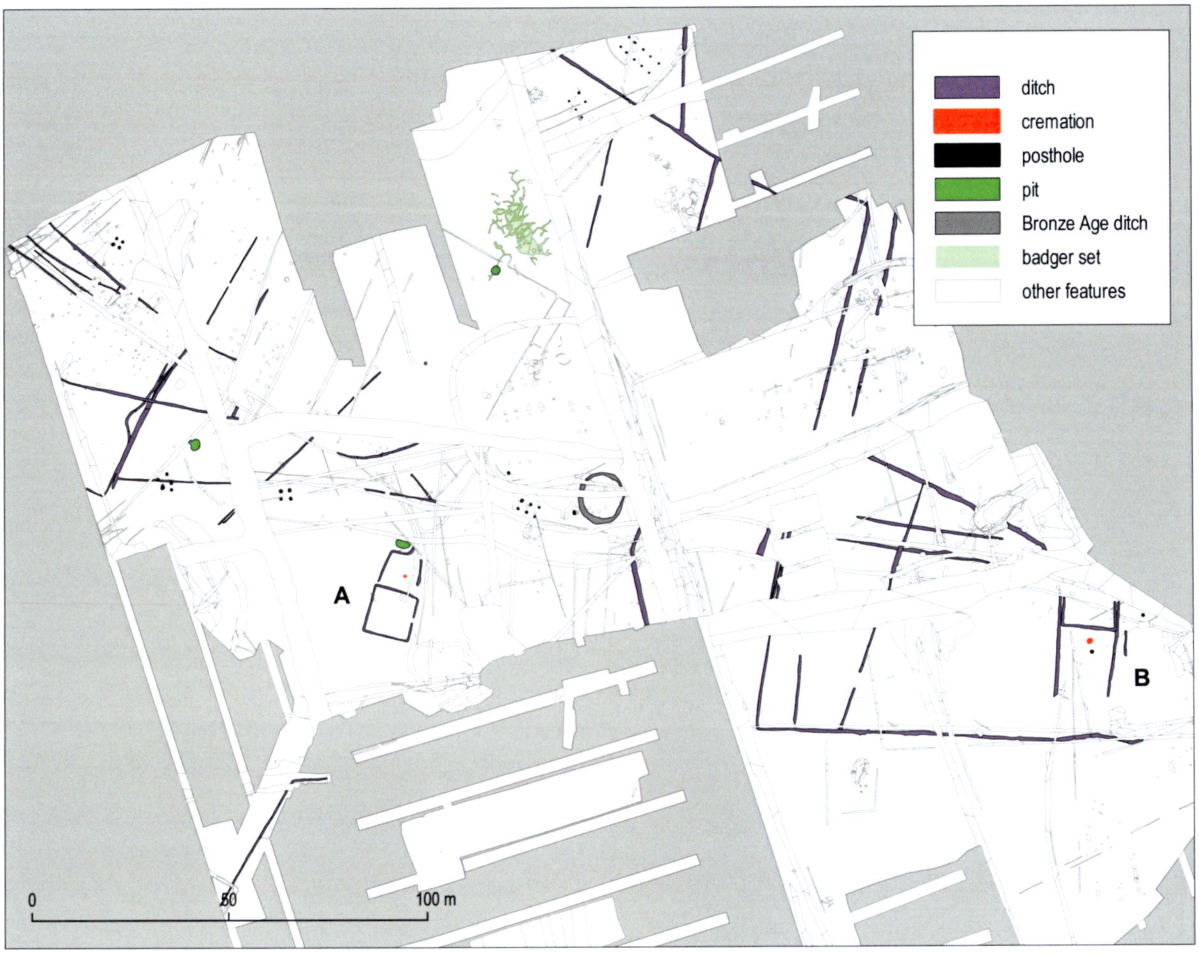

Figure 6.5. Part of the excavation plan of Ronse-Pont West (courtesy of Solva, after De Graeve 2020, figure 72).

In Ursel, most of the cremation graves date to the 1st century BCE and the 1st century CE. Several of the cremation graves cut over the upper fills of the rectangular ditches. As not all of the cremations were dated, it is presently not known whether any of the graves are contemporary to the rectangular ditches. The ditches in Ursel revealed few datable finds. Only five pottery shards were recovered from ditch A. Most finds were recovered from the top phase of ditch B: around 100 pottery shards and thirty pebbles the size of sling shots. Ditch C contained some lithic fragments and seven pottery shards, which could be roughly dated to the Iron Age.

None of the finds in the ditches in either of the sites indicate a use of the structures over a prolonged period of time. In Ursel, the ditches were likely consecutive rather than contemporary. A new one was dug when needed, making it likely the ditches were not open features for long. Their utilisation was ephemeral. Likewise, in Dendermonde-Hoogveld no evidence of ditch maintenance was found. Parts of the structures may have been added in a sequential order, and depositions in the ditch could

have been unique events that were contemporaneous to the construction of the ditch. An interpretation of the use of the rectangular ditches as a 'cult place' is therefore unsustainable. Yet, the function of the enclosure is unlikely to have been limited to the incorporation of a barrow. Instead, the purpose must have been the inclusion of the ancestral spirit(s) that were thought to reside within the barrow into the Late Iron Age arrangement of the location and the activities that took place there.

6.3.2 Respecting the ancestors

In both Ursel and Dendermonde-Hoogveld the ancestral spirits that resided in the Bronze Age barrow were managed by surrounding the place by a ditch. In the preceding part of this chapter I suggested this was done to include or incorporate the spirit into the Late Iron Age use of the location. The Iron Age people apparently felt related to the place and its residing spirits, or force a claim to the land in this way. However, there is another possible explanation. What if the ditch was meant to manipulate the spirit in a different manner, such as confining it to the enclosed space? The two interpretations of the rectangular ditch around the barrow do not have to be mutually exclusive. Even when the spirit was not confined by an enclosure, the barrow was still a place to be respected. Long-term elements in the landscape such as barrows could potentially mark a transition zone, emphasising continuity and constituting social anchorage (Løvschal 2014).

In Ronse-Pont West a large excavation revealed 4000 years of landscape use. In the Late Iron Age the landscape was divided by ditches, while several smaller structures, such as granaries, indicated settlement activities (De Graeve 2020, 183-338). As house plans and wells were absent and only a few pits were found, the core of the settlement seems to have been just outside of the excavation area. The ditch systems are interpreted as fields belonging to different farm yards. Notably, the ditch systems seem to take the central position of an older Middle Bronze Age A barrow into account (*Ibid.*, 117-131). The features belonging to two former badger setts north of the Bronze Age barrow (fig. 6.5, light green) could be an indication that more barrows used to be there, as badgers seem to have a preference for making their homes in barrows (e.g. Bourgeois, Cherretté & Meganck 2001; Doorenbosch 2013, 191; De Graeve et al. 2014; Bowden et al. 2014).

The Bronze Age ring ditch is respected by a ditch system to the west and one to the east. Both ditch systems are attached to a rectangular or square ditch 'annex'. To the west (fig. 6.5, A), the rectangular structure had an opening of 1m wide on the east side (De Graeve 2020, 281-285). Scattered in the fill of the ditch some charcoal was found, along with one small fragment of burned bone and pottery. The pottery consisted of large slabs of a situla in one location (not specified in the report) and part of a ribbed bowl in another, both heavily secondarily burned. The material could be typologically dated to the 3rd-2nd century BCE (*Ibid.*, 284). A cremation burial was found in a mole burrow 3.2m north of structure A, dating to 4th-3rd century BCE (*Ibid.*, 288-294). The rectangular structure attached to the eastern ditch system, was only partly documented as it was cut by more recent features (fig. 6.5, B). If any pottery was found in association with this ditch, it was not mentioned in the report (De Graeve 2020, 287). A cremation grave just south of structure B was more intact, accompanied by a couple of pots. The remains could be dated to the 2nd or early 1st century BCE.

Both structures A and B seem to have been positioned so that they physically connected a grave and a rectangular structure to the east and the west field systems. The Iron Age constructors made an effort to emphasise their attachment. In contrast, both of the field systems seem to 'respect' rather than include the Bronze Age ring ditch as if the Iron Age people preferred to include their own ancestors buried near the rectangular structures over the

ancient 'mythical' spirit(s) that resided in the barrow. The barrow functioned as a so-called point of 'articulation' in the landscape (Løvschal 2014). This situation is comparable to the site of Aalter-Woestijne, where a line of Bronze Age monuments is respected by the Iron Age use of the landscape. Both the Bronze Age barrows as well as the Iron Age rectangular structures had their predefined place in these landscapes. This topic will be further explored in Ch.7.2.

In the western Picardie region (northwest France) Late Iron Age cemeteries are found to be incorporated in field systems in a similar manner as the graves in Ronse. Small scale cremation cemeteries are situated on borders between field systems, sometimes at the end of a path, and enclosed by a ditch that is connected to a larger field system (Buchez 2011). Buchez (2011) remarks how the graves are 'enclosed but outside of the main enclosure' in a separate smaller enclosure. The layout in Ronse, and that of several other sites mentioned hereafter (see Ch.6.3.3 and Ch.6.4), seems to fit in this regional tradition.

6.3.3 Burial enclosures

In the Middle Iron Age there is a clear relationship between rectangular ditched structures and cremation cemeteries as all of the structures were found with graves

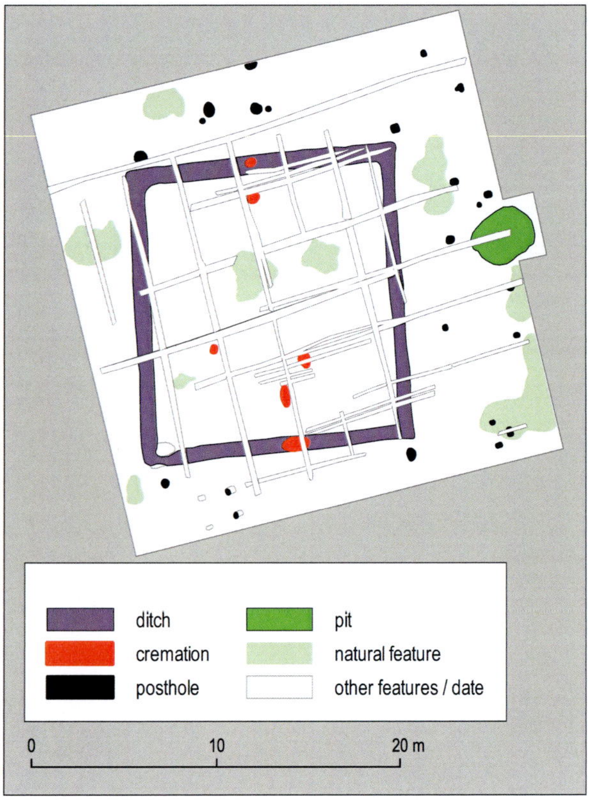

Figure 6.6. The excavation plan of Knesselare-Westervoorde (after Vermeulen & Hageman 1997, figure 2).

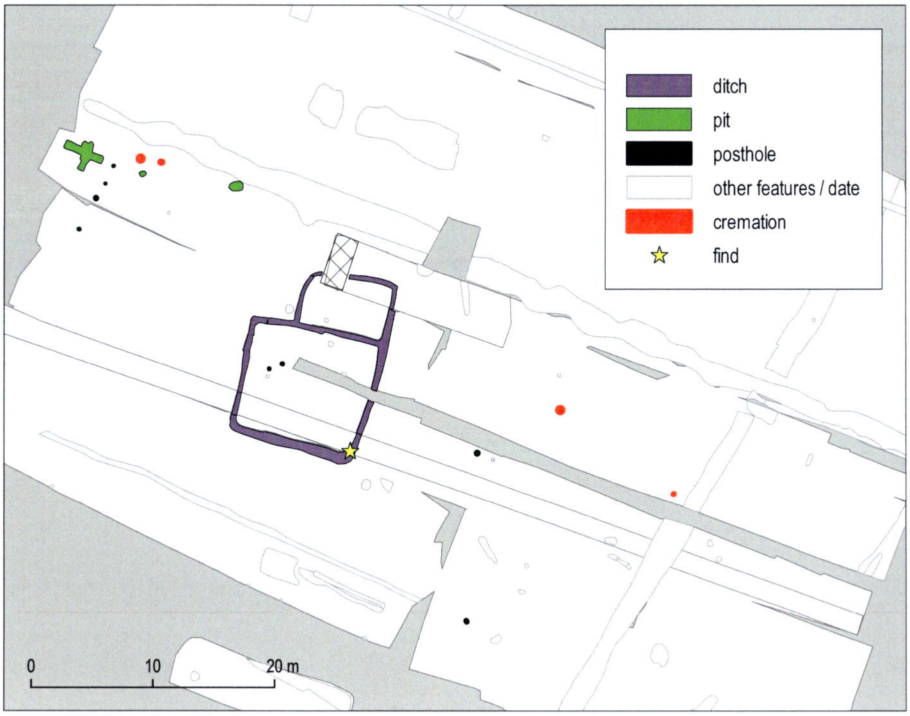

Figure 6.7. Part of the excavation plan of Haren-Groenstraat (after Knippenberg 2013, figure 7.1 and Schurmans 2011, figure 10).

in the vicinity. This tradition continues into the Late Iron Age. In Knesselare a Late Iron Age rectangular structure was found several tens of metres from the Roman road, but with a different orientation (fig. 6.6). The fill of the ditch showed two phases, of which the lower one filled in over a period of weeks or months after the ditch was dug (Vermeulen & Hageman 1997). Enclosed by the structure four poorly preserved cremation graves were found. Additionally, both in the northern and the southern ditch cremation remains were found. These were both dug in the ditch fill before it was entirely filled. The ditch seemed to have been used for a short period of time, mostly to accommodate several cremation graves. The feature could therefore be interpreted as a cemetery demarcation.

In the ditch 60 Late Iron Age pottery shards were found (*Ibid.*). In one of the large postholes north of the midsection of the rectangular structure a large fragment of an upside down pot was found. The pot was of a similar date as the pottery from the ditch. Numerous postholes were discovered around the structure (*Ibid.*). The fill of the postholes resembled the appearance of the ditch. Most noticeable were four postholes near the corners.

Very few of the Late Iron Age rectangular ditches actually entirely enclosed a cemetery. Some are found enclosing a few graves, while more contemporary graves are found outside of the ditch. For example in Haren, a larger and a smaller rectangular structure were found, connected to each other (fig. 6.7). The relative shallow position of the Iron Age features underneath the top soil caused them to be damaged by ploughing activities (Van

der Leije & Knippenberg 2013). As a result cremation remains inside the ditch could have been destroyed.

In the southeast corner of the larger rectangular ditch rim fragments of a Late Iron Age pot and a slingshot bullet were found (Meurkens 2013; fig. 6.7, star). Four cremation graves were spread out over the excavation area: two 15-30m east of the rectangular structure and two 20m northwest, two of which were dated to the Early to Middle Iron Age. The graves were found incomplete due to their shallow position. The ditch structure in Haren is interpreted by Van der Leije & Knippenberg (2013, 82-83) as a burial monument based on its limited size and the burials in the vicinity. However, given that at least two of the burials are older, they may be unrelated to the structure.

As usual, the lack of graves could be attributed to poor preservation. Mierlo-Hout was such an example, as most of the cremation remains were not preserved on the site. How many graves were associated with the ditch, whether positioned outside or enclosed within, remains unknown. In Ursel the graves were preserved, but their contemporaneity to the ditch is unclear. It is evident that the ditch was not respected for long after its construction. In Ronse, the graves seemed to have been deliberately positioned outside of the rectangular ditch. Summarising, graves are more often positioned outside of the ditch than within. A rectangular ditch was apparently not requisite to accommodate a cremation cemetery. However, sometimes the rectangular ditch did seem to have its primarily purpose as a cemetery demarcation. This was certainly the case in for example the cemeteries

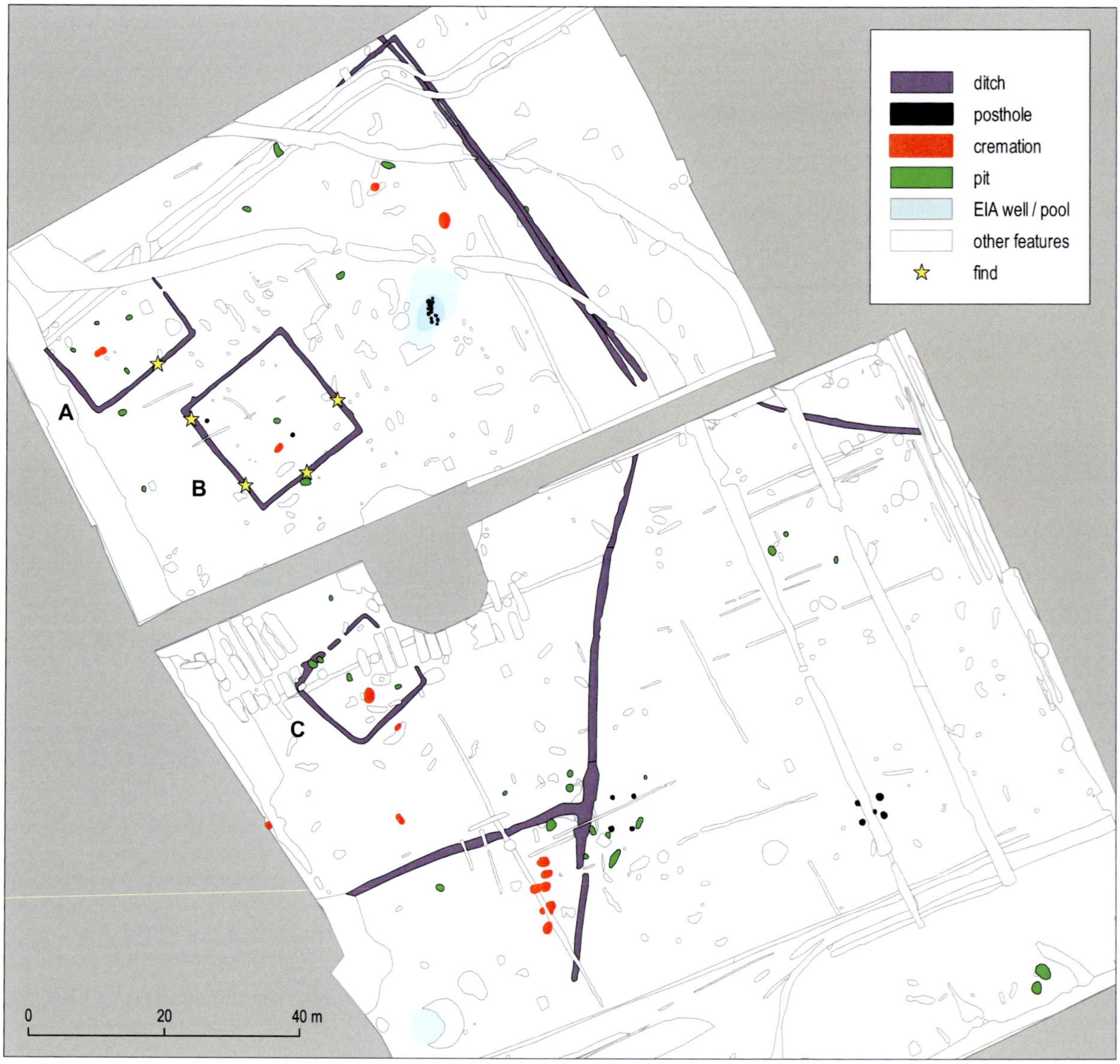

Figure 6.8. Part of the excavation plan of Oostvleteren-Kasteelweg (after Demey 2013, figure 6.1 and 7.1).

of Acy-Romance, although even there not all graves were enclosed by the ditches.

A more nuanced picture of the use of burial enclosures in the Late Iron Age emerges from the site of Oostvleteren-Kasteelweg (fig. 6.8). The excavation of the site revealed three rectangular and several contemporary linear ditches dividing the landscape (Demey 2013, 66-87; Demey *et al.* 2013). All three rectangular ditches enclosed one grave and several pits. If the excavation would have covered only the three rectangular structures, the conclusion that the local burial tradition was to enclose a cremation by a rectangular ditch could easily have been drawn. In actuality, the larger excavation area revealed that the burial tradition was more varied. Two 'flat' cremation graves (within a surrounding feature) were found northeast of the rectangular structures

and one more to the south. These were all situated within the same division of the landscape. Linear ditches seem to indicate the boundary of the cemetery to the east. Another cluster of graves was found south of the T-junction of linear ditches. These were positioned close together and in a (northern) corner of the field system.

Three aspects about this arrangement stand out. The first is that the graves again appear to be arranged in relation to a field system, and the second is that a feature surrounding the grave was not meant for everyone. Only three people were buried in an enclosure, while the others were placed near a junction of ditches, or on their own. An underlying reason for this preferential treatment such as age or gender is difficult to determine. For many cremation remains neither sex or age could be

RECTANGULAR STRUCTURES IN THE LATE IRON AGE   107

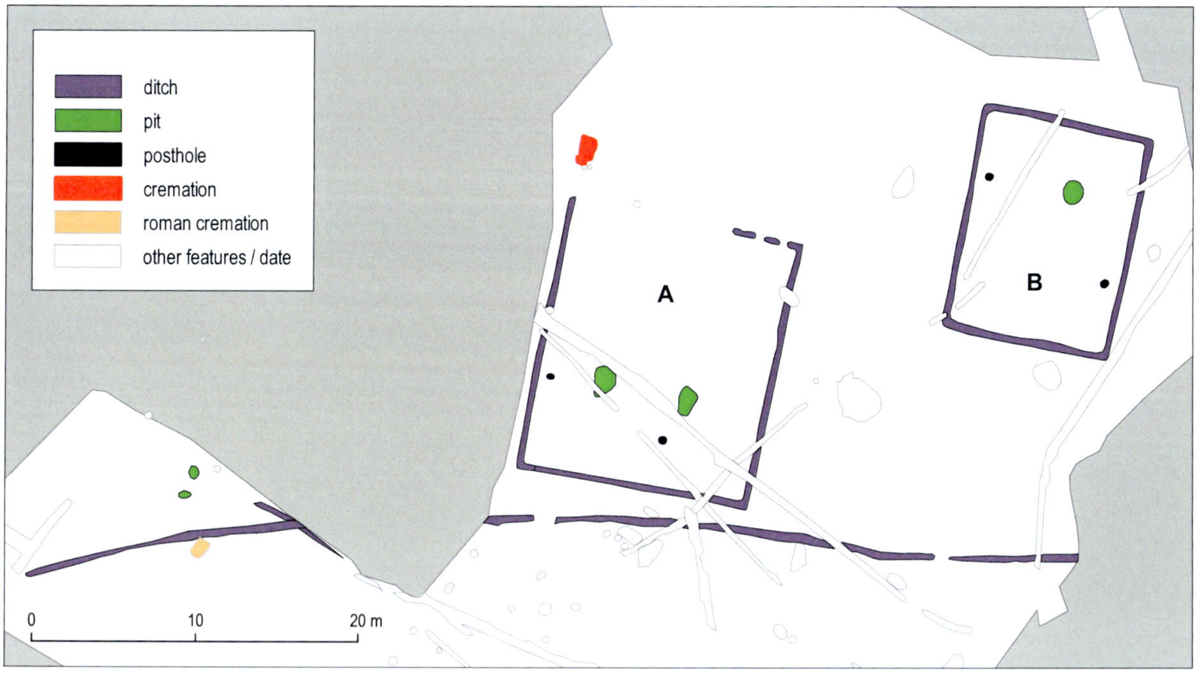

Figure 6.9. Part of the excavation plan of Erembodegem Zuid IV phase 3 zone 1 (after Verbrugge, De Graeve & Cherretté 2011, plate 3; digital site plan courtesy of SOLVA).

established. Some of the 'flat' graves belonged to women and children, although at least one adult male was among them (Demey 2013, 109). Notably, the only grave of a younger child, aged 2-8, was the only one without pottery as a grave gift. Besides physical conditions, sociocultural factors such as status in life, membership of a social group, or manner of death could have instigated a difference in interment.

The third noticeable aspect is that the rectangular ditches were used for additional activities besides the placement of cremation remains. All three rectangular structures portray a similar arrangement: a cremation grave with (burned) grave goods representing the main burial in the southern part of the enclosed space, along with additional depositions in the ditch in the form of pottery or charcoal concentrations with small amounts of burnt pottery (Demey 2013, 109). Also, pits were dug and post were placed in the enclosed space. The pits held mostly charcoal. Apparently burned material as well as deposited pottery form the remaining evidence in the archaeological record of activities connected to the rectangular structures.

Likewise, in Erembodegem, two rectangular structures were found adjacent but not connected to a long linear ditch, near a single cremation grave (Van de Vijver, Wuyts & Cherretté 2009; Verbrugge, De Graeve & Cherretté 2011). The layout resembles the site of Oostvleteren-Kasteelweg with pits and postholes enclosed by both rectangular structures, although the lack of a grave inside is a notable difference (fig. 6.9). In Oostvleteren the rectangular

structures could be perceived as burial enclosures, but for the two in Erembodegem this interpretation cannot be substantiated. The only (undated) grave was found a couple of meters north of structure A.

The shallow remains of ditch A revealed a relative 'large amount' of pottery fragments (Vijver, Wuyts & Cherretté 2009). The pottery dates Late La Tène, possibly transitional period to Early Roman. Ditch B delivered 'a limited amount' of pottery fragments. The exact numbers were not published. Two pits in the interior of feature A are situated 6m from the south side and 4m from each other in a symmetrical layout (*Ibid.*). Both pits were approximately 1.35m long and 80cm deep. The multiple layered fill of the western pit contained some burned bone and pottery fragments. The eastern pit merely contained pottery. The only other features in the interior of both structures were two postholes. Structure B also enclosed a pit containing charcoal. Thirty meters to the southwest another Iron Age ditch was found that resembled the rectangular structures (Verbrugge, De Graeve & Cherretté 2011, 23). It was interpreted as one side remaining from a rectangle. Near the ditch, 26m south of structure A, fragments of a circular ditch were found, dating to the Middle Bronze Age A (Verbrugge, De Graeve & Cherretté 2011, 19).

The enclosed charcoal pits are interpreted as graves containing pyre remains despite the fact that no cremation remains were identified (Vijver, Wuyts & Cherretté 2009). No interpretation of the enclosures was offered in either of the reports. The structures seem to conveniently accommodate the pits, implying the function of these pits is intertwined with that of the ditches. As the only verifiable grave was found *outside* of the structures, an interpretation as a burial enclosure seems unlikely. The grave could be a later addition.

A similar stray grave was found in Maastricht, in between two parallel ditches at least 60m long and 16-17m apart (Hazen & Blom 2015; see Appendix). The only two contemporary features possibly related to these large dividing features, were a small four posted structure and the cremation grave. The parallel ditches were

Site	Ditch date in century BCE	Main structure size (m)	Graves	Posts / pits inside	Ditch width (cm) x depth (cm)	Ditch cross section	Finds in ditch
Alveringem-Eikhoek/ Hoogstade	2nd-1st?	13.6 × 10.8, 12.7 × 9.8	None	Multiple	85 × 35, 70 × 16	Bowl	A lot of pottery
Barneveld-Harselaar-west	2nd-1st	10.3 × 8.2	None	Multiple	60-90 × 34	Shallow	Pottery
Cuijk-Ewinkel	2nd-1st?	12+ x 8+	None	2 posts	150 x ?	?	Pottery, stones, fibula, slag, burned loam, wet stones, spindle whorl, glass bracelet
Dendermonde-Hoogveld	2nd-1st half 1st	24 × 18	Outside? (1)	2 structures	70-100 × 20-30	Shallow	Pottery, charcoal
Erembodegem-Zuid-IV	1st?	16 × 14, 13 × 11	Outside (1)	1-2 pits, 2 posts	30 x few cm, 45 x few cm	Shallow	Pottery
Harelbeke-Evolis	2nd-1st	11.5 × 10	None	2-3 posts	50 × 10-20	Shallow	Pottery
Haren-Groenstraat	2nd-1st	10.5 × 8.5, 7.2 × 4.7	Outside (4?)	2 posts	25-90 × 10-25	Shallow	Pottery
Knesselare-Westervoorde	2nd-1st	15.6 × 14.8	Inside (4), ditch (2)	None	100 × 52	Bowl / V	Pottery
Kontich-Alfsberg	1st?	59 × 46, 37 × 29	None	Multiple	800 × 400, 60 × 40	V / U	Pottery
Kortrijk-Morinnestraat west	2nd half 4th-2nd	11 × 10	None	2 pits	40 × 20	Shallow	Pottery, spindle whorl
Kortrijk-Morinnestraat east	2nd-1st	10.5 × 9.5	None	2 posts	60-80 × 10	Shallow	Pottery, spindle whorl
Maastricht-A2 Landgoederen Route	2nd-1st half 1st?	60+ x 17	Inside (1)	4 post structure	200 × 70	?	None?
Mierlo-Hout-Ashorst	2nd-1st	85 × 21	Ditch (2)	2-4 posts/pits?	175 × 75	V	None?
Odijk-Singel	2nd-1st	7.5 × 6.5	None	Unclear	70-80 × 30	Bowl	Pottery, bones, metals, slags, burned loam
Oedelem-Wulfsberge	2nd half 4th-2nd	11 × 10, 12 × 11	Outside?	4 posts	? x 10-20, ? x 50	Shallow	Pottery
Oegstgeest-Rijnvaert	2nd-1st	20.1 × 6.4-6.8	None	2 posts	20-50 × 35	Bowl / V	Pottery
Oostvleteren-Kasteelweg	2nd-1st	17 x ?, 18 × 18, 14 × 14	Inside (3), outside (10)	2-4 posts/pits	60 × 29, 100 × 22, 70 × 28	Bowl	Pottery, grinding stone, iron nail
Oss-Brabantstraat	1st	31 × 23	None	Contemporaneity unclear	20-40 × 40	U	Pottery, 2 pcs cremation
Oss-Ussen R2	2nd-1st	20.8 × 10.4-15.6	None	6 posts?	60-200 × 35-60	Bowl	Pottery, spindle whorl, tephrite, animal bone
Oss-Westerveld R57	2nd-1st	46 × 37	None	5 posts	200 × 40-70	Bowl / V	Pottery, grinding stone, iron slags, nail, animal bones
Rijkevorsel-Wilgenlaan	1st?	13.2 × 13.2	None	1-4 posts?	20 x ?	U	Pottery
Ronse-Pont West	3rd-2nd	12.1 × 11.6	Outside (1)	None	50 × 20	Shallow	Pottery
Ursel-Rozestraat	1st?	A 14 x ?, B 47.5 × 16, C 15 x ?	Inside (55), ditch (6), outside (7)	4 posts	50 × 50, 150 × 60, 170 × 110	U	Pottery

Table 6.1. Overview of Late Iron Age rectangular structures.

interpreted by Hazen and Blom (2015, 203) as a cult place or a burial monument. As neither of these suggestions can be substantiated due to a lack of associated finds and lack of a contemporary context, an interpretation as a field system may be more evident. The four-posted structure seems to support a utilisation of the space as arable land. The physical characteristics of the ditches resemble the large rectangular structure in Mierlo even though the contextual information does not.

Examples such as Oostvleteren illustrate that rectangular structures cannot be defined as common cemetery demarcations in the Late Iron Age. Most were of a temporary nature and did not strictly enclose the burial(s). Even though these example seem related to graves, their presence was commonly not required. This use of the rectangular ditches in respect to graves is a continuation from the Middle Iron Age, except that, as is demonstrated below, the utilisation of the structures diversifies even further.

6.4 Rectangular structures and field systems

The use of ditches for various purposes not only intensifies in the Late Iron Age, the features also became of a more temporary nature (Løvschal 2014). Cross sections over

ditches show that during the Middle Iron Age rectangular ditches generally had a V-shape with a depot of up to 1m and a width of about 2m (Table 5.1). This size diminishes in the Late Iron Age (Table 6.1). Their cross section was more often bowl-shaped and shallower, while ditches also became longer and were used for all sorts of purposes: not only rectangular structures, but settlement boundaries, defensive earthworks, surrounding graves and above all, land divisions. The emphasis was on quantity rather than on the quality of the features. As the number of ditches increased, perhaps time to make them was limited and their ephemeral visibility sufficed for their use.

6.4.1 Rectangular structures in fields

As the increased role of boundaries and linear land divisions becomes apparent in the Late Iron Age, likewise space in the landscape is claimed for rectangular structures and burial grounds. In the Middle Iron Age sites of Itteren, Boechout, Brecht, Aalter and possibly Kooigem rectangular structures were found to be connected to field systems. With the intensification of land divisions in the Late Iron Age, all rectangular structures were connected to or situated near a linear ditch. In Oedelem, two rectangular ditches were found as a seemingly integral part of a field system (Bourgeois, Cherretté & Meganck 2001; Cherretté

Figure 6.10. Part of the excavation plan of Oedelem-Wulfsberge (after Bourgeois et al. 2001, figure 2; Cherretté & Bourgeois 2002, figure 1; De Reu & Bourgeois 2013, figure 5).

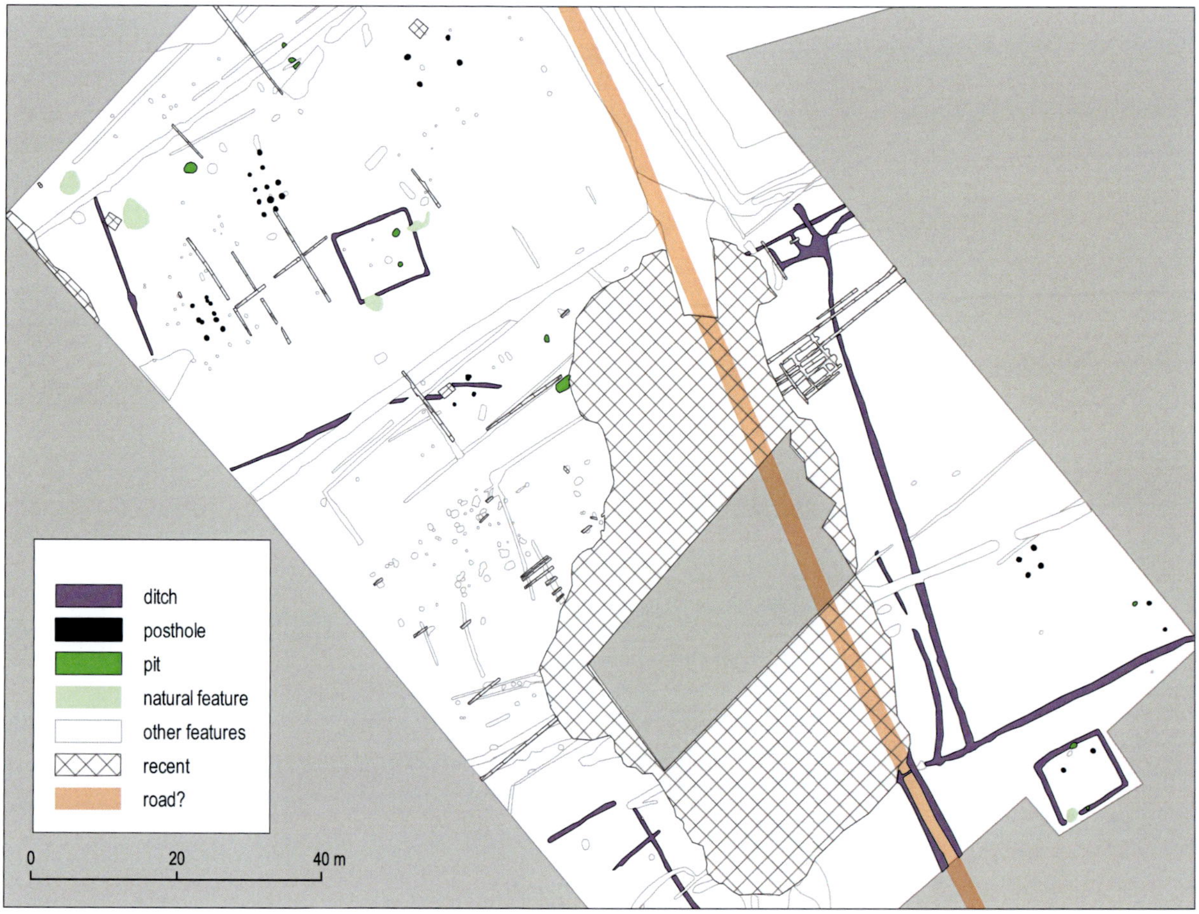

Figure 6.11. Part of the excavation plan of Kortrijk-Morinnestraat, showing the western rectangular ditch (left) and the eastern one (right) (after Apers 2017, appendices 8 and 13).

& Bourgeois 2002; Cherretté & Bourgeois 2003; De Reu & Bourgeois 2013). One of the rectangular structures is crossed over by a linear ditch, the other is in-between two linear ditches (fig. 6.10). This arrangement seems to have been made around the time when the linear ditches were dividing the land. The rectangular diches were most likely here first, positioned near older Bronze Age circular diches. The Bronze Age features on this location were not entirely respected nor incorporated. Rather, the Late Iron Age features seem to have been positioned as to deliberately redefine the landscape, without doing too much damage to the old monuments. It mattered to build the rectangular structures on this exact location. The act expressed the manner in which the Iron Age people conceptualised the barrows and the residing ancestral spirits.

The rectangular structures in Oedelem are interpreted as funerary monuments, by association with the burial mounds, and by analogy with similar monuments, although conclusive evidence for this is lacking (Cherretté & Bourgeois 2003). The state of preservation of the site complicates the interpretation as none of the presumed

burial structures held any graves. In contrast to Ursel and Dendermone-Hoogveld, the rectangular structures do not enclose the older barrows. The constructors instead chose to connect to the barrows in a more subtle manner, by a slight overlap of one corner. The two linear ditches dividing the barrow landscape in segments are notable, each segment containing a rectangular structure and one or more circular ones. Only one of the structures is physically connected to the linear ditches, but the connection to the field division is evident nonetheless. Given the number of granaries found in the field to the north, the space was in use as farmland and arable land was nearby.

Several rectangular structures that were discovered in fields illustrate the proposition that they held an intrinsic value that did not require a grave. In Kortrijk two such structures were found, only 105m apart (Apers 2017). The ditch of the western structure contained a charcoal rich fill on the northwest side (*Ibid.* 2017, 47-48; fig. 6.11, left). Apart from tree fells on the south and the east side of the ditch, it appeared uninterrupted. In the ditch 310 pottery

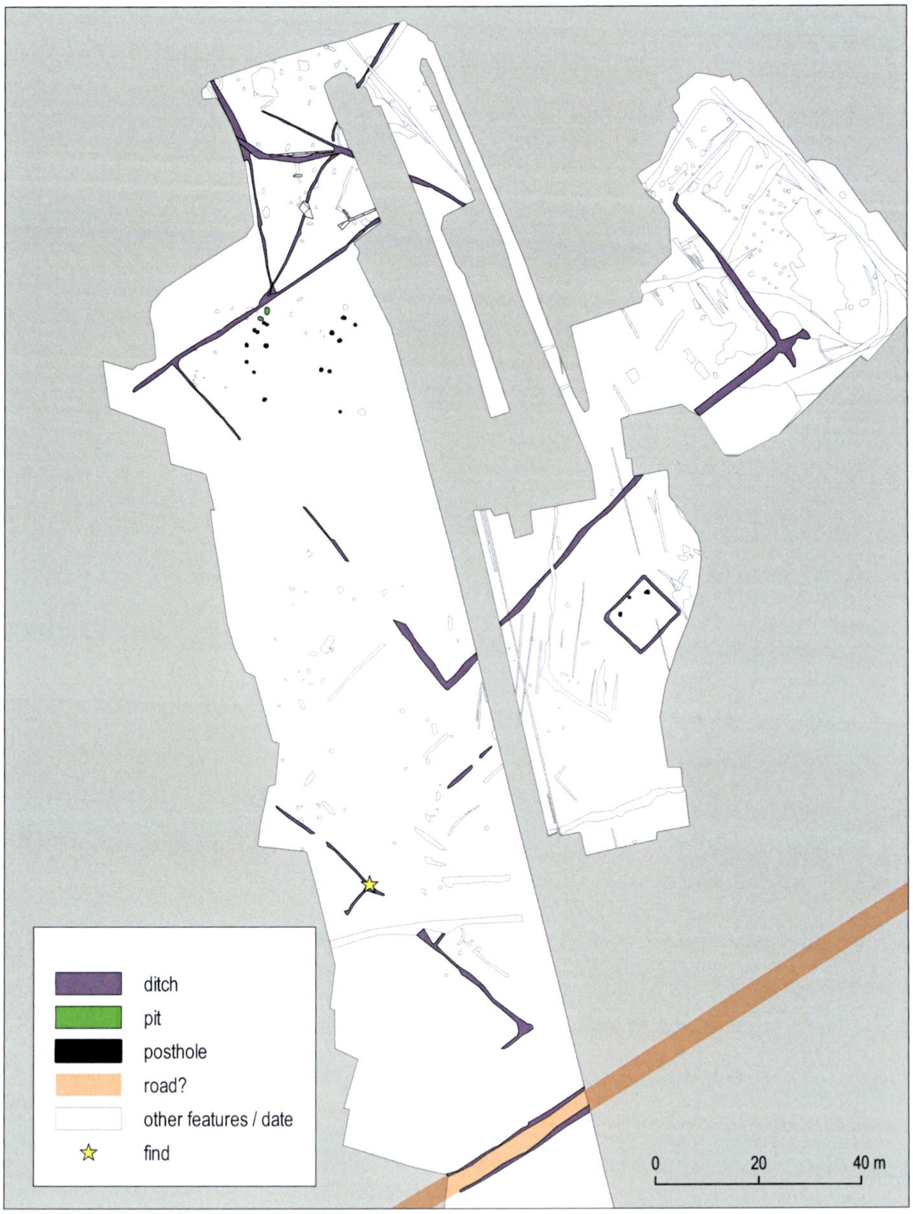

Figure 6.12. Part of the excavation plan of Harelbeke-Evolis zone 1 (after De Logi et al. 2008, figure 14 and Messiaen et al. 2009, figure 1).

fragments of at least ten different pots, a spindle whorl and part of a sandstone grinding stone were found (Apers 2017, 48-51). Most of the pottery derived from the north and south sides of the ditch.

The second structure was slightly smaller and less well preserved, but otherwise showed remarkable similarities (fig. 6.11, right). Despite the shallow depth of the ditch, 204 pieces of pottery were recovered from it, including two fragments of spindle whorls (Apers 2017, 53-55). Like the western structure, most (but not all) pottery was found in the north and south sides of the ditch. In the vicinity other structures were documented, mostly four posted granaries dating to the Late Iron Age indicating the area was used for agriculture (*Ibid.*).

A comparable rectangular structure was found in Harelbeke, 450m north of Kortrijk (fig. 6.12). The relation between the sites will be discussed in Ch.7.3. The structure measured 11.5 × 10m and lay parallel to a field system of linear ditches (De Logi *et al.* 2008, 18).

The pottery assemblage found in the rectangular ditch fill was deemed 'too complete, too much, and too uniform' to belong to ordinary settlement deposits (De Logi *et al.* 2008, 19). The 411 shards were concentrated in the south corner and in the fill of the southeast side (Messiaen *et al.* 2009). The pottery description suggests a single bulk-deposit. Enclosed by the rectangular ditch three postholes were found, positioned in a symmetrical layout (Messiaen *et al.* 2009). Along with the size of the structure, the positions of the postholes bare a notable resemblance to the structures in Kortrijk, which both have two pits or postholes lined out. Another pottery concentration of 577 shards (fig. 6.12, star) was found on the junction of ditches in the southwest of the excavation, contemporary to the rectangular ditch (Messiaen *et al.* 2009).

Based on the pottery finds in the ditch fill, the rectangular ditch in Harelbeke was interpreted as a 'rural cult place' by De Logi *et al.* (2008, 39-41). However, the structure, in accordance to the pottery, likely represents an act that was performed once. As such, a designation as a cult place is unlikely. The construction of this structure had a different purpose. The discovery of the pottery deposition on the linear ditch junction is relevant as it links the act to the ditch system, and possibly to the land ownership and the crops grown on the land. It is conceivable that these fields, or rather what they contained, needed protection or good fortune set in motion by this offering. The addition of the rectangular structure could likewise have had a function in a 'ritual of exchange', confined within the (symbolic) boundary that the ditch was meant to represented.

The appearance of this kind of enclosure suggests a temporary utilisation in connection to the linear land divisions, possibly reflecting an action that was performed only once, of which the pottery deposition was a part. As there is no contemporary house in the vicinity, the pottery in the ditch cannot be attributed to settlement waste. Instead, the pottery was brought, possibly broken on the location, and subsequently deposited there.

Abovementioned sites provide some insight in the use of rectangular structures in relation to field systems. Rectangular ditches are found both attached to or positioned alongside linear ditches that divide the landscape in the Late Iron Age. The structures seem to have their place in the landscape dependent on the linear ditches. Conceivably, the rectangular ditches confirmed or reinforced the divisional function of the linear ditches. As suggested for the Middle Iron Age site of Brecht (Ch.5.2), the rectangular burial monument was added to a field system to establish a physical connection to the land. It may have served a purpose as a land claim or spiritual protection. This relationship will be further explored in the three case studies in chapter 7. The purpose of the structure may have remained similar to examples enclosing or near a grave: the protection and/or fertilization of the land or a signature of ownership, by means of the housing of an auspicious spirit, related soul or ancestor. The creation of the rectangular ditch, possibly in combination with a (pottery) deposition in the ditch, was deemed sufficient to serve this purpose.

6.5 Diverse use and variable contexts of rectangular structures

One of the objectives of this chapter was to test the hypothesis that rectangular structures designated as 'cult places' became detached from burial grounds in the Late Iron Age. Examples like Kortrijk and Harelbeke suggest that rectangular structures were indeed built in other environments than near graves. In fact, the available data

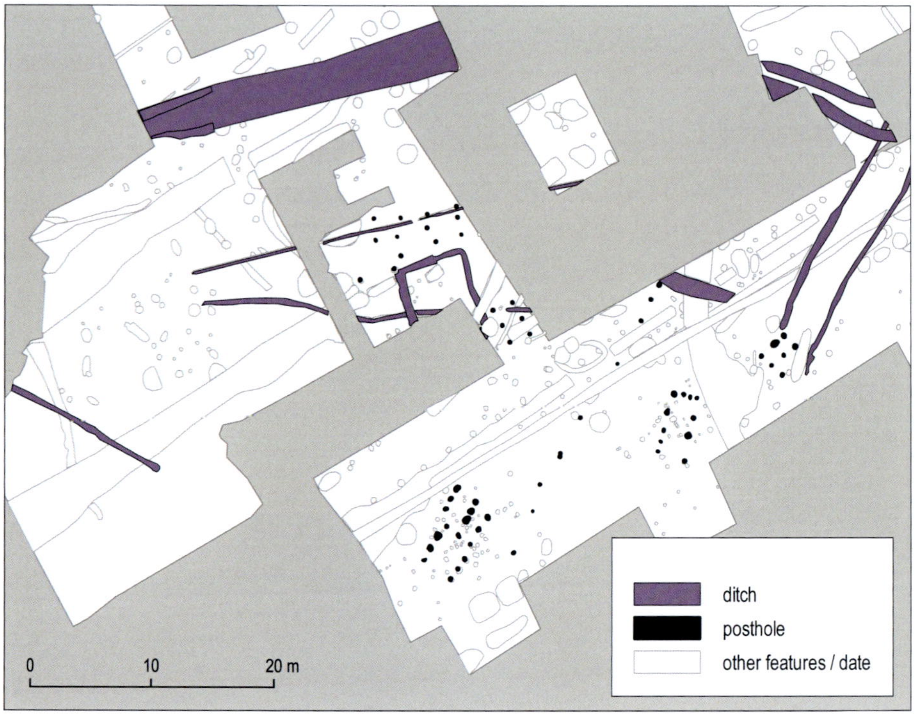

Figure 6.13. Part of the excavation plan of Odijk-Singel (after Lohof 2000, figures 3-5 and Schurmans & Verhelst 2007, figure 6.2a).

indicates that a majority of the Late Iron Age rectangular structures (56%) were found without any graves in the vicinity. For some of the sites it is possible that the state of preservation played a role. Graves may have been eroded, ploughed, or cleared. However, other sites show that the rectangular structures were never related to a cemetery or even a single grave. These structures were not made as a cemetery demarcation or a burial enclosure, or even an enclosed space for burial related acts such as a place for the performance of the actual cremation. Instead, rectangular structures were discovered in a variety of locations, an indication their function may have been more diverse than initially assumed.

6.5.1 Rectangular structures in settlements

In Britain, shrines, as Iron Age rectangular structures are generally called there, were mostly found near settlements (Hargrave 2018, 202). In the Low Countries this is rarely the case for rectangular structures. Only the Middle Iron Age structures of Oss-Ussen R49 and R50 were found in a settlement context. All of the others were related to or in the vicinity of a cemetery. The emphasis shifts slightly in the Late Iron Age. Many Late Iron Age rectangular structures that were not related to graves were found in

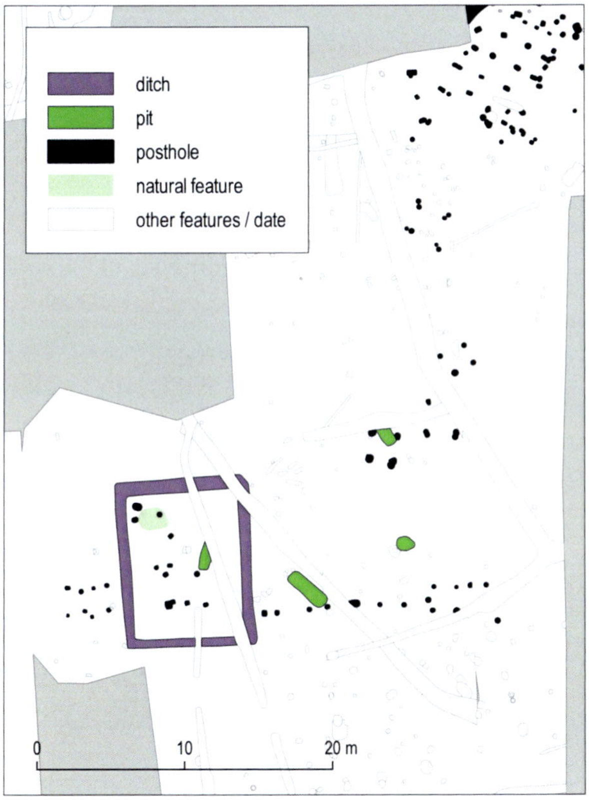

Figure 6.14. Part of the excavation plan of Barneveld-Harselaar-West-west (after Brouwer 2013; digital site plan courtesy of BAAC).

or near settlements. Settlement features are defined in this chapter as house plans, farm yards or outhouses. A cluster of postholes or the presence of one or more pits is not considered a settlement feature, as their function and the relation to the rectangular structure is unclear.

An example of a rectangular structure as part of a Late Iron Age settlement was found in Odijk (Schurmans 2007, 40; fig. 6.13). The ditch contained a concentration of finds in the fill, including 19.3 kg of typical Late Iron Age pottery on the north side, which was 25% of the entire Iron Age pottery complex found at the site (Van Kerckhove 2007). Other finds from this location are bones, metals, slags and burned loam (Schurmans 2007).

No features were found enclosed by the rectangular ditch, although it was not fully excavated. In the vicinity, several straight or slightly curved ditches also date to the Late Iron Age, of which the largest are interpreted as settlement boundaries (Schurmans 2007, 45). The structure was interpreted by Schurmans (2007, 40) as a possible 'ritual' enclosure based on the pottery deposition, although he argues that the pottery could have originated as settlement waste as the structure is situated within a settlement and could have enclosed a storage facility. The fact that the structure was only partly excavated, and on two separate occasions, makes any interpretation uncertain. The arrangement of the settlement in the Late Iron Age, and which features are concurrent, is somewhat muddled by the fragmented excavation. The structure appears to be aligned with the field system and some of the outhouses. If it is related to these features, the ditch might indeed have had a drainage function around a storage facility.

The situation in Odijk resembles another side in the northern region of the research area. In Barneveld, a rectangular structure was found in between granaries (Brouwer 2013, 72-73; fig. 6.14).

In the ditch fill 31 pottery fragments were found (Brouwer 2013, 72). Going by Brouwer's description, these fragments were spread throughout the ditch and in different fills. There is a higher chance for this sparse material to be settlement waste, than the large deposit found in Odijk. Several postholes and a pit were identified enclosed by the ditch (*Ibid.*, 72). Due to a lack of finds their date is unknown. Around the ditch several four-posted structures were documented, interpreted as granaries and further north, a Late Iron Age house plan was found. None of the pits were described in the report.

The site was interpreted as a 'cult place' near a settlement (Brouwer 2013, 72). However, as in Odijk, the function of the structure could be related to granaries or a storage facility. A surrounding ditch may have served to protect the grain from rodents or other wildlife. Alternatively, or in addition, the ditch may have provided spiritual protection. The distinction between these could

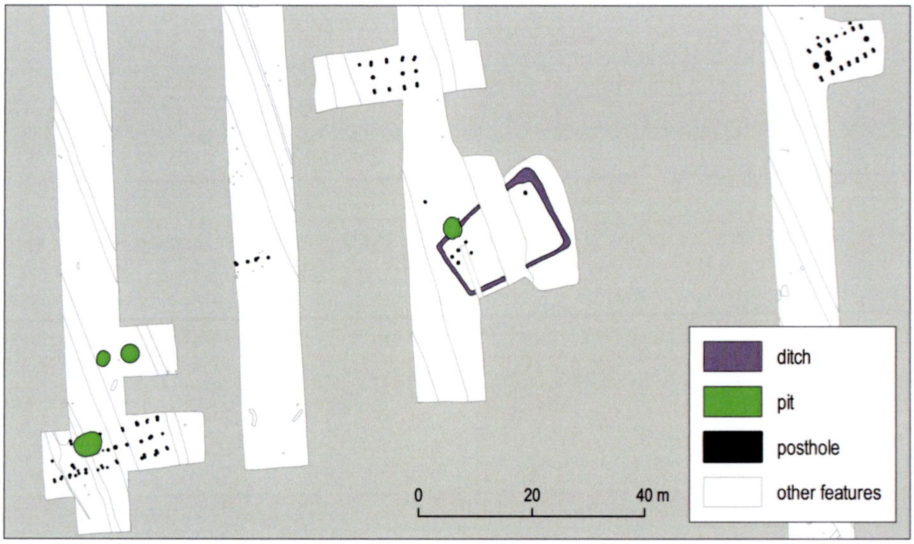

Figure 6.15. Part of the excavation plan of Oss-Ussen, structure R2 (based on original field data; Leiden University).

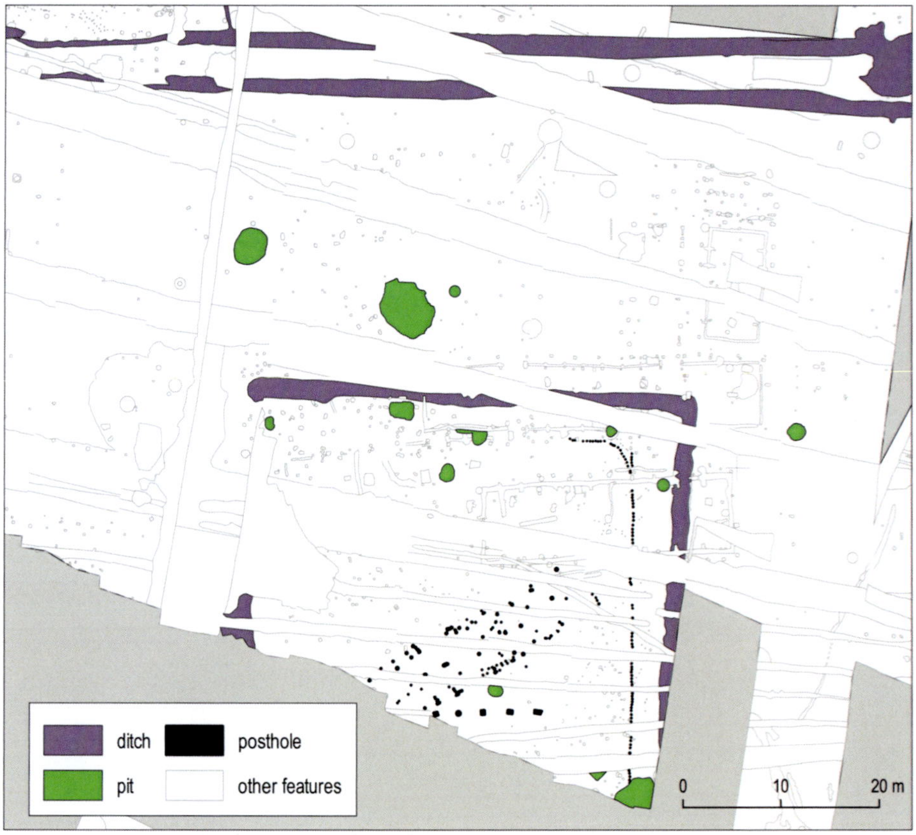

Figure 6.16. Part of the excavation plan of Oss-Ussen Westerveld, structure R57 (original field data, courtesy of Leiden University). The two ditches on the top of the figure belong to the Roman settlement phase.

have been neglectable to Iron Age people. No evidence to substantiate that assumption was found in Barneveld. The pottery deposition in Odijk however, is disproportionally large for the settlement and could be interpreted as an (additional) protective measure.

In between several Late Iron Age houses in Oss-Ussen, a trapezium shaped structure was found (fig. 6.15). Six postholes were found in the interior, that belonged to a

small structure (Van der Sanden 1998, 317). As a large recent ditch ran straight through the centre of the structure other associated features might be missing.

In the fill of the ditch 68 pottery fragments were found, along with part of a spindle whorl, and small amounts of tephrite and animal bone (Van der Sanden 1998, 317). The pottery could probably be dated to the Late Iron Age (De Leeuwe & Jansen 2018). On the northwest side a 90cm deep pit was dug over the ditch. It could be argued that this pit was of a later date, but, as in the Oss-Ussen structure R25/26, it is likely that the pit was dug in this location deliberately. At the bottom of the pit a pot was found placed upside-down. The upper fill of the ditch showed a bowl-shape that may have been an open feature for a while and yielded 200 pottery shards also dating to the Late Iron Age.

Oss-Ussen R2 was likely a structure with a short utilisation. In fact, the data thus far suggests that most rectangular structures in the Low Countries were only in use for a short time. The context of the structures or the dimensions seem to have little influence on the duration. One debatable large example was found in Oss-Westerveld. Only parts of the west, north and east side were excavated, making the structure at least 46×37m (fig. 6.16; Van der Sanden 1998, 318-319). The cross sections showed a variable fill, some with a laminated or humic first phase (De Leeuwe & Jansen 2018; see Appendix).[16] This may be interpreted as a fill that accumulated over time, instead of a short-lived and fast filled-in feature. Considering the size of the ditch, it yielded relatively few finds (Van der Sanden 1998, 332-333; De Leeuwe & Jansen 2018). A total of 347 pottery shards (of which 47 Roman) were recovered, along with a miniature bowl, a grinding stone, iron slags, a nail, and bones from cattle, sheep/goat, pig and dog. It is unknown in which phases of the ditch fill this material originated and whether the whole ditch was searched.

All along the inner east side of the structure and part of the northeast side, a row of postholes was found (Van der Sanden 1998, 318-319). This palisade was parallel to the ditch, so association can be assumed. None of the pits could be related with the rectangular structure, but it has been suggested a row of five postholes on the south side of the interior was associated because of the similarity in orientation. A Late Iron Age house plan was also found in the centre of the interior, with a northeast-southwest orientation (Schinkel 1998, 159; Wesselingh 2000, 169 – note 18). Contemporaneity between the rectangular structure and the house is uncertain as both features were difficult to date. A *terminus ante quem* for the rectangular structure was provided by a house plan crossing over the ditch on the east side, that was dated by dendrochronology to the end of the 1st century BCE to the beginning of the 1st century CE (Jansma 1995, 132; Wesselingh 2000, 99, 169 – note 17). The rectangular structure is situated inside the much larger Roman settlement boundary, also rectangular, that consisted of two parallel ditches (fig. 6.16, partly visible on the top side of the figure; see Appendix fig. A.36-2). The structure was initially interpreted as an 'open air sanctuary' (Slofstra & Van de Sanden 1987) and later suggested as a structure built for a single event, a

'foundation ritual' preceding the use of the settlement (Wesselingh 2000, 123-128). Neither interpretation can be substantiated by finds or field observations. According to the French model, the use of the place as a sanctuary would require material depositions. Also, the ditch was clearly filled in different phases which is generally an indication that it was an open feature for a prolonged time. It is possible that a structure built for a single event was left open and subsequently filled in different phases shortly after, although difficult to prove. As the ditch encloses a Late Iron Age house it could be interpreted as the boundary of a farmyard, although the different orientation is a discrepancy. The exact alignment with the much larger settlement ditches of the Roman Era suggests it may have been a direct predecessor.

In contrast, a similar ditch that was only partly excavated in Cuyck-Ewinkel produced a lot more finds (see Appendix). The ditch could be followed at least 12m to the southeast and 8m to the southwest. Just cleaning the surface of the ditch produced 700 pieces of pottery, weighing almost 9 kg (Ball, Arnoldussen & Van Hoof 2001, 61-63; Ball & Arnoldussen 2002). The ditch was initially interpreted as a burial monument or a settlement ditch (Ball, Arnoldussen & Van Hoof 2001, 61-63), but on account of the associated finds an explanation as a 'ritual enclosure' was suggested later (Ball & Arnoldussen 2002).

6.5.2 Structural elements

Rectangular structures in or near a settlement could have served different functions. Barneveld, Odijk and Oss-Ussen R2 may be ditches around a storage facility, similar to the structures in Kortrijk and Harelbeke, while a larger ditch such as Oss-Westerveld could be perceived as a settlement or farmyard boundary. The physical characteristics of a rectangular structure combined with the context provide evidence for its use. At the start of Ch.6.4 it became apparent that most Late Iron Age ditches did not have a large cross section (table 6.1). Unlike the German *Viereckschanzen*, their purpose was clearly not to create a physical barrier preventing people, cattle or wildlife to cross. Rather, they opposed a visual, but often temporary, demarcation in the landscape. There are exceptions, of which Kontich-Alfsberg is unique for the Low Countries.

The most prominent feature of the excavations in Kontich-Alfsberg was a 7-8m wide and 4m deep moat (fig. 6.17; Annaert 1995/1996). On the inside of the moat, at a constant distance of 4m, a narrow rectangular ditch was documented (Annaert 1993). It can be interpreted as a bedding trench that once held a wooden planked or wattle work wall. This type of ditch is also known from house constructions from the second half of the Late Iron Age onwards, as the outer walls of the houses were placed in a narrow trench (Schinkel 1998, 120, 193-199; Fokkens 2019a; De Vries 2021, 43-47).

---

16   Field data, University Leiden depot.

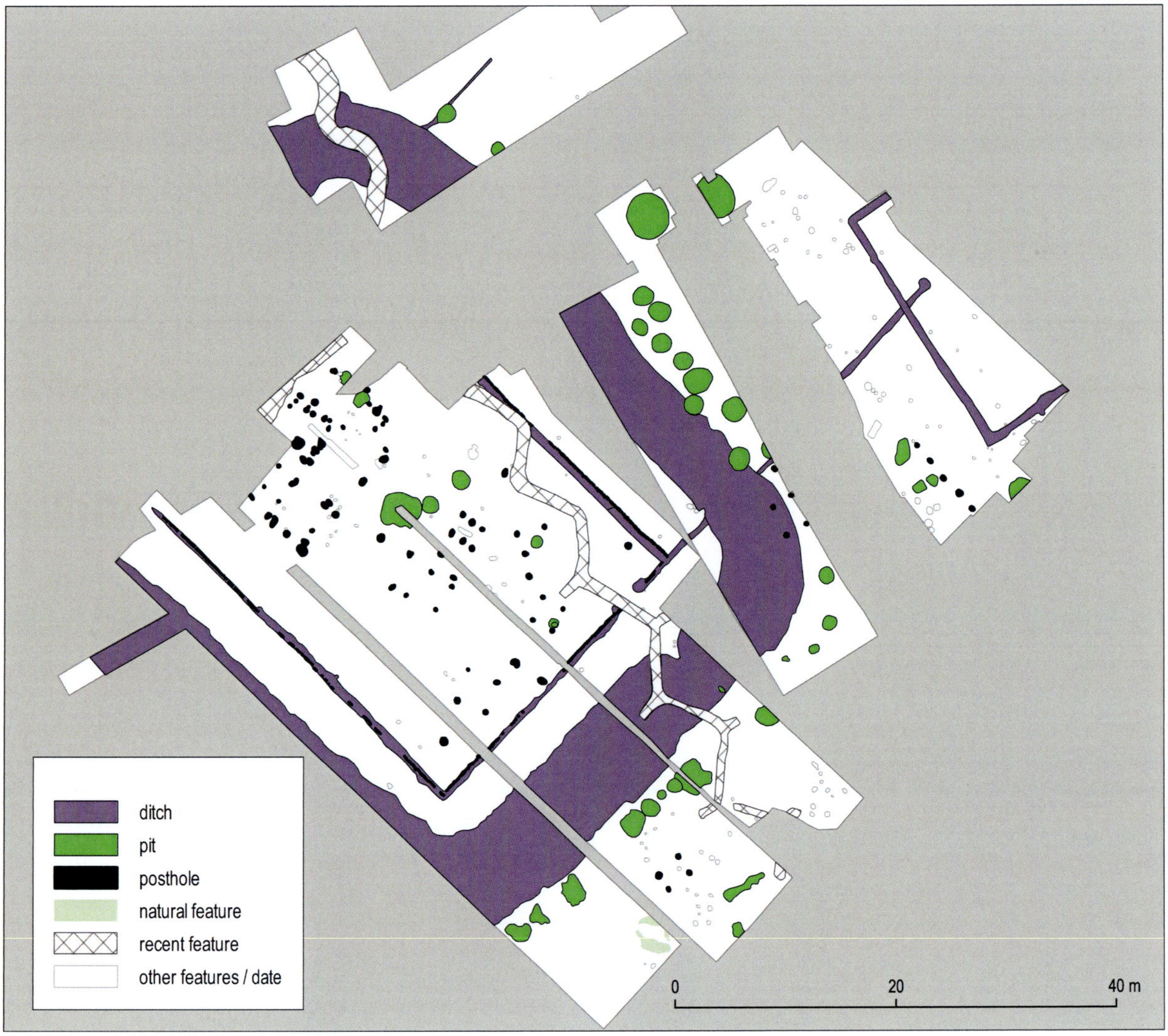

Figure 6.17. The excavation plan of Kontich-Alfsberg (after Annaert 1993, figure 3 and 5; Annaert 1995, plate 1).

Between the moat and the wall would have been a bank, formed by the soil from the moat. These construction elements together raised a formidable defensive structure.

In the interior of the ditch many postholes and several pits were found. Annaert (1993) interpreted these features as a Middle Iron Age settlement based on pottery finds, predating the ditch and moat. The exception is the larger building on the northwest side, which according to Annaert (1993; 1995) was contemporary to the ditch or the moat, based on the similar orientation. The charred remains in the postholes indicated the building was burned down, an event that, based on a single pottery fragment, took place in Early Roman times. By then the moat had been filled in. The fact that hardly any features in the excavation overlap, the empty region between the moat and the ditch, combined with the poor dating of the features, allows a Middle to Late Iron Age date for both the ditch and the moat.

Annaert (1995/1996) made a chronology mainly based on the orientation of features, and concluded that the site was used as a settlement in the Middle Iron Age, an open air sanctuary in the Late Iron Age (comprising of the bedding trench and a few posts in a cross setting), and some sort of fortified home with a function resembling a *Viereckschanze* during the Roman invasion at the end of the Iron Age. Based on an assumed Middle Iron Age *terminus post quem* and a Roman *terminus ante quem*, I placed this site in this chapter. The whole site with the unusually large moat preceded by a palisade has all the appearances of a fortification, probably originating in the Iron Age. The presence of a building, pits and granaries in the enclosed space seems to support this hypothesis, as does the location choice on a relatively high location. Most other rectangular structures in the research area were

RECTANGULAR STRUCTURES IN THE LATE IRON AGE   117

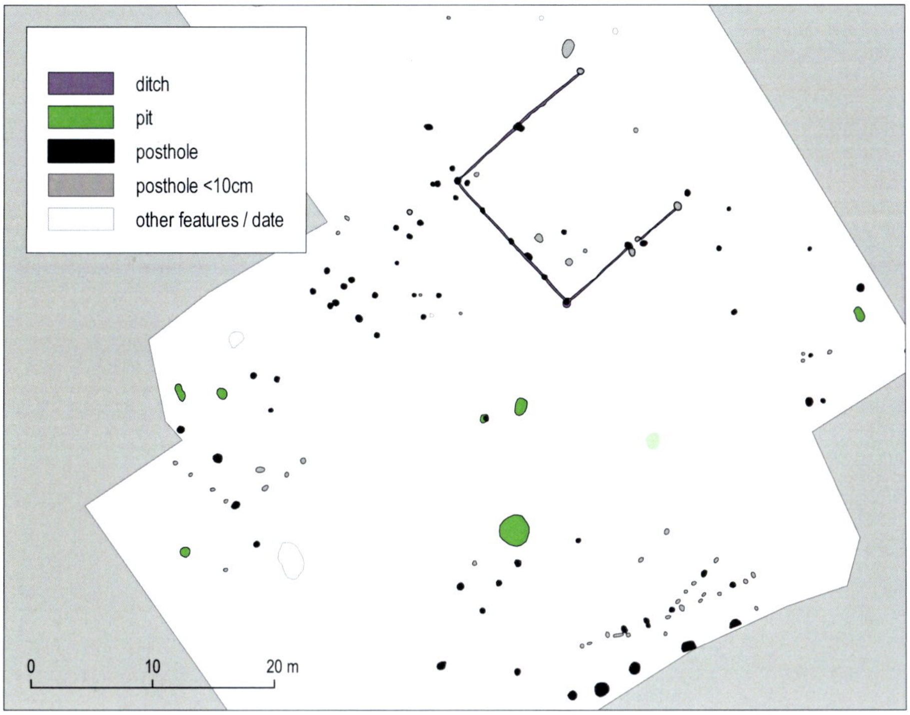

Figure 6.18. Part of the excavation plan of Rijkevorsel-Wilgenstraat (after Van Liefferinge, Smeets & Fockedey 2013, figure 17 and 18).

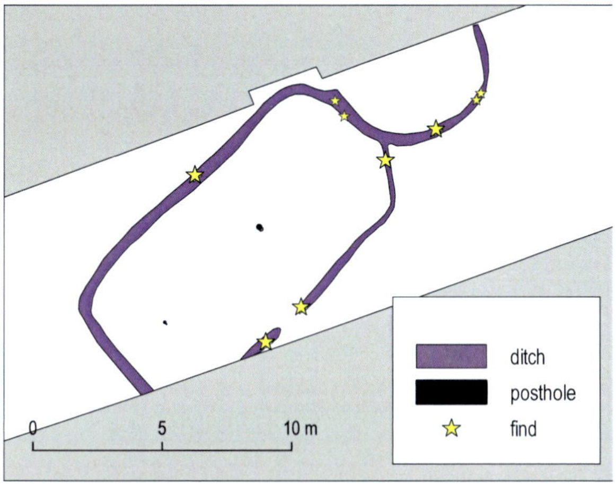

Figure 6.19. Part of the excavation plan of Oegstgeest-Rijnvaert (after Van de Geer 2017, figure 5.2).

found on a transitional place, commonly on a slope, or in a transitional area from dry to wetter lands, not on the highest point. The comparison to *Viereckschanzen* is only justified in the sense of a defensive structure, as the dimensions and features are different and *Viereckschanzen* are a phenomenon specific for southern Germany. A comparison to settlement enclosures found in England (Ch.3.4.3) may be more appropriate.

Bedding trenches as a structural element are found in other Late Iron Age structures. As structures with this type of ditch represent an entirely different building tradition,

rectangular structures with a bedding trench likely served a different function from the 'regular' rectangular structures with an open ditch. The purpose of a bedding trench is a wall, which is usually built to enclose a space entirely. A rectangular structure in Rijkevorsel consisted of posts on the corners and in the middle of the sides, placed in a narrow bedding trench (fig. 6.18). The east side was poorly preserved and parts are missing. On the south side a 60cm interruption is flanked by four more postholes, indicating an entrance.

A few fragments (4 grams in total) of burned bone were found in the interior, just above the excavating surface, the likely remains of a cremation burial (Van Liefferinge, Smeets & Fockedey 2013, 23-24; Smits 2013). The ditch and the posts in Rijkevorsel only yielded five pieces of pottery (Van Liefferinge, Smeets & Fockedey 2013, 28-31). Despite this low number they could be dated to the Late Iron Age. A 20cm deep pit on the west side of the excavation held three looming weights, also dating to the Iron Age. The structure was suggested to be a burial monument (*Ibid.* 2013, 23). Indeed, the few crumbs of cremation remains hint at a grave, but a wall as a surrounding feature is unusual. The size and the lack of central postholes indicate it was an open, roofless structure. In contrast to most other structures in this thesis that have symbolic boundaries in the form of a ditch that could easily be crossed, this structure consisted of a physical barrier. Given the settlement context, it could have functioned as a livestock pen. A rectangular structure in Ruiselede similar to the one in Rijkevorsel yielded two cremation burials

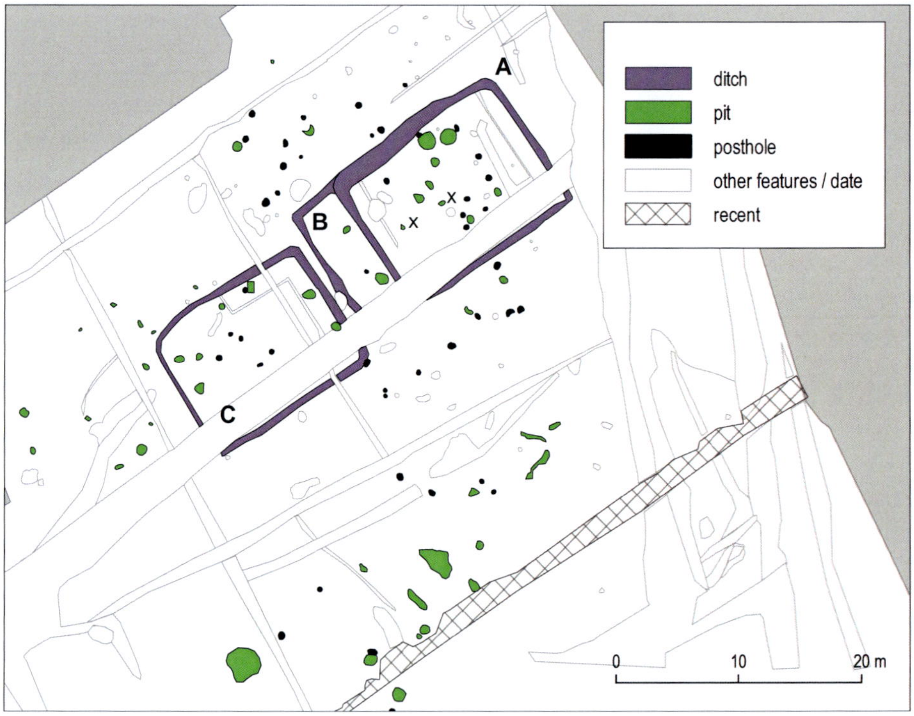

Figure 6.20. Part of the excavation plan of Alveringem-Eikhoek (after Vanoverbeke 2012, appendix 1 and 2).

in the interior and eight more adjacent to the east side of the structure, all dating to the Roman era (Deconynck & Beek 2010). Another similar looking structure in Baarle Randweg – site 13 was situated in a settlement, in-between several granaries, and had no association with graves (Van der Veken 2020, 555-558). The example in Baarle was a perfect square of 18.6 × 18.6m, with equally narrow bedding trenches. It was discovered in between several small outhouses and near a larger building with the same orientation.

Besides defensive measures and wall foundations, ditches could also be used for drainage. This has already been suggested for rectangular structures in field systems, but a settlement context is also a possibility. A structure in Oegstgeest was the subject of several considerations. It consisted of two parts: a rectangular and a connected round ditch on the northeast side (fig. 6.19; Van de Geer 2017, 15-20). In the middle of the south side of the rectangular part there was an interruption of the ditch of around 1m wide, suggesting an entrance. On the west side of the round ditch another interruption was documented.

In the fill of the ditches 538 pieces (5.6 kg) of Late Iron Age pottery were found (Van de Geer 2017, 23). Most of the pottery was found in five concentrations (Fig. 6.19, stars). The largest concentration was uncovered on the south side of the circular ditch, where the remains of at least four pots were found on the bottom of the ditch. Apart from pottery, a concentration of burned clay was found (Most eastern star in fig. 6.19) and three small fragments of animal bone. Van de Geer (2017, 23-31) considered three

options for the structure: a ditch surrounding a storage facility, or a ditch surrounding a house, or function as a cult place. Based on regional analogies, an interpretation as a burial monument was not opted, as comparable structures were never associated with graves. Some of the similar structures on other sites were found connected to a field system, which was interpreted as an arrangement to improve drainage (Van Londen 2006, 32-34). As the ditch in Oegstgeest appeared to have contained water, a drainage function is a likely possibility. The enclosed space would have been raised in order to keep the floor dry (Van de Geer 2017, 24). The possibility that the enclosed space used to contain a house would explain the pottery depositions, as well as the opening and the two posts (*Ibid.* 2017, 25-28). Substantiated by the regional research by Van Londen (2006), and the arguments by Van der Geer (2017, 24-29), a function as a sort of small settlement mound is the most likely interpretation. This is only a valid argument for the West Lowlands region, as the ditches found here are demonstrated to have contained water. Nearly all other sites mentioned in this chapter are situated in well drained sandy soils.

6.5.3 A place for deposition

Even though most Late Iron Age sites mentioned in this chapter have one or more pottery concentrations or deposited finds in the rectangular ditch, one site stands out. As was the case for the Middle Iron Age sites of Kooigem and Oss-Ussen R25/26, the Late Iron Age site of Alveringem held an exorbitant amount of deposited pottery, more than all of the other sites in this chapter combined. In a 0.5 ha excavation, two rectangular structures were found next to each other (Vanoverbeke 2012, 15-36; Vanoverbeke & Clerbaut 2012). The northeast structure seems to consist of two phases, a rectangular ditch (A) overlapping another ditch (B) on the west side (fig. 6.20). A total of 72.4 kg of pottery was found within the ditches of the two structures, the majority in the northwest sides of structures A and C (Vanoverbeke 2012, 25; Vanoverbeke & Clerbaut 2012). Additionally, two small pits enclosed by structure A (Fig. 6.20, indicated with 'x' next to them) were found to be filled with pottery fragments (Vanoverbeke & Clerbaut 2012). Other pits contained charcoal and some burned animal bone fragments.

The site was described as eroded and the features as difficult to differentiate with vague and shallow postholes and pits (Vanoverbeke & Clerbaut 2012). Human remains, in whatever form of burial tradition, could have been lost post-deposition. However, among the many features that were documented not a single trace of cremation remains were found. Conceivably, this was not a cemetery.

The pottery deposition in structure A held the remains of at least 352 individual vessels (Vanoverbeke & Clerbaut 2012). If this was deposited in one instance, the deposition represents an event that involved an entire community. It also seems that the act of depositing was preceded by the digging of the ditch. At separate events, ditches B and C were added, accompanied by their own depositions. Evidently, the rectangular ditch and the pottery deposition are part of the same custom. These were not the only actions performed on the site. Other pits were dug, to accommodate at least two more pottery depositions. Also, there is evidence of fires, of which the remains were disposed of in pits. All of the actions, offerings and burning things, remind us of attempts to exchange with the spirit world, a form of communication.

The publication of the site was unfortunately limited and a detailed description of the associated features is missing. Additional questions could be answered by an analysis of the pottery: was all the pottery broken on the location or was it already broken when it arrived there? Was the pottery spread out or left in specific locations? Does it show signs of secondary burning?

Secondarily burned pottery was found on another site: Oss-Brabantstraat. The pottery was found in the upper fill of four pits on the site. All four started out as a well in the Middle Iron Age (De Leeuwe 2011, 31-44). By the Late Iron Age, the wells were filled in until a bowl shaped pit remained. In all

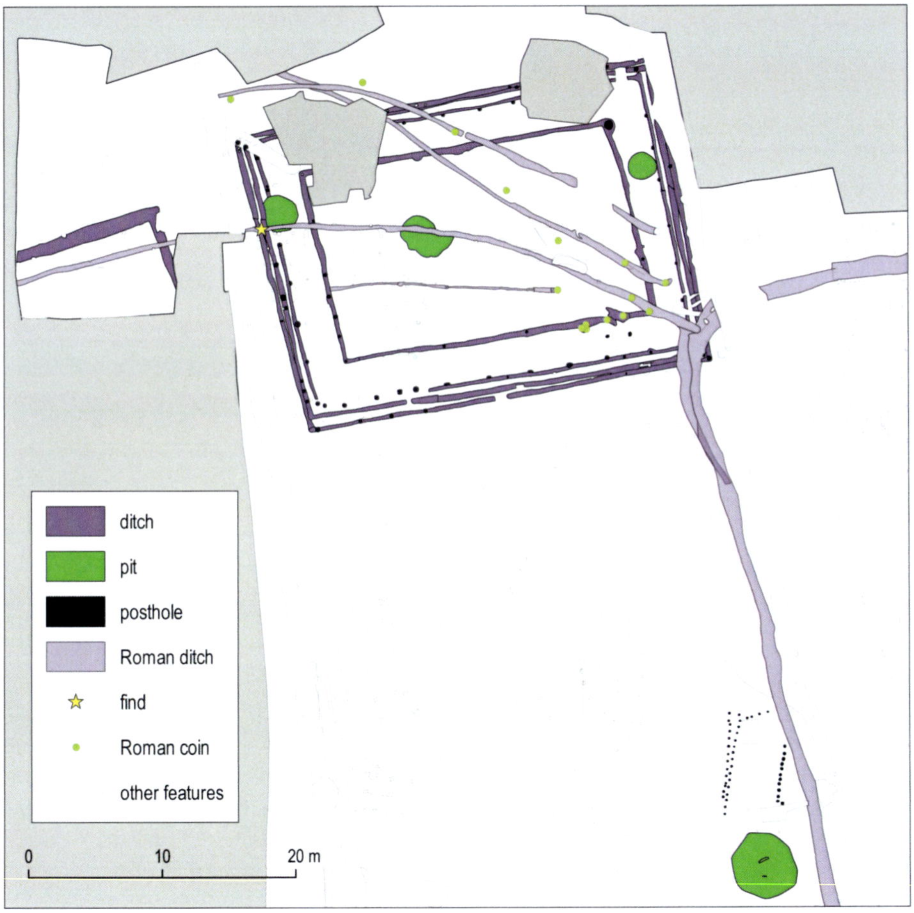

ditch

pit

posthole

Roman ditch

find

Roman coin

other features

0   10   20 m

Figure 6.21. Part of the excavation plan of Oss-Brabantstraat (after De Leeuwe 2011, figure 2).

three cases the pits were lined with a layer of burned loam, charcoal and/or secondarily burned pottery. Apparently, these pits were used as some sort of open-air fire place.

The use of the pits as a fire place may predate the construction of a 31m long and 23m wide rectangular structure on the site (fig. 6.21). The positioning of the features suggests the pits were still in use or at least visible at the time (De Leeuwe & Jansen 2018). Three of the former wells were enclosed by the structure, while a fourth remained situated 36m to the south. This fourth one was used as a

receptacle into the Roman Era, as a so-called typical Roman glass 'Melon' bead was found in the upper fill.

The rectangular structure consisted of bedding trenches. This type of ditch served as a foundation trench for a wall, so these were never open features (De Leeuwe 2011, 51-63). Three bedding trenches shape the outer parts of the structure, representing at least two different phases of walls. A post on the southeast corner still contained a fragment of wood that was ^{14}C-dated to 92 calBCE-53 calCE, providing a *terminus ante quem* for

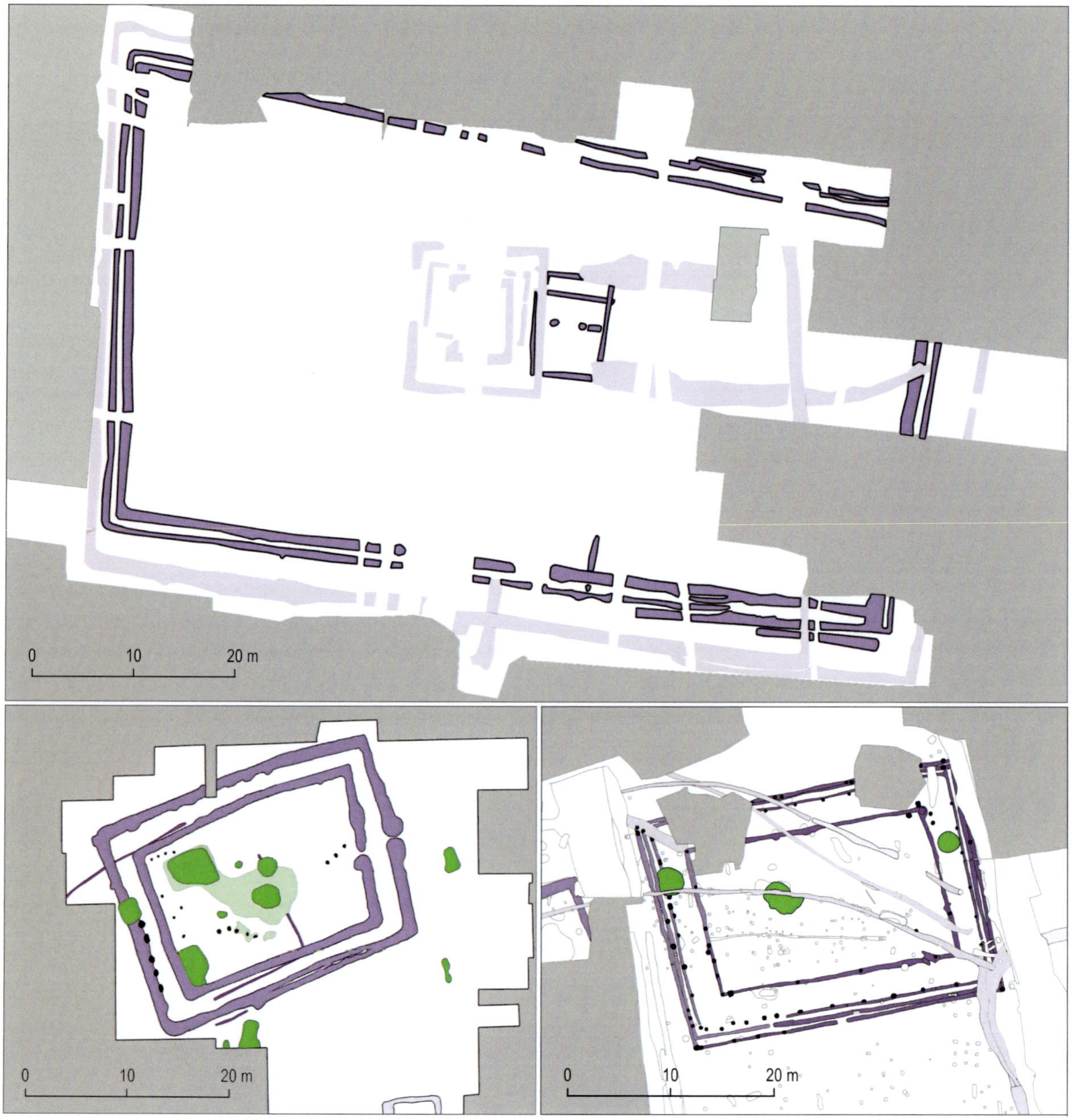

Figure 6.22. Plan of Oss-Brabantstraat (bottom right) compared to Elst-Westeraam (top; after Van Enkevort 2007, figure 6) and Villeneuve-au-Châtelot (bottom left).

RECTANGULAR STRUCTURES IN THE LATE IRON AGE   121

the construction of the final phase of the structure (De Leeuwe & Jansen 2018). The inner ditch had a V-shaped cross section indicating it was likely an open feature.

In in the 1st-2nd century CE, the planked or wattle-work walls were removed upon demolition of the rectangular structure, as a new ditch system was built over (De Leeuwe 2011, 69-74; ditches diagonally and in the lower right corner of fig. 6.21). This new ditch system belonged to the Roman settlement of Westerveld, 300m to the west (Wesselingh 2000, 123-126; Fokkens 2019b; see also Ch. 6.22, Ch. 7.2, and Appendix fig. A.36-2). Spread out over the diagonal ditches fourteen Roman coins were found (see Appendix fig. A.36). These coins are interpreted as a deposition at the time the rectangular structure was demolished, originating in the southwest corner where the entrance would have been (De Leeuwe & Jansen 2018). This is similar to conclusions based on analogies where coins are found near the entrance.[17] The 1st-2nd century coins form a sizable depot for the Oss region.

Other than the finds from the (former well-)pits that the rectangular structure enclosed, few other finds could be related to the structure. In the rectangular ditches a total 230 fragmented pieces of pottery were found, two cremated human bone fragments, one iron nail, and a few stones (De Leeuwe 2011, 51-63). The only notable Iron Age find was a piece of a glass La Tène bracelet.

Due to the construction method, the rectangular structure in Oss-Brabantstraat is distinctly different from most other rectangular structures in this chapter. Bedding trenches were found in other rectangular structures, like Rijksevorsel and Liessel, but those likely served as cattle pens. The different phases indicate that the rectangular structure in Oss-Brabantstraat was in use for a longer time period. The Early Roman phase of Elst-Westeraam has a comparable construction (Van Enckevort 2007). In Elst-Westeraam a Roman cult place was documented with a bedding ditch that included a remaining section of the original wooden plank wall (Van Enckevort & Heirbaut 2007). The wood could be dated by means of dendrochronology to 38-39 CE. The initial construction resembles Oss-Brabantstraat in the use of the parallel narrow bedding trenches. The ditches in Elst cover a much larger area, of c. 80 × 40m, in later phases replaced by a single slightly shorter and wider ditch (fig. 6.22). The interior held a separate smaller ditched structure that was succeeded in c. 100 CE by a Gallo-Roman temple.

Another site that the rectangular structure in Oss-Brabantstraat resembles is Villeneuve-au-Châtelot (Ch. 3.2.4). The size, the general lay-out of the rectangular ditches, and even the orientation of the sites are comparable. The main differences are the number of finds and the utilisation period. Whereas Villeneuve-au-Châtelot and Elst-Westeraam were used and modified well into Roman times, the use of Oss-Brabantstraat seems to stop abruptly, visualized by the Roman coin deposition and the traversing of the Roman field system over the old bedding trenches. In Ch. 8.7 I will evaluate this situation. On the basis of the different phases of Oss-Brabantstraat, the 'abandonment offering' in the form of the coin depot, in combination with the similarities to the other sites, the structure can be interpreted as a cult place.

6.6 Synthesis: the varied use of rectangular structures in the Late Iron Age

All of the Middle Iron Age sites were in some fashion related to one or more contemporary graves. This is no longer the case in the Late Iron Age. Of the 23 Late Iron Age sites discussed in this chapter 13 sites (57%) are not associated with a cemetery or even have any burials in the vicinity (table 6.1). The hypothesis that rectangular ditches gradually become detached from cemeteries in the Late Iron Age can be verified by the data. Many of the rectangular structures are close to a settlement, and some, as Ussen R2 and Barneveld for example, were found adjacent to a house plan. The large structure in Oss-Westerveld even surrounds a Late Iron Age house plan.

Not only did the location where the rectangular structures were placed change in the Late Iron Age, but also the nature of the ditch itself. Whereas in the Middle Iron Age the V-shaped cross section was most dominant, in the Late Iron Age a narrower and shallower bowl-shape is more common. The diminished dimensions could be the result of poor preservation, or more likely, the ditches were shallower to begin with. Compared to the Middle Iron Age examples the ditch lost some of its physical appearance. The fact that the structures were made, in a particular chosen location, accompanied by pottery depositions, seems to indicate that mere presence of the feature prevailed over carefully groomed physical aspects. Physicality literally did not matter anymore, unless it was for a defensive purpose.

In the 1st century BCE a ditch with a U-shaped cross section is introduced for the cult place in Brabantstraat. This was a construction to accommodate a wall made of wood or wattle work: a bedding trench. This type of feature served in various buildings: for walls of houses (Schinkel 1998, 194-195; Fokkens 2019, 51), in Kontich as a possible form of defensive structure (rectangular structure type 4), in Rijkevorsel as a possible cattle pen (type 7), and in Oss-Brabantstraat and Elst-Westeraam as the demarcation of a cult place (rectangular structure type 5). The bedding trench had multiple applications in the Late Iron Age. In general it can be stated that during the Late Iron Age the use of ditches increases, while their temporary nature also becomes more evident.

Ditches are used for a diversity of purposes, both in structures as well as in field systems and for structuring

---

17   Demierre et al. (2019) for French examples and Score et al. (2011) for Hallaton in England; see also Ch. 3.4.2 and fig. 3.17.

Type of site	Century BCE	Weapons	Pottery	Animal bones	Human bones	Statues	Ditch (and bank)	Context
Square ditch as burial surrounding feature (type 1)	6th-1st	-	-	-	-	-	+	Cemetery
Rectangular ditched structure (type 2)	2nd-1st	-	+ / +++	+	-	-	+	Cemetery
Defensive structure (Kontich-Alfsberg) (type 4)	2nd-1st	?	?	?	?	?	+++	Settlement
Rectangular (walled) cult place (Oss-Brabantstraat) (type 5)	1st	-	++	+?	+?	-	-/+	Settlement?
Smaller rectangular structure in/ near field system (Odijk, Kortrijk, etc.) (type 6)	4th-1st	-	+ / ++	-	-	-	+	Fields / single burial?
Cattle pen (Rijkevorsel-Wilgenstraat) (type 7)	7th-1st	-	-	-	-	-	-/+	Settlement

Table 6.2. Types of rectangular structure and related finds and features For the Late Iron Age in the Low Countries (- = none; + = few, ++ = relatively common / reasonable amount, +++ = many / large).

the landscape. On some sites the relation of rectangular structures to a field system becomes apparent through the physical connection (rectangular structure type 6), as in Ursel, Ronse, and Oedelem. In other sites the structures are found parallel and/or near a field system, as in Erembodegem, Kortrijk, Oostvleteren, Odijk, and Harelbeke. There are regional differences in the use of ditches for landscape structuring (Løvschal 2014). In the southwest region of the research area, field systems are more often attached to a rectangular structure. The increase in ditches and land divisions in this region is related to the northwest French tradition, where different types of enclosures are in use simultaneously (Buchez 2011; Buchez 2011a).

The relation to fields or to land in general, can be construed as a claim to the land or a request for protection by ancestral spirits. The expanding importance of a visual link with the land is consistent with the theory of increasing population density in the Late Iron Age. Whatever the cause was in the Late Iron Age, increased pressure on land tenure resulted in land divisions, expressed in the Low Countries by the digging of linear ditches. In chapter 8 I will elaborate on this topic further.

One remarkable detail can be found in the structures of Erembodegem, Kortrijk, Alveringem, Harelbeke, Oegstgeest, Oss-Ussen R52 and possibly Ursel, Oedelem, and Dendermonde: these structures all have two to five postholes in the enclosed space aligned along one of the sides. What these rows of posts represent may be crucial to the use of these structures. The posts could have been interconnected, creating a simple structure such as wooden board, or they could have been used to span something (ropes, hides, etc.). Alternatively, the posts were some sort of wooden totems, similar to the anthropomorphic figures found in Oberdorla, or the

standing wooden statues as suggested by Poux (2019). Both interpretations are potentially linked to ancestral worship. The postholes can be interpreted as the subterranean remainder of some sort of above ground location marker for the place, similar in function to the Malagasy standing stones.

6.7 Conclusion

This chapter set out to test the hypothesis that 'cult places became increasingly detached from cemeteries in the Late Iron Age'. Indeed, rectangular structures seem to be increasingly built away from cemeteries, although most of these structures do not qualify as cult places. The structures are related to other contexts than cemeteries, partly because rectangular structures were used for more diverse purposes in the Late Iron Age, which is consistent with the increased use of ditches in general. Land and spaces had to be delimited and structured. Most rectangular structures that were examined in this chapter could be perceived as a place for deposition, commonly associated with pottery depots and sometimes related to graves, field systems, older barrows, or pits. Similar to Middle Iron Age sites they are often positioned on a slope, likely better described as the transitional area between wet and dry. The significance of the location in the landscape and the relation to other features will be the topic of chapter 7. There are only two sites that with a reasonable degree of confidence can be interpreted as cult places: Oss-Brabantstraat and Alveringem. As the site probably had a construction date in the 1st century BCE, Oss-Brabantstraat inadvertently supports an argument by Derks (1996, 143-144) on the earliest introduction of cult places in the Low Countries. Based on the evidence, Alveringem seems to be a revisited location for depositions, although the site deserves further research as the pottery assemblage needs a thorough analysis.

7

The environment and context of rectangular structures

7.1 Introduction

One of the fundamental questions around which this thesis revolves is how the rectangular structures were used in the Iron Age. Their use is also directly related to the places that were chosen to build these structures in the landscape. From the previous chapters it becomes apparent that the earlier examples are all related to cemeteries and graves, while in the Late Iron Age the structures are more frequently detached from the burial context.

Only a few excavations or combined excavations have produced a sufficiently extensive data set of Iron Age features to allow an archaeological analysis on a landscape level. In this chapter several sites with rectangular structures are explored on a larger scale to allow for a broader and diachronic interpretation of their context. This approach aims to explain the position of the rectangular structures in the landscape and their connection to contemporary and older, at the time still visible, features. By including landscape elements such as relief, rivers, and Bronze Age barrows, a diachronic understanding of the Iron Age environment is developed, in which the rectangular structures had their place.

7.2 Aalter-Woestijne

The individual Bronze and Iron Age elements found in the landscape of Aalter-Woestijne are discussed the Appendix. In this section, the formation processes that led to that complex landscape will be discussed. The structure discussed in Ch.5.4.1 was not the only rectangular structure found in Aalter. Two rectangular structures were excavated, from two different time periods, both related to a linear ditch. In the case of the oldest structure, a more square-shaped ditch, it is overlapped by a ditch that probably dates to the Middle Iron Age. Fig. 7.1 (top left) shows the initial situation in the Early Iron Age to the beginning of the Middle Iron Age. The square structure is situated near several urnfield features. No linear ditches structure the landscape yet. Several Bronze Age features are situated on a higher ridge to the east. Thereafter, a double ditch with a palisade (ditch 4) was built, that crossed over the square structure on its north side (fig. 7.1, top right). This palisaded double ditch seemed to have a contemporaneous counterpart to the north of the site (ditch 2), flanking an open area in between.

The younger, rectangular structure discussed in chapter 5, overlaps a linear ditch (ditch 3) that also likely dates to the Middle Iron Age (fig. 7.1, lower right). The rectangular structure dated to the 4th-3rd century BCE. As it overlaps another linear ditch, it serves as a *terminus post quem* for the ditch system to which it was the last addition. The latter also seemed to have a counterpart to the north, ditch 1 (fig. 7.1, below).

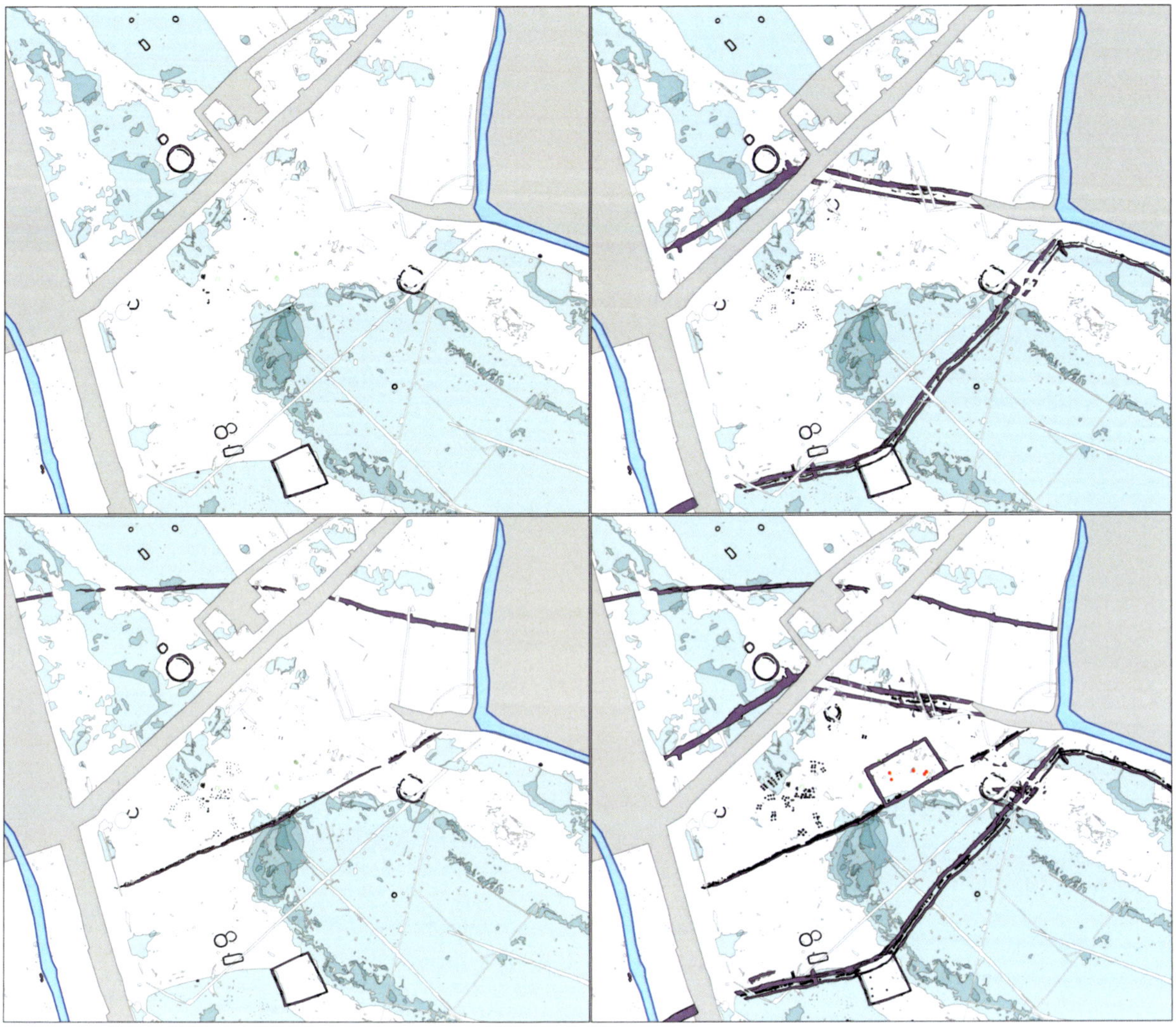

Figure 7.1. Landscape development in Aalter-Woestijne. First phase (top left), second and third phase (top right: ditch 2 and 4, or lower left: ditch 1 and 3) and fourth phase (lower right). White: higher sand ridges; green: depressions; dark: ditches and posts; grey: not excavated; the courses of the two brooks (blue) are approximations (based on De Groote & Van de Vijver 2019, 9-42).

How are we to interpret the undeniable relationship between the rectangular structures and the linear ditches? Two possibilities can be explored.

First, the square and the rectangular ditch attributed a certain quality to the linear ditches. By creating a rectangular structure, the enclosed space could be used for burials or given to the ancestors. This action could add an intrinsic value to the rectangular ditch, which extended to connected (linear) ditches. Initially, the square ditch was an open feature, evident by its laminated bottom fill. The top fill was more homogenous, an indication of a faster closure (Van de Vijver *et al.* 2019, 131). It was probably dug in the Early to Middle Iron Age and was still visible at the time the linear ditch system was dug, incorporating most of the north side of the square ditch. The makers of double linear ditch 4 even made an effort in the form of

a small detour to ensure the incorporation of the square structure. The square structure and/or the space within maintained its meaning that was important to the people making the linear ditch systems. We must assume the younger rectangular structure had an intrinsic quality similar to the square structure. It was dug over another linear ditch system (ditch 3) probably not long after linear ditches 1 and 3 were made. This newer rectangular structure was deemed necessary, perhaps replacing the older one in its function, or assigning a value to linear ditch 3 and/or the ditch system (ditch 1 and 3).

A second possibility is that the rectangular ditch made practical use of the linear ditch and vice versa. It is entirely conceivable that, even for the most experienced of diggers, digging a ditch was a laborious activity. Most of these ditches were quite wide and deep and many cubic metres

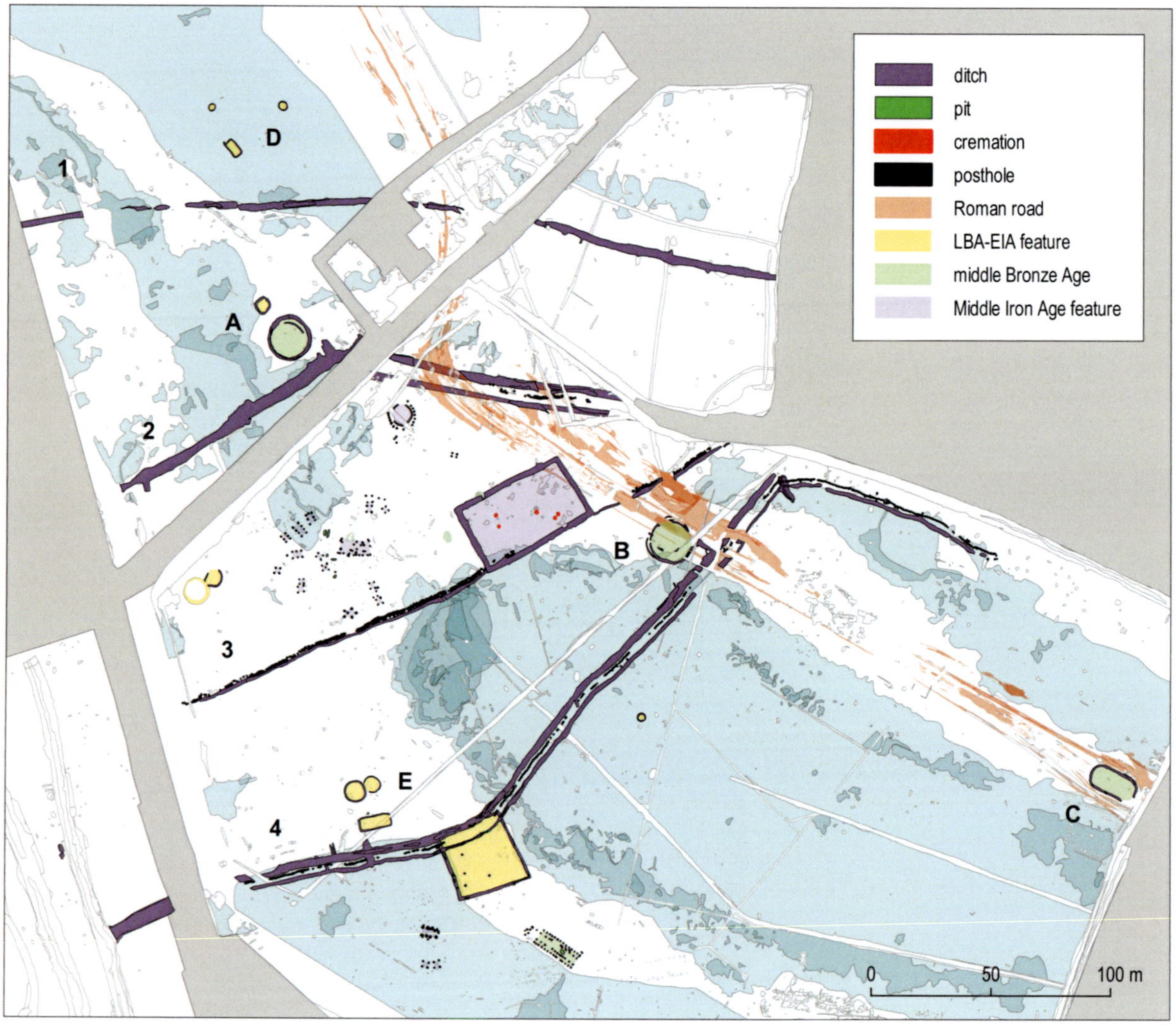

Figure 7.2. Bronze and Iron Age features and Roman road in Aalter Woestijne, based on De Groote & Van de Vijver (2019); figures and interpretation, combined with primary field data (courtesy of Agentschap Onroerend Erfgoed Vlaanderen and De Vlaamse Waterweg).

would have to be moved. The maximum depth likely correlates with the height of a man and how deep he could dig (including the waste heap) without having to exit the ditch during the process. He would have been standing on the narrow flat strip on the bottom of the ditch. In plotting a course for linear ditch 4, it might have been conceivable to incorporate the already (somewhat remaining) open north side of the square ditch and thereby saving the effort of having to dig around 25m in length of at least one stretch. It is noteworthy that at this point ditch 4 changes direction 35 degrees from nearly west-east to southwest-northeast. Likewise, ditch 3 was used as one side of the rectangular ditch in the 3rd century BCE. In the Medieval Period many centuries later, the Iron Age ditches were apparently still visible and even then some were reused and redug to serve as part of the field system around a

late or post-medieval castle (De Groote *et al.* 2019). Reusing older ditches may have been an old and practical strategy.

7.2.1 Function of the linear ditches

Leaving aside the relationship between the structures for the moment, what was the function of the linear ditch systems? The ditch systems are situated between the Woestijnebeek and the Grottebeek, two brooks flanking the west and the east sides of the site (fig. 7.1, blue). Clearly the four ditch systems were made to enclose the space between them and the two brooks. It seems unlikely the ditch systems were used at the same time as they were not symmetrical. Instead, the systems seem to form two pairs: ditch two 2 and 4, and ditch 1 and 3 (fig. 7.2, numbers). Without precise dates it is not possible to establish which system was made first, but the relation to the older square structure indicates that ditches 2 and 4 may be the older pair. Given there were two sets of ditches, one a replacement of the other, the linear ditches and accompanying palisades were only in use for a limited period in the Middle Iron Age. This was before the rectangular structure was added in the 3rd century BCE. Van de Vijver et al. (2019, 149) suggests either an interpretation as a defensive system or as a system bordering a spiritual space.

Ditches 2 and 4 both consist of a double ditch with a palisade in between. In both ditch 2 and ditch 4 the northern ditch was wider and deeper than the southern one. Ditch system 4 bends towards the southeast on the east side, parallel to the course of the Grottebeek brook. On the west side, system 4 extends into a medieval or even post-medieval ditch on the other side of the road (fig. 7.2, 'Watermolenstraat'). The canalised Woestijnebeek served as the basis for the eastern moat of the castle (De Groote et al. 2019, 278), in which this ditch seems to end. It is notable that both Bronze Age barrows A and B, as well as the small rectangular ditch of cluster E are positioned at the same distance north of ditch systems 2 and 4, all around 5-7m. Added to the fact that ditch 4 overlaps the square structure, it could be concluded ditch system 2 and 4 were laid out while taking into account, or using as reference points, all the pre-existing Bronze Age and Early Iron Age features. On the east side, the ditch systems converge at the point where the current brook bends north. On the west side the ditches are a maximum of 180m apart. The space between ditches 2 and 4 and the brooks covers almost 4 hectares.

Ditches 1 and 3 display a similar arrangement, just further to the north. These also converge in the brook to the east, enclosing a slightly larger area, over 4.3 hectares. Specifically ditch systems 1 and 3 seem to have been laid out so that they cross the higher ground between the brooks. Both are singular ditches, although ditch 3 had a palisade to the north side consisting of two to three layers of posts placed closely together. It is possible the palisades of ditch system 1 were not preserved, or instead of a palisade, ditch system 1 could have had another type of palisade that is no longer visible, such as a row of (thorn) bushes or hedges.[18]

The ditch systems may have had a defensive function, although it seems unlikely a couple of ditches and a palisade would endure in a conflict for long. Alternatively, the ditch systems functioned as a cattle corral. The enclosed space could have served to keep animals in and perhaps at the same time keep unwanted intruders out, such as cattle thieves or wolfs.

---

18   Hedges were also suggested for ditches in Oss (Fokkens 2019b, 193; Fokkens 2019c; 83; Van As & Fokkens 2019, 343-344). Thorn bushes are for example used in East-Africa in a *boma* (*kraal* or corral) to keep the cattle safe from lions at night (e.g. Patterson 1973 [1907]).

7.2.2 Incorporation of rectangular structures

Returning to the previous discussion, the role of the structures in this structured landscape can be evaluated. Most likely the square structure predates the ditch systems and the rectangular structure was made after the ditch systems lost their function. Both structures were positioned near settlement features. In the case of the square structure it may be related to three or four settlement features and the rectangular structure is positioned at a distance of 30-40m east of at least 17 settlement features, mostly granaries. Despite the number of granaries, little evidence was found of agriculture in the immediate vicinity. Pollen samples from the ditch of the rectangular structure and ditch 4 revealed an area of heathland and woods (Van de Vijver et al. 2019, 143-145). During the use of ditch 4, forests gave way to heather, a vegetation type that commonly develops through grazing. The pollen spectra of the area clearly indicate a human presence, possibly in the form of animal husbandry. The heather development was temporarily interrupted by a phase of forest restoration with mainly young pines, shortly before the dated level (4th-3rd century BCE). Thereafter the heather re-established, as well as grasslands (Ibid., 144-145). The pollen spectrum of the rectangular ditch indicates a developed heathland. It is conceivable the storage of grain and other harvested crops was confined to the protected space between the ditch systems, together with the livestock, while the actual farmland was located elsewhere in the area.

Taking into consideration the dispersed position of the features in the landscape, both the square and the rectangular ditch could have served as burial grounds for their respective settlements nearby. Of the rectangular structure we know it was used as a cemetery, as five graves were found in the interior. For the square structure we can only assume. Notably the square structure was on the outside of the cattle pen, while the rectangular one was on the inside. This may be an indication that the pen was no longer in use when the rectangular structure was made.

Concluding, the ditch systems probably had a function as a reinforced cattle pen. A similar palisade ditch was found in Hever (see Ch.5.3.5), although the cemetery there was not connected. The square structure held few pottery shards (Van de Vijver et al. 2019, 131), and their characteristics or distribution is not described in the report. The pottery deposition in the southwest corner of the rectangular structure was interpreted as votive offer that was made directly after the digging of the ditch (see Ch.5.4.1). Assuming these structures once contained burials and were thought to house the spirits of relatives or ancestors who provided protection or claim to the land, an incorporation of these monuments to the land was deemed an essential asset, giving value and attributing a quality to the ditch systems and the protected, enclosed area. The incorporation of the Bronze Age barrow in the Iron Age ditch system in Ursel (Ch.6.2.1) can likewise be construed as a gesture whereby the ancestors who resided in those place were added to the field systems and the narrative of the place.

7.3 Harelbeke and Kortrijk

The excavations in Harelbeke in 2007 (De Logi *et al.* 2008) and in Kortrijk in 2015 (Apers 2017) both produced Iron Age rectangular structures (fig. 7.3). All three structures had similar dimensions (11 × 10m, 10.5 × 9.5m, and 11.5 × 10m) and yielded a comparable amount of pottery (respectively 310, 204, and 441 shards). In the two structures in Kortrijk, most of the pottery was found in the northwest and southeast ditch fills. In the Harelbeke structure this concerned the southeast side as well as the south corner of the fill. All three structures had a ditch of a limited size: 0.4-0.6m wide and 10-20cm deep.

Another remarkable resemblance concerns the features enclosed by the rectangular structures. The structure in Harelbeke had three posts and in Kortrijk-Morinnestraat West two pits or postholes positioned along the northwest side, which was the side of a ditch system. The Kortrijk-Morinnestraat East structure had two posts along the northeast side. Notably, the latter dated earlier than the other two, 4th to 2nd century BCE verses 2nd to 1st century BCE.

A similar setup with two or more posts in the enclosed space of a rectangular structure was observed in other excavations. In Oostvleteren (Ch.6.2.3), all the three structures held a post or pit arrangement. In Erembodegem (Ch.6.3.2), both structures held exactly two posts, although in a different orientation. In Alveringem (Ch.6.5.1) the structures were found to contain several posts, possibly not contemporary. In Rijkevorsel (Ch.6.4.9) at least two post were found in the interior, and in Oegstgeest (Ch.6.5.5) two posts stood at the centreline of the structure. All of these structures were dated to the Late Iron Age, and the associated posts were placed 3-6m apart.

7.3.1 Ditch systems

In the excavation of Harelbeke the rectangular structure was associated with several ditch systems (Ch.6.9). Most ditches had the same orientation as the rectangular structure, either parallel or perpendicular. Some of the ditches could be dated to the Late Iron Age based on pottery. The east corner of the system that shows a slightly different orientation was interpreted as part of a medieval ditch system, possibly reusing an older Iron Age ditch (De Logi *et al.* 2008, 23-24). The excavator of the site in Kortrijk interpreted most of the ditches on that site as medieval (Apers 2017, 100-102). Specifically the broader

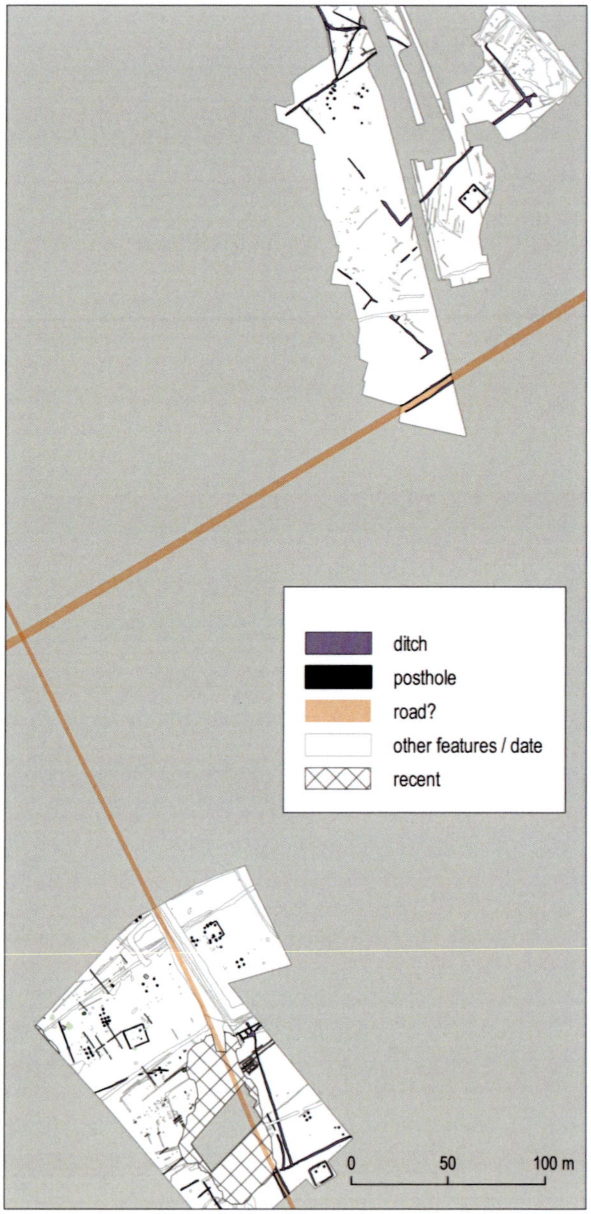

Figure 7.3. Iron Age features in the excavations of Harelbeke and Kortrijk (after De Logi et al. 2008, figure 14 and 51, Messiaen et al. 2009, figure 1 and Apers 2017, appendices 8 and 13).

ditches could be dated by pottery finds. The function of the medieval ditch system was interpreted as a division system for fields and water drainage (Apers 2017, 126). Many smaller ditches yielded no datable finds. In fig. 7.3 I have assigned some of these undated ditches to the Iron Age, mostly based on their orientation. The assumed Iron Age ditch system in Kortrijk has a slightly different orientation (north by northwest) than the ditch system in Harelbeke (northwest). The same applies to the corresponding rectangular structures.

7.3.2 Roads

The ditch systems in Harelbeke and Kortrijk principally consist of single linear ditches except for two locations. On the far south side of the excavation in Harelbeke and the far south side of the excavation in Kortrijk, a set of parallel ditches have been found. In Harelbeke the parallel ditches were interpreted as the flanks of a Late Iron Age road (De Logi *et al.* 2008, 35-36). The ditches were a maximum of 1m wide and 3.5m apart. In an excavation pit 350m to the northeast similar features were found, thought to be part of the same road. The parallel ditches on the southern end of the Kortrijk excavation are also about 1m wide and resemble the road in Harelbeke. Unfortunately, these features are not described in the report. With a distance of 2m on average the ditches in Kortrijk are closer together, making the road in between narrower. It is conceivable that the road takes a 90 degree turn somewhere north of Kortrijk, to continue its course to the northeast, or to connect to the Harelbeke road in a crossing or T-junction. In fig. 7.3 the course of the roads is hypothetically extended (fig. 7.3, red). In the Kortrijk excavation the northern part of the road is probably covered by more recent features. More recently, another set of parallel ditches was discovered in an excavation 200m further north of Harelbeke (Jennes 2019). That road runs parallel to the road in Harelbeke. That same excavation also yielded a pit with a pottery deposition (Geerts 2022). The deposition consisted of the shards of four pots that may have been new and especially made for the occasion. The pit also yielded a layer of charcoal. It is conceivable pottery was especially made to use it in depositions (*Ibid.*).

There is an alternative explanation for the double parallel ditches. In Oss double parallel ditches are interpreted as settlement enclosures or features encompassing arable land in which livestock was kept (Fokkens 2019b, 190-196). Their fill indicates they were used only for a short period. Due to the limited depth above the groundwater levels the ditches do not hold water permanently. The space in between the ditches may have held a wall or a hedge, but no evidence of this was found, making a function as a defensive system difficult to prove. If the ditch systems in Harelbeke and Kortrijk were used as enclosures they might not be connected as suggested in fig. 7.3. The rectangular structures are located at a short distance from the roads, 14 to 28m in Kortrijk and 60m in Harelbeke.

7.3.3 Iron Age landscape use in the Harelbeke-Kortrijk region

In Kortrijk-Morinnestraat pollen samples aided in the reconstruction of an open Late Iron Age to Early Roman landscape of grasslands and farmlands (Caspers & Van Asch 2017).[19] Among the grasses were pollen of buttercup and clover, typical for grazed meadows. Analysis also showed dung fungi in the samples, supporting the use of the landscape for animal husbandry. The livestock included sheep, indirectly indicated by the spindle whorls found in the rectangular structures and the spring scissors that may be used in sheep shearing (Apers 2017, 128). Iron Age burials seem to be missing from the archaeological record, but one Roman period cremation grave was found. The grave was located 25m southeast of the northern rectangular structure in Kortrijk (*Ibid.* 2017, 60-61).

The farmstead on the north side of the Kortrijk excavation is one of the earliest structures in the landscape. It is contemporary to the nearest rectangular structure, both dating in the Middle to Late Iron Age. Amidst the outhouses, the rectangular structure seems to have a regular place on the farmyard. Could the structure have served a farm related function? Understanding what the posts were used for seems critical for the interpretation of these rectangular structures. The two posts in the interior could have served to hang something in between, support a wall, a rack or drying goods. In this context it is conceivable a cowhide was stretched and dried in between the posts, in order to make leather for example. This might require a distance of several metres between the posts where the hide is stretched and worked. These quotidian functionalities give no explanation for the presence of the rectangular ditch surrounding the place of action. Given the limited depth it is unlikely the ditch held water, but it could have served to drain water from the interior. If the posts represent a haystack, draining the place would be essential.

It is likely that after the use of the structure near the settlement, the other two rectangular structures were made, possibly as a replacement. At this time, in the 2nd or 1st century BCE, the field system was extended. The road may have been a later addition, as it crosses between the house and some of the other structures.

The rectangular structures in Kortrijk and Harelbeke were needed in different locations, in between the fields. The posts in the enclosed space seem to indicate a practical use of the structure, related to agricultural activities. The ditch around them would have served as drainage. At the same time, pottery was deposited in the ditches. As the rectangular structures are not directly situated in the vicinity of a house, we must assume the pottery was brought to these structures deliberately and therefore represents an act of deposition. In relation to the northwest French tradition of incorporating

---

19   The pollen sample was taken in a large loam extraction pit in the centre of the excavation. The date of this pit is probably Roman to medieval (Apers 2017, 104-112). The sample was carbon dated to 169 calBCE-16 calCE (95.4% probability calibration, seeds, RICH-23411: 2056 ± 32 BP).

small cremation cemeteries in the field systems (Buchez 2011; Buchez 2011a), the rectangular structures could have housed one or more cremation graves that have since disappeared. Alternatively, the rectangular structures housed ancestral spirits without the presence of the remains.

7.4 Oss-Ussen

Even though Oss-Ussen has been a thoroughly published site, the relationship between the settlements, the cemeteries and the alleged cult places have never been fully explored. In the first half of the 4th century BCE two out of the three

settlements were abandoned and moved to two new locations (Schinkel 1998, 170-171). The old settlements that had been inhabited since the Early Iron Age were on the north and northeast sides of the excavated area (*Ibid.* 1998, 65, figure 59; figure 7.4, A and B). The newer Middle Iron Age settlements are to the east and southeast (*Ibid.*, 102, figure 95; figure 7.4, C and D).

Simultaneously, a similar shift in settlement relocation was observed in Oss-Mikkeldonk several hundred meters to the northwest of Ussen (Fokkens 2019c; Fokkens 2019b, figures 11.6 and 11.7). The relocation of the settlements to

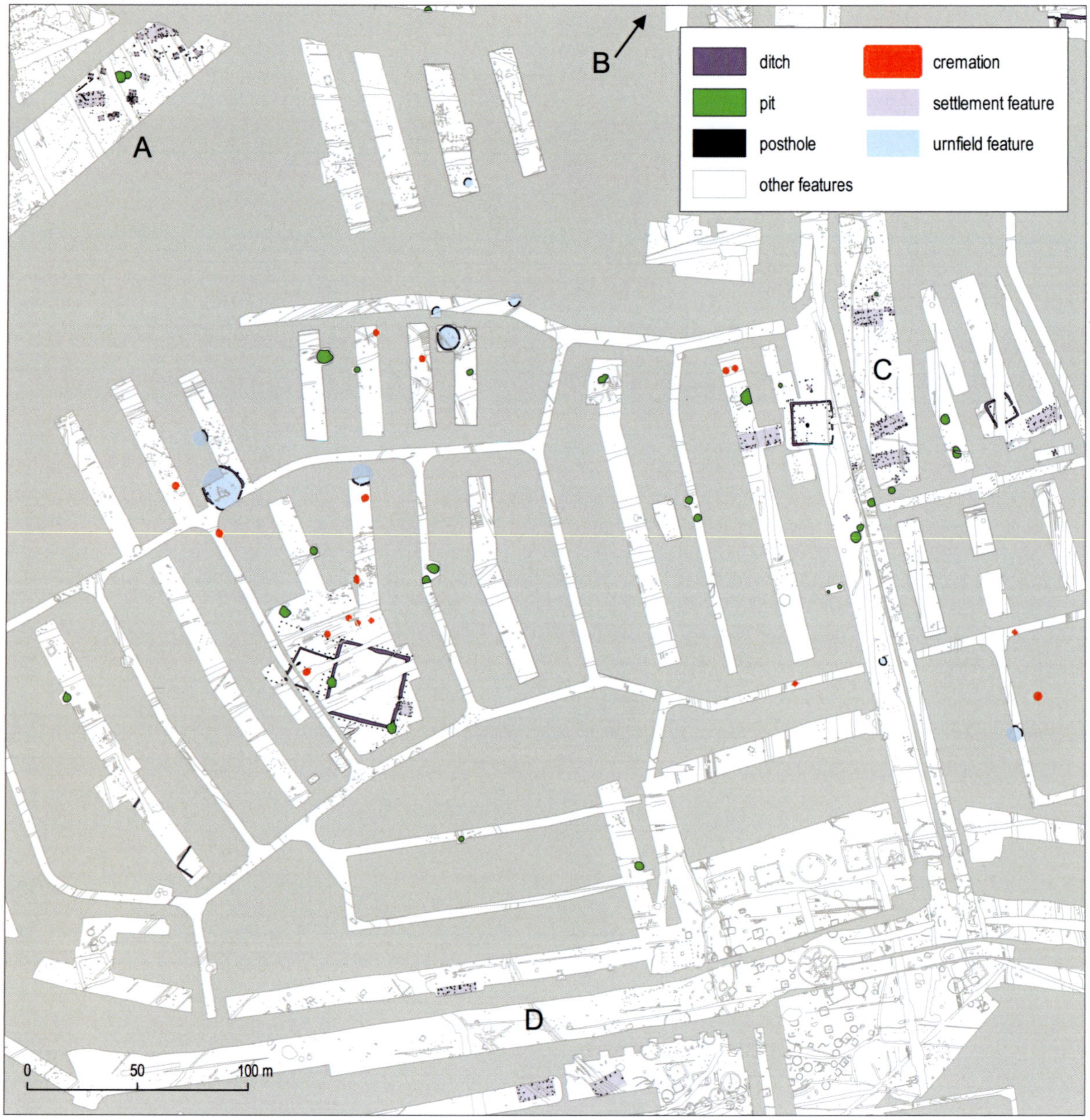

Figure 7.4. Middle Iron Age features around R25/26 and R49 in Oss-Ussen (after Schinkel 1998, multiple figures). R: surrounding feature number; F: flat cremation grave number; A-D: Early to Middle Iron Age settlements.

Figure 7.5. Middle Iron Age settlement C (after Schinkel 1998, figure 65).

slightly higher, more inland sites could be attributed to the increased influence of the Meuse river to the north (Schinkel 1998, 171; Fokkens 2019b).

7.4.1 Early to Middle Iron Age cemetery

Besides the underlying reason for the location shift, the location choice of the settlements in regard to contemporary burials and surrounding structures is notable. The area in between settlements A and B and settlement D is an elongated strip of land orientated roughly northeast to southwest. It was used as a cemetery during the Early and Middle Iron Age (Van der Sanden 1998). In the Late Iron Age and Roman era the cemeteries shifted to the northwest and southeast. In total sixteen flat cremation graves were found (fig. 7.4, F), along with nine circular and four rectangular surrounding features (fig. 7.4, R). Large parts were not excavated so the original number of graves is undoubtedly higher as the cemetery easily spans several hundred metres in length (Ibid.). None of the circular ditches or the interior space actually yielded any cremation remains, but it is assumed these were features surrounding a grave. A possible explanation for the missing remains could be that they were placed in a barrow, slightly elevated, and

were therefore subsequently destroyed by ploughing in contrast to the flat graves where the remains were placed in a pit (which in theory could also have been covered by a barrow). In fact, the only cremation grave found within a surrounding feature was the one in the smaller rectangular structure of R25/R26.

Two of the circular ditches could be dated through pottery to the Early Iron Age (R16 and R31), as well as two flat cremation graves in the vicinity (F15 and F17). R16 showed signs of animal burrowing, an indicator for the former presence of a barrow (Ibid., 324). Semi-circle R55 was overcut by a pit dating to 325-250 BCE, and therefore dates to the Early or Middle Iron Age. Cremation grave F23 was dated to the Middle Iron Age by an intact bowl standing in the pit. Apart from R25/R26 and R49, the other surrounding features and cremation remains were not dated. Six other surrounding features were found on the south side of settlement A.[20] None of these were properly dated, although an Early Iron Age was suggested (Schinkel 1998, Map 3 Early Iron Age).

---

20   These features (R29 and R37-R41) are not highlighted in figure 7.6.

7.4.2 Settlement C and rectangular structures R49 and R50

Five houses of a type called '4A' make up settlement C (Schinkel 1998, 74).[21] This relatively small house type is characterised by alternating wall and inner posts, and a two-aisled interior (Schinkel 1998, 193; Verwers 1972, 63-94). It is also known as a 'Haps' type and was in use in the region between approximately 375 and 250 BCE. The houses are situated around structures R49 and R50. R49 was marked as a possible cult place based on the high amount of pottery in the ditches (Van der Sanden 1994, 210; also see Ch.5.15). The pottery from R49 dated the structure in the last phase of the Middle Iron Age, 325-250 BCE (Van der Sanden 1994; 1998). R50 on the other hand yielded only few finds: a 2.5cm long fragment of an iron rod and 15 shards in the northwest corner, unfortunately not enough to date the feature. As was the case with R26 and R2, a recent ditch ran straight through the centre of R50 destroying a possible cremation grave. Still, the similarities between R49 and R50 are striking. R50 seems a smaller version of R49; a ditch with an interruption on the east side and postholes on the inside (fig. 7.5). Both are positioned in-between houses, distinctly outside of the cemetery.

R49 has a similar orientation to the house west of it and almost similar to the northern and southern houses of the settlement. R50 lies parallel to the eastern most and the centrally located house. Concluding, it appears R49 and R50 are part of this settlement, and likely represent two phases given the orientations. What could have been their function so near the houses? A cautious interpretation as a cult place has been suggested (Van der Sanden 1994; Schinkel 1998, 110; De Leeuwe & Jansen 2018): a central place in the settlement for communal activities; although a burial monument (or both) could not be excluded. Schinkel (1998, 110) further suggests each settlement could have had their own cult site, although he considers R25/R26 a more likely candidate as a central place for cult activities.

Another possibility is that R49 and R50 served as animal pens, which would explain the fencing on the inside and the size of the entrances. The ditch could have served for keeping the interior dry and clean. Examination of botanical remains found in Iron Age features and buildings in Ussen revealed an environment severely affected by humans (Bakels 1998). Mostly seeds and pollen from crops in fields and gardens were found, and some from plants growing in wastelands and along paths. No water plants or fruit trees were growing in the vicinity of the settlements, only a few trees such as the occasional oak, and a moderate number of grasses. Grasslands were probably further away in the Meuse valley. The settlements would have been mostly surrounded by arable lands. The plant spectrum shows little change during the Iron Age indicating continuity, save for an increase in grasslands in the Late Iron Age. In settlements a few hundred meters further north, such as Mikkeldonk, the farmyards were quite wet (Bakels 2019). Pollen and seeds analysis indicate heavily 'polluted' and much trodden open areas also containing few trees. Digging ditches to keep an area dry seems like a rational solution.

Assuming these structures were animal pens, what kind of animals would have been in there? Analysis of several thousand animal remains showed that cattle and horses were popular in Ussen during the Iron Age (Lauwerier & IJzereef 1998). These animals might have been grazing in pastures closer to the river though, as concluded by the plant remains analysis. Possibly the horses and/or cattle were brought inside the pen at night or on occasions. R49 had an interior space of 237 m² which would serve such a purpose. Some pigs and sheep were also kept. Sheep would have been out in a flock on some heathlands, perhaps even grazing in between the barrows of the urnfield. Pigs however, are commonly kept in a pen. R50 had an inner surface of 59 m². It is conceivable pigs could have been kept in this space. In general, a pig needs about 5 m² of space per pig, but the space needs to slope towards the sides to keep it clean.[22] The fence needs to be sturdy. This poses a problem for the pig pen interpretation. In R50 the posts are spaced 3.7m apart and the 80cm wide entrance is only flanked by one post. This is not a proper fence for this purpose. R49 is actually better suitable as an animal pen, with the posts 2.5-2.8m apart and a 2.3m wide entrance, although given the finds related to this structure and the granary inside, R49 was (also?) used for other purposes.

7.4.3 The central position of rectangular structure R25/R26

At the same time, rectangular structure R25/R26 is situated in an entirely different setting from R49 and R50. Where the latter are associated with a settlement, R25/R26 is associated with a cemetery that had been used since the Early Iron Age. Dating to the last phase of the Middle Iron Age, R25/R26 seems to be the latest addition to the cemetery before it was abandoned in favour of other locations (Schinkel 1998, figures 143 and 144). R25/R26 has a central location in regard to the settlements which are all 100-250m removed. In relation to the cemetery the structure is situated on the south side, respecting all the

---

21   The house furthest to the west is not dated. Schinkel assumes a Late Iron Age date for it (Schinkel 1998, 74). As not all houses were contemporary in the settlement, typologically the house plan looks like a Haps type and the orientation is similar, I have included it here. It may be the latest addition to the settlement.

22   By modern standards at least; information from: https://www.nda.agric.za/docs/Infopaks/housing.htm

graves including the older urnfield participants, which would still have been visible at the time of construction. In the Late Iron Age, settlements moved mainly northeast and southwest, and four cemeteries were in use, lying 90m west, 140m southwest, 270m southeast and 350m east of R25/R26. R25/R26 maintained its central position. In the Late Iron Age and Roman era the landscape was demarcated and divided by long linear or curved ditches. The ditches respect the position of R25/R26, suggesting the structure maintained its intrinsic value for a long time after its use.

7.4.4 Iron Age landscape use in Oss-Ussen

In the Early Iron Age urnfields served as a fixed location around which settlements were periodically moved (Roymans & Fokkens 1991; Schinkel 1998, 167-170; Gerritsen 2003, 256-258). A cemetery provided the social identity for local groups, ensuring the relationship with a specific area of land and all of the ancestors. The cemetery in Oss-Ussen was used for a long time. After urnfield type burials went out of fashion, flat cremation burials were added without burial monuments. The burial ground expended until the 3rd century BCE when large monument R25/26 was constructed. R25/26 may have replaced the role of burial monuments as a central place in burial ceremonies. As most flat cremation burials are left undated, this hypothesis is difficult to test. The settlements north of the cemeteries in Oss occupied more or less the same territory as their predecessors until the first half of the 4th century BCE (Schinkel 1998, 170-179; Fokkens 2019, 189-192). Thereafter settlements were established in different locations. In the Late Iron Age, the settlements were moved again to more permanent locations occupied by an increased number of people, and often surrounded by a ditch system. It is conceivable that structure R25/26 was made by the inhabitants of contemporary settlements C and D, to the east and south of the cemetery. As mentioned earlier, the incitement for building the structure may be related to the changed burial customs. The changed settlement location could be a second motivation as the land was still connected to their ancestors in the cemetery. The burial customs may well have involved the offering or breaking of pottery of which large amounts were found in R25/26. The different pits which held the pottery could have been made on separate occasions. Other contemporary pits were found in the vicinity of the structure. Two of these, 35m north of R25/25, and one 40m to the northwest, were dated to the second half of the Middle Iron Age (Schinkel 1998, 290). Perhaps the location of the pit was not bound to the structure, but rather to the proximity of the graves. The pits 35m north were interpreted as a watering hole (for cattle) and a well (Schinkel 1998, 74). However, given the unusual setting of these features within the cemetery, this interpretation may need reconsidering.

7.5 Diachronic landscape use and the rectangular structure

The three case studies in this chapter provide significantly different contextual settings for rectangular structures. In Aalter, the rectangular structures were physically integrated into the prevailing field systems. One structure preceded the field system, while another was the successor of a second field system, making the structures an integral part of the formation process of the local pastural landscape. The landscape in Harelbeke-Kortrijk was similarly demarcated by linear ditches aligned along the roads. Rectangular structures of an explicit type were embedded in this formalised setting, at seemingly regular intervals. In Oss the landscape developed around an urnfield cemetery, encircled by fields and settlements that regularly changed location. Two interconnected rectangular structures were the central focal point of the cemetery and at the same time two other structures were in use within a settlement, distinctly placed in between the houses.

Each of these structures had their intrinsic social designation, whether a cemetery, field system or a settlement, assumingly related to a variable specialised function. The contextual differences are notable, but there are also similarities worth considering. In all of the three case studies multiple structures appear, that each have a role in the landscape. Clearly there is causality between the excavated area and the number of rectangular structures found. It transpires that these structures are not so unique after all. Conceivably, where there is one, more can be expected. In some instances, as is the case for Aalter, the structures are consecutive. In both the Oss and Harelbeke-Kortrijk regions multiple rectangular structures seem to have been in use simultaneously. In Oss, the contrasting contexts suggests that the structures likely had different functions, while in Harelbeke-Kortrijk their uniformity and comparable setting suggests all three structures were used for the same purpose.

Another common denominator to consider is the relation of the rectangular structures to boundaries as defined by Løvschal (2014). She described a diachronic approach to complex organisational devices relating to the landscape, starting with material lines of linear landscape markers in the late Neolithic or Bronze Age, developing into process-related boundaries or large-scale demarcations in the Iron Age. In Aalter, the barrow alignment on the ridge is an example of such a line. Bronze Age barrows are often respected in the Iron Age and incorporated into field systems. In Ronse-Pont West (see Ch.6.4.8), the extensive pattern of Late Iron Age linear ditches covers the entire area, except a space around the barrow. Barrows were not the only markers that were integrated into the Iron Age landscape. In Oss and Aalter the rectangular structures were built in the Middle Iron

Age before the linear ditch systems were put in place. The field systems thereafter were laid out in such a manner that ensured the integration of the older features into the functionality of the linear field system. The incorporation of the rectangular structures when the landscape is structured does not inevitably result in the field system having the same orientation, as demonstrated in Aalter where the linear ditches are at a 90-degree angle to the barrow alignment. Løvschal (2014) explains this as an articulated and ephemeral boundary, not a formalised and fixed one. The arrangement in Aalter certainly had a temporary character, not only with changing field systems but simultaneously the construction of a replacement rectangular structure.

All rectangular structures, whether barrows or otherwise can be perceived as 'existing man-made elements in the landscape [...] that would have been associated with certain ideas of the past and possibly also a given right to particular areas with ancestors buried inside them.' (Løvschal 2014, 739). In conclusion, rectangular ditches were positioned in prominent and often strategic locations within the landscape. Similar to older barrows, urnfields, and cemeteries, the rectangular structures were sometimes assimilated into field systems and settlements. The rectangular ditches had their own intrinsic value, or a practical purpose, depending on their position and their relation to preceding and succeeding features in the landscape. In all cases the diachronic contextual approach proves essential for the interpretation of the structures. In the next chapter I will explore the topic of the intrinsic value of the structures further.

8

The function of a rectangular structure

8.1 Introduction

In the previous chapters I discussed how rectangular structures are defined in different regions of Northwest Europe (Ch.3), how the relation of the structures to burials changed throughout the Iron Age of the Low Countries (Ch.4-Ch.6), and how their place in the Iron Age landscape developed (Ch.7). Different types of rectangular structures were in use, distinguishable from each other by their size, appearance, associated finds, and their context. Many were used as symbolic boundaries, not physical obstacles, while others served as defensive structures or surrounding cattle pens. Each site that contained one or more of these structures went through its own intrinsic processes, related to observable trends in the burial customs, settlement patterns and field systems.

In Ch.5.5 I distinguished three different types of rectangular structures that were in use during the Middle Iron Age in the Low Countries: one used in relation to wet depositions, a larger 'rectangular ditched structure', and a burial surrounding feature. The latter is commonly a square ditch, but can also have other forms. In chapter 6.6 it transpires that by the Late Iron Age no less than six types of rectangular structure were in use synchronously. The Late Iron Age types include one for defensive purposes, smaller rectangular structures related to field systems, and the introduction of the 'walled' cult place. Additionally, at least since the Early Iron Age, rectangular structures were occasionally used as cattle pens or settlement surrounding features. The types are summarised in table 8.1.

For most of these types the function can be deduced from their description. However, this is not the case for types 2 and 6, the types most commonly interpreted by excavators as 'cult places'. In this the range of possible functions for rectangular structures will be explored, working towards an interpretation of type 2 and 6 structures. Why did people construct these labour intensive structures? An understanding of the generative principles that instigated the emergence of this phenomenon is essential.

Type 2 structures were found throughout the research area, below the great rivers (fig. 8.1). A slight division between the east and the west of the research area can be distinguished, with most of the type 6 structures in the western part. It would seem field systems are more prominent in the west of the Low Countries. I will conclude this chapter with a reflection on the type 2 and type 6 structures (Ch.8.6), and of the type 5 structure of the Brabantstraat that initiated the research topic of this thesis and will make a suggestion on the motivation for the construction of this particular unusual rectangular structure in Oss (Ch.8.7).

8.2 The rectangular structure as a functional earthwork

Except for the post-setting in Someren and the stone pavements on the Kops Plateau, all structures in this thesis consist of at least one ditch. The activity of digging ditches

Type	Interpretation	Characteristics	Examples
1	Burial surrounding feature	Commonly less than 10m, square, shallow bowl shaped cross section of ditch, none or few finds, surrounding a grave (although sometimes eroded)	Destelbergen-Beekeinde, Meteren-Plantage, Oosterhout-De Contreie, Someren-Waterdael III, Weert-Laarvelt
2	Rectangular ditched structure as a provisional communication place	At least 15-20m in length, pottery deposition(s), commonly V-shaped cross section ditch, (sometimes) related to graves that are enclosed or nearby	Aalter-Woestijne, Alveringem, Boechout-Mussenhoevelaan, Born-Koeweide, Dendermonde-Hoogveld & Oud Klooster, Erembodegem, Gronsveld, Haren-Groenstraat, Hever-Stationsstraat, Itteren-Emmaus, Knesselare, Mielo-Hout-Ashorst, Nijmegen-Kops Plateau, Oss-R2, -R25/26, Oss-Ussen R49, Ursel
3	Wet deposition place	Many finds in a watery context	Houten-Castellum
4	Defensive structure	Very large cross section of the ditch (unpassable without a bridge), palisade or bank inside, settlement features inside	Kontich-Alfsberg
5	Walled cult place	U-shaped cross section for the ditch (bedding trench), multi-phased, pits with burned/broken material	Oss-Brabantstraat
6	Rectangular structure related to field system	Approximately 10-15m long, pottery deposition, field system nearby, sometimes related to a grave	Brecht-Akkerweg, Harelbeke-Eviolis, Kortrijk-Morinnestraat, Odijk, Oedelem-Wulfsberge, Oostvleteren-Kasteelweg, Ronse-Pont West
7	Cattle pen or settlement feature	U-shaped cross section for the ditch (bedding trench), few or no finds	Barneveld-Harselaar-west, Liessel-Willige Laagt, Loon op Zand-Kraansvense Heide, Oss-Westerveld R57, Oss-Ussen R50, Oegstgeest-Rijnvaert, Rijkevorsel-Wilgenlaan

Table 8.1. Types of Iron Age rectangular structures found in the Low Countries.

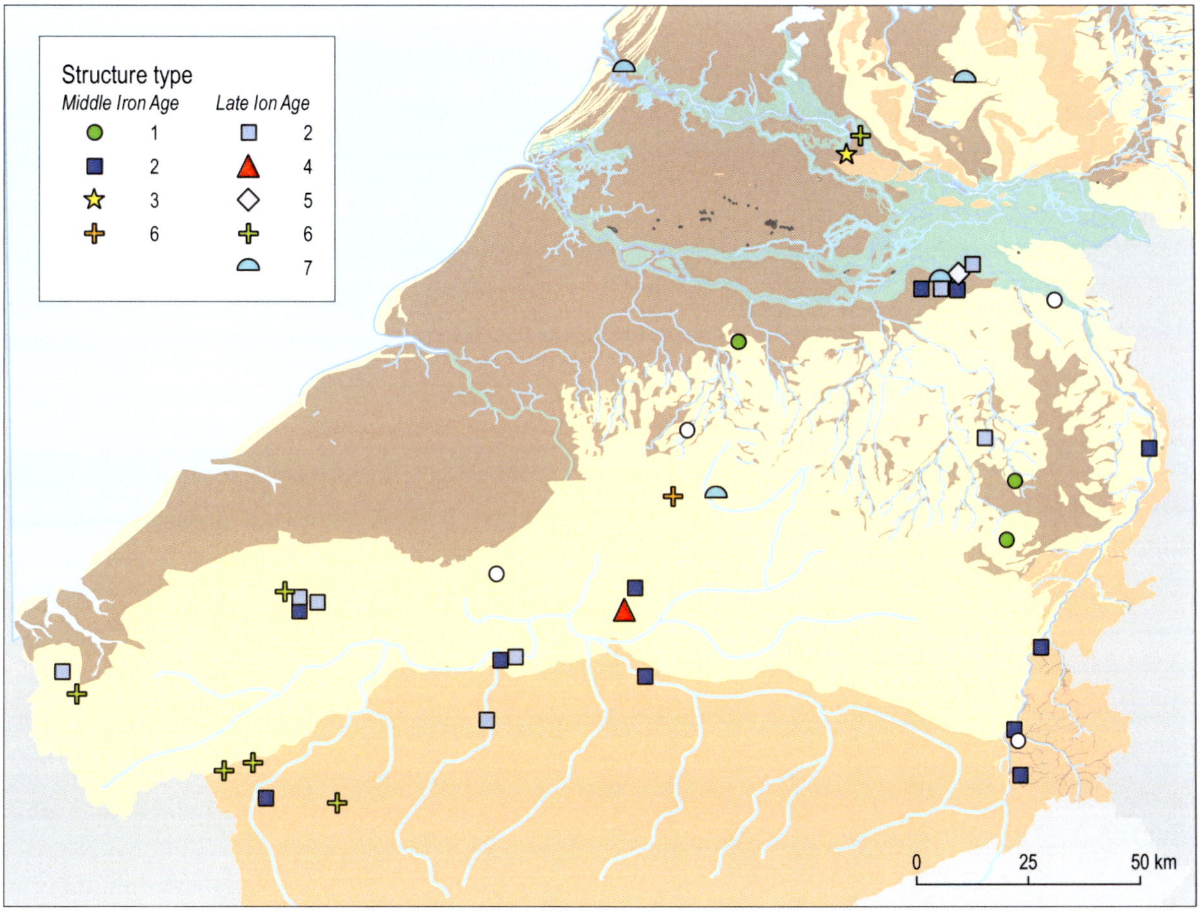

Figure 8.1. Distribution map of Middle and Late Iron Age structures by type.

intensifies almost exponentially during the Iron Age. Specifically in the later Iron Age ditches become a multi-purpose feature, structuring, and in some places dominating, the landscape.

On a basic level ditches serve a purpose for drainage, as a defensive structure, or as symbolic boundaries (e.g. Løvschal 2014; Brestel 2017, 35-53). A ditch can even be the unintended by-product of the construction of a bank or a barrow. The drainage type is arguably the most common. Ditches made for water management were used everywhere in the Iron Age, especially in the Low Countries: in field systems bordering meadows and arable land, road sides, and around houses, farm yards and other structures. Drainage ditches have their origins in the Neolithic. Band ceramic houses of the 5th millennium BCE used to have drainage ditches along the long walls in order to manage the water coming down from the roof (Van de Velde & Van Wijk 2014). Digging a ditch is a simple yet labour-intensive solution to drain or collect water. Several rectangular structures in this thesis have a ditch for which a drainage function may be a possible interpretation. These are shallow features that could have functioned to drain for example the cattle pen or storage facility that it surrounded. This includes the Early Iron Age settlement features in Liessel (Ch.4.3.1) and Loon op Zand (Ch.4.3.2), Middle Iron Age features R49 and R50 in Oss (Ch.5.5.1 and Ch.7.4), and the Late Iron Age structures in the Harelbeke-Kortrijk area (Ch.7.3), as well as the one in Odijk (Ch.6.4.7). In assigning a drainage function to a rectangular ditch, the enclosed space is also designated a practical profane purpose as a consequence. Whatever was kept, stored, housed or made within the enclosure, had to be kept as dry as possible. In this scenario, the soil coming out of the ditches would conceivably have been deposited on the enclosed space, enhancing the draining effect by raising the ground.

8.2.1 Field boundaries and landscape structuring

Ditches bordering fields and meadows were not common on a larger scale until the Iron Age, although a range of other types of fences and boundaries were applied in the Bronze Age (Løvschal 2020). In the Late Bronze Age and Early Iron Age, fields were often surrounded by banks instead of ditches, as found in Celtic fields (e.g. Spek et al 2003; Kooistra & Maas 2008; Spek et al. 2009, 11; Theunissen 2009; Arnoldussen, Schepers & Maurer 2016; Nielson & Dalsgaard 2017). Celtic fields typically consist of 20 to 40m square, interconnected small plots separated by banks, covering several hectares altogether. The general configuration of this parcelled landscape and its superficial resemblance to some Iron Age cemeteries such as in Raalte, led Groenewoudt (2011) to the theory that the shape inspired rectangular cult places. This theory is highly

unlikely for several reasons. First, none of the structures in this thesis displayed any relation to Celtic fields, nor have any Celtic fields been found in the vicinity. Celtic fields as a mostly northern phenomenon, are situated in different geographical regions than the rectangular structures (compare fig. 1 in Arnoldussen, Schepers & Maurer 2016 to the maps in this thesis). Also, banks as opposed to ditches are a different cognitive as well as visual experience. Nielson & Dalsgaard (2017) suggested that the banks were created using soil originating from neighbouring fields, not from digging a ditch. Further on in this chapter, I will demonstrate that the digging of a ditch and thereby creating a fissure in the earth was a significant part of the act. And finally, few finds related to Celtic fields can be interpreted as offerings (relating to a cult).

The parcelled landscape of the Celtic fields of interconnected squares, may have been merely the result of the applied method of agriculture. In ploughing a field the curvature of the land dictates the shape of the arable plot. In the Low countries the limit would often have been dictated by both water and forests rather than hills and rocks. The pulling of the plough in furrows conceivably results in a rectangular field, inherent to the process. Some Celtic fields were in use during the Iron Age and even into the Roman Era (Theunissen 2009), a synchronous development to the increased use of ditches for land divisions in other regions. This contemporaneity indicates there are regional differences, as proposed by Løvschal (2014).

On a larger scale linear ditches were used to structure landscapes. Middle Iron Age sites such as Aalter-Woestijne, Brecht-Akkerweg, Kooigem-Bos, Dendermonde-Oud Klooster, and to a lesser extent Itteren-Emmaus and Hever-Stationsweg, are exhibiting linear features that indicate the landscape was being divided. Plots were delineated and areas structured. This phenomenon seems to be particularly developing in the Middle Iron Age. By the Late Iron Age, sites such as Ronse-Pont West, Oostvleteren-Kasteelweg, the Harelbeke-Kortrijk area, Erembodegem, and Oedelem-Wulfsberge, manifest that landscape structuring was well established by then. Ditches were used to indicate where the roads, farmlands, cemeteries, and other assigned areas had their place in the landscape. The emergence of chiefdoms in the Late Iron Age is a generative principle mentioned for land divisions, as privatising property gains weight and therefore land demarcations become important (Gibson 2007).

8.2.2 Defences

Ditches for water management of arable land were often of a limited size, smaller than the modern-day equivalent generally applied in the Low Countries. When dug for defensive purposes however, their size could take impressive dimensions. As demonstrated in chapter 3.3.1, a ditch of 4-6m wide and 2.5m deep probably sufficed as an effective defensive measure in *Viereckschanzen*, but in oppida ditches could reach to even larger proportions. In the oppidum of Maiden Castle in England, an almost continual modification process for over 300 years resulted in ditch constructions of 12-15m wide and over 6m deep (Sharples 1991, 63-67, fig. 50).

Notably, the cross section of a ditch made for defensive purposes is often V-shaped, while the smaller drainage ditches were more irregularly bowl-shaped. This shape may have been inherent of the digging method rather than the result of an intentional act, although conceivably as a defensive measure a V-shaped ditch is likely to be more effective. The seemingly excessively large ditch that was partially excavated in Kontich-Alfsberg could be perceived as a defensive structure. In this aspect it is comparable to the *Viereckschanzen*. If indeed the structure in Kontich was a defensive structure, it is quite unique for the region. The motivation for its construction on this particular location can only amount to guesswork, although the obvious incentive would be a (local) conflict.

8.2.3 House and settlement ditches

Another application of ditches can also be found in Kontich-Alfsberg, preceding the large ditch. The narrow appearance and straight sides define it as a bedding trench: a foundation trench for a wall. Often this type of ditch holds few finds, as it was not meant as an open feature unlike other ditches. Bedding trenches are rarely found in rectangular structures in the Iron Age. Apart from Kontich, Oss-Brabantstraat was the only other site where this type of ditch was used. It seems the bedding trench was (re-)introduced towards the end of the Iron Age, and in the Roman Era thereafter became a regular building method applied in house constructions (Slofstra 1991, 139; Schinkel 1998, 120-127; Fokkens 2019a, 50-51).

Finally, ditches were used to define settlements. Boundaries delimiting settlements seem to be predominantly a Late Iron Age and Roman phenomenon, generally consisting of a single or a double ditch system. These surrounding ditch systems are unlikely to have had a defensive function (Fokkens 2019b, 193-197; Jansen 2021a). Generally, ditches with this function were only about 1m wide and relatively shallow, only containing water after heavy showers. In theory a wall or hedge could have been situated next to the ditch, although evidence of this was never found. Fokkens (*Ibid.*, 193) further remarks that some of the settlement ditches show evidence of maintenance and would have enclosed not only the houses, but also some arable land and space were livestock could be corralled. The entrance often resembled a funnel, another indication

the enclosures were used for channelling and herding cattle (*Ibid.*, 196). In conclusion, surrounding settlements with a ditch, and including for example a hedge, would suffice to keep cattle confined during the night.

8.2.4 The temporality of a ditch

With the exception of bedding trenches, ditches as functional earthworks were meant to remain open features, otherwise their function diminishes. When not maintained, a ditch will be overgrown and refilled as sediments start to shift in the slopes and plants root within days or weeks of construction, specifically in the soft soils of the Low Countries. Many ditches therefore have an ephemeral character (Løvschal 2014). This seems to apply not only to ditches in larger field systems, but also to the rectangular structures that are the subject of this thesis.

None of the structures in this thesis portray convincing evidence of re-digging of the ditches, of successive phases, or of maintenance. Pedological and palynological research of the ditches of the rectangular enclosure in Aalter, provided evidence that the ditches were dug down to a level above the groundwater, remained open for a period no longer than a few weeks, and subsequently closed up by filling them in completely (Langohr & Fechner 1993). In rare cases however, traces of wooden plank lining have been found in ditches, as was also documented in the site of Gournay-sur-Aronde. These were used in some V-shaped ditches with the intention of prolonging the ditch as an open feature. A Bronze Age ring ditch in Aalter is one of the oldest examples (Van de Vijver *et al* 2019a, 84). There, 20cm wide vertically placed planks were used to reinforce the lower sides. The ring ditch would have surrounded a barrow and central grave, neither of which remained at the time of excavation. Clearly, this ditch was not merely a by-product of the barrow construction, it had an additional symbolic value as a depression in the soil.

The significance of the dimensions of the ditch in a rectangular structure as a physical obstacle diminishes during the course of the Iron Age. In the Middle Iron Age rectangular structures tended to be made out of ditches with a remaining width of 150cm and 70cm deep on average (table 5.1). By the Late Iron Age the remains of ditches of rectangular structures average around 90cm wide by only 35cm depth (table 6.1). Once constructed, the value of the feature was established, possibly affirmed by a deposition in the ditch, and thereafter needed no further maintenance to assure sustained perceptibility. In the Late Iron Age the ditches generally became shallower and thereby more ephemeral. Whereas in the Middle Iron Age over half of the documented rectangular ditches have a V-shaped cross section, by the Late Iron Age only a few were still constructed in this fashion (compare table 5.1 and table 6.1). A bowl or randomly generated shape becomes common, with less attention to physical appearances or durability.

Evidently, the rectangular structures were not meant to last. If people had a perception of having created a permanent place, it was merely cognitive. Either the act of digging the ditch or making a boundary surrounding a designated space was the intention. Once it was done, the space and/or the ditch kept their symbolic meaning even when the visibility diminished. This act of creating a rectangular ditch was performed only on exceptional occasions. When a structure was needed an additional ditch was made, as was the case in for example Koeweide, Itteren, Kemzeke, Aalter, Alveringem, and Boechout, but the original ditch was never redug. Notably, several of the structures were reused in the Roman Era as burial grounds. In Itteren for example, the place was not used for at least two or three centuries, before in the late 2nd century CE over a dozen new burials were added, also within the rectangular ditch, but not in the second cemetery to the north. Apparently, this place was still visible as a burial ground after all this time, despite the transient character of the ditches and the fact that the site could have been completely overgrown after that time. Perhaps a wall next to the ditch would have helped create this type of lasting visibility, or the cognitive perception of the place was transferred through generations.

8.2.5 The concept of a rectangle

Not only are most of the structures in this thesis made of a ditched earthwork, they are also mostly rectangular. Wait (1985, 156) noted a bias in the selection of Iron Age rectangular structures in Britain as shrines, for the only reason that their rectangular shape opposed the commonly round domestic features such as houses, even though their construction method was the same. However, the binary opposites in form remain notable. Throughout the Bronze and Iron Age on the British Isles houses were round, and so were the religious structures from the Neolithic onwards. All henge monuments portray a round setting, their purpose interpreted as alignments with the equinoxes and/or solstices (e.g. Bradley 1998). It is conceivable this reflects the shape of the houses. Parker Pearson & Ramilisonina (1998) interpret the stone monuments that may have been perceived as the places for the dead; the spirits of the deceased were housed there, while wooden examples were reserved for the living. Could this concept apply to structures on the near continent as well? In Northwest Europe houses have always been rectangular. Rectangular ditches, or long barrows / long graves, developed in urnfields as some of the oldest features. It has been suggested by Roymans & Kortlang (1999, 45) that long graves held a prominent position in the mortuary customs of the Lower Rhine Urnfield Culture based on several observations. Roymans

& Kortlang (1999, 45-49) suggested that long graves were meant for adults, predominantly males, possibly the heads of a family and founders of the cemetery. The shape of the long grave was meant to symbolise a house, reflecting the basic family-unit, and ensuring the continuity between the world of the living and the dead. Based on another observation, Roymans & Kortlang (1999, 45) state that in contrast to barrows, long graves sometimes contain rich ceramic material. One particular long grave in Weert held the shards of at least 14 pots found at the bottom of the ditch (Verwers 1975, 26-31; Verlinde 1987, 245, 253 as cited by Roymans & Kortlang 1999). These pottery depositions were attributed by Roymans & Kortlang (1999, 45) to 'special ritual activities, probably feasting'.

The square or the rectangular shape emerged because an underlying meaning that was applied by the people who made these monuments dictated or required this particular form. In the Neolithic and Bronze Age, burial monuments in the Low Countries were generally not rectangular. Passage graves as well as barrows were round or oval, or even key-hole shaped. Several square monuments dating to the Middle Bronze Age in the Northwest of the Netherlands (Jezeer & Roessingh 2019, 330-341) were exceptions. No human remains were found in these monuments, but an interpretation as a burial monument is probable nonetheless. These early examples of rectangular structures provide proof of concept of an idea that was not common until the Middle Iron Age. Perhaps rectangular structures can be attributed to founders in the Late Bronze Age and Early Iron Age, but not until the later Iron Age these structures become detached from graves. The shape could have been applied to people who had a divergent manner of death, or a special role in society or way of life, such as a hunter or a blacksmith (e.g. Freeman & Pankhurst 2003; Jørgensen 2012). This social role also entails outsiders or social outcasts, a theory that is also proposed for Iron Age inhumation burials and sacrificial victims found in peat bogs and storage pits (Van der Sanden 1990; 1996; Lambot 1998; Aldhouse-Green 2006, 15; Hargrave 2018, 184). However, recent evidence based on isotope analysis indicates that in the Low Countries unburned Iron Age skeletal remains are usually locals (Kootker et al. 2018; Kootker 2022). Analysis of human cremation remains from graves generally indicates that neither gender or age was the motivation for the construction of a rectangular (burial) monument as all categories are represented. The absence of age or gender discrimination was previously apparent in urnfields, where the cremation remains of both sexes and of all age categories were interred in equal numbers, either with or without an urn (Louwen 2021, 114). Concluding, the construction of rectangular structures related to graves is more likely related to the manner of death or the social role in a community, not to age, gender, or outsiders.

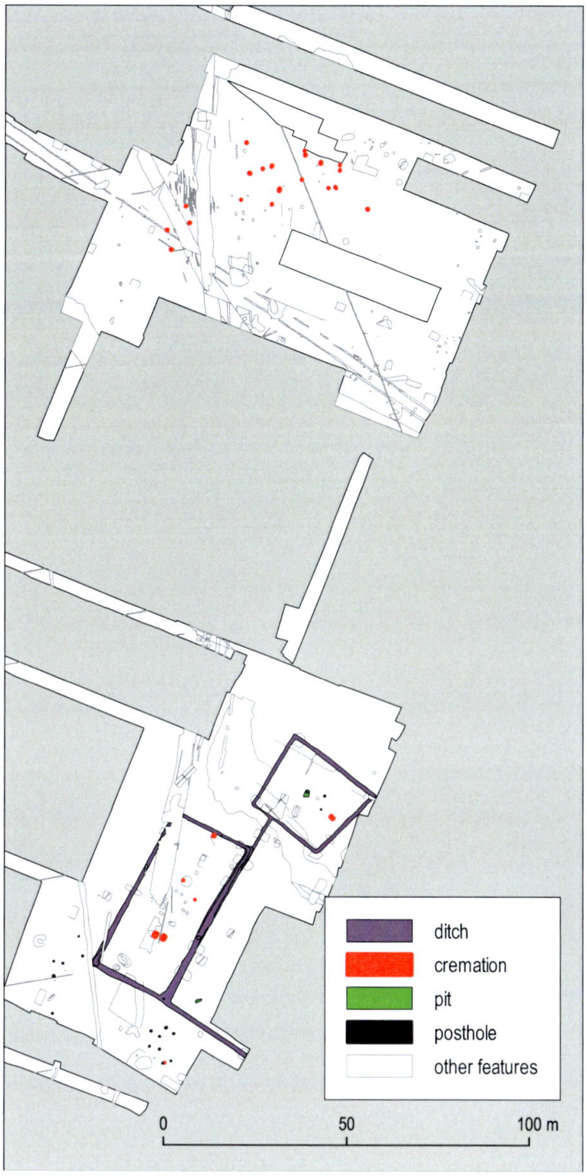

Figure 8.2. Excavation plan of both cemeteries at Itteren-Emmaus (After Meurkens & Tol 2011, figures 6.1, 6.11 and 8.3).

8.3 The rectangular structure as a cemetery demarcation

The relation between rectangular ditches and burials is undeniable. On the Kops Plateau, a path of cobbles was used to materialise this connection into a permanent, visual element (Fontijn 2002a). However, it was not until the Middle Iron Age that the use of larger rectangular structures became more widespread. Nearly all rectangular structures from this period either surrounded or were placed in the direct vicinity of a cremation cemetery. Their connection to graves may be apparent, but it was not the sole purpose for their construction. The ditch was not

merely a cemetery demarcation. In Itteren for example, two large rectangular structures surrounded only a few contemporary graves, while a larger cremation cemetery was situated 150m to the north without a demarcation (fig. 8.2; Ch.5.2.2; Meurkens & Tol 2011). What if it was never the primary intention to accommodate many graves inside the rectangular structures? Why were there two cemeteries in use, in close proximity of each other, at the same time? There is a possibility two different communities with different burial traditions placed their cemeteries in close proximity. However, this does not explain the absence of graves within one cemetery, the one 'protected' by a ditch, while most of the graves appear to be present in the other, 'unprotected' cemetery. An alternative explanation is that these separate burial grounds represent different conceptual positions, or different societal roles, for people in the Iron Age. Manner of death in addition to identity may be related to this difference in burial traditions.

In Ch.5.4.1 I proposed the rectangular structures in Itteren are ephemeral structures made for a temporary purpose, one added after another. These monuments were only meant for a special occasion or a select group of people. More people were interred within the normal burial grounds to the north. As both the rectangular structure cemeteries and the northern cremation cemetery held the graves of women, men and children (Meurkens & Tol 2011, 70-74), neither age or gender was the decisive factor when it came to the choice of burial grounds. Again, the choice therefore is most likely to be related to manner of death or social role.

As not all Iron Age cemeteries had a large rectangular structure, clearly a rectangular structure was needed only on certain occasions. Also, the graves were commonly not confined to the inner space of the enclosure. This seems to be a regional phenomenon. In northern France for example, the Late Iron Age village of Acy-Romance portrays a notable contrast between the inhumation burials in pits that were found inside the village and the 'ordinary' cemeteries outside (Ch.3.2.5; Lambot 1998; Lambot & Méniel 2000). The latter involved different cemeteries where people were interred according to the regular cremation custom. That was not the only contrast. The cremation cemeteries were surrounded by a ditch while the pit burials were not. Whatever the ditch symbolised, it was deemed unnecessary for the dead people in the pit burials.

The fact that burial customs in Acy-Romance involved creating a boundary between the space used for a cemetery and the outside world has relevance. In a cult place, temple, church, synagogue, or mosque the structure facilitates the communication with one or more deities. Conceivably, ditched structures, whether round or rectangular, were used in burial customs for a similar purpose. As most Iron Age cremation graves are not situated inside a structure,

142   BEFORE TEMPLES

Site	Ditch date in century BCE	Pottery	Spindle whorl	Glass	Sling shot bullet	Bone / crem.	Stones	Metal	Char-coal	2nd burned
Poperinge-Koestraat	11th	1 whole pot, 2 in fragments, on the westside								
Nijmegen-Kops Plateau	9th-7th?	-						1 axe, NE side		
Kooigem-Bos	5th-mid 4th	9130 fragments. inside + depot in fill on the westside								
Dendermonde-Oud Klooster	5th-1st	217 NW ditch, incl. 2 situla-shaped pots								
Zundert-Akkermolenweg	5th-1st	145 fragments, SE side								X
Brecht-Akkerweg	5th?	173 fragments								
Kemzeke-Kwakkel	5th	154 fragments (A) 400 fragments (B)						Bracelet		
Born-Koeweide	4th-early 2nd	310 fragments								
Itteren-Emmaus	4th-early 2nd	NW corner 1 pot, west 1 pot, 95 mostly SW corner								X
Oss-Ussen R25/26	4th-early 2nd	1229 fragments in ditches, 2085 in pits, SE and W	X				X	Slags		
Houten-Castellum	4th-3rd?	35 fragments, more in ditch pits	1 in pit			3 in pits	13			Chopped
Oss-Ussen R49	4th-3rd?	1100 fragments	X		X	X	X			
Aalter-Woestijne	4th-3rd	6 pots, SW corner		Bead		X			X	X
Hever-Stationsstraat	4th-3rd.	63 fragments								
Lomm-Hoogwatergeul	4th-2nd.	305 fragments			1	78		Roman fibula		
Kortrijk-Morinnestraat west	Late 4th-2nd	310, mostly NW and SE	1				1			
Oedelem-Wulfsberge	Late 4th-2nd	'some pottery' (A)								
Boechout-Mussenhoeve-laan	4th-1st	819 in total: 43 (A), 360 (B), 226 (C), 190 (D)		Bracelet			X	3 nails		
Gronsveld-Duijsterstraat	3rd-2nd	6 fragments					X			
Ronse-Pont West	3rd-2nd	Some pottery				1				X
Alveringem-Eikhoek/ Hoogstade	3rd-1st?	5113 fragments on NW sides (A, C)								
Kontich-Alfsberg	3rd-1st?	8 fragments (narrow ditch)								
Rijkevorsel-Wilgenlaan	3rd-1st?	5 fragments								
Harelbeke-Evolis	3rd-1st	411 fragments, SE corner								
Haren-Groenstraat	3rd-1st	Pot in SW corner				1				
Oss-Ussen R2	3rd-1st	68 fragments in ditch, 200 in pit W + 1 upside down pot	1			X	1			
Oss-Westerveld R57	3rd-1st	347 fragments, 1 miniature bowl				X	1	Slags, 1 nail		
Dendermonde-Hoogveld	2nd-1st half 1st	19 fragments				X	X		X	
Cuijk-Ewinkel	2nd-1st?	700 fragments at least	1	Bracelet			X	Fibula, slag		
Barneveld-Harselaar-west	2nd-1st	31 fragments								
Knesselare-Westervoorde	2nd-1st	60 fragments								
Kortrijk-Morinnestraat east	2nd-1st	204 fragments	2							
Odijk-Singel	2nd-1st	468 fragments on N-side				X		Slags, metals		
Oegstgeest-Rijnvaert	2nd-1st	538 fragments, mostly S/SE side				3				
Oostvleteren-Veurnestraat / Kasteelweg	2nd-1st	30 fragments (A), a bowl, a pot, fragments of 1 pot (B), 10 (C)					X			X
Erembodegem-Zuid-IV	1st BCE (- 1st CE?)	'large amount' (A), 'limited amount' (B)								
Oss-Brabantstraat	1st BCE – 1st CE	230 fragments		Bracelet		2	X	1 nail		
Ursel-Rozestraat	1st BCE – 1st CE	5 fragments (A), 100 fragments (B), 7 fragments (C)					X			

Table 8.2. Summary of finds related to rectangular ditches dating to the Iron Age from oldest to youngest; 'x' is present, but exact numbers unknown.

Century BCE	Dominant burial customs	Grave goods (incl. urn)	Pottery deposition in rect. structures	Wet depositions	Structure type						
					1	2	3	4	5	6	7
7	Cremation	++	-	++	-	+	-	-	-	+	+
6	Cremation / inhumation	+	-	++	+	-	-	-	-	+	+
5	Cremation / inhumation	+++	++	+	-?	+	-?	-	-	+	-
4	Cremation	+	++	+	+	+	+	-	-	+	-
3	Cremation	+	++	+	+	++	+	-	-	-	-
2	Cremation	+	++	+	+	++	+	+?	-	-	+
1	Cremation	+	+?	++	++	++	+	+	+	-	+

Table 8.3. Iron Age practices throughout the centuries in the Low Countries (- = none; + = few, ++ = relatively common, +++ = many). Structures types: see table 8.1.

not even in urnfields, apparently communication (either with deities or spirits) was commonly not required or did not need the facilitation of a rectangular structure. In cemeteries the intended communication was likely not with a deity, but with the spirit of the deceased. Perhaps making a boundary created a place for the spirit of the deceased to reside in or return to when needed, a home for, or place of communication. Sometimes long dead (mythical?) ancestors were included, by literally incorporated the barrow within the ditch system, as in for example Dendermonde-Hoogveld and Ursel. In this way the spirits of the ancestors that were already present could be involved in the communication or invoked.

In the Late Iron Age the emphasis shifts towards rectangular structures that are no longer verifiably related to burials, and new types emerges (type 4, 6, and 7). The larger rectangular structures dating to the Late Iron Age become increasingly detached from cemeteries, as more and more are not related to any graves, while the use of causeways was entirely abandoned by the 3rd century BCE, even though watery depositions continue and even intensify again during the 1st century BCE. Seemingly, the enclosures were erected for a slightly different reason, not directly related to burials but rather as a derivative of the burial customs and the corresponding belief system. The find assemblage may shed some light on that.

8.3.1 Associated finds

Pottery is easily the most dominant find category in the excavation of Iron Age sites. In virtually all sites discussed in this thesis pottery was found in or related to the ditch of the rectangular structure. For thirty-nine sites the finds spectrum is summarised in table 8.2.[23]

Four sites (10%) immediately stand out for their large amount of pottery found related to the rectangular structures, namely Kooigem, Alveringem, and two in Oss. The quantity of pottery found in those sites totals to thousands of shards per structure. Fourteen (35%) more sites contain several hundred pieces of pottery. In Odijk and Cuijk, they add up to a considerable weight, indicating that the assemblage consisted of large fragments that were likely broken on the spot. The other sites have moderate amounts of pottery, ranging from a few to over a hundred shards per site (45%). Lomm is counted among the latter, as the number of shards is considered low compared to the large size of the ditch, although not the entire ditch was searched.

In eleven excavation reports the location of where the pottery was found in the ditch is stated. Both the northwest and southeast corners or – sides seem to be most common. Southwest, west or north sides/corners are occasionally used for depositions. The exception is the northeast side, which is never mentioned. The only deposition known on the northeast side is the Late Bronze Age-Early Iron Age axe found on the corner of the structure on Kops Plateau in Nijmegen. This site is also the only exception where no pottery deposition was related to the ditch, although this may be attributed to the type of ditch.

In at least five sites the pottery fragments were secondarily burned and in Houten the pottery seemed to have been deliberately chopped. Other finds were also made of fired clay, such as spindle whorls and slingshot bullets. Metals and other materials are uncommon in rectangular structures in the Low Countries. The metals are usually limited to a few nails; other objects are rare. Houten is the only structure that was associated with an iron weapon: a spearhead. This is an exception, as none of the other structures contained any weapons besides the occasional slingshot bullet. Clearly, none of the other structures can be interpreted as war trophies reflecting the northern French sanctuaries. Neither does the find assemblage seems to represent an entire community. Exceptions may be the large depositions in Kooigem, Alveringem, and in Oss-Ussen R25/26.

---

23   Urnfield sites or sites that yielded no finds related to the rectangular structure(s) were left out.

In conclusion, rectangular structures generally contain one or more depositions of pottery in the ditch. The pottery is often found near the bottom, indicating it was deposited shortly after the construction of the ditch. The disposition must therefore be related to the initiation of the structure. Pottery depositions associated with rectangular structures occur consistently throughout the Middle and Late Iron Age. In the 5th century BCE this occurred in the vicinity, indicating the grounds may have been initiated before the construction of the structure. In Brecht, Houten, and Itteren pits containing Early La Tne-type whole pots were discovered (see also Ch.8.5.1). This reminds us of the 'pit of the vases' in Gournay-sur-Aronde, that was excavated adjacent to the sanctuary. In Kooigem, Kemzeke, and possibly in Dendermonde-Oud Klooster, similar Early La Tène depositions were found at the bottom of the ditch. In subsequent centuries, depositions commonly involved breaking the pottery first, and/or secondarily burning it, before depositing in the ditch. Towards the end of the Iron Age, pottery depositions in rectangular structures subside, probably in favour of a renewed interest in depositions in wet places and in other contexts such as cult places (e.g. Jansen, Van der Linde & Fokkens 2002; Roymans 2004; Jansen & Jacques 2014). Generally, trends of depositions do not seem related to the development and use of particular types of rectangular structures (table 8.3).

8.4 The rectangular structure as a symbolic boundary

Before inferring the function of the rectangular structures, the aspects of the Iron Age belief system that set in motion the construction of these structures must be considered. Often the emphasis of Iron Age religion is on the gods or the deities that were worshipped (e.g. Wait 1985, 195-199; Brunaux 1986, 69-80; Roymans 1990, 49-92; Randsborg 1995, 76-80; Derks 1996; Aldhouse-Green 2001; 2016; Van den Broeke 2005). These gods were thought to be omnipresent in different parts of the Iron Age world view and cosmology, and could be contacted through interaction at liminal places. Deposits in watery environments were probably aimed at a deity that resided there, just like acts of exchange involving sacrifice were aimed at a fertility deity when it came to the cultivation of crops (Wait 1985, 262-263; Randsborg 1995, 75; Bradley 2005, 165-177). The rectangular structures however, were related to burials, certainly initially, and therefore part of the burial customs. Their construction was not aimed at the gods, but rather at the dead and the ancestors. The ancestral 'worship' or 'cult' basically revolves around the belief in the soul. Wait (1985) tried in a holistic approach to involve the soul as the main component of the Iron Age belief system, connected to the use of secondary mortuary customs, such as the manipulation of partly decomposed remains. Based on ethnographic research he concluded that the concept of a

belief in the soul involved four closely linked aspects: that the soul is immortal; that death is considered a liminal, transitional process instead of an event; that the body and soul exist in parallel as the fate of both are linked; and a belief in the 'otherworld', a place where the soul goes after death has been finalised by the destruction or deposition of the body (*Ibid.*, 250). In this context the act of cremation has a logical place. The transitional process is not complete until after the destruction of the body. Likewise, gifts intended for the deceased in the afterlife have to be destroyed in order to ensure transfer to the realm of the spirits, or to enable the spirit to use the object.

8.4.1 Formulation of the afterlife

The burial tradition is an event structured by the living, by the mourners (e.g. Brück 2006; Louwen 2021, 236). At that moment they are in charge of what happens to the body of the deceased and as a consequence they can also manipulate what happens to the soul. In cremation, the regular burial process in the Iron Age, the soul is set free to join the ancestors or to reincarnate. Clearly, in inhumations this was not the case. According to Wait (1985, 250) inhumations were designed to retain the soul at the place of burial. It was captured inside the body. Sometimes additional measures ensured the fixation of the soul in a certain place, the likely scenario for peat bodies that were pinned down in a bog (Van der Sanden 1990). In the worldview of the Iron Age people, the belief in the soul would not have been perceived as part of a formal religion. Rather, as Bradley (2005, 120) implied when he described how sacred and profane are two layers exactly superimposed, having a soul was part of their reality, an integral part of life and of human existence. The soul was thought be located in the head and when people died, something happened to that soul.

The occurrence that instigated the making of a rectangular ditch is related to this belief in an immortal soul. Several clues transpire from the former chapters as to what this occurrence entailed. First, a rectangular ditch was related to one or more burials and only constructed under specific conditions, for a minority of society. The majority of the population were buried in cremation cemeteries not demarcated by a ditch. Since the ditch was intended as a temporary feature, the conclusion must be that the event that triggered its construction was rare. Another feature, not previously discussed, is that these ditches are nearly always continuous. In fact, care is taken to ensure the uninterrupted character of the feature. In Lomm and Kooigem for example, a small bridge probably spanned the ditch to provide an entrance, while an interruption of the ditch would have been more economic to make. When there is an opening it is narrow, as can be perceived in the northern ditch of Boechout and in the first phase of Oss-Brabantstraat. Likewise, in Gournay-sur-Aronde efforts were taken to ensure the entrance was actually over a pit, thereby forcing the users of the sanctuary to use a bridge (Brunaux, Méniel & Poplin 1985, 67-68). Most sites however, show no sign of a bridge. A person could step over the ditch, as these limited-sized features were symbolic rather than physical boundaries. Finally, the act involved an object of exchange. The constant type of deposition found in connection to all of these structures, is pottery.

Pottery depositions can be considered as more personal than other types of Iron Age depositions, such as animal remains (Kok 2008, 70-71). Pottery is specifically household related, deposited by (direct) family members. Large numbers of weapons or animal bones are conceivably the result of a community cooperation or of elite individuals, sometimes the residue of a gathering or feast (e.g. Brunaux 1986; Browning 2011; Hargrave 2018, 54, 151-152). The rectangular structures in the Low Countries are specifically linked to pottery depositions, commonly not the result of large community gatherings. Exceptions may be the extravagantly large deposits in Oss-Ussen R25/26, Kooigem, and Alveringem.[24] What do these pottery depositions mean in this context and how are they related to the belief in the soul? Individual depositions may be intended to bind the soul to the household whose pottery it was, or provide a place resembling the former home; a safe and familiar place for the spirit. Perhaps the pottery was meant to lure the ancestral spirits into residing in the place of deposition or to return there when they needed to do so, as for example when a communication exchange was required. This type of exchange was often related to a requirement or protection, sometimes referred to as a 'fertility ritual' (Wait 1985, 262-263; Brunaux 1986, 91-93). The deposition was a request for a favour from the spirit.

In houses, pottery was being deposited in postholes before the construction was fixed in place, assumingly to protect the house. Van den Broeke (2005) called these 'foundation offerings'. Often the deposited pottery had been secondarily burned before deposition, a sign that the material was intended for the spirits. Perhaps the spirit of an ancestor could be bound to the house in this manner or be invoked upon on occasions, in order for good fortune and protection. Pottery depositions are polyhydric, as a multi-faceted link between the spirit world and the living.

Perhaps the way we regard 'abandonment sacrifices' also needs to be reconsidered. Under the assumption that broken and burned pottery represents a link to a dead relative, or the soul of a deceased, then perhaps a pottery deposition in an abandoned house is meant to bind the soul of a person who died there to that place. Specifically

on occasions when a person died what was considered a 'bad death', the place could have become a taboo. The reason for the deposition, or even for the house move, could be the underlying superstition.

8.4.2 Monuments without remains

What we are left with is an ephemeral, continuous structure, containing depositions made by direct relatives of the deceased. Assumingly, the continuous nature of the ditch had a similar function as the pottery: to contain or accommodate the soul or spirits of one or more dead people. In the Middle Iron Age all rectangular structures were related to burials, even if not all of the burials were enclosed by it. The ditch itself is nearly always V-shaped in cross section and of a substantial size. This changes in the course of the Late Iron Age, from the 2nd century BCE onwards. The ditch generally diminished in size, became shallower and increasingly a symbolic boundary rather than a physical one. Both the appearance and the dimensions of the structures became of less importance. A similar trend is noticeable in the orientation of the structures. The Early and Middle Iron Age structures had a prevailing orientation around the northeast to southwest, while the Late Iron Age structures seem to have no preferred orientation (fig. 8.3).

So while there are some diachronic developments, the structures portray significant synchronic variation. Different shapes and sizes are used at the same time and likely with variable functions.

Also, rectangular structures are progressively more often constructed without a relation to burials. In, for example, the structures of Alveringem, Dendermonde-Hoogveld, and Erembodegem cremation graves do not seem to be missing. These were not particularly badly eroded sites. Rather, the more likely explanation is that they never contained Iron Age graves. These structures did contain pottery deposits though. Apparently the spirits could be asked to reside, be attracted to, or return to this symbolic place, this artificially constructed 'house', even when their physical body was elsewhere. The soul would know where to go by guidance of the familiar pottery from their (former) household.

The absence of a body would make these monuments *de facto* a cenotaph. The word derives from the Greek for 'new tomb'. An example is the Cenotaph in London, a monument for fallen World War I soldiers, particular ones whose body was never repatriated. More generally, a cenotaph is a monument over an empty grave, for a person who died elsewhere and whose body is missing, or whose body has since been moved. The use of a cenotaph is an ancient concept, that likely emerged long before the Iron Age. Examples are known as early as the Neolithic, as was suggested for 15% of graves in the Bulgarian cemetery of Varna, dating to 4600-4300 BCE (Chapman *et al* 2006). In

---

24   The pottery assemblage of the latter two sites has unfortunately not been fully studied and the deposition as a whole is therefore poorly understood.

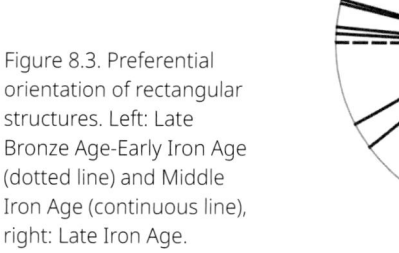

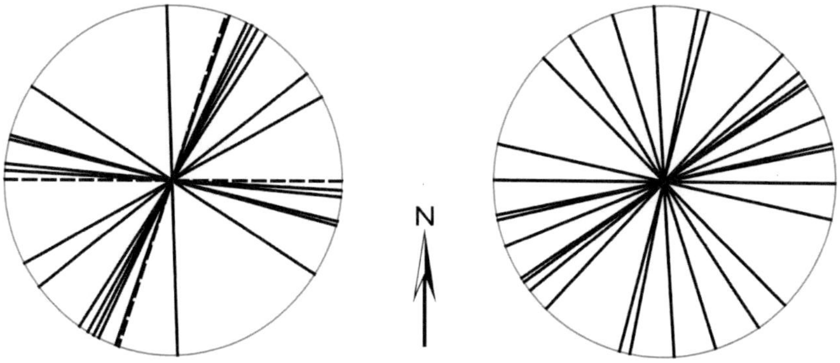

Figure 8.3. Preferential orientation of rectangular structures. Left: Late Bronze Age-Early Iron Age (dotted line) and Middle Iron Age (continuous line), right: Late Iron Age.

the Varna cemetery the same type of objects were found in graves with a body as well as in ones without. According to Fontijn (2019, 71) this implies that the objects in question could represent the concept of an (absent) person.

8.4.3 The impact of conflict

Assuming the rectangular ditches were fundamentally made to commemorate or communicate with dead or missing persons, or to be more precise, to bind the soul of a missing or dead person to a specific place, who would these structures represent? The absence of a missing body could be considered a special 'manner of death'. As in World War I, conflict would be the obvious main reason for people to go missing, followed perhaps by kidnapping. In the Low Countries, conflict in the Iron Age is an elusive concept as hillforts, mass graves, or other indications of fights are mostly absent in the archaeological record. The only direct evidence are weapon finds. To illustrate the distribution and numbers, Iron Age weapon finds in the Netherlands are plotted as an example (fig. 8.4). Swords and lance heads dominate, most of which derive from the great rivers. Gündlingen swords represent a specific Early Iron Age type of which seven were found in major rivers, seven in a burial context and one in a marsh (Fontijn 2002, 155-157). In the Low Countries this type of sword represents a new practice of deposition in the burial context at the time, as well as possibly the first type of sword to have been used in mounted warfare (*Ibid.*, 171-172). Both bronze and iron specimens are known.

Provided these weapons were not merely made for display or to be deposited, they must have been made to fight with and be used in combat. Societies in the Low Countries were mostly made up of dispersed small settlements with little discernible social differentiation, in the Late Iron Age clustering locally into somewhat larger settlements as the number of farmsteads increased while they were positioned closer together (Jansen & Van As 2012; Jansen 2021, 273-274). These settlements of clustered houses had a more permanent and fixed position,

sometimes emphasised by a surrounding settlement ditch. This 'dispersed settlement notion' elicits an image as an uneventful and peaceful society. In reality, we are aware that Iron Age societies were varied as the settlements and farms were not all similar, and the amount of arable land or number of livestock varied. Also, not everyone was a farmer. Craft specialisations developed into different social roles, sometimes forced by circumstances as not all attempts at farming were successful. Iron Age society contained more trades than farming, people who provided other services, such as blacksmiths, shamans, potters, hunters, workers paid in kind, perhaps even warriors or people skilled in combat who could be called upon when needed (by a tribal chief?). Inevitably, this would include people, like cattle thieves and raiders, who found it easier to take than to create. The palisaded ditches in Aalter and Hever, as well as settlement ditches and cattle corrals, suggest the creation of protective areas where livestock can be kept for protection. Also, trade routes and commodities change from time to time, social systems are adjusted accordingly, and land is increasingly claimed and demarked by boundaries. In an increasingly hierarchical society this must have resulted in the occasional conflict. It is conceivable that warriors who returned from a battle sacrificed their weapons in a river in exchange for their safety, for peace, or for victory. As a consequence, other warriors did not return as their bodies remained on the battlefield or they were kidnapped. From an Iron Age perspective, their souls were at risk of getting lost, or taken hostage, maybe eternally wandering without finding their way home. Relatives left behind may have tried to manipulate these lost souls into returning home, by providing a place to reside and a beacon to aim for. The closed ditch outlined the symbolic location of the spiritual house, while the pottery deposits formed the guideline. The excavations at Ribemont-sur-Ancre (Brunaux et al. 2003, 37) and Saumeray (Hamon *et al.* 2002) provided analogies here. Both these sites yielded two differently shaped structures, one of them containing more weaponry,

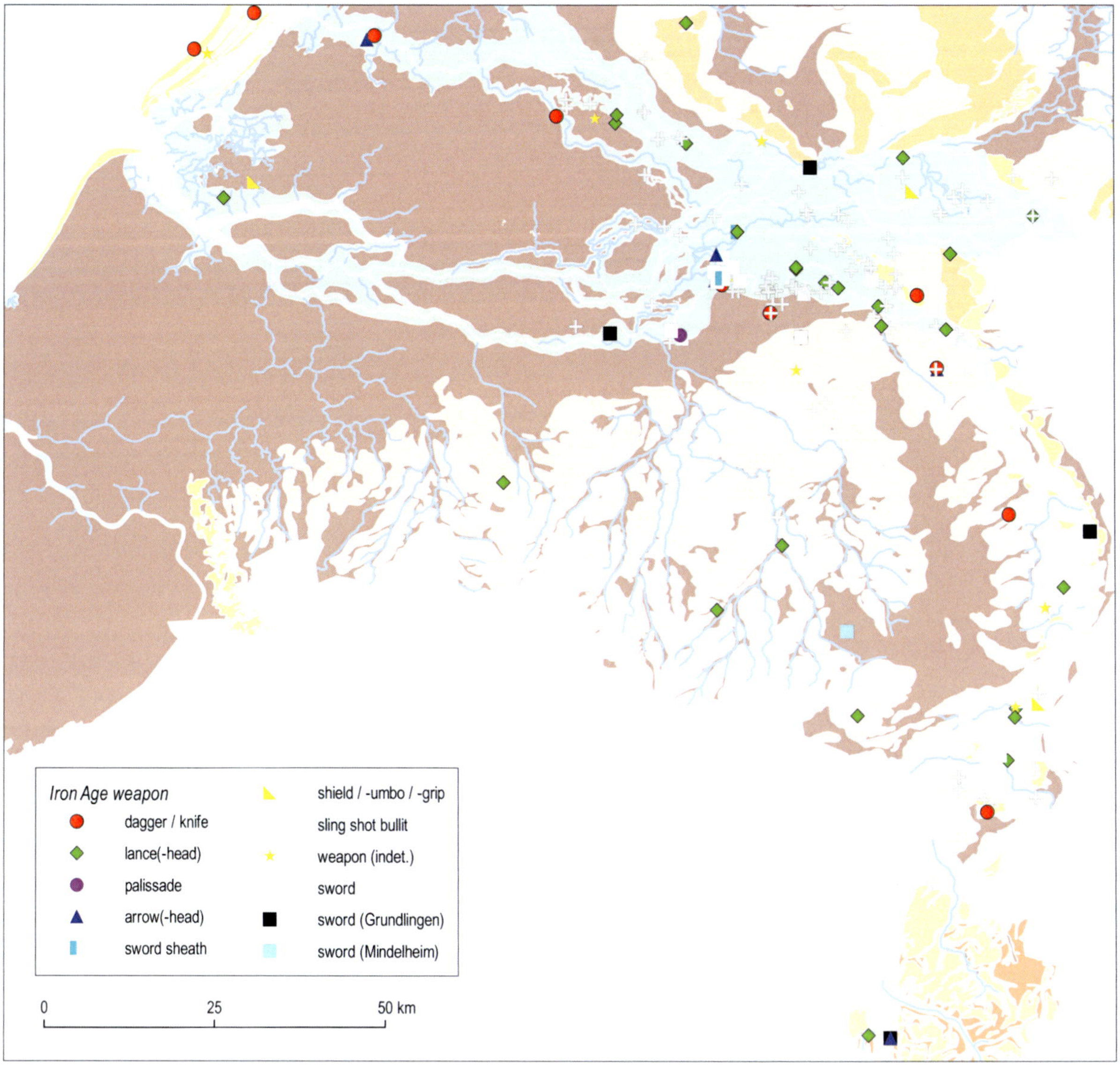

Figure 8.4. Map of the southern Netherlands with the known locations of Iron Age weapon finds plotted on the palaeographic map of the Netherlands of around 250 BCE (source: Archis; RCE). Soils: brown: peat; green: clay; yellow and beige: sand.

while the other held more pottery depositions (Ch.3.2.2). The structure containing the pottery is suggested to have been used for funerary rites, or intended as a memorial for the fallen friendlies, while the other is related to the remains of the battle, the enemy, or the defeated party. The fact that the structures at these sites were of a temporary nature is also relevant. Most rectangular structures in the Low Countries seem to have a short utilisation. Pottery deposits in the Low Countries structures are dominantly on the southeast, southwest, west, and northwest sides of the structures (see table 8.1). This orientation could be attributed to the direction of the sunrise or sunset, although conceivably the side was randomly chosen, or possibly, this was the

direction in which the people who were commemorated here disappeared.

In the sites of Aalter-Woestijne, Kemzeke, Itteren, Born, Oss-Ussen R25/26, Ursel, Dendermonde-Hoogveld, Haren, Alveringem, and Boechout appendixes or additions were attached to the main structure. This could have been roughly at the same time. Generally, the temporal difference between the main structure and the additions seems slight, making synchronicity or diachronicity difficult to determine. In line with the previous theory, these additions are conceivably meant for other missing people, possibly from other households, or made on separate occasions. Additional cremation burials, often positioned outside of the main structure, could be attributed to relatives seeking a connection to the missing relative, fellow tribesman, or ancestor. Alternatively, the rectangular ditch was not only created for missing people, but still related to the manner of death, perhaps in rare cases of what was considered a 'bad death'.

To summarise, the rectangular ditch was likely made for people who died a 'special' death, such as people who went missing. By making an artificial home for their soul, a place for the spirit was created, where at the same time commemoration and communication with the ancestors could take place. Not only were additional burials added, but other actions may have been performed after the enclosed space was created, to further communicate with the spirits of the ancestors that resided there.

8.5 The rectangular structure as a deposition space

Once a rectangular structure of type 2 or 6 was created and the depositions were in place, the structure was left to erode and overgrow, or possibly even filled in by hand. However, the place that was created was rarely forgotten. The space kept its value even after the visibility faded. This is illustrated by the fact that some of these sites were reused in the Roman era. The Roman graves in Itteren were added precisely within the boundaries of the Iron Age structure. In Lomm, the cemetery was continuously used until into the Roman era. Some of the Roman graves were even placed in the top layer of the ditch fill, as was the case in Dendermonde-Oud Klooster. In Dendermonde-Hoogveld Roman cremation graves were added just outside of the structure, as was the case in Poperinge. Apparently the space could keep its symbolic value for centuries.

The construction of the rectangular ditch and the associated pottery depositions are by no means the only action performed in these places. Further archaeological evidence is provided in the form of pits, posts, and other depositions. In this manner, when a space is repeatedly used for actions, it sustains its value. Indicating it as a cult place however, may be overemphasising the way in which these locations were regarded by Iron Age people. The cognitive perception of these places may have been one of the occasional 'mode of exchange' when the desire to communicate with the residential spirits of the ancestors arose, not a place to pay tribute to the gods.

8.5.1 Pits

The reason why most excavations reveal a large number of pits is simple: they were used for a wide variety of uses. Pits were dug for latrines, watering holes, for storage, mining, to accommodate specific craftworks, or for example dig in a post, or bury a person or another animal.

Only a limited number of motivations for pit creation are not related to houses, farmyards, farming, or animal husbandry. These include burials, acts of a religious nature, warfare, and natural causes. Not only the shape of the pit and the characteristics of the fill are requisite for the correct interpretation, but also the context is essential. For example the pits near structure R25/R26 in Oss-Ussen were interpreted as settlement features by Schinkel (1998, 267-297) on the basis of their contents even though the context is a burial ground. Perhaps the reason for the presence of these features in specific locations needs to be reconsidered. Many pits related to the rectangular structures of types 2 and 6 were devoid of finds. The oldest example was found in Poperinge, where a shaft-like pit with a possible wooden lining was found under the ditch (Van der Linde & Kalshoven 2017, 44-46). In Born-Koeweide a number of pits were found within the ditch system and in the direct vicinity, although none held any datable material. In some excavation reports it transpires that pits are an underappreciated type of feature. None of the pits around the structure in Dendermonde-Hoogveld or in Barneveld were described in the report, while in Lomm nearly half of the pits were not sectioned.

A total of 19 rectangular structures contained pits that could probably be associated with the use of the enclosed space (table 8.4). In contrast, urnfield monuments or later structures surrounding graves (type 1 rectangular structures), rarely have associated pits enclosed. One of the few exceptions are the three structures in Oostvleteren. For type 2 rectangular structures, enclosed pits are a reasonably common feature. Most of the pits contain finds. Pottery was customary, along with burned material in the form of burned loam, burned animal bones, charcoal or secondarily burned pottery. In some cases material may have been burned on the spot. Gerritsen (2003, 97-102) interpreted pits in settlements with burned material as the residue of a feast in honour of the ancestors. During the habitation phase of a house this was done in order to ensure the well-being of the farm and its inhabitants, while after abandonment the motivation was to symbolise closure.

In Lomm, pits were found to be generally bowl-shaped in cross section and rich with charcoal. Likewise, the structure in Oss-Ussen R49 contained a shallow pit that looked like a burn-spot. In Erembodegem, the multiple layered fill of the western pit contained some burned bone and pottery fragments, possibly indicating that the act of burning material was a repeated event here. Structure B on that site also enclosed a pit that contained charcoal. Oss-Brabantstraat contained a bowl-shaped pit coated with a layer of secondary burned pottery and another pit with a layer of burned loam and charcoal, conceivably the result of separate events. In Cuijk, the pit northwest of the ditch contained a lot of charcoal and some burned loam. An older Early Iron Age pit in the centre of one of the rectangular structures in Itteren held a layer of burned material, including the shards of five secondary

Site	Date in century BCE	Pits inside	Finds	Pits outside	Finds	Post structures
Poperinge-Koestraat	11th	1 shafted pit under ditch				
Nijmegen-Kops Plateau	11th-7th?	At least 3	EIA pottery	Several	EIA pottery, some secondarily burned, a large iron knife	Row on inside of ditch
Kooigem-Bos	5th-mid 4th	1 in ditch	Seven 4th-3rd century pots, cremation remains, charcoal, a bronze buckle, a fibula fragment, stone bracelet fragments			Large structure in NE-corner
Brecht-Akkerweg	5th?			1	Several 5th century BCE pots	
Kemzeke-Kwakkel	5th					2 posts?
Born-Koeweide	4th-early 2nd	Several?		Several?		6 posted; possibly another
Itteren-Emmaus	4th-early 2nd	1	Five secondary burned EIA pots			2 posts?
Oss-Ussen R25/26	4th-early 2nd	1 animal burial, 2 pits in ditch	Large amount of pottery, some secondarily burned	Several?		2 posts inside? post rows on outside; structure on outside
Houten-Castellum	4th-3rd?	6 in ditch	Stone fragments, human skull, deer antlers, pottery, fragments of animal bones, wood, charcoal, an iron ring, burned loam	Several	A variety of objects, large 5th century pot	
Oss-Ussen R49	4th-3rd?	1	Burn spot			Posts on inside of ditch; 2 posts; 4 posted
Hever-Stationsstraat	4th-3rd					4 posted
Lomm-Hoogwatergeul	4th-2nd	17?	Charcoal			Rows in inside; 3-, 4-, and 6-posted structure
Kortrijk-Morinnestraat west	2nd half 4th-2nd					2 posts
Oedelem-Wulfsberge	2nd half 4th-2nd					4?-posted
Boechout-Mussenhoevelaan	4th-1st	1	Pottery			4-, 6- posted
Gronsveld-Duijsterstraat	3rd-2nd	3?	Burned loam? Few pottery shards	1	Large pit with cremation grave and burned loam	
Alveringem-Eikhoek/Hoogstade	3rd-1st	Multiple	Pottery, charcoal, burned animal bone			Multiple posts, structures unclear
Harelbeke-Evolis	3rd-1st					3 posts
Haren-Groenstraat	3rd-1st					2 posts
Mierlo-Hout	3rd-1st	Several?				
Oss-Ussen R2	3rd-1st	1 in ditch	Upside down pot, other pottery			5?-posted
Oss-Westerveld R57	3rd-1st	Relation unclear				Post row
Dendermonde-Hoogveld	2nd-1st half 1st			Multiple	Not reported	Row on inside; structure
Cuijk-Ewinkel	2nd-1st?			1	Charcoal, burned loam	2 posts
Barneveld-Harselaar-west	2nd-1st	1	Not reported			Small structure?

Table 8.4. Rectangular structures with associated pits, post settings and post structures.

Site	Date in century BCE	Pits inside	Finds	Pits outside	Finds	Post structures
Maastricht-A2	2nd-1st					4-posted
Knesselare-Westervoorde	2nd-1st				Upside-down pot in posthole	Posts near corners on outside
Kortrijk-Morinnestraat east	2nd-1st	2	Pottery, charcoal			2 posts
Oegstgeest-Rijnvaert	2nd-1st					2 posts
Oostvleteren-Kasteelweg	2nd-1st	2 to 4 per structure	Charcoal and burned loam	Several	EIA well	
Erembodegem-Zuid-IV	1st BCE (- 1st CE?)	1 to 2	Burned bone, pottery, charcoal			2 posts per structure
Oss-Brabantstraat	1st BCE – 1st CE	3 reused pits	Secondarily burned pottery, burned loam, charcoal			Relation unclear
Ursel-Rozestraat	1st BCE – 1st CE					Small row on inside?

Table 8.4. Continued.

burned pots. The symbolic significance related to this pit may have initiated the construction of the rectangular structures on this location.

On other sites material that was already burned may have been brought to the place. Near the Kops Plateau structure a pit was found containing pottery, some of it secondarily burned, together with a large iron knife. The pit with the knife also contained the rim of a large pot that was deliberately placed upright and covered with cobbles. In the pit related to the Oss-Ussen R2 structure, a pot was found placed upside-down at the bottom. Complete pots represent rare finds in pits; mostly the pottery was found broken. In for example Alveringem, two small pits in structure A were entirely filled with pottery fragments, while others contained charcoal or burned animal bone fragments.

The only wet deposition site related to a rectangular structure known in the Low Counties (Houten-Castellum) portrays multiple pits and the largest variety of objects. Several shaft like pits were found associated with the structures. The objects they contained were habitually fragmented, such as grinding stone fragments, a piece of a human skull and deer antlers, a whole human cranium, pottery and a spindle whorl, fragments of cattle, sheep/goat, and pig bones, fragments of wood, charcoal, an iron ring, some burned loam, and several stones. This variety in depositions corresponds with similar practices in the wetlands of the Oer-IJ area in the northwest of the Netherlands (Kok 2008).

In relation to rectangular structures, the pits represent additional actions. In Itteren, this may have been performed before the construction of the ditch. This was also likely to be the case in sites where pits containing a 5th century BCE pottery deposition were found in proximity to the subsequent rectangular structure. The

function of these features is likely analogous to the pottery depositions in the ditch. A pit was dug presumably with the intention of depositing an offering of exchange. In these specific 5th century BCE pits, it was not (yet) habitual to break or burn the pottery.

Thereafter, the gift was often broken and/or burned in order to enable transmitting it to the realm of the dead or the 'otherworld'. Brunaux (1985, 123-125) and Aldhouse-Green (2002, 129-135) refer to this act as gifting to the underworld, to chthonic gods or spirits that could only be reached by digging a pit. For the Low Countries the act was more likely aimed at the (direct) ancestors rather than deities. Specifically the act of burning indicates the recipient of the exchange is the soul of an ancestor rather than a deity or god. Diachronic developments in this practice show little variation. The act of burning material and depositing (or burning) it in a pit as an offering was customary throughout the Iron Age and into the Roman period (e.g. Van Enckevort 2007, 25-29).

8.5.2 Postholes and enclosed structures

Postholes are often the only remains of buildings or other above ground structures. Consistency in excavated house plans has resulted in a reasonable understanding of what Iron Age houses looked like. For the structures found in and around the rectangular structures that are the subject of this thesis this is more problematic, even though more than half of the rectangular structures contained two or more postholes (table 8.4). The actual above ground construction that would have interconnected the posts is mostly subject to speculation. Isolated postholes, small groups of posts, or rows could even represent some sort of totems, like the anthropomorphic figures found in Oberdorla (Behm-Blancke et al. 2003). This interpretative problem is illustrated by the enigmatic post row that was reconstructed for the structure in Gournay-sur-Aronde. In 1985, Brunaux, Méniel & Poplin published a theory that three pits and four postholes dating to the earliest phase of the sanctuary were situated precisely in the geometric centre of the enclosure, forming two perpendicular axes pointing at four cardinal points and in line with a group of sacrificial pits. This theory initiated a search within rectangular structures in the Low Countries by Slofstra & Van der Sanden (1987) for similar aligned rows of features. They found such an alignment on the Roman site of Hoogeloon, where they reconstructed a north-south alignment of pits and a perpendicular east-west alignment that consisted of a row of posts, on the north side (not centralised) within a rectangular ditched enclosure. The structure as a whole was interpreted as an open air sanctuary. This interpretation of Hoogeloon was later discarded by Hiddink (2014, 248-262). He reinterpreted the posts and pit row as part of a Roman settlement structure and the rectangular ditch as a possible Middle Iron Age burial feature. The actual cremation burials would have been eroded. The date of the ditch, along with any associated features, remains doubtful and the site is therefore not included in this thesis.

None of the sites in this thesis display post alignments directed at cardinal points or perpendicular to other features. The only post rows were found aligned with the ditch on the inside (Lomm, Nijmegen-Kops Plateau, Oss-Ussen R49, Oss-Westerveld R57, and Dendermonde-Hoogveld), or on the outside (Oss-Ussen R25/26). In Oss-Brabantstraat a row of posts was placed in the bedding trench type ditch, undoubtably in support of a wall. These rows seem to belong to a construction of which the purpose was related to the function of the ditch as a visual and physical boundary. The posts were often placed a few metres apart, and would have supported planking or a fence of sorts, emphasising the enclosure. This statement is supported by the observation that, on the sites where documentation of the entire feature was possible, all of the above-mentioned sites have an entrance. On sites without post alignments along the ditch no entrances were documented. Evidently, an entrance was *needed* in these enclosed structures, to allow access. In all other structures, where the ditch is a continuous feature, a visitor could easily step over the ditch.

Isolated posts were found on the corners on the Knesselare structure for example. Their function remains more elusive. In chapter 7.3 a practical explanation was suggested for two posts separated by several metres: they could have served to hang something in between, support a wall, a rack, or drying goods, such as working a cowhide. Twelve structures contained two posts, sometimes accompanied by larger structures (table 8.4). In many of the sites, a profane interpretation like that does not suffice, as I have already established a function of the whole structure as part of the burial customs. Another explanation is needed. As four or six-posted structures are nearly as common, it is conceivable that the two posts were also part of a slightly more complex structure. Perhaps two other posts were not founded as deep, and as a result left no features after the top soil layer was ploughed. A small structure thus constructed resembles a 'house of the dead', used in burials for, for example, excarnation or preparing the body for cremation. A small structure or platform could naturally have been used in a ceremonial act that elude us for the moment. Excarnation is a recurring subject in discussions on Iron Age burials and histological evidence has been presented by several studies (Booth & Madgwick 2016; Panhuysen 2017).

Only a few sites contain larger, more complex structures related to the ditch. In both Kooigem and Oss-Ussen R25/R26 a structure of many posts was found on the east side. In Oss, the structure was positioned on the outside of the ditch, adjacent to the entrance. In Kooigem, the structure spans over the ditch in the northeast corner. In Ch.5.3.6 a bridge within an entrance building was suggested for this structure. The two structures were related to the entrance as if the building represented a liminal place and by passing though and/or over a person could enter the realm of the spirit world. As such an effort was made, these structures represent more permanent places that were visited on multiple occasions.

8.6 The rectangular structure as a liminal place

In-between the world of the living and the other world in which spirits, deities, and animated supernatural powers resided, a changeover zone was part of the worldview of Iron Age people. This zone could be a physical place, a bodily transition, or cognitive experience performed on different levels. An example is the burial customs, in which, according to Iron Age perception, the transition of the soul after death takes place by cremating the body in a 'rite of passage'. The soul becomes a spirit in a process that is entirely manipulated by the living. The living control where the spirit is housed and allow it to become an ancestor by administrating the correct procedures. Cremation is only one way in which the body and soul of the deceased could be manipulated (table 8.5).

In order to communicate with the spirits or the ancestors measures had to be taken, such as creating a space for communication in a liminal place, enabled by personal items, and applying a certain level of liminality to the living. Some form of physical boundary had to be crossed. This could include stepping over a ditch, crossing a bridge, or passing through a gate. When this boundary is crossed, the 'spiritual' space can be entered. This entering may have involved other customs, ones that did not leave any archaeological evidence.

Treatment of the body	→	Intended treatment of the soul		
Cremation	→	Passage, becoming an ancestor, reincarnation		
Inhumation, submersion (peat bog)	→	No passage, torment, sacrifice in exchange for benefit of the community, safeguarding the location		
Decapitation	→	Captivity, kidnapping for ransom, punishment		
Missing in action	→	Wandering/lost, homeless, unable to communicate or join the ancestral home	→	Create liminal place for communication and residence

Table 8.5. Iron Age manipulations of the spirit of the deceased.

	Type 1	Type 2	Type 3	Type 4	Type 5	Type 6	Type 7	Total
On a slope	4	7				4	2	17
Near water		2						2
On edge / near top of ridge	2	5		1		3	3	14
Flat area		7			1		1	9
Water edge			1					1
Loam-sand transition		1						1
Total	6	22	1	1	1	6	6	44

Table 8.6. Location of rectangular structures per type (based on 44 structures). See table 8.1 for the definition of the types.

In Madagascar for example, upon entering a sacred space this action required taking of your footwear.

Both the physical and the cognitive perceptions were addressed when a rectangular structure was positioned in the landscape. Structures of types 2 and 6 were not randomly or conveniently built in the vicinity of settlements. In fact, the location of the settlements in relation to the structures seems predominantly irrelevant. Rather, the rectangular structures are positioned on a deliberately chosen *liminal location*. This will be substantiated in Ch.8.6.1.

The connection with the landscape was important for the living as well as the dead. As pointed out by Louwen (2021, 237-238), in the Late Bronze Age and Early Iron Age the dead were not only burned, their cremated remains were also buried in urnfields, thereby tying their last physical form to a place with a long history. Practices changed over time, probably related to socio-cultural changes and adaptations to the prevailing worldview of Iron Age society, while the belief in ancestors remained constant. Monuments were the places where the souls of the ancestors resided. On Kops Plateau, the relation between the rectangular structure and the ancestral barrows was materialised by a cobble path (Fontijn & Cuijpers 1999). This relation to ancestral places was also clearly visible in Ursel and Dendermonde-Hoogveld, where the older Bronze Age barrows were literally incorporated in the Iron Age structures. Inclusion of the (mythical) ancestors was sometimes a decisive factor for the location choice (Gerritsen 2003, 167).

8.6.1 In-between the high-low dichotomy

Most sites in this thesis are located on a slight slope. The Low Countries, specifically the sandy and loamy soils, are not entirely flat. At present, the original wavy-relief character of these soils has been mostly equalised by millennia of farming, but in the Iron Age the relief would have been more pronounced. These slight height differences were noticed and while the higher grounds were used for barrow landscapes (Bourgeois 2013), the slopes were used as liminal places. In for example Aalter, the use of the slight relief is clearly evident by the barrows on the ridge and the rectangular structures lower down towards the brooks. Urnfields may have occupied variable positions near barrow sites and on open heathlands, as well as on (slight) slopes, or in a brook valley (De Mulder 2011, 22-24). The location of the rectangular structures is predominantly on a slope (39%), on or near the top of a dune, levee, cuesta, hill or plateau (32%), or on a flat area (20%), near water (table 8.6). In contrast to findings from research in England (Hargrave 2018, 137), there is no preferential slope side discernible. Rectangular structures were made on south (Nijmegen, Kortrijk-west, Harelbeke, Alveringem, Mierlo), southwest (Cuijk), north (Boechout, Rijkevorsel), east (Brecht, Kortrijk-east, Haren) and west (Kooigem, Oegstgeest, Odijk) facing slopes.

Sometimes these transitional areas are also defined by the soil type. In for example Erembodegem, the site is located on the border between the loamy and the sandy soils, similar to Dendermonde-Hoogveld where the transitional area from sand to the loamy sand probably separates the drier from the latter, more wet area. In the Low Countries where the land tends to be quite flat, water plays an important role in the draining of arable lands as well as in Iron Age liminality and depositional practices. Slopes, such as river levees, inevitably emphasise the transition from dryer soils to wet areas, as they tend to end in creeks, rivers and peaty areas, a transition that would be visual by the difference in vegetation. As a result, the sites are often bordered or in the vicinity of small streams in a relatively unpronounced valley (Erembodegem, Kemzeke, Hever, Cuijk), or situated on the terrace of a large river (Lomm, Itteren, Born), where the difference between wet and dry land, and between higher and lower grounds, would have been clearly defined by both relief and vegetation.

As early as Wheeler (1928), the location of sanctuaries was frequently noted on hill-tops, and in certain cases near pools or springs. Fauduet (1993, 102) summarised that geographically around 80% of Roman sanctuaries in France were built on a hilltop or a slope, the remainder in a valley, most likely near a fork in the river or a bridge. Moore (2007) found that rectilinear enclosures dating to 400-200 BCE, a characteristic feature for the Cotswolds and West Midlands in England, were often placed at junctions of earlier field systems.

Summarised, the rectangular structures were constructed in liminal zones, on a slope between high and low grounds, a place where commonly the dry landscape transitioned into a wetter environment. This intentional positioning likely aided the communication with the spirits that resided there. Initially, the ditch is an important feature in this process although in itself not substantial enough to prevent a physical entry. It was perhaps meant to keep the dead contained, certainly not to keep the living out. As a result, the ditch did not have to be substantial in size of even remain visible, in a process of conceptualisation. As time progressed during the Iron Age, the effort that was made to construct the ditch was lessened. Middle Iron Age ditches have larger cross sections on average, than Late Iron Age examples.

The enclosed space was where the spirits resided. In type 2 or type 6 structures, the ditch would have served to hold these spirits in place and facilitated the communication with them through offerings. Possibly, the spirits could be summoned there, even when the actual body was absent. The ditch was not maintained as a durable feature, but made for an occasion. Once made, the ditch lost its use, although the liminal space it had created remained. Even for centuries after, into the Roman Era as testified by the additional burials (confirmed in Itteren, Lomm, Dendermonde-Hoogveld, Dendermonde-Oud-Klooster, Erembodegem, and Mierlo-Hout), these liminal spaced could keep their intrinsic value. The use of the site as a burial ground after centuries have passed suggests that the site was not overgrown by plants and trees. Apparently there was still something visible or marked that was being preserved and the place being kept an open space.

8.7 Epilogue: evaluating Oss-Brabantstraat

In two previous publications I defined the structure in Oss-Brabantstraat as a cult place (De Leeuwe 2011; De Leeuwe & Jansen 2018). Now I would like to reflect on that interpretation. What makes this site a cult place? Gournay-sur-Aronde as Brunaux has presented it, complies with our idea of an Iron Age cult place. This site has been in use for a long period of time, visible by its many alterations. Pits, ditches, posts, and even a wall were added, adjusted or removed in different phases. The site must therefore have been revisited on a number of occasions. The number of finds certainly attributes to our perception of a cult place. Thousands of weapons, pottery, and animal and human remains deposited in certain designated areas of the ditch accumulate to another visible testimony of the long utilisation of the place as an offering site. A clearly defined set of conventions formed the basis of these archaeological remains.

Only a few of these characteristics can be recognised in Oss-Brabantstraat. First, the three pits in the interior can be interpreted as offering places. As customary to the Low Countries, the offerings would more likely have been aimed at ancestral spirits rather than at the chthonic deities. And second, the outer boundary was rebuilt at least once. In both phases there was a wall on the outside, placed in a bedding trench, preventing people from looking in. This is a distinctly different building tradition for a rectangular structure. The construction represents a break in the tradition of using rectangular ditches as open symbolic features. Clearly, another set of conventions shaped the basis for this structure. The analogous Early Roman structure in Elst-Westeraam indicates this invention is related to a Roman influence. The structure at the Brabantstraat likely dates slightly earlier, coinciding with the period of Caesar's conquests of Gaul and Belgium. How does the structure at the Brabantstraat fit into this timeframe?

At this point we have to take into account the identity of the people who built the structure. In the Late Iron Age, Oss was inhabited by multiple coexisting settlements in the vicinity, each consisting of a group of 20 to 50 people in close contact with other groups (Schinkel 1998, 174-179; Roymans & Gerritsen 2002; Fokkens 2019; Jansen 2021, 339-341). According to Caesar, a tribe named the Eburones inhabited a large part of the Low Countries in the 1st century BCE. Due to a shortage of grain in Gaul, Caesar was forced to spread out his army and he stationed five cohorts in the territory of the Eburones, in the region between (or near?) the Rhine and the Meuse (Gallic Wars, V, 24, trans. Macdevitt 2012).

Presumably this included Oss and the surrounding area, where rumours of a well-organised advancing army must have preceded the invasion for at least a couple of years. In subsequent battles the Eburones were defeated, and after the Gallic Wars the region was inhabited by different tribes that supported the Roman occupation (Roymans 2004).

This depopulation is not immediately apparent from the settlement patterns in Oss that seem to testify of continuation into the Roman Period rather than of disruption (Schinkel 1998, 186; Jansen & Van As 2012; Fokkens 2019, 192-193). However, there are some indications that another (new) group of people may have been involved. Schinkel (1998, 184-204) used 123 house plans in Oss-Ussen to formulate a typology in which he described a continuous use of several house types from the Late Iron Age into the Roman Period. Additionally, he also noted that '... that new houses were constructed at a previously built-over site only from the Late Iron Age onwards and especially in the Roman period' (*Ibid.*, 189) and several new types of house types emerge in the Roman Period (*Ibid.*, 166). A new building tradition was used alongside an old one in one existing settlement, succeeded an old tradition in another settlement, and was used in a newly founded settlement. The settlement of Oss-Westerveld, situated 200m west of Oss-Brabantstraat, was in use in the Late Iron Age and grew to a larger size in the 1st century CE with nine to eleven contemporary houses (Wesselingh 2000, 71-170). However, the houses dating to the end of the 1st century BCE crossed over their Iron Age predecessors. Wesselingh (2000, 197) further notes that 'Unfortunately the process of change cannot be followed, because the last half of the 1st century BCE is virtually undetectable in the archaeological data.' In Oss-Schalkskamp, a settlement ditch dating to the transitional phase into the Roman Period was built over a Late Iron Age grave (Wesselingh 2000, 175-177; Fokkens 2019, 98-99). Fokkens (2019, 98) points out that burial monuments were generally respected, so apparently the new inhabitants of Oss-Schalkskamp had no memories or considerations for their predecessors, an indication that the later people were not related and were new arrivals. These changes can be interpreted as an internal local adjustment influenced by the subsequent Roman occupation, or, perhaps more likely, construed as a new group of people moving in, in the latter half of the 1st century BCE.

At the same time, a large deposition of weapons ended up in Kessel-Lith (Roymans 2004, 103-193). Arguably, the site in Kessel could be related to contemporary events, as the place where defeated warriors ended up, although the human remains of that site have not been dated. The finds and characteristics of the material suggests acts of deposition took place here, making an interpretation as a wet deposition place a likely scenario.

Regardless, an invasive force such as the one that Caesar imposed must have had a profound impact on the local communities and their resources. Conceivably, subsequent events could have instigated the construction of a rectangular structure. Perhaps some of the fallen warriors and their gear ended up in Kessel, while many of their relatives were left in Oss. The structure in the Brabantstraat was constructed at the time of these events and could have been made to commemorate or communicate with the missing and fallen men in battle. As new people arrived in the region, perhaps in the course of the 1st century CE or thereafter, the old monument was broken down and eventually built over.

9

Conclusion

9.1 Iron Age beliefs

People in the Iron Age are commonly associated with their belief in a pantheon of gods, which they did not worship at temple-like structures as the Romans did. The structures that are the subject of this thesis are usually interpreted in accordance with that assumption. In the Low Countries there is no evidence for rectangular structures dating to the Iron Age that were dedicated to one or more gods. There is evidence however, that foremost Iron Age people believed in ancestors and therefore in spirits and the soul. Ancestral worship is an ancient tradition in the Low Countries, evidence of which dates back to the Bronze Age and the Neolithic. In accordance with a Bayesian 'Odds-model' approach, it can be argued that the archaeological evidence is better suited to a belief in the ancestors than to a belief in the gods.

A belief in the soul results in a complex system of practices and traditions. This creed became most relevant upon death, when the soul was believed not to die with the body. Louwen (2021, proposition 1) recently proposed that 'Graves from archaeological contexts should primarily be read as the material precipitation of the transition made by the decedent to whatever new role she or he was envisioned to occupy'. In the present study I would like to take this proposition one step further and state that the material precipitation of Iron Age religion in archaeological contexts, specifically the burial context, is often better explained as the result of the belief in the soul by the next of kin, whose main concern was what happened to that soul after death. A belief in the soul has a range of profound consequences for both the dead and the living, which stretches beyond ancestral worship. What happened to the soul mattered to Iron Age people and many of their actions can be explained from this point of view. The soul became a spirit that could reincarnate in a new body, haunt, dwell, linger, and maybe even be held captive by an enemy. A large part of this must have depended on the manner of death and the treatment of the corpse, and specifically their head. The head was believed to be the place where the soul of a person resides.

Cremation was obviously the preferred final rite of passage for the recently deceased in the Iron Age. Perhaps this ensured a life after death, a peace of mind, the spirit entering the realm of the ancestors, or the safeguarding of a reincarnation. On occasion people were sacrificed, by drowning, strangulation or burning, or their remains ended up maimed and sometimes decapitated, in a place of sacrifice. Including excarnation, inhumation, and/or mutilation in the treatment of a dead body was likely motivated by the belief that the soul could be manipulated. The spirits of these sacrificed or defeated humans were not meant to find their way home or take their place among the ancestors. They were meant to be bound to a place. It is conceivable that other animals were thought to have a soul. In that respect, for example the remains a dog deposited in a certain place like the entrance at Hallaton, may have been intended to function as a guardian spirit.

CONCLUSION   157

9.2 Warriors and missing persons

The initial subject of this thesis is a certain type of rectangular structure found in the Low Countries. In table 8.1 they were named 'type 2' and 'type 6' rectangular structures. Other rectangular structures can be interpreted as cattle pens, features surrounding graves, defensive structures, or drainage ditches for houses, outhouses or settlements. Type 2 or 6 rectangular structures can be roughly defined as:

- a larger type of Iron Age structure, consisting of an open ditch measuring at least 15-20m in length, commonly without an interruption, commonly V-shaped in cross section,
- a rectangular ground plan,
- often related to several cremation graves (to a lesser extent in the Late Iron Age),
- sometimes related to field systems or Bronze Age barrows
- generally related to one or more pottery depositions.

Admittedly, this is still a vague and ambiguous definition, but variety is also characteristic. Apparently, these structures were only made to a limited set of rules allowing for local adjustments. In order to begin to understand what the rectangular structures that are the subject of this study were made for, I start with the assumption that the belief in the human soul is at the basis of the motivation for many Iron Age acts. To Iron Age people, having a soul was as logical and intrinsic to the human body as having a heart. When a death happened at home, the treatment of the body was according to the preferred burial rite: cremation. The soul became a spirit that could then be guided to whatever place it was supposed to go, reincarnate or join the realm of the ancestors. However, what happened to people who died under less preferred circumstances, like warriors who died in battle or kidnapped women, who never returned home? We know where some of these conquered warriors ended up: mutilated and deposited, perhaps after being on display, in the waters of Lake Neuchatel at La Tène or perhaps in the River Meuse near Kessel-Lith, decapitated with their skull on display in Houten-Castellum, with their headless body on display in the sanctuary at Ribemont-sur-Ancre, or their decomposed remains deposited in a ditch in Gournay-sur-Aronde. This was assumingly the treatment of the corpses of the enemy and not of survivors or fallen friendlies when they were brought home. The latter could be cremated if that was the preferred rite of passage. Often these sacrifices are interpreted as offerings to the gods (e.g. Brunaux 1986, 69-80; Roymans 1990, 49-92; Randsborg 1995, 76-80; Derks 1996; Aldhouse-Green 2001; 2016; Van den Broeke 2005), but from an ancestral perspective they can be interpreted as related to a taboo, a superstition, or some manipulation of the soul.

Besides Kessel-Lith and Houten, none of the Iron Age sites in the Low Countries display indications of the treatment of conquered enemies or other masses of unlucky souls, but we do know where many of their weapons ended up: in the water. Regardless of who they belonged to, the large numbers of weaponry depositions indicate a certain degree of unrest and conflict. Even the dispersed settlement communities that made up the Low Countries experienced conflicts during the Iron Age. The region was reasonably densely populated, probably comparable to other northwest European regions. So here too, there must have been threats and tensions that created situations in which people did not return home. Indications of conflicts, apart from the above mentioned skeletal evidence and weapon depositions, are found in this region in the form of linear ditches used as land divisions, sometimes accompanied by palisades, and slingshot bullets.

What did the next of kin do when a relative did not return home? Where did they believe their soul went to in such a situation? From the practices of Malagasy peoples we learned that it can be useful to have a place for spirits to aim for when they are lost. Like the monoliths that serve as a guide, a place where a spirit can reside and the next of kin can communicate. I would like to consider in this thesis that the rectangular structures that are at the core of this study primarily served a similar purpose. Clearly a rectangular structure was commonly not needed to demark a cemetery and even when it was, the ditch was not meant to stay visible indefinitely. A rectangular structure was constructed only under certain circumstances, it was meant to be transient, and not necessarily related to a grave. As burials are absent in some of these structures, so might the person or persons have been for whom the monument was intended: a kind of cenotaph for (a) missing person(s). Generally, it was not meant as a permanent monument where mourners kept returning to, but the construction of the structure did give the place a lasting meaning. The cremation graves found related to some of the structures could belong to relatives who died at a later time, in an attempt to reconnect to the ancestral spirits of their relatives.

Pottery was found in virtually all rectangular structures, sometimes in large amounts. On rare occasions a whole pot was deposited, or even a depot of pots. A pit with whole pots seems to be a phenomenon that was primarily practiced in the 5th-early 4th century BCE. In rectangular structures from about 400 BCE, a deposition was made after the construction of the ditch, at the bottom of the ditch, and sometimes subsequent depositions were made in pits. Specifically the depositions in pits often contained (secondarily) burned material. Broken objects, specifically pottery, symbolises the life cycle (Kok 2008, 175-176). Both pottery and nails can bind people, so perhaps these objects were thought to attach a spirit to a certain place. As a logical extension, it would make sense not only to break, but also to secondarily burn the pottery as burning could transfer an object to the realm of the dead. Another point raised by Kok (2008, 70-71) was the symbolic value of pottery in offerings as a representation of an individual or a family. As the most common objects in rectangular structures, pottery seems to indicate the connection of a particular family to their dead (or missing) relative. Perhaps the pottery does not exactly represent the person, but rather aids in the communication with the deceased, or is meant to bind a spirit to their former 'home'. The location of the pottery in the ditch was relevant, the northwest and southeast sides being the most common. This could be related to the sunrise and the opposite side. Also, the location where the structures were built seems deliberately chosen to assist in the communication with the dead, as they are found in liminal places, positioned between the (relatively for Low Countries) high and low grounds, or wet and dry areas. Conceivably, the sunrise also symbolised a liminal place, between dark and light, or life and the afterlife.

9.3 A place for communication

The digging a rectangular ditch and depositing pottery in it in order to guide a spirit may have been a tradition that was particular for the Low Countries. In other regions of Northwest Europe, a ditch could have a more permanent function. In France, they formed boundaries for cemeteries or served as depositories in sanctuaries. The continuation of the ditch without interruptions may have a similar symbolic value, to prevent spirits from crossing this boundary, or to emphasise the designated place. In this way the souls of the sacrificed warriors in Ribemont could not leave to haunt their victors who mutilated their bodies after death and took their heads. In the same manner the ditch was uninterrupted in Gournay and could only be entered over a bridge. However, even though the underlining beliefs are similar these structures were made for different purposes. As Lejars (2001) suggested, the structures have a variety of functions, and differences are also a regional phenomenon. Regional studies such as Aalter-Woestijne and Oss show that even within a local Iron Age community rectangular structures served a variety of functions, most of which were of a temporary nature.

Not only did the construction of a ditch had meaning in demarking a certain area, the rectangular shape was significant. The shape contrasted with natural forms and may have reflected the essence of a house or, more symbolically, a home. The ditch may have served to keep or guide spirits in, while the rectangular shape was an aid to this purpose. Even though it was not a requirement, the rectangular shape was used on most occasions and

contrasted the round shape that was so familiar from ditches around barrows from the Late Neolithic onwards. The idea of the rectangular ditch as a 'house for spirits' seems to have it origins in the late Urnfield tradition as suggested by De Laet (1966) and Fontijn (2002b). Rectangular ditches in the Low Countries first occurred during the Urnfield period. In general, in an urnfield, the ditch around the grave could demark a place for both the body and the soul of the deceased to reside and perhaps the accompanying pottery or the urn as a vessel provided a connection to the living relatives (Louwen 2021, 177-182). As many urnfield graves did not have a surrounding feature, this was not perceived as an essential part of the burial tradition. Towards the final phases of urnfields, the rectangular ditch might have been considered a stronger expression of this home and the conditions under which it was used, had changed.

The function of the rectangular structures is a regional specific phenomenon for the Low Countries below the riverine area (mid-southern Netherlands and Belgium apart from the Ardennes). In this description the rectangular ditch is defined as a larger structure, at least 15-20m in length, not the type surrounding single graves. This type of structure can be perceived as a regional sociocultural adjustment to certain (stressful) situations, comparable to human sacrifices in bogs as a North European custom, and depositing human remains in storage pits as a phenomenon found in northern France and England (fig. 2.7). The rectangular structures in the Low Countries cannot be defined as cult places or sanctuaries, like some of the structures found in France. Apart from the structure in Kooigem, they do not adhere to the description by classical writers of a sacred place with heaps of the spoils of war inside. They were not intended to be in use for an extended period, nor did they commonly serve a recurring deposition act, as the number and type of deposited objects in most structures indicate. In the Low Countries the numbers and types of objects do not compare to the 'archetype' cult place. The theory proposed in this thesis is that the structures in the Low Countries were made *for a specific occasion*. Their primary purpose was not to communicate to chthonic gods or other deities, but rather to communicate with and shelter spirits of dead or missing relatives. There are exceptions. Oss-Brabantstraat is one of these, as the ditches do not represent a temporary demarcation but rather provide a bedding trench for a more permanent wall. This was a different type of rectangular structure, as the internal space was confined and closed off to the outside. Oss-Brabantstraat has more resemblance to a French sanctuary, particularly Villeneuve-au-Châtelot, than any of the other Iron Age structures found in the Low Countries. The site in Oss can therefore be considered as a cult place. Burned pottery on this site might indicate a similar function as the other rectangular structures, although the construction with a wall was different and it was rebuilt at least once and subsequently destroyed. Also, the three enclosed pits could be interpreted as receptacles for recurring attempts to communicate with a chthonic deity, or equally plausible, with dead relatives. The structure in Oss-Brabantstraat probably signifies the end of the Iron Age, just before or at the time of the arrival of the Roman army. The use of the place could have been related to conflict, and built to commemorate, or communicate with relatives, fallen warriors, or the missing. Notably, the structure was destroyed and built over in the Roman Era, unlike similar structures in Villeneuve-au-Châtelot and Elst-Westeraam. With the end of the Iron Age, the construction of the larger rectangular structures with their pottery depositions seems to diminish in the Low Countries, perhaps in favour of temples and (supra-)local open-air sanctuaries. In this respect, the rectangular structures were the predecessors of the Roman cult places, even though their meaning was different and they were likely related to a separate set of religious beliefs.

9.4 Some answers and more questions

This study primarily set out to research *(1) Which finds and features can be related to an Iron Age rectangular structure in the Low Countries?*' In chapter 3 I defined what a cult place or sanctuary in theory looks like, based on the northern French examples. Through analysis of the data in chapters 4 to 8 the conclusion followed that most rectangular structures in the Low Countries are not like the northern French examples. In the Low Countries they are defined by a rectangular ditch of at least 15-20m in length. The feature had a limited monumentality and was not meant to last, even though it was commonly of a substantial size which must have taken a reasonable effort to make. It had a limited sustainability, as it was dug and then left to fill in gradually or even closed deliberately a short time after. Pottery is the most common type of find in all of these structures. In some structures such as Kooigem, Oss-R25/26, and Alveringem pottery was found in great amounts. For most sites however, it seems that a modest deposition sufficed. As a settlement context is rare for these structures, it is unlikely the pottery finds are the result of the 'normal' residual precipitation of settlement material. These pots or potshards were brought to the site for a reason that served a 'spiritual' purpose. In some cases a whole pot was left, although this seems predominantly an early La Tène phenomenon. In the oldest structure dating to the Late Bronze Age a small example was placed at the bottom of the ditch. In the 5th-early 4th century BCE it was a custom to leave a depot containing a collection of pots, as found in Kooigem, Itteren, Gournay, and Brecht. All sites thereafter contain mostly intentionally broken pottery. Besides breaking, the pottery was sometimes burned. Both methods of treatment are common for transferring earthly materials to the world of the dead or a place where spirits are thought to reside, a place where only deactivated objects are recognized.

This leads me to the second research question: *(2) How were these rectangular structures used in Iron Age?* In most cases the rectangular structures were of a temporary nature and subsequently refilled or left to fill by natural processes. The rectangular ditch was made for or on a specific, singular occasion. It was made in a liminal place, on a slope between high and low or between wet and dry places. This was done so that it could serve as a liminal place to aid communication between the world of the living and the realm of the dead. On some sites additional ditches were constructed, but existing ditches were never redug. Some remained visible until the Roman Era. As all rectangular structures contain pottery depositions, pottery is the most significant indication of the use of these structures and typical for the social group that made these depositions. From previous studies we understand that pottery is a personal sacrifice, in contrast to large numbers of community offerings as found in the French sanctuaries. As pottery is considered representative of a family or household level, this type of deposition fits best into the dispersed farmyards or small scale settlement societies we envision for the Iron Age in the Low Countries.

The people who sacrificed the pottery in a temporary receptacle represented by a ditch or a pit, were trying to communicate with a family member, someone close to the surviving relatives. Apparently this did not necessarily involve the physical remains of the family member actually being there. Specifically in the Late Iron Age over half of the rectangular structures were not verifiably related to graves. Only the spirit or soul of the deceased had to be there to communicate. The rectangular ditch may have aided this purpose in the sense that it provided a place for souls to reside and above all a place for the surviving kin to commemorate or communicate. The short duration of the utilisation of these structures indicates that this communication was an incidental matter rather than a prolonged process. This also suggests a communication with the recently deceased rather than the distant ancestors, although the latter may have been included. A rectangular structure was made on particular occasions as only a few cemeteries have one and some are found unrelated to cemeteries. The diversity in the construction of these monuments indicates that there was only a vague idea of what it should look like and only a few conventions that the structure had to adhere to. This is in contrast to for example the uniformity of German *Viereckschanzen*.

(3) The socio-cultural function these structures served within Iron Age societies was likely related to the manner of death and/or the social role of the deceased. Perhaps the

structure was made when family members went missing and never returned, which would explain the examples without burials. Surviving family members could have chosen to be buried there at a later date, so their souls could be reunited in death. In some cases, as for example in Lomm, Itteren, Boechout, and Dendermonde, this resulted in a cemetery that was in use for a much longer period and by more than one family, until the dead finally became ancestral spirits. On rare occasions additional acts were performed there, involving small buildings and pits. The pits were sometimes used to burn material, presumably in an attempt of communication with the spirit(s) that resided there.

The earliest rectangular structures appear in the Late Bronze Age, but not until the Middle Iron Age do they become more common. This leads to research question *(4) what the environmental and social context was of these rectangular structures and whether it changed over time?* Until the 3rd century BCE the rectangular structures are almost exclusively associated with cremation graves. The graves did not have to be within the boundaries of the structure, sometimes they were positioned outside. In the Late Iron Age the structures become increasingly detached from cemeteries to the point that more than half of them can no longer be associated with graves. In contrast to examples found in England, the Low Countries rectangular structures were rarely situated in the vicinity of a settlement. Instead, the structures were positioned in a physical liminal zone, between the relatively highest and the lowest ground, between the settlements and the arable land or the grazing pastures, where dry land transitions into wetlands.

Based on the above description, the rectangular structures in the Low Countries cannot (5) be identified as the cult places described by classic writers such as Caesar and Diodorus in the final stages of the Iron Age. No large amounts of finds that were initially 'heaped into piles' were found in the Low Countries rectangular structures, nor can they be described as a place 'where warriors came to sacrifice captured animals'. Exceptions may be the large pottery deposit in Kooigem and the wet deposition site in Houten-Castellum, where an abundance of animal bones were found along with human skulls that had been on display.

A clear hiatus in this thesis is an encompassing overview of cemeteries dating to the Middle and Late Iron Age. As these were generally small cemeteries, and the graves have few or no goods or surrounding features, do we often miss them in excavations? Are more situated in the vicinity of a rectangular structure as was the case in Itteren? Furthermore, the large pottery depositions in Alveringem and Kooigem need analysis. Why did these sites exhibit such an overabundance of broken pottery? Neither pottery depositions (mostly found in settlements) in the research area, or depositions in wet places such as rivers has been studied sufficiently. An overview of Iron Age deposition sites is needed here. Additional research on these topics would give a better understanding of synchronous developments in the later Iron Age and provide a more thorough context for the rectangular structures and their associated depositions. By addressing these topics, the current research questions become more approachable and some of the theories launched in this thesis could be tested.

I will conclude this thesis with a request for future studies of the Iron Age to consider what is factually represented by ancestral worship. In the Iron Age belief system, actions were often the result of cognitive values related to the intrinsic presence of ancestral spirits, in contrast to the more conscious belief in the pantheon of omnipresent gods or deities. For the latter there is no demonstrable archaeological evidence in the Low Countries before the construction of Roman temples in the 1st century BCE. The farmer communities that made up the Low Countries during the Iron Age occasionally dealt with conflicts and misconduct, resulting in loss of life and people going missing, and inevitably in the manipulation of the souls of those involved by both the victors as well as the next of kin, who considered the ones that never returned home.

References

Aldhouse Green, M. 2006 [2001]. *Dying for the Gods: Human Sacrifice in Iron Age and Roman Europe.* Stroud: Tempus Publishing Limited.

Aldhouse-Green, M. 2015. *The Celtic myths, a guide to the ancient gods and legends.* London: Thames & Hudson.

Aldhouse-Green, M. 2018. Formal religion. In: C. Haselgrove, K. Rebay-Salisbury & P.S. Wells (eds.), *The Oxford Handbook of the European Iron Age.* DOI: 10.1093/oxfordhb/9780199696826.013.1.

Almagro-Gorbea, M. & A. Lorrio 1993. La tête humaine dans l'art Celtique de la péninsule Ibérique. In: J. Briard & A. Duval (eds.), *Les représentations humaines du Néolithique à l'Âge du Fer. Actes du 115e Congrès National des Sociétés Savantes.* Paris: Éditions du C.T.H.S., 219-237.

Altman, N. 2019 [2017]. *Sacred Trees.* New York: Gaupo Publishing.

Annaert, R. 1993. Een Viereckschanze op de Alfsberg te Kontich (prov. Antwerpen): meer dan een cultusplaats. *Archeologie in Vlaanderen 3,* 53-125.

Annaert, R. 1995/1996. De Alfsberg te Kontich (prov. Antwerpen). Eindrapport. *Archeologie in Vlaanderen* 5, 41-68.

Apers, T. 2017. Archeologische opgraving Kortrijk Morinnestraat (prov. West-Vlaanderen). *Monument Vandekerckhove Basisrapport* 2017.20, Ingelmunster.

Arcelin, P. & J.-L. Brunaux 2003. Un état des questions sur les sanctuaires et les pratiques cultuelles de la gaule celtique. *Gallia* 60, 5-8.

Armit, I. 2012. *Headhunting and the Body in Iron Age Europe.* Cambridge: Cambridge University Press.

Arnold, B. 2009. La Tène, entre Néolithique et Moyen Âge: un contexte topographique dynamique. In: M. Honegger, et al. (eds.), *Le site de La Tène: bilan des connaissances – état de la question. Actes de ta Table ronde internationale de Neuchâtel, J-3 novembre 2007.* Neuchâtel: Office et musée cantonal d'archéologie, 19-28.

Arnoldussen, S. & W.K. van Zijverden 2004. Culemborg-Den Heuvel. Bronze Age remains and Iron Age settlement traces next to a break-through channel in the Schoonrewoerd stream ridge. *Lunula*

Archaeologia Protohistorica 12. Brussels: Cellule Archéologie des Âges des Métaux, 59-71.

Arnoldussen, S. 2008. *A living Landscape. Bronze Age settlement sites in the Dutch river area (c. 2000-800 BC).* [PhD-dissertation Leiden University]. Leiden: Sidestone Press.

Arnoldussen, S., M. Schepers & A. Maurer 2016. Celtic fields in Brabant: wat stuifmeel en zaden kunnen vertellen. *Paleo-aktueel* 27, 23-31.

Baetsen, S. 2011. Menselijk bot. In: L. Meurkens & A.J. Tol (eds.), Grafvelden en greppelstructuren uit de ijzertijd en Romeinse tijd bij Itteren (gemeente Maastricht). *Archolrapport* 144. Leiden: Archol BV, 153-167.

Baetsen, W. & R. de Leeuwe 2022. Fysisch-antropologisch onderzoek. In: R. de Leeuwe (ed.), Plangebied Jochem Janszplantsoen en Singel te Odijk, gemeente Bunnik; proefsleuvenonderzoek en een archeologische opgraving van een midden ijzertijd en vroegmiddeleeuwse vindplaats. *RAAP-rapport* 5708. Weesp, 185-188.

Bakels, C.C. 1998. Fruits and seeds from the Iron Age settlements at Oss-Ussen. In: H. Fokkens (ed.), The Ussen project: the first decade of excavations at Oss. *Analecta Praehistorica Leidensia* 30. Leiden: Leiden University Press, 337-348.

Bakels, C.C. 2019. Vegetation and crops in Oss-North. In: H. Fokkens, S. van As & R. Jansen (eds.), The Oss-Noord Project – the second decade of excavations at Oss 1986-1996. *Analecta Praehistorica Leidensia* 48. Leiden: Leiden University Press, 127-153.

Bakx, R. & I. Bourgeois 2021. Een langdurige funeraire traditie? Nieuwe dateringen werpen nieuw licht op de site Boechout-Mussenhoevelaan (prov. Antwerpen, België). *Lunula Archaeologia Protohistorica* 29. Brussels: Cellule Archéologie des Âges des Métaux, 49-55.

Bakx, R. 2018. Funeraire monumenten en een waterkuil uit de midden- en late ijzertijd. In: R. Bakx, J. Verrijckt & M. Smeets (eds.), Het archeologisch onderzoek aan de Mussenhoevelaan te Boechout. *Archeo-rapport* 456. Tienen: Studiebureau Archeologie bvba, 57-88.

Bakx, R., J. Verrijckt & M. Smeets 2018. Het archeologisch onderzoek aan de Mussenhoevelaan te Boechout. *Archeo-rapport* 456. Tienen: Studiebureau Archeologie bvba.

Ball, E.A.G. & S. Arnoldussen 2002. Grootschalig karteren onderzoek in het Land van Cuijk (NL): een nieuw potentieel voor het bestuderen van langtermijnprocessen in de metaaltijden. *Lunula Archaeologia Protohistorica* 10. Brussels: Cellule Archéologie des Âges des Métaux, 7-12.

Ball, E.A.G., S. Arnoldussen & L. van Hoof 2001. Aanvullend Archeologisch Onderzoek in de Heeswijkse Kampen te Cuijk. *Archolrapport* 5. Leiden: Archol BV.

Bataille, G. 2007. Un nouveau protocole d'analyse des grands ensembles de mobiliers métalliques sur la base de la N.M.I. L'exemple du sanctuaire laténien de La Villeneuve-au-Châtelot (Aube). In: P.-Y. Milcent (ed.), *L'économie du fer protohistorique: de la production à la consommation du métal*, actes du XXVIIIe colloque de l'AFEAF de Toulouse des 20-23 mai 2004, *Aquitania*, suppl. 14/2. Bordeaux, 365-380.

Behm-Blancke, G., H. Jacob, S. Dušek, B. Lettmann, & Thüringisches Landesamt für Archäologische Denkmalpflege 2003. *Heiligtümer der Germanen und ihrer Vorgänger in Thüringen: Die Kultstätte Oberdorla: Forschungen zum alteuropäischen Religions- und Kultwesen. Teil 1: Text und Fototafeln, Weimarer Monographien zur Ur- und Frühgeschichte*, Bd. 38. Stuttgart: Theiss.

Behm-Blancke, G., S. Dušekand, H. Jacob, H. Ullrich & H. Eberhardt 2002. *Heiligtümer der Germanen und ihrer Vorgänger in Thüringen – Die Kultstätte Oberdorla: Forschungen zum alteuropäischen Religions- und Kultwesen, Teil 2: Katalog der Heiligtümer und Funde*, Weimarer Monographien zur Ur- und Frühgeschichte, Bd. 38, 2. Stuttgart: Theiss.

Beke, F. & A.C. van den Dorpel 2015. Resten van rituele handelingen en begravingen uit de Bronstijd, IJzertijd en Romeinse periode. Archeologische opgraving te Poperinge 'Zwijnlandstraat'. *Ruben Willaert bvba Rapport*, Brugge.

Beke, F., D. Teetaert, G. De Mulder & S. Reniere 2017. Rituelen langs een oude rivierloop: deposits uit de Brons- en IJzertijd te Poperinge Zwijnlandstraat (prov. West-Vlaanderen, België). *Lunula Archaeologia Protohistorica* 25. Brussels: Cellule Archéologie des Âges des Métaux, 31-36.

Bell, C. 1992. *Ritual theory, ritual practice*. New York, N.Y., [etc.]: Oxford University Press.

Bell, C. 2009. *Ritual: perspectives and dimensions* ([New ed.] / [forew. by Reza Aslan]). Oxford [etc.]: Oxford University Press.

Benigni, H., B. Carter, & E. Ua Cuinn, 2003. *The Myth of the Year, Returning to the Origing of the Druid Calendar.* Maryland: University Press of America.

Beniot, F. 1955. Le monde de l'au-delà dans les représentations celtique. *Ogam* 7, Rennes.

Bernhard, H. 1986. Militärstationen und frührömische Besiedlung in augusteisch-tiberischer Zeit am nördlichen Oberrhein. *Landesdenkmalamt Baden-Württemberg (Hrsg.), Studien zu den Militärgrenzen Roms III.* 13. Internationaler Limeskongreß-Aalen 1983. Forschungen und Berichte zur Vor- und Frühgeschichte in Baden-Württemberg 20. Stuttgart, 105-121.

Biel, J. 2007. Fürstensitze. Das Modell Wolfgang Kimmigs vor dem Hintergrund neuer Ausgrabungs- und Forschungsergebnisse. *Fundberichte aus Baden-Württemberg* 29, 235-254.

Birley, A.R. 1999. Trans. Tacitus, *Germania*. Oxford: University Press.

Bittel, K., S. Schiek & D. Muller 1990. *Die Keltischen Viereckschanzen – Atlas archäologischer Geländedenkmäler in Baden-Württemberg 1*, Stuttgart: Theiss.

Bloo, S. & P. Weterings 2017. Prehistorisch en Romeins aardewerk. In: C.M. Van der Linde & M. Kalfshoven (eds.), Cultusplaats in de achtertuin Sporen uit de late bronstijd tot en met de nieuwe tijd in Poperinge (Koestraat). *BAAC-report* A-13.0116. 's-Hertogenbosch: BAAC BV, 69-78.

Bogaers, J.E.A.T. & P.J.J.Stuart 1971. *Deae Nehalenniae: gids bij de tentoonstelling Nehalennia de Zeeuwse godin, Zeeland in de Romeinse tijd, Romeinse monumenten uit de Oosterschelde.* Leiden: Rijksmuseum van Oudheden.

Bogaers, J.E.A.T. 1955. *De Gallo-Romeinse tempels te Elst in de Over-Betuwe.* [PhD-dissertation Nijmegen University]. 's-Gravenhage: Staatsdrukkerij- en Uitgeverijbedrijf.

Booth, T.J. & R. Madgwick 2016. New evidence for diverse secondary burial practices in Iron Age Britain: A histological case study. *Journal of Archaeological Science* 67, 14-24.

Boreel, G. 2017. Fysische geografie. In: J. van Renswoude & D.S. Habermehl (eds.), Opgravingen te Houten-Castellum. Bewoning langs een restgeul in de IJzertijd, Romeinse tijd en Vroege Middeleeuwen. *Zuidnederlandse Archeologische Rapporten* 65. Amsterdam: VUhbs archeologie / Vrije Universiteit, 35-88.

Bos, J.A.A. & F.S. Zuidhoff 2015. Paleografische ontwikkeling van het landschap. In: P.L.M. Hazen, E. Drenth & E. Blom (eds.), Tien millennia bewoningsgeschiedenis in het Maasdal, van jachtkamp tot landgoed langs de A2 bij

Maastricht. *ADC Monografie* 17. Amersfoort: ADC-Archeo-Projecten, 196.

Bosquet, D. & D. Preud'homme 2000. Découverte d'une enciente laténienne à Hannut, au lieu dit "Trommelveld" (Lg.). *Lunula Archaeologia Protohistorica* 8. Brussels: Cellule Archéologie des Âges des Métaux, 79-87.

Bouman, M.T.I.J. 2012. Fysisch geografisch onderzoek. In: W. Jezeer & L.P. Verniers (eds.), De Plantage: een nieuwe wijk, een rijk verleden. Een archeologische opgraving op De Plantage in Meteren (gemeente Geldermalsen). *ADC-rapport* 2713. Amersfoort: ADC-Archeo-Projecten 21-42.

Bourgeois, L. (ed.) 1999. *Le sanctuaire rural de Bennecourt (Yvelines), Du temple gaulois au temple gallo-romain.* Maison des Sciences de l'Homme. Documents d'archéologie française 77, Paris.

Bourgeois, Q.P.J. & S. Arnoldussen 2006. Expressing monumentality: some observations on the dating of Dutch Bronze Age barrows and houses. *Lunula Archaeologia Protohistoria* 14. Brussels: Cellule Archéologie des Âges des Métaux, 13-26.

Bourgeois, J. & J. Rommelaere 1991. Bijdrage tot de kennis van het Meetjesland in de metaaltijden. De opgravingen te Ursel (1986-1989) en Aalter (1989-1990). *Appeltjes van het Meetjesland* 42, 59-88.

Bourgeois, J. 1991. Enclos et nécropole du second âge du fer à Kemzeke (Stekene, Flandre orientale). Rapport provisoire des fouilles 1988. *Scholae Archaeologicae* 12, Gent.

Bourgeois, J., B. Cherretté & M. Meganck 2001. Kringen voor de doden. Bronstijdgrafheuvels te Oedelem-Wulfsberge (W.-Vl.). *Lunula Archaeologia Protohistorica* 9. Brussels: Cellule Archéologie des Âges des Métaux, 23-27.

Bourgeois, J., J. Semey & J. Vanmoerkerke 1989. Ursel. Rapport provisoire des fouilles 1986-1987.Tombelle de l'âge du bronze et monuments avec nécropole de l'âge du fer. *Scholae Archaeologicae* 11, Gent.

Bourgeois, Q.P.J., 2013. *Monuments on the horizon. The formation of the barrow landscape throughout the 3rd and 2nd millennium BC.* [PhD-dissertation Leiden University]. Leiden: Sidestone Press.

Bowden, M., E. Jamieson, N. Linford, P. Linford, A. Payne & Z. Edwards 2014. Netheravon Barrows, Figheldean, Wiltshire: Report on Analytical Earthwork and Geophysical Surveys, April and May 2014. *English Heritage Research Report Series* 77. London: English Heritage.

Bradley, R. 1998. *The Passage of Arms: Archaeological Analysis of Prehistoric Hoards and Votive Deposits* [2nd Revised edition]. Oxford: Oxbow Books.

Bradley, R. 2002. Death and the regeneration of life: a new interpretation of house urns in Northern Europe. *Antiquity* 76.6 (292), 372-377.

Bradley, R. 2005. *Ritual and Domestic Life in Prehistoric Europe.* Abingdon: Routledge.

Bradley, R. 2017. *A geography of offerings – Deposits of valuables in the landscapes of Ancient Europe.* Oxford: Oxbow Books.

Bremmer, J. 1983. *The early Greek concept of the soul.* Princeton, New Yersey/Guildford, Surrey: Princeton University Press.

Brestel, T.J. 2017. Die Ausgrabungen in Manching-Süd von 1990-2009, studien zur siedlungsstruktur und befestigungsanlage des oppidums. *Manching Band* 21. Wiesbaden: Reichert Verlag.

Brijker, J. & C. Moolhuizen 2012. De vorming van het landschap. In: W. Roessingh & E. Blom (eds.), Graven op De Contreie. Bewoningsgeschiedenis van de Houtse Akkers te Oosterhout, van de Bronstijd tot en met de Slag om het Markkanaal. *ADC-rapport* 2750 / *Monografie* 14, 35-48, Amersfoort: ADC Archeo-Projecten.

Brinkkemper, O. & L. Van Wijngaarden-Bakker 2005. All-round farming. Food production in the Bronze Age and the Iron Age. In: L.P. Louwe Kooijmans, P.W. van den Broeke, H. Fokkens, A.L. van Gijn (Eds.). *The Prehistory of the Netherlands.* Amsterdam, 491-512.

Brouwer, M.C. (ed.) 2013. Op die saelwehr staende een huijs – Sporen van erf Klein Harselaar met middeleeuwse voorgangers en een nederzetting uit de ijzertijd te Barneveld, Harselaar West-west. *BAAC-rapport* A-11.0390. 's-Hertogenbosch: BAAC BV.

Browning, J. 2011. The animal bones. In: V. Score, J. Browning & University of Leicester Archaeological Services (eds.), Hoards, hounds and helmets: A conquest-period ritual site at Hallaton. Leicestershire. *Leicester archaeological monographs* 21. Leicester: University of Leicester Archaeological Services, 103-135.

Brück, J. 1999. Ritual and rationality: some problems of interpretation in European Archaeology. *European journal of Archaeology* 2, 313-344.

Brück, J. 2006. Fragmentation, personhood and the social construction of technology in Middle and Late Bronze Age Britain. *Cambridge Archaeological Journal* 16.2, 297-315.

Brunaux, J.-L., P. Méniel & F. Poplin 1985. Troisième partie. Les structures du sanctuaire. *Revue archéologique de Picardie.* Numéro spécial 4, 53-93.

Brunaux, J.-L. & P. Méniel 1983. Le sanctuaire de Gournay-sur-Aronde (Oise): structures et rites, les animaux du sacrifice. *Revue archéologique de Picardie* 1-2, 165-173.

Brunaux, J.-L. 1975. Fouille de sauvetage à Gournay-sur-Aronde (Oise). *Revue archéologique de l'Oise* 6, 27-31.

Brunaux, J.-L. 1980. Un sanctuaire gaulois à Gournay-sur-Aronde (Oise). *Gallia* 38, fascicule 1, 1980, 1-25.

Brunaux, J.-L. 1983. Les sanctuaires celtiques et leurs depots. *L'Art Celtique en Gaule*, Catalogue d'exposition. Dieppe, 80-83.

Brunaux, J.-L. 1986. *Les Goulois – Sanctuaires et rites.* Paris: Errance.

Brunaux, J.-L. 1995. Religion gauloise et religion romaine. La leçon des sanctuaires de Picardie. *Cahiers du Centre Gustave Glotz* 6, 139-161.

Brunaux, J.-L. 1996. *Les religions gauloises. Rituels celtiques de la Gaule indépendante.* Paris: Errance.

Brunaux, J.-L. 1996a. Chronologie et histoire: les lieux de culte dans la genèse du Belgium. In: T. Lejars (ed.), Le Nord de la Gaule et la chronologie du second Âge du Fer, actes de la table ronde de Ribemont-sur-Ancre, oct. 1994. *Revue archéologique de Picardie* 3/4. Amiens, 209-221.

Brunaux, J.-L. 1997. Les sanctuaires celtiques de Gournay-sur-Aronde et de Ribemont-sur-Ancre, une nouvelle approche de la religion gauloise. *Comptes rendus des séances de l'Académie des Inscriptions et Belles-Lettres* 141.2, 567-600.

Brunaux, J.-L. 1998. Un monumental trophée celtique à Ribemont-sur-Ancre (Somme). In: J.-L. Brunaux, G. Leman-Delerive & C. Pommepuy (eds.), *Les rites de la mort chez les Celtes du Nord*, Actes de la Table Ronde des 4 et 5 décembre 1997 à Ribemont-sur-Ancre. Revue Archéologique de Picardie, 107-113.

Brunaux, J.-L., M. Amandry, V. Brouquier-Reddé, L.-P. Delestrée, H. Duday, G. Fercoq du Leslay, T. Lejars, C. Marchand, P. Méniel, B. Petit & B. Rogéré 1999. Ribemont-sur-Ancre (Somme). Bilan preliminaire et nouvelles hypotheses. *Gallia* 56, 177-283.

Buchez, N. 2011. La Protohistoire ancienne. Recherche et fouille de sites de l'âge du Bronze à La Tène ancienne sur les grands tracés linéaires en Picardie occidentale. Questions méthodologiques et résultats scientifiques. *Revue archéologique de Picardie* 3-4, 121-199.

Buchez, N. 2011a. La Protohistoire récente – état de la documentation et principaux résultats issus de la fouille des sites funéraires de La Tène moyenne à La Tène finale sur les grands tracés linéaires en Picardie occidentale. In: *Revue archéologique de Picardie* 3-4, 267-334.

Buchsenschutz, O. 1984. Structures d'habitats et fortifications de l'âge du Fer en France septentrionale, *Mémoires de la Société Préhistorique Française* 18.

Buitenhuis, H. & H. Halici 2002. Archeozoölogie, in: Milojkovic, J. & Smits, E. (eds.), Archeologie in de Betuweroute, Lage Blok, een nederzettingsterrein uit de Midden-IJzertijd bij Meteren (gemeente Geldermalsen). *Rapportage Archeologische Monumentenzorg* 9. Meppel: Krips, 149-178.

Bullivant, S., M. Farias, J. Lanman & L. Lee 2019. *Understanding Unbelief, Atheists and agnostics around the world, Interim findings from 2019 research in Brazil, China, Denmark, Japan, the United Kingdom, and the United States,* University of Kent.

Cadoux, J.-L. & J.L. Massy 1970. Ribemont-sur-Ancre: Etudes. *Revue du Nord* 52.207, 469-511.

Cadoux, J.-L. 1982. L'ossuaire gaulois de Ribemont-sur-Ancre (Somme). Campagne de 1982. *Revue archéologique de Picardie* 3/4, 12-13.

Cadoux, J.-L. 1982a. Les fouilles du sanctuaire gallo-romain de Ribemont-sur-Ancre (Somme): un bilan (1966-1981). *Revue archéologique de Picardie* 4, 136-144.

Carpentier, L. 2015. Un axe de recherche pour l'origine des temples à plan centré en Gaule romaine: une nouvelle analyse fonctionnelle des espaces. *Annales de Janua 3.*

Caspers, M. & N. Van Asch 2017. Palynologisch onderzoek van Kortrijk Morinnestraat. In: T. Apers (ed.), Archeologische opgraving Kortrijk Morinnestraat (prov. West-Vlaanderen). *Monument Vandekerckhove Basisrapport* 2017.20. Ingelmunster, appendix 6.

Chapman, J., T. Higham, V. Slavchev, B. Gaydarska & N. Honch 2006. The Social Context of the Emergence, Development and Abandonment of the Varna Cemetery, Bulgaria. *European Journal of Archaeology* 9(2-3), 159-183. DOI: 10.1177/1461957107086121.

Chaume, B. & W. Reinhard 2003. Les statues de Vix: images héroïsées de l'aristocratie hallstattienne. Die lusitanisch-galläkischen Kriegerstatuen. Actes du colloque international du 18-19 janvier 2002 à Lisbonne. *Madrider Mitteilungen* 44, 249-268.

Chaume, B. & W. Reinhard 2009. La céramique du sanctuaire hallstattien de Vix "les Herbues". In: B. Chaume (ed.), *La céramique hallstattienne de France orientale: approches typologique et chrono-culturelle,* colloque international de Dijon, 21/22 nov. 2006. Dijon: Editions Universitaires dijonnaises, 27-50.

Chaume, B. & W. Reinhard 2011. Les statues du sanctuaire de Vix-Les Herbues dans le contexte de la statuaire anthropomorphe hallstattiene. *Documents d'Archéologie Méridionale* 34, 293-310.

Chaume, B. 2001. *Vix et son territoire à l'Age du fer: fouilles du mont Lassois et environnement du site princier.* Montagnac: Editions Monique Mergoil.

Chaume, B. 2011. *Vix (Côte-d'Or), Une Résidence Princière Au Temps De La Splendeur D'Athènes, Archéologie en Bourgogne.* Chatillon-sur-Seine: Musée du Pays Châtillonnais Trésor de Vix.

Chaume, B., W. Reinhard & G. Wustrow 2007. Les dépôts de l'enclos cultuel hallstattien de Vix « les Herbues » et la question des enceintes quadrangulaires. *Bulletin de la Société préhistorique française* 2, 343-367.

Cherretté, B. & J. Bourgeois 2002. Palenkrans uit de midden-bronstijd en nederzettingspsorten uit de late ijzertijd te Oedelem-Wulfsberge, W.-Vl. *Lunula Archaeologica Protohistorica* 11. Brussels: Cellule Archéologie des Âges des Métaux, 13-15.

Cherretté, B. & J. Bourgeois 2003. Oedelem-Wulfsberge 2002: grafmonumenten uit de brons- en ijzertijd (W.-Vl.). *Lunula Archaeologica Protohistorica* 11. Brussels: Cellule Archéologie des Âges des Métaux, 33-36.

Clémençon, B. & P.M. Ganne 2009. Toutatis chez les Arvernes: les graffiti à Totates du bourg routier antique de Beauclair (communes de Giat et de Voingt, Puy-de-Dôme). *Gallia* 66.2. Archéologie de la France antique, 153-169.

Clerbaut, T. 2012. Vondstmateriaal gerelateerd aan de ijzertijdfase. In: R. Vanoverbeke (ed.), Archeologische opgraving aan de Eikhoek te Hoogstade, gemeente Alveringem. *BAAC Vlaanderen Rapport* 30. Gent: BAAC Vlaanderen, 23-27.

Collins, J. 1984. *The European Iron Age.* London: Batsford.

Collins, J. 1989. Viereckschanzen, enceintes carrées et lapins en Angleterre. In: O. Buchenschutz & L. Olivier (eds.), *Les Viereckschanzen et let encienties quadrilaterales en Europe Celtique*, Actes du IXe Colloque de l'A.F.E.A.F. Chateaudun, 16-19 mal 1985, Association Française pour l'Etude de l'Age du Fer. Paris: Editions Errance, 15-20.

Collins, J. 1993. Die Oppidazivilisation. In: H. Dannheimer & R. Gebhard, *Das keltische jahrtausend. Katalog zur Ausstellung Rosemheim*, Mainz: Ph. con Zabern, 102-106.

Cooremans, B. 1995. Macrobotanisch onderzoek. in: R. Annaert (ed.), De Alfsberg te Kontich (prov. Antwerpen). Eindrapport. *Archeologie in Vlaanderen* 5, 53-55.

Cosyns, P. 2013. Een Romeinse tempel aan de Keverstraat, Tongeren. *Signa* 2, 35-39.

Couderc, P. & K. Sillander (eds.) 2012. *Ancestors in Borneo Societies. Death, transformation, and social immortality.* Copenhagen: NiAS Press.

Crease, S.M.E. 2015. *Re-thinking ritual traditions: interpreting structured deposition in watery contexts in Late Pre-Roman Iron Age and Roman Britain.* [PhD-dissertation UCL]. London.

Crossland, Z. 2014. *Ancestral encounters in highland Madagascar: material signs and traces of the dead.* New York: Cambridge University Press.

Crossland, Z. 2018. "I make this standing stone to be a sign" Material presence and the temporality of the trace in highland Madagascar. In: S. Souvatzi, A. Baysal and E.L. Baysal (eds.), *Time and History in Prehistory.* Abingdon; New York: Routledge, 229-249.

Cunliffe, B. 1984. Danebury: An Iron Age Hillfort in Hampshire. Vol. 1, The excavations 1969-1978: the site, *CBA Research Report* 52. DOI:10.5284/1000332.

Cunliffe, B. 1992. Pits, preconceptions and propitiation in the British Iron Age. *Oxford Journal of Archaeology* 11.1, 69-83.

Cunliffe, B. 1995. Danebury: An Iron Age Hillfort in Hampshire. Vol. 6, A Hillfort community in Perspective, York, *CBA Research Report* 102. DOI:10.5284/1000332.

Cunliffe, B. 1999. *The Ancient Celts.* London: Pinguin Books.

Cunliffe, B., P. Farrell & M. Dee 2015. A happening at Danebury hillfort – but when? *Oxford Journal of archaeology* 34.4, 407-414.

De Cock, S. 1987. Het Archeologisch onderzoek te Kooigem-Kortrijk. *Westvlaamse Archaeologica* 3.1, 3-15.

De Graeve, A. (ed.) 2020. Ronse Pont West, 4000 jaar leven in een dynamisch landschap. *Solva Archeologie Rapport* 150. Sint-Lievens-Houtem: Solva.

De Graeve, A., E. Du Rang, C. Van Heche, A. Verbrugge & B. Cherretté 2014. Een kringgreppel en dassenburchten te Ronse Pont-West (prov. O.-Vl., België). *Lunula Archaeologia Protohistorica* 22. Brussels: Cellule Archéologie des Âges des Métaux, 37-40.

De Groote, K. & M. Van de Vijver (eds.) 2019. Aalter Woestijne, Een geschiedenis van meer dan 5000 jaar, *Relicta Monografieën* 18. Brussel: Archeologie, Monumenten-, en landschapsonderzoek in Vlaanderen.

De Groote, K., E. Schynkel, F. De Buyser, A. Lentacker, A. Ervynck, E. Thieren & W. Van Neer 2019. Het Woestijnegoed en het kasteel van Woestijne. In: K. De Groote & M. Van de Vijver (eds.), Aalter Woestijne, Een geschiedenis van meer dan 5000 jaar. *Relicta Monografieën* 18. Brussel: Archeologie, Monumenten-, en landschapsonderzoek in Vlaanderen, 269-343.

De Grooth, M.E.Th. 1998. De duur en exploitatie. In: P.C.M. Rademakers (ed.), *De prehistorische vuursteenmijnen van Rijckholt-St. Geertruid.* Maastricht: Werkgroep Prehistorische Vuursteen mijnbouw/Nederlandse Geologische Verenging Afd. Limburg.

De Laet, S.J. 1966. Van grafmonument tot heiligdom – beschouwingen over de oorsprong van het Kelto-Romeins Fanum met vierkantige cella. *Mededelingen van de Koninklijke Vlaamse Academie van België, Klasse der Letteren* 28.2. Brussel: Paleis der Academiën.

De Laet, S.J., H. Thoen & J. Bourgeois 1985. De opgravingen te Destelbergen / Eenbeekeinde in het raam van de vroegste geschiedenis van de stad Gent, I. De voorgeschiedenis. *Handelingen der Maatschappij voor Geschiedenis en Oudheidkunde te Gent, Nieuwe Reeks* 39, 3-35.

De Leeuwe, R. & N. Prangsma 2011. Sporen en structuren. In: D.A. Gerrets & R. de Leeuwe (eds.), Rituelen aan de Maas-Lomm Hoogwatergeul fase II, een archeologische opgraving, *ADC-rapport* 2333, Amersfoort, 79-112.

De Leeuwe, R. & R. Jansen 2018. Space becomes a ritualised place. Five Iron Age and Early Roman period cult places in Oss (Netherlands). *Metaaltijden 5. Bijdragen in de studie van de metaaltijden.* Leiden: Sidestone Press, 175-189.

De Leeuwe, R. 2007. Twee grafheuvels in het prehistorisch dodenlandschap van Oss-Zevenbergen, circa 1800-500 v.Chr. In: R. Jansen & L.P. Louwe Kooijmans (eds.), *10 Jaar Archol – Van contract tot wetenschap.* Leiden: Archol BV, 205-220.

De Leeuwe, R. 2011. Een cultusplaats in Oss. Opgraving van een nederzetting en een cultusplaats aan de Brabantstraat. *Archolrapport 123.* Leiden: Archol BV.

De Leeuwe, R. 2022. The Mandible of Odijk. The varied contexts of unburnt human remains in the Middle Iron Age. *Metaaltijden 9. bijdragen in de studie van de metaaltijden.* Leiden: Sidestone Press, 115-126.

De Leeuwe, R. (ed.) 2022a. Plangebied Jochem Janszplantsoen en Singel te Odijk, gemeente Bunnik; proefsleuvenonderzoek en een archeologische opgraving van een midden ijzertijd en vroegmiddeleeuwse vindplaats. *RAAP-rapport* 5708. Weesp: RAAP Archeologisch Adviesbureau.

De Logi, A., L. Messiaen, K. Sturtewagen, & T. Bruyninckx 2008. Kortrijk/Harelbeke Evolis (prov. West-Vlaanderen), *Monument Vandekerckhove Rapport* buiten reeks.

De Mulder, G. & J. Putman 2006. Een status quaestionis van het archeologisch onderzoek op de Kemmelberg. In: *De Kemmelberg en verwante elitesites in Centraal en West-Europa (6de-5de eeuw): perspectieven voor toekomstig onderzoek/The Kemmelberg and related elite sites in Central and Western Europe (6th-5th century): perspectives for future research,* 19-23. Ieper-Kemmel.

De Mulder, G., 2011. *Funeraire rituelen in het Scheldebekken tijdens de late bronstijd en de vroege ijzertijd. De grafvelden in hun maatschappelijke en sociale context.* [PhD-dissertation Ghent University]. Gent: Gent University Press.

De Mulder, G., C. Snoeck, D. Tys, M. Vercauteren, M. Boudin, E. Warmenbol, G. Capuzzo, K. Salesse, C. Sabaux, S. Dalle, E. Stamataki, A. Sengeløv, M. Hlad, R. Annaert, B. Veselka & I. Kontopoulos 2020. The Late Iron Age cemetery of Kemzeke/Kwakkel (prov. of East-Flanders, Belgium): first radiocarbon dates on cremated bone and new insights in the funerary practices of the Iron Age. *Lunula Archaeologia Protohistorica* 28. Brussels: Cellule Archéologie des Âges des Métaux, 133-137.

De Navarro, J.M. 1972. *The finds from the site of La Tene, vol. 1, Scabberds and swords found in them. London.* Oxford: Oxford University Press.

De Reu, J. & J. Bourgeois 2013. Bronze Age barrow research in Sandy Flanders (NW Belgium): an overview. In: D.R. Fontijn, A.J. Louwen, S. van der Vaart & K. Wentink (eds.), *Beyond Barrows – Current research on the structuration and perception of the prehistoric landscape through monuments.* Leiden: Sidestone Press, 155-194.

De Reu, J., G. de Mulder, M. van Strydonck, M. Boudin & J. Bourgeois 2012. 14C Dates and Spatial Statistics: Modeling Intrasite Spatial Dynamics of Urnfield Cemeteries in Belgium Using Case Study of Destelbergen Cemetery. *Radiocarbon* 54.3-4, 635-648.

De Rijck, A. 2019. Vierkant, verheven en vereeuwigd. Archeologisch onderzoek aan de Akkerweg te Brecht (Provincie Antwerpen, België). *Lunula Archaeologia Protohistorica* 27. Brussels: Cellule Archéologie des Âges des Métaux, 101-106.

De Rijck, A. 2020. Archeologisch onderzoek van inheemse funeraire en bewoningssporen uit de ijzertijd te Brecht, Akkerweg (Provincie Antwerpen). *ABO Archeologische rapporten* 976, Aartselaar.

De Vries, K. 2021. *Settling with the norm? Norm and variation in social groups and their material manifestations in (Roman) Iron Age (800 BC-AD 300) settlement sites of the northern Netherlands.* [PhD-Dissertation Groningen University]. Leiden: Sidestone Press.

Delestrée, L.-P. 2001. L'or du trophée Laténien de Ribemont-sur-Ancre (Somme), témoin d'une bataille oubliée. *Revue numismatique, 6e série – Tome* 157, 175-213.

Demey, D. 2012. Archeologisch onderzoek te Oud Klooster (Dendermonde). *Ruben Willaert bvba rapport.* Sijsele: Ruben Willaert bvba.

Demey, D. 2012a. Archeologisch vooronderzoek Koestraat (Poperinge). *Ruben Willaert bvba rapport* 12. Sijsele: Ruben Willaert bvba.

Demey, D. 2013. Archeologisch onderzoek Oostvleteren Kasteelweg-Nieuwe Begraafplaats. *Ruben Willaert bvba rapport* 62. Sijsele: Ruben Willaert bvba.

Demey, D., F. Beke, J. Smet, L. Ryckebusch & W. De Clercq 2013. Een grafveld op de overgang van IJzertijd naar Romeinse tijd: opgravingen langs de Kasteelweg te Oostvleteren (gem. Vleteren, W.-Vl.). *Signe* 2, 53-55.

Demierre, M., G. Bataille & R. Perruche 2019. Faciès mobiliers et espaces rituels: les ensembles des sanctuaires laténiens du IVe au Ier siècle av. J.-C.. In: P. Barral & M. Thivet (eds.), *Sanctuaires de l'âge du Fer. Actes du 41e colloque international de l'Association française pour l'étude de l'âge du Fer (Dole, 25-28 mai 2017), Collection AFEAF* 1, 331-342.

Derieuw, M. 2009. *Romanisatie van het religieuze landschap. Rurale en suburbane heiligdommen in de civitates Nerviorum en Tungrorum.* [MA-thesis]. Gent: Universiteit Gent.

Derks, T. & N.G.A.M. Roymans 2009. Ethnic Constructs in Antiquity: the role of power and tradition. *Amsterdam Archaeological Studies* 13. Amsterdam: Amsterdam University Press.

Derks, T. 1996. Goden, tempels en rituele praktijken: de transformatie van religieuze ideeën en waarden in Romeins Gallië. [PhD-dissertation Amsterdam University]. *Amsterdam Archaeological Studies* 2. Amsterdam: Amsterdam University Press.

Derks, T. 2002. Roman imperialism and the sanctuaries of Roman Gaul. *Journal of Roman Archaeology* 15. 541-545. Cambridge: Cambridge University Press.

Didier, B. & J.-L. Cadoux 1982. Les thermes du sanctuaire gallo-romain de Ribemont-sur-Ancre (Somme). *Gallia* 40.1, 83-106.

Diepeveen-Jansen, M. 2001. People, Ideas and Goods – New perspectives on 'Celtic barbarians' in Western and Central Europe (500-250 BC). [PhD-dissertation, Amsterdam University]. *Amsterdam Archaeological Studies* 7. Amsterdam: Amsterdam University Press.

Doorenbosch, M. 2013. *Ancestral heaths: reconstructing the barrow landscape in the central and southern Netherlands.* [PhD-dissertation Leiden University]. Leiden: Sidestone Press.

Drury, P.J. 1980. Non-classical religious buildings in Iron Age and Roman Britain: a review. In: W.J. Rodwell (ed.), Temples, churches and religion: recent research in Roman Britain, with a gazetteer of Romano-Celtic temples in continental Europe. *BAR* 77, 45-78.

Durkheim, E. 1995 [1912]. *The elementery forms of religious life.* A new translation by K.E. Fields. New York: the Free Press.

Duval, A., C. Lyon-Caen & S. Lourdaux (eds.) 1994. *Vercingétorix et Alésia: Saint-Germain-en-Laye, Musée des antiquités nationales, 29 mars-18 juillet 1994.* Paris: Éditions Réunion des Musées Nationaux.

Earle, T., J. Ling, C. Uhnér, Z. Stos-Gale & L. Melheim 2015. The political economy and metal trade in Bronze Age Europe: understanding regional variability in terms of comparative advantages and articulations. *European Journal of Archaeology* 18.4, 633-657.

Edelstein, L. & I.G. Kidd 1972. *Posidonius 1, The fragments.* Cambridge: Cambridge University Press.

Fauduet, I. 1993. *Les temples de tradition celtique en Gaule romaine.* Paris: Collection des Hesperides.

Fauduet, I. 2010. *Les temples de tradition celtique.* Paris: Nouvelle édition revue et augmentée.

Fechner, K. & R. Langohr 1993. Bodemkundige gegevens en interpretatie. In: R. Annaert (ed.), Een Viereckschanze op de Alfsberg te Kontich (prov. Antwerpen): meer dan een cultusplaats, *Archeologie in Vlaanderen* 3, 85-94.

Fercoq du Leslay, G. 1996. Chronologie et analyse spatiale à Ribemont-sur-Ancre (Somme). *Revue archéologique de Picardie* 3-4, 189-208.

Fercoq du Leslay, G. 2000. L'apport des fossés de Ribemont-sur-Ancre (Somme) à la chronologie et à l'interprétation du site. *Revue archéologique de Picardie* 1-2, Les enclos celtiques – Actes de la table ronde de Ribemont-sur-Ancre (Somme), 113-146.

Fercoq du Leslay, G., G. Bataille & C. Chaidron 2019. Évolution des pratiques rituelles laténiennes et de leurs contextes: le cas du sanctuaire de Ribemont-sur-Ancre (Somme). In: P. Barral & M. Thivet, *Sanctuaires de l'âge du Fer. Actes du 41e colloque international de l'Association française pour l'étude de l'âge du Fer (Dole, 25-28 mai 2017), Collection AFEAF* 1, 291- 311.

Fernández-Götz, M. & D. Krausse 2016. Early Centralisation Processes North of the Alps. Fortifications as symbols of Power and Community Identity. In: P. Fontaine & S. Helas (eds.), *Fortificazioni arcaiche del Latium vetus e dell'Etruria meridionale.* Brussels / Rome: Belgisch Historisch Instituut te Rome, 267-286.

Fernández-Götz, M. & N.G.A.M. Roymans 2015. The Politics of Identity: Late Iron Age Sanctuaries in the Rhineland. *Journal of the North Atlantic* 8. 18-32. DOI: 10.3721/037.002.sp803.

Fernández-Götz, M. 2014. Identity and Power: The Transformation of Iron Age Societies in Northeast Gaul. *Amsterdam Archaeological Studies* 21. Amsterdam: Amsterdam University Press.

Fernández-Götz, M. 2018. Urbanization in Iron Age Europe: Trajectories, Patterns, and Social Dynamics. *Journal of Archaeological Research* 26, 117-162.

Fichtl, S. 2013. Les agglomérations gauloises de la fin de l'âge du Fer en Europe celtique (IIIe-Ier siècle av. J.-C.), In: D. Garcia (ed.), *L'habitat en Europe celtique et en Méditerranée préclassique – Domaines urbains.* Paris: Errance, 1-24.

Fichtl, S. 2018. Urbanization and oppida. In: C. Haselgrove, K. Rebay-Salisbury & P.S. Wells, *The Oxford Handbook of the European Iron Age.* DOI: 10.1093/oxfordhb/9780199696826.001.0001.

Fitzpatrick, A.P. & A.B. Powell 1997. The Late Iron Age Religious Site. In: A.P. Fitzpatrick (ed.), Archaeological Excavations on the Route of the A27 Westhampnett Bypass, West Sussex, 1992. Volume 2: the Cemeteries. *Wessex Archaeology Report* 12. Salisbury: Wessex Archaeology, 13-241.

Fitzpatrick, A.P. (ed.) 1997. Archaeological Excavations on the Route of the A27 Westhampnett Bypass, West Sussex, 1992. Volume 2: the Cemeteries. *Wessex Archaeology Report* 12. Salisbury: Wessex Archaeology.

Fockedey, L. & R. Bakx 2018. Lithostratigrafische en bodemkundige opbouw. In: R. Bakx, J. Verrijckt & M. Smeets, Het archeologisch onderzoek aan de

Mussenhoevelaan te Boechout. *Archeo-rapport* 456. Tienen: Studiebureau Archeologie bvba, 18-27.

Fokkens, H. & R. Jansen 2004. *Het vorstengraf van Oss. Een archeologische speurtocht naar een prehistorisch grafveld.* Utrecht: Matrijs.

Fokkens, H. (ed.) 1998. The Oss-Ussen Project – the first decade of excavations at Oss. *Analecta Praehistorica Leidensia* 30. Leiden: Leiden University Press.

Fokkens, H. 2002. Vee en voorouders: centrale elementen uit het dagelijks leven in de bronstijd. In: H. Fokkens & R. Jansen (eds.): *2000 jaar bewoningsdynamiek. Brons- en ijzertijdbewoning in het Maas-Demer-Scheldegebied.* Alblasserdam: Haveka, 125-148.

Fokkens, H. 2013. Post alignments in the barrow cemeteries of Oss-Vorstengraf and Oss-Zevenbergen. In: D.R. Fontijn, A.J. Louwen, S. Van der Vaart & K. Wentink (Eds.), *Beyond Barrows. Current research on the structuration and perception of the Prehistoric landscape through monuments.* Leiden: Sidestone press. 141-155.

Fokkens, H. 2019. Introduction to the project. In: H. Fokkens, S. van As & R. Jansen (eds.), The Oss-Noord Project – the second decade of excavations at Oss 1986-1996. *Analecta Praehistorica Leidensia* 48. Leiden: Sidestone Press, 15-26.

Fokkens, H. 2019a. Chronology and typology of structures. In: H. Fokkens, S. van As & R. Jansen (eds.), The Oss-Noord Project – the second decade of excavations at Oss 1986-1996. *Analecta Praehistorica Leidensia* 48. Leiden: Sidestone Press, 39-60.

Fokkens, H. 2019b. Oss-North: a synthesis. In: H. Fokkens, S. van As & R. Jansen (eds.), The Oss-Noord Project – the second decade of excavations at Oss 1986-1996. *Analecta Praehistorica Leidensia* 48. Leiden: Sidestone Press, 183-211.

Fokkens, H. 2019c. Excavations in the Mikkeldonk district. In: H. Fokkens, S. van As & R. Jansen (eds.), The Oss-Noord Project – the second decade of excavations at Oss 1986-1996. *Analecta Praehistorica Leidensia* 48. Leiden: Sidestone Press, 61-87.

Fokkens, H., B. Veselka, Q.P.J. Bourgeois, I. Olalde & D. Reich 2017. Excavations of Late Neolithic arable, burial mounds and a number of well-preserved skeletons at Oostwoud-Tuithoorn: a re-analysis of old data. In: H. Kamermans & C.C. Bakels (eds.), *Exerpta Archaeologica Leidensia II: Analecta Praehistorica Leidensia* 47. Leiden: Faculty of Archaeology, Leiden University, 95-150.

Fokkens, H., R. Jansen & I.M. van Wijk (eds.) 2009. Het grafveld Oss-Zevenbergen: een prehistorisch grafveld ontleed. *Archolrapport* 50. Leiden: Archol BV.

Fokkens, H., S. van As & R. Jansen (eds.) 2019. The Oss-Noord Project – the second decade of excavations at Oss 1986-1996. *Analecta Praehistorica Leidensia 48.* Leiden: Sidestone Press.

Fontijn, D.R. & Q.P.J. Bourgeois 2008. Houses and barrows in the Low Countries. In: S. Arnoldussen & H. Fokkens (eds.), *Bronze Age Settlements in the Low Countries.* Oxford: Oxbow Books. 41-57.

Fontijn, D.R, S. van der Vaart & R. Jansen (eds.) 2013. *Transformation through destruction. A monumental and extraordinary Early Iron Age Hallstatt C barrow from the ritual landscape of Oss-Zevenbergen.* Leiden: Sidestone Press.

Fontijn, D.R. & A.G.F.M. Cuijpers 1999. Prehistoric stone circles, stone platforms and a ritual enclosure from Nijmegen. *Berichten van de Rijksdienst voor het Oudheidkundig Bodemonderzoek* 43, 33-67.

Fontijn, D.R. & L. Amkreutz 2018. Het verzonken zwaard van Ommerschans. In: L. Heerma van Voss, M. 't Hart, K. Davids, K. Fatah-Black, L. Lucassen & J. Touwen (eds.). *Wereldgeschiedenis van Nederland, Amsterdam.* Ambo/Anthos, 39-43.

Fontijn, D.R. 1996. Socializing landscape: Second thoughts about the cultural biography of urnfields. *Archaeological Dialogues* 3, 77-87.

Fontijn, D.R. 2002. Sacrificial Landscapes. Cultural biographies of persons, objects and 'natural' places in the Bronze age of the Southern Netherlands, 2300 -600 BC. [PhD-dissertation Leiden University]. *Analecta Praehistorica Leidensia* 33-34. Leiden: Leiden University Press.

Fontijn, D.R. 2002a. Het ontstaan van rechthoekige 'cultusplaatsen'. In: H. Fokkens & R. Jansen (eds.), *2000 jaar bewoningsdynamiek. Brons- en ijzertijdbewoning in het Maas-Demer-Scheldegebied.* Alblasserdam: Haveka, 149-172.

Fontijn, D.R. 2019. *Economies of destruction : how the systematic destruction of valuables created value in Bronze Age Europe, c. 2300-500 BC.* London / New York: Routledge.

Fontijn, D.R., A.J. Louwen, S. van der Vaart & K. Wentink (eds.) 2013. *Beyond Barrows. Current research on the Structuration and perception of the prehistoric landscape through monuments.* Leiden: Sidestone Press.

Frazer, J.G. 2012 [1911]. *Taboo and the Perils of the Soul.* The Golden Bough, The Third Edition, Volume 3. New York: Cambridge University Press.

Freeman, D. & A. Pankhurst 2003. *Peripheral people: the excluded minorities of Ethiopia.* London: Hurst & Co.

Frézouls, E. 1975. Circonscription de Champagne-Ardenne, La Villeneuve-au-Châtelot. *Gallia* 33, fascicule 2, 398-402.

Furholt, M. 2003. Die absolutchronologische Datierung der Schnurkeramik in Mitteleuropa und Südskandinavien. *Universitätsforschungen zur prähistorischen Archäologie* 101. Bonn: Dr. Rudolf Habelt GmbH.

Gassmann, P. 2007. Nouvelle approche concernant les datations dendrochronologiques du site éponyme de La Tène (Marin-Epagnier, Suisse). *Annuaire d'archéologie suisse* 90, 75-88.

Gassmann, P. 2009. Inventaire exhaustif des datations des bois provenant du site de La Tène. In: M. Honegger, et al. (eds.), *Le site de La Tène: bilan des connaissances – état de la question. Actes de ta Table ronde internationale de Neuchâtel, J-3 novembre 2007*. Neuchâtel: Office et musée cantonal d'archéologie, 49-55.

Geerts, R.C.A. 2022. Voor een rite vervaardigd? Een interessante aardewerkdepositie uit Kortrijk (België). In: J. van der Leije, E.H.L.D. Norde, B.J.W. Steffens & K.M. de Vries (eds.), *Metaaltijden 9, bijdragen in de studie van de metaaltijden*. Leiden: Sidestone Press, 97-104.

Gerrets, D.A. & R. de Leeuwe (eds.) 2011. Rituelen aan de Maas-Lomm Hoogwatergeul fase II, een archeologische opgraving. *ADC-rapport 2333*. Amersfoort: ADC-Archeo-Projecten.

Gerritsen, F. 2003. Local Identities. Landscape and community in the late prehistoric Meuse-Demer-Scheldt region. [PhD-dissertation University of Amsterdam]. *Amsterdam Archaeological Studies* 9. Amsterdam: Amsterdam University Press.

Gerritsen, F.A. & N.G.A.M. Roymans 2006. Central places and the construction of tribal identities: The case of the Late Iron Age Lower Rhine Region. In: C. Haselgrove (Ed.), *Celtes et Gaulois, l'Archéologie face à l'Histoire, 4: les mutations de la fin de l'âge du Fer. Actes de la table ronde de Cambridge, 7-8 juillet 2005*. Glux-en-Glenne: Bibracte, Centre archéologique européen, 251-266.

Gheysen, K. & G. De Mulder 2010. Een bronstijdgrafheuvel in de ruilverkaveling Merksplas (provincie Antwerpen, België). *Lunula Archaeologia ProtohistoricaI* 18. Brussels: Cellule Archéologie des Âges des Métaux, 49-55.

Giles, M. 2007. Refiguring rights in the Early Iron Age landscapes of East Yorkshire. In: C. Haselgrove & R. Pope (eds.), *The Earlier Iron Age in Britain and the near continent*. Oxford: Oxbow Books, 103-118.

Glasbergen, W. 1954. Barrow excavations in the Eight Beatitudes. The Bronze Age cemetery between Toterfout & Halve Mijl, North Brabant. II. The Implications. *Palaeohistoria* 3, 1-204.

Glob, P.V. 2004 [1965]. *The bog people: Iron-Age man preserved*. New York: New York Review Books.

Gluckman, M. 1962. *Essays on the rituals of social relations*. Manchester: Manchester University Press.

Goguey, R. 1968. *De l'aviation à l'archéologie. Rechercher sur les techniques et les méthodes de l'archeologie aérienne: Alésia-Vix et quelques sites archéologiques en Bourgogne*. Paris: Technip.

Goussard, É., B. Lambot, M. Pieters & B. Squevin 2019. Le phénomène des dépôts de miniatures d'armes dans les sanctuaires celtes: réflexions à partir de l'exemple des Rèmes. In: P. Barral & M. Thivet (eds.), *Sanctuaires de l'âge du Fer. Actes du 41e colloque international de l'Association française pour l'étude de l'âge du Fer (Dole, 25-28 mai 2017), Collection AFEAF* 1, 313-330.

Greatorex, C. 2003. Living on margin? The Late Bronze Age landscape of the Willingdon Levels. In: D. Rudling (ed.), *The Archaeology of Sussex to AD 2000*. Brighton: University of Sussex Department of Continuing Education , 89-100.

Green, M.J. 1997 [1992]. *Dictionary of Celtic Myth and Legend*. London: Thames and Hudson.

Grimes, R.L. 1999. Jonathan Z. Smith's Theory of Ritual Space. *Religion* 29:3, 261-273. DOI:10.1006/reli.1998.0162.

Grimes, R.L. 2014. *The craft of ritual studies*. Oxford: University Press.

Groenewoudt, B. 2011. Curves turning into squares. Late Prehistoric landscape change and the changing morphology of ritual structures. Causality? Assessment of evidence. *Landscape History* 32.2.

Groot, M. & M. van Haasteren 2017. Dierlijk bot. In: J. van Renswoude & D.S. Habermehl (eds.), Opgravingen te Houten-Castellum. Bewoning langs een restgeul in de IJzertijd, Romeinse tijd en Vroege Middeleeuwen. *Zuidnederlandse Archeologische Rapporten* 65. Amsterdam: VUhbs archeologie / Vrije Universiteit, 687-733.

Gysseling, M. 1960. *Toponymisch woordenboek van België, Nederland, Luxemburg, Noord-Frankrijk en West-Duitsland (vóór 1226)*. Belgisch Interuniversitair Centrum voor Neerlandistiek, Bouwstoffen en studiën voor de geschiedenis en de lexicografie van het Nederlands VI. deel 1, A-M. Brussel: Belgisch Interuniversitair Centrum voor Neerlandistiek.

Habermehl, D.S. & A. Sinke 2017. Speciale deposities uit de ijzertijd en Romeinse tijd. In: J. van Renswoude & D.S. Habermehl (eds.), Opgravingen te Houten-Castellum. Bewoning langs een restgeul in de IJzertijd, Romeinse tijd en Vroege Middeleeuwen. *Zuidnederlandse Archeologische Rapporten* 65. Amsterdam: VUhbs archeologie / Vrije Universiteit, 398-409.

Habermehl, D.S. 2022. Gewoon bijzonder. Archeologisch onderzoek naar speciale depositiepraktijken rond huis en erf (neolithicum-nieuwe tijd). *Nederlandse Archeologische Rapporten* 79. Amersfoort: Rijksdienst voor het Cultureel Erfgoed.

Haffner, A. 1995. *Heiligtümer und Opferkulte der Kelten*. Stuttgart: Theiss.

Hanks, B. 2008. The past in later prehistory. In: A. Jones (ed.), *Prehistoric Europe : theory and practice*. Malden, Mass., [etc.]: Wiley-Blackwell, 255-284.

Hargrave, F. 2018. *Ritual and Religious Sites in Later Iron Age Britain with particular reference to Eastern England*. [PhD-dissertation University of Leicester]. Leicester.

Harrell, S. 1979. The Concept of Soul in Chinese Folk Religion, *The Journal of Asian Studies* 38. 3, 519-528.

Hazen, P.L.M. & E. Blom 2015. Bewoningssporen uit de ijzertijd. In: P.L.M. Hazen, E. Drenth & E. Blom (eds.), Tien millennia bewoningsgeschiedenis in het Maasdal, van jachtkamp tot landgoed langs de A2 bij Maastricht, *ADC Monografie* 17, Amersfoort: ADC Archeo-Projecten, 195-236.

Heeren, S. 2014. De vindplaats Maren-Kessel/Lith: van heiligdom naar legerkamp. In: R. Jansen (ed.), *De archeologische schatkamer Maaskant, Bewoning van het noordoost-Brabantse rivierengebied tussen 3000 v. en 1500 n.Chr.* Leiden: Sidestone Press, 253-267.

Heim, J. 1991. Première contribution palynologique â l'étude du site archéologique de Kemzeke-Kwakkel (comm. de Stekene, Flandre orientale). *Scholae Archaeologicae* 12. Gent, 29-34.

Hessing, W. & P. Kooi 2005. Urnenvelden en brandheuvels – Begraving en grafritueel in late bronstijd en ijzertijd. In: L.P. Louwe Kooijmans *et al.* (eds.), *Nederland in de Prehistorie*. Amsterdam: Bakker, 631-654.

Hessing, W.A.M. 1993. Ondeugende Bataven en verdwaalde Friezinnen?: enkele gedachten over de onverbrande menselijke resten uit de ijzertijd en Romeinse tijd in West- en Noord-Nederland. In: E. Drenth, W.A.M. Hessing & E. Knol (eds.), Het tweede leven van onze doden. *Nederlandse Archeologische Rapporten* 15. Amersfoort: Rijksdienst voor Oudheidkundig Bodemonderzoek, 17-40.

Heunks, E. 2011. Resultaten fysisch-geografisch onderzoek. In: L. Meurkens & A.J. Tol (eds.), Grafvelden en greppelstructuren uit de ijzertijd en Romeinse tijd bij Itteren (gemeente Maastricht). *Archolrapport* 144. Leiden: Archol BV, 45-60.

Heunks, E. 2013. Landschappelijk kader en resultaten landschappelijk onderzoek. In: S. Knippenberg (ed.), Neolithicum en ijzertijd in de Maaskant, Opgravingen van een midden-neolithische nederzetting en een midden- en late ijzertijd crematiegrafveld te Haren (N-Br.). *Archolrapport* 214. Leiden: Archol BV, 23-33.

Hiddink, H.A. & E. de Boer (eds.) 2011. Opgravingen in Waterdael III bij Someren 1. Grafvelden en begravingen uit de IJzertijd en Romeinse tijd. *Zuidnederlandse Archeologische Rapporten* 42. Amsterdam: VUhbs archeologie / Vrije Universiteit.

Hiddink, H.A. 2003. Het grafritueel in de Late IJzertijd en Romeinse tijd in het Maas-Demer-Scheldegebied, in het bijzonder van twee grafvelden bij Weert. *Zuidnederlandse Archeologische Rapporten* 11. Amsterdam: Archeologisch Centrum Vrije Universiteit.

Hiddink, H.A. 2012. Bewoning uit de latere prehistorie. In: E. De Boer & H.A. Hiddink (eds.), Opgravingen in Waterdael III bij Someren 2. Bewoningssporen uit de latere prehistorie, de Vroege en Volle Middeleeuwen. *Zuidnederlandse Archeologische Rapporten* 50. Amsterdam: VUhbs archeologie / Vrije Universiteit, 57-68.

Hiddink, H.A. 2014. De Romeinse villa-nederzetting op de Kerkakkers bij Hoogeloon (Noord-Brabant). *Zuidnederlandse Archeologische Rapporten* 53. Amsterdam: VUhbs archeologie / Vrije Universiteit.

Hiddink, H.A. 2014a. Huisplattegronden uit de late prehistorie in Zuid-Nederland. In: A.G. Lange, E.M. Theunissen, J.H.C. Deeben, J. van Doesburg, J. Bouwmeester & T. de Groot (eds.), *Huisplattegronden in Nederland. Archeologische sporen van het huis*. Amersfoort: Rijksdienst voor het Cultureel Erfgoed, 169-207.

Hillam, J. 2003. Tree-ring analysis of the causeway timbers. In: N. Field & M. Parker Pearson (eds.), *Finkerton – An Iron Age Timber Causeway with Iron Age and Roman Votive offerings*. Oxford: Oxbow Books, 25-37.

Holzer, V. 2019. Rites et architectures dans les sanctuaires celtiques du complexe cultuel de Roseldorf (Basse-Autriche). In: P. Barral & M. Thivet (eds.), *Sanctuaires de l'âge du Fer. Actes du 41e colloque international de l'Association française pour l'étude de l'âge du Fer (Dole, 25-28 mai 2017)*, Collection AFEAF 1, 149-162.

Hondius-Crone, A. 1955. *The Temple of Nehalennia at Domburg*. Amsterdam: Meulenhoff.

James, S. 2018. Warriors, war, and weapons; or arms, the armed, and armed violence. In: C. Haselgrove, K. Rebay-Salisbury & P.S. Wells (eds), *The Oxford Handbook of the European Iron Age*. DOI: 10.1093/oxfordhb/9780199696826.013.1.

Jansen, R. & F. Jacques 2014. De 'vergeten' vindplaats Haren-Spaanse Steeg. Een riviercultusplaats uit de late ijzertijd. In: R. Jansen (ed.), *De archeologische schatkamer Maaskant. Bewoning van het Noordoost-Brabantse rivierengebied tussen 3000 v. en 1500 n.Chr.* Leiden: Sidestone Press, 235-251.

Jansen, R. & H. Fokkens 2002. Een korte biografie van Oss-Horzak, een lokale gemeenschap tussen Maaskant en Heikant. In: H. Fokkens & R. Jansen (eds.), *2000 jaar bewoningsdynamiek. Brons- en ijzertijdbewoning in het Maas-Demer-Scheldegebied*. Alblasserdam: Haveka BV, 315-340.

Jansen, R. & S. van As 2012. Structuring the landscape in Iron Age and Roman period (500 BC – AD 250): the multi-period site Oss-Horzak. In: C.C. Bakels & H. Kamermans (eds.), The End Of Our Fifth Decade. *Analecta Praehistorica Leidensia* 43/44. Leiden: Leiden University Press, 95-115.

Jansen, R. 2007. Bewoningsdynamiek op de Maashorst, van neolithicum tot 'Nistelre'. In: R. Jansen (ed.), Bewoningsdynamiek op de Maashorst (deel 2), De bewoningsdynamiek van Nistelrode van laat-neolithicum tot volle middeleeuwen. *Archolrapport* 48. Leiden: Archol BV, 541-570.

Jansen, R. 2018. Zwerven erven? Locatiekeuze en bewoningsdynamiek in oostelijk Noord-Brabant tussen 1500 v.Chr. en circa 0. In: E. A. G. Ball & R. Jansen (eds.), Drieduizend jaar bewoningsgeschiedenis van oostelijk Noord-Brabant: synthetiserend onderzoek naar locatiekeuze en bewoningsdynamiek tussen 1500 v.Chr. en 1500 n.Chr. op basis van archeologisch onderzoek in het Malta-tijdperk. *Nederlandse Archeologische Rapporten* 61. Amersfoort: Rijksdienst voor het Cultureel Erfgoed, uitgever, 197-282.

Jansen, R. 2021. *Verleden als Leidraad, IJzertijdbewoning en landschapsinrichting in noordoostelijk Noord-Brabant in verleden én heden.* [PhD-dissertation Leiden University]. Leiden: Sidestone Press.

Jansen, R. 2021a. Verleden in het Verleden. Bewoning en landschapsinrichting in de ijzertijd in noordoostelijk Noord-Brabant. In: R. Jansen, *Verleden als Leidraad, IJzertijdbewoning en landschapsinrichting in noordoostelijk Noord-Brabant in verleden én heden.* Leiden: Sidestone, 293-428.

Jansen, R., C. van der Linde & H. Fokkens 2002. Archeologisch onderzoek Hertogswetering. Een cultusplaats aan de Maaskant. *Archeologische Rapporten Maaskant* 7 / *Archolrapport* 7. Leiden: Archol BV.

Janson, S. 2000. Keltische Viereckschanzen, vorgeschichtiche Kult- und Opferplätze? Argumente Pro und Kontra, *GRIN Verlagsprogramm*, Document Nr. V78931.

Janssens, M. 2007. Plangebied Regenwaterbuffers te Gronsveld en Rijckholt, gemeente Eijsden, archeologisch vooronderzoek: een bureau- en inventariserend veldonderzoek (verkennende fase). *RAAP-notitie* 2504. Weesp: RAAP Archeologisch Adviesbureau.

Janssens, M. 2008. Plangebied regenwaterbuffers (deelgebieden 1 en 2) te Gronsveld en Rijckholt, gemeente Eijsden: archeologisch vooronderzoek: een waarderend veldonderzoek (proefsleuven). *RAAP-rapport* 1652. Weesp: RAAP Archeologisch Adviesbureau.

Jennes, N. 2019. Sporen en structuren. In: R.C.A. Geerts, N. Jennes, F.R.P.M. Miedema & C. Moolhuizen (eds.), Landindeling uit de IJzertijd/Vroeg-Romeinse periode onder het industrieterrein, Een archeologische opgraving te Evolis 76, Kortrijk. *VEC Rapport* 82. Geel: Vlaams Erfgoed Centrum, 39-58.

Jensen, J. 2002. *Danmarks oldtid – Bronzealder.* Copenhagen: Gyldendal.

Jezeer, W. & L.P. Verniers 2012. De Plantage: een nieuwe wijk, een rijk verleden. Een archeologische opgrvaing op De Plantage in Meteren (gemeente Geldermalsen). *ADC-rapport* 2713. Amersfoort: ADC Archeo-Projecten.

Jezeer, W. & W. Roessingh 2019. Sporen uit de Bronstijd. In: A.J .Tol & W. Roessingh (eds.), Archeologie langs de Westfrisiaweg, Opgravingen van vindplaatsen uit de late prehistorie, middeleeuwen en Nieuwe tijd in het tracé van de Westfrisiaweg. *ADC-rapport* 5000 / *Archolrapport* 461. Amersfoort: ADC Archeo-Projecten / Leiden: Archol BV, 319-345.

Jezeer, W. 2015. Middeleeuwse bewoningssporen en een ritueel landschap uit de ijzertijd. Een archeologische opgraving aan de Stationsstraat te Hever (Gemeente Boortmeerbeek). *VEC Rapport* 31. Leuven: Vlaams Erfgoed Centrum bvba.

Joffroy, R. 1954. La tombe de Vix (Côte-d'Or). *Monuments et mémoires de la Fondation Eugène Piot 48,* fascicule 1, 1-68.

Joffroy, R. 1960. *L'Oppidum de Vix et la civilisation Hallstattienne finale dans l'Est de la France.* Paris: Publications de l'Université de Dijon XX, Société les Belles Lettres.

Jones, H.L. 1927. *The geography of Strabo. IV: [Book VIII-IX].* Cambridge, Mass. : London: Harvard University Press; Heinemann.

Jope, E.M. 1971. The Witham shield. *The British Museum Quarterly* 35.1/4, 61-69.

Jørgensen, R. 2012. The Social and Material Context of the Iron Age Blacksmith in North Norway. *Acta Borealia* 29.1, 1-34. DOI:10.1080/08003831.2012.678718.

Jud, P. & K.W. Alt 2009. Les ossements humains de La Tène et leur interprétation. In: M. Honegger, et al. (eds.), *Le site de La Tène: bilan des connaissances – état de la question. Actes de ta Table ronde internationale de Neuchâtel, J-3 novembre 2007.* Neuchâtel: Office et musée cantonal d'archéologie, 57-63.

Kaeser M.-A., 2012. Les interprétations du site de La Tène: des interférences et des parasitages significatifs. In: A. Testart (ed.), *Les armes dans les eaux: questions d'interprétation en archéologie.* Paris: Errance, 53-72.

Kaeser, M.-A. 2017. La Tène, nouvelles recherches, nouvelles interprétations. *Antiquités* 8, 48-59.

Kanael, G. & T. Lejars 2009. Quel avenir pour l'étude du site de La Tène? In: M. Honegger, et al. (eds.), *Le site de La Tène: bilan des connaissances – état de la question. Actes de ta Table ronde internationale de Neuchâtel, J-3 novembre 2007*. Neuchâtel: Office et musée cantonal d'archéologie, 263-273.

Kaul F. 2011. The Gundestrup Cauldron: Thracian Art, Celtic Motifs. *Etudes Celtiques* 37, 81-110.

Kaul, F. 1995. Ships on bronzes. In: O. Crumlin-Pedersen & B. Munch Thye (eds.), *The Ship as Symbol in Prehistoric and Medieval Scandinavia: Papers from an International Research Seminar at the Danish National Museum, Copenhagen, 5th-7th May 1994*. Copenhagen: Nationalmuseet, 59-70.

Kaul, F. 1998. *Ships on bronzes: a study in Bronze Age religion and iconography. National Museum Studies in Archaeology and History* 3.1. Copenhagen: National Museum.

Kaul, F. 2004. Der sonnenwagen von Trundheim. In: H. Meller (ed.), *Der geschmiedete Himmel – Die weite Welt im Herzen Europas vor 3600 Jahren*. Stuttgart: Landesmuseum für vorgeschichte Halle, 54-57.

Kerkhof, P.A. 2016. Nehalennia -taalkundige oplossing voor een Zeeuws raadsel. *Neerlandistiek, Online tijdschrift voor taal- en letterkundig onderzoek* 25-10-2016.

Kimmig, W. 1969. Zum Problem späthallstättischer Adelssitze. In: K.H. Otto & J. Herrmann (eds.), Siedlung, Burg und Stadt. Studien zu ihren Anfangen, *Deutsche Akademie der Wissenschaften zu Berlin, schriften der Sektion für Vor- und Frühgeschichte* 25. Berlin: Deutsche Akademie der Wissenschaften, 95-113.

King, A.C. & Soffe G. 1994. The Iron Age and Roman temple on Hayling Island. In A.P. Fitzpatrick & E.L. Morris (eds.), *The Iron Age in Wessex- recent work*. Salisbury: Trust for Wessex Archaeology, 114-116.

King, A.C. & Soffe, G. 2013. *A Sacred Island: Iron Age, Roman and Saxon Temples and Ritual on Hayling Island. Hayling Island Excavation Project*. Winchester: University of Winchester.

Kline, A.S. 2014 (trans.). Lucan. *The Civil War (Pharsalia)*. https://www.poetryintranslation.com/.

Kluiving, S.J. 2005. De fysische geografie en geologie van de Heeswijkse Kampen. In: E.A.G. Ball & E.N.A. Heirbaut (eds.), Cuijk-Heeswijkse Kampen: een landschap vol archeologie. Proefsleuven en Opgravingen in de jaren 2003-2004. *Archolrapport* 39. Leiden: Archol BV, 23-34.

Knight, D. 2007. From open to Enclosed: Iron Age landscapes of the Trent Valley. In: C. Haselgrove & T. Moore (eds.), *The Later Iron Age in Britain and the Near Continent*. Oxford: Oxbow Books, 190-218.

Knippenberg, S. 2009. De vondsten van natuursteen. In: A.J. Tol (ed.), Graven en nederzettingsresten uit de late prehistorie en volle middeleeuwen. Een archeologisch onderzoek te Weert-Laarveld. *Archolrapport* 127. Leiden: Archol BV, 79-80.

Knippenberg, S. 2013. Neolithicum en ijzertijd in de Maaskant. Opgravingen van een midden-neolithische nederzetting en een midden- en late ijzertijd crematiegrafveld te Haren (N-Br.). *Archolrapport* 214. Leiden: Archol BV.

Kok, M.S.M. 2008. *The homecoming of religious practice – And analysis of offering sites in the wet low-lying parts of the landscape in the Oer-IJ area (2500 BC – AD 450)*. [PhD-dissertation Amsterdam University]. Rotterdam: Lima.

Kooi, P.B. 1979. *Pre-Roman urnfields in the north of the Netherlands*. [PhD-dissertation Groningen University]. Groningen: Wolters-Noordhoff/ Bouma's Boekhuis BV.

Kooistra, L.I. 2017. Botanische materialen. In: J. van Renswoude & D.S. Habermehl (eds.), Opgravingen te Houten-Castellum. Bewoning langs een restgeul in de IJzertijd, Romeinse tijd en Vroege Middeleeuwen. *Zuidnederlandse Archeologische Rapporten* 65. Amsterdam: VUhbs archeologie / Vrije Universiteit, 747-788.

Kooistra, M.J. & G.J. Maas 2008. The widespread occurrence of Celtic field systems in the central part of the Netherlands. *Journal of Archaeological Science* 35, 2318-2328.

Kootker, L.M. 2022. Isotopenonderzoek. In: R. de Leeuwe (ed.), Plangebied Jochem Janszplantsoen en Singel te Odijk, gemeente Bunnik; proefsleuvenonderzoek en een archeologische opgraving van een midden ijzertijd en vroegmiddeleeuwse vindplaats. *RAAP-rapport* 5708. Weesp: RAAP Archeologisch Adviesbureau, 222-228.

Kootker, L.M., C. Geerdink, P.W. van den Broeke, H. Kars & G.R. Davies 2018. Breaking Traditions: An Isotopic Study on the Changing Funerary Practices in the Dutch Iron Age (800-12 bc). *Archaeometry*, 60.3, 594-611. DOI:10.1111/arcm.12333.

Krämer, W. 1958. *Manching, ein vindelikisches Oppidum an der Donau, Neue Ausgrabungen in Deutschland*. Berlin: Gebrüder Mann.

Krist, J.S. (ed.) 2005. Archeologische opgraving Mencia Sandrode-Akkermolenweg te Zundert, een grafveld uit de Late Bronstijd en Midden-Ijzertijd. *Synthegra Rapport* 2003-145. Hoog-Keppel: Synthegra Archeologie bv.

Kuijpers, M.H.G. 2008. *Bronze Age metalworking in the Netherlands (C. 2000-800BC). A research into the preservation of metallurgy related artefacts and the social position of the smith*. Leiden: Sidestone Press.

Kuijpers, M.H.G. 2015. Contradicting Context: Understanding Early Bronze Axes from the Perspective of Production. In: P. Suchowska-Ducke, S. Scott Reite & H. Vandkilde (eds.), Forging

Identities. The Mobility of Culture in Bronze Age Europe: Volume 1. *British Archaeological Reports* S2771, 203-212.

Kurtz, D.C. & J. Boardman 1971. *Greek Burial Customs.* London: Thames & Hudson.

Lambot, B. & P. Méniel 2000. Le centre communautaire et cultuel du village gaulois d'Acy-Romance dans son contexte régional. Rites et espaces en pays celte et méditerranéen. *École Française de Rome* 276, 7-139.

Lambot, B. 1998. Les morts d'Acy-Romance (Ardennes) à La Tène finale – Pratique funéraires, aspects religieux et hiérarchie social. In: G. Leman-Delerive (ed.), *Les Celtes: rites funéraires en Gaule du Nord entre le VIe et le Ier siècle avant Jésus-Christ – recherches récentes en Wallonie: exposition, Tournai, Maison de la Culture.* Namur: Ministère de la région wallonne, Direction de l'archéologie, Études et documents. Fouilles 4, 75-87.

Lammers, S. 2017. Preface. In: R.C.G.M. Lauwerier, M.C. Eerden, B.J. Groenewoudt, M.A. Lascaris, E. Rensink, B.I. Smit, B.P. Speleers & J. van Doesburg (eds.), Knowledge for Informed Choices. Tools for more effective and efficient selection of valuable archaeology in the Netherlands. *Nederlandse Archeologische Rapporten* 55. Amersfoort: Cultural Heritage Agency of the Netherlands, 5.

Langohr, R. & K. Fechner 1993. The digging and filling of Iron Age monument ditches in the sandy area of north-west Belgium: the pedological and palaeo-environmental approach. *Lunula Archaeologia Protohistorica* 1. Brussels: Cellule Archéologie des Âges des Métaux, 45-50.

Lanting, J.N. & J. van der Plicht 2001. De 14C-chronologie van de Nederlandse pre- en prototohistorie IV: bronstijd en vroege ijzertijd. *Palaeohistoria* 43, 117-262.

Lanting, J.N. & J. van der Plicht 2006. De 14C-chronologie van de Nederlandse pre- en prototohistorie V: midden- en late ijzertijd. *Palaeohistoria* 47/48 (2005/2006), 241-427.

Lauwerier, R. & G. IJzerreef 1998. Livestock and meat from the Iron Age and Roman period settlements at Oss-Ussen (800 BC-AD 250). In: H. Fokkens (ed.), The Ussen Project: the first decade of excavations at Oss. *Analecta Praehistorica Leidensia* 30. Leiden: Leiden University Press, 349-367.

Lawson, A.J. 2007. *Chalkland: an archaeology of Stonehenge and its region.* East Knoyle: Hobnob Press.

Lejars, T. 1999. Le Mobilier métallique d'epoque Gauloise. In: J.-L. Brunaux *et al.* (eds.), Ribemont-sur-Ancre (Somme). Bilan preliminaire et nouvelles hypotheses. *Gallia* 56. Annex II, 241-253.

Lejars, T. 2001. Les installations cultuelles celtiques, Un aperçu de la recherche en France. In: S. Vitri &

F. Oriolo (eds.), *I Celti in Carnia e nell'arco alpino centro orientale (atti della giornata di studio).* Trieste, 245-277.

Lejars, T. 2007. Lieux de culte et pratiques votives en Gaule à La Tène ancienne. In: C. Mennessier-Jouannet, A.-M. Adam & P.-Y. Milcent (eds.), *La Gaule dans son contexte Européen aux IVe et IIIe s. av. n.è., Actes du XXVIIe colloque international de l'Association Française pour l'Etude de l'Âge du Fer (Clermont-Ferrand, 29 mai-1er juin 2003).* Thème spécialisé, Publication 5140 CNRS, Archéologie des sociétés méditerranéennes.

Leman Delerive, G. 2000. Enclos funéraires et cultuels dans la partie septentrionale de la Gaule Belgique. In: *Revue archéologique de Picardie 1-2. Les enclos celtiques – Actes de la table ronde de Ribemont-sur-Ancre (Somme)*, 67-76.

Lewis, M.J.T. 1966. *Temples in Roman Britain.* Cambridge: University Press.

Lohof, E. 2000. Archeologisch onderzoek op de locatie Singel/Schoudermantel te Odijk, gemeente Bunnik (plangebieden Peek en Singel West). *ADC-rapport* 60. Bunschoten: ADC.

Louwen, A. 2021. *Breaking and making the ancestors : piecing together the urnfield mortuary process in the Lower-Rhine-Basin, ca. 1300-400 BC.* [PhD dissertation, Leiden University]. Leiden: Sidestone Press.

Louwen, A. 2022. *From assessment to Excess: the sheer abundance of urnfield data in the Lower-Rhine basin.* Paper presented on EAA, Budapest, session 366.1.

Løvschal, M. 2014. Emerging boundaries: Social Embedment of Landscape and Settlement Divisions in Northwest Europe during the First Millenium BC. *Current Anthropology* 55.6, 725-750.

Løvschal, M. 2020. The logics of enclosure: deep-time trajectories in the spread of land tenure boundaries in late prehistoric northern Europe. *Journal of the Royal Anthropological Institute (N.S.)* 26, 365-388.

Macdevitt, W.A. 2012. (Trans.) Julius Caesar. *The Gallic Wars.* Memphis: Bottom of the Hill Publishing.

Macdonell, A.A. 1900. The ancient Indian conception of the soul and its future state, *The Journal of Theological Studies* 1.4, 492-506.

Mansfeld, G. 1989. Les Vieckschanzen dans le Bade-Würtemberg. In: O. Buchsenschuts & L. Olivier (eds.), *Les Viereckschanzen et les enceintes quadrilaterales en Europe celtique. Actes du IXe Colloque de IAF.E.AF. Chateaudun, 16-19 mal 1985, Association Française pour l'Etude de l'Age du Fer.* Paris: Editions Errance, 27-36.

Marion, S. 2005. Les occupations protohistoriques du sanctuaire de La Bauve à Meaux (Seine-et-Marne). In: *L'âge du Fer en Île-de-France, XXVIe colloque de L'AFEAF, thème régional. Tours: Fédération pour l'édition de la Revue archéologique du Centre de la*

France. *Supplément à la Revue archéologique du centre de la France* 26, 85-95.

Martens, E. 2007. Archeologie in het meetjesland, *Erfgoed Leeft* 3, Ekloo.

Martin, E. 1993. Settlements on Hill-tops: Seven Prehistoric Sites in Suffolk. *East Anglian Archaeology* 65. Ipswich: Suffolk County Planning Department.

Mathys, M. 2009. *De quartiaire geologische geschiedenis van het Belgisch Continentaal Plat, zuidelijke Noordzee.* [PhD-dissertation Gent University]. Gent.

Meffert, M. 2014. Het provinciaal archeologisch landschap Maaskant. In: R. Jansen (ed.), *De archeologische schatkamer Maaskant, Bewoning van het noordoost-Brabantse rivierengebied tussen 3000 v. en 1500 n.Chr.* Leiden: Sidestone Press, 65-83.

Megaw, J.V.S. 2003. Celtic foot(less) soldiers ? An iconographic note. *Gladius*, 23, 61-70.

Meijlink, B.H.F.M. 2002. Synthese. In: Meijlink, B.H.F.M. & P. Kranendonk (eds.), *Archeologie in de Betuweroute: Boeren, erven, graven. De boerengemeenschap van De Bogen bij Meteren (2450-1250 v. Chr.).* Meppel: Krips, 753-835.

Meller, H. 2004. Der Himmelsscheibe von Nebra. In: H. Meller (ed.), *Der geschmiedete Himmel – Die weite Welt im Herzen Europas vor 3600 Jahren,* Landesmuseum für vorgeschichte Halle. Stuttgart: Theiss, 22-31.

Meniel, P. 1991. Les animaux dans les sanctuaires Gaulois du nord de la France. In: Brunaux, J.-L. (ed.). Les sanctuaires celtiques et leurs rapports avec le monde méditerranéen: actes du colloque de Saint-Riquier: 8 au 11 novembre 1990 and organisés par la direction des Antiquités de Picardie et l'UMR 126 du CNRS. *Archéologie aujourd'hui, Dossiers de protohistoire* 3, 257-267.

Meniel, P. 2010. Histoire de l'alimentation carneé dans la village gaulois d'Acy-Romance (2e-1er BC Ardennes, France). *SAGVNTVM Extra* 9, 57-68.

Mertens, J. 1968. Een Romeins tempelcomplex te Tongeren. *Kölner Jahrbuch für Vor- und Frühgeschichte* IX, 1967-1968, 101-106.

Messiaen, L., A. De Logi, K. Sturtewagen & T. Bruyninckx 2009. Late ijzertijd/vroeg Romeinse sporen te Kortrijk-Evolis (Provincie West-Vlaanderen, Belgie). *Lunula Archaeologia Protohistorica* 17. Brussels: Cellule Archéologie des Âges des Métaux, 213-216.

Mestdagh, B. & E. Taelman 2008. Archeologisch onderzoek Ursel-Rozestraat. 6 oktober tot 16 december 2008. *KLAD-rapport* 9. Aalter: Kale-Leie Archeologische Dienst.

Mestdagh, B. & R. Bakx 2020. Ceramische slingerkogels in nederzettingscontexten. Recente vondsten in Oostvleteren, Waregem (prov. West-Vlaanderen) en Borsbeek (prov. Antwerpen) (Belgie). *Lunula Archaeologia Protohistorica* 28. Brussels: Cellule Archéologie des Âges des Métaux, 139-143.

Mestdagh, B. 2008. *Een rijk maar onvolledig verleden, Status questiones van het archeologisch onderzoek naar de ijzertijdsite van Kooigembos (West-Vlaanderen).* MA-thesis Gent University. Gent.

Meurkens, L. & A.J. Tol 2011. Grafvelden en greppelstructuren uit de ijzertijd en Romeinse tijd bij Itteren (gemeente Maastricht). *Archolrapport* 144. Leiden: Archol BV.

Meurkens, L. 2011. Sporen en structuren uit de prehistorie en Romeinse tijd. In: L. Meurkens & A.J. Tol (eds.). Grafvelden en greppelstructuren uit de ijzertijd en Romeinse tijd bij Itteren (gemeente Maastricht). *Archolrapport* 144. Leiden: Archol BV, 61-98.

Meurkens, L. 2011a. Prehistorisch aardewerk en objecten van gebakken klei. In: L. Meurkens & A.J. Tol (eds.). Grafvelden en greppelstructuren uit de ijzertijd en Romeinse tijd bij Itteren (gemeente Maastricht). *Archolrapport* 144. Leiden: Archol BV, 103-120.

Meurkens, L. 2013. Aardewerk uit de late prehistorie. In: S. Knippenberg (ed.), Neolithicum en ijzertijd in de Maaskant, Opgravingen van een midden-neolithische nederzetting en een midden- en late ijzertijd crematiegrafveld te Haren (N-Br.). *Archolrapport* 214. Leiden: Archol BV, 83-84.

Meurkens, L. 2016. Aardewerk en keramische vondsten uit de prehistorie en Romeinse tijd. In: J. Van der Leije (ed.), Onderzoek naar bewoning en grafritueel uit de late bronstijd en ijzertijd in plangebied Koeweide, Proefsleuvenonderzoek en opgraving in deelgebied Klein Trierveld, vindplaats 2 & 55 (gemeente Sittard-Geleen). *Archolrapport* 271. Leiden: Archol BV, 75-87.

Meysami-Azad, S. 2017. *Reincarnation in Abrahamic Religions.* MA Thesis in Theology and Religious Studies, Leiden University Centre for the Study of Religion (LUCSoR), Leiden: Leiden University.

Milcent, P.-Y. 2017. The Atlantic Early Iron Age in Gaul. In: A. Lehoërff & M. Talon (eds.). *Movement, Exchange and Identity in Europe in the 2nd and 1st Millennia BC beyond Frontiers.* Oxford: Oxbow Books, 79-98.

Moore, T. 2006. The Iron Age. In: N. Holbrook & J. Jurica (eds.), Twenty-five years of Archaeology in Gloucestershire: A review of new discoveries and new thinking in Gloucestershire, South Gloucestershire and Bristol 1979-2004, Cirencester: *Cotswold Archaeology BGAR* 3, 61-96.

Moore, T. 2007. The early to later Iron Age transition in the Severn-Cotswolds: enclosing the household? In: C. Haselgrove & R. Pope (eds.), *The Earlier Iron Age in Britain and the Near Continent.* Oxford: Oxbow Books, 259-278.

Morris, B. 2006. *Religion and anthropology, a critical introduction.* Cambridge: University Press.

Müller, D. 1999. Topographische Lage der Viereckschanzen. In: G. Wieland (ed*.), Keltische Viereckschanzen – Einem Rätsel auf der Spur.* Stuttgart: Theiss.

Müller, F. 1993. Kultplätze und Opferbräuche. In: H. Dannheimer & R. Gebhard (eds.), *Das keltische Jahrtausend.* Mainz am Rhein: Von Zabern, 177-188.

Müller, F.M. 1892. *Natural religion.* The Gifford Lectures delivered before the University of Glasgow in 1888. London: Longsman, Green and Co.

Murray, M. 1995. Viereckschanzen and feasting: socio-political ritual in Iron Age central Europe. *Journal of European Archaeology 3.2,* 125-152.

Nielson, N.H. & K. Dalsgaard 2017. Dynamics of Celtic fields – A geoarchaeological investigation of Øster Lem Hede, Western Jutland, Denmark. *Geoarchaeology 32,* 414-434.

Nieuwhof, A. 2008. Restanten van rituelen. In: A. Nieuwhof (ed.), De Leege Wier van Englum. Archeologisch onderzoek in het Reitdiepgebied. *Jaarverslagen van de vereniging voor terpenonderzoek* 91. Groningen: Tienkamp en Verheij, 79-115.

Nieuwhof, A. 2015. *Eight human skulls in a dung heap and more Ritual practice in the terp region of the northern Netherlands 600 BC – AD 300.* [PhD-dissertation University of Groningen]. Groningen.

Norde, E.H.L.D. 2018. Ongrijpbare graven. Het grafritueel in de midden- en late ijzertijd op de Gelderse en Overijsselse zandgronden. *Metaaltijden 5, Bijdragen aan de studie van de metaaltijden.* Leiden: Sidestone Press, 113-136.

Nouwen, R. 1997. Tongeren en het land van de Tungri (31 v.Chr.-284 n.Chr.). *Maaslandse Monografieën* 59. Leeuwarden / Mechelen: Eisma B.V.

Oldfather, C.H. 1939. (trans.) *Diodorus of Sicily: in ten volumes. III: Books IV (continued) 59-VIII.* London : Cambridge, Mass.: Heinemann; Harvard University Press.

Palmer, J. 2009/2010. *Het roodbeschilderde aardewerk van de Kemmelberg: technotypologie, verspreiding en socio-ideologische context.* [Unpublished MA-thesis Gent University]. Gent.

Panhuysen, R. 2017. Menselijk bot. In: J. van Renswoude & D.S. Habermehl (eds.), Opgravingen te Houten-Castellum. Bewoning langs een restgeul in de IJzertijd, Romeinse tijd en Vroege Middeleeuwen. *Zuidnederlandse Archeologische Rapporten* 65. Amsterdam: VUhbs archeologie / Vrije Universiteit, 735-745.

Parker Pearson, M. & N. Field 2003. The Fiskerton artefact assemblage. In: N. Field & M. Parker Pearson (eds.), *Fiskerton, An Iron Age timber causeway with Iron Age and Roman votive offerings.* Exeter: the Short Run Press, 173-178.

Parker Pearson, M. & Ramilisonina 1998. Stonehenge for the ancestors: the stones pass on the message. *Antiquity* 72, 308-326.

Parker Pearson, M. 2003. *The archaeology of death and burial.* Stroud: Sutton Publishing Limited.

Patterson, J.H. 1973 [1907]. *The Man-eaters of Tsavo, and other African adventures.* London and Glasgow: Fontana Books.

Pauli, L. (ed.). 1980. *Die Kelten in Mitteleuropa: Kultur, Kunst, Wirtschaft. Salzburger Landesaustellung 1 Mai-30 Sept. 1980 im Keltenmuseum Hallein, Österreich.* Salzburg: Amt der Salzburger Landesregierung, Kulturabteilung.

Périchon, R. 1987. L'imagerie Celtique d'Aulnat (1). In: C. Bemont, B. Delplace, K. Fischer, K. Gruel , K. Peyre & J.-C. Richard (eds.), *Mélanges offerts au Dr J.-B. Colbert de Beaulieu.* Paris: Le Léopard d'Or, 677-695.

Pfister, C. 2000. Die keltischen Viereckschanzen in der Schweiz. *Efodon-Synesis* 7.

Piette, J. 1979. Villeneuve-au-Châtelot-Les Grèves. In: E. Frézouls (ed.), Circonscription de Champagne-Ardenne. *Gallia* 37.2, 417-419.

Piette, J. 1981. Villeneuve-au-Châtelot-Les Grèves. In: E. Frézouls (ed.), Circonscription de Champagne-Ardenne. *Gallia* 39.2, 397-399.

Piette, J. 1983. Villeneuve-au-Châtelot-Les Grèves. In: E. Frézouls (ed.), Circonscription de Champagne-Ardenne. *Gallia* 41.2, 368-371.

Planck, D. 1982. Eine neuentdeckte keltische Viereckschanze in Fellbach-Schmiden, Rems-Murr-Kreis: Vorbericht der Grabungen 1977-1980, mit beiträgen von H.E. Bleich, U. Körber-Grohne und B. Becker. *Germania* 60, 105-172.

Pope, R. 2021. Re-approaching Celts: Origins, Society, and Social Change. *Journal of Archaeological Research* 30, 1-67. DOI:10.1007/s10814-021-09157-1.

Poux, M. 2019. Huius sunt plurima simulacra: l'absence de statues de culte dans les sanctuaires gaulois. In: P. Barral & M. Thivet (eds.), *Sanctuaires de l'âge du Fer. Actes du 41e colloque international de l'Association française pour l'étude de l'âge du Fer (Dole, 25-28 mai 2017), Collection AFEAF* 1, 221-240.

Prangsma, N.M. 2008. Lomm Hoogwatergeul fase 1 (gemeente Arcen en Velden). Een archeologische opgraving. *ADC-rapport* 1344. Amersfoort: ADC Archeo-Projecten.

Pryor, F. 2001.*The Flag Fen basin: archaeology and environment of a fenland landscape.* London: England Heritage.

Randsborg, K. 1995. *Hjortspring: Warfare and sacrifice in Early Europe.* Århus: Aarhus University Press.

Reichenberger, A. & M. Schaich 1996. Vorbericht zur Ausgrabung der Viereckschanze von Plattling-Pankofen, Lkr. Deggendorf. In: K. Schmotz (ed.), *Vorträge des Niederbayerischen Archäologentages* 14, 83-153.

Reichenberger, A. 1986. Zum Stand der Ausgrabungen in einer keltischen Viereckschanze bei Wiedmais. Vorträge d. 4. Niederbayer. *Archläologentages Deggendorf* 1985, 99-105.

Reichenberger, A. 1993. Zur Interpretation der latenezeitlichen Viereckschanzen. *Jahrbuch des Römisch-Germanischen Zentralmuseums* (JRGZM) 40, 353-396.

Reyns, N., H. Verbeeck & J. Bruggeman (eds.) 2018. Archeologisch onderzoek op de Steenakker en het Kapelleveld te Kontich, Synthese van de opgravingscampagnes op de site Kontich-Kazerne tussen 1964 en 1993. *AVRA Monografie* 3. Leuven: Peeters.

Robb, J.E. 2002. Fysische antropologie. In: B.H.F.M. Meijelink & P. Kranendonk (eds.), *Archeologie in de Betuweroute: Boeren, erven, graven. De boerengemeenschap van De Bogen bij Meteren (2450-1250 v. Chr.).* Meppel: Krips, 667-688.

Roessingh, W. & A.J. Tol. (eds.) 2019. Archeologie langs de Westfrisiaweg, Opgravingen van vindplaatsen uit de late prehistorie, middeleeuwen en Nieuwe tijd in het tracé van de Westfrisiaweg. *ADC-rapport* 5000 / *Archolrapport* 461. Amersfoort: ADC Archeo-Projecten / Leiden.

Roessingh, W. & E. Blom (eds.) 2012. Graven op De Contreie. Bewoningsgeschiedenis van de Houtse Akkers te Oosterhout, van de Bronstijd tot en met de Slag om het Markkanaal. *ADC-rapport* 2750 / *Monografie* 14. Amersfoort: ADC Archeo-Projecten.

Roessingh, W. 2018. *Dynamiek in beeld. Onderzoek van Westfriese nederzettingen uit de bronstijd.* [PhD-dissertation Leiden University]. Leiden: Sidestone Press.

Roessingh, W., E. Drenth, R. Geerts, E. Smits, E. Lohof & B.J. Kromhout 2012. Een urnenveld uit de Late Bronstijd –Midden-IJzertijd. In: W. Roessingh & E. Blom (eds.), graven op De Contreie. Bewoningsgeschiedenis van de Houtse Akkers te Oosterhout, van de Bronstijd tot en met de Slag om het Markkanaal. *ADC-rapport* 2750 / *Monografie* 14. Amersfoort: ADC Archeo-Projecten, 57-106.

Roessingh, W., E. Drenth, R. Geerts, J. Brijker, C. Moolhuizen, L. Verniers, M. Melkert & J. van dijk 2012a. Bewoning in de IJzertijd. In: W. Roessingh & E. Blom (eds.), graven op De Contreie. Bewoningsgeschiedenis van de Houtse Akkers te Oosterhout, van de Bronstijd tot en met de Slag om het Markkanaal. *ADC-rapport* 2750 / *Monografie* 14. Amersfoort: ADC Archeo-Projecten, 107-146.

Roymans, N.G.A.M. & A. Tol 1993. Noodonderzoek van een dodenakker te Mierlo-Hout. In: N.G.A.M. Roymans & F. Theuws (eds.), *Een en al zand: twee jaar graven naar het Brabantse verleden.* 's-Hertogenbosch: Stichting Brabantse Regionale Geschiedbeoefening, 42-56.

Roymans, N.G.A.M. & F. Gerritsen 2002. Landschap, ecologie en mentaliteit. Het Maas-Demer-Scheldegebied in een lange-termijn perspectief. In: H. Fokkens & R. Jansen (eds.), *2000 jaar bewoningsdynamiek. Brons- en ijzertijdbewoning in het Maas-Demer-Scheldegebied.* Alblasserdam: Haveka BV, 371-406.

Roymans, N.G.A.M. & F. Kortlang 1999. Urnfield symbolism, ancestors and the land in the Lower Rhine region. In: F. Theuws & N. Roymans (eds.), Land and Ancestors. Cultural dynamics in the urnfield period and the middle ages in the southern Netherlands. *Amsterdam Archaeological Studies* 4. Amsterdam: Amsterdam University Press, 33-61.

Roymans, N.G.A.M. & H. Fokkens 1991. Een overzicht van veertig jaar nederzettingsonderzoek in de Lage Landen. In: H. Fokkens & N. Roymans (eds.), Nederzettingen uit de bronstijd en de vroege ijzertijd in de Lage Landen. *Nederlandse Archeologische Rapporten* 13. Amersfoort: Rijksdienst voor Oudheidkundig Bodemonderzoek, 1-19.

Roymans, N.G.A.M. & H. Hiddink 1991. Nederzettingssporen uit de bronstijd en vroege ijzertijd op de Kraanvense Heide te Loon op Zand. In: H. Fokkens & N. Roymans (eds.), Nederzettingen uit de bronstijd en de vroege ijzertijd in de Lage Landen. *Nederlandse Archeologische Rapporten* 13. Amersfoort: Rijksdienst voor Oudheidkundig Bodemonderzoek, 111-127.

Roymans, N.G.A.M. & T. Derks 1994. De tempel van Empel: Een Herculesheiligdom in het woongebied van de Bataven. *Graven naar het Brabantse verleden* 2. s-Hertogenbosch: Stichting Brabantse regionale geschiedbeoefening,.

Roymans, N.G.A.M. & T. Derks 2014. Rural cult places and the symbolic construction of supralocal communities. In: N. Roymans, T. Derks & H. Hiddink (eds.), The Roman villa of Hoogeloon and the archaeology of the periphery. *Amsterdam Archaeological Studies* 22. Amsterdam: Amsterdam University Press, 229-243.

Roymans, N.G.A.M. 1990. Tribal societies in northern Gaul: an anthropological perspective. [PhD-dissertation Amsterdam University]. *Cingula* 12. Amsterdam: Universiteit van Amsterdam, Albert Egges van Giffen Instituut voor Prae- en Protohistorie.

Roymans, N.G.A.M. 1991. Late Urnfield Societies in the Northwest European plain and the expanding networks of Central European Hallstatt groups. In: N.G.A.M. Roymans & F. Theuws (eds.), Images of the past, studies on ancient societies in North-Western Europe. *Studies in prae- en protohistorie* 7. Amsterdam: Amsterdam University Press, 9-89.

Roymans, N.G.A.M. 2004. Ethnic identity and imperial power. The Batavians in the early Roman empire. *Amsterdam Archaeological Studies* 10. Amsterdam: Amsterdam University Press.

Roymans, N.G.A.M. 2007. Understanding social change in the Late Iron Age Lower Rhine region. In C. Haselgrove, & T. Moore (Eds.), *The Later Iron Age in Britain and beyond*. Oxford: Oxbow Books, 478-491.

Roymans, N.G.A.M. 2009. Hercules and the construction of a Batavian identity in the context of the Roman empire. In: T. Derks & N. Roymans (eds.). The Role of Power and Tradition. Ethnic Constructs in Antiquity. *Amsterdam Archaeological Studies* 13. Amsterdam: Amsterdam University Press, 219-238.

Samson, A.V.M. 2006. Offshore finds from the Bronze Age in North-western Europe: the shipwreck scenario revisited. *Oxford Journal of Archaeology* 25.4, 371-388.

Schaich, M. 1998. Zur Ausgrabung der Viereckschanze von Pocking-Hartkirchen, Lkr. Passau. In: K. Schmotz (ed.), *Vorträge des Niederbayerischen Archäologentages* 16, 157-196.

Schiek, S. 1985. Eine neue keltische Viereckschanze bei Ehningen, Kreis Böblingen. *Arch. Ausgr. Baden-Württemberg* 1984, 78-82.

Schinkel, C. 1998. Unsettled settlement, occupation remains from the Bronze Age and the Iron Age at Oss-Ussen. The 1976-1986 excavations. In: H. Fokkens (ed.) 1998, The Oss-Ussen Project – the first decade of excavations at Oss. *Analecta Praehistorica Leidensia* 30. Leiden: Leiden University Press, 5-305.

Schlosser, W. 2004. Der Himmelsscheibe von Nebra – Astronomische untersuchungen. In: H. Meller (ed.), *Der geschmiedete Himmel – Die weite Welt im Herzen Europas vor 3600 Jahren, Landesmuseum für vorgeschichte Halle*. Stuttgart: Theiss, 44-47.

Schurmans, M. & E. Verhelst (eds.) 2007. Oudheden uit Odijk. Bewoningssporen uit de late ijzertijd, Romeinse tijd en Merovingische tijd aan de Singel West/Schoudermantel. *Zuidnederlandse Archeologische Rapporten* 30. Amsterdam: VUhbs archeologie / Vrije Universiteit.

Schurmans, M. 2007. Sporen en structuren. In: M. Schurmans & E. Verhelst (eds.), Oudheden uit Odijk. Bewoningssporen uit de late ijzertijd, Romeinse tijd en Merovingische tijd aan de Singel West/Schoudermantel. *Zuidnederlandse Archeologische Rapporten* 30. Amsterdam: VUhbs archeologie / Vrije Universiteit, 23-59.

Schurmans, M.D.R. 2011. Inventariserend Veldonderzoek door middel van proefsleuven in het plangebied Haren Groenstraat, gemeente Oss. *Zuidnederlandse Archeologische Notities* 231. Amsterdam: VUhbs archeologie / Vrije Universiteit.

Schwarz, K. 1959. *Atlas der Spätkeltischen Viereckschanzen Bayrens*. München: Bayerisches Landesamt für Denkmalpflege.

Schwarz, K. 1975. *Die Geschichte eines keltischen Temenos im nördlichen Alpenvorland, Ausgrabungen in Deutschland*. Mainz: Gefördert von der deutschen Forschungsgemeinschaft 1950-75 1/1, 324-358.

Score, V., J. Browning & University of Leicester Archaeological Services 2011. Hoards, hounds and helmets: A conquest-period ritual site at Hallaton, Leicestershire. *Leicester archaeological monographs* 21. Leicester: University of Leicester Archaeological Services.

Sharples, N.M. (ed.) 1991. Maiden Castle: Excavations and Field Survey 1985-6. *English Heritage Archaeological Report* 19. London: English Heritage.

Sievers, S. & H. Wendling 2014. Manching – A Celtic oppidum between Rescue Excavation and Research. In: C. von Carnap-Bornheim (ed.), *Quo Vadis? Status and future perspectives of long-term excavations in Europe*. Neumünster/Hamburg: Wachholtz verlag-Murmann Publishers, 137-152.

Sievers, S. 2010. Die waffen aus dem oppidum von Manching. *Manching Band* 17. Wiesbaden: Reichert Verlag.

Sinke, A. 2017. Speciale deposites uit de ijzertijd. In: J. van Renswoude & D.S. Habermehl, (eds.), Opgravingen te Houten-Castellum. Bewoning langs een restgeul in de IJzertijd, Romeinse tijd en Vroege Middeleeuwen. *Zuidnederlandse Archeologische Rapporten* 65. Amsterdam: VUhbs archeologie / Vrije Universiteit, 399-406.

Slofstra, J. & W.A.B. van der Sanden 1987. Rurale cultusplaatsen in de Romeinse tijd in het Maas-Demer-Scheldegebied. *Analecta Praehistorica Leidensia* 20. Leiden: Leiden University Press, 125-168.

Slofstra, J. 1991. Changing settlement systems in the Meuse-Demer-Scheldt Area during the Early Roman period. In: N.G.A.M. Roymans & F. Theuws (eds.), Images of the past, studies on ancient societies in North-Western Europe. *Studies in prae- en protohistorie* 7. Amsterdam: Amsterdam University Press, 131-198.

Smeets, M. & V. Vander Ginst 2013. Het archeologisch vooronderzoek aan de Stationsstraat te Boortmeerbeek (Hever). *Archeo-rapport* 180. Kessel-Lo: Studiebureau Archeologie.

Smith, A. 2001. *The Differential Use of Constructed Sacred Space in Southern Britain, from the Late Iron Age to the 4th Century AD*. [PhD-dissertation University of Wales Collage]. Parkway: ProQuest LLC.

Smits, E. 2004. Crematieresten. In: G. Tichelman (ed.), Archeologisch onderzoek in het kader van De Maaswerken, Inventariserend veldonderzoek (IVO), waarderende fase. Koeweide Klein-Trierveld, vindplaatsen 44, 46-47 en 55. *ADC-rapport* 306. Amersfoort: ADC Archeo-Projecten, 77-78.

Smits, E. 2009. Het onderzoek van crematieresten. In: A.J. Tol (ed.), Graven en nederzettingsresten uit de late prehistorie en volle middeleeuwen. Een archeologisch onderzoek te Weert-Laarveld. *Archolrapport* 127. Leiden: Archol BV, 47-54.

Smits, E. 2013. Het fysisch-antropologisch onderzoek. In: N. Van Liefferinge, M. Smeets & L. Fockedey (eds.), Het archeologisch onderzoek in Rijkevorsel-Wilgenstraat. *Archeo-rapport* 159. Kessel-Lo: Studiebureau Archeologie bvba, 33-37.

Sørensen, M.L.S. & K.C. Rebay 2008. The impact of 19th century ideas on the construction of 'urnfield' as a chronological and cultural concept. In: A. Lehoërff (ed.), *Construire le temps. Histoire et méthodes des chronologies et calendriers de derniers millénaires avant notre ère et Europe occidentale. Actes du XXXe colloque international de Halma-Ipel, UMR 8164 (CNRS, Lille 3, MCC), 7-9 décembre 2006, Lille.* Bibracte: Centre archéologique européen, 57-67.

Spek, T., M. Snoek, W. van der Sanden, M. Kosian, F. van der Heijden, L. Theunissen, M. Nijenhuis, H. Vroon & K. Greving 2009. Archeologische waardering van Celtic fields in Drenthe – Een verkennend methodologisch onderzoek. *Rapportage Archeologische Monumentenzorg* 141. Amersfoort: Rijksdienst voor het Cultureel Erfgoed.

Spek, T., W. Groenman-van Waateringe, M. Kooistra & L. Bakker 2003. Formation and land-use history of Celtic fields in north-west Europe -an interdisciplinary case study at Zeijen, The Netherlands. *European Journal of Archaeology* 6.2, 141-173.

Stead, I.M. 1996. *Celtic Art in Britain Before the Roman Conquest.* [2nd edition]. London: British Museum.

Stuart, P. 2003. *Nehalennia – Documenten in steen.* Goes: De Koperen Tuin.

Ter Schegget, M. 1999. Late Iron Age human skeletal remains from the river Meuse at Kessel: a river cult place? In: F. Theuws & N.G.A.M. Roymans (eds.), Land and Ancestors. Cultural dynamics in the Urnfield period and the Middle Ages in the Southern Netherlands. *Amsterdam Archaeological Studies* 4. Amsterdam: Amsterdam University Press, 199-240.

Ter Wal, A. 2012. Houten Castellumterrein, proefsleuvenonderzoek, *BAAC rapport* A-08.0412. DOI: 10.17026/dans-z8a-xbnf.

Ter Wal, A. 2013. Zundert Randweg – locatie III, Inventariserend veldonderzoek door middel van proefsleuven. *BAAC rapport* A-12.0211. 's-Hertogenbosch: BAAC BV.

Ter Wal, A. 2013a. Gemeente Zundert, Plangebied Verlengde Hofdreef, Opgraving. *BAAC rapport* A-12.0143. 's-Hertogenbosch: BAAC BV.

Termote, J. 1987. De Keltische Hoogtenederzetting van Kooigembos. De opgravingscampagne 1986, *Westvlaamse Archaeologica* 3, 61-72.

Theunissen, E.M. 1999. *Midden-Bronstijdsamenlevingen in het zuiden van de Lage Landen. Een evaluatie van het begrip 'Hilversum-cultuur'.* [PhD-dissertation Leiden University]. S.l.: s.n.

Theunissen, L. 2009. Inleiding, probleemstelling en werkwijze. In: T. Spek, M. Snoek, W.A B. van der Sanden, M. Kosian, F. van der Heijden, L. Theunissen, M. Nijenhuis, H. Vroon & K. Greving (eds.), Archeologische waardering van Celtic fields in Drenthe. *Rapportage Archeologische Monumentenzorg* 141. Amersfoort: Rijksdienst voor het Cultureel Erfgoed, 9-14.

Theunissen, M. 1993. Het grafveld van Rijckevorsel/ Helhoekheide. 700-400 BC. *Lunula Archaeologia Protohistorica* 1. Brussels: Cellule Archéologie des Âges des Métaux, 41-44.

Theuws, F. & N.G.A.M. Roymans (eds.) 1999. Land and Ancestors. Cultural dynamics in the urnfield period and the middle ages in the southern Netherlands. *Amsterdam Archaeological Studies* 4. Amsterdam: Amsterdam University Press.

Tichelman, G. 2004, Archeologisch onderzoek in het kader van De Maaswerken, Inventariserend veldonderzoek (IVO), waarderende fase. Koeweide Klein-Trierveld, vindplaatsen 44, 46-47 en 55. *ADC-rapport* 306. Amersfoort: ADC Archeo-Projecten.

Tol, A.J. 1999. Urnfield and settlement traces from the Iron Age at Mierlo-Hout. In: F. Theuws & N.G.A.M. Roymans (eds.), Land and Ancestors. Cultural dynamics in the Urnfield Period and the Middle Ages in the Southern Netherlands. *Amsterdam Archaeological Studies* 4. Amsterdam: Amsterdam University Press, 87-132.

Tol, A.J. 2009. Graven en nederzettingsresten uit de late prehistorie en volle middeleeuwen. Een archeologisch onderzoek te Weert-Laarveld. *Archolrapport* 127. Leiden: Archol BV.

Tracey, J. 2012. New evidence for Iron Age burial and propitiation practices in Southern Britain. *Oxford Journal of Archaeology* 31.4, 367-379.

Tuin, B.P. 2008. Menselijke resten. In: Nieuwhof, A. (ed.) 2008. De Leege Wier van Englum, Archeologisch onderzoek in het Reitdiepgebied. *Jaarverslagen van de Vereniging voor het Terpenonderzoek* 91. Groningen: Tienkamp en Verheij, 187-248.

Turner, V. 1967. *The forest of symbols, aspects of Ndembu Ritual.* Itheca and London: Cornell University Press.

Tylor, E.B. 1873. *Primitive culture: researches into the development of mythology, philosophy, religion, art, and custom.* [2nd ed.]. London: Murray.

Ulrich, H. 2003. Menschliche skelettreste aus der germanischen Kultstätte von Oberdorla. In: G. Behm-Blancke, H. Jacob, S. Dušek, B. Lettmann & Thüringisches Landesamt für Archäologische Denkmalpflege (eds.), *Heiligtümer der Germanen und ihrer Vorgänger in Thüringen: Die Kultstätte Oberdorla: Forschungen zum alteuropäischen Religions- und Kultwesen. Teil 1: Text und Fototafeln, Weimarer Monographien zur Ur- und Frühgeschichte, Bd.* 38. Stuttgart: Theiss, 128-153.

Van As, S. & H. Fokkens 2019. Features in the Schalkskamp quarter. In: H. Fokkens, S. van As & R. Jansen (eds.), The Oss-Noord Project – the second decade of excavations at Oss 1986-1996. *Analecta Praehistorica Leidensia* 48. Leiden: Sidestone Press, 301-345.

Van As, S., A. Tol & R. Jansen (in prep). *Opgraving Mierlo-Hout Ashorst / Snippenscheut.* Leiden: Leiden University.

Van Beek, R. 2006. Het grafritueel in Oost-Nederland tussen de Vroege IJzertijd en de tweede eeuw AD (ca. 500 BC-100 AD). *Lunula Archaeologia Protohistorica* 14. Brussels: Cellule Archéologie des Âges des Métaux, 61-69.

Van Beek, R. 2010. *Reliëf in tijd en ruimte: Interdisciplinair onderzoek naar bewoning en landschap van Oost-Nederland tussen de vroege prehistorie en middeleeuwen.* [PhD-dissertation Wageningen University]. Leiden: Sidestone Press.

Van de Geer, P. 2011. La Tène-glas. In: L. Meurkens & A.J. Tol (eds.). Grafvelden en greppelstructuren uit de ijzertijd en Romeinse tijd bij Itteren (gemeente Maastricht). *Archolrapport* 144. Leiden: Archol BV, 149-152.

Van de Geer, P. 2014. La Tène-armringen uit de Maaskant. Verspreiding en interpretatie. In: R. Jansen (ed.), *De archeologische schatkamer: bewoning van het noordoost-Brabantse rivierengebied tussen 3000 v. en 1500 n.chr.* Leiden: Sidestone Press, 373-385.

Van de Geer, P. 2017. Een cultusplaats uit de late ijzertijd? Opgraving van een greppelstructuur in plangebied Rijnvaert, te Oegstgeest. *Archolrapport* 337. Leiden: Archol BV.

Van de Velde, P. & I.M. van Wijk. 2014. De huizen van de bandkeramiek (LBK) in Nederland. In: A.G. Lange, E.M. Theunissen, J. van Doesburg, J.H.C. Deeben, J. Bouwmeester, T. de Groot (eds.), *Huisplattegronden in Nederland: archeologische sporen van het huis.* Havertown: Barkhuis, 29-60.

Van de Vijver, M. & K. De Groote 2016. *Rapportage van het archeologisch onderzoek te Aalter-Woestijne, zones 1 en 3 (prov. Oost-Vlaanderen).* Brussel: Onderzoeksrapport Agentschap Onroerend Erfgoed.

Van de Vijver, M., F. Wuyts & B. Cherretté, 2009. Bronstijd- en ijzertijdsporen te Erembodegem: cirkels, rechthoeken en kuilen (Aalst, provincie Oost-Vlaanderen, België). *Lunula Archaeologia Protohistorica* 17. Brussels: Cellule Archéologie des Âges des Métaux, 15-22.

Van de Vijver, M., H. Vandendriessche, A. Storme, K. Deforce & K. Quintelier 2019a. Bronstijd. In: K. De Groote & M. Van de Vijver (eds.), Aalter Woestijne, Een geschiedenis van meer dan 5000 jaar. *Relicta Monografieën* 18. Brussel: Archeologie, Monumenten-, en landschapsonderzoek in Vlaanderen, 81-115.

Van de Vijver, M., H. Vandendriessche, A. Storme, K. Deforce, K. Quintelier & P. Cosyns 2019. IJzertijd. In: K. De Groote & M. Van de Vijver (eds.), Aalter Woestijne, Een geschiedenis van meer dan 5000 jaar. *Relicta Monografieën* 18. Brussel: Archeologie, Monumenten-, en landschapsonderzoek in Vlaanderen, 117-149.

Van den Broeke, P.W. 1987. De dateringsmiddelen voor de IJzertijd van Zuid-Nederland. In: W.A.B. van der Sanden & P.W. van den Broeke (eds.), Getekend Zand. Tien jaar archeologisch onderzoek in Oss-Ussen. *Bijdragen tot de studie van het Brabants Heem* 31. Waalre: Stichting Brabants Heem, 23-44.

Van den Broeke, P.W. 2002. Een vurig afscheid? Aanwijzingen voor verlatingsrituelen in ijzertijdnederzettingen. In: H. Fokkens & R. Jansen (eds.), *2000 jaar bewoningsdynamiek. Brons- en ijzertijdbewoning in het Maas-Demer-Scheldegebied.* Alblasserdam: Haveka, 45-61.

Van den Broeke, P.W. 2005. Gaven voor de goden -Riten en cultusplaatsen in de metaaltijden. In: L.P. Louwe Kooijmans *et al., Nederland in de prehistorie.* Amsterdam: Bakker, 659-677.

Van den Broeke, P.W. 2012. *Het handgevormde aardewerk uit de ijzertijd en Romeinse tijd van Oss-Ussen. Studies naar typochronologie, technologie en herkomst.* [PhD-dissertation Leiden University]. Leiden: Sidestone Press.

Van den Broeke, P.W. 2014. Inhumation burials: new elements in Iron Age funerary ritual in the southern Netherlands. In: A. Cahen-Delhaye & G. De Mulder (eds.), *Des espaces aux esprits: l'organisation de la mort aux âges des Métaux dans le nord-ouest de l'Europe.* Namur: Institut du Patrimoine wallon, Service publications, 161-183.

Van den Broeke, P.W. 2015. Het verlatingsritueel: een poging tot reconstructie. In: E.A.G. Ball & S. Arnoldussen (eds.), *Metaaltijden 2, Bijdragen in de studie van de metaaltijden.* Leiden: Sidestone Press, 83-100.

Van den Broeke, P.W. 2017. Beschrijving van het ijzertijdaardewerk uit de geselecteerde referentiecontexten. In: J. van Renswoude & D.S. Habermehl (eds.), Opgravingen te Houten-Castellum. Bewoning langs een restgeul in de IJzertijd, Romeinse tijd en Vroege Middeleeuwen. *Zuidnederlandse Archeologische Rapporten* 65. Amsterdam: VUhbs archeologie / Vrije Universiteit, 146-217.

Van den Dikkenberg, L. 2018. *Interactions, elites and inconspicuous burials Interregional connections and changes in the burial ritual in the Meuse-Demer-Scheldt area and neighbouring Dutch and German riverine areas in the Middle Iron Age (500-250 BCE).* [unpublished MA thesis Leiden University]. Leiden.

Van den Dikkenberg, L. 2020. Middle Iron Age (500-250 BC) cemeteries in the Southern-Netherlands, the Rhineland and Flanders. In: M. Hendriksen, E. Norde & N. de Vries (eds.), *Metaaltijden 7. Bijdragen in de studie van de metaaltijden.* Leiden: Sidestone Press, 69-79.

Van der Leije, J. & L. Meurkens 2016. Synthese. In: L. van der Leije (ed.), Onderzoek naar bewoning en grafritueel uit de late bronstijd en ijzertijd in plangebied Koeweide, Proefsleuvenonderzoek en opgraving in deelgebied Klein Trierveld, vindplaats 2 & 55 (gemeente Sittard-Geleen). *Archolrapport* 271. Leiden: Archol BV, 107-121.

Van der Leije, J. & S. Knippenberg 2013. Crematiegrafveld uit de ijzertijd. In: S. Knippenberg (ed.), Neolithicum en ijzertijd in de Maaskant, Opgravingen van een midden-neolithische nederzetting en een midden- en late ijzertijd crematiegrafveld te Haren (N-Br.). *Archolrapport* 214. Leiden: Archol BV, 77-86.

Van der Leije, J. 2016. Onderzoek naar bewoning en grafritueel uit de late bronstijd en ijzertijd in plangebied Koeweide, Proefsleuvenonderzoek en opgraving in deelgebied Klein Trierveld, vindplaats 2 & 55 (gemeente Sittard-Geleen). *Archolrapport* 271. Leiden: Archol BV.

Van der Linde, C.M. & D.R. Fontijn 2011. Mound 1 – a monumental Iron Age barrow. In: D.R. Fontijn, Q. Bourgeois & A. Louwen (Eds.), *Iron Age Echoes. Prehistoric land management and the creation of a funerary landscape -the "twin barrows" at the Echoput in Apeldoorn.* Leiden: Sidestone Press, 33-64.

Van der Linde, C.M. & M. Kalfshoven 2017. Cultusplaats in de achtertuin Sporen uit de late bronstijd tot en met de nieuwe tijd in Poperinge (Koestraat). *BAAC-rapport* A-13.0116. 's-Hertogenbosch: BAAC BV.

Van der Linde, C.M. 2009. Het prehistorische aardewerk van Weert-Laarveld. In: A.J. Tol (ed.), Graven en nederzettingsresten uit de late prehistorie en volle middeleeuwen. Een archeologisch onderzoek te Weert-Laarveld. *Archolrapport* 127. Leiden: Archol BV, 59-72.

Van der Meer, W. 2017. Resultaten van het archeobotanisch onderzoek. In: C.M. van der Linde & M. Kalfshoven (eds.), Cultusplaats in de achtertuin Sporen uit de late bronstijd tot en met de nieuwe tijd in Poperinge (Koestraat). *BAAC-rapport* A-13.0116. 's-Hertogenbosch: BAAC BV, 127-132.

Van der Sanden, W.A.B. & P.W. Van den Broeke (eds.) 1987. Getekend Zand: 10 jaar archeologisch onderzoek in Oss-Ussen. *Bijdragen tot de studie van het Brabantse Heem* 31. Waalre.

Van der Sanden, W.A.B. 1987. Oss-Ussen: de grafvelden. In: W.A.B. van der Sanden & P.W. van den Broeke (eds.), Getekend zand, Tien jaar archeologisch onderzoek in Oss-Ussen, *Bijdragen tot de studie van het Brabantse Heem* 31, Waalre, 69-80.

Van der Sanden, W.A.B. 1990. Veenlijken, offers in het veen? In: W.A.B. van der Sanden (ed.), Mens en moeras: veenlijken in Nederland van de bronstijd tot en met de Romeinse tijd. *Archeologische monografieën van het Drents Museum* 1, Assen, 204-229.

Van der Sanden, W.A.B. 1994. De funeraire en aanverwante structuren. In: K. Schinkel (ed.), *Zwervende erven.* Leiden: Leiden University Press, 199-218.

Van der Sanden, W.A.B. 1996. *Through Nature to Eternity: the Bog Bodies of Northwest Europe.* Amsterdam: Batavian Lion International.

Van der Sanden, W.A.B. 1998. Funerary and related structures at Oss-Ussen. In: H. Fokkens (ed.), The Oss-Ussen Project – the first decade of excavations at Oss. *Analecta Praehistorica Leidensia* 30. Leiden: Leiden University Press, 307-336.

Van der Vaart-Verschoof, S. & R. Schumann 2017. Differentiation and globalization in Early Iron Age Europe, Reintegrating the early Hallstatt period (Ha C) into the debate. In: R. Schumann & S. van der Vaart-Verschoof (Eds.), *Connecting Elites and Regions.* Leiden: Sidestone Press, 9-27.

Van der Vaart-Verschoof, S. 2017. *Fragmenting the chieftain: a practice-based study of Early Iron Age Hallstatt C elite burials in the Low Countries.* [PhD-dissertation Leiden University]. Leiden: Sidestone Press.

Van der Veken, B. 2020. Een raadsel uit de IJzertijd – vindplaats 13. In: J.F. van der Weerden, B. Van der Veken & M.P.J. Janssens (eds.), Tienduizend jaar gedeelde bewoningsgeschiedenis in Baarle. Definitief archeologisch onderzoek in het tracé van de randweg Baarle, gemeenten Baarle-Hertog en Baarle-Nassau (In opdracht van de provincie Noord-Brabant). *RAAP-rapport* 3375. Weesp: RAAP Archeologisch Adviesbureau, 551-566.

Van der Weyden, T.J.S.M. 2013. *Nijmegen Kops plateau: A Roman fort.* Nijmegen: Bureau Archeologie en

Monumenten Gemeente Nijmegen. DOI: 10.17026/dans-znx-zrhj.

Van Dijk, X.C.C. 2009. Plangebied regenwaterbuffer Duijsterstraat te Gronsveld, gemeente Eijsden; een archeologische opgraving. *RAAP-rapport* 1763. Weesp: RAAP Archeologisch Adviesbureau.

Van Dorselaer, A. 1974. *Resultaten van zes opgravingscampagnes op de Kemmelberg.* Brussel: Nationale Dienst voor Opgravingen.

Van Enckevort, H. & E. Heirbaut 2007. De Romeinse Cultusplaats. In: H. van Enckevort (ed.) 2007. De Romeinse cultusplaats. Een opgraving in het plangebied Westeraam te Elst-Gemeente Overbetuwe (Gld.). *Archeologische Berichten Nijmegen* 5. Nijmegen: Gemeente Nijmegen, 15-30.

Van Enckevort, H. & K. Zee 1996. *Het Kops Plateau: Prehistorische grafheuvels en een Romeinse legerplaats in Nijmegen.* Abcoude: [Amersfoort]: Uniepers; Rijksdienst voor het Oudheidkundig Bodemonderzoek.

Van Enckevort, H. (ed.) 2007. De Romeinse cultusplaats. Een opgraving in het plangebied Westeraam te Elst-Gemeente Overbetuwe (Gld.). *Archeologische Berichten Nijmegen* 5. Nijmegen: Gemeente Nijmegen.

Van Giffen, A.E. 1945. Oudheidkundige aantekeningen over Drentsche Vondsten XII. *Nieuwe Drentsche Volksalmanak* 63. Assen, 69-134.

Van Ginkel, E. 2015. Caesar was here... Or was he? Mediahype rond een massamoord. *De Erfgoedstem* 14-12-2015. https://erfgoedstem.nl/caesar-was-in-kessel/.

Van Haaster, H. 2011. Pollen- en macrorestenonderzoek. In: L. Meurkens & A.J. Tol (eds.), Grafvelden en greppelstructuren uit de ijzertijd en Romeinse tijd bij Itteren (gemeente Maastricht). *Archolrapport* 144. Leiden: Archol BV, 175-188.

Van Kerckhove, J. 2007. Aardewerk. In: M. Schurmans & E. Verhelst (eds.), Oudheden uit Odijk. Bewoningssporen uit de late ijzertijd, Romeinse tijd en Merovingische tijd aan de Singel West/Schoudermantel. *Zuidnederlandse Archeologische Rapporten* 30. Amsterdam: VUhbs archeologie / Vrije Universiteit, 60-89.

Van Liefferinge, N., M. Smeets & L. Fockedey 2013. Het archeologisch onderzoek in Rijkevorsel-Wilgenstraat. *Archeo-rapport* 159. Kessel-Lo: Studiebureau Archeologie bvba.

Van Londen, H. 2006. *Midden-Delfland: the roman native landscape past and present.* [PhD-Dissertation Amsterdam University]. Amsterdam: Amsterdam University Press.

Van Renswoude, J. & D.S. Habermehl (eds.) 2017. Opgravingen te Houten-Castellum. Bewoning langs een restgeul in de IJzertijd, Romeinse tijd en Vroege Middeleeuwen. *Zuidnederlandse Archeologische Rapporten* 65. Amsterdam: VUhbs archeologie / Vrije Universiteit.

Van Renswoude, J. 2017. Sporen, structuren en fasering. In: J. van Renswoude & D.S. Habermehl (eds.), Opgravingen te Houten-Castellum. Bewoning langs een restgeul in de IJzertijd, Romeinse tijd en Vroege Middeleeuwen. *Zuidnederlandse Archeologische Rapporten* 65. Amsterdam: VUhbs archeologie / Vrije Universiteit, 89-142.

Van Renswoude, J., D.S. Habermehl & A. Sinke, 2017. Catalogus. Opgravingen te Houten-Castellum. Bewoning langs een restgeul in de IJzertijd, Romeinse tijd en Vroege Middeleeuwen. *Zuidnederlandse Archeologische Rapporten* 65. Amsterdam: VUhbs archeologie / Vrije Universiteit, 931-1118.

Van Vilsteren, V.T. 1989. Heilige huisjes. Over de interpretatie van vierpalige structuren bij grafvelden. *Westerheem* 38.1, 2-10.

Van Wijk, I., H. Fokkens, D.R. Fontijn, R. de Leeuwe, L. Meurkens, A. van Hilst & C. Vermeeren 2009. Resultaten van het definitieve onderzoek. In: H. Fokkens, R. Jansen & I.M. van Wijk (eds.), Het grafveld Oss-Zevenbergen: een prehistorisch grafveld ontleed. *Archolrapport* 50. Leiden: Archol BV, 69-140.

Van Zijverden, W. 2007. Fysische geografie. In: M. Schurmans & E. Verhelst (eds.), Oudheden uit Odijk. Bewoningssporen uit de late ijzertijd, Romeinse tijd en Merovingische tijd aan de Singel West/Schoudermantel. *Zuidnederlandse Archeologische Rapporten* 30. Amsterdam: VUhbs archeologie / Vrije Universiteit, 11-22.

Van Zoolingen, R.J. (ed.) 2010. Een Cananefaatse cultusplaats. Inheems-Romeinse bewoning aan de Lozerlaan, *Haagse Oudheidkundige Publicaties* 12, Den Haag: Gemeente Den Haag.

Van Zoolingen, R.J. 2011. Rural cult places in the civitas Cananefatium. *Journal of Archaeology in the Low Countries* 3-1/2, 5-30.

Vandecatsye, S. & K. Laisnez 2009. Een toekomstige industriezone met een Keltisch-Romeins verleden. Basisrapportage omtrent het archeologisch onderzoek van Hoogveld-J te Sint-Gillis-Dendermonde. *Archaeological Solutions bvba Rapportage* 2009 / 01. Dendermonde: DDS.

Vanoverbeke, R. & T. Clerbaut 2012. Twee (rituele?) late ijzertijd-monumenten te Alveringem-Hoogstade (prov. West-Vlaanderen, Belgie). *Lunula Archaeologia Protohistorica* 20. Brussels: Cellule Archéologie des Âges des Métaux, 189-193.

Vanoverbeke, R. 2012. Archeologische opgraving aan de Eikhoek te Hoogstade, gemeente Alveringem, *BAAC Vlaanderen Rapport* 30, Gent: BAAC Vlaanderen.

Venclova, N. 1989. Mšecké Žehrovice, Bohemia: excavations 1979-88. *Antiquity* 63(238), 142-146. DOI:10.1017/S0003598X00075669.

Venclova, N. 1997. On enclosures, pots and trees in the forest. *Journal of European Archaeology 5.1*, 131-150.

Verbrugge, A. & A. De Graeve 2010. Aalst (Erembodegem) Zuid IV Fase 3 Archeologisch vooronderzoek, proefsleuvenonderzoek. *Solva rapport 22.* Aalst: Solva.

Verbrugge, A., A. De Graeve & B. Cherretté 2011. Erembodegem Zuid IV Fase 3 Archeologisch onderzoek. *Solva rapport* 27. Aalst: Solva.

Verhart, L. 2006. *Op zoek naar de Kelten – Nieuwe archeologische ontdekkingen tussen Noordzee en Rijn.* Utrecht: Mattrijs / Limburgs Museum.

Verlinde, A.D. 1985. Die Gräber und Grabfunde der späten Bronzezeit und frühen Eisenzeit in Overijssel, IV. *Berichten van de Rijksdienst voor het Oudheidkundig Bodemonderzoek* 35, 231-411.

Verlinde, A.D. 1987. *Die Gräber und Grabfunde der späten Bronzezeit und frühen Eisenzeit in Overijssel.* [PhD-dissertation Leiden University]. S.l.: s.n.

Vermeulen, F. & B. Hageman 1997. Een rituele omheining uit de late ijzertijd te Knesselaere (O.-Vl.). *Lunula Archaeologia Protohistorica* 5. Brussels: Cellule Archéologie des Âges des Métaux, 29-33.

Verwers, G.J. 1972. Das kamp veld in Haps in Neolithicum, Bronzezeit und Eisenzeit. *Analecta Praehistorica Leidensia* 5. Leiden: Leiden University Press.

Verwers, G.J. 1973. Over de rand van de ijzertijd. *Westerheem* 22, 10-15.

Verwers, G.J. 1975. Urnenveld en nederzetting te Laag Spul, gem. Hilvarenbeek, prov. Noord-Brabant. *Analecta Praehistorica Leidensia* 8. Leiden: Leiden University Press, 23-43.

Vos, P. & S. de Vries 2013. *2e generatie palaeogeografische kaarten van Nederland (versie 2.0).* Deltares, Utrecht. Downloaded on 20-12-2019 from www.archeologieinnederland.nl.

Vouga, P. 1923. *La Tène: monographie de la station.* Leipzig: Hiersemann.

Wagenvoort, H. 1971. Nehalennia and the souls of the dead. *Mnemosyne* 24.3, 273-292.

Wait, G.A. 1985. Ritual and Religion in Iron Age Britain. *BAR British Series* 149 (i). Oxford: B.A.R.

Wait, G.A. 1985a. Ritual and Religion in Iron Age Britain. *BAR British Series* 149 (ii). appendices. Oxford: B.A.R.

Walker, L. 1984. Population and behaviour: deposition of the human remains. In: B. Cunliffe (ed.), Danebury: An Iron Age Hillfort in Hampshire. Vol. 2, The Excavations 1969-1978: the Finds. *CBA Research Report* 52b. London: Council for British Archaeology, 442-462.

Waterbolk, H.T. 1962. Hauptzuge der eisenzeitliche Besiedlung der nordlichen Niederlanden. *Offa 19*, 9-46.

Waterbolk, H.T. 1977. Walled enclosures of the Iron Age in the north of the Netherlands. *Palaeohistoria* 19, 97-137.

Wells, P.A. 1993. Settlement, economy, and cultural change at the end of the European Iron Age: excavations at Kelheim in Bavaria, 1987-1991. *Archaeological series / International Monographs in Prehistory* 6. Ann Arbor, Mich.

Wells, P.A. 1995. Identities, material culture, and change: 'Celts' and 'Germans' in late-Iron-Age Europe. *Journal of European Archaeology* 3.2, 169-185.

Wells, P.A. 2001. *Beyond Celts, Germans and Scythians: Archaeology and Identity in Iron Age Europe.* London: Duckworth.

Wells, P.A. 2011. The Iron Age. In: S. Milisauskas (ed.), *European Prehistory: A Survey.* Dordrecht: Springer, 405-460.

Wendling, H. & K. Winger 2014. Aspects of Iron Age Urbanity and Urbanism at Manching. In: M. Fernández-Götz, H. Wendling & K. Winger (eds.), *Paths to Complexity, Centralisation and Ubanisation in Iron Age Europe.* Oxford: Oxbow Books, 132-139.

Wendling, H. 2013. Manching reconsidered: new perspectives on settlement dynamics and urbanization in Iron Age Central Europe. *European Journal of Archaeology* 16.3, 459-490.

Wendling, H. 2019. Un sanctuaire sans architecture: la zone à offrandes du centre de l'oppidum de Manching. In: P. Barral & M. Thivet (eds.), *Sanctuaires de l'âge du Fer. Actes du 41e colloque international de l'Association française pour l'étude de l'âge du Fer (Dole, 25-28 mai 2017), Collection AFEAF 1,* 163-175.

Wesselingh, D. 2000. *Native neighbours: local settlement system and social structure in the Roman period at Oss (the Netherlands).* [PhD-dissertation Leiden University]. Leiden: Leiden University Press.

Wheeler, R.E.M. 1928. A "Romano-Celtic" Temple near Harlow, Essex, and note on the type. *The antiquaries Journal* 8, 300-326.

Whimster, R. 1989. *The emerging past.* London: Royal Commission on Historic Monuments of England.

Wieland, G. (ed.) 1999. *Keltische Viereckschanzen: einem Rätsel auf der Spur.* Stuttgart: Theiss.

Wieland, G. 1995. Die spätkeltischen Viereckschanzen in Süddeutschland – Kultanlagen oder Rechteckhofe?. In: A. Haffner (ed.), *Heiligtümer und Opferkulte der Kelten.* Stuttgart: Theiss, 85-99.

Wieland, G. 1995a. Opferschachte oder Brunne? *Archäologie in Deutschland* 4, 26-29.

Wieland, G. 1996. *Die Spätlatènezeit in Württemberg: Forschungen zur jüngeren Latènekultur zwischen Schwarzwald und Nördlinger Ries*. Stuttgart: Theiss.

Wigley, A. 2007. Rooted to the spot: the "smaller enclosures" of the later first millennium BC in the central Welsh Marches. In: C. Haselgrove & T. Moore (eds.), *The Later Iron Age in Britain and Beyond*. Oxford: Oxbow Books. 173-189.

Willems, W.J.H. & L.I. Kooistra 1991. Early Roman camps on the Kops Plateau at Nijmegen (NL). In: V.A. Maxfield & M.J. Dobson (eds.), *Roman Frontier Studies 1989. Proceedings of the XVth International Congress of Roman Frontier Studies*. Exeter: University of Exeter Press, 210-214.

Willems, W.J.H. 1996. Een Romeins legerkamp op het Kops Plateau te Nijmegen / Ein römisches Militärlager auf dem Kops Plateau in Nijmegen. In: L.J.F. Swinkels (ed.), *Een leven te paard. Ruiters uit de Lage Landen in het Romeinse leger / Reiten für Rom. Berittene Truppen an der römischen Rheingrenze*. Nijmegen: Provincie Gelderland; [Köln]: Landschaftsverband Rheinland, 28-31.

Witte, N. 2012. Deurne, Liessel Plangebied "Willige Laagt", Inventariserend veldonderzoek door middel van proefsleuven en opgraving van een ingericht boerenerf uit de vroege ijzertijd. *BAAC-rapport* A-10.0280. 's-Hertogenbosch: BAAC BV.

Wolf, A.P. 1974. Gods, ghosts and ancestors. In: A.P. Wolf (ed.), *Religion and ritual in Chinese society*. Stanford: Stanford University Press, 131-182.

Woodward, A. 1992. *Shrines and sacrifice*. English Heritage, London: B.T. Batsford Ltd.

Yperman, W. & M. Smeets 2018. Het archeologisch vooronderzoek aan de Akkerweg te Brecht. *Studiebureau Archeologie bvba Archeo-rapport* 441. Tienen: Studiebureau Archeologie.

Yü, Y.-S. 1987. "O Soul, Come Back!" A Study in The Changing Conceptions of The Soul and Afterlife in Pre-Buddhist China. *Harvard Journal of Asiatic Studies* 47.2, 363-395.

Zuidhoff, F.S. & J.A.A. Bos 2011. Landschap en vegetatie Lomm Hoogwatergeul fase II. In: D.A. Gerrets & R. de Leeuwe (eds.), Rituelen aan de Maas-Lomm Hoogwatergeul fase II, een archeologische opgraving. *ADC-rapport* 2333. Amersfoort: ADC Archeo-Projecten, 27-62.

Zuidhoff, F.S. & J.A.A. Bos 2015. Landschap en vegetatie. In: P.L.M. Hazen, E. Drenth & E. Blom (eds.), Tien millennia bewoningsgeschiedenis in het Maasdal, van jachtkamp tot landgoed langs de A2 bij Maastricht. *ADC Monografie* 17. Amersfoort: ADC Archeo-Projecten, 195-236.

CATALOGUE OF RECTANGULAR STRUCTURES IN THE LOW COUNTRIES

Aalter-Woestijne (B)

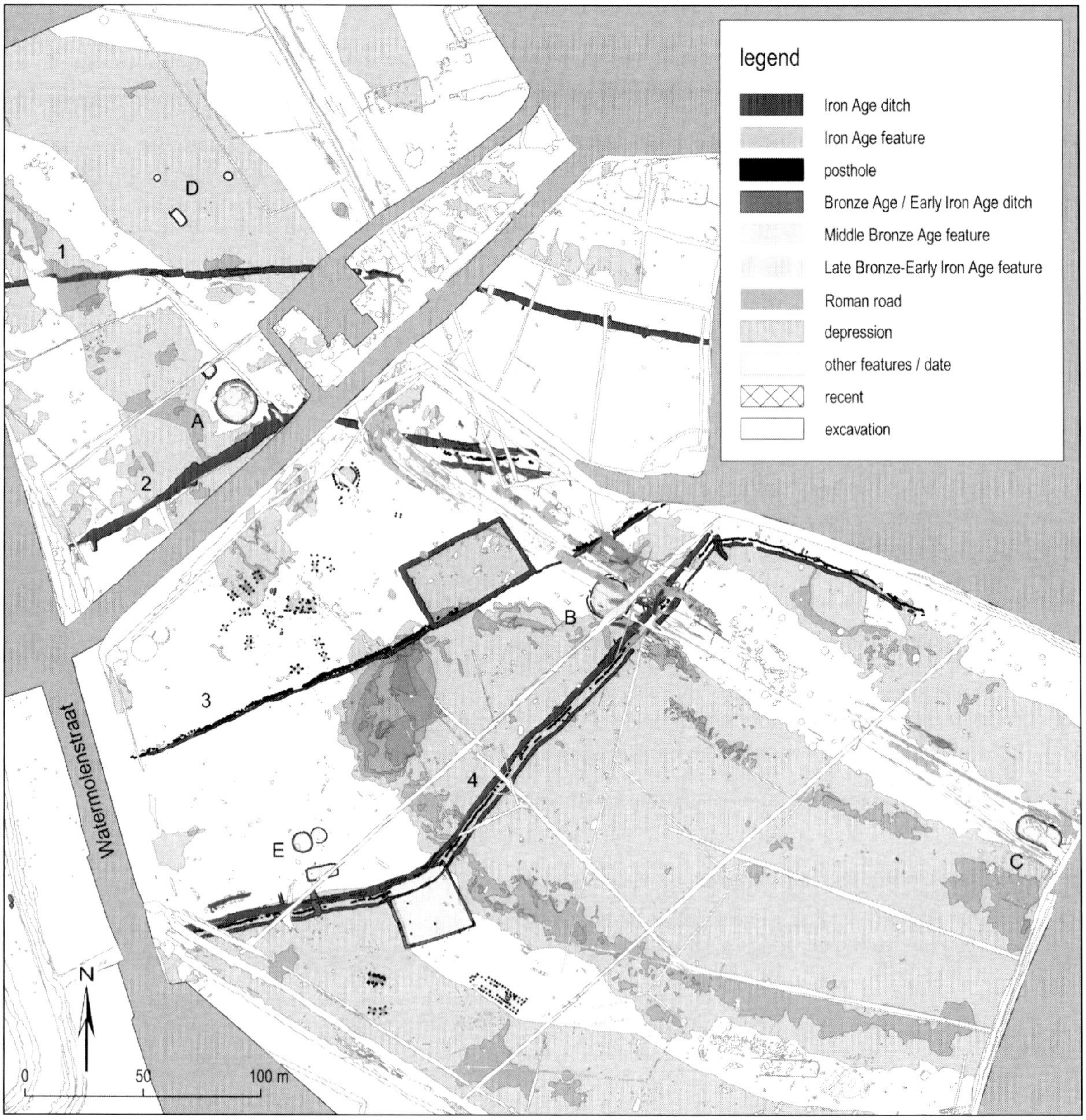

Figure A.1. Bronze and Iron Age features and a Roman road in Aalter Woestijne, based on De Groote & Van de Vijver (2019); figures and interpretation, combined with primary field data (courtesy of Agentschap Onroerend Erfgoed Vlaanderen and De Vlaamse Waterweg). For colour version see fig. 7.2.

The excavation of the site of Aalter Woestijne revealed an extensive Bronze and Iron Age configuration of features and finds. The oldest find was a single Middle Palaeolithic Levallois point. Thereafter, a spread of microliths, flint tools and pottery that was found in depressions and tree fells revealed human activities in the Mesolithic and Neolithic (Vandendriessche & Crombé 2016). The earliest anthropogenic features date to the Bronze Age, more specifically postholes, a Middle Bronze Age B house plan, burial monuments, pits, and cart tracks (Van de Vijver et al. 2016, 67-100; Van de Vijver et al. 2019, 81-115). From the Iron Age, large ditch systems accompanied by palisades subdivide the landscape (Van de Vijver et al. 2019, 117-149).

Rectangular structure

The first rectangular structure was excavated as a separate entity in 1989 (Bourgeois & Rommelaere 1991). It measured 48 by 27 m, with a 2m wide uninterrupted ditch (fig. 5.4). Originally the ditch would have been sizable, with 90 to 200cm depth at the time of construction (Langohr & Fechner 1993). It was dug down to the ground water level, where the ditch was at least 50cm wide at the bottom making a slight V-shape in cross-section.

Finds

The ditch could be dated to the 4th-3rd century BCE on the basis of pottery and charcoal (370-170 calBCE[25]) (Bourgeois & Rommelaere 1991; Vijver et al. 2016, 114). Research of the ditch fills suggested that not only was it deliberately closed shortly after construction, the podzol layers of the soil that were taken out during construction were returned in the ditch in the same stratigraphical order (Langohr & Fechner 1993). The fill of the ditch consisted of a layer of larger and small lumps of loamy sand at the bottom, suggesting some trampling and a thicker layer of humic soil on top containing charcoal layers and burned bone (Bourgeois & Rommelaere 1991).

Associated features

The rectangular structure exactly overlaps a linear ditch on the south side (Van de Vijver et al. 2019, 117-149). Two short rows of postholes were found parallel to the ditch inside the south east corner of the structure (Bourgeois & Rommelaere 1991). These turned out to be part of a much larger palisade along the ditch on the south side (Van de Vijver et al. 2019, 125-127). Several (five?) poorly preserved, undated and not described cremation graves were found and at least two large tree fells, of which one overlaps the ditch. On the site plan of 1991 many 'burn spots' are indicated, not documented in the later (re-)excavation. In the southwest corner of the ditch, a depot was discovered consisting of six secondarily burned and unburned pots, and some calcified bone on a layer of charcoal (Bourgeois & Rommelaere 1991). The pottery is typologically dated to the 3rd century BCE. Other finds are a small blue glass bead with yellow lines and fragments of a pottery dish in the ditch fill.

Landscape

The site is situated near the top of a sand ridge, on the edge of the Hoge Kale depression (Bourgeois & Rommelaere 1991; Langohr & Fechner 1993). On a more local scale, the structure is situated on the slight slope from an elevation to a depression south of the structure. The landscape in Aalter-Woestijne was in use for over a millennium before the construction of the rectangular structure in the 3rd century BCE (De Groote & Van de Vijver 2019). Documentation of the heights of the excavation level and the difference in soil horizons provides insight into the use of the relief of the landscape. The structure is an integral part of the landscape organisation (figure A.1).

Woestijne in the Middle Bronze Age

Bronze Age features dominate the higher grounds of the landscape. Avoiding the depressions on either side, three prominent Bronze Age burial monuments were built on the narrow sandy ridge forming a line that crosses the landscape from northwest to southeast. One of the monuments had an oval shaped ditch (fig. A.1, C) and two had a circular ditch (fig. A.1, A and B) with a diameter of around 17m (Van de Vijver et al. 2019a). These barrow monuments would have been tactically positioned on the ridge to guarantee visibility (Bourgeois 2013, 107). Nothing of the barrows, human remains, or of accompanying grave goods remained. Only soil colourations betrayed the former presence of a barrow. Monument B was the oldest, consisting of three phases visible by three different overlapping circular ditches, all with a sharp V-shape in cross-sections. The first phase yielded no dateable material. The second phase could be dated to 1867-1622 calBCE by two pieces of charcoal from the bottom fill of the ditch, and the final phase to 1631-1459 calBCE.[26]

Great effort was taken to ensure the ditch of monument A remained an open feature after it was dug. The sides had been lined by planking, consisting of planks of 20cm wide on average. The planks must have remained in situ as the wood had coloured the sand into dark stripes. The ditch was on average 1.3m wide and 63cm deep, with sides at a 45 degree angle and a flat bottom. Three ^{14}C-dates of charcoal from the bottom of the ditch gave a range of dates between 1500 and 916 calBCE.[27]

Oval structure C, 190m southeast of structure C, was of a similar age more precisely dated by four pieces of charcoal to 1501-1224 calBCE (Van de Vijver et al. 2019a,

---

25   95.4% probability calibration date of charcoal of alder wood, RICH-20850: 2190 ± 33 BP.

---

26   Second phase: 95.4% probability calibration, charcoal from the lowest fill, RICH-20477: 3405 ± 33 BP. Third phase: 95.4% probability calibration, charcoal from the lowest fill, RICH-20480: 3278 ± 34 BP (Van de Vijver et al. 2019a, table 4.5).

27   95.4% probability calibrations, charcoal from the lowest fill, RICH-20595: 3145 ± 31 BP, RICH-20608: 2988 ± 33 BP, RICH-20548: 2841 ± 33 BP (Van de Vijver et al. 2019a, table 4.5).

Structure Location	Feature	Cross-section (width x depth)	Finds	Date
A	5.5m ø circular ditch	0.83m x 64 cm	5 pieces of pottery	788-430 calBCE (2σ calibrations, charcoal, RICH-20610: 2500 ± 30 BP; RICH-20550: 2469 ± 32 BP)
D	7.2 × 3.7m ditch	0.4m x 19 cm	124 gr cremation remains	1728-1111 calBCE (2σ calibrations, calcined bone and charcoal, RICH-20474: 3331 ± 32 BP; RICH-20982: 3172 ± 33 BP; RICH-20873: 2989 ± 35 BP)
D	2.6-2.8m ø ditch	0.2m x ?	None?	Roman?
D	3.4-3.8m ø ditch	0.4m x ?	None?	Roman?
E	8.2m ø circular ditch	0.5-0.6m x 30 cm	None?	405-210 calBCE (2σ calibration, charcoal, RICH-20899: 2283 ± 33 BP)
E	6.8m ø circular ditch	0.3m x 15 cm	None?	Late Bronze Age – Early Iron Age based on typology?
E	13.4 × 5.2m ditch	0.5-0.7m x 40 cm	'a few' pieces of pottery	Late Bronze Age – Early Iron Age based on typology?

Table A.1. Smaller ditched structures in Aalter-Woestijne and their characteristics (based on Van de Vijver & De Groote 2016 and Van de Vijver *et al.* 2019).

table 4.5). The 19.8 × 9.6m structure was flanked by a road on both sides that was in use in the Roman era, but possibly in existence since the Bronze Age.[28]

A rectangular three-aisled house plan was found south of the barrows, also situated on a higher ridge parallel to the barrows and the ridges (figure 7.2, green rectangle below). Five ^{14}C-dates on charcoal from the postholes all calibrated between 1660 and 1200 BCE.

Late Bronze Age and Early Iron Age structures

Almost due south of the rectangular structure discussed in §5.4.1, another almost square structure was found (figure 7.2, yellow square below). Unlike the former, this square structure was crossed over by two ditches and a palisade. It measured 29.5 × 30m and seems to have an orientation parallel to linear ditch system 3 and the rectangular structure. The ditch was 1.15m wide on average and 54cm deep (Van de Vijver & De Groote 2016, 107; Van de Vijver *et al.* 2019, 129-131). The cross-sections showed a V-shape with a flattish bottom and a laminated fill indicating it was an open feature for a prolonged period (visible in Van de Vijver *et al.* 2019, figures 5.26 and 5.28). Three ^{14}C-dates place the structure principally in the Late Bronze Age, 1265-753 calBCE[29], although a few pottery shards indicated a date in the Iron Age (Van de Vijver & De Groote 2016, 107). The pottery is not described in detail or in precise numbers in either one of the reports, yet the drawings of some of the pieces indicate that the assemblage

at least comprises of a miniature bowl, ten rim fragments and several decorated pieces (Van de Vijver *et al.* 2019, figure 5.44). According to the digital excavation plan, four postholes were found in the interior of the square ditch. These are neither dated nor described.

Several smaller structures were found resembling urnfield features (fig. A.1, D, E and the small circular ditch northwest of A). Some were carbon dated with varying results (table A.1). None of the urns remained, but the larger one of the circular ditches at location E held some cremated remains in the centre (undated) and the rectangular structure at location D had cremation remains in the northwest side of the ditch fill. Others were interpreted as an urnfield feature based on their appearance. At least two small circular ditches (figure A.1, D), approximately 3m in diameter, were not mentioned in the report. As these also resemble urnfield features I have included them here even though a Roman date is a possibility. A single flat cremation grave was found 12m north of the small circular ditch A (Van de Vijver *et al.* 2019, 131-132). The cremated remains were dated to 777-510 calBCE.[30]

Linear ditch systems

Four large linear ditch systems cross the excavated terrain from west to east. In figure A.1 they are numbered 1 to 4, from north to south. Dating the ditches and placing them in chronological order proved to be a challenge (table A.2). These large open features would have served as artefact traps for a long time. Both older and younger material found their way into the fill layers. As unavoidable obstacles in the local landscape, the ditches were overcut by many later features mixing up the already diverse assemblage even more. All four ditch systems yielded

---

28 The Bronze Age version of the road would not have crossed over the monuments, but was likely next to them, while the Roman road seems to go over.

29 95.4% probability calibrations, charcoal, RICH-20586: 2958 ± 33 BP, RICH-20863: 2758 ± 34 BP and 91.9% probability calibration, charcoal RICH-20603: 2593 ± 32 BP (Van de Vijver & De Groote 2016, 119).

30 95.4% probability calibration, calcined bone, RICH-20540: 2488 ± 29 BP.

Ditch system	Length (m)	Features	Cross-section (width x depth)	Finds	Date
1	322	Ditch	2.77m x 77 cm	Pottery, glass La Tène bracelet fragment	Late Iron Age?
2	220	Ditch Double palisade Ditch	3.14m x 94 cm 1.97m x 74 cm	'A lot of pottery' [a]	Middle to Late Iron Age? (511-372 calBCE and 199-45 calBCE[b])
3	252	Double/triple palisade Ditch	1.09m x 35 cm	Pottery	Middle to Late Iron Age?
4	391	Ditch Single palisade Ditch	2.75m x 96 cm 1.29m x 59 cm	Pottery	Middle to Late Iron Age? (1108-389 calBCE based on four out of six 14C-dates)

[a] No precise numbers are mentioned in the reports in regards to the amount of pottery found.

[b] 95.4% probability calibrations, charcoal, RICH-20622: 2346 ± 30 BP and RICH-20600: 2100 ± 31 BP (Van de Vijver *et al.* 2019, table 5.4).

Table A.2. Linear ditches in Aalter-Woestijne and their characteristics (based on Van de Vijver & De Groote 2016 and Van de Vijver *et al.* 2019).

charcoal that was carbon dated. For ditch systems 1, 3 and 4 the ^{14}C-dates resulted in a large spread ranging from Neolithic to Roman and even post-Medieval. Only ditch system 2 resulted in two non-overlapping Iron Age dates (table A.2). The ^{14}C-dates for ditch system 4 resulted in six non-overlapping dates, four of which were sequential from the Late Bronze Age to the Middle Iron Age.

Linear ditch 1 could be documented over a length of 322m. The eastern part of the ditch was redug and reused in the Medieval Period (Van de Vijver *et al.* 2019) thereby demonstrating it was still visible at the time. The same applies for the western part of ditch 2. It had also been reused and at a deeper excavation level near barrow A the older ditch was observed along with several postholes. The northern ditch of ditch system 4 also seems to have had a small reused part. This is discussed in chapter 7.2.6.

Other Iron Age structures

In different places of the excavated area Iron Age structures were found. I will highlight a selection here. Only 14m southwest of the square ditch eight postholes of a small building were found (Van de Vijver *et al.* 2019, 121). The building measured at least 6.5 × 3.5m and could be carbon dated to the Early to Middle Iron Age.[31] Two or three four-posted granaries accompanied it. Further north, in the area between ditch systems 2 and 3, a cluster of small structures was found. The cluster consisted of at least 16 or 17 granaries positioned around a larger structure. Most granaries were four-posted, measuring 2 × 2 m, five had six posts and one had eight. The larger structure consisted of an unclear configuration of posts. It measured approximately 11 × 5.5m. A few small pieces of pottery were found in the postholes that could be dated no more accurately than 'Iron Age'. Two ^{14}C-dates

from charcoal found in the postholes of two of the granaries resulted in 542-390 calBCE and 359-92 calBCE.[32] These dates are contemporary to the carbon date results from ditch system 2 (see table A.2).

North of the cluster of small structures, less than 40m northwest of the rectangular structure and only 6m from ditch system 2, lay a circular ditch with a post circle around it. The ditch measured 8m in diameter and was only 0.45m wide and 18cm deep (Van de Vijver *et al.* 2019, 87-89). The incomplete post circle had a diameter of 11 m, consisting of posts set on average 1m apart. One charcoal sample from the ditch was dated to 401-210 calBCE.[33] Another sample dated in the post-Medieval Period.

Interpretation differences

The assignment of the features to a certain time period as I have shown on the map in Figure A.1 differs in a number of ways from the interpretation of the excavators (De Groote & Van de Vijver 2019). A narrow ditch oblique to ditch 2 and enclosing a terrain in which barrow A is located, is interpreted in the report as an Iron Age feature even though some Roman pottery was found in the fill and the ^{14}C-dates cover a period from the Late Neolithic to the Roman era (Van de Vijver *et al.* 2019, 117). Also, a nine-posted outhouse on the north side of the enclosed terrain is considered typical for the Roman era, and other similar narrow ditches in the excavation are assigned to the Roman era. These arguments, along with the difference in ditch-type (it is much narrower than the other linear Iron Age ditches), gave enough doubt in order not to allocate

---

[31] 95.4% probability calibration, charcoal, RICH-20472: 2391 ± 31 BP (Van de Vijver *et al.* 2019, table 5.4).

[32] 92.1% probability calibration, charcoal, RICH-20879: 2376 ± 34 BP and 95.4% probability calibration, charcoal, RICH-20476: 2155 ± 33 BP (Van de Vijver *et al.* 2019, table 5.4).

[33] 95.4% probability calibration, charcoal, RICH-20629: 2274 ± 32 BP (Van de Vijver & De Groote 2016, table 10).

the ditch to the Iron Age. I reassigned the ditch to the Roman Era (or later), so it is not included in figure A.1.

The road that is indicated as a Roman feature in figure A.1 has been in use for a long time, possibly from the Bronze Age onwards (Van de Vijver *et al.* 2019a, 102-103). As most documented cart tracks seem to cross over the Bronze and Iron Age features, I have chosen not to include it as an Iron Age feature. However, the course of the road is indicative for the high ridge, and for that reason it is included in figure A.1.

The burial monument with the circular ditch and post circle, have been interpreted in the report by Van de Vijver *et al.* (2019a) as a Bronze Age feature based on the typology of barrow types. The monument is included here as an Iron Age feature based on one of the ^{14}C-dates and recent research by Louwen (2021).

Type of structure
2

Alveringem-Eikhoek/Hoogstade (B)

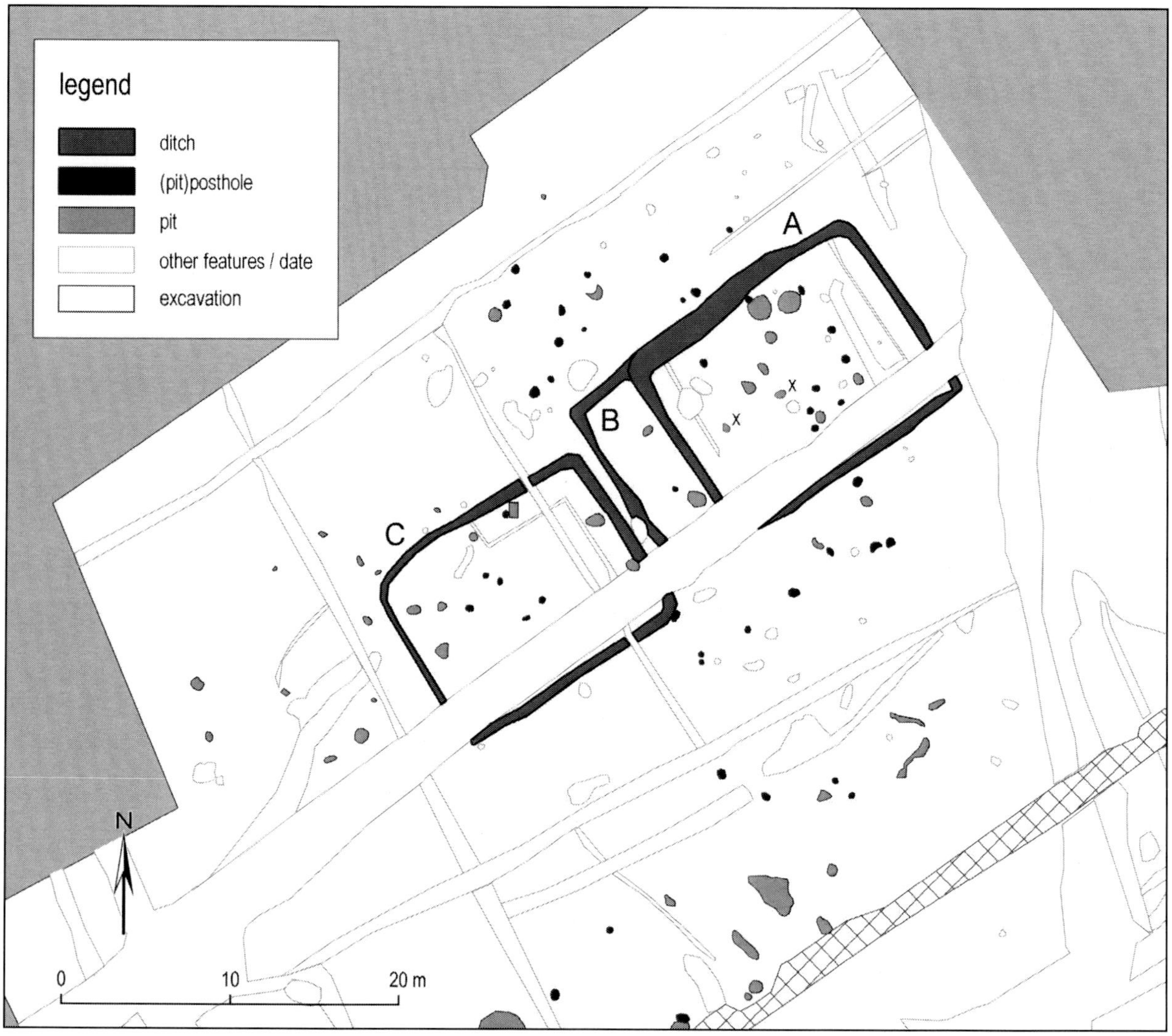

Figure A.2. Part of the excavation map for Alveringem-Eikhoek/Hoogstade. (after Vanoverbeke 2012, appendix 1 and 2). For colour version see fig. 6.20.

In a 0.5 ha excavation in the Belgium county of Alveringem, two rectangular structures were found next to each other (Vanoverbeke 2012, 15-36; Vanoverbeke & Clerbaut 2012).

Rectangular structures

The northeast structure seems to consist of two phases, a rectangular ditch (A) overlapping another ditch (B) on the west side (fig. A.2). Ditch A measured 13.6 × 10.8m. Ditch B would have added another 3.6m in length. The width was 0.5-0.85m and the depth 21-35cm. A sample from ditch A was carbon dated to 348-52 calBCE.[34] Ditch C had similar dimensions of 12.7 × 9.8 m, with a poorly preserved 0.25-0.7m wide and 6-16cm deep ditch. A sample from ditch C dated 361-175 calBCE.[35] Both ditches had a bowl-shaped cross-section.

---

34   95.4% probability calibration, charcoal, Ua-43277: 2125 ± 30 BP.
35   95.4% probability calibration, charcoal, Ua-43276: 2187 ± 30 BP.

Finds

A staggering amount of pottery (72.4 kg) was found within the ditches of the two structures, the majority (5113 pieces; MNI = 352) in the northwest sides of both structures A and C (Vanoverbeke 2012, 25; Vanoverbeke & Clerbaut 2012). This was 88.3 % of the total amount of pottery found on the site. A full pottery analysis has not been published, but a short summery was published as dating to the Late Iron Age (Vanoverbeke & Clerbaut 2012).

Associated features

Two small pits enclosed by structure A (Fig. A.2, indicated with 'x' next to them) were "entirely filled with pottery fragments" (Vanoverbeke & Clerbaut 2012).[36] Two large pits enclosed on the north side of structure A were 20 and 35cm deep and filled with (some?) charcoal. Another small pit yielded possible burned animal bone fragments. Many other pits and postholes were found inside and out of the rectangular structures. The fill of the features resembled the appearance of the ditches, typified by a vague outline and a shallow depth (Vanoverbeke 2012, 18-20). Ditch C had two pits (or postholes?) in the interior space evenly distributed along the sides (unknown for the southeast side). No datable material was found in the pits and they are not described in detail in the report. Likewise, two pits were found in the interior space of ditch B. The pits were 15cm and 30cm deep and flat bottomed. South of ditches A and B a row of postholes is situated around 4m from the southern ditch, seemingly connecting it to the southeast corner of ditch C. Additionally, several postholes were found in the interior spaces of the ditches. Similar to the row of posts, these were unfortunately not described in the report other than noted as 'postholes' (Vanoverbeke 2012, appendix 2, feature list).

Landscape

The site is situated on sandy loam soil, on the plateau of Izenberge (Vanoverbeke 2012, 13-14; Vanoverbeke & Clerbaut 2012). The slightly wavy terrain would have had a more pronounced relief in the Iron Age. The site is located on a slope 8-9m above sea level, between the 11-13m high point of the plateau, and the 3m low point of a small river valley 700m to the south.[37]

Type of structure

2

---

36   Actual number of pottery shards not mentioned.

37   Information from height map: https://nl-be.topographic-map.com/maps/g9vu/Vlaanderen

Barneveld-Harselaar-west (NL)

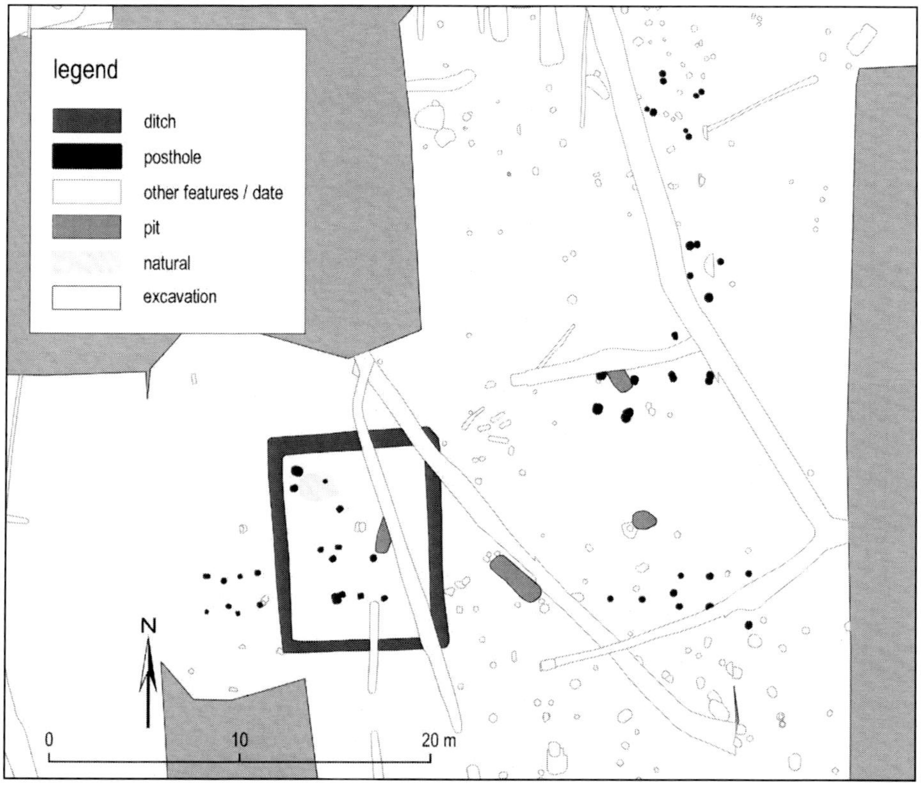

Figure A.3. Part of the excavation map for Barneveld-Harselaar-west. (after Brouwer 2013; digital site plan courtesy of BAAC). For colour version see fig. 6.14.

Several excavations took place in advance of the development of a large 21 ha industrial area in Barneveld (Brouwer 2013). In 2011 just over 2 ha was excavated in irregular shaped pits revealing Iron Age settlement features.

Rectangular structure

One rectangular structure of 10.3 × 8.2m was suggested as a cult place (*Ibid.*, 72-73; fig. A.3). The continuous ditch was 60-90cm wide and 34cm deep. The fill of the ditch had three phases, of which the lower two consisted of thin layers and the upper phase was brown-grey blotched. The upper fill was dated to 174-4 BCE.[38]

Finds

In the ditch fill 31 pottery fragments were found (Brouwer 2013, 72).

Associated features

Several postholes were identified in the interior of the ditch (*Ibid.*, 72). Due to a lack of finds their date is unknown. In the northwest corner a tree fell was documented. The feature contained charcoal from an elder tree that was carbon dated to the Bronze Age.[39] Around the ditch several four-posted structures were documented, interpreted as granaries. To the north a Late Iron Age house plan was found. None of the pits were described in the report. The site is described as a cult place near a settlement (Brouwer 2013, 72).

Landscape and context

These Iron Age features were situated on the lower flank of a sand ridge (*Ibid.*, 61). The terrain slopes gently from the ridge on the east of the site (elevation 10m above sea level) to the west into the valley of a stream 2.5m lower. The top of the ridge was inhabited from the Late Medieval Period onwards. The context of the rectangular structure could be described as near or in a settlement.

Type of structure

7

---

38 95.4% probability calibration, material and lab sample number not stated in report, 2075 ± 25 BP.

39 Lab sample number not stated in report, 3415 ± 30 BP.

Boechout-Mussenhoevelaan (B)

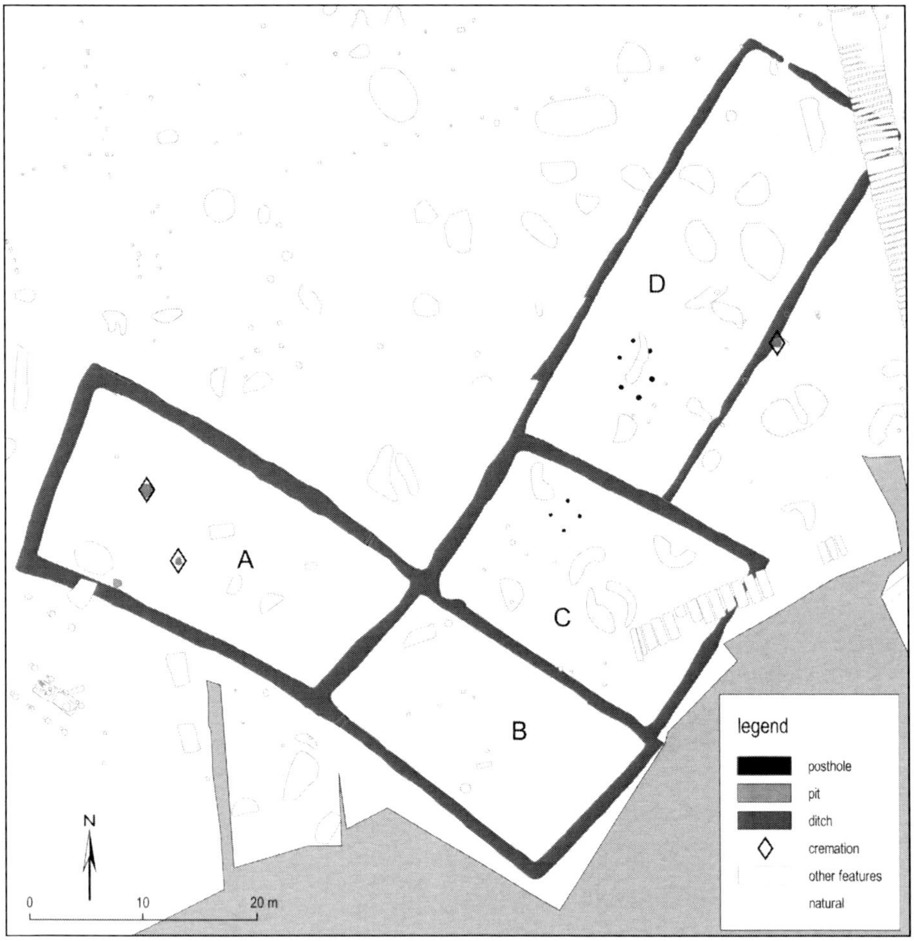

Figure A.4-1. Part of the excavation plan of Boechout-Mussenhoevelaan (after Bakx, Verrijckt & Smeets 2018, figures 5.1, 5.3, 5.5 and 5.9; digital plan courtesy of R. Bakx, Studiebureau Archeologie bvba). For colour version see fig. 5.6.

As the result of a 2 ha large excavation in Boechout, an Early Iron Age settlement was found, the remains of a Middle to Late Iron Age cemetery and two large ditch systems (Bakx, Verrijckt & Smeets 2018; Bakx & Bourgeois 2021). The most impressive ditch system consisted of four connected rectangular ditches (fig. A.4-1).

Rectangular structures

The ditches were continuous, apart from one 50cm wide interruption on the north side of ditch D. From west to east the dimensions were (approximately) 31.9 × 15.6m (structure A), 24.8 × 14.7m (structure B), 23.9 × 16.9m (structure C), and 39.3 × 15.5m (structure D).

Structure A had V-shaped ditches in cross-sections, while structures B, C and D had bowl shaped cross-sections (Bakx et al. 2018). The fill consisted of two phases. The ditches were continuous, apart from one 50cm wide interruption

on the north side of ditch D. Structure A has a width of 1.05-1.50m and a depth of 64-75cm. In most places the cross-sections of the ditch appears V-shaped (fig. A.4-2). The ditches of structures B and C are between 0.70 and 1.26m wide, and 38-52cm deep with a bowl shaped cross-section (Bakx et al. 2018). The fill consisted of two phases. Structure D had somewhat narrower ditches with a width of 0.5-1.2m and shallower with a depth of 23-47cm. The cross-sections also showed a bowl-shape with a rounded to flat bottom. In sections of the junctions, structure D looks to overlap structure C and in turn structure C overlaps B. The junctions of A and B were not sectioned. It can be concluded that B is older than C, and D is the youngest of the three.

Finds

The largest parts of the rectangular ditches were searched for finds (Bakx 2018). In total 819 fragments of Middle and

Figure A4-2. Cross section of structure A in the northwest corner (Bakx *et al.* 2018, fig. 5.8).

Late Iron Age pottery were found, 43 of which in structure A, 360 in structure B, 226 in structure C, and 190 in structure D. The pottery seemed spread out in the ditches fills rather than concentrated. Other finds included three pieces of a burnt glass La Tène bracelet in a ditch of structure B, a variety of natural stones (number not indicated in report), and three iron nails. A spot in the interior of structure A (fig. A.4-1, indicated as pit) contained a concentration of pottery shards belonging to a Middle to early Late Iron Age pot. Two fragments of molten bronze, one fragment of a bronze needle and a bronze coin were found in the vicinity of the ditches. Spread out over the interior spaces of the structures some cremation remains were found. One of these found in the southeast ditch of structure B was dated to 356-64 calBCE.[40]

Associated features

Three cremation graves were found, two of which were in structure A and one was just outside the eastern ditch of structure D (Bakx *et al.* 2018). One of the cremations in structure A belonged to an adult aged 30-60 years, dated to 387-205 calBCE.[41] The cremation overcutting ditch D was dated 198-47 calBCE.[42] In the fill of ditch D loose cremation remains were dated to the Middle Bronze Age (Bakx & Bourgeois 2021). The north side of ditch B/ south side of C delivered cremation remains that dated to the Late Iron Age.

In the interior of structure D six postholes were documented belonging to either one or two separate structures. In the interior of structure C a four-posted structure was found. About 50m east of structure D, two parallel ditches with the same orientation were found. The ditches were 12.6m apart, 27.3 and 21.8m long and slightly curved.

Bakx *et al.* (2018, 98-100) give several possible interpretations for the ditch system, without a preference for one or another: the large monuments were only built for high-status individuals or families, founders' graves that demonstrate the unity of a group and emphasise a claim to the land visible to outsiders, a cult place, or a straightforward cemetery enclosure. The latter suggestion is accompanied by the comment that this hypothesis does not explain the occurrence of multiple ditches.

Landscape

The site is located on the gentle northern slope of the Boom cuesta, an asymmetrical sandy ridge (Fockedey & Bakx 2018). The higher ground of the ridge, 25m above sea level, is several kilometres to the southwest, while the terrain towards the north and east slopes down to 9m above sea level. The two ditch systems were found halfway down the slope, at a level of around 14m above sea level. The site was reasonably well preserved and covered by a layer of ploughed soil enriched with sods (Bakx *et al.* 2018, 26, 154). Pollen analysis of a sample from a nearby Middle Iron Age watering pit showed open grass lands and fertilizer fungal spores (*Ibid.*, 84-88).

Type of structure

2

---

40   95.4% probability calibration, cremated bone, KIK-15215/RICH-26055: 2149 ± 28 BP.

41   95.4% probability calibration, cremated bone, KIK-13289/RICH-24118: 2236 ± 29 BP.

42   95.4% probability calibration, cremated bone, KIK-13290/RICH-24117: 2100 ± 30 BP. In the report this is stated as another feature, but it later transpired the samples were switched (pers. comm. R. Bakx).

Born-Koeweide (NL)

Figure A.5. Part of the excavation plan for Born/Koeweide (after Van der Leije 2016). For colour version see fig. 5.7.

The structure in Born was found in an excavation of 1.5 ha that also revealed features and structures belonging to a Late Bronze – Early Iron Age settlement (Van de Leije 2016).

Rectangular structures

The ditch system consists of two connected rectangular ditches (Van de Leije 2016, 62-70). One of the ditches (A) has a trapezium shape of 43.5m by 25/19.5m (fig. A.5). A smaller ditch (B) of 20.8m by 14.5m is attached to it. The lower part of ditches was filled with brown silty clay resembling the matrix, while the upper fill was greyer in colour. Additionally, the bottom fill of the smaller structure showed thin layers, an indication that it was an open feature for a while after construction. The large ditch was 85-170cm wide and 80-100cm deep, with a V-shape and a flat bottom. In the southwest corner the depth was only is 50 cm, due to a gravel layer. The

smaller ditch was 100-160cm wide with a maximum depth of 78cm. It also had a V-shape, but with a rounded/bowl-shaped bottom.

There was no evidence of what was done with the content of the ditch after it was dug and the structure seemed to consist of one phase. The smaller structure was probably slightly younger than the larger rectangular structure, based on the depth and the fill of the ditches (Van de Leije 2016, 69). Two 14C-dates of charcoal from the lower ditch fill resulted in 366-192 calBCE and 382-203 calBCE.[43] The upper fill was almost the same date: 369 to 174 calBCE.[44] A carbon date of the actual

---

43 95.4% probability calibrations, resp. Poz-68687: 2200 ± 30 BP and Poz-70592: 2225 ± 35 BP (Van der Leije 2016, 70).

44 95.4% probability calibration, Poz-70594: 2195 ± 35 BP (Van der Leije 2016, 70).

bottom of the ditch resulted in Late Bronze Age. The ditch structures are interpreted as cemeteries, also used for ancestral worship or remembrance (Van der Leije & Meurkens 2016).

Finds

Only 310 sherds were found in the rectangular ditches, half of which were indeterminable small pieces (Meurkens 2016). The pottery is a mix of Late Bronze Age to Early Iron Age material and (Middle to) Late Iron Age. Given the 14C-dates, the later period material is thought to be representable for the construction period of the structure and the older component is considered as surface scatter from an earlier settlement that got mixed in when the ditches were dug. All the post-constructions are assumed to be part of a Late Bronze to Early Iron Age settlement (Van der Leije 2016, 55-62), although the structure within the rectangular ditch was not dated.

Associated features

Three cremation graves were found, two of which inside the ditch system. The latter were small (1.4 grams and 26.4 grams) and without grave goods (Tichelman 2004, 48-50; Smits 2004). The third grave was found 2m north of the ditches (Van de Leije 2016, 63-65). The cremation remains were deposited in a 10cm deep, round pit, accompanied by a bowl. A bone fragment was carbon dated to 407-234 calBCE.[45] The burned remains were probably of a male of at least 40 years old, who had suffered from malnutrition (Velseka 2016). Originally there might have been more cremation graves, but they were not conserved on the site (Van de Leije 2016, 107). The shallow depth of the features below the surface level probably caused them to be absorbed in the top soil due to ploughing. Despite the number of pits that were found inside the ditch system and in the vicinity, none could be associated with the ditches by lack of datable material. Most are presumed to be part of the Late Bronze Age to Early Iron Age settlement phase of the site.

Landscape

The site is located on the Geistingen terrace, a lower terrace of the river Meuse 200m from the river plain (Van der Leije & Meurkens 2016). In the Iron Age the distance to the river itself would have been less than 500m. The site is situated on a small local elevation of roughly 90 by 70m which would have been a noticeable place in the landscape, in between the lower lying river and the higher terraces. The soil consists of clay layers, 30 to 300cm thick, deposited at high water levels in the Early Holocene.

Type of structure

2

---

45   95.4% probability calibration, Poz-68685: 2300 ± 30 BP (Van der Leije 2016, 70).

Brecht-Akkerweg (B)

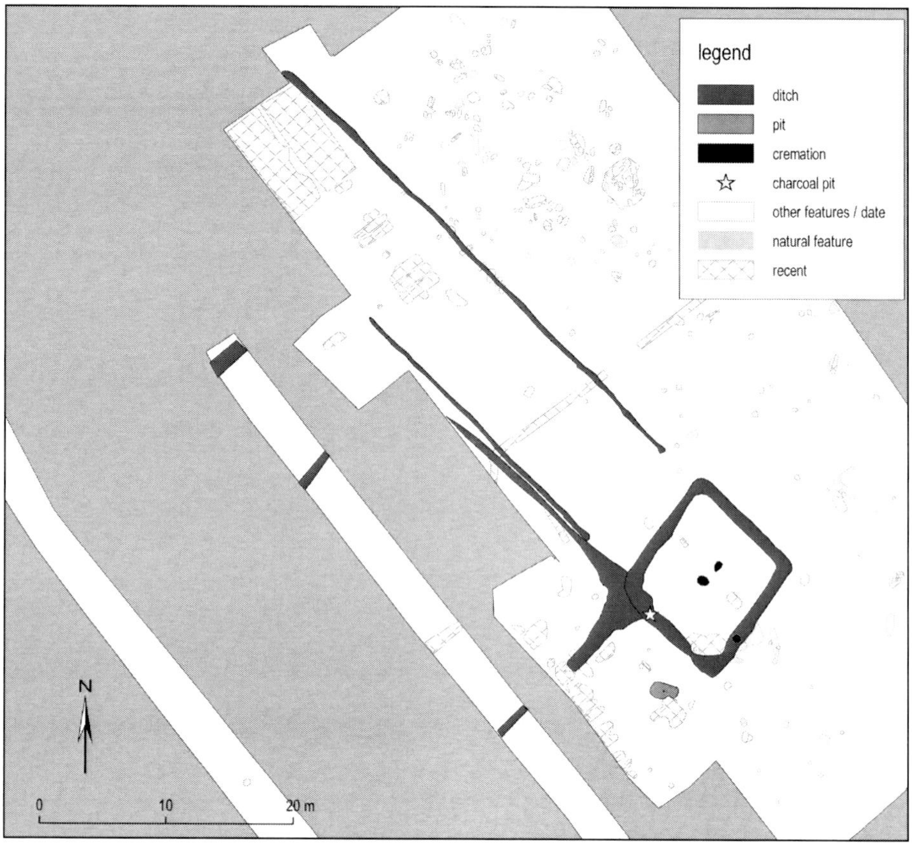

Figure A.6. Part of the excavation plan for Brecht-Akkerweg (after De Rijck 2020, fig. 43, fig. 48; digital excavation plan courtesy of A. de Rijck / ABO).

The name 'Brecht' derives from the Germanic word 'brakti', which refers to a hill or mountain (De Rijck 2019; 2020, 19). The village of Brecht is indeed situated on top of a hill and the site itself is on another local height.

Rectangular structure

Within the excavated area the surface slopes up to the west, where the preservation of the features became poor due to deep ploughing. On the east side Late Iron Age settlement features were found and a 10m square ditch (De Rijck 2020, 46-56). The latter structure was seemingly dug around a central cremation grave (fig. A.6). Cross sections of the square ditch showed a bowl shape of 20-40cm deep. The ditch could be dated to the Middle Iron Age based on pottery found in the fill, although the exact quantity or location is not stated in the report.

Finds and Associated features

Two other cremation graves were found, both without charcoal and at a relatively high excavation level (De Rijck 2019; Yperman & Smeets 2018, 18). Due to the high stratigraphical position it is conceivable that other graves were destroyed by ploughing. Another possible grave was found on the south side of the square ditch. 2 meters southwest of the square ditch a deep oval pit was discovered (De Rijck 2019). At the bottom of the pit 173 shards were found belonging to several initially complete pots. Most were of Marne type pottery, dating to the 5th century BCE.

The pit also contained cremation remains, although it is not stated in the report if these also derive from the bottom of the pit. The excavator leaves the option open that the pit is contemporary to the ditches and the older pottery was some sort of heirloom offering. Besides the cremation remains, the central grave contained charcoal and burned animal bones (De Rijck 2020, 46-61). Linear ditches extend from the square structure at least 40m in the north direction and 5m to the west.

The square ditch was more or less contemporary to the linear ones (De Rijck 2020, 59), and assumingly, so were the cremation graves. The linear ditches are interpreted by De Rijck (2019; 2020, 58) as drainage, or possibly part of a long barrow.

Landscape

The terrain consists of moderately dry to dry sandy soils, on the flank of a ridge (Yperman & Smeets 2018, 2-6). Just north of the site another excavation revealed a Bronze Age, Iron Age and Roman settlement and cemetery. The height difference within the site is 0.5 m, sloping down to the east.

Type of structure

6

Cuijk-Ewinkel (NL)

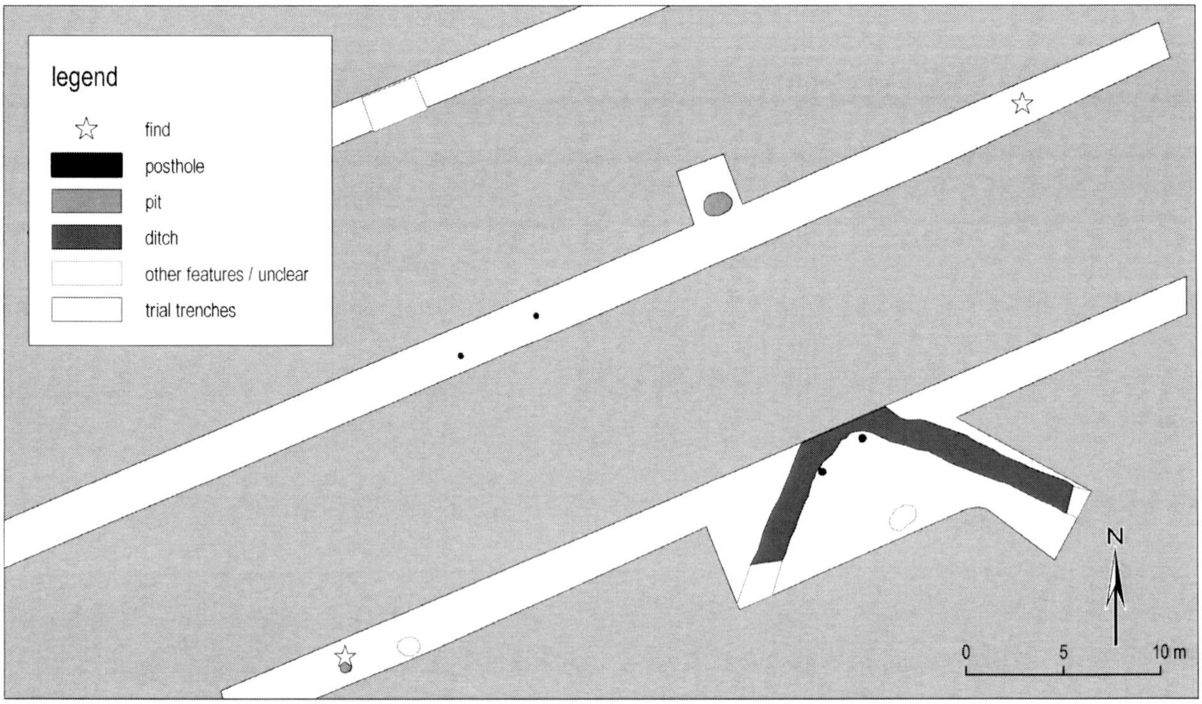

Figure A.7. Part of the trial trench plan of Cuijk-Ewinkel (after Ball, Arnoldussen & Van Hoof 2001, figure 58).

The ditch was initially interpreted as a burial monument or a settlement ditch (Ball, Arnoldussen & Van Hoof 2001, 61-63), but on account of the associated finds an explanation as a 'ritual enclosure' was suggested later (Ball & Arnoldussen 2002). Any additional comments on my part will similarly amount to speculation. The inclusion within this thesis is mainly based on the relatively large number of finds in the ditch, as well as some remarkable depositions in the vicinity, which can be interpreted as depositions.

Rectangular (?) structure

The ditch could be followed at least 12m to the southeast and 8m to the southwest. It was approximately 1.5m wide and has not been sectioned for the reason that it was part of a preliminary investigation.

Finds and Associated features

Just cleaning the surface of the ditch produced 700 pieces of pottery, weighing almost 9 kg (Ball, Arnoldussen & Van Hoof 2001, 61-63; Ball & Arnoldussen 2002). The material looked weathered. Some pieces could be dated to the Late Iron Age. Other finds from the upper fill of the

ditch included stones, an iron fibula, slag, burned loam, several wet stones, a spindle whorl and a piece of a dark purple glass bracelet. Next to the pit west of the ditch half a (possibly Roman) grinding stone was found (fig. A.2, left star). The pit northwest of the ditch contained a lot of charcoal and some burned loam. Just over 16m northeast of the ditch 30 kg of natural stones were found (fig. A.7, right star).

Landscape

The area around the site in Cuijk consists of an old terrace of the river Meuse, partly covered by river dunes and loamy soils (Kluiving 2005). In between the sandy ridges the lower parts are filled with loamy sand (Ball, Arnoldussen & Van Hoof 2001, 58-60). To the southwest the terrain slopes down towards a residual meander gully. To the northwest lies the top of a sandy ridge.

Part of a rectangular ditch was discovered during a large scale trial trench project in 2000 and 2001 (Ball, Arnoldussen & Van Hoof 2001; Ball & Arnoldussen 2002). As this part of the 105 ha large planning area was left undeveloped, the site was never further excavated and information remains limited.

Type of structure
Undetermined

Dendermonde-Hoogveld (B)

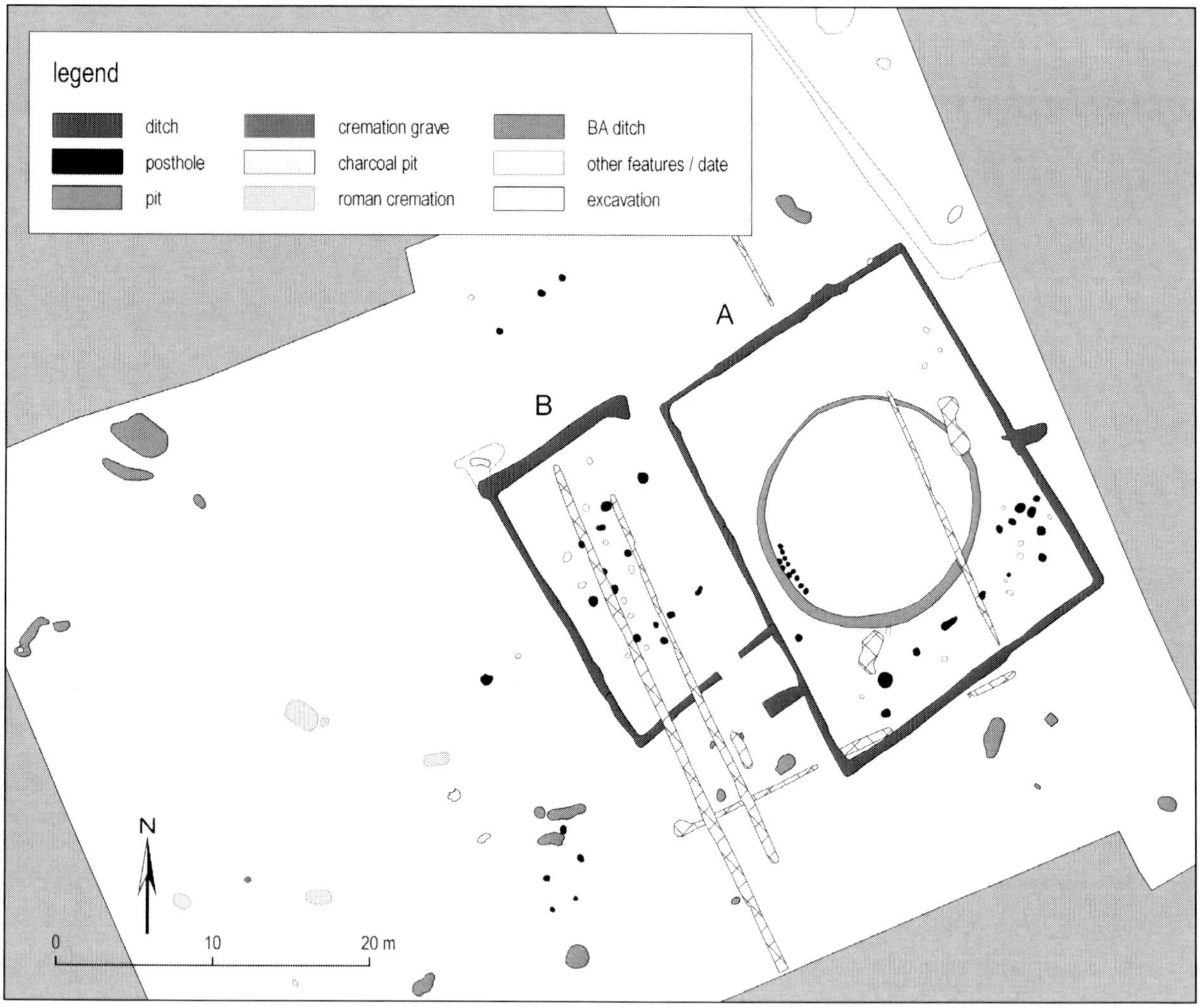

Figure A.8. Part of the excavation plan of Dendermonde-Hoogveld (after Vandecatsye & Laisnez 2009). For colour version see fig. 6.4.

Approximately 5 km east of the Middle Iron Age site of Dendermonde-Oud Klooster (§5.4.3), other rectangular structures were constructed around a Middle Bronze Age barrow (figure A.8).

Rectangular structures

The largest ditch (A) measured 24 × 18m (Vandecatsye & Laisnez 2009, 22-23). A maximum ditch depth of 30cm remained with a fill that was much darker on the east side around a bulge, coloured by a concentration of charcoal. Ditch B measured 18 × 11m and had the same depth as structure A. The interruption on the northeast side is interpreted as an intentional

entrance; the interruption on the south side was caused by poor preservation (*Ibid.* 2009, 22-23). The fill of ditch B has a charcoal concentration in the northwest corner.

Finds

The fill of ditch B has a charcoal concentration in the northwest corner. The charcoal rich fill on the east side of structure A also produced a large amount of cremation remains and 19 fragments of pottery (*Ibid.* 2009, 22-23). The east side fill could be dated to the Late

Iron Age by a piece of charcoal (205-55 calBCE)[46] and a burned bone (207-57 calBCE)[47]. On the west side small amounts of cremated remains were found in the ditch fill. The circular ditch was dated by concentrations of Bronze Age pottery that were found in the lower fill on the northwest and south side. Charcoal from the same layer was carbon dated to 1665-1502 calBCE.[48]

Associated features

The most prominent associated feature is the circular Bronze Age ditch of 14m in diameter, within structure A. The Bronze Age ditch also had a remaining depth of 20-30cm (*Ibid.* 2009, 12-15). South of the circular ditch, within the area enclosed by ditch A, a row of postholes was found. The features of the main row were well preserved to a depth of about 60cm deep, indicating that they were once part of a substantial structure. The postholes yielded no finds, but one could be dated by a piece of charcoal from an oak to 361-121 calBCE[49], an older date than the rectangular ditch. Another short row of postholes was found inside the circular ditch on the west side. Their setting suggests a relation with the ditch or a barrow. These postholes were less visible and preserved to a maximum depth of 20cm. In the interior of structure B, eleven postholes were found and another eleven possible postholes. Six cremation graves were found west of the structures, of which five were dated to the Roman era and one to the Early to Middle Iron Age. The cremation remains of the latter were dated twice with different results.[50] One additional Roman cremation grave was found within structure B. Seven other features in the vicinity were possible graves, and contained only a charcoal concentration (figure 6.4, yellow features). Several pits were found around the rectangular ditches. These were not described in detail in the report. Other Iron Age features are spread out over the excavated area, among which are a well and several granaries (*Ibid.* 2009, 48).

The description of the charcoal pits that were found in the vicinity is not reported. The postholes enclosed by the ditches were vaguely interpreted by Vandecatsye & Laisnez (2009, 23) as 'ritual structures', possibly connected to a 'Celtic death cult'. A reference or possible reconstruction was not presented to support this statement. In Fig. A.8 I have taken the liberty of redefining a small charcoal pit in the western enclosure as a posthole. The enclosed structure becomes more clearly visible through this modification, enabling two types of reconstruction. One is

that the postholes represent several smaller structures or several phases of one smaller structure, or more likely, the posts represent a larger structure that was open towards the barrow.

Landscape

Hoogveld is situated in the transitional area from sand to loamy sand (Vandecatsye & Laisnez 2009, 8). The general characteristic of the local soil is a moderately wet sandy loam with a blotched and crumbled B-horizon.

Type of structure

2

---

46   91.4% probability calibration, charcoal, KIA-45050: 2125 ± 25 BP.
47   88.2% probability calibration, calcined bone, KIA-45072: 2130 ± 25 BP.
48   95.4% probability calibration, charcoal, KIA-45065: 3305 ± 35 BP.
49   95.4% probability calibration, charcoal, KIA-45067: 2175 ± 30 BP.
50   KIA-45070: 2475 ± 30 BP and KIA-45071: 2370 ± 30 BP.

Dendermonde-Oud Klooster (B)

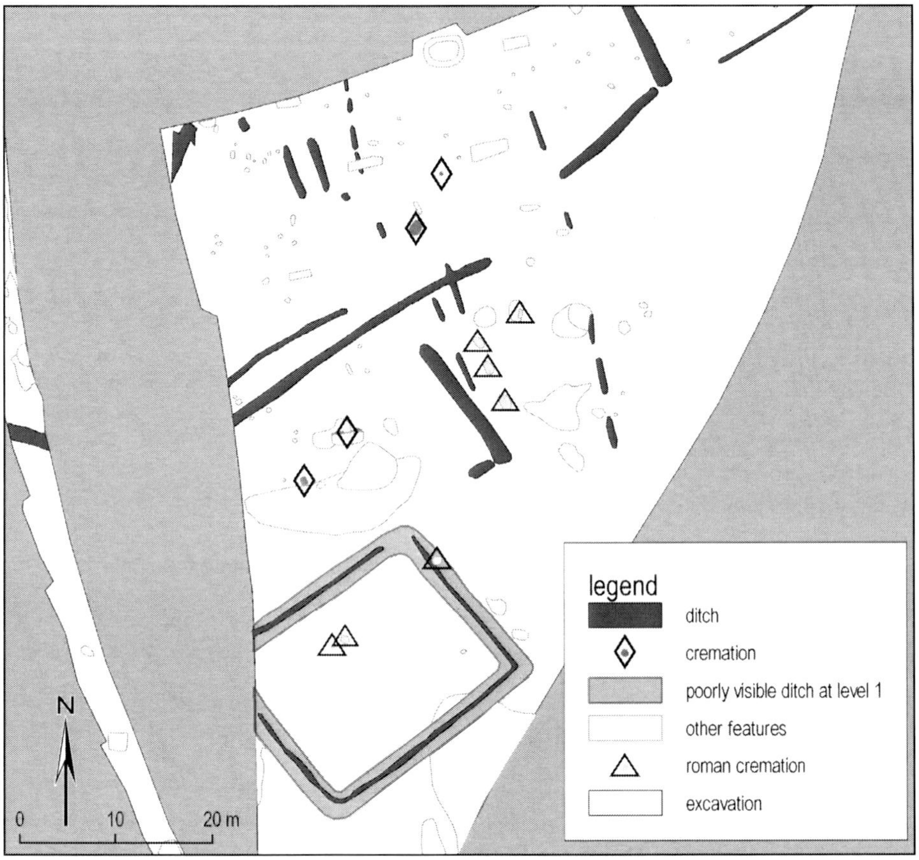

Figure A.9. Part of the excavation plan of Dendermonde-Oud Klooster (after Demey 2012). For colour version see fig. 5.12

The excavation in Dendermonde revealed a rectangular ditch and several fragments of a ditch system. An interpretation as *Viereckschanze* or *enclos cultuel* was proposed based on its shape and associated finds and features (Demey 2012, 29-32).

Rectangular structure

The structure is a rectangular ditch measuring 27 by 23 m, orientated from the southwest to the northeast (fig. A.9). The west corner of the structure was outside the research area and has not been excavated. The position of the site on the brown loamy sand of Flanders resulted in bad preservation and poor visibility of archaeological features. As a result, some features were documented as fragments, as for example several parts of the same ditch. The rectangular ditch was barely visible at the excavation level (fig. 5.12, light purple), but the bottom was better preserved (fig. A.9, dark purple). It seemed uninterrupted with a maximum width of 2.25m and 0.9m deep. The cross-section had a rounded, tapered (V-shaped?) profile.

Finds

In the rectangular ditch 117 pottery fragments were found, in addition to the 100 fragments that were found at the excavation surface while uncovering the structure (Demey 2012, 29-32). Most finds were collected on the northwest side, including the deposit of two situla-shaped pots dating between 400 and 150 BCE. A burnt bone found near the pottery concentration was carbon dated 395-206 calBCE.[51] Finds at the southern end of the annex ditch consisted of pottery, two grinding stone fragments, a sandstone and a large conical loom weight. At the northern end of the ditch fill a layer of charcoal was discovered, possibly representing a secondary deposition (Demey 2012, 31).

---

51   95.4% probability calibration, SUERC-37634/GU25769: 2255 ± 30 BP.

Associated features

Several ditches and remains thereof, were found north of the rectangular ditch (Demey 2012, 29-32). Only one could be dated as a contemporary, a fragment found northeast of the rectangular structure. The orientation suggests these two features were once connected, perhaps as some sort of annex. Four features have been interpreted as remains of contemporary cremation graves, even though two contained no bone fragments. One of the graves furthest to the north is an oval shaped pit with a deposition of charcoal and a large burned pottery dish dating 400-150 BCE. Additionally, at least seven Roman period cremation graves could be identified. One of the Roman cremation graves was found in the top of the ditch fill.

Landscape

The site is situated in the Dender valley, on the south-western flank of a height, a slightly elevated area surrounded on the western and northern sides by an old meander (Demey 2012, 6).

Type of structure

2

Destelbergen-Eenbeekeinde (B)

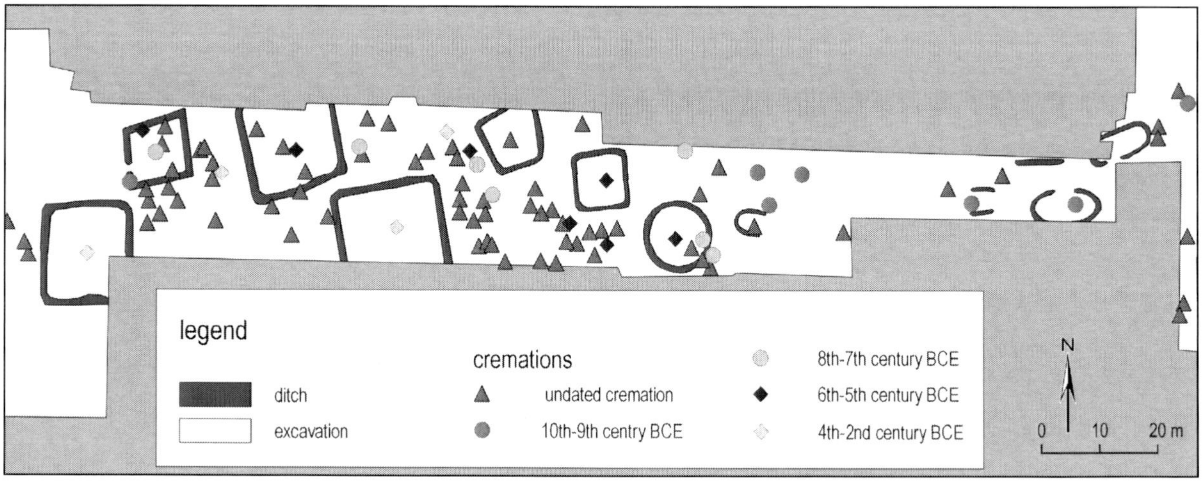

Figure A.10. Part of the excavation plan of the urnfield of Destelbergen. The structure interpreted by De Laet as a cult place is the second from the left (after De rue *et al.* 2012, figure 2 and Table 3, dates based on the 'weighted average mean of the probability density function of the calibrated date calBCE'). For colour version see fig. 4.3.

At first glance the cemetery in Destelbergen seems to be a regular medium sized urnfield, excavated between 1960 and 1984 (De Laet 1966; De Laet *et al.* 1985). The urnfield cemetery contained 105 graves. Four types of graves could be distinguished: cremation remains in an urn, cremation inside and outside of the urn mixed with charcoal from the pyre, cremation without an urn, and cremation remains with the pyre charcoal deposited in the top fill of a pit. Only twelve graves had a peripheral structure in the form of a ditch. One ditch was round, six were square(-ish) and five were parts of long barrows (fig. A.10). Twenty-six graves were carbon dated to determine the chronology and utilisation of the cemetery (De Rue *et al.* 2012). The long barrows and associated graves on the east side of the cemetery date to the Late Bronze Age, the others to the Early and Middle Iron Age. Apparently the cemetery spread out towards the west during its use.

Rectangular structure

The interpretation of the only square ditch with an opening as a cult place, after its excavation in the 1960s, is illustrative of the fact that it was the first square ditch to be excavated in an urnfield at the time and was also one with multiple graves (fig. A.10, top left ditch). The structure in question had a slightly diamond shaped square with sides of 11.6m in length, 1.2m wide (De Laet 1966). On the west side was an opening of 1.2m wide. The cross-section of this particular square ditch is not described, although a

similar feature on the site portrays a rounded bottom (De Laet 1985, fig. 5).

Finds and Associated features

The diamond shaped ditch enclosed five cremation graves and one in the ditch itself just south of the entrance (De Laet 1966). The grave situated in the exact centre of the structure, is assumed to be the reason for its construction. It consisted of a decorated urn with cremation remains placed in a shallow pit. The cremated remains were carbon dated to 783-517 calBCE, making it the oldest grave in the centre of a square ditch (De Mulder 2011, 167-170; De Rue *et al.* 2012).[52] Curiously the structure contained an older grave. Since this was the only grave not on the east side of the cemetery dating to the Late Bronze Age De Rue *et al.* (2012, 644) assume this grave was exhumed from another part of the cemetery and reburied in the ditch of the square monument, just south of the entrance. This provenance is debatable as there is no evidence, as for example in the form of an empty pit, so the urn and its cremation remains could also have come from another cemetery or from some entirely different place such as a house.

---

52 95.4% probability calibrated date, cremated bone, KIA-34892: 2495 ± 30 BP. Other graves in the centres of square ditches dated: 2320 ± 30 BP (KIA-34887), 2405 ± 40 BP (KIA-37706), 2215 ± 30 BP (KIA-30042), and 2450 ± 30 BP (KIA-37707).

Landscape

The site is situated on the slope near the left bank of the River Schelde, between the interfluvial plain of the river and the sandy ridges of the Schelde Valley (De Laet *et al.* 1985).

Type of structure

1

Erembodegem-Zuid-IV, phase 3, zone 1 (B)

Figure A.11. Part of the excavation plan of Erembodegem Zuid IV phase 3 zone 1 (after Verbrugge, De Graeve & Cherretté 2011, plate 3; digital site plan courtesy of SOLVA). For colour version see fig. 6.9.

The two rectangular structures found in Erembodegem were excavated in 2007 as one the first parts of a much larger project initiated by the development of an industrial estate. The structures were mentioned in an article by Van de Vijver, Wuyts & Cherretté (2009) and some of the results including the carbon dates were later incorporated in a report on additional excavations of the area (Verbrugge, De Graeve & Cherretté 2011).

Rectangular structures

The western structure (A) measured 16 × 14m (Van de Vijver, Wuyts & Cherretté 2009; fig. A.11). Due to the poor preservation state of the feature most of the north side was missing. The western structure (A) measured 16 × 14m. The ditch was only 0.25-0.30m wide and very shallow. Due to the poor preservation state of the feature most of the north side was missing. Charcoal obtained from the ditch fill dated to 371-199 calBCE.[53] Structure B was slightly better preserved measuring 13 × 11m. Its width was 0.25-0.45 m; the remaining depth also very shallow. Despite the depth, two samples were carbon dated from the fill of the ditch, with a combined result of 351-49 calBCE.[54]

Finds

The shallow remains of ditch A revealed a relative 'large amount' of pottery fragments (Vijver, Wuyts & Cherretté 2009). The pottery dates Late La Tène, possibly transitional period to Early Roman. Ditch B delivered 'a limited amount' of pottery fragments. The exact numbers were not published.

---

53 95.4% probability calibration, charcoal, 10cm below excavation level, KIA-43546: 2210 ± 30 BP.

54 95.4% probability calibrations, charcoal, 10cm below excavation level, KIA-43547: 2140 ± 25 BP and KIA-43549: 2115 ± 30 BP.

Associated features

Two pits in the interior of feature A are situated 6m from the south side and 4m from each other in a symmetrical layout (Vijver, Wuyts & Cherretté 2009). Both pits were approximately 1.35m long and 80cm deep. The multiple layered fill of the western pit contained some burned bone and pottery fragments. The eastern pit merely contained pottery. The only other features in the interior of both structures were two postholes. A couple of meters north of structure A an undated cremation grave was found. Structure B also enclosed a pit. It contained charcoal dating to 360-116 calBCE.[55] Thirty metres to the southwest another Iron Age ditch was found in 2011 that resembled the rectangular structures (Verbrugge, De Graeve & Cherretté 2011, 23). It was interpreted as one side remaining from a rectangle. Near the ditch, 26m south of structure A, fragments of a circular ditch were found, dating to the Middle Bronze Age A (Verbrugge, De Graeve & Cherretté 2011, 19). The enclosed charcoal pits are interpreted as graves containing pyre remains despite the fact that no cremation remains were identified (Vijver, Wuyts & Cherretté 2009).

Landscape

The area is located on the border between the loamy and the sandy soils, characterised by low hills and small stream valleys (Vijver, Wuyts & Cherretté 2009). The excavation is situated on the reasonably flat southern flank of the valley of the Molenbeek (Verbrugge, De Graeve & Cherretté 2011, 10). The loamy soil of the excavation surface is a dark brown colour that in most places resembles the B-horizon above, limiting the visibility of features (Verbrugge & De Graeve 2010.).

Type of structure

2

---

55   95.4% probability calibration, charcoal, 10cm below excavation
      level, KIA-43543: 2170 ± 30 BP.

Gronsveld-Duijsterstraat (NL)

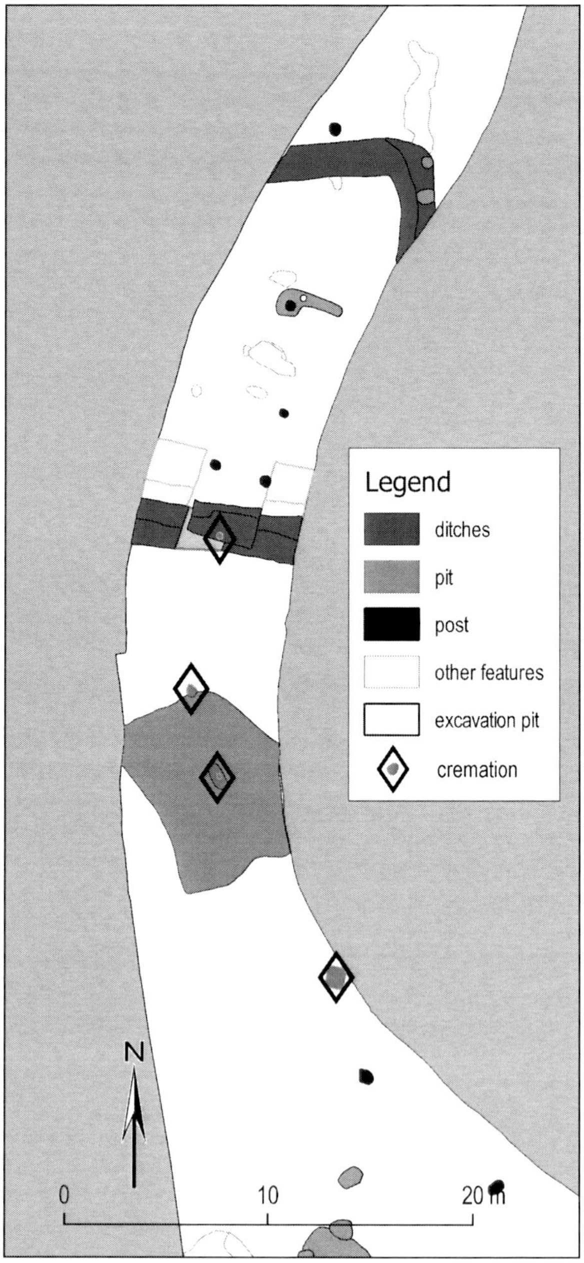

Figure A.12. Part of the excavation plan of Gronsveld-Duijsterstraat (after Van Dijk 2009). For colour version see fig. 5.11.

The odd-shaped excavation pit in Gronsveld was induced by a plan for a new water reservoir.

Rectangular structure

In the narrow pit one corner and part of three sides of a rectangular structure were unearthed (fig. A.12). Despite the incompleteness of the structure the ditches almost certainly belonged to the same structure with a width of about 14m (Van Dijk 2009, 43-45).

Finds

In a preliminary trial trench part of the south side of the structure was excavated. It contained a cremation grave with calcite bone fragments alongside two iron nails (Janssens 2008, 17). The undated cremation was placed in the top fill of the ditch.

Associated features

Three further cremation graves were uncovered south of the rectangular structure (Van Dijk 2009, 39-43; fig. A.12). Unfortunately none of the graves were carbon dated. Two of these contained some burned loam and several pieces of pottery, one contained an iron fibula typical for the Middle La Tène-period (ca. 250-150 BCE) and another grave contained several flint objects. One grave was in the middle of a large shallow pit. This pit was approximately 8 by 9m and contained 275 pieces of burned loam (3 kg), three stones and eleven flints artefacts. Flint may seem an unusual find in Iron Age features, but on this site it was littered with it. The abundance of flint can be explained by the proximity to the famous Rijckholt mines just over 1 km away, which produced during its prehistoric use a staggering 15 million kilos of flint material (Van Dijk 2009, 77; De Grooth 1998). Although the Iron Age represents the final stage of flint use, the sheer availability of artefacts at the site provoked the reuse of tools. Inside the structure only one pit was excavated, which could have served as a large posthole. Only four pieces of pottery were recovered from the fill. Three postholes were found on the south side of the inner space. Two small pits seem to have been dug in the fill of the ditch on the northeast side.

In the top fill of the ditch flints, stones, burned loam and six pottery pieces were found. These finds probably ended up in this fill much later as the culture layer above formed. On the basis of finds from several pits in the vicinity the site is dated to the Middle Iron Age (Van Dijk 2009, 5).

Some of the features could be representative of settlement activity and at the same time yield depositions. Van Dijk (2009, 80-91) brought forward an interpretation as a burial monument based on the cremation in the ditch, while leaving the possibility of a cult place open.

Landscape

The site is situated two-thirds down a slope with the higher löss plateau to the east and the Meuse valley to the west (Van Dijk 2009, 22). The location is relatively flat and unaffected by erosion. A colluvium covers the top 65 to 80cm of the site, thereby protecting the features from ploughing (Janssens 2007).

Type of structure

2?

Harelbeke-Evolis (B)

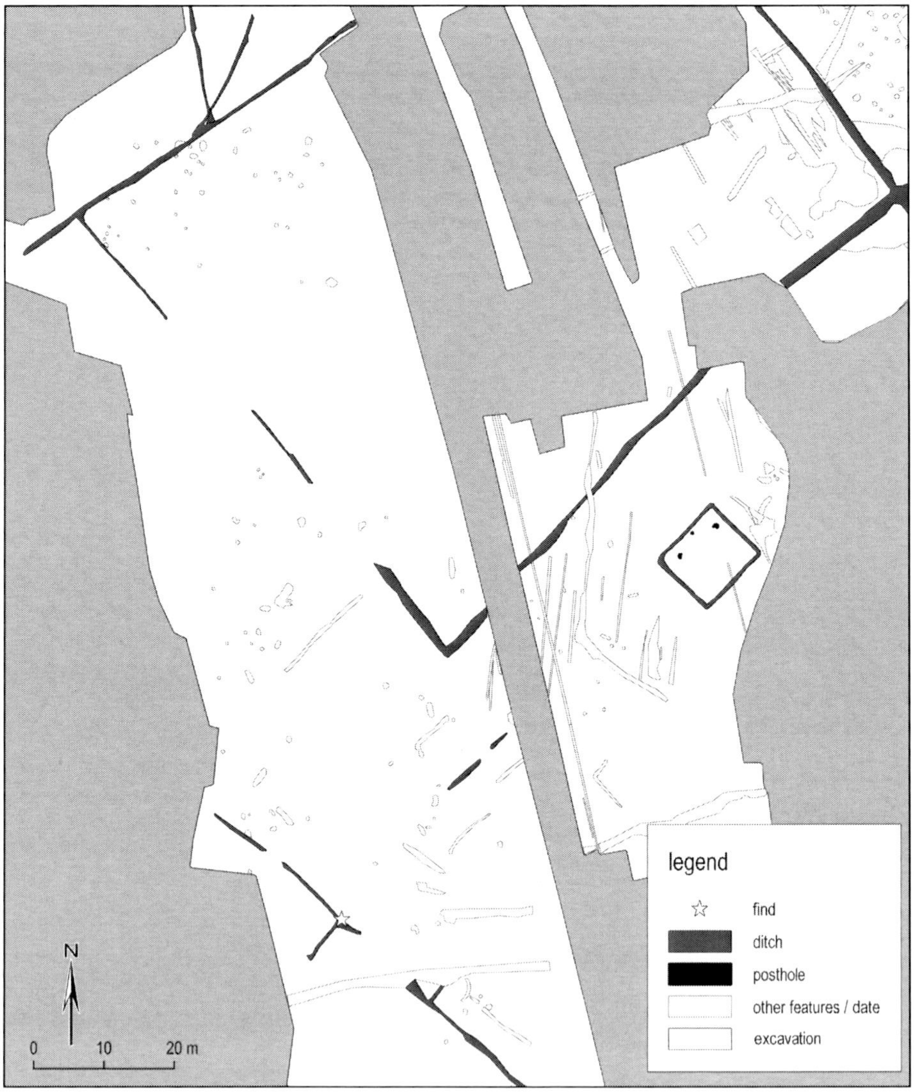

Figure A.13. Part of the excavation plan of Harelbeke-Evolis zone 1 (after De Logi *et al.* 2008, figure 14 and Messiaen *et al.* 2009, figure 1). For colour version see fig. 6.12.

The development of a 48 ha large industrial area was preceded by an archaeological trial trench project and several excavated areas of 2.5 ha in total (De Logi *et al.* 2008; Messiaen *et al.* 2009). The site of Kortrijk is 450m to the south (§6.4.1). The relation between the sites is discussed in §7.3. The large scale of the excavation provided insight in Late Iron Age to Early Roman land division systems. Besides the long linear ditches, a rectangular structure was found (fig. A.13).

Rectangular structure

The structure measured 11.5 × 10m and lay parallel to one of the linear ditches (De Logi *et al.* 2008, 18). No settlement features were found, apart from several postholes and two

pits on the west side (De Logi *et al.* 2008, 30). One of the pits contained 'a lot of pottery', which remained unspecified in the report.

Finds

The pottery assemblage found in the rectangular ditch fill was deemed 'too complete, too much and too uniform' to belong to ordinary settlement deposits (De Logi *et al.* 2008, 19). The 411 shards were concentrated in the south corner and in the fill of the southeast side (Messiaen *et al.* 2009). Pottery found in linear ditches prove their contemporaneity to the rectangular ditch. Near the junction of ditches in the southwest of the excavation (fig. A.13, star) a concentration of 577 shards of pottery were found dating to the Late Iron Age-Early Roman era (Messiaen *et al.* 2009).

Associated features

Enclosed by the rectangular ditch three postholes were found, positioned in a symmetrical layout (Messiaen *et al.* 2009). All three postholes had a remaining depth of around 30cm. The posts would have been 3.5m apart. Just 15m northwest of the rectangular ditch, a large rectangular ditch system of 89m by 78m was documented (De Logi *et al.* 2008, 19-29). The width of the linear ditches was approximately 0.7-0.8m and the remaining depth in the best preserved places around 40cm. The cross-sections showed a relatively shallow inclined V-shape with a flattish bottom. Charcoal from the ditch was dated to 198-47 calBCE (Messiaen *et al.* 2009).[56] The ditch connects at an oblique angle to another ditch on the northwest side. The southwest ditch system no longer connects, but still shows a similar orientation.

Based on the pottery finds in the ditch fill, the rectangular ditch was interpreted as a 'rural cult place' by De Logi *et al.* (2008, 39-41).

Landscape

The terrain is on a gradual slope, with the highest point a few hundred meters to the northwest at 33m above sea level, sloping down to the south and east to around 22m (De Logi *et al.* 2009, 6). The soil consists of brown sandy loam, with a 50-60cm thick upper layer that shows severe bioturbation phenomena causing poor preservation of the features.

Type of structure

6

---

56   95.4% probability calibration, charcoal, KIA-35561: 2100 ± 30 BP.

Haren-Groenstraat (NL)

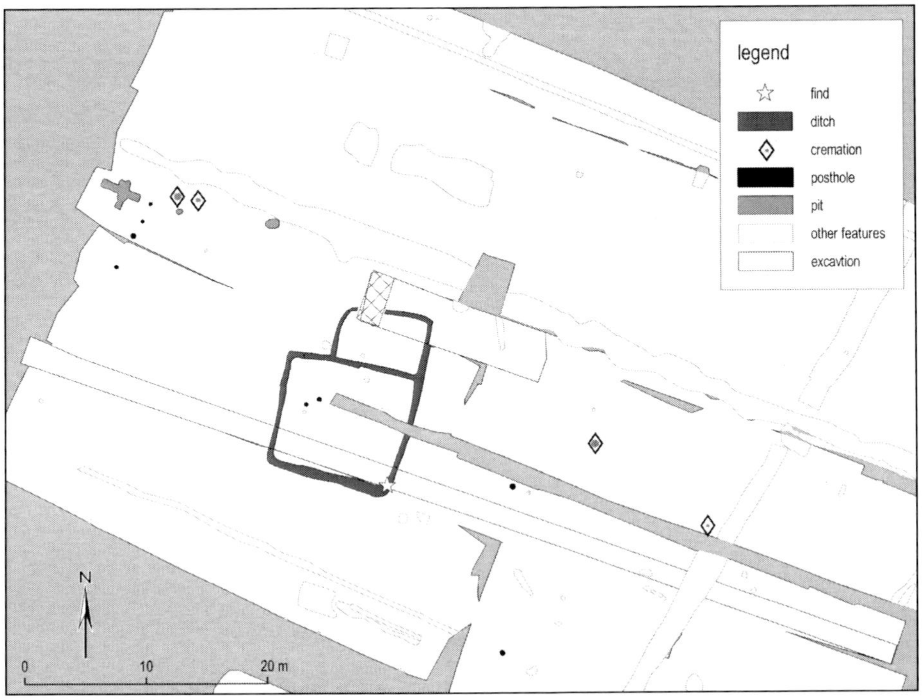

Figure A.14. Part of the excavation plan of Haren-Groenstraat (after Knippenberg 2013, figure 7.1 and Schurmans 2011, figure 10). For colour version see fig. 6.7.

The site of Haren-Groenstraat was selected for excavation because of Neolithic finds in the test trenches (Knippenberg 2013, 7). The main excavation method was in 50×50cm squares that were sieved in 5cm thick layers. The Iron Age component of the site was an unexpected by-catch.

Rectangular structures

The ditches of an Iron Age enclosure were found in the trial trenches, but for some reason were thought to date to the post-Medieval period (Schurmans 2011, 21). A short broad trench was dug through the northern part of the structure and a long narrow one through the southern part. The relative shallow position of the Iron Age features underneath the top soil caused them to be damaged by ploughing activities (Van der Leije & Knippenberg 2013). A larger and a smaller rectangular structure were found, connected to each other (fig. A.14). The larger rectangle measured 10.5 by 8.5m and the smaller one north of it just 7.2 by 4.7m. The width of the ditches varied between 25 and 90 cm, while the remaining depth was only 10 to 25cm.

Finds

In the southeast corner of the larger rectangular ditch rim fragments of a Late Iron Age pot and a slingshot bullet were found (Meurkens 2013; fig. A.14, star). Due to the trial trench running through it only part of the pot remained, near the excavation surface.[57] The bottom of the pot might have been near the bottom of the ditch. In the trial trench over the southern ditch two Iron Age pottery fragments were found, but the exact location is not mentioned in the report (Schurmans 2011, 24-25).

Associated features

One posthole was found inside the ditch. Four cremation graves were spread out over the excavation area, two 15 to 30m east of the rectangular structure and two 20m northwest. The graves were found incomplete due to their shallow position. Only the underside of small pits with a cremation remained. In one grave the fragmented bottom of an urn was found. Carbon dating of two cremated remains resulted in 732-397 calBCE and 522-383 calBCE.[58]

Landscape

The site is situated on the eastern edge of a Pleistocene river dune (Heunks 2013). The dune is slightly elevated

---

57 Pers. comm. S. Knippenberg.

58 95.4% probability calibrations, BETA-326227: 2400 ± 35 BP and BETA-326229: 2360 ± 30 BP.

compared to the surrounding alluvial plain. To the east lies an extinct gully of the Haren river belt, a predecessor to the Meuse that became inactive by the Early Bronze Age.

The ditch structure in Haren is interpreted by Van der Leije & Knippenberg (2013, 82-83) as a burial monument based on its limited size and the burials in the vicinity. However, these burials can be dated to the Middle Iron Age, so they may be unrelated to the structure.

Type of structure
2

Hever-Stationsstraat (B)

Figure A.15-1. Part of the excavation plan of Hever-Stationsstraat. (after Jezeer 2015). For colour version see fig. 5.8.

The oldest features in the excavation in Hever are two Bronze Age pits situated within a half circular ditch. A large rectangular enclosure crossed over the other half of the circular ditch (fig. A.15-1).

Rectangular structure

The length of the rectangular is approximately 38m (centre to centre) and the width is approximately 15m. The ditch has a width of about 1.6m and a recorded depth of 25-45cm and V-shaped in cross section. The filling of the trench was brown-grey to dark brown-grey. According to Jezeer (2015, 20) the ditch filled in three stages (fig. A.15-2, left). However, when compared to

a similar feature (fig. A.15-2, right) it is possible that the ditch contained another, deeper fill that was not excavated. Also, Jezeer concluded the ditch was redug several times. This is not apparent from the cross-section depicted in the report.

Finds

Compared to other sites, the rectangular structure in Hever contained few pottery shards and was very shallow. Only 63 pieces of pottery were collected, mostly deriving from the southwest corner and the northeast corner respectively, where the pottery was found scattered over a small area (*Ibid.*, 21). The half circular ditch enclosed within

Figure A.15-2. Cross section of the rectangular ditch (left; source: Jezeer, 2015, figure 15) and the slightly bend ditch (right; source: Jezeer, 2015, figure 17).

the rectangular ditch contained a complete dish, which was placed at the bottom, dating between 450 and 375 BCE (fig. 5.8, yellow star).

Associated features

Just over 50m west of the rectangular structure another large ditch was found. It slightly curves from southwest to northeast over a distance of at least 40m. The ditch had a similar appearance to the rectangular feature (fig. A.15-2, right). It also seem to have filled in different stages (Jezeer 2015, 22). Adjacent, a palisade was found with an interruption on the north side. A pit is positioned in front of this 'opening'. No description of this pit was included in the report.

A total of 23 cremation graves were found, of which only four were carbon dated (Jezeer 2015, 26-33). Most were clustered east of the rectangular structure; six were inside the rectangle structure with a seventh in the ditch. One grave lay on the far west side of the excavation. Two centrally located graves within the rectangular structure were carbon dated to 401-209 calBCE and 376-201 calBCE.[59] Two graves from the eastern cluster dated earlier, 731-397 calBCE and 413-232 calBCE.[60]

Another feature that can be associated to the rectangular structure was a four-posted structure in the north side of the interior, measuring 3m x 1.8m. The eastern postholes of this structure contained a lot of charcoal. No finds were recovered from the postholes, but the association was based on the orientation and central position within the rectangle. A single gram worth of cremation remains was found in the southwest posthole. It is unknown whether any Iron Age pits or other types of features were found in- or outside the rectangular structure. These were not mentioned in the report.

The two Bronze Age pits measured 1 to 1.2m in length and were dated on the basis of a loom weight and a flint arrow head to the Early to Middle Bronze Age. Some pottery fragments were also recovered but could not be accurately dated. Two other circular ditches were found, of which the one 30m to the east was only partly uncovered, while the one 77m to the west was entirely excavated.

Landscape

The site in Hever lies on a relatively flat area that drains into a brook 300m to the east (Smeets & Vander Ginst 2013). The soil consists of loamy sand, is quite waterlogged and covered by a thick anthropogenic humid A-horizon.

Type of structure

2

---

59   95.4% probability calibrations, resp. KIK-10414: 2273 ± 32 BP and KIK-10415: 2216 ± 32 BP.

60   95.4% probability calibration of resp. KIK-10416: 2394 ± 32 BP and KIK-10417: 2310 ± 32 BP.

Houten-Castellum (NL)

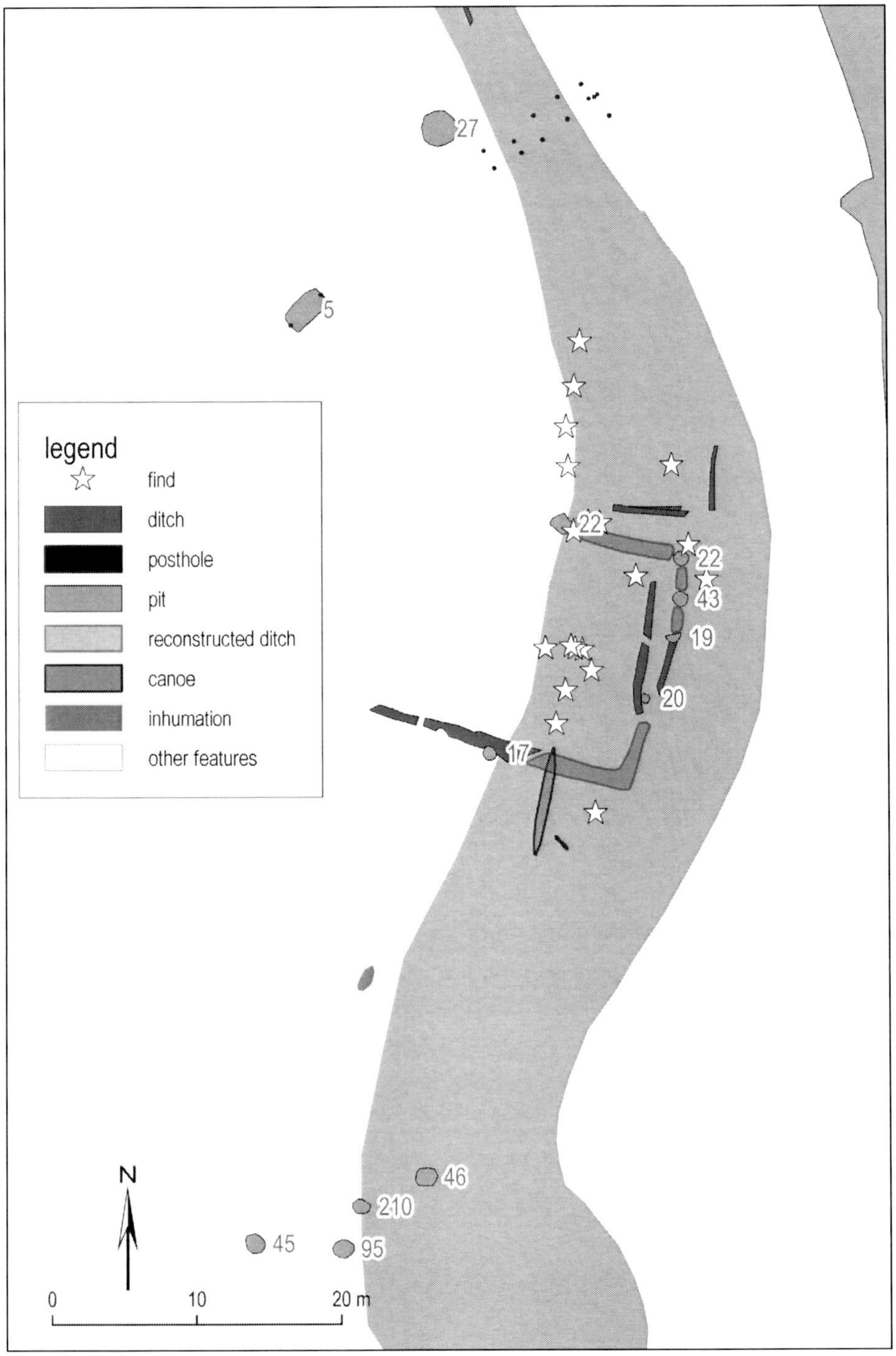

Figure A.16. Part of the excavation plan of Houten-Castellum displaying the residual channel (light blue) Middle Iron Age features and some of the associated finds. The posts of one of the small bridges can be seen near pit 27. For colour version see fig. 5.2.

In contrast to most of the other sites discussed here, Houten-Castellum is characterised by a wet environment. During the Iron Age several small river channels were active in the area (Van Renswoude & Habermehl 2017).

In the Middle and Late Iron Age most on site activities were related to a particular residual channel. The remains of two small bridges were found with two fish hoop nets between them. The best preserved bridge was 8m long and 1.4 wide, the base consisting of 10 posts. Most of the posts were made of alder and some had a remaining length of 1m in situ. The bridge was carbon dated to the 5th century BCE (Van Renswoude 2017, 111-113). Further south, an inhumation grave was discovered along with an rectangular structure that was interpreted as a place for ancestor worship (fig. A.16).

Rectangular structure

The rectangular structure was reconstructed after the excavation, as the excavation took place in different pits complicating the documentation of the feature as a whole (Van Renswoude et al. 2017, 1115). It measured approximately 18 by 16m and was positioned half in the residual channel and half on the river bank (Van Renswoude 2017, 115). On the bank the ditch was 10 to 20cm deep, sloping down to the channel 70cm lower, where it had a depth of 60cm.

Finds

In the best documented southern ditch only 35 pottery shards and 13 bone fragments were found (Van Renswoude et al. 2017, 986). The pottery was just enough to date the feature to the late Middle Iron Age. This amount was relatively small in comparison to the layers of the channel, where a total of 81221 pieces of Middle Iron Age pottery were found and 118 ceramic objects (mostly loom weights, spindle whorls and slingshot bullets) and 344 Iron Age metal objects, of which 132 dated to the Middle Iron Age. At least 41 pots were deliberately destroyed by chopping off the bottom (Habermehl & Sinke 2017). Middle Iron Age layers contained 24382 bones of which 2588 were analysed (Groot & Van Haasteren 2017). They belonged mostly to cattle, along with sheep/goat and some pig, horse, red deer, wild cat and grey seal. Nearly all finds originated from the south side of the excavation, not near the two bridges, but rather around the rectangular structure and also south of that.

Middle Iron Age iron objects (fig. A.16, stars) that were found in the rectangular structure were a needle, two fibulae, a ring, two belt hooks, and a spear head. Just outside the structure more iron objects were recovered, among which were three more needles, two fibulae, a clamp, five belt hooks and two other spear heads. Several Middle Iron Age pits were documented, both in the ditch and in the vicinity of the structure. Pits 19-22 and 43 are

situated in line with the ditches of the enclosure (Van Renswoude 2017). The pits are between 56 and 106cm deep with straight sides like a shaft and contained some unusual finds. Pit 19 contained a 1.8 kg heavy fragment of a grinding stone while in pit 20 a piece of a human skull and deer antlers with use-wear traces on them were found. Pit 22 revealed a whole human cranium, pottery and a spindle whorl, and pit 43 yielded another large grinding stone fragment. The skull from pit 22, along with a skull found in the channel, showed damage that could be ascribed to displaying them on a stake: both craniums were damaged by a force or tool from below (Panhuysen 2017).

Associated features

An inhumation grave was found only 17m south of the rectangular structure. It held the remains of a 18 to 22 year old individual on its side in a crouched position (*Ibid.* 2017). Due to erosion parts were missing. No grave goods were found. The grave could be dated between 350 and 250 BCE, so possibly contemporary to the rectangular structure.

Pit 5 northeast of the enclosure turned out to be a shallow (10 cm) rectangular pit of 3.2 by 1.7 m, with four posts at the corners (Van Renswoude 2017). This pit would have been covered by a light roof. Pit 27 near the southern small bridge was also quite large. The diameter measured around 2.25m and the depth was 84cm containing a total of six consecutive fills. It held 189 pieces of pottery and 53 fragments of bone. Pits 45, 46 and 95 south of the structure contained few finds despite their reasonable size, except for pit 210 that uncovered 335 pieces of pottery, 74 fragments of bone (cattle, sheep/goat and pig), 27 fragments of wood, 6 pieces of charcoal, an iron ring, some burned loam and several stones. Both pit 95 and pit 210 had a shaft-like appearance comparable to the pits in between the ditches.

The most remarkable find was a 7m long dugout canoe, made of alder wood. It would appear the canoe was found directly underneath the southern ditch of the structure, at a slightly deeper level. The association with the rectangular structure is unclear and not described by the excavators. On the bases of the layer it was found in, the object most likely dates to the 5th century BCE, although the cabon date suggests it is older.[61]

The rectangular structure is interpreted as a enclosure used for an ancestral or death cult (Van Renswoude & Habermehl 2017, 881-883). Also, four human skeletal remains had cutting marks and a further five displayed gnaw marks, both indications of excarnation (Panhuysen 2017). The four-posted structure over pit 5 could have served such a purpose. At least three human skulls, possibly four, and an inhumation grave

---

61   95.4% probability calibration, Poz-81647: 2273 ± 32 BP.

could be attributed to the Middle Iron Age (*Ibid.* 2017, 741, table 15.3). Other human skeletal remains were found, but no overview of their date or their context is given in the report. Some finds are interpreted as depositions, among those a rare large pot typical for the period 450-400 BCE (Sinke 2017). It was found along with a piglet skeleton and a burned spindle whorl and basically proves this was a site used for depositions since the 5th century BCE.

Landscape

Each residual channel represents an active period of the main channel of the Houten current belt. (Ter Wal 2012, 52). The residual channels suggest a strong migration of the actively meandering main channel, where meandering bends were cut off from time to time. The site is located on the western edge of a strip of sand deposits within the Houten Channel Belt (Boreel 2017). The environment on the banks of the channel during the Middle Iron Age are described as swampy (Van Renswoude 2017, 115). The landscape was open, with spread out patches of trees and some dispersed willows and alders next to the channel (Kooistra 2017). Nearby there would have been fields and grass lands.

Type of structure

3

Itteren-Emmaus (NL)

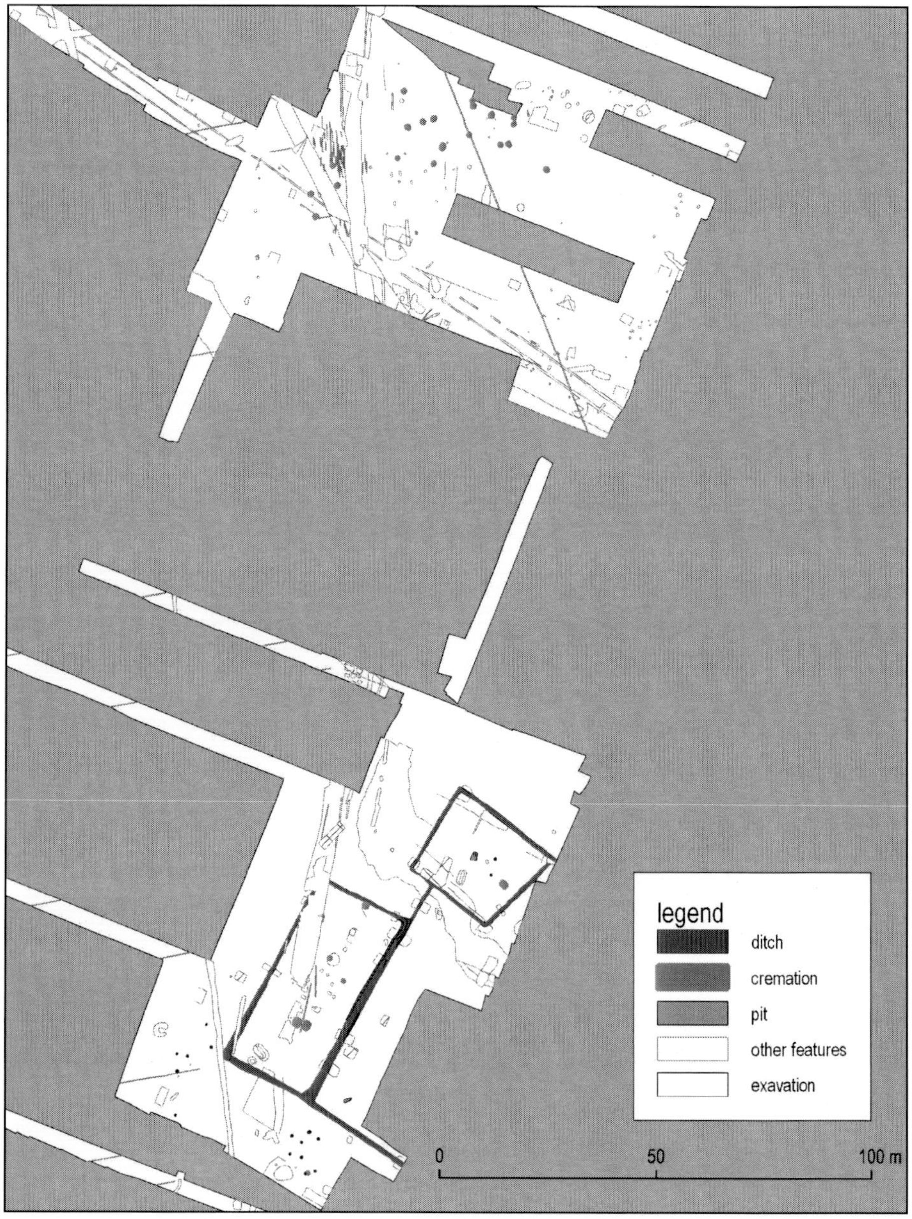

Figure A.17-1. Excavation plan of both cemeteries at Itteren-Emmaus (After Meurkens & Tol 2011, figures 6.1, 6.11 and 8.3). For colour version see fig. 8.2.

The excavation of Itteren-Emmaus consists of two separate locations (Meurkens & Tol 2011).

The northern site revealed twenty cremation graves dating to the Middle to Early Late Iron Age (Meurkens 2011). The cremated bone fragments were placed in a small pit, sometimes with some of the charred pyre remains. At least twelve adults were identified, of which two or three females and five possible males, as well as three juveniles and two toddlers.

Rectangular structures

The largest rectangular structure was partly destroyed by an old road that crossed it from north to south (fig. A.17-1). It measured 47 × 22 m, and consisted of a V-shaped ditch of 70cm deep that was maximum 170cm wide (Meurkens & Tol 2011, 70-71). Charcoal from the top fill provides a terminus ante quem (end date) of 374-162 calBCE for the construction of the ditch.[62]

Another better preserved structure was trapezium shaped and had a cross sections showing a V-shaped ditch of maximum 120cm wide and 80cm deep, with a narrow flat bottom (Meurkens & Tol 2011, 61-62; fig. A.17-2). The ditch seemed to have filled in two phases. The bottom fill consisted of thin layers of sediments, showing that the ditch gradually filled. The upper half filled faster, as it had a 'cleaner' appearance. Two 14C-dates revealed a contemporary structure, as charcoal collected from the bottom and the top of the ditch dated to 383-186 calBCE.[63] A third linear ditch apparently connecting the two rectangular ones could be followed over a distance of 57m northeast to southwest, where it continues its course at a 90 degree angle to the southeast over at least 26m (Meurkens 2011). The larger rectangle seems to cut over the linear ditch that had a fill that looked similar to that of the trapezium ditch.

Finds

In the northwest corner of the trapezium ditch a deposit of pottery fragments was found, probably belonging to a single pot (Meurkens 2011a). In the centre of the west side of the same structure an almost complete pot was found that appeared to be secondarily burned. The grave inside the trapezium belonged to a woman aged 20-40 years who died between 387 and 204 calBCE (Meurkens 2011, 73-77; Baetsen 2011).[64]

The large rectangular and the linear ditch only held 95 fragments of pottery combined. Most of that originated in a pottery concentration at the southwest corner of the large rectangle where the linear ditch bends to the southeast. The pottery dated to the 3rd or 2nd century BCE.

Associated features

Six Iron Age cremation graves were found at this location, confined within two large rectangular connected ditches (fig. A.17-1). As both cemeteries are contemporary they could be considered as a whole, but given the distance between them I review the southern one as a separate site for now.

Of the cremation graves five were found in the large rectangular structure and one in the trapezium. The two large cremation graves in the southern half of the large ditch contained mostly charcoal, the others only cremation remains (Meurkens 2011, 77-78). Burials in the

Figure A.17-2. Cross section of the trapezium shaped ditch (source photo: Archol B.V.).

large rectangle were dated between 386 and 163 calBCE.[65] One of the graves belonged to a man aged 30-50 (figure A.17-1, centre, next to Roman cremation) and one to a child (Baetsen 2011). The others could not be determined. Associated pottery and La Tène bracelets limits the date of these graves to the latter half of the 3rd century BCE (Meurkens 2011, 74-77; Van de Geer 2011).

At the northern location a round pit with a layer of burned material was also found, containing among other finds the shards of at least five secondary burned pots. It measured 85cm in diameter, had a depth of 30cm and was carbon dated to 780-417 BCE (Meurkens 2011a, 93-94).

Landscape

The site is situated on the transitional area where a relatively high part of the Meuse valley slopes down to a lower laying area with several channels (Heunks 2011). During the Iron Age the lower areas would have been prone to occasional flooding, mostly unfit for habitation or farming activities. The border between wet and dry, and between higher and lower grounds would have been clearly defined by both relief and vegetation. Pollen analysed from the lower fill of the large rectangular ditch pointed towards the edge of a forest or an open forest (Van Haaster 2011). This included alders that would have been near the water, and hazels that would have been on the higher grounds. Pollen of grasses was also included, indicating a use of grassland.

Type of structure

2

---

62   Calibration with 93.8% probability; Poz-36376: 2180 ± 35 BP.

63   95.4% probability calibration of the top Poz-36378: 2205 ± 35 BP and the bottom Poz-36415: 2210 ± 35 BP.

64   95.4% probability calibration, cremated bone, Poz-36214: 2230 ± 30 BP.

65   95.4% probability calibrations, cremated bone, resp. Poz-36215: 2210 ± 40 BP, Poz-36216: 2175 ± 30 BP, and Poz-38436: 2220 ± 40 BP.

Kemzeke-Kwakkel (B)

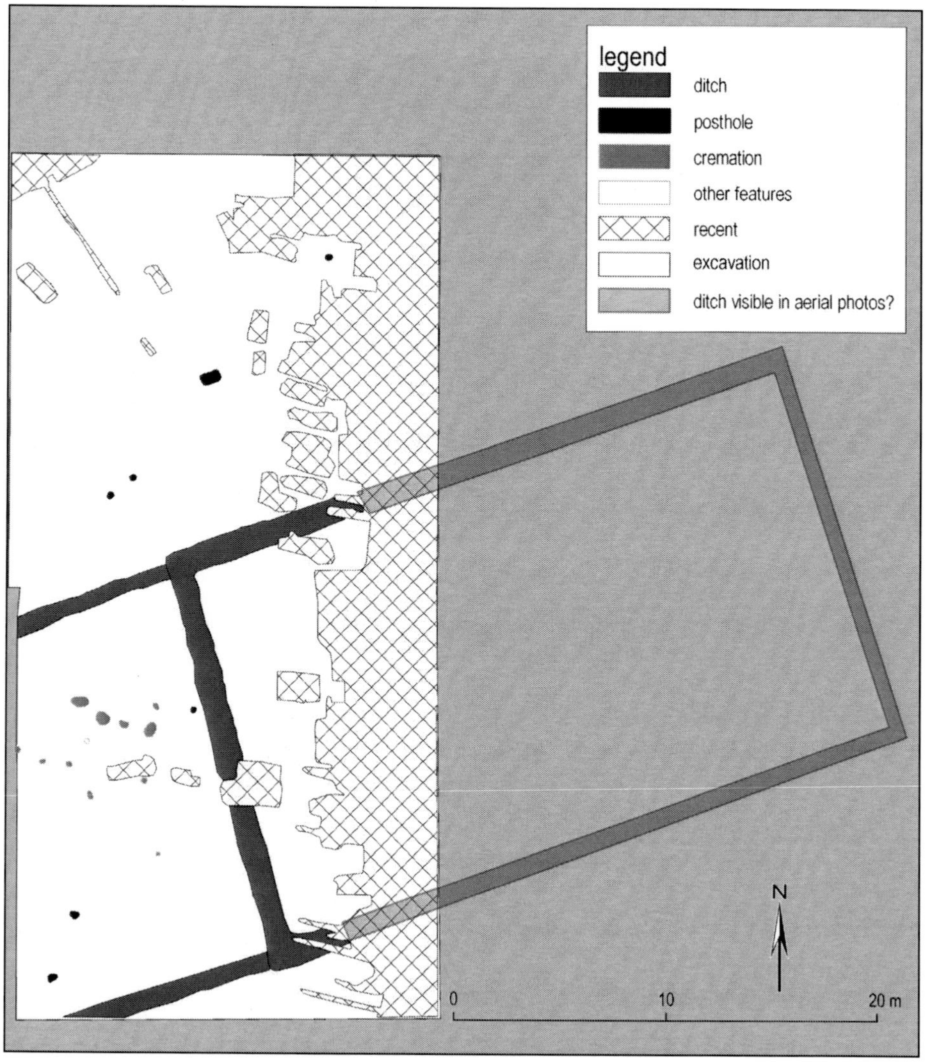

Figure A.18. The excavation plan of Kemzeke-Kwakkel, with the supposed eastern part based on the description and aerial photographs (after Bourgeois 1991).

The excavation area was selected on the basis of aerial photos (Bourgeois 1991). A rectangular feature was recognised from the air and the western part of it excavated in 1988 (fig. A.18). Subsequent fieldwork was planned but never executed.

Rectangular structures

The limited excavation of 1988 revealed two structures. On the west side two parallel ditches were excavated over a short distance. These two ditches seem to make out one structure of about 18.5m wide (structure A), while a U-shaped ditch on the east side represented the second one (structure B).

The ditches of structure A were filled in two different phases. The bottom layer showed humic layers alternating with thin layers of leached grey white sand. The top fill consisted of relatively homogeneous brown sand rich in humus and bioturbation.

Finds

Most of the finds from structure A were uncovered in the upper fill of the ditches: 154 pottery shards and several fragments of iron bracelets (Bourgeois 1991). The pottery could typologically be dated to the Early La Tène period, between 475 and 400 BCE.

Structure B was of a later date than A as it cuts over. The northern ditch could be followed for about 10 m, but the eastern part of the structure was severely disturbed. Judging by the aerial photo, originally the structure was a rectangle of around 30m in length by a width of 19m. About 400 sherds were found in the upper fill of structure B, but these were too fragmented for an accurate date. No carbon dating was executed. The three stage fill of the ditch had a yellow-brown humic layer on the bottom, then a layer of yellow ferric sand and at the top a thick homogeneous grey-black layer. According to Bourgeois (1991, 38) soil sample analysis shows that the ditches of structure B were not open for very long, apparently after only a few days or weeks the ditches were filled in and the monument was erased from the landscape. The statement concerning the fast filling of the ditches is insufficiently substantiated by the evidence presented in the article by Bourgeois (1991) or in the palynological contribution by Heim (1991). The cross sections show different layers, which are interpreted as different phases in which the ditches were filled (Bourgeois 1991, fig. 11; Heim 1991). Bourgeois seems to have based his hypothesis on the evidence presented in the pedological and palynological analysis of Aalter (see §5.4.1; Langohr & Fechner 1991).

Associated features

Twelve cremation graves were found between the ditches of structure A (Bourgeois 1991). Originally this could have been a higher number as with some graves only a few centimetres remained. Eight of the cremation remains were placed in a small pit mostly without grave goods and four accompanied by some burned pyre wood. One grave contained a bowl and a situla shaped vase that could be dated to the Early La Tène period, one contained several iron nails and another had a different type of bowl typical for the 5th century BCE. The excavators initially assumed all graves dated to the 5th century BCE, but additional research revealed a prolonged use of the cemetery as two graves were dated to 204-51 calBCE and 161 calBCE-20 calCE (De Mulder *et al.* 2020).[66] Other than the graves, only several postholes were documented. They did not contain any material.

Landscape

The last Middle Iron Age site of this type is situated on a small sandy ridge, with a northeast to southwest orientation only 1 or 2m elevated over the nearby fields (Bourgeois 1991). To the northwest, the site is bordered by small stream, the Brandakkerbeek. Analysis of pollen from in the lower fill of the ditch shows a mixed deciduous forest, dominated by lime, alder and hazel and some plum, oak, maple and holly, and a few grasses and ferns (Heim 1991).

Type of structure
Undetermined

---

66   95.4% probability calibrations, cremated bone, resp. RICH-27017: 2116 ± 27 BP, RICH-27056: 2046 ± 25 BP.

Knesselare-Westervoorde (B)

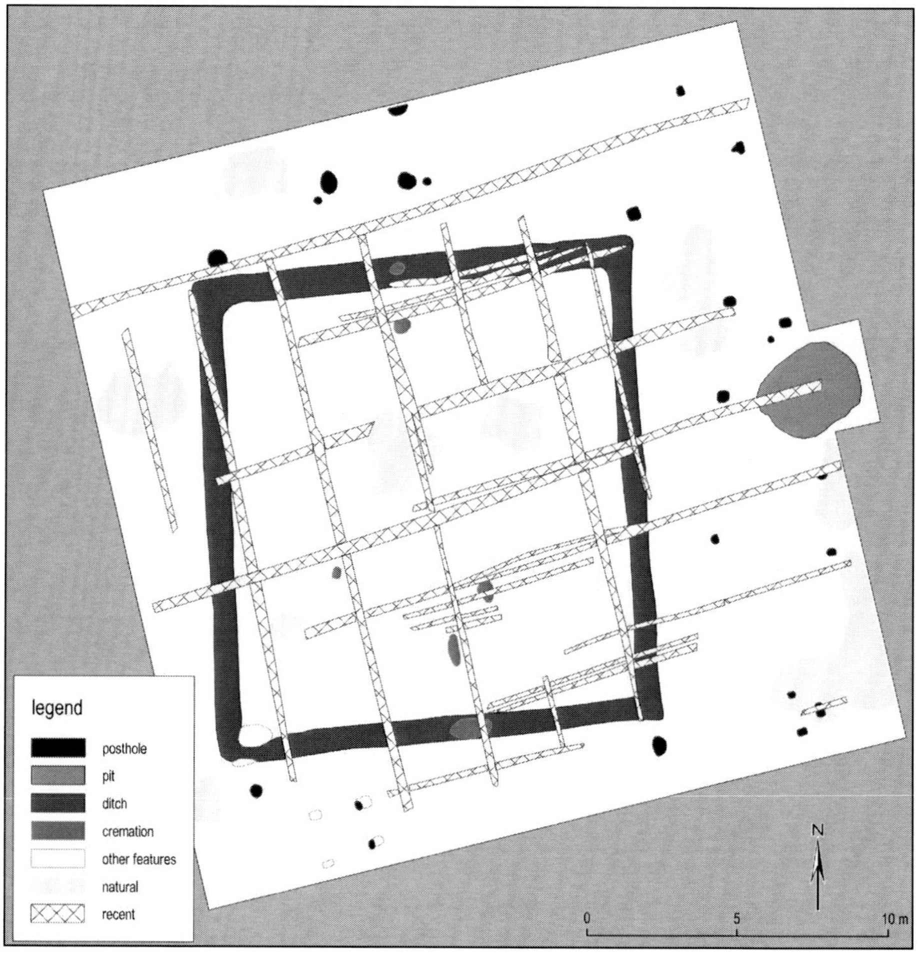

Figure A.19. The excavation plan of Knesselare-Westervoorde (after Vermeulen & Hageman 1997, figure 2). For colour version see fig. 6.6.

The excavation of the Westervoorde site in Knesselare is only known by a four page publication (Vermeulen & Hageman 1997) and an aerial photo by J. Semey (Martens 2007, 33). The excavation in 1996 was focused on the rectangular structure, as it was noticed on aerial photos as part of a project surveying a Roman road (Vermeulen & Hageman 1997). As a result only a limited area around the structure was excavated. The structure was interpreted by Vermeulen and Hageman (1997) as a 'ritual enclosure'.

Rectangular structures

The rectangular structure was found several tens of metres from the Roman road, but with a different orientation. It measured 15.6 × 14.8m (fig. A.19). The ditch was 0.7-1.0m wide, and showed a variable bowl- or V-shaped profile in cross-sections. The remaining depth was 26-52cm. The fill of the ditch showed two phases, of which the lower one

filled in over a period of weeks or months after the ditch was dug (*Ibid.* 1997).

Finds

In the ditch 60 pottery shards were found (*Ibid.* 1997). The pottery could be dated to the Late Iron Age. The cremation on the south side in the ditch yielded 42 pottery shards.[67] After publication of the article, charcoal from the ditch was dated to 166 calBCE -20 calCE.[68] In one of the large postholes north of the midsection of the rectangular structure a large fragment of an upside down pot was

---

67 These 42 were probably included in the 60 named earlier, but this is not entirely clear from the article.

68 95.4% probability calibration, charcoal, KIK-689/UtC-5373: 2050 ± 30 BP.

found. The pot was of a similar date as the pottery from the ditch.

Associated features

Numerous postholes were discovered around the structure (*Ibid.* 1997). The fill of the postholes resembled the appearance of the ditch. Most noticeable were four postholes near the corners of the ditch. Given the limited size of the excavation, no other structures could be identified. In the interior of the structure four poorly preserved cremation graves were found. Additionally, both in the northern and the southern ditch cremation remains were found. These were both dug in the ditch fill before it was entirely filled. In and outside of the rectangular structure several tree fells were documented. As these could not be dated, their association to other features is unknown. East of the structure a large 3.5m pit was found. The pit was 70cm deep and appeared to have been an open feature for a substantial length of time, visible by thin and humic layers. The top fill contained chunks of iron concretions and 300 fragments of Early Roman miniature pots and small beakers.

Landscape

The excavation surface was reasonably flat, about 400m away from the steep edge of the Ursel cuesta (*Ibid.* 1997). The soil consisted of loamy sand with a high groundwater level.

Type of structure

2

Kontich-Alfsberg (B)

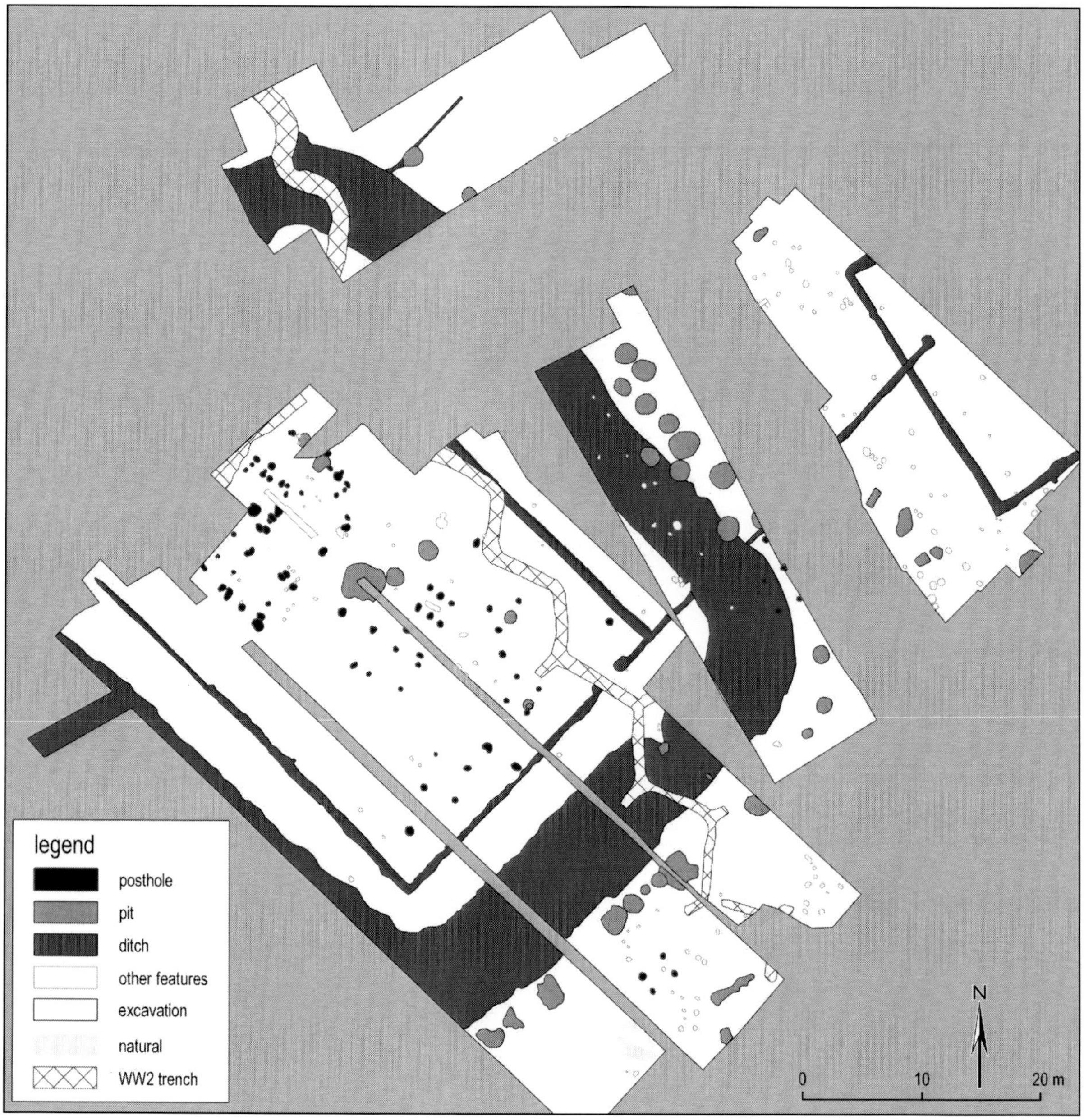

Figure A.20. The excavation plan of Kontich-Alfsberg (after Annaert 1993, figure 3 and 5; Annaert 1995, plate 1). For colour version see fig. 6.17.

The Alfsberg in Kontich is a complex site, even more so as a result of the limited size of the excavations that took place in 1972-73, 1990-92 (Annaert 1993) and 1995 (Annaert 1995/1996).

Rectangular structures

The most prominent feature of the excavations was a 7-8m wide and 4m deep moat that was entirely filled in by the beginning of the Roman era (fig. A.20; Annaert 1995/1996). On the inside of the moat, at a constant distance of 4 m, a narrow rectangular ditch was documented (Annaert 1993). In cross-sections it appeared U-shaped with steep sides and a flat bottom, a cross-section that is interpretable as a bedding trench. The fill of this feature showed the impressions of small posts (6-10cm diameter) forming a palisade which had been fixed in position by filling the ditch with sand from one side and iron concretion lumps from the other. When the moat was dug, the soil was probably deposited on the inside, creating a bank (Annaert 1993). The presence of a bank was assumed on the basis of features resembling badger setts in the empty area between the moat and the palisade ditch.

Finds

The fill of the narrow palisade ditch only yielded eight pieces of pottery, but as an extension of the palisade is overlapped by the moat, it must predate the construction of the moat (Annaert 1993, Annaert 1995/1996). The moat was much richer in finds, but only three sections were made, and the finds only came from the top two layers dating to the early Roman era. As the result of the originally steep sides (60-65 degrees), the lower part of the moat filled quite fast, mainly soil that slid down to a stable equilibrium at an angle of 32-39 degrees (Fechner & Langohr 1993). No construction date is known for the moat and no carbon dates are available for the site.

Associated features

In the interior of the ditch many postholes and several pits were found. Based on pottery finds, Annaert (1993) interpreted these features as a Middle Iron Age settlement, predating the ditch and moat. The exception is the larger building on the northwest side, which according to Annaert (1993; 1995) was contemporary to the ditch or the moat, based on the similar orientation. The charred remains in the postholes indicated the building was burned down, an event that, based on a single pottery fragment, took place in Early Roman times. The fact that hardly any features in the excavation overlap, the empty region between the moat and the ditch, combined with the poor dating of the features makes a Middle to Late Iron Age date for the ditch as well as the moat possible. A large pit in the centre of the enclosed interior yielded Roman pottery in the fill, as did the few pits that were sectioned on the outside along with the part of another rectangular ditch on the east side of the excavation (Annaert 1993; Annaert 1995/1996). The pits on the outside were interpreted as silos based on shape and content (seeds).

Landscape

The site is situated on a cuesta with a northeast to southwest orientation (Annaert 1993). The southern flank slopes down gently towards a stream, while the northern slope is steeper and ends 10m lower in a swampy area. The soil consists of loamy sand that harboured a reasonably open natural landscape in the (Late?) Iron Age with an alder forest and some hazel, oak, lime and beech trees (Fechner & Langohr 1993; Cooremans 1995). Much of the sand on the site has disappeared over the centuries due to erosion and quarrying (Annaert 1995/1996).

Type of structure

4

Kooigem-Bos (B)

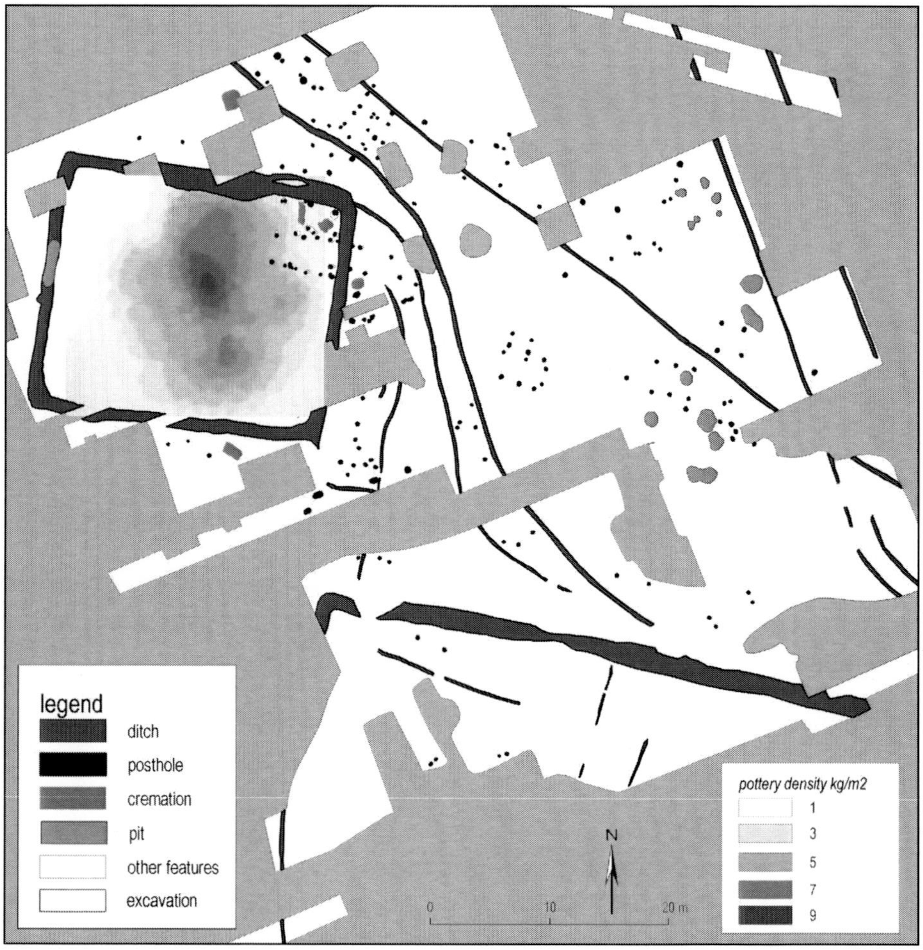

Figure A.21-1. Largest part of the available excavation plan of Kooigem Bos (based on excavation data in the RAMS depot, Waarmaarde). For colour version see fig. 5.3.

The Kooigem Bos site was excavated in fragments in the 1980s and 1990s (Mestdagh 2008, 24-29). Unfortunately not all parts were properly documented or published due to the involvement of amateur archaeologists and their quarrel with the professionals. In 1986 a rectangular structure was uncovered that remains the best described part of the site (Termote 1987).

Rectangular structures

It consisted of a rectangular ditch of 25.5m by 21.5m measured on the outside (fig. A.21-1). The width of the ditch varied from 1.1m on the west side to 2m on the north side, at a maximum depth of around 85cm. The cross-section was mainly V-shaped, filled in two main phases.

The ditch had a primary fill, a sort of colluvium layer at the bottom, that had formed when the ditch was still an open feature. The secondary fill was a much thicker humic layer containing many finds. The uniform character of the second fill looked like it was filled in one instant (Termote 1987, 63). The original surface was probably around 20cm higher than the recorded one.

Finds

Inside the western ditch a depot and cremation remains were found during a dig in 1985. A victim of circumstance, no drawings or pictures of this find in situ are available. Termonte (1987) notes that the pit in which the depot was found was dug into the second fill of the ditch. The depot / grave held seven nicely decorated, archaeologically complete pots, along with some cremation remains, charcoal, a bronze buckle, a fibula fragment and two stone bracelet fragments. The depot could be described as a typical 'Groupe de la Haine' depot (Mestdagh 2008, 39). A piece of charcoal from the pit was carbon dated

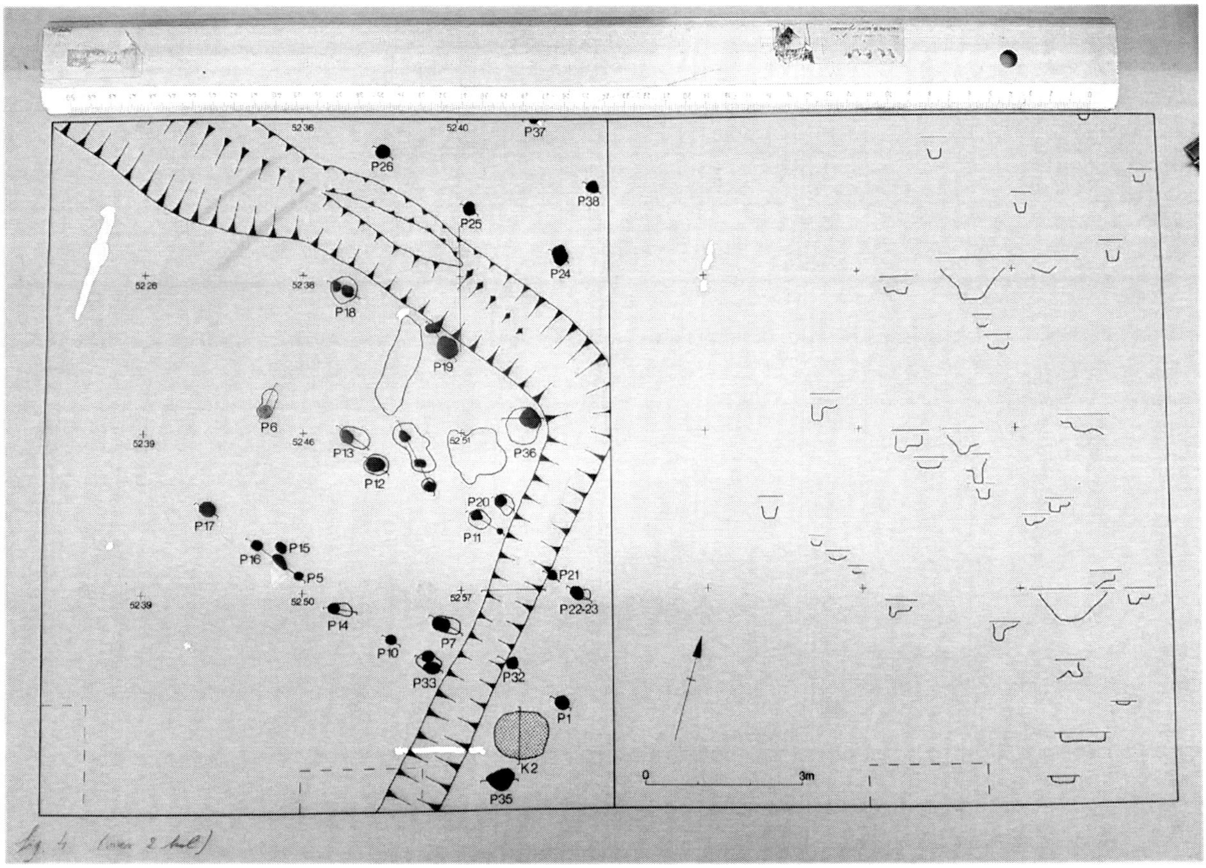

Figure A.21-2. Sections of the structure in the northeast corner and the rectangular ditch (Termote 1987, figure 4; source RAMS depot).

to 538-198 calBCE.[69] Typologically the pottery could be dated to 350-275 BCE (Termote 1987).

The thin primary fill of the ditch contained fragments of burned loam and charcoal and some pottery sherds (Termote 1987). The secondary fill was much richer in finds. Both fills can be dated to the late Hallstatt period to early La Tène (5th to mid-4th century BCE) based on the finds. In the soil layer above the recorded feature surface, inside of the rectangular ditch, a large quantity of pottery sherds (N=9130) were found, dating to the same period as the finds from the secondary fill of the ditch. Fragments of pots found 5 to 7m apart could be refitted. Termote (1987) interprets this as some sort of spoil heap of deposited material, based on the spatial spread, with the largest density in the centre of the structure (fig. 5.3, shaded). 67% belonged to pots of the situla type. The remainder of the pottery consisted of bowls and dishes, and a minority of beakers. A relative small amount of the pottery was decorated with geometric patterns. Furthermore two miniature (drinking?) bowls were found, several spinning

and weaving weights, along with an early example of a sling bullet (Mestdagh & Bakx 2020).

A large ditch southeast of the rectangular one allegedly belongs to another, larger rectangular structure although lack of documentation prevents testing this hypothesis (Mestdagh 2008, 34-35). Finds from this ditch have a contemporary date. No finds are known from the narrower ditches that cross the excavation pits on the east side. Their cross sections were documented in an earlier campaign and showed a width of 40 to 58 cm, by a depth of 38 to 64cm (De Cock 1987).

Associated features

In the northeast corner a post setting was found, related to the rectangular ditch (Termote 1987). This was likely a small building of approximately 5.4 by 5.4m (fig. A.21-1). The southern half of this building, made of two parallel rows of posts, might have connected to some sort of bridge over the ditch on the east side. The northern half of the building stood on the northeast corner and covered two shallow cremation graves.

Other cremation graves were positioned outside to the east, south and north of the rectangular ditch. On the

---

69 95.4% probability calibration, IRPA-802 (1987), Koninklijk Instituut voor het Kunstpatrimonium: 2300 ± 60 BP.

east side outside the ditch a row of postholes 2m apart was discovered, possibly leading up to the entrance. Further east, a cluster of pits contained mostly pottery (contemporary to the pottery associated with the ditch) and burned material (De Cock 1987). Some of the pits looked like former storage pits and were interpreted by De Cock (1987) as part of settlement features.

Another pit south of the rectangular structure uncovered burned pieces of loam and some pottery. The pit had a completely flat bottom and was nearly 2m long. Many pits are indicated on field drawing in the consulted archive as cremation graves (fig. 5.3, red), but none of the cremation remains have been described.

Directly to the north an alleged Iron Age settlement is located and 50 to 100m to the southeast a Roman one. Several excavations provided dates for these locations but not enough information for the type of site (Mestdagh 2008, 24-29). A further 100m south another large rectangular structure was excavated, indicated on the site map as a 'gallo-Roman building' (Termote 1987). The structure measured approximately 30 by 20m and had a stone base of about 1m wide (information from drawing in the RAMS Archive). As this part of the site remains unpublished, the function of this building is unknown.

Landscape

The site is situated on a forested and relatively high hill, a prominent location in the landscape. The hill is the southwest end of a plateau, stretching out towards the northeast. The terrain slopes down (30+ m) to the west and south into several river valleys. The rectangular structure lies near the top of a hill, on the flank where the western slope starts (Termote 1987). The height difference within the structure shows this transitional location; on the east side the structure surface is 2m higher than on the west side.

Type of structure

2

Kortrijk-Morinnestraat East (B)

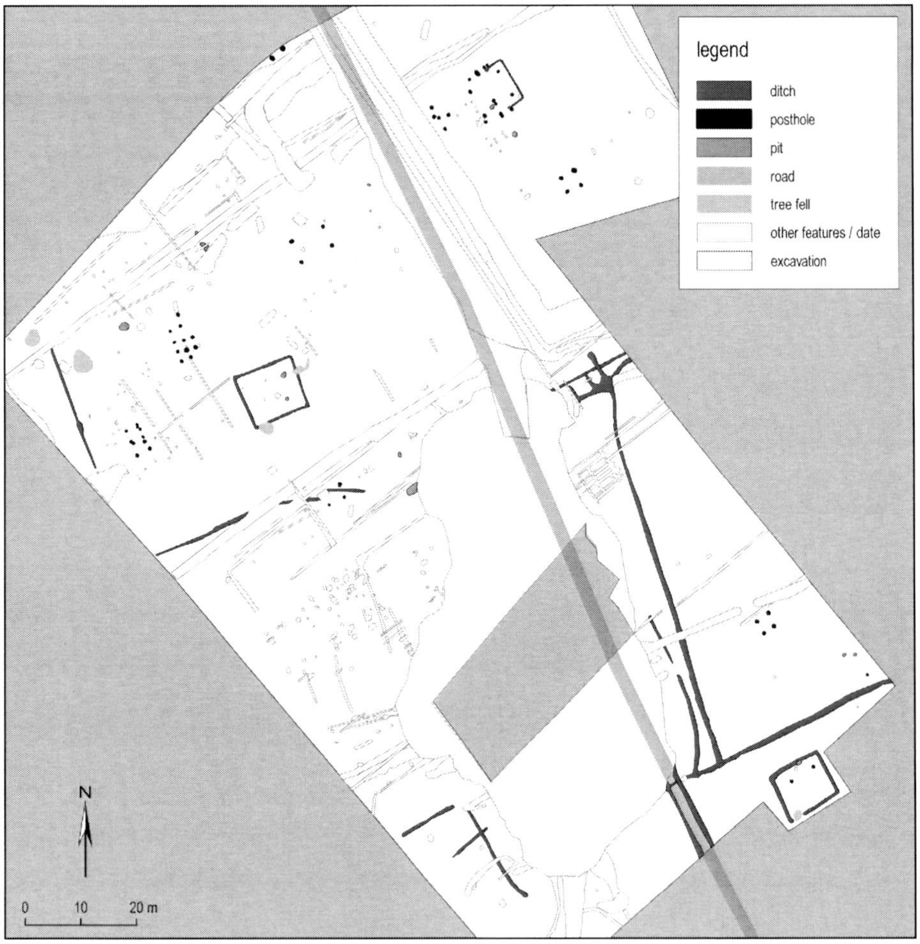

Figure A.22. Iron Age features in the excavation of Kortrijk-Morinnestraat (after Apers 2017, appendix B29 and B30). For colour version see fig. 6.11.

Along the Morinnestraat in Kortrijk a 1.6 ha large excavation revealed two similar structures.

Rectangular structure

With 10.5 × 9.5m the eastern structure was slightly smaller and less well preserved than the western structure (fig. A.22) The preservation was less, as the 0.6-0.8m wide ditch only had a remaining depth of 10cm. Notably on the south side another tree fell was documented, approximately on the same location of the ditch as documented on the western structure.

Finds

Despite the shallow depth of the ditch, 204 pieces of pottery were recovered from it, including two fragments of spindle whorls (Apers 2017, 53-55). Like the western structure, most (but not all) pottery was found in the

northwest and southeast ditches. Charcoal from the ditch was dated somewhat younger than the western structure to 161-1 calBCE.[70]

Associated features

Two postholes were found near the north side of the interior of the ditch 4.8m apart, preserved to a depth of 20 and 42cm (*Ibid.* 2017, 55). Two pits were found underneath the ditch. One in the middle of the northwest side was 70cm deep and contained a lot of charcoal. Another pit underneath the southeast ditch was 20cm deep and held 31 pieces of pottery. The only other structure in the vicinity was an undated four-posted structure 25m to the north. A small pit in the east corner of the excavation

---

70   95.4% probability calibrations, RICH-23145.1.1/-.1.2: 2060 ± 22 BP.

yielded a reasonable amount of pottery and an iron tool that resembled spring scissors (Apers 2017, 45-46).

Landscape

The soil profile on the east side of the excavation showed a 20cm thick iron-rich B-horizon (*Ibid.* 2017, 33-34). This layer was not present on the west side. The terrain on the east side was 0.8m lower. Several outhouses and part of a house plan were found on the north and west side of the excavation (fig. A.22). The house plan on the north side of the excavation consists of a bedding trench on the northeast side and several posts in the interior resembling a three-aisled house (Apers 2017, 37-40). The southwest side is less defined, as some posts and specifically the wall construction seem to be missing. Three 14C-dates place the building in 401-120 calBCE.[71] At least six or seven outhouses can be recognised, one of which was found more isolated on the southeast side of the excavation. The latter could be carbon dated to 406-215 calBCE.[72] All settlement features have the same orientation as the rectangular structures and the assumed course of the road.

Type of structure

6

---

71 95.4% probability calibrations, charcoal from postholes, RICH-23153: 2276 ± 29 BP; RICH-23151: 2172 ± 28 BP; RICH-23144: 2187 ± 30 BP (Apers 2017, table 1 and appendix 1).

72 95.4% probability calibration, charcoal from a posthole, RICH-23146: 2293 ± 32 BP (Apers 2017, table 2 and appendix 1).

Kortrijk-Morinnestraat West (B)

The second structure was excavated 105m northwest of the Morinnestraat East ditch (Apers 2017, 52).

Rectangular structure

The western structure measured 11 × 10m (*Ibid.* 2017, 47-48; figure A.22). The ditch was 0.4m wide and about 20cm deep in cross-sections. The northwest side contained a charcoal rich fill. Apart from tree fells on the south and the east side of the ditch, it appeared uninterrupted. The rectangular structure is interpreted as either a sanctuary, based on the pottery deposition, or possibly a burial monument, albeit with the grave missing (*Ibid.* 2017, 57).

Finds

In the ditch 310 pottery fragments were found, of at least ten different pots, and a spindle whorl (Apers 2017, 48-51). Most of the pottery was found in the northwest and southeast sides of the ditch. Besides pottery, part of a sandstone grinding stone was also found. The charcoal from the ditch was dated to 361-115 calBCE.[73]

Associated features

Two pits with a distance of 4m between them were found enclosed by the ditch (*Ibid.* 2017, 47). Both were 40cm deep and yielded no finds. In the vicinity other structures were documented, mostly four posted granaries dating to the Late Iron Age (*Ibid.* 2017, appendix 13). The structure to the northwest of the ditch had four 60cm deep founded posts (*Ibid.* 2017, 61).

Landscape

The site is situated on a sandy loam area in between the rivers Leie and the Schelde, characterised by alluvial deposits and depressions (Apers 2017, 7-9). The terrain slopes down from south to north. Within the excavated area there is a 2.4m height difference.

Type of structure

6

---

[73]   95.4% probability calibrations, RICH-23150: 2183 ± 29 BP and RICH-23147: 2167 ± 29 BP.

Liessel-Willige Laagt (NL)

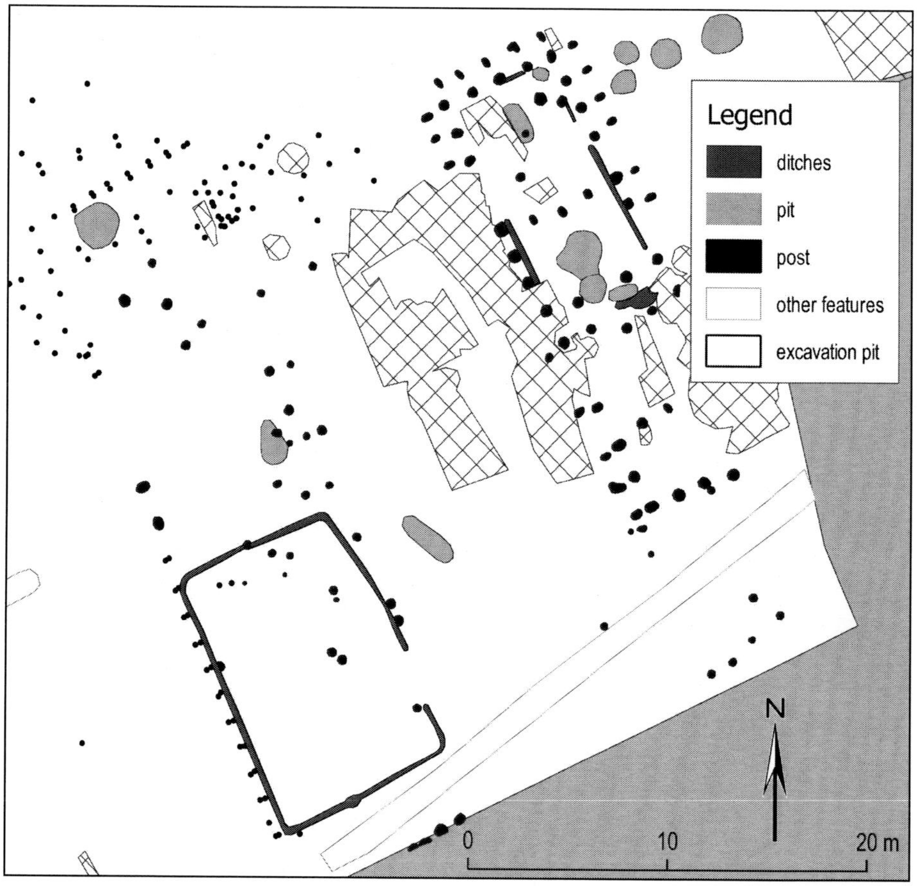

Figure A.24. Section of the excavation plan of Liessel-Willige Laagt (based on: Witte, 2012, figure 3.30). For colour version see fig. 4.8.

The excavation in 2010 of an Early Iron Age site in Liessel revealed a settlement with mainly settlement associated features (Witte 2012). The rectangular structure was interpreted as a possible cattle pen, although the possibility of a 'ritual' significance for the inhabitants of the farmstead was suggested by Witte (2012, 38).

Rectangular structure
The enclosure consisted of a rectangular ditch, measuring 19 by 8 meters (Witte 2012). Its narrow appearance of 40cm wide (at a remaining depth of 35cm) suggests that it functioned as a bedding trench accommodating a wattle work wall.

Finds
Two fragments of pottery were recovered from the ditch fill. Flanking the opening on the east side three postholes were found. These might have belonged to posts that were part of a fence gate.

Associated features
Next to the west side of the ditch a row of double posts was found. This construction is thought to have been either part of the pen or part of the farmyard, narrowly enclosing the pen. The space inside of the ditch was mostly empty, apart from a few (unpublished) postholes.

Apart from the house plan two outhouses, two fences and a rectangular ditched structure were found.

Landscape
The site was located on a cover sand ridge. The context of the rectangular feature is the settlement of which it seems to be an integral part. No cemetery remains are known in the vicinity. A near complete large house plan of a type that is fairly common for the Early Iron Age (Schinkel 1998, 190-191; Hiddink 2014a; Fokkens 2019a) was positioned on a farmyard with similarly orientated features.

Type of structure
7

Lomm-Hoogwatergeul (NL)

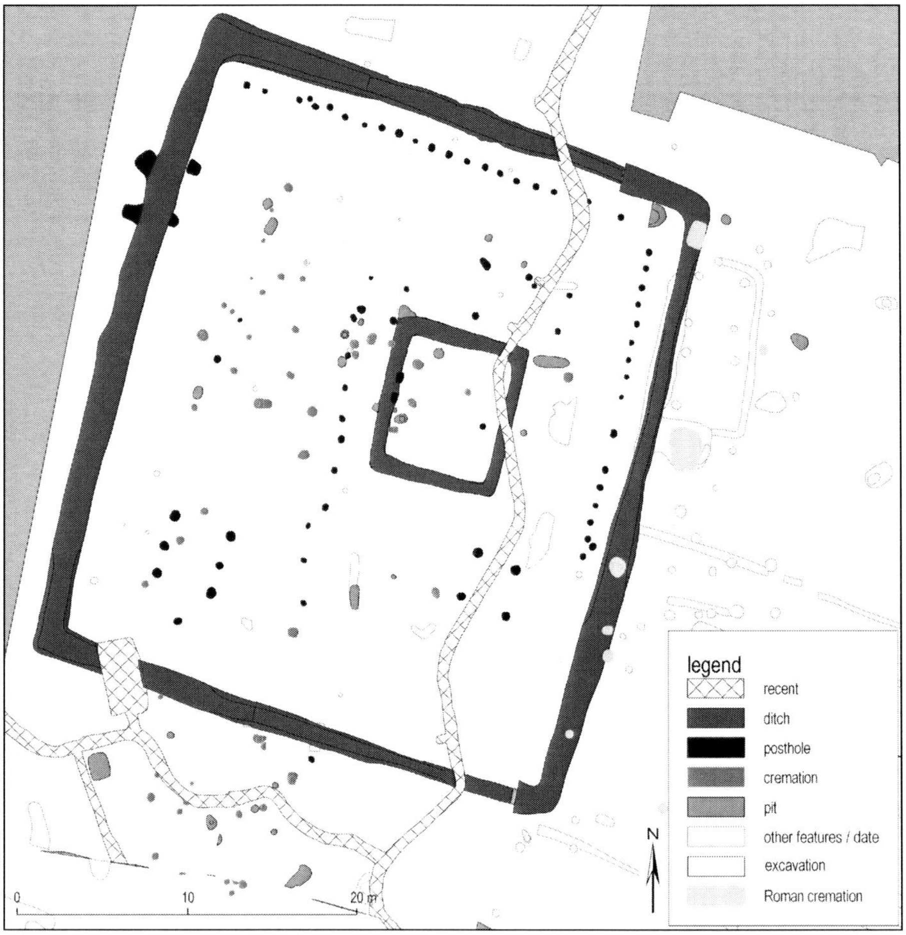

Figure A.25.1. Part of the excavation plan of Lomm-Hoogwatergeul with Iron Age features and Roman graves (after Gerrets & De Leeuwe 2011). For colour version see fig. 5.9.

legend
- recent
- ditch
- posthole
- cremation
- pit
- other features / date
- excavation
- Roman cremation

Figure A.25-2. Cross-sections of the large ditch (left) with a two stage fill, and the small ditch inside (right), Source photos: ADC Archeoprojecten.

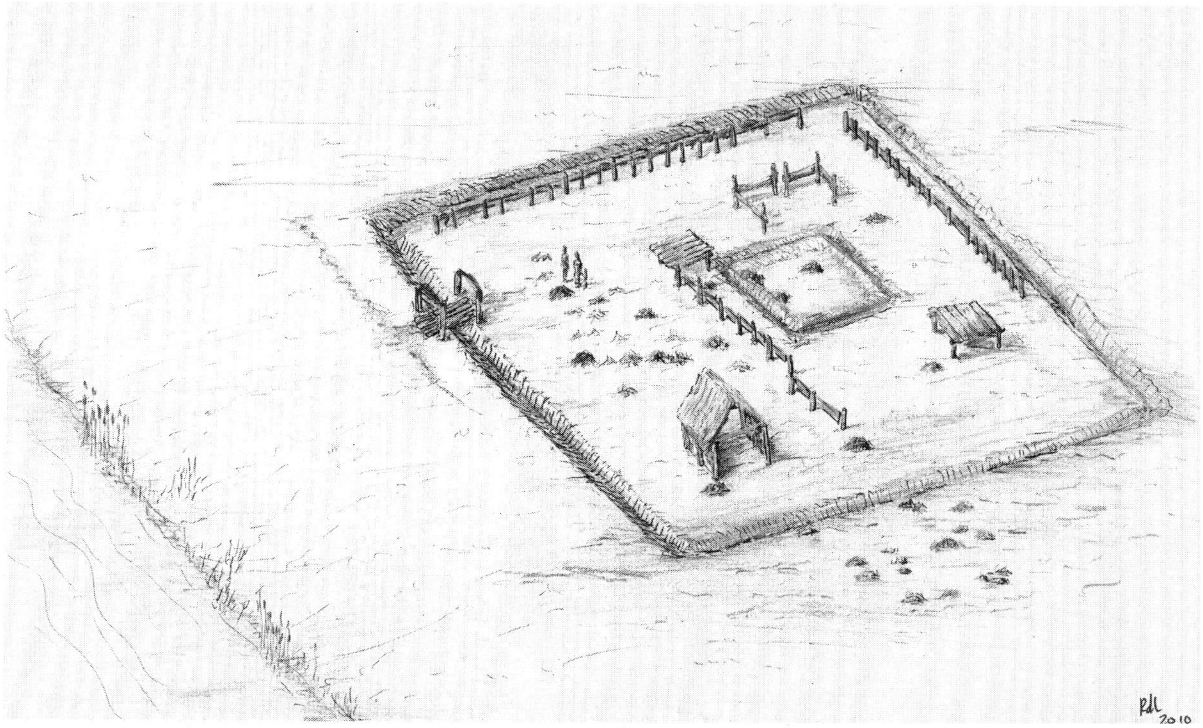

Figure A.25-3. A reconstruction of Lomm-Hoogwatergeul.

The site in Lomm-Hoogwatergeul contains a large enclosure that was interpreted as a 'local cult place' (Gerrets & De Leeuwe 2011; Roymans & Derks 2014). The site owes this interpretation to the demonstrable long use of the site as a burial ground and the multiple structures in the enclosed space that appeared to have been used for various activities (fig. A.25-1).

Rectangular structure

The structure was excavated in 2008. The large rectangular ditch measured approximately 38 by 33.5m (De Leeuwe & Prangsma 2011; fig. 5.9). The cross section was V-shaped with a maximum depth of 80cm and narrow flattish bottom (fig. A.9, left). The fill of the ditch consisted of two to four layers, probably representing at least two phases. The oldest layer was only visible in a few places and filled with clean loamy sand. It would appear this part of the ditch filled in relatively fast after construction.

Finds

Parts of the ditches were sieved. This resulted in a limited number of finds. The large ditch uncovered 305 pieces of fragmented and weathered pottery, a sling shot bullet, a Roman fibula and 78 cremation fragments. In the small ditch 34 cremation fragments were found. More finds were discovered as grave goods, such as burned glass fragments, pottery, bronze objects and animal bones. The oldest dated grave belonged to an adult, carbon dated

to 393-205 calBCE.[74] It was found close to the centre of the large ditch. The grave also contained the fragments of three glass arm rings, dating it more precisely to the 3rd century BCE.

The lowest layer in most places has a flat bottom and contains some charcoal. A carbon date of this charcoal resulted in 376 to 171 calBCE.[75] The upper fill was much later, probably Late Iron Age to Roman Era, as several Roman grave were found on top of the east side of the ditch.

Associated features

Many features seem to be associated with the large rectangular ditch, most noticeable a smaller rectangular ditch inside (De Leeuwe & Prangsma 2011). The small ditch measured 9 by 8m and was about 1m wide and 30cm deep. The fill of the small ditch seemed similar to the bottom fill of the large one (fig. A.25-2, right). Other features were visible by postholes. In the interior of the large ditch this included a six-posted structure in the southwest part, two four-posted structures, two three-posted structures, two rows of posts along the inside of the ditch on the north and east sides and one or two rows just west of the longitudinal axis. Four larger postholes, two on either side of the ditch, on

---

74   95.4% probability calibration, cremated bone, SUERC-28703: 2245 ± 35 BP.

75   95.4% probability calibration, charcoal from the bottom of large ditch, SUERC-28708: 2190 ± 35 BP.

the northwest side, seem to indicate an entrance. Perhaps some sort of small bridge of the ditch was positioned here. A total of 61 cremation graves were found, and more cremation fragments in the ditch fills. Two graves could be dated to the Middle Iron Age, four to the Middle to Late Iron Age (of which one south of the large ditch), eleven to the Late Iron Age and nine to the Roman era. The other graves could not be dated. The Roman graves are clustered on the east side of the (then filled in) large ditch. The Iron Age graves were positioned inside and south of the large ditch. In and around the ditch 31 pits were found, of which unfortunately only 17 were sectioned. Most pits were bowl-shaped in cross section and rich with charcoal. Their position in between the cremation graves suggests fill of (part of) the cremation pyre remains.

In the vicinity, 200-300m away, an Early to Middle Iron Age settlement is situated. Besides three house plans, hundreds of pits were excavated, among which several pits were discovered with pottery depositions (Prangsma 2008, 20; De Leeuwe & Prangsma 2011, 82-83). One charcoal rich pit held 15 kg of Early to Middle Iron Age pottery. Another pit held 172 shards of secondarily burned pottery and 1.5 kg burned loam.

Landscape

The site is part of a much larger research area situated next to the river Meuse. A 72 hectare large planning area was selected for widening the river to prevent future flooding in the region (Gerrets 2011). The site was situated on the east bank of the Meuse, on the sandy clay deposits only about 50m away from the water edge. The area is a wide, slightly wavy terrace only 1 to 2m elevated above the water level (Zuidhoff & Bos 2011, fig. A.25-3). The position of the river would have been similar in late prehistory (Gerrets & De Leeuwe 2011, 302). During the Iron Age the Meuse valley was mostly covered by deciduous forest dominated by oak trees (Zuidhoff & Bos 2011).

Type of structure

2

Loon op Zand-Kraanvense Heide (NL)

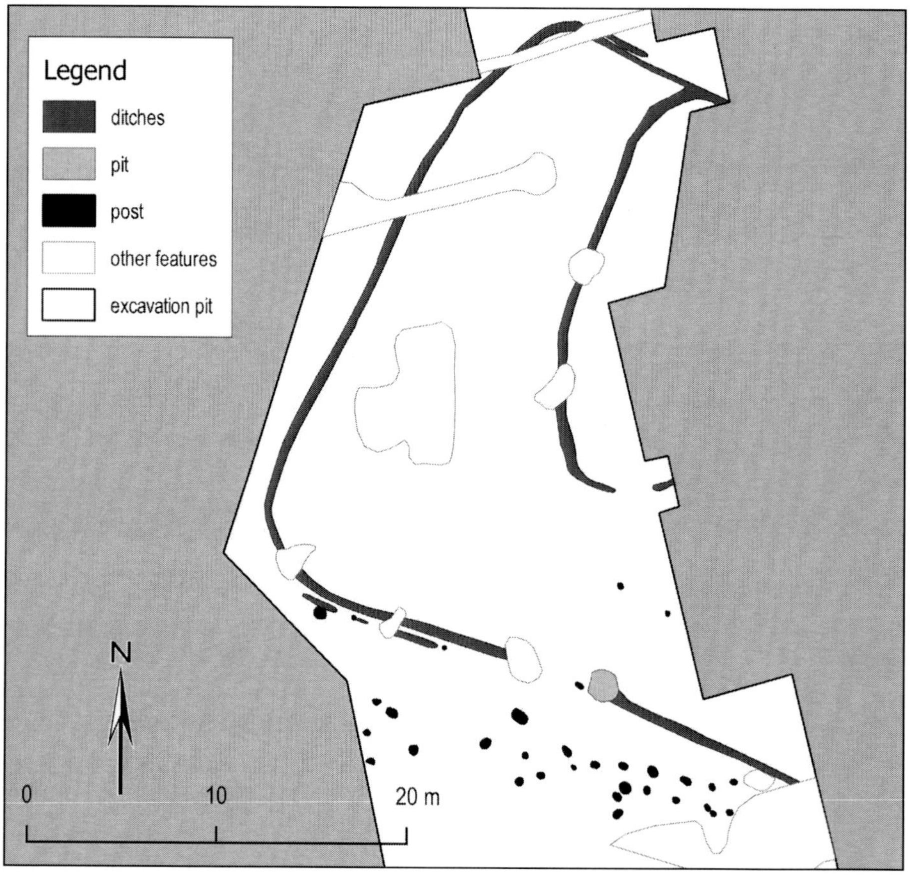

Figure A.26. Excavation plan of Loon op Zand (after Roymans & Hiddink 1991, figure 15). For colour version see fig. 4.9.

The site on the Kraanvense Heide was discovered in 1987 by members of the AWN (the Netherlands Archaeological Society). The site was subsequently excavated in 1988 before it would disappear under a new provincial road.

Rectangular structure

The structure seems to consist of an outer and an inner construction (fig. A.26). The outer ditch was made of a 30cm wide trench with a remaining depth of just 10 to 40cm (Roymans & Hiddink 1991). The structure measured about 32m NNE to SSW and at least 31m on the south side, measured WNW to ESE. The eastern part was not excavated. Connected to the north inside was another narrow ditch of similar dimensions. The width of the ditch was around 35cm and a depth of 15 to 50cm with steep sides. This oval shaped ditch had a length of 19m and a width of at least 8.5m. The narrow ditch with the steep sides led the excavators to the conclusion this had once held a palisade, although no post impressions were observed in the ditch fill. The larger outside ditch had an opening of at least 2.5m on the south side and the inner one an opening of around 1.9m on the southeast side. A round pit flanked the south entrance on the east side.

Finds

A total of 50 pottery shards from the ditch date the structure in the Late Bronze Age to Early Iron Age.

Associated features

Many post holes were found both inside and south of the structure of which it is unclear how they relate to the ditch (Roymans & Hiddink 1991).

Further to the south, a settlement was found consisting of at least five house plans, eleven outhouses and several storage pits. It was occupied from the Middle Bronze Age to Early Iron Age. On the north side of the excavation, 50m from the nearest house plan, the features of an enclosure were found interpreted by Roymans & Hiddink (1991, 124) as either a cattle pen or a cult place.

Landscape

The site was located on the western end of the Loonse and Drunense Duinen, a large area of inland dunes and cover sand ridge (Roymans & Hiddink 1991). To the west the ridge starts to slope down.

Type of structure

7

Maastricht-A2 Landgoederen Route (NL)

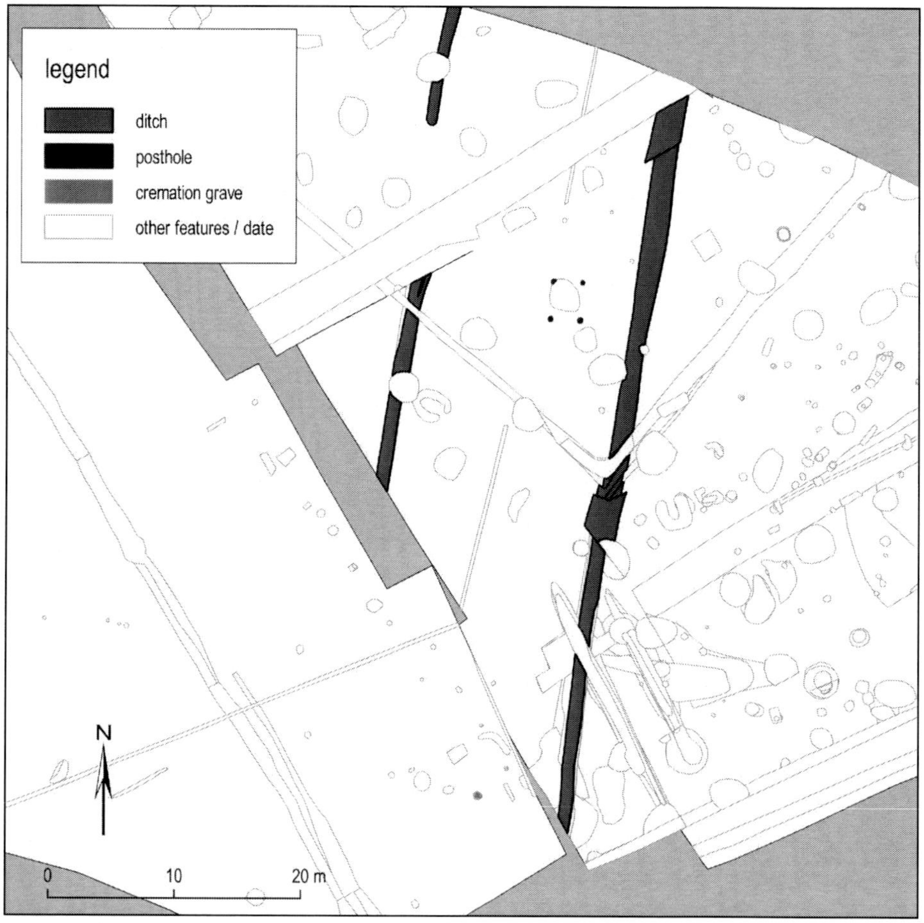

Figure A.27. Part of the excavation plan of Maastricht-Landgoederen (after Hazen & Blom 2015, figure 7.2).

A double ditch structure was documented in a part of a project expanding the A2 highway, where few other Iron Age features were found (Hazen & Blom 2015). The parallel ditches were interpreted by Hazen and Blom (2015, 203) as a cult place or a burial monument.

Rectangular structure

Two parallel ditches were dated to the Iron Age on the basis of the divergent orientation from the Roman features (among which a large Roman road with a WSW-ENE orientation). They could be followed for over 60m in length within the excavation and 147m if an observation in a trial trench to the north is taken into account (fig. A.27, trial trenches to the north not depicted). The ditches were positioned 16-17m apart and had a width of around 2m and a depth of 60-70cm. The fill of the ditches consisted of a thin layered phase at the bottom that seemed to have formed by rainfall. The phase

at the top had a uniform appearance. The fill was difficult to recognise in places and the western ditch was missed in several excavation pits. Based on the appearance of the fill Hazen and Blom (2015, 200) suggested that the ditches were not open features for a prolonged period.

Finds

No finds were recovered from either of the ditches.

Associated features

A four posted structure of 3.2 × 2.6m had the same orientation as the ditches (Hazen & Blom 2015, 199). The postholes were poorly preserved at a depth of 8cm. Both the ditches and the four postholes were devoid of finds. On the south side of the excavation a cremation grave was found. Originally this may have been positioned in between the ditches. The cremation was placed in a 25cm deep pit filled with charcoal and calcined bone fragments of human, dog, pig and cow, along with two pots (Hazen & Blom 2015). One of the pots was secondarily burned and incomplete. The remains were dated between 201-46 calBCE.[76]

Landscape
The site in Maastricht is situated on an inactive part of the floodplain of the river Meuse, with higher river terraces to the east (Bos & Zuidhoff 2015). During the Iron Age, the landscape around the site became more open, with fields, meadows and brushwood replacing the deciduous forest. West and north of the site a small residual Early Holocene channel would have made a depression in the landscape (Zuidhoff & Bos 2015).

Type of structure
Undetermined

---

76   95.4% probability calibration, cremated bone, SEURC-37649: 2105 ± 30 BP.

Meteren-De Plantage (NL)

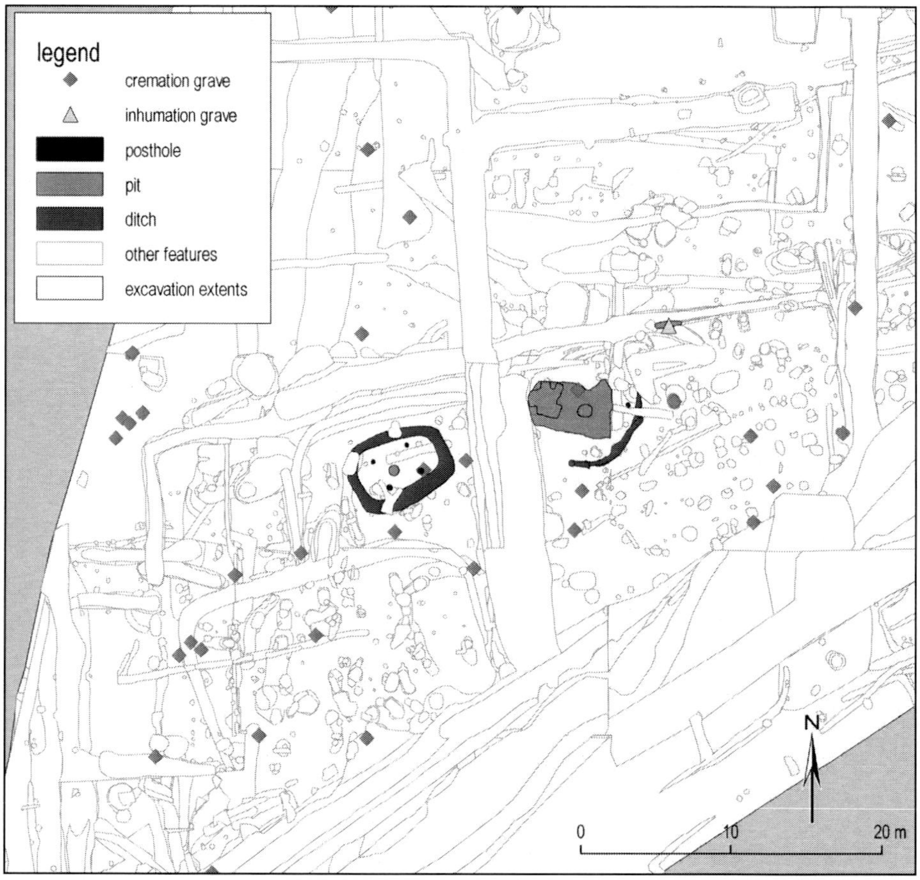

Figure A.28. Part of the excavation plan of Meteren-Plantage (based on: Jezeer & Verniers, 2012). For colour version see fig. 4.4.

A few of the oldest finds and features in Meteren-De Plantage dated to the Neolithic, succeeded by an inhumation grave dating to the 13th to 11th century BCE (Jezeer & Verniers 2012, 43-58). Most of the excavation area however covered an Early to Middle Iron Age cemetery.

Rectangular-ish structure

Amidst the graves was an oval ditch with an overall length of 6.8m and a maximum width of 5m (fig. A.28). The ditch had a flat bottom and straight sides with a maximum remaining depth of 50cm. In the enclosed space four posts of a small structure were found along with a 14cm deep, bowl-shaped pit in the central region. Initially the feature was suggested to be a cult place because of its central position in the cemetery, although later the interpretation changed to a long barrow (Jezeer & Verniers 2012, 59-62).

Finds

No finds were directly associated with the oval structure apart from a cremation grave that was found 20cm above one of the postholes. A Bronze Age date was suggested solely based on the stratigraphical position and a resemblance to equally poorly dated sites.

Associated features

The oval ditch structure was situated within an Early to Middle Iron Age cemetery with 44 cremation graves containing a minimum of 58 individuals and one inhumation. None of those graves had a structure around it or contained any charcoal remains of the pyre. All age categories were represented, with a relative high number of young individuals with 47% under 19 years old (Lemmers 2012). The use of the cemetery can be dated to the 6th to 5th century BCE (Jezeer & Verniers 2012, 93-98).

An inhumation grave was found 16m northeast of the oval structure (fig. A.28, triangle). It belonged to a woman in her thirties and could be dated to the 5th century BCE. In between the inhumation grave and the oval structure a charcoal pit was found, 5.5m long and 3m wide (fig. A.28, indicated as large pit). It looked like fire(s) had been burning in this location. Around the charcoal pit part of a circular ditch was found, also dated to the 6th or 5th century BCE by some associated pottery.

The four-posted structure within the oval enclosure was interpreted by Jezeer & Verniers (2012, 59-60) as a funerary house. The charcoal spot 10m to the east was probably the place of the general pyre.

Landscape

The site in Meteren was positioned on slightly higher river bank deposits, flanked by a former active river belt (Bouman 2012).

Type of structure

1

Mierlo-Hout-Ashorst / Snippenscheut (NL)

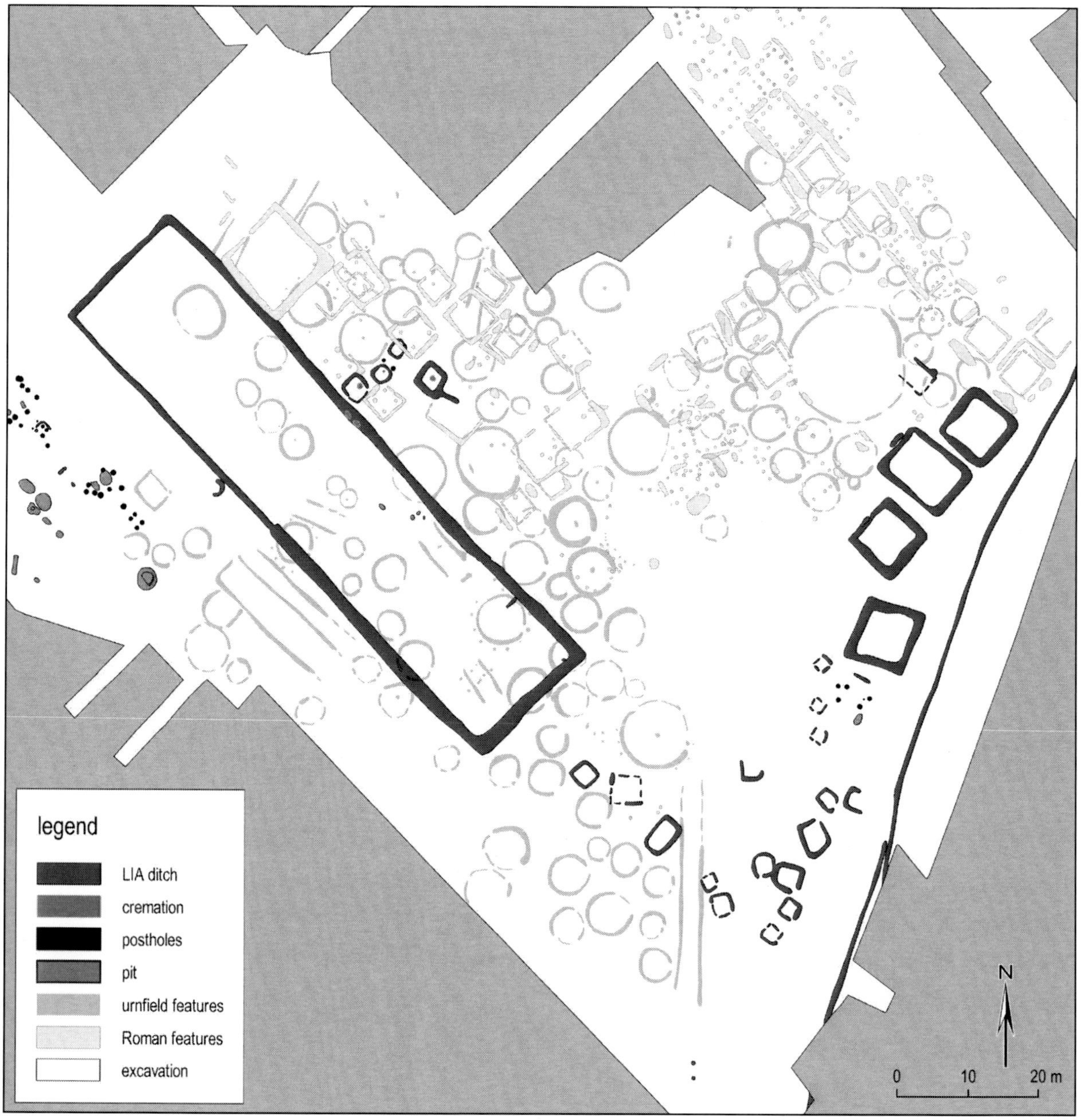

Figure A.29. Part of the excavation plan of Mierlo-Hout (after Van As, Tol & Jansen in prep.). For colour version see fig. 6.2.

In the Late Iron Age, an Early to Middle Iron Age urnfield was reused as burial grounds (Roymans & Tol 1993; Tol 1999; Van As, Tol & Jansen in prep.).

Rectangular structure

A large, 85m long rectangular structure was apparently the first feature to be constructed in the Late Iron Age after a hiatus of about three centuries (Tol 1999; Van As, Tol & Jansen in prep.). It measured 85 × 21m and consisted of a ditch with a V-shaped cross-section of 75cm deep and 1.75m wide.

On the southeast side of the ditch, the 'footprint' of a former bank was visible as podzol formations. The soil from the ditch seemed to have been deposited on the inside of the ditch, forming a bank. Over time the soil slid back into the ditch, still visible by the asymmetrical ditch fill on all sides of the structure. The ditch would have been an open feature for a prolonged period of time accumulating thin layers of sand at the bottom, followed by a thicker podzolised phase. Charcoal from the bottom of the ditch was dated to 545-400 calBCE[77], but given the ditch crossed over several older structures the charcoal could have derived from one of those.

Finds

No finds are associated with the large structure.

Associated features

The cemetery was in a poor state of preservation. For the Late Iron Age-Roman phase only twenty cremation graves were found, opposed to 94 structures. Two poorly preserved cremation graves were found in the ditch on the north side (fig. A.29). Only the south and east part of the cemetery are more or less contemporary to the large rectangular structure (Van As, Tol & Jansen in prep.). The structure was preceded a few centuries earlier by an urnfield that was in use from circa 750 to 450 BCE (Tol 1999). The large rectangular ditch was constructed straight over and around several of the older burial monuments, while none of the Late Iron Age or Roman graves were enclosed by it. The large structure was succeeded by many graves in the Roman era. The cemetery is bordered by an undated ditch on the southeast side, marking the transitional region from the sand ridge on which the cemetery is situated, to the lower wet zone (Van As, Tol & Jansen in prep.). Both phases of the cemetery seem to respect a Middle Bronze Age barrow with a ring ditch on the east side, situated on the highest part of the sand ridge.

Landscape

The cemetery is situated on the southeast flank of a sand ridge, edging the lower and wetter landscapes.

Type of structure

2

---

77   84.3% probability calibration, or 733-400 cal BCE for 95.4% probability, charcoal, GrA-56398: 2405 ± 30 BP.

Nijmegen-Kops Plateau (NL)

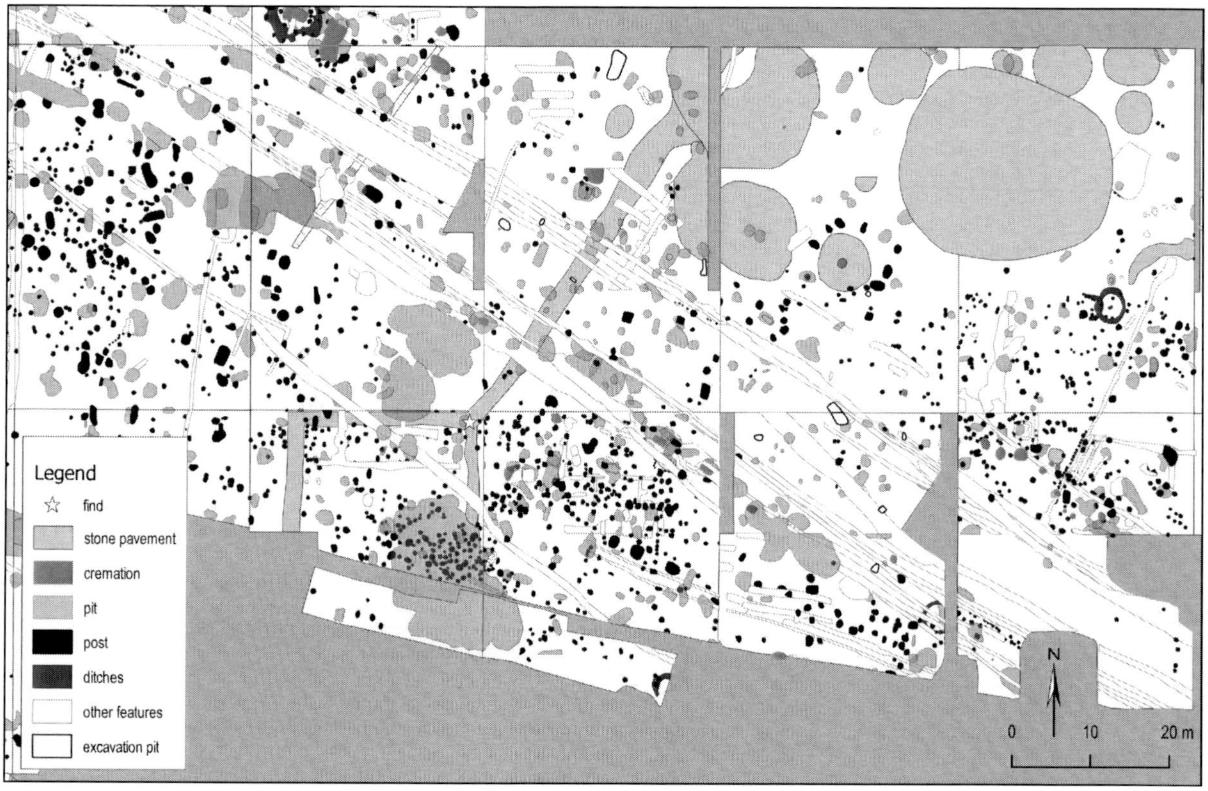

Figure A.30. Section of the excavation plan of Kops Plateau (Van der Weyden 2013, Odyssee project open access data; Fontijn & Cuijpers 1999, figure 3 and 14). For colour version see fig. 4.5.

An area of 8 hectares of the Kops Plateau was excavated between 1986 and 1995. The site is best known as a Roman military camp (Willems & Kooistra 1991; Willems 1996). Most features are attributable to the Roman occupation, but unfortunately many were never described in detail in an excavation report. The published data only gives a general overview of the site and only the most remarkable finds. Even though the raw excavation data was made available recently, a general description of the features and a synthesis based on those is still missing. This is specifically crucial in the interpretation of the multitude of pits and postholes. Their number is comparable to that of an oppidum such as Danebury or Manching. As a result not many structures were reconstructed or dated and it remains uncertain which postholes and pits belong to the structure under review here.

Under the stones of four of the pavement structures several post holes and pits were observed, but the stone platforms were mostly preserved and not further

excavated (Fontijn & Cuijpers 1999). Two stone circles contained a cremation grave in the centre. For most of the stone platforms it is assumed these were covered by a mount (Fontijn & Cuijpers 1999, 43-45). One smaller stone platform was surrounded by pits in which some Middle Bronze Age pottery was found. In the soil above four of the platforms Late Bronze Age-Early Iron Age cremation urns were found, interpreted as secondary graves. According to Fontijn & Cuijpers (1999, 45-48) a Middle to Late Bronze Age date for the stone platforms is likely on the basis of pottery finds.

Rectangular structure

A 42m long and 80cm wide stone path connects the second largest stone platform to a rectangular enclosure southwest of it (fig. A.30). This enclosure consists of a stone pavement of 1.5 to 2m wide, marking a rectangular space of 24m by at least 15m (Fontijn & Cuijpers 1999). According to the excavators, the stone pavement was probably placed in a shallow ditch. Part of the south section was destroyed in the Roman period, and another part is situated outside the excavation area, making it impossible to determine whether the shape is either U-shaped or a complete rectangle.

Finds

The most notable find associated with the stone enclosure in Nijmegen is a bronze socketed axe among the stones on or in the northwest corner, on the exact location where the corner joins the path to the stone platforms (fig. A.30, star). The type of axe is typical for the second half of the Late Bronze Age to the Early Iron Age (Fontijn 2002, 162). Commonly such axes are known from depositions in wet places and hoards in the Late Bronze Age, making the location of the deposition within the rectangular enclosure on the Kops Plateau an exception (Fontijn 2002a, 157-162).

Associated features

The cobble path connection to the platforms (or former barrows) suggests a certain degree of simultaneity, with a time difference between the phenomena of no more than a few generations. The path is interpreted as a possible procession route from the rectangular marked space to the barrows, comparable to post settings and allées (Fontijn & Cuijpers 1999, 59; Fontijn 2002a). Fontijn (2002b, 160-162) pointed out that the rectangular cobble shape marked a symbolic enclosed space where actions could take place and even suggested an ancestral cult, encompassing a ceremony in which the recently deceased were almost literally included among their real or acclaimed ancestors.

Landscape

As the name suggests, the Kops Plateau is a natural height with a flattish top encompassing an area of 11 hectare above the town of Nijmegen (Van Enckevort & Zee 1996; Fontijn 2002a). The structure was situated at the edge of the plateau. According to Fontijn (Fontijn & Cuijpers 1999, 55; Fontijn 2002a, 157) the edge of the plateau would have prevented the rectangular shape extending beyond 7 to 8m south.

Type of structure

Undetermined

Odijk-Singel (NL)

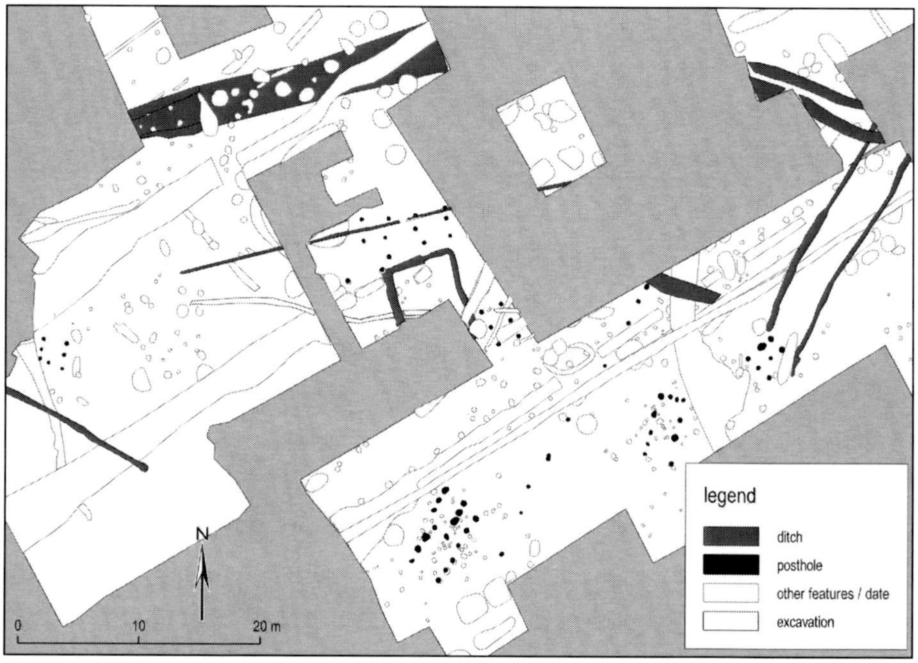

Figure A.31. Part of the excavation plan of Odijk-Singel (after Lohof 2000, figures 3-5 and Schurmans & Verhelst 2007, figure 6.2a). For colour version see fig. 6.13.

The excavated parts along the Singel in Odijk were limited to the roads and house foundations of a future residential and industrial estate in 2000 and 2005 (Lohof 2000; Schurmans & Verhelst 2007, 3). This strategy led to a rather fragmented excavation plan (figure A.31). The site has been inhabited since the Middle Iron Age (Lohof 2000, 11; De Leeuwe 2022).

Rectangular structure

On the south side of the excavation a rectangular structure was found, measuring 7.5 × 6.5m (Schurmans 2007, 40). The southwest corner of the structure was not excavated and the eastern part had a deeper excavating surface, excavated in 2000, than the western one that was excavated in 2005. This resulted in a difference in width and depth for the ditch on both sides (depth on the west side 18-30cm versus 7-12cm on the east side). Charred residue on a pottery shard from the ditch was dated to 170 calBCE-4 calCE.[78]

Finds

The ditch contained a concentration of finds in the fill on the north side (Schurmans 2007). This includes 468 pieces

(19.3 kg) of typical Late Iron Age pottery (Van Kerckhove 2007). Other finds from this location are bones, metals, slags and burned loam (Schurmans 2007). The description of these finds is unclear as find lists are not included in either one of the reports (the connection between find numbers and feature numbers is missing), and the specialists only state find numbers.

Associated features

Most features dating to the Late Iron Age were clustered on the south side of the excavation (Schurmans 2007). No features were found in the interior of the rectangular ditch. In the vicinity, several straight or slightly curved ditches and ten small structures interpreted as granaries were documented. Right next to the ditch on the east side was a (minimal) six-posted example covering a surface of at least 3 × 1.75m. One of the posts is crossed over by a feature dated Roman to Early Medieval. The granaries were dated solely by their orientation, but the ditches were more accurately dated. A large ditch north of the rectangular structure is interpreted as a settlement boundary feature. The ditch is 2.2-4.5m wide and nearly 1m deep. It dates to 197-45 calBCE.[79]

---

78   95.4% probability calibration, residue on pottery POZ-12958: 2060 ± 30 BP.

79   95.4% probability calibrations, residue on pottery POZ-12848: 2110 ± 22 BP and animal bone POZ-12849: 2095 ± 30 BP.

Overall, based on pottery and carbon dates, the linear ditches are slightly older than the rectangular one (Van Kerckhove 2007, table 7.1).

Landscape

The site is situated on a relatively high bank of an old meander belt (Van Zijverden 2007). The soil consists of layers of laminated sand and sandy clay, sloping down to the west.

Type of structure

6

Oedelem-Wulfsberge (B)

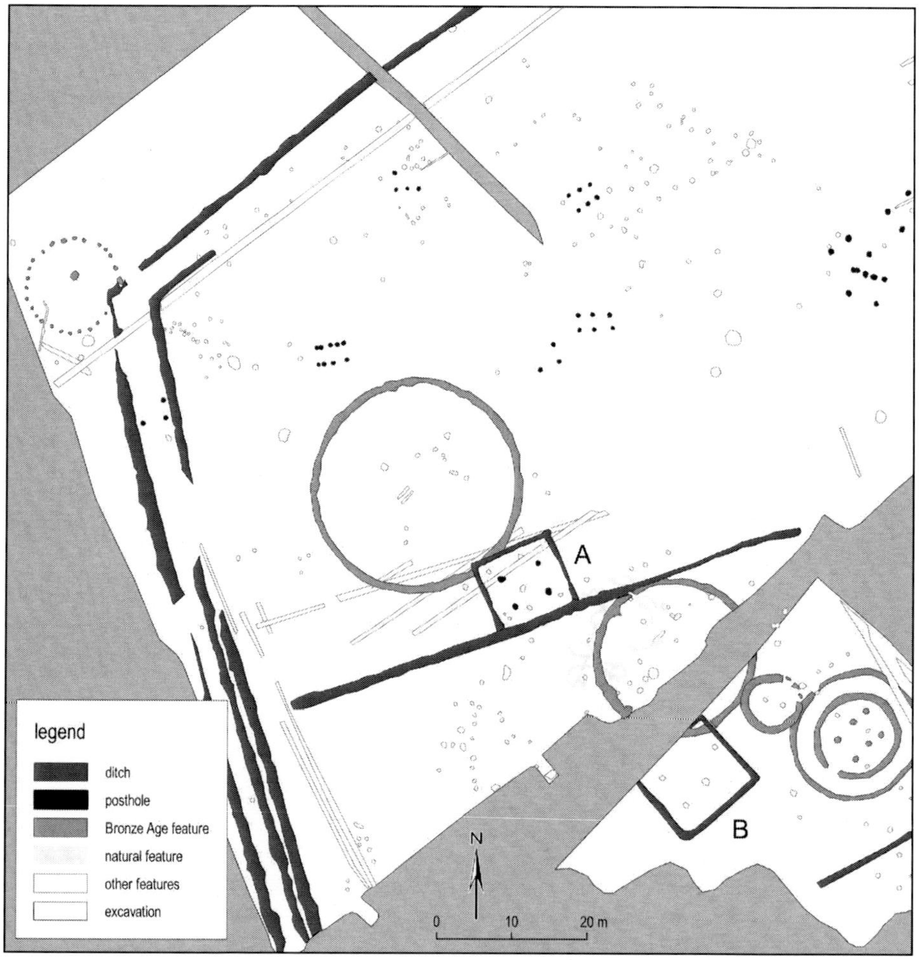

Figure A.32. Part of the excavation plan of Oedelem-Wulfsberge (after Bourgeois *et al.* 2001, figure 2; Cherretté & Bourgeois 2002, figure 1; De Reu & Bourgeois 2013, figure 5). For colour version see fig. 6.10.

The excavations from 2000 to 2002 in Oedelem took place as part of an ongoing scientific project by Gent University to increase knowledge of the chronology and duration of Bronze Age barrow cemeteries (Bourgeois, Cherretté & Meganck 2001; Cherretté & Bourgeois 2002; Cherretté & Bourgeois 2003; De Reu & Bourgeois 2013). The presence of the barrows was visible on aerial photos by their circular ditch. Besides the barrows, several Iron Age features were revealed in the excavations.

Rectangular structures

Two rectangular ditches were found, both crossing over a circular ditch with one corner (fig. A.32; *Ibid.* 2001; Cherretté & Bourgeois 2003). The northwest rectangular ditch (A) measured 11 × 10m and the southeast ditch (B) 12 × 11m. Ditch A had a remaining depth of 10-20cm (Bourgeois, Cherretté & Meganck 2001), while ditch B was

better preserved at a depth of 50cm on the south and west sides (Cherretté & Bourgeois 2003).

One of the ditches was dated to 356-112 calBCE.[80] Generally, the rectangular structures are thought to have the same date as the linear ditches: Late Iron Age to Early Roman (*Ibid.* 2003). The rectangular structures are interpreted to have a 'ritual' or funerary function, by association with the burial mounds, and by analogy with similar monuments, although conclusive evidence for this is lacking (Cherretté & Bourgeois 2003).

---

80 95.4% probability calibration, charcoal from 75cm below surface, KIK-2780/KIA-21206: 2160 ± 25 BP. Unknown which ditch as the feature numbers were not published.

Finds

Some pottery was found in the fill of ditch A and the postholes in the interior (Bourgeois, Cherretté & Meganck 2001). The amount or exact location was not stated in the report.

Associated features

The site is dominated by the oldest features: the Bronze Age barrows and their circular ditches with diameters up to 28m (*Ibid.* 2001). The barrows were probably still visible when the rectangular structures at their base were dug, although not the circular ditches. Ditch A is in turn crossed over by a linear ditch at the south side that contained pottery dating to the Late Iron Age to Early Roman era. The linear ditch was found to have a maximum depth of 50 cm, getting shallower to the west until it disappears entirely. On the west and north side, the cemetery is flanked by two to three linear parallel ditches. These contained Iron Age pottery. Several small four and six-posted structures were found dispersed over the area. Four postholes were also found in the interior of ditch A, at an evenly spaced distance from the ditch and set in a 4 × 4.8m square.

Landscape

The two largest barrows were positioned at the highest location in the area, on a slightly elevated sandy ridge between a depression in the east and a lower laying clay area in the west (Bourgeois, Cherretté & Meganck 2001). The site is situated at the bottom of the southern slope of a cuesta.

Type of structure

6

Oegstgeest-Rijnvaert (NL)

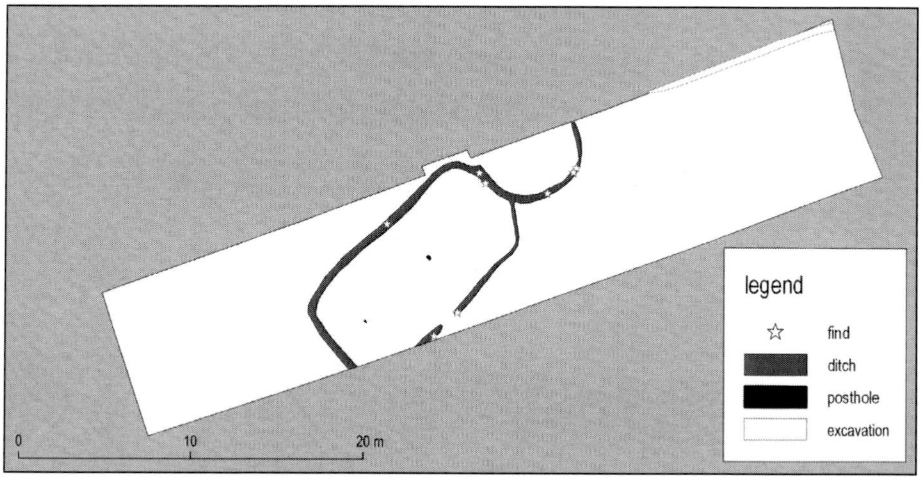

Figure A.33. Part of the excavation plan of Oegstgeest-Rijnvaert (after Van de Geer 2017, figure 5.2). For colour version see fig. 6.19.

The construction of a new road instigated an archaeological project in Oegstgeest, the only site in this thesis located in the west of the Netherlands. During the Iron Age, the site was situated on a dry river bank of the Old Rhine (Van de Geer 2017, 15-20). An unusual structure came to light for which one possible interpretation was a cult place.

'Rectangular' structure

The structure measures 20.1m x 6.4-6.8m and consists of two parts: a rectangular structure and a connected round ditch on the northeast side (figure A.33). In the middle of the south side of the rectangular part there was an interruption of the ditch of around 1m wide. The width of the ditches is only 0.2-0.5m and the depth a maximum of 35cm showing a bowl- or slight V-shape in cross-sections. On the west side of the round ditch another interruption was documented. The fill showed a thin dark humic-rich clay layer on the bottom containing charcoal and pottery. The rest of the fill was more uniform in colour, and contained some charcoal, seemingly the result of a gradual filling. Unfortunately space was limited and the structure could not be entirely excavated.

Finds

In the fill of the ditches 538 pottery pieces (5.6 kg) were found (Van de Geer 2017, 23). Most of the pottery was found in five concentrations (Fig. A.33, stars). The pottery could be typologically dated to the Late Iron Age, 200-1 BCE (*Ibid.* 2017, 31-38). The largest concentration was uncovered on the south side of the circular ditch, where the remains of at least four pots were found on the bottom of the ditch. Apart from pottery, a concentration of burned clay was found (Most eastern star in fig. A.33) and three small fragments of animal bone.

Associated features

In the interior of the ditch two postholes were uncovered (*Ibid.* 2017, 22). Preservation was minimal as the posthole in the middle of the east side was 16cm deep, while of the one on the west side only 1cm remained. No other prehistoric features were found in the vicinity.

Landscape

The soil consists of laminated silty clay and sand layers with a vegetation horizon. The top of the bank lies on the east side of the excavation pit, lowering 15cm at the place of the ditches and sloping further down to the west (Van de Geer 2015).

Type of structure

7

Oosterhout-De Contreie (NL)

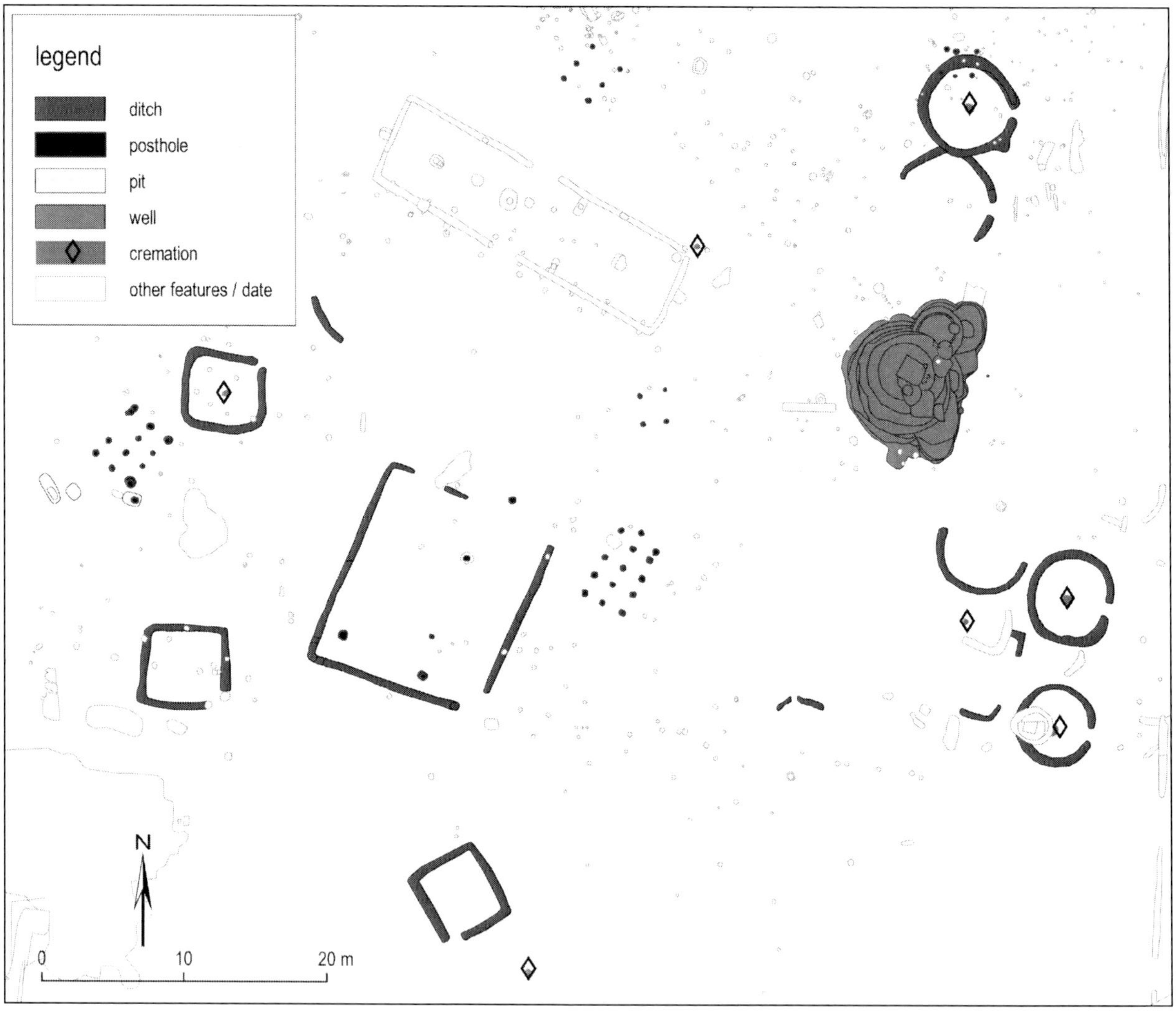

Figure A.34. Part of the excavation plan of Oosterhout-Contreie (after Roessingh *et al.* 2012).

The 14 ha large excavation in Oosterhout in 2010 revealed part of a Late Bronze Age to Middle Iron Age urnfield with at least 200 burial structures and 88 associated cremation graves (Roessingh *et al.* 2012). 35 of the surrounding features were square. One larger rectangular structure was suggested by Roessingh *et al.* (2012, 72-73) as a possible cult place (fig. A.34).

Rectangular structure

The larger square structure measured 13,1 × 14,5m. The ditch was 50cm wide and on average 18cm deep. Due to the shallow depth of the excavation surface, the preservation of the ditch and other features in the vicinity was poor.

Finds

A Middle Iron Age date is proposed for the structure on the basis of its shape and position within the cemetery, as no associated finds were recovered (Roessingh *et al.* 2012, 103).

Associated features

Due to the poor preservation it is impossible to determine if the monument originally housed cremation remains (Roessingh *et al.* 2012). As some of the other square ditches nearby also lacked cremation graves, this might be the case. Two separate cremation remains were found in the vicinity, 20m north and 20m south. Four postholes or pits were found enclosed by the ditch, but these were not described in the report.

Relatively few burial structures could actually be dated, but the data suggests that the oldest graves were positioned in the southwest and had no grave structure (*Ibid.* 2012). Graves with a circular ditch date from the Late Bronze Age to the Middle Iron Age, the somewhat larger examples being the older ones. Three square ditches could be dated to the Middle Iron Age and one to the Early Iron Age. Several graves without a surrounding structure in the southeast area could also be dated to the Middle Iron Age. Directly next to the ditch on the east side a large granary with a possible Late Iron Age date was situated. A large well or pit dating to the Early to Middle Iron Age was found 20m to the northeast. The bottom of the 1.4m deep well would have been under water. It shows many phases and usage over a long period. 53 pottery shards and one whole pot were found in the fills. Middle and Late Iron Age settlement features have been found spread out over the terrain, of which 13 are Middle Iron Age house plans (Roessingh *et al.* 2012a). The nearest Middle Iron Age houses to the large rectangular structure are 40m to the west and 90m to the east, one of which was built over a square grave structure.

Landscape

Within the excavation surface an almost 2m height difference was documented (Brijker & Moolhuizen 2012). The higher grounds are to the south and west where the larger part of the urnfield is located, the lower grounds to the north and east, where most of the Iron Age house plans were found (Blom & Roessingh 2012, 244). Halfway along this elevation the larger rectangular structure was situated.

Type of structure

1

Oostvleteren-Kasteelweg (B)

Figure A.35. Part of the excavation plan of Oostvleteren-Kasteelweg (after Demey 2013, figure 6.1 and 7.1). For colour version see fig. 6.8.

The excavation revealed three rectangular and several contemporary linear ditches dividing the landscape (Demey 2013, 66-87). Of the northern structure three sides were preserved, the fourth northwest side was obscured by a subsequent Roman ditch (fig. A35, A. For colour version see 6.8).

Rectangular structures
Of the northern structure three sides were preserved, the fourth northwest side was obscured by a subsequent Roman ditch (fig. A.35, A). The southeast side of ditch A was 17m and at the excavation surface 0.6m wide. The cross-section showed a uniform fill, and an on average 29cm deep bowl-shape. Nearby, the second

structure (B) measured nearly 18 × 18m square. The ditch was wider (0.7-1.0 m) and shallower (average 22 cm) than structure A, although the fill looked similar. The third, 14m square structure (C) was situated 25m south of structure B. The south side of structure C was best preserved with a ditch of 0.7m wide and 28cm deep. The northeast side was disturbed by later features.

Finds
In the fill of ditch A, on the southeast side, a concentration of pottery was found on the bottom of the ditch spread out over 2m in length (Demey 2013, 66-87; fig. A.35, star). Half of the 30 shards showed traces of secondary burning. In the fill of ditch B the west, south and east sides contained

finds (fig. A.35, stars). The west side yielded a grinding stone made of lime-sandstone, near the south corner a bowl standing upright on the bottom was found, and the east side yielded a sandstone next to a pottery bowl. In the middle of the southeast side fragments of a pot were found on the bottom of the ditch fill, resembling the deposition in ditch A. The fill of ditch C was less rich in finds. In the south corner of the ditch ten pottery shards were found.

Associated features

The interior of ditch A yielded four shallow pits and one cremation of an adult of 23-40 years old (Demey 2013, 66-87). The cremation could be dated to 171-1 calBCE.[81] The pits contained some charcoal in the fill, in two of them this was supplemented with a small amount of cremated bone. Ditch B enclosed several postholes and the cremation remains of an adult of 23-40 years old, possibly a male. The most visible posthole lay near the centre of the structure and had a remaining depth of 15cm. The dating of the cremation grave resulted in an older date than the grave within ditch A: 355-60 calBCE.[82] The southeast side of ditch B crosses over part of a 1.5 × 1.0m large pit. The fill of the 35cm deep pit contained charcoal and burned loam. In the interior of structure C a cremation grave was crossed over by a recent feature. The scant remains could not be dated or analysed. Two shallow pits nearby contained charcoal deposits. Other cremation graves were spread out over the west side of the terrain. Linear ditches seem to indicate the boundary of the cemetery to the east. A cluster of six graves was found south of the T-junction of the linear ditches. One of these graves could be dated to 353-64 calBCE.[83] Other contemporary features include two four-posted structures and a well that had its first use in the Early Iron Age. East of structure B lies an 11m long shallow 'pool' or depression with a post setting in the centre dating to 732-403 calBCE.[84]

As Demey (2013, 109) points out, all three rectangular structures are arranged in a similar manner: a cremation grave and pottery representing the main burial in the southern part of the enclosed space, along with additional acts in the form of charcoal concentrations with small amounts of burnt pottery and structured pottery depositions. In order to determine why some deceased received a surrounding feature and additional depositions while others did not, a thorough analysis is needed. Even though the excavators made a considerable effort to date

and analyse all of the graves, for many cremation remains sex or age proved difficult to determine. Some of the plainer graves belonged to women and children, although at least one adult man was among them (Demey 2013, 109). Notably, the only grave of a younger child, aged 2-8, was the only one without pottery as a grave gift.

Landscape

The site is situated on an old terrace of the river IJzer, covered with fine loamy sand (Demey 2013, 26-31). The brownish colour of the soil complicates the identification of archaeological features. The area is part of the northern edge of a sand-loam region, where it slopes down gently to the river valley. As a result, the soil in the southern part of the excavation is dry and sandy, and on the north side loamier.

Type of structure

6

---

81   95.4% probability calibration, burned bone, SEURC-46816: 2068 ± 26 BP.

82   95.4% probability calibration, burned bone, SEURC-46815: 2147 ± 29 BP.

83   95.4% probability calibration, burned bone, SEURC-44254: 2143 ± 26 BP.

84   95.4% probability calibration, charcoal, SEURC-44255: 2413 ± 26 BP.

Oss-Brabantstraat (NL)

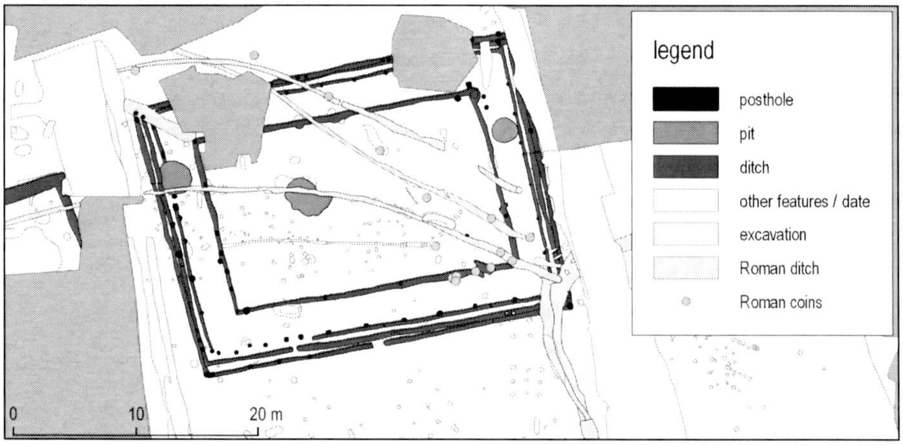

Figure A.36-1. Part of the excavation plan of Oss-Brabantstraat (after De Leeuwe 2011, figure 2). For colour version see fig. 6.21.

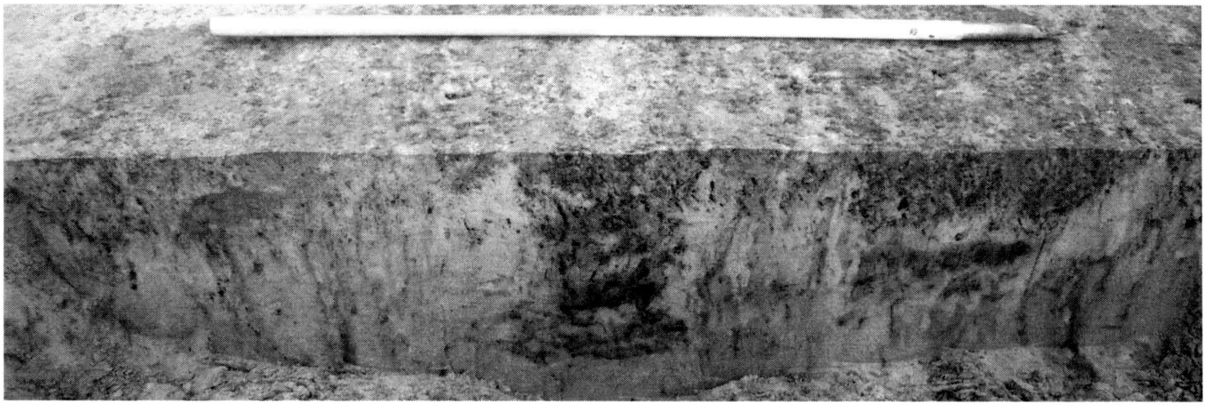

Figure A.36-2. Cross-section over two of the bedding trenches.

The geographical location for the Brabantstraat in Oss is near the Ussen region where four other rectangular structures were found. Excavations took place in 2008 and 2010, covering an area of nearly 1 ha. A Late Iron Age house plan was documented on the south side of the excavation (De Leeuwe 2011, 45-51).

Rectangular structures

On the north side of the excavated area, 100m from the house, a rectangular structure was found that contained multiple phases. The 31 × 23m structure that occupied the site in the Late Iron Age was built with bedding ditches for wall foundations (De Leeuwe 2011, 51-63; De Leeuwe & Jansen 2018). These ditches were not meant to lay open, but were narrow (0.2-0.4 m) with straight sides (maximum 40cm deep) to accommodate a wall (fig. A.36-2). Three bedding ditches seem to shape the outer

part of the structure, representing at least two different phases of the structure (De Leeuwe 2011, 51-63). The outermost ditch had an interruption on the south side and several posts in the ditch. The post on the southeast corner still contained a fragment of wood that was carbon dated to 92 calBCE -53 calCE, providing a terminus ante quem for the construction of the final phase of the structure (De Leeuwe & Jansen 2018).[85] The next two ditches, partly overlapped by the outermost ditch, probably belonged to the initial phase of the structure. This phase had a 35cm narrow entrance on the southeast side. The innermost ditch was different. It showed a V-shape in cross-sections and a uniform coloured fill. While the lumpy blotched fill of the outer ditches seemed to have accumulated over a

---

85 95.4% probability calibration, wood, GRN-31711: 2020 ± 25 BP.

Figure A.36-3. Large scale excavated area in Oss (data: Leiden University depository & Archol BV). Upper right: Oss-Brabantstraat, below left: Oss-Ussen R49, upper left: Oss-Ussen R57.

short period, like it was filled in in one instance, the filling of the inner ditch took longer. The planked or wattle-work wall must have been removed upon demolition of the structure, after which the outer ditch was filled in. This event occurred in the Roman era, as a new ditch system was built over the structure (De Leeuwe 2011, 69-74; ditches diagonally and in the lower right corner of figure A.36-1).

Finds

The number of finds from the ditches was meagre, as is to be expected of a ditch that was not built as an open feature. In total 230 very fragmented pieces of pottery were found, two human cremation bone fragments, one iron nail and a few stones (De Leeuwe 2011, 51-63). The only notable Iron Age find was a piece of a glass La Tène bracelet that was found on the crossing between a rectangular and a roman ditch (figure 6.21, star). Spread out over the diagonal ditches fourteen Roman coins were found. These coins are interpreted as a deposition at the time the rectangular structure was demolished, originating in the southwest corner (De Leeuwe & Jansen 2018). The coins form a sizable depot for the Oss region.

Associated features

Even though many features were documented in the interior of the rectangular structure, few can be positively associated with it. At least five four-posted structures were found, that probably belong to the farm yard of a Middle Iron Age house situated 45m to the south (De Leeuwe 2011, 31-43). Four other features can be considered. In between the outer and inner ditch two wells were found, and near the centre of the rectangular structure a third well (figure 6.21, indicated as pits). The well in the centre could be dated by the dendrochronology of the remains of a construction at the bottom to 446 ± 7 BCE. All three wells seemed to have had a second use as a large bowl shaped pit of 40 to 60cm deep (De Leeuwe & Jansen 2018). In all three features the upper fill appeared to have been open for a longer period. The bowl shape of the pit on the west side was coated with layer of secondary burned pottery (213 pieces, 1.7 kg). Due to the burned state the pottery was difficult to date, but 4th to 3rd century BCE was suggested even though some might have a later date (De Leeuwe 2011, 79-93). The bowl pit near the centre contained a lot of burned loam and charcoal (De Leeuwe 2011, 51-63). The bowl pit on the east side was empty, but appeared to have been an open feature for a while, visible by iron oxidation. It is unfortunate that the top fill of the three pits was never carbon dated. It was not considered as an option at the time.

The corner of a possible predecessor was found 7m west of the rectangular structure. This ditch had a V-shaped cross-section and a 47cm deep three phase fill, of which the lower one had filled up fast. 41 pieces of pottery dated it likely to the Late Iron Age. Unfortunately space was too limited to investigate the ditch further.

Landscape

Oss is for the most part located on an extensive cover sand plain. To the north are the lower-lying clay areas near the Maas. The drainage of the soil is particularly favourable in this transition from sand to clay area, which is why this area has traditionally been regarded as very suitable long-building soil (De Leeuwe 2011, 11). On a more local scale the area appears quite flat. The site is approximately 200m east of the (subsequent) Roman Era settlement of Westerveld (fig. A.36-3).

Type of structure

5

Oss-Ussen R2 (NL)

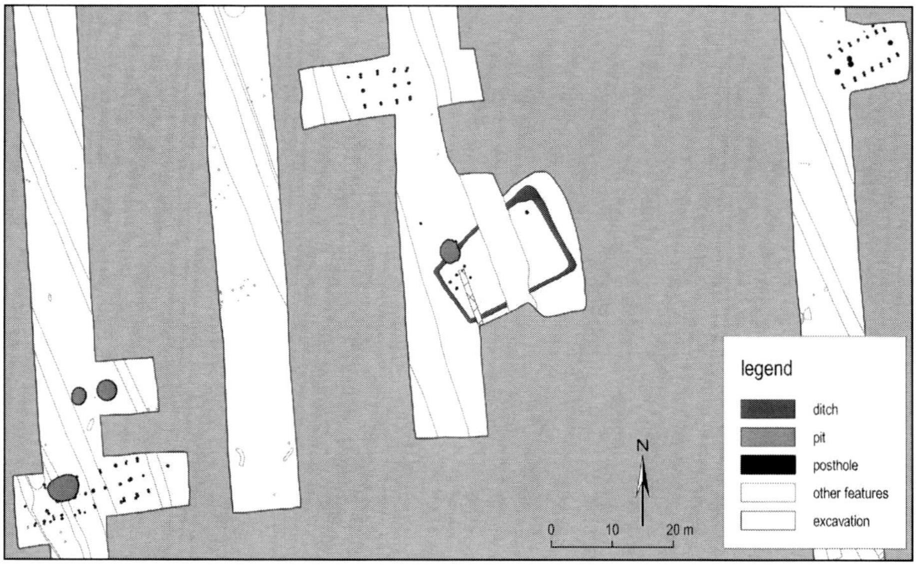

Figure A.37. Part of the excavation plan of Oss-Ussen, structure R2 (based on original field data; Leiden University). For colour version see fig. 6.15.

Structure R2 was excavated in 1978 as part of the Ussen project (Van der Sanden 1998, 317, 321-322). Three Late Iron Age houses were excavated, to the west, north and east within a 60m radius from structure R2 (De Leeuwe & Jansen 2018). Unfortunately the area was only partly excavated leaving large spaces archaeologically void, but the context can likely be described as a settlement (figure 6.15).

Rectangular structures
The trapezium shaped structure was 20.8m long, with a ditch that varied in width (0.6-2.0 m) and in depth (35-60 cm). The cross-sections were bowl-shaped to irregular (De Leeuwe & Jansen 2018).

Finds
In the fill of the ditch 68 pottery fragments were found, along with part of a spindle whorl, and small amounts of tephrite and animal bone (Van der Sanden 1998, 317). The pottery could probably be dated to the Late Iron Age (De Leeuwe & Jansen 2018).

Associated features
Six postholes were found in the interior (Van der Sanden 1998, 317). As a large recent ditch ran straight through the centre of the structure, some other associated features might be missing. On the northwest side a 90cm deep pit was dug over the ditch. At the bottom of the pit a pot was found placed upside down. The upper fill of the ditch showed a bowl-shape not unlike the pits in the Brabantstraat structure that may have been an open feature for a while. The fill yielded 200 pottery shards dating to the Late Iron Age.

Landscape
See Oss-Brabantstraat.

Type of structure
2

Oss-Ussen R25/R26 (NL)

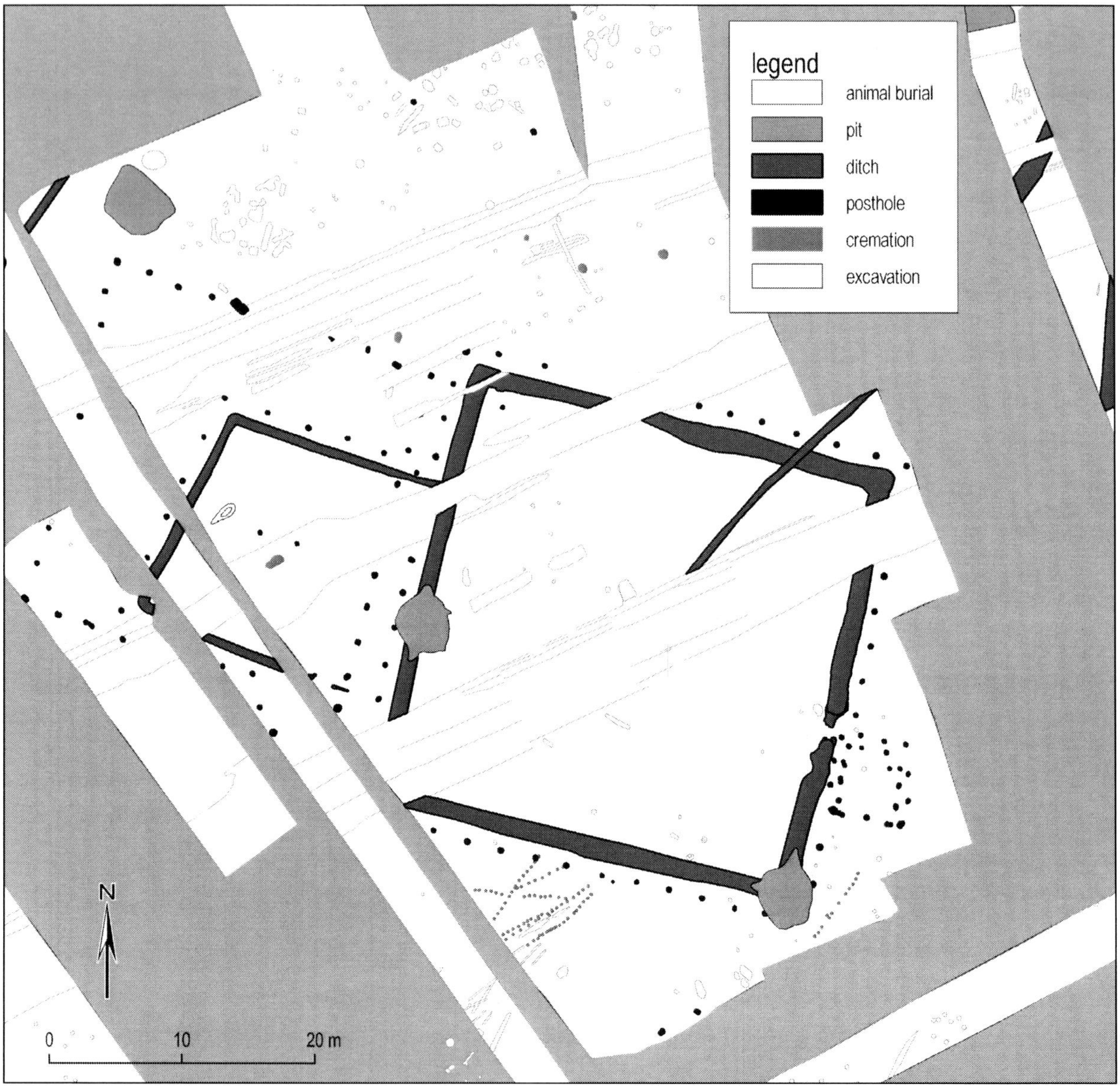

Figure A.38. Part of the excavation plan of Oss-Ussen with R25/R26 (after data from the library of the University Leiden). For colour version see fig. 5.10.

The residential area of Ussen was extensively excavated during the late 1970s and early 1980s (Fokkens 1998, 1-4). Ussen lies in a transitional area between the valley of the river Meuse to the north and west and the sandy soils to the east and south (Schinkel 1998, 12). In late prehistory the river would have been about 2.5 km to the north. The region is reasonably flat with fairly wet soils.

Rectangular structure

The structure designated as R25/R26 was first described in an article on open air cult places by Slofstra & Van der Sanden (1987) and since then used by many authors as an archetypical open-air cult place example. It consists of two connected rectangular ditches and post settings (fig. A.38). The larger ditch is a square measuring 32.5m by 33.5m with a distinctly V-shaped cross section (De Leeuwe & Jansen 2018). The initial and largest structure was called R26 ('Ritual structure' number 26). It has a square ditch with an inner surface of circa 916 m2. The ditch would initially have been an open feature of at least 2 to 2.5m wide at the surface and around 1m deep (*Ibid.*). Outside of the ditch posts were placed at a distance of 2.5 to 2.8m. Most unfortunately, a recent ditch runs straight through the centre destroying any central features that might have been there. An opening in the ditch (or entrance) appears on the east side. At the excavation level the ditch was 1.2 to 2.2m wide. It had a V-shaped cross section and was around 70cm deep. Postholes were found to be evenly placed (2.5-2.8m apart) on the outside of the ditch. The smaller western addition, of which the annex ditch had an inner surface area of circa 270 m2, was named R26a. The remainder of this ditch was around 0.4 to 0.8m wide, only maximum 30cm deep and slightly bowl shaped in cross section. The posts outside this ditch were placed at a slightly wider spacing, 3.0-3.3m. Postholes were found on the outside of the ditch as well as in a wider square setting. It contained a cremation grave in the centre, holding just 7 grams of cremation remains. Third, R25 is a final phase consisting of a square palisade on the west side of R26, with posts set at the same distance as around R26, measuring a surface area of around 605 m2. Nothing was found in the centre.

Finds

A relatively large amount of pottery was found in the ditches (1229 fragments) and pits (1792 fragments in the south eastern one and 283 fragments in the western one) (Slofstra & Van der Sanden 1987; Van der Sanden 1998, 325). The pottery assemblage was found with fragments of loom weights, spindle whorls, iron slags and pieces of stone, resembling regular settlement deposits (Van den Broeke 2012, 340). The structure was dated based on the pottery assemblage and a radiocarbon date of a piece of wood found in the southern pit 371-179 calBCE (Van den Broeke 2012, 34).[86] The pottery from the pits could be dated to 350-250 BCE.

Associated features

Several features can be associated with the structures. Just east of R26 is a small post structure called S164 that was initially interpreted as an outhouse or granary (Schinkel 1998, 263), and reinterpreted as part of R25/26 (De Leeuwe & Jansen 2018). S164 is aligned along the ditch of R26 and the surface partly overlaps with the posts of the palisade. Both ends of the ditch at the entrance appear to have been modified at least once, indicating multiple phases there.

On the south side, five palisades of small posts representing different phases are positioned to stop at the posthole row of the large structure. Two pits were made in the ditch. The one in the southeast corner had a depth of 95cm and the one on the mid-west side was 140cm deep (Van der Sanden 1998, 282-312). Inside the smaller structure a cremation grave was found and in the vicinity at least seven cremation graves were excavated (Schinkel 1998, sheet 15; see also §7.4). All of these are very shallow pits of 6 to 20cm in depth, with only few cremation remains of weights varying between 1 and 98 grams per grave. Like many other funerary structures in Oss, the graves appeared incomplete and severely eroded (Van der Sanden 1998, 319). Other features in the vicinity are pits P117, P119 and P120 (Schinkel 1998, 290). P117 is interpreted as a pit; the latter two are respectively a well and a watering hole. These features have the same date as P098 and P118. Pit P116 directly north of R25 dates to the Early Iron Age. Unfortunately the cremation remains were never dated or examined.

Landscape
See Oss-Brabantstraat.

Type of structure
2

---

86   95.4% calibration of wood, GrN-11132: 2200 ±35 BP.

Oss-Ussen R49 (NL)

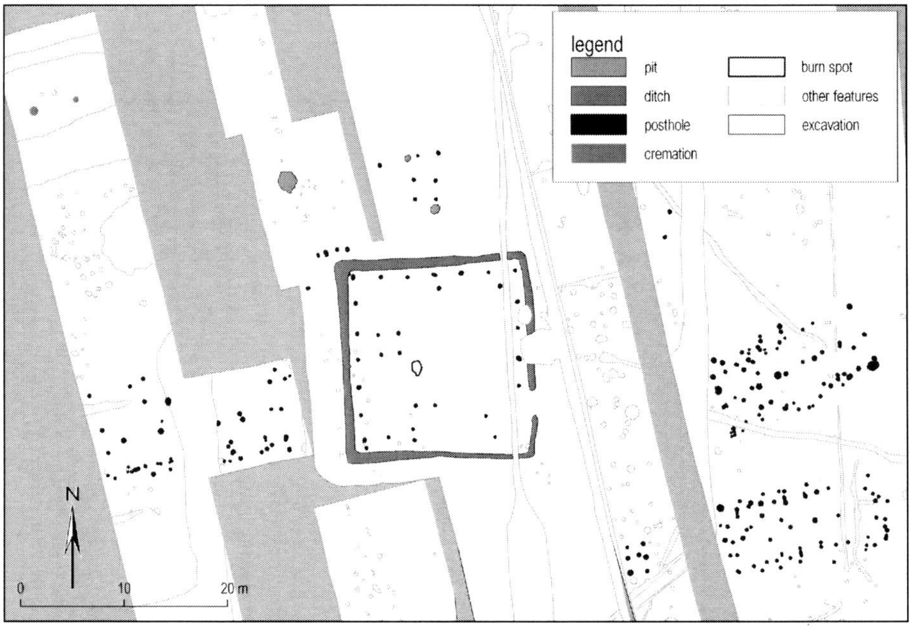

Figure A.39. Part of the excavation plan of Oss-Ussen with R49 (after Van der Sanden 1998, figure 20; depository of the University Leiden). For colour version see fig. 5.13.

In 1978, one year before R25/R26, another somewhat smaller rectangular structure was excavated in Ussen. Like R25/R26 it consists of a ditch and a post setting (fig. A.39).

Rectangular structure

The ditch measured 18.5 by 19 m, was bowl-shaped in the cross-section, 50cm deep and around 1m wide at the excavation level. The ditch shows a 2.1m wide interruption on the southeast side. Postholes were only found along the east, north and west sides, at a distance of 2.4 to 2.9m.

Finds

Inside the ditch fill over 1100 pottery fragments were found (of which 75% in the western half), along with several sling shot bullets, a spindle whorl, some small stones and burned and unburned animal bones (Van der Sanden 1998, 315-316, 330-331). Some pottery fragments from different locations in the ditch could be refitted. One posthole contained 87 secondarily burned fragments of pottery and the other 20 fragments. The structure is situated 195m north of R25/R26 (De Leeuwe & Jansen 2018). The context of the location will be discussed in more detail in §7.4.

Associated features

Two postholes were found on the north-south centre line within the enclosed area (Van der Sanden 1998, 330-331). A four-posted structure was found on the west side of the interior of the structure, and another a few metres north of the ditch, accompanied by other postholes and pits. A shallow pit in the west-centre looked like a burn-spot. Two undated cremation graves were found 29m to the northwest. To the west a Middle or Late Iron Age house plan was found, and to the east two more Middle Iron Age house plans (Schinkel 1998, 103-105, 216-219).

Landscape

See Oss-Brabantstraat.

Type of structure

2

Oss-Westerveld R57 (NL)

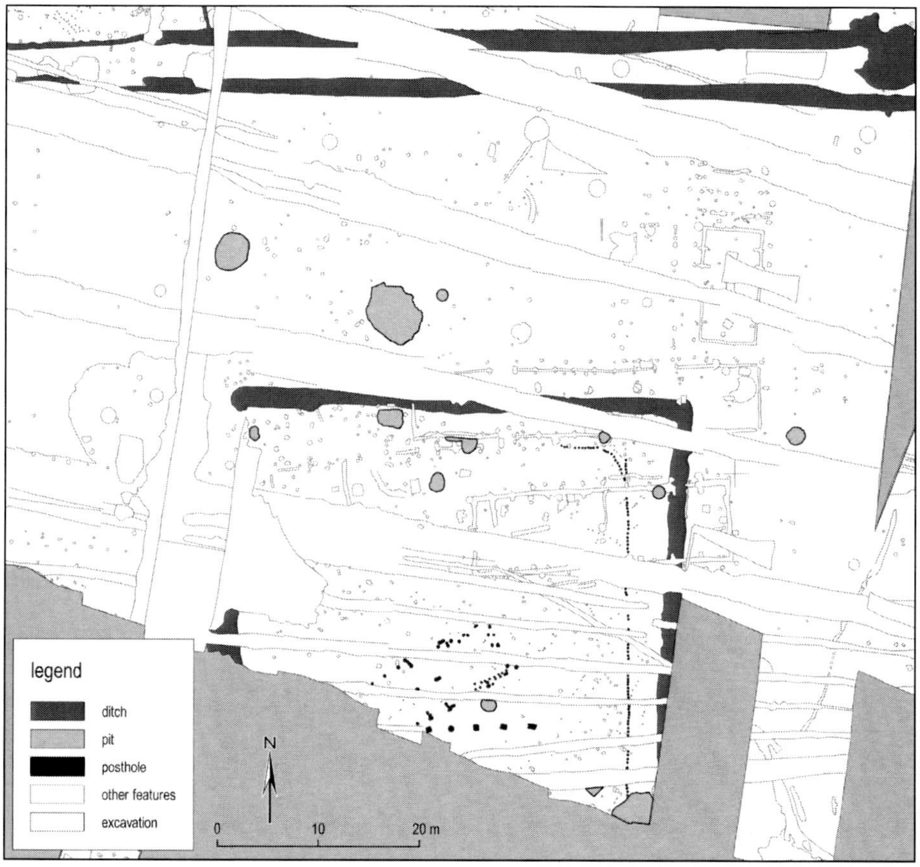

Figure A.40-1. Part of the excavation plan of Oss-Ussen Westerveld, structure R57 (original field data, courtesy of Leiden University). For colour version see fig. 6.16.

legend

■ ditch
■ pit
■ posthole
□ other features
□ excavation

N

0   10   20 m

Figure A.40-2. Cross section over the ditch of R57 (photo: University Leiden depository).

The largest rectangular structure with a Late iron Age date in Oss was excavated in 1983 (Van der Sanden 1998, 318-319, 332-333). The geographical location for R57 is similar to the situation described for the Middle Iron Age site of R25/R26. All five Oss sites included in these chapters are relatively close to each other, within 1.3 km, on the west side of the city (De Leeuwe & Jansen 2018). R57 is the only site directly linked to the Roman settlement of Westerveld, as it is situated within the large settlement ditches, even though as explained above it predates the use of the settlement.

Rectangular structure

Only parts of the west, north and east side were excavated, making the structure at least 46 × 37m (fig. A.40-1; Van der Sanden 1998, 318-319). The cross-section was bowl shaped to a shallow V-shape with a flattish bottom (De Leeuwe & Jansen 2018). The fill had a variable appearance, some with a laminated or humic first phase.[87] This may be interpreted as a fill that accumulated over time instead of a short-lived and quickly filled-in feature. The cross-section measured 200cm wide by 40-70cm deep (fig. A.40-2).

Finds

Considering the size of the ditch, it yielded relatively few finds (Van der Sanden 1998, 332-333; De Leeuwe & Jansen 2018). A total of 347 pottery shards (of which 47 Roman) were recovered, along with a miniature bowl, a grinding stone, iron slags, a nail and bones from cattle, sheep/goat, pig and dog. It is unknown in which phases of the ditch fill this material originated and whether the whole ditch was investigated.

Associated features

All along the inner east side of the structure and part of the northeast side, a row of small posts was found (Van der Sanden 1998, 318-319). This palisade was parallel to the ditch, so association can be assumed. None of the pits could be associated with the ditches of the rectangular structure, but it has been suggested a row of five postholes on the south side of the interior could be associated because of the similarity in orientation of the row. A Late Iron Age house plan was found in the centre of the interior, with a northeast-southwest orientation (Schinkel 1998, 159; Wesselingh 2000, 169 – note 18). Contemporaneity between the rectangular structure and the house is uncertain as both features were difficult to date. A house plan crossing over the ditch on the east side was dated by dendrochronology to the end of the 1st century BCE to the beginning of the 1st century CE (Jansma 1995, 132; Wesselingh 2000, 99, 169 – note 17). R57 itself is situated inside the much larger Roman settlement boundary, that consisted of two parallel ditches (figure A.36-3).

Landscape

See Oss-Brabantstraat.

Type of structure

7

---

87   Field data, available at the University Leiden.

Poperinge-Koestraat (B)

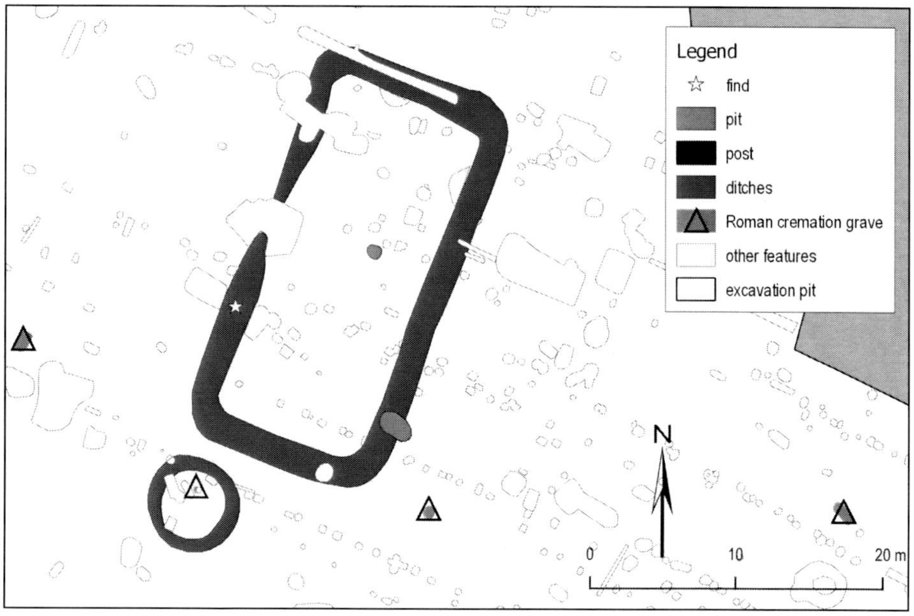

Figure A.41. Section of the excavation plan of Poperinge (after Van der Linde & Kalshoven 2017). For colour version see fig. 4.7.

The last site with a cemetery context to be discussed in this chapter lies on the southwestern edge of the research area, near the border with France.

Rectangular structure

The main excavated structure on this site consisted of a rectangular ditch of 28 by 13.7 m, measured on the outside (Van der Linde & Kalshoven 2017, 40). At the excavation level the ditch was 1.70m to 2.05m wide (fig. A.41). It had a V-shaped cross section and a bowl shaped bottom and a maximum depth of 126cm. According to Van der Linde & Kalshoven (2017, 40-47) the appearance of the fill layers suggests the ditch was an open and dry feature, with the groundwater level below the bottom. They suggest the ditch filled gradually in different phases and no attempts were made for redigging. If there was an opening in the ditch it would have been on the west side. This cannot be stated for certain due to a local recent disturbance of the soil at that location.

The excavators reconstructed the ditch as originally having had a total depth of 1.8m and a width of around 3m (Van der Linde & Kalshoven 2017, 40-47). On the north side some colluvium was found in the ditch fill indicating the soil from the ditch was used to make a wall on the outside and possibly also on the inside. Six samples were carbon dated from the lower and central fills of the ditch, indicating the ditch must have been dug between 1258-911 BCE and filled during the centuries

after.[88] This sizable ditch would have been visible for a long time, possibly still in the Roman era, until it was filled and built over in the later medieval times.

Finds

Finds that can be directly associated with the Late Bronze Age structure are scarce. During the trial trenches on the site of Poperinge, a nearly complete pot was found standing upright near the bottom of the ditch (Demey 2012, 17). The cup-shaped piece of pottery is identified as a *Henkeltasse*, a type typical for the Late Bronze Age or Early Iron Age (Demey 2012, 17; Bloo & Weterings 2017, 73). As the pot seems to be placed at the bottom of the ditch deliberately, it was interpreted by the excavators to be an offering (Demey 2012, 14-15).

A total of 120 shards of pottery were found in the ditch, belonging to a bowl and two pots most likely dating to the Late Bronze Age. Most pottery was found on the south side of the monument, in the corners, and on the west side of the ditch close to what might have been the entrance. Finds from the ditch also included 35 quite large sandstones, that were interpreted as deliberately broken

---

88   Lower fill: 95.4% calibrated dates, charcoal, Poz-81785: 2945 ± 30 BP; Poz -81787: 2870 ± 30 BP; Poz -81791: 2835 ± 30 BP. Central fill: 95.4% calibrated dates, charred nutshell, Poz -81788: 2755 ± 30 BP; charred fruit pit, Poz -81789: 2835 ± 30 BP; charcoal, Poz -81790: 2935 ± 30 BP.

(Van der Linde & Kalshoven 2017, 110). In, or rather under the ditch on the southeast side, a shaft-like pit was found. Its remaining depth was 1.1m below the bottom of the ditch (Van der Linde & Kalshoven 2017, 44-46). The walls of this feature were probably covered by a wooden lining. The shaft was slightly wider than the ditch and contained no finds. The bottom of the shaft was above the groundwater level.

Analysis of macro-botanical samples of the ditch fill demonstrated remains of plants with edible nuts or fruits, namely hazel, hawthorn, blackberry and oak. According to Van der Meer (2017) this assemblage of plants deviates from samples in contemporary settlements. Especially hawthorn is mentioned for its use in burial rituals, while the act of cutting a hawthorn was thought to bring bad luck (De Cleene & Lejeune 2000, 725-733, cited by Van der Meer 2017).

Associated features

The large rectangular ditch at Poperinge remains a rather enigmatic feature without contemporary parallels in the region. The circular ditch to the south may be of a later Iron Age date (Bloo & Weterings 2017). The context with the later burials indicates a connection to the burial ritual, but a ditch of this size does not resemble known urnfield features. If radiocarbon dating and pottery had not been so decisive for a Late Bronze Age date, in my view a Roman interpretation would be more obvious as the best analogy is probably a large rectangular structure excavated at Dinther-Retsel measuring as 34 by 17m (De Leeuwe 2006,

25-27; Moesker et al. 2012, 65-67). It was situated in a Late Iron Age and Roman cremation cemetery containing many square and round ditches of different shapes and sizes. The 2.5m wide ditch had a distinct V-shaped cross section and was 145cm deep and its construction was dated by OSL-samples between 46 and 97 CE (Moesker et al. 2012, 65-67). A possible Roman link for the Poperinge structure is the pit in the centre of the monument and the Roman graves. The pit contained 147 pieces of Roman pottery and fragments of iron nails along with a thick layer of burned soil and charcoal. This pit was marked as a possible deposition feature (Van der Linde & Kalshoven 2017, 51-52).

Landscape

The site is situated on the edge of a higher elongated strip of land parallel to the natural relief of the terrain, in prehistory flanked by two creek valleys (Demey 2012; Van der Linde & Kalshoven 2017). In the valleys two deposition sites were found (Beke & Van den Dorpel 2015; Beke et al. 2017). One of the depositions was a secondary burned Middle Bronze Age bucket urn containing charred grains, two stones and a flint scraper tool. The excavator proposed they symbolised two grinding stones as part of an 'agricultural ritual depot'. Another depot was found, consisting of five complete early La Tène pottery dishes (probably 5th century BCE based on the style combined with a ^{14}C-date).

Type of structure

Undetermined

Ronse-Pont West (B)

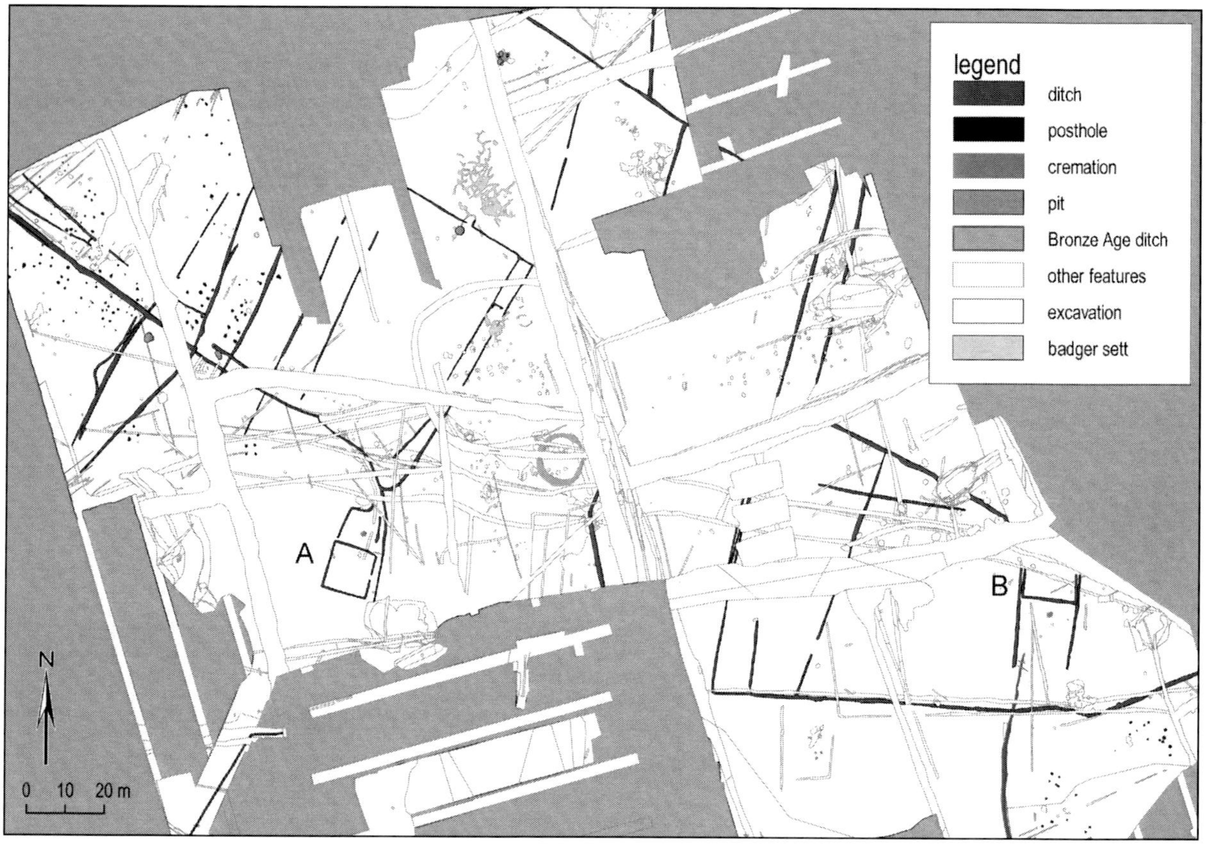

Figure A.42. Part of the excavation plan of Ronse-Pont West (courtesy of Solva, after De Graeve 2020, figure 72). For colour version see fig. 6.5.

In Ronse a large excwavation revealed 4000 years of landscape use. In the Late Iron Age the landscape was divided by ditches, while several smaller structures, such as granaries, indicated settlement activities (De Graeve 2020, 183-338). As house plans and wells were absent and only a few pits were found, the core of the settlement seems to have been just outside of the excavation area. The ditch systems are interpreted as fields belonging to different farm yards.

Rectangular structures

Two structures were interpreted as burial or 'ritual' enclosures (*Ibid.* 2020, 287). The structure on the west side measured 12.1 by 11.6m (figure A.42, A). The ditch was only 0.5m wide and 20cm deep. It had an opening of 1m wide on the east side (*Ibid.* 2020, 281-285).

The second rectangular structure, on the east side, was only partly documented as it was cut by more recent features (figure A.42, B).

Finds

Scattered in the fill of the ditch of the west structure some charcoal, one small fragment of burned bone, and pottery was collected. The pottery consisted of large slabs of a situla in one location (not specified in the report) and part of a ribbed bowl in another, both heavily secondarily burned. The material could be typologically dated between circa 300 and 120 BCE (*Ibid.* 2020, 284).

If any pottery was found in association with the ditch of the the second rectangular structure, it was not mentioned in the report (De Graeve 2020, 287).

Associated features

A cremation burial was found in a mole burrow, just 3.2m north of structure A, dating to 380-200 BCE, slightly older than the structure (De Graeve 2020, 288-294). The situation resembles the more intact cremation grave just 3.6m south of structure B, where the cremation remains were accompanied by a couple of pots. The remains could be dated to the 2nd or early 1st century BCE by combining the pottery and a carbon date.[89]

Several ditches seem to be related to the rectangular structures. For structure A, the ditch system connects to the north, enclosing the grave. For structure B the enclosure is flanked by two ditches that extend south, also in the direction of the grave. Notably, the ditch systems seem to take the central position of an older Bronze Age barrow into account (De Graeve 2020, 117-131). Charcoal from the lower fills of the circular ditch indicated a Middle Bronze Age A date for the monument. A pit near the centre of the circular ditch contained Early Iron Age pottery, although this is interpreted as a secondary use of the barrow. The features belonging to two former badger setts north of the Bronze Age barrow (figure 6.5, light green) could be an indication that more barrows used to be there, as badgers seem to have a preference for making their homes in barrows (i.e. Bourgeois, Cherretté & Meganck 2001; Doorenbosch 2013, 191; De Graeve *et al.* 2014; Bowden *et al.* 2014).

Landscape

The area extends across a hill (+40m TAW), just south of the highest hilltops of the Flemish Ardennes (De Graeve *et al.* 2014). The highest point is centrally located in the research area.

Type of structure

6

---

89   95.4% probability calibration, burned bone, RICH-22739: 2141 ± 32 BP.

Rijkevorsel-Wilgenlaan (B)

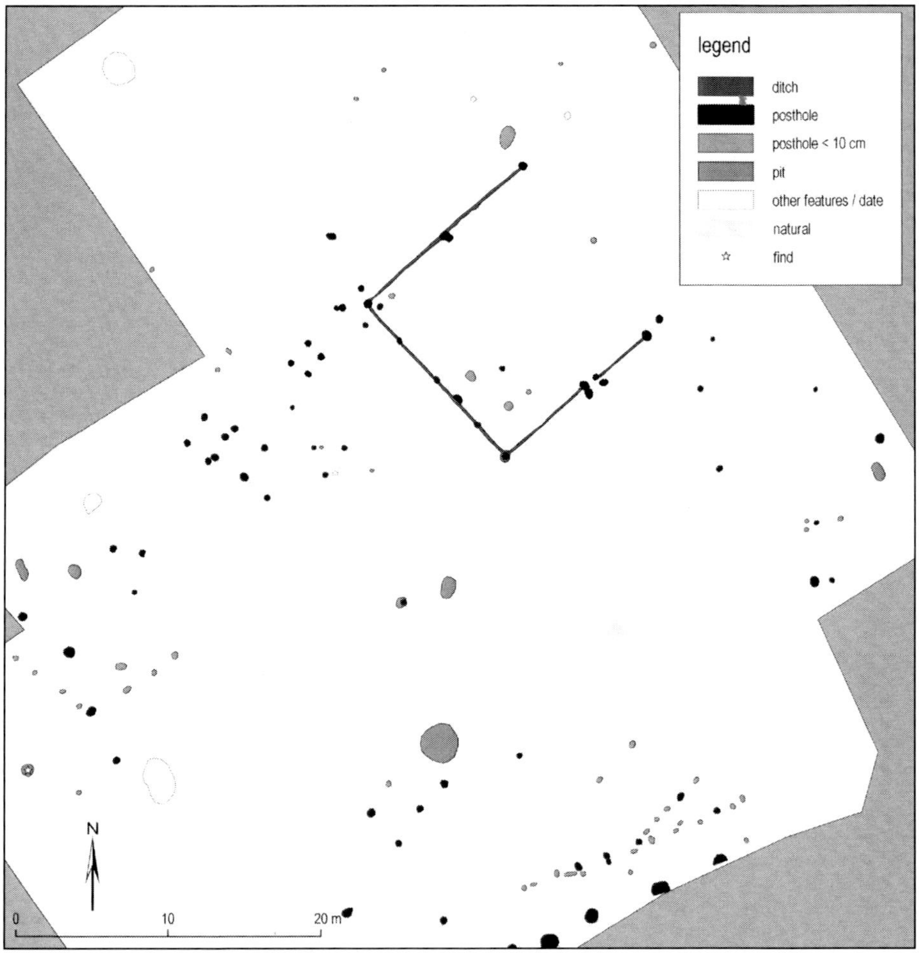

Figure A.43. Part of the excavation plan of Rijkevorsel-Wilgenstraat (after Van Liefferinge, Smeets & Fockedey 2013, figure 17 and 18). For colour version see fig. 6.18.

In 2012 a square structure was excavated in Rijksevorsel (Van Liefferinge, Smeets & Fockedey 2013, 21-26; figure 6.18).

Rectangular structure

The structure consisted of posts on the corners and in the middle of the sides, placed in a narrow bedding trench of about 20cm wide. The remaining depth of the ditch is not mentioned in the report. As the east side seems to be missing, it might not have been preserved. On the south side a 60cm interruption is flanked by four more postholes, indicating an entrance.

Finds

The rectangular structure including the posts only yielded five pieces of pottery (Van Liefferinge, Smeets & Fockedey 2013, 28-31). Despite this low number they could be dated to the Late Iron Age. Only 171 pieces of pottery were found on the entire site, 98 of which were Roman and could be related to a house plan on the south side of the excavation. No carbon dates are available for the site.

Associated features

In the interior four postholes were found on the south side and two on the west side (Van Liefferinge, Smeets & Fockedey 2013, 21-26). One of the postholes on the west side might be part of a four-posted structure. Several undated four-posted structures cluster around the west corner and further west of the rectangular structure. A few fragments (4 grams in total) of burned bone were found in the interior, just above the excavating surface, the likely remains of a cremation burial (Van Liefferinge, Smeets & Fockedey 2013, 23-24; Smits 2013). A rectangular structure in Ruiselede similar to the one in Rijkevorsel yielded two cremation burials in the interior and eight more adjacent to the eastside of the structure, all dating to the Roman era (Deconynck & Beek 2010).

A 20cm deep pit on the west side of the excavation held three looming weights, also dating to the Iron Age.

Landscape

The excavation was situated on a loamy sand area, on a terrain sloping down at a 1% angle towards the north (Van Liefferinge, Smeets & Fockedey 2013, 9-17). In some places the original podzol soil was intact. To the east lies a small stream. An Early to Middle Iron Age cemetery was found 3.4 km to the south (Theunissen 1993).

Type of structure

7

Someren-Waterdael III (NL)

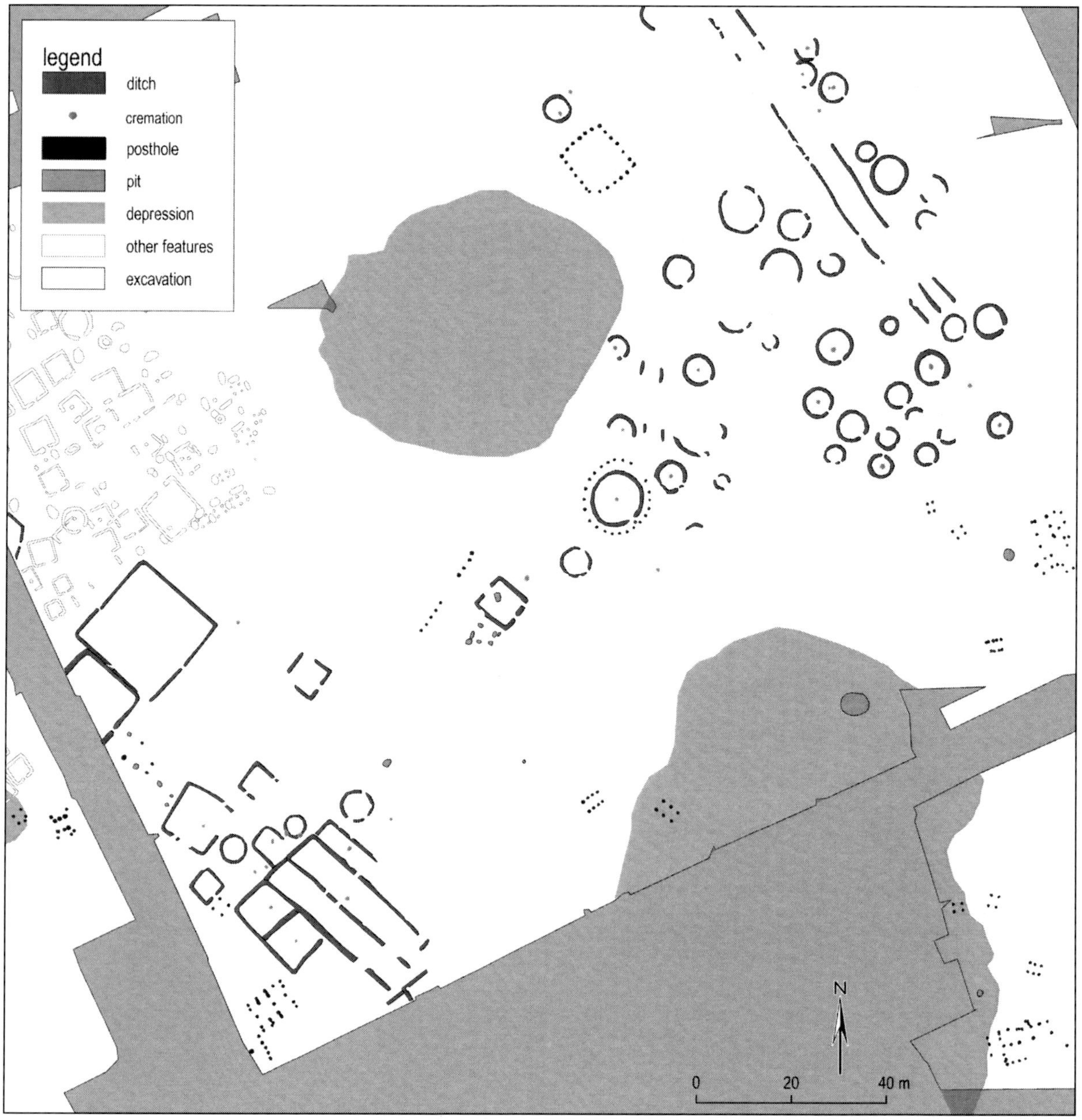

Figure A.44. Middle Iron Age and adjacent features in the Someren-Waterdael III cemetery (based on Hiddink & De Boer 2011, figure 6.1 and plate 30; Hiddink 2012, figure 4.2 and 4.3).

In the Waterdael residential area of Someren large scale excavations have been part of the development since the 1990s (Hiddink & De Boer 2011). Expansion of the residential area brought about another 14 ha excavation in 2006-2007. The excavation revealed a large urnfield cemetery that reveals the changing use of burial structures from the Early Iron Age to the Late Roman period.

Rectangular structure

The structure cautiously suggested by Hiddink & De Boer (2011, 127-128) to be a cult place concerns a square post setting amidst burial structures dating mainly to the Early and Middle Iron Age (fig. A.44, near the top). It measures 11.8 × 10.8 m, consisting of seven postholes on each side, including the corners (Hiddink & De Boer 2011, 263-264). The remaining depth of the postholes was only 4-26cm. As the structure was nearly devoid of finds, it was dated on the basis of the location, orientation and physical appearance of the features.

Associated features

The archaeological remains were poorly preserved. Only 30% of the burial structures could be associated with cremation remains (Hiddink & De Boer 2011, 120). The burial 7m north of the square post setting was carbon dated to 542-385 BCE (Hiddink & De Boer 2011, 264).[90] A total of 325 graves and burial structures were documented, of which 83 were dated or allocated Early to Middle Iron Age (Hiddink & De Boer 2011, 111-116). The three large rectangular ditches contained no datable material or a grave and the remaining depth of the ditch varied between 5 and 35cm. Like many features the ditches could not be dated accurately. Their suggested date is the Middle Iron Age. One grave is dated to the Middle to Late Iron Age and the rest to the Late Iron Age and Roman era. Of the Early to Middle Iron Age structures, 44 (53%) had a circular ditch, most of which had an interruption on the southeast side and 21 structures were rectangular (Hiddink & De Boer 2011, 123-127). This was in contrast to the Late Iron Age and Roman part of the cemetery, when square ditches were the norm (75-80%) (Hiddink & De Boer 2011, 139). Middle Iron Age settlement features were found to the east and south of the cemetery, the nearest house plans lying approximately 70 to 100m away (De Boer & Hiddink 2012, 10-14; Hiddink 2012, 59-68; fig. A.44 lower right corner). One piece of loam was found in the square post setting and one pottery fragment (Hiddink & De Boer 2011, 127-128). The latter was considered intrusive. One separate cremation grave was found to the northeast of the post setting.

Landscape

The site is situated on sandy soils flanked by two small rivers, the Aa and the Dommel (Hiddink & De Boer 2011, 87-110). The area shows local depressions of several decimetres depth (shaded areas in fig. A.44). The cemetery is located circa 500m west of the highest point of a sandy ridge on a very gentle slope (Hiddink & De Boer 2011, 35-36). The height difference from the top of the ridge to the river valley 2 km southwest of the site is 5 to 6m.

Type of structure

1

---

90   92.7% probability calibration, cremated bone, GrA-43339: 2370 ± 35 BP.

Weert-Laarvelt (NL)

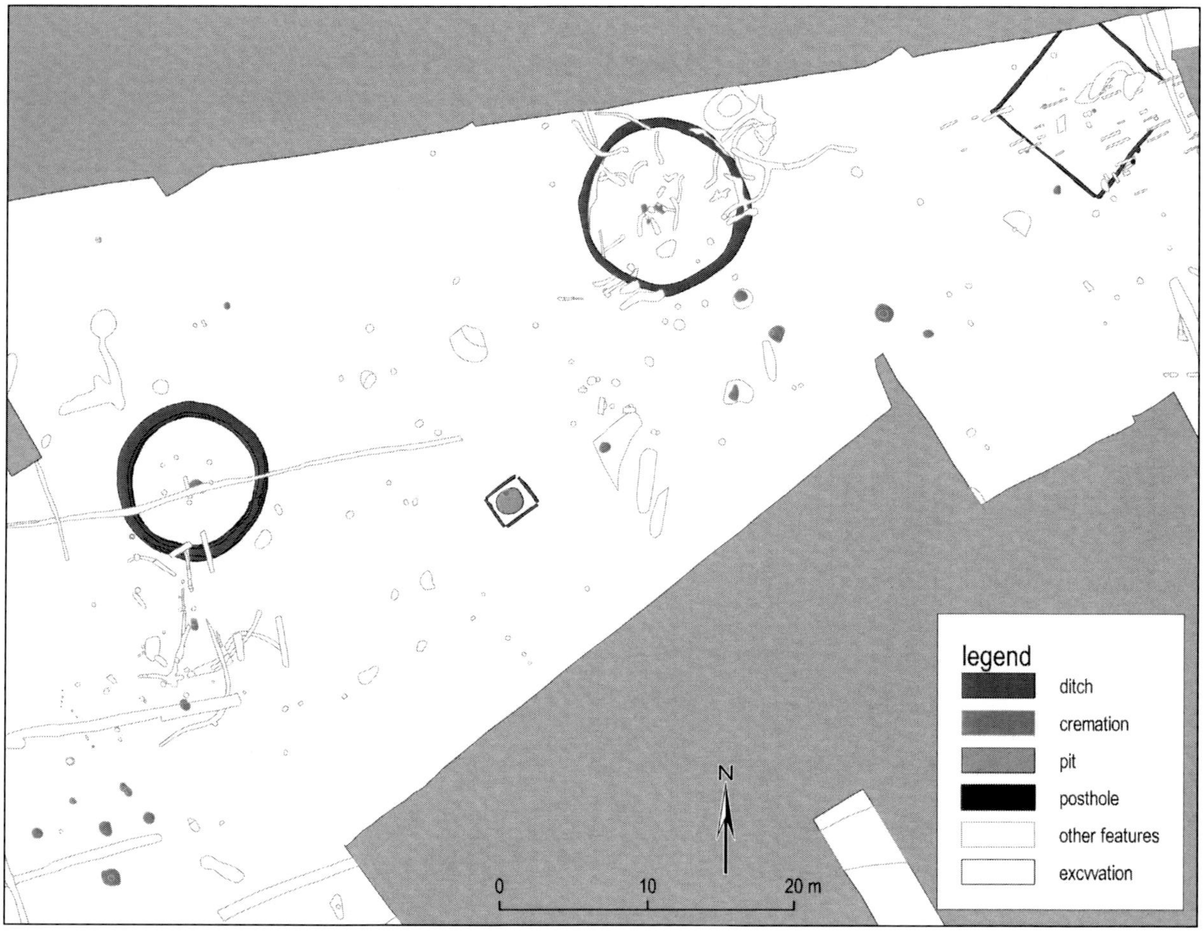

Figure A.45. Part of the excavation plan of Weert-Laarveld (after Tol 2009).

Weert-Laarvelt is a well preserved and reasonably complete example of a Middle to Late Iron Age cemetery. Spread out over an area of 100m long and around 30m wide, 23 cremation graves were found (Tol 2009, 85). Four of these were positioned within one of the ditch structures and the rest were without a surrounding feature (fig. A.45). The two round structures were both around 11m in diameter. The ditch would have surrounded a barrow, its former presence indicated by soil discolorations and animal burrows (Tol 2009, 37-38). Inside the circular ditches two juveniles were buried, 3-7 years and 9-12 years (Smits 2009).

Rectangular structure

The square 9 by 9m ditch was damaged by ploughing activities. On three corners of the monument postholes

were found as well as in the middle of the southeast ditch. Just outside of the southwest ditch another five postholes were positioned. The remains in the centre belonged to a 20 to 30 year old man and dated 410 to 200 calBCE.[91]

Finds

Only 162 pieces of pottery were found, mostly in the graves. A meagre two pieces were found in the ditches (Van der Linde 2009). Six graves contained metal objects, including three complete belt hooks. In between the human cremation remains, animal bones of sheep/goat and pigs were found in nine graves (Smits 2009). The

---

91   95.4% probability calibration, cremated remains, Poz-25933: 2290 ±35 BP.

CATALOGUE OF RECTANGULAR STRUCTURES IN THE LOW COUNTRIES   277

eastern circular ditch revealed 30 pieces of grinding stone interpreted as a deposition (Knippenberg 2009).

Associated features

The other grave in the square monument also belonged to an adult and dated 760-410 BCE.[92] The small square ditch measured 2.9 by 2.5m and also had postholes in the corners and a fifth posthole on the northeast side. Inside the small ditch a charcoal spot was found and a cremation grave with the remains of a 30 to 60 year old person. Out of the 23 cremation remains, 14 were carbon dated of which 12 resulted in circa 400-200 BCE (Tol 2009, 30-39). A 5th century BCE grave that belonged to a 20-60 year old woman was positioned just outside of the square ditch, making it appear as if the ditch was constructed in this location to include only the older male burial.

Landscape

The site is situated on a narrow sandy ridge a couple of meters above the surrounding area (Tol 2009, 81). During the Iron Age this was a favourable location for arable land, in contrast to the swampy lower areas.

Type of structure

1

---

92 95.4% probability calibration, cremated remains, Poz-25931: 2405 ±35 BP and Poz-25931: 2460 ±35 BP.

Ursel-Rozenstraat (B)

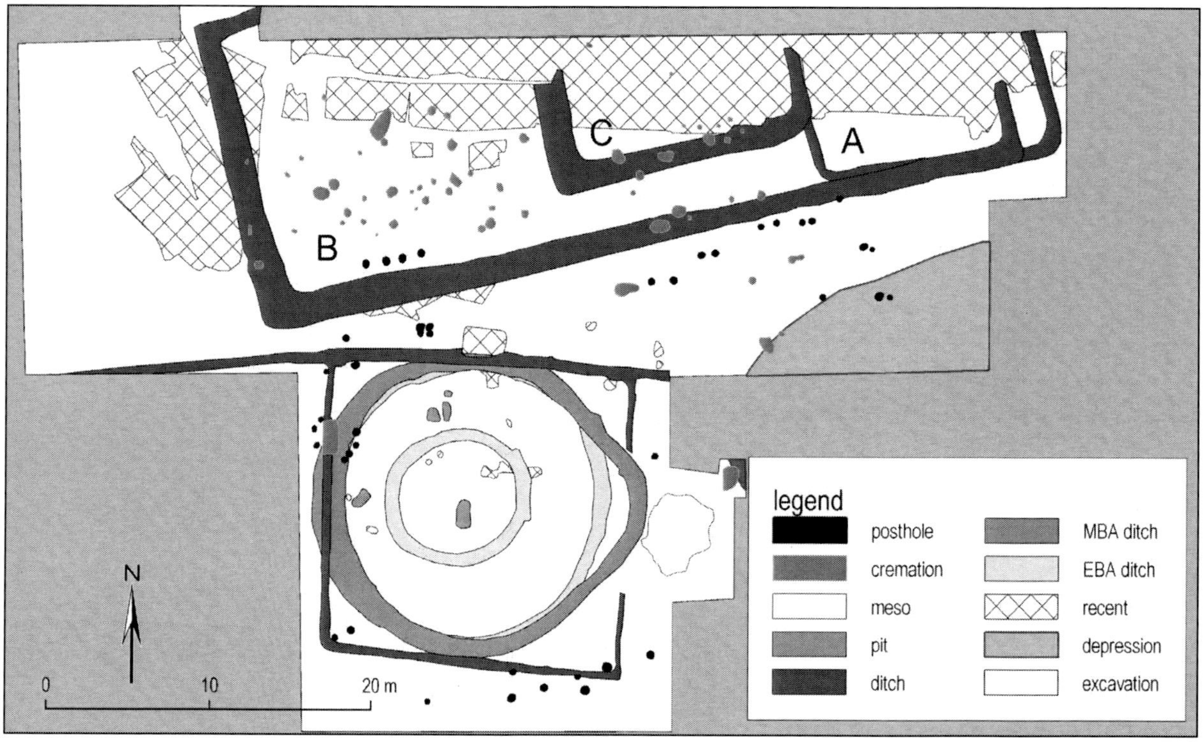

Figure A.46. The excavation plan of the cemetery in Ursel (based on Bourgeois & Rommelaere 1991). For colour version see fig. 6.3.

Adjacent to a Bronze Age tumulus three rectangular Iron Age structures were found (Bourgeois, 1998; Bourgeois *et al.* 1989).

Rectangular structures

The oldest was the most eastern ditch (fig. A.46, A). The north side of the structure was disturbed, but the length was 14m on the south side. The ditch was about 0.50m wide and 50cm deep with oblique walls and a flat bottom. The largest enclosure (B) measured a length of 47.5m (Bourgeois *et al.* 1989). 47.5m long and 16m wide (Bourgeois *et al.* 1989). The ditch was best preserved on the west side, where it had a width of 1.5 m, also with straight sides 60cm deep and a flat bottom. Ditch C could be contemporary to large ditch B. It had a maximum width of 1.70m and was conserved for nearly 110cm deep. In cross sections the walls were oblique and the bottom narrow and flat. The different layers of the fill can be subdivided into two phases, similar to ditch A and B. The bottom phase had a clean appearance.

Finds

Only five pottery shards were recovered from ditch A. Most finds were recovered from the top phase of ditch B: around 100 pottery shards and thirty pebbles the size of sling shots. Ditch C contained some lithic fragments and seven pottery shards, which can roughly be dated to the Iron Age.

Associated features

Several (pairs of) postholes can be associated with the rectangular structures, although the limited size of the excavation prevents an interpretation of their context. A total of 68 cremation graves have been found (Bourgeois, 1998). Most of these date to the 1st century BCE and the 1st century CE. Several of the cremation graves cut over the upper ditch fill. Crucially, one of the cremation graves that had been dug in the ditch fill on the west side, could be carbon dated to 390-108 calBCE.[93] According to the

---

93   95.4% probability calibration, charcoal, IRPA-987: 2200 ± 50 BP.

researchers, the rectangular ditches were no longer visible when the site was used for the necropolis (Bourgeois *et al.* 1989). It is difficult to tie the use of the site along the Rozenstaat in Ursel to a specific period in late prehistory. Apart from a Mesolithic hearth, the oldest features are a smaller circular ditch of 7.5m in diameter around a grave (indicated as pit in fig. A.46) that was entirely eroded by ploughing and a larger one of about 17m in diameter (Bourgeois, 1998; Bourgeois & Rommelaere 1991; Bourgeois *et al.* 1989). The smaller circular ditch was 0.7m wide and 40cm deep and its appearance suggested it was filled shortly after it was dug. Two charcoal fragments from the smaller ditch date to the Early Bronze Age. The larger ditch was 1m wide and 30-60cm deep and probably surrounded a tumulus that covered the inner circular ditch. Based on pottery and radiocarbon dates the outer ditch was redug in the Early Iron Age and made egg-shaped with an extension to the east. This egg-shaped ditch was dug deeper than the initial circular one. The lower fill was comparable to that of the earlier ditches and seemed to have been filled in shortly after it had been dug. The upper fill looked like it gradually accumulated. No grave or finds could be associated with this phase. In a third phase a narrow ditch about 17.5m square was dug in the same place, cutting over the circular monument on all four sides and a row of five posts on the south side (Bourgeois 1998; Bourgeois *et al.* 1989). Like the egg-shaped ditch, the square ditch cannot be associated with a grave. The square ditch was shallow and badly eroded. It is assumed to be a demarcation of the Bronze Age monument, constructed at a time when the tumulus was still visible, isolating it from the rest of the landscape. On the north side the narrow square ditch is connected to another east-west orientated narrow ditch. Unfortunately no finds could be associated with the square ditch surrounding the round ones. The square ditch was overcut by a Roman cremation grave.

The presence of an extensive ditch system was demonstrated by an excavation 200m to the south (Mestdagh & Taelman 2008). This field system might have originated in the Middle Iron Age.[94] How it connected to the rectangular structures remains a hiatus for future research to fill.

Landscape
The pedological landscape of the Ursel region is a complex patchwork of sand, silty sand, light sandy loam and clay (Langohr & Pieters, 1989). The relief is almost flat with some slight depressions, rising towards the north. The site is located on a well-drained cover sand area, at the bottom of a very gradual slope bordering a broad depression. Pollen analysis from the Early Iron Age ditch showed an environment that was about 70% covered with forest at the time, mostly with hazel and alder trees, changing in the Later Iron Age to around 50% coverage in favour of heathland (Bourgeois & Rommelaere 1991).

Type of structure
2

94   Charcoal from a ditch, KIA-39823: 2370 ± 20 BP.

Zundert-Akkermolenweg (NL)

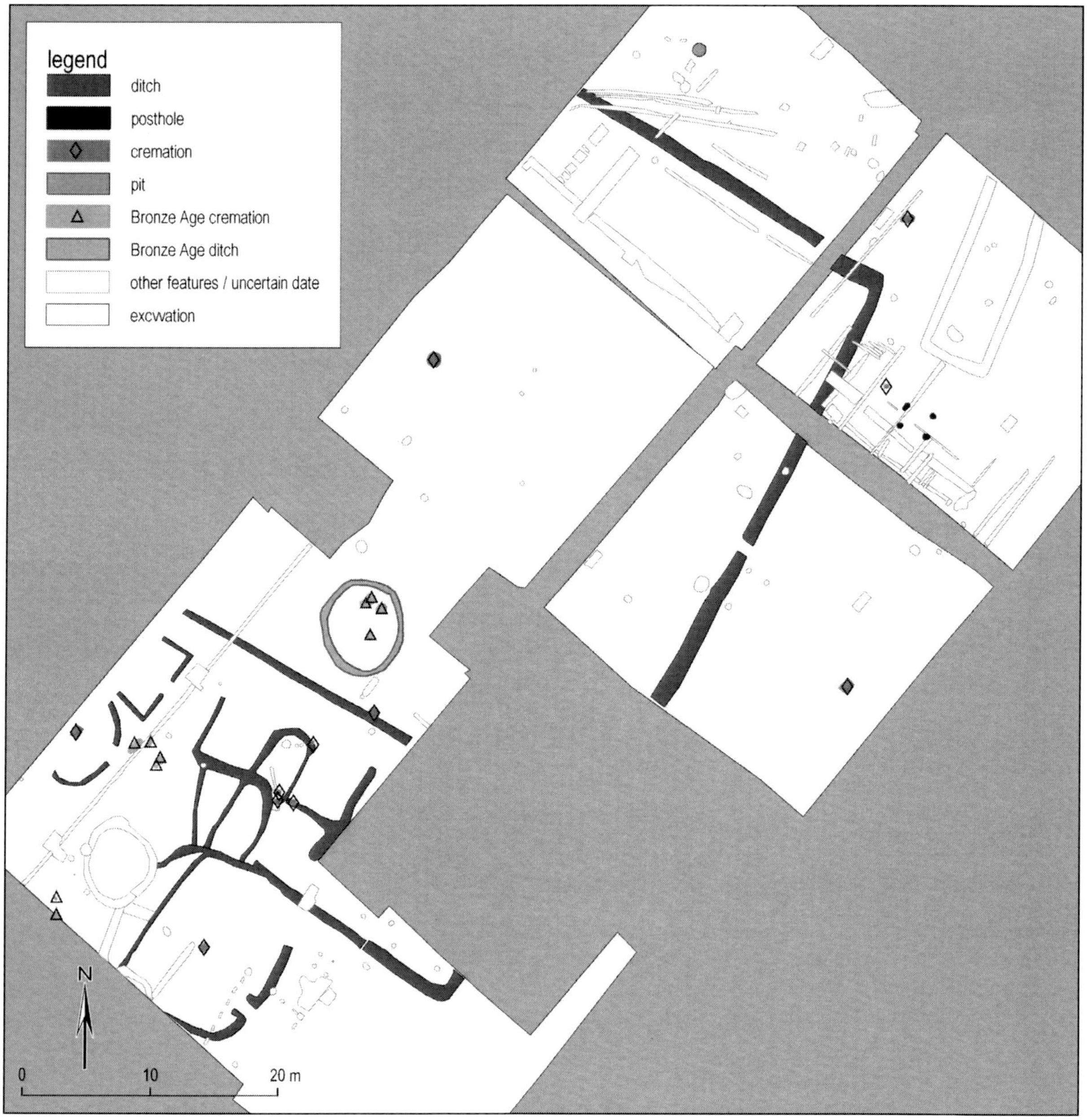

Figure A.47. Part of the excavation plan of Zundert-Akkermolenweg (based on Krist 2005, appendix 1-3).

The excavation of the site in Zundert was executed in different phases and two excavation surfaces in 2003 (Krist 2005). This resulted in a somewhat vague description of the excavated features. In 2012 additional fieldwork revealed some of the surrounding area (Ter Wal 2013; 2013a). Ditches and cremation graves from the Late Bronze Age to the Middle Iron Age were represented (fig. A.47).

Rectangular structure

The largest ditch is interpreted as a cult place and described as a 48m square feature (Krist 2005, 66-77).

CATALOGUE OF RECTANGULAR STRUCTURES IN THE LOW COUNTRIES   281

However, only the northeast corner and a possible south side were excavated. Provided the southern ditch is indeed part of the same structure, it measures 48m southwest to northeast (Krist 2005) or 64m depending on which ditch is connected. The other dimension is entirely uncertain. The ditch was approximately 1m wide at the excavation surface and the depth 80cm. It was not described in the excavation report whether this referred to the first or second excavation level, or what shape the cross-section of the ditch had. An interruption of the ditch was documented on the east side.

Finds

In the large ditch 145 pottery fragments were found, mostly near the southern end of the interruption on the east side (Krist 2005, 68). About 37% of the pottery was secondarily burned.

Associated features

A total of 35 cremation graves were found, of which 12 could be dated to the Late Bronze Age and 14 to the Middle Iron Age, some through association (Krist 2005, 48-56). Several smaller ditches could be dated to the Middle Iron Age, like the graves on the basis of pottery typology. None of the smaller ditches are accurately described in the report, or where the associated pottery originated. These ditches are therefore only partially shaded in fig.

A.47. Judging by the excavation plan, there seems to be a network of small connected features. One grave, dug into the top of the ditch fill on the south side, was carbon dated to the 1st century BCE. Another grave found in a semi-circular feature on the west side of the excavation pit date between 475 calBCE and 52 calCE.[95] The circular ditch within the large ditch could be dated to the Late Bronze Age. The other circular ditch is assumed to be Bronze Age by its appearance. As this date remains uncertain, it is not so indicated in fig. A.47. No pits were described in the report.

The excavation report of Zunder-Akkermolenweg is chaotic. The maze of ditches at the south side of the excavation resembles an animal den. Without actually having seen the situation it is difficult to conclude from the report what is a manmade feature and what is not. The large rectangular ditch was incomplete and the relation to other ditches is unclear.

Landscape

The site in Zundert is located on top of a sand ridge with a northwest-southeast orientation (Krist 2005, 80). The micro-relief is not described in the report.

Type of structure

Undetermined

---

95   95.4% probability calibration, charcoal, R.J. Van de Graaf laboratorium, sample 187: 2187 ± 104 BP.